E–Business Applications for Product Development and Competitive Growth:
Emerging Technologies

In Lee
Western Illinois University, USA

BUSINESS SCIENCE REFERENCE

Hershey · New York

Director of Editorial Content:	Kristin Klinger
Director of Book Publications:	Julia Mosemann
Acquisitions Editor:	Lindsay Johnston
Development Editor:	Myla Harty
Publishing Assistant:	Julia Mosemann
Typesetter:	Michael Brehm
Production Editor:	Jamie Snavely
Cover Design:	Lisa Tosheff

Published in the United States of America by
Business Science Reference (an imprint of IGI Global)
701 E. Chocolate Avenue
Hershey PA 17033
Tel: 717-533-8845
Fax: 717-533-8661
E-mail: cust@igi-global.com
Web site: http://www.igi-global.com/reference

Copyright © 2011 by IGI Global. All rights reserved. No part of this publication may be reproduced, stored or distributed in any form or by any means, electronic or mechanical, including photocopying, without written permission from the publisher. Product or company names used in this set are for identification purposes only. Inclusion of the names of the products or companies does not indicate a claim of ownership by IGI Global of the trademark or registered trademark.

Library of Congress Cataloging-in-Publication Data

E-business applications for product development and competitive growth :
emerging technologies / In Lee, editor.
    p. cm.
  Includes bibliographical references and index.
    ISBN 978-1-60960-132-4 (hbk.) -- ISBN 978-1-60960-134-8 (ebook) 1.
Electronic commerce. 2. Information technology--Management. 3. New products.
4. Technological innovations--Management. I. Lee, In, 1958-
  HF5548.32.E17369 2011
  658.5'7502854678--dc22
                        2010046732

British Cataloguing in Publication Data
A Cataloguing in Publication record for this book is available from the British Library.

All work contributed to this book is new, previously-unpublished material. The views expressed in this book are those of the authors, but not necessarily of the publisher.

Table of Contents

Detailed Table of Contents

Chapter 1

Frank Schlemmer, Queen's University of Belfast, Northern Ireland
Brian Webb, Queen's University of Belfast, Northern Ireland

It has been suggested that the Internet can be used to leverage a firm's strategic assets. However, empirical research on complementarity is still rare and frequently inconclusive, especially in the context of small and medium-sized enterprises. We propose a theoretical framework with the independent variables business resources, dynamic capabilities and IT assets. Survey data of 146 small firms suggest that the Internet is complementary with business resources and dynamic capabilities but not with IT assets. Therefore, the framework may enable small firm managers to create competitive advantage by identifying strategic assets that are complementary with the Internet. Furthermore, our research our research highlights the threat of an over-investment in IT assets

Chapter 2

Jaume Franquesa, Kent State University, USA
Alan Brandyberry, Kent State University, USA

This study explores the relevant dimensions of organizational slack in small and medium enterprises (SMEs) and investigates their impact on adoption of different types of information technology (IT) innovations. Using recent data from a representative sample of 2,296 U.S. SMEs, we find that the slack-innovation relationships previously described in larger firms do not hold well for SMEs. Our results show potential slack (measured as access to external credit) to be a strong predictor of technology adoption in SMEs. By contrast, available slack appeared not to be a significant factor in SME innovation adoption. Moreover, the direction of the effects of potential slack was moderated by the capital-intensity of the innovation. In particular, e-commerce, which required lesser financial resources for SME adoption, was found to be pursued by those with lesser potential slack. We argue that, in some cases, innovation adoption may represent a form of "bricolage" by resource constrained SMEs.

Jun Li, University of New Hampshire, USA
Michael Merenda, University of New Hampshire, USA
A.R. (Venky) Venkatachalam, University of New Hampshire, USA

Previous research has largely ignored how business process digitalization across the value chain enhances firm innovation. This paper examines the relationship between the extensiveness of business process digitalization (BPD) and new product development (NPD) in a sample of 85 small U.S. manufacturers. Scores of extensiveness was derived from the number of adopted e-business practices regarding inter and intra-firm activities such as: customer and supplier services (computer-aided design and manufacturing), employee services (education/training), and industry scanning (technology sourcing). We found that (1) NPD is positively related to the extensive use of BPD, and (2) the relationship between NPD and the extensiveness of BPD is stronger in more mature firms than that in younger firms. We conclude that small and medium-sized enterprise (SME) production innovation strategies are positively associated with the strategic use of BPD and span spatial, temporal, organizational, and industry boundaries thus aiding SME global competitiveness.

Susan J. Winter, Portland State University, USA
Connie Marie Gaglio, San Francisco State University, USA
Hari K. Rajagopalan, Francis Marion University, USA

Firms employ information and communication technology (ICT) in their pursuit of competitive growth and the productivity-related business value that accrues from its use is widely acknowledged. However, the organizational literature has long recognized that operational efficiency and productivity are not the only factors required for corporate success. One of the primary tasks facing firm leaders is the management of external stakeholders' impressions of the firm that enable it to gain access to external resources. This paper explores this additional symbolic dimension of ICT business value by investigating how and when the simple possession and use of ICT itself might create favorable impressions of the firm, yielding business value and competitive growth over and above its effects on operational efficiency and productivity. Using qualitative and inductive methods, we identify established and emerging ICTs' additional symbolic meanings for potential customers and develop a model of the judgment process through which ICT affects corporate images. When assessing the business value of ICT savvy managers should consider both efficiency and organizational image. Implications for theory, practice, and future research are discussed.

Dag H. Olsen, University of Agder, Norway
Tom R. Eikebrokk, University of Agder, Norway

This article examines the relationship between training, competence and performance of small and medium-sized enterprises (SMEs) in the context of e-business. Literature review combined with a triangulation of qualitative and quantitative methods were used to investigate these relationships. Data about e-business competences and performance in 339 SMEs in three European countries was combined with data about training supply from 116 providers of e-business related training. The empirical findings document a positive relationship between training, competence and performance and show that training explains variances in e-business competences and performance in terms of efficiency, complementarities, lock-in and novelty. The research has both theoretical and practical implications. It contributes to theoretical development by lending support to the idea that methodological issues are an important reason behind the lack of empirical support frequently reported in the literature. The study has practical implications for public policy makers, training suppliers and SME managers.

Mehruz Kamal, The College at Brockport, State University of New York, USA
Sajda Qureshil, University of Nebraska at Omaha, USA
Peter Wolcott, University of Nebraska at Omaha, USA

The use of Information and Communication Technologies (ICTs) by Small and Medium Sized Enterprises (SMEs) have the potential to enable these businesses to grow through access to new markets and administrative efficiencies. However, the growth of the smallest of these SMEs which are micro-enterprises is hindered by their inability to adopt ICTs effectively to achieve competitive advantage. This paper investigates how micro-enterprises can adopt ICTs to grow and achieve competitiveness. This investigation of a set of seven micro-enterprises took place through an interpretive field study in which action research was used to diagnose and treat the micro-enterprises with interventions through a process of "Information Technology (IT) Therapy". This process involved providing individualized IT solutions to pressing problems and opportunities and the development of a longer-term IT project plan, customized for each of the businesses. The increase in competitiveness of these micro-enterprises was assessed using the Focus Dominance Model and their growth through a modified model of micro-enterprise growth based on the resource based view of the firm. This research also contributes with a unique set of skills and experiences that ITD innovators can bring in helping micro-enterprises achieve sustained growth and competitive advantage.

    Linda Little, Northumbria University, UK
    Pam Briggs, Northumbria University, UK

Certain privacy principles have been established by industry, e.g. the U.S. Public Policy Committee of the Association for Computing Machinery (USACM). Over the past two years, we have been trying to understand whether such principles reflect the concerns of the ordinary citizen. We have developed a method of enquiry which displays a rich context to the user in order to elicit more detailed information about those privacy factors that underpin our acceptance of ubiquitous computing. To investigate use and acceptance, Videotaped Activity Scenarios specifically related to the exchange of health, financial, shopping and e-voting information and a large scale survey were used. We present a detailed analysis of user concerns, firstly in terms of a modified Hertzberg model that identifies a set of constructs that might reflect user-generated privacy principles, secondly those factors likely to play a key role in an individuals cost-benefit analysis, and thirdly, longer-term concerns of the citizen in terms of the impact of new technologies on social engagement and human values.

    Heng Xu, The Pennsylvania State University, USA

Information privacy is at the center of discussion and controversy among multiple stakeholders including business leaders, privacy activists, and government regulators. However, conceptualizations of information privacy have been somewhat patchy in current privacy literature. In this paper, we review the conceptualizations of information privacy through three different lenses (information exchange, social contract and information control), and then try to build upon previous literature from multiple theoretical lenses to create a common understanding of the organization-consumer information interaction in the context of Business-to-Consumer electronic commerce (B2C e-commence). We argue that consumers' privacy beliefs are influenced by the situational and environmental cues that signal the level of privacy protections in a particular environment. The framework developed in this research should be of interest to academic researchers, e-commerce vendors, legislators, industry self-regulators, and designers of privacy enhancing technologies.

    Edward J. Szewczak, Canisius College, USA
    Coral R. Snodgrass, Canisius College, USA

This article examines the role of the business associate of healthcare providers (BAHP) in the National Health Information Network. Current Health Insurance Portability and Accountability legislation has little to say about BAHPs and their potential impact on medical information privacy. For the good of the business enterprise, managers who are BAHPs or who supervise BAHPs need to be aware of the potential pitfalls of ignoring medical information privacy and take a proactive stance in protecting medical information privacy within the National Health Information Network. Among the approaches that managers can adopt include creating legal contracts between a business and BAHPs, proactively adopting more effective transmission security technologies, and insuring that BAHPs properly dispose of medical information after their use. Such proactive approaches will help to insure that the business is protected against a serious data breach that may result in popular and/or legal challenges to the business.

Chapter 10

Siani Pearson, Hewlett Packard Research Labs, UK
Damien Allison, Imagini Europe Limited, UK

Organisations are under pressure to be compliant to a range of privacy legislation, policies and best practice. At the same time many firms are using privacy as a key differentiator. There is a clear need for high-level management and administrators to be able to assess in a dynamic, customisable way the degree to which their enterprise complies with these. We outline a solution to this problem in the form of a model-driven automated privacy process analysis and configuration checking system. This system models privacy compliance constraints, automates the assessment of the extent to which a particular computing environment is compliant and generates dashboard-style reports that highlight policy failures. We have developed a prototype that provides this functionality in the context of governance audit; this includes the development of software agents to gather information on-the-fly regarding selected privacy enhancing technologies and other aspects of enterprise system configuration. This approach may also be tailored to enhance the assurance provided by existing governance tools, and to provide increased feedback to end users about the degree of privacy and security compliance that service providers are actually providing.

Chapter 11

Davide Rossi, University of Bologna, Italy
Elisa Turrini, University of Bologna, Italy

Model-driven methods are always welcome when developing complex applications. Their availability is usually related to the problem domain that has to be addressed and to the software architectures that have to be supported. Process-aware Web applications are arguably the prominent examples of applications in which multi-user, coordinated work takes place and are, as the web evolves towards a Business System, strongly emerging as one of the main types of Web-applications.In this article we propose a model-driven approach to process-aware Web applications based on a graphical process modeling and execution language that eases the development process (from the design to the implementation) by promoting an effective separation of concerns.Driven by an emerging class of applications, the Web is evolving into a Business System. Web-based business applications allow the participation of several actors to complex enterprise-wide (or even multi-enterprise) business processes and pose new challenges to the software designers and software architects. The design models have to address both navigational and process-based interactions; the software architecture has to provide the components to enact the process and has to define how these components interoperate with the other components of the Web applications. In this paper we show how, promoting an effective separation of concerns, a process modeling language and its enactment engine can be used in the modeling and implementation of process-aware Web applications.

Chapter 12

Bernard Espinasse, Aix-Marseilles University, France
Sébastien Fournier, Aix-Marseilles University, France
Fred Freitas, Universidade Federal de Pernambuco, Brazil
Shereen Albitar, Aix-Marseilles University, France
Rinaldo Lima, Universidade Federal de Pernambuco, Brazil

Due to Web size and diversity of information, relevant information gathering on the Web turns out to be a highly complex task. The main problem with most information retrieval approaches is neglecting pages' context, given their inner deficiency: search engines are based on keyword indexing, which cannot capture context. Considering restricted domains, taking into account contexts, with the use of domain ontology, may lead to more relevant and accurate information gathering. In the last years, we have conducted research with this hypothesis, and proposed an agent- and ontology-based restricted-domain cooperative information gathering approach accordingly, that can be instantiated in information gathering systems for specific domains, such as academia, tourism, etc. In this chapter, we present this approach, a generic software architecture, named AGATHE-2, which is a full-fledged scalable multi-agent system. Besides offering an in-depth treatment for these domains due to the use of domain ontology, this new version uses machine learning techniques over linguistic information in order to accelerate the knowledge acquisition necessary for the task of information extraction over the Web pages. AGATHE-2 is an agent and ontology-based system that collects and classifies relevant Web pages about a restricted domain, using the BWI (Boosted Wrapper Induction), a machine-learning algorithm, to perform adaptive information extraction..

Chapter 13

Flavius Frasincar, Erasmus University Rotterdam, The Netherlands
Jethro Borsje, Erasmus University Rotterdam, The Netherlands
Leonard Levering, Erasmus University Rotterdam, The Netherlands

This chapter describes Hermes, a framework for building personalized news services using Semantic Web technologies. The Hermes framework consists of four phases: classification, which categorizes news items with respect to a domain ontology, knowledge base updating, which keeps the knowledge base up-to-date based on the news information, news querying, which allows the user to search the news with concepts of interest, and results presentation, which shows the news results of the search process. Hermes is supported by a framework implementation, the Hermes News Portal, a tool that enables users to have a personalized access to news items. The Hermes framework and its associated implementation aim at advancing the state-of-the-art of semantic approaches for personalized news services by employing Semantic Web standards, exploiting and keeping up-to-date domain information, using advanced natural language processing techniques (e.g., ontology-based gazetteering, word sense disambiguation, etc.), and supporting time-based queries for expressing the desired news items.

Chapter 14

Ranjit Goswami, Indian Institute of Technology, Kharagpur, India
S. K. De, Indian Institute of Technology, Kharagpur, India
B. Datta, Indian Institute of Technology, Kharagpur, India

E-business adoption towards creating better stakeholders' values in any business organization should begin with corporate home pages, which is equivalent of the online identity of the physical firm. This paper, by taking two snapshot pictures of corporate homepages, one in 2005 and another in 2007, analyses e-business adoption levels in fifteen publicly-listed Indian firms of three different sizes and five sectors from four external stakeholders (Customers, Suppliers/Alliances, Shareholders and Society/Community) perspectives. We also measure overall e-business readiness levels from four stakeholders' perspectives in 2005 and 2007, and analyze the adoption as per Stages of Growth model. The measurement is based on presence of various categories of interactions, as commonly perceived, between the firm and respective stakeholder group.

Chapter 15

Ruiliang Yan, Indiana University Northwest, USA
John Wang, Indian Montclair State University, USA

With the explosive growth of online sales, multi-channel retailers are increasingly focused on finding ways of integrating the online channel with traditional retail stores. The need for the development of effective multi-channel strategies is strongly felt by the retailers. The present research normatively addresses this issue and using a game theoretic approach, derives optimal strategies that maximize profits under different competitive market structures. Managerial implications are discussed and probable paths of future research are identified.

Chapter 16

Zakaria Maamar, Zayed University, UAE
Philippe Thiran, University of Namur, Belgium
Jamal Bentahar, Concordia University, Canada

This chapter discusses the structure and management of communities of Web services from two perspectives. The first perspective, called coopetition, shows the simultaneous cooperative and competitive behaviors that Web services exhibit when they reside in the same community. These Web services offer similar functionalities, and hence are competitive, but they can also cooperate as they are sharing the same savoir-faire. The second perspective, called competition, shows the competition that occurs not between Web services but between communities of Web services. These communities are now associated with similar functionalities. To differentiate such communities, a competition model based on a set of metrics is discussed in this chapter as well.

Research into the determinants of online auction prices has tended to group them into buyer factors, seller factors and site factors. A case is presented which recounts how a $30 handbag was sold for $ 22,750 in an online auction shortly after a national sport event. Analysis of the case indicates that, in addition to the three groups of factors already identified, other factors can exert a considerable influence on the final auction price. A model is proposed which depicts five groups of factors impacting the final price: buyer factors, seller factors, site factors which are expanded to include timing of the auction, and site brand strength; product factors which include product features, brand strength, and brand extension/association; and promotion, which includes media publicity. While not all factors will impact on every auction, due consideration should be accorded each of them by both buyers and sellers.

This study was conducted to help understand the factors involved in building a successful website. A national survey of professionals in the areas of website design and development were contacted. Based on past published writings in the literature eight factors were identified as critical to the success of website functionality. The factors that are consistently posited in the literature are: 1) Entertainment and Visual Appeal, 2) Reliability, 3) Cost Reductions Attained, 4) Back-End Processes Enabled, 5) Personalization, 6) Information Quality, 7) User Empowerment, and 8) Privacy/Security. Study results are based on the analysis of 349 responses and provide support for the research hypotheses.

Chapter 19

In this paper, the authors adapt a value chain analysis framework used in the music industry and apply it to the television industry, in order to probe the television value creation and distribution mechanisms and examine how they were affected by technology. More specifically, they examine how viewers can effectively become producers by repositioning themselves in the value chain and the implications of such a shift. Their discussion takes place in the context of a case study, that of Current TV, in order to illustrate in practice the opportunities and implications for the content producers, the broadcasters, and the viewers themselves.

Chapter 20

There has been considerable Research into the usage of the Internet for Business-to-Business (B-to-B) marketing activities in recent years. The need to understand how and why B-to-B companies utilize the Internet is important for researchers and practitioners alike. This study combines Davis' model-the Technology Acceptance Model (TAM)- and Roger's Theory- the Innovation diffusion Theory (IDT) to understand the process of Internet adoption for marketing purposes. It makes a comprehensive review of information technology, information systems, and marketing literature to locate factors that predict Internet use for marketing purposes. Moreover, it extends both TAM and IDT to find out factors that affect relative advantage, ease of use and compatibility of using the Internet for B-to-B marketing activities. Using a sample of 123 UK companies utilize the Internet, we found a substantial positive effect of the proposed factors on the Internet usage for B-to-B marketing activities.

Preface

INTRODUCTION: WEB 2.0 TECHNOLOGIES FOR COMPETITIVE ADVANTAGES

Recently, the Web paradigm shifted from the business-centered to user-centered one. This paradigm shift has become known as "Web 2.0", coined by Tim O'Reilly in 2004 (O'Reilly, 2007). Since then, Web 2.0 has become a Web platform as a method to quickly reach a large pool of consumers. Web 2.0 has changed the nature of a user from a content consumer to a content generator. In contrast, the pre-Web 2.0 era is characterized by read-only websites and proprietary web applications. Web 2.0 brought about a variety of interactive community-based initiatives that leverage data, harness distributed intelligence, and utilize a rich multimedia (O'Reilly, 2005). These community-based initiatives include collaborative advertising (e.g., Google AdSense), P2P file sharing (e.g., BitTorrent), and user-generated content (e.g., Wikipedia), and social bookmarks (e.g., del.icio.us, Digg), to name a few. The contribution of Internet users to the content creation of the websites has been dubbed "user generated content" (UGC). While technological distinctions between Web1.0 and Web 2.0 are often not clear in some areas, the social and technological environment for positive user participation and interactivity epitomizes Web 2.0.

Many companies saw the potential benefits of Web 2.0 and began to capitalize on it. This extension of Web 2.0 to the industries is dubbed as "enterprise 2.0" (McAfee, 2006b). The user-generated contents are used to understand customers' preferences and to support instantaneous, custom-tailored customer experiences (e.g., Amazon's book reviews, Blockbuster's movie recommendations). The wisdom of crowds is another business area which utilizes the aggregation of information in groups (e.g., the sales forecast at HP through prediction markets and 'Connect and Develop' platform at Procter & Gamble). Crowdsourcing is also explored in business such as product developments to leverage the Web-based mass collaboration (e.g., Pepsi's marketing campaign in early 2007 which allowed consumers to design the look of a Pepsi can).

While no single economic theory can fully explain the sources of value creation of e-business (Amit & Zott, 2001), the potential of value creation in e-business may be derived from four interrelated dimensions: efficiency, complementarities, lock-in, and novelty. In a similar vein, values derived from Web 2.0 may be assessed from these four dimensions. Barney (1991) suggested that advantage-creating resources must have four conditions: value, rareness, inimitability, and non-substitutability. As Web 2.0 technologies are now widely available and easily substitutable, early adopters' advantage will be rapidly eroded. Small or large, firms that constantly create unique value of Web 2.0 through superior management skills, innovation, and business process reengineering are likely to enjoy sustainable competitive advantage.

The main purposes of this preface are to review literature on Web 2.0, to explore a typology of Web 2.0 technologies and to suggest future research directions. This preface proceeds as follows: Section

2 presents a literature review on Web 2.0. Section 3 develops a typology of Web 2.0 applications in businesses. Finally, Section 4 concludes with managerial implications and future research directions.

LITERATURE REVIEW

Principles of Web 2.0

Web 2.0 refers to the multitude of new ways that the Internet is used as a platform for developing and hosting software applications and developing and exchanging digital contents by the businesses and users. Web 2.0 has already had great impacts on the ways that people interact and businesses operate. Popular Web 2.0 applications include social networking sites, videos and images sharing, wikis, blogs, and social bookmarking. While many researchers have presented often confusing and conflicting opinions on the characteristics of Web 2.0, the following seven principles exemplify Web 2.0 (O'Reilly, 2005, 2006).

1) The Web as Platform

The Web serves as a platform which is loosely tied together by a set of protocols, open standards, and agreements for cooperation. Web 2.0 connects services to each other and harnesses the power of the users. Web as a platform can *leverage a massive variety of customer-self services and unique data via users' interaction and participation, expanding from the center to the edges of Web space and from the head to the long tail of the population.*

2) Harnessing Collective Intelligence

As users contribute new contents to the Web, the web of connections and associations among users grows stronger as a result of their collective activities. Collective intelligence is formed out of massive user participation and collaboration via the Web. Innovative Web business models such as social bookmarking and online encyclopedias take advantage of the *network effects:* the more people participate in generating and refining contents, the more useful they become to the users. Collective Intelligence *contributes to the market success* of Web 2.0 adopters.

3) Data as the Next "Intel Inside"

The competitive advantage of Web 2.0 that adopters inherit comes from superior data management. Successful e-commerce business models utilize some type of specialized data. Those data might be about products, events, customers, location, or maps. As evidenced by innovative e-commerce companies such as Google, eBay, and MapQuest, the control over exclusive databases can lead to market dominance and sustainable competitive advantage.

4) End of the Software Release Cycle

Software in the Web 2.0 era must be understood as a service, not as a product, which has to be operated daily with users as co-developers. Google's or Yahoo!'s expertise in daily operations is as important as expertise in their new product development. These companies will cease to exist if they cannot operate daily. The daily operations run on Web-based software, which is constantly being developed and upgraded. In the spirit of the open source development practices, *users must be treated as co-developers.* The perpetual beta is a Web 2.0 software release strategy in which the product is developed in the open, with new features slipstreamed in on a monthly, weekly, or even daily basis.

5) Lightweight Programming Models (LPMs)

A simple pragmatism in application development is touted. Google Mashup and RSS have become one of the most widely deployed web services because of its simplicity, while most other complex web services have yet to achieve wide adoption. The lightweight programming models (LPMs) intentionally maintain low barriers to *create a network of loosely coupled systems.* Other features of LPMs include *syndication of data and design for "hackability" and remixability.*

6) Software above the Level of a Single Device

Web 2.0 is no longer limited to the PC platform. Software can be accessed by PCs, servers, handhelds, and other mobile devices via various Web platforms. iTunes is an example of the software developed above the level of a single device. This application seamlessly reaches from the mobile device to a massive back-end server, with the PC acting as a local cache and control station (O'Reilly, 2005). TiVo is another good example of a multi-device application. It can seamlessly transfer shows from a server to PC, and then to mobile device.

7) Rich User Experiences

Success of the Web applications depends on a satisfied user experience. Rich user experiences of Web applications will come from PC-equivalent interfaces and interactivity. Google's AJAX is a technology which brings rich user experience by delivering full scale applications.

Web 2.0 Technologies

A recent McKinsey (2008) survey indicates that "a growing number of companies remain committed to capturing the collaborative benefits of Web 2.0." According to Forrester Research (2009), the investments in Social Media are expected to grow by more than 15 percent annually over the next five years despite the current recession. The following discusses major Web 2.0 technologies including social networking sites, blogs, folksonomies, and wikis.

1) Social Networking Sites

Social networking sites (SNS) use the Web-based technologies to allow individuals to form or maintain online social connections and share their skills, talents, knowledge, and/or preferences with other members. Boyd and Ellison define social networks as "web-based services that allow individuals to (1) construct a public or semi-public profile within a bounded system, (2) articulate a list of other users with whom they share a connection, and (3) view and traverse their list of connections and those made by others within the system" (2007 p. 211). While every social networking site requires its members to create a profile, each site has different purposes and targets certain user population. For example, Facebook focuses on students' friend networks, while LinkedIn focuses business networks, and MySpace focuses on special interest topics such as movies and hobbies. Recently, these SNS are expanding their business models and are competing with each other.

Firms began to use SNS in a variety of ways. Many firms leverage their own internal SNS to increase efficiency in the workplace (Middleton, 2008). SNS also facilitate recruiting and connecting potential contributors for distributed innovation processes (Cash et al., 2008). As hiring tools, SNS enable recruiters to view the manner in which candidates behave in an online setting and the type of people they socialize with (Henricks, 2009). Firms can also use social networks to engage in direct market research (Henricks, 2009) and to maintain a positive relationship with customers (Parise et al., 2008). LinkedIn's new service, Company Groups, allows all of a company's employees to subscribe to a single private Web forum where they can talk to one another, share ideas, and ask company-related questions.

2) Blogs

Blogs are online journals that are characterized by short entries and regular updates. Blogs are inherently flexible and can be used for a variety of purposes, ranging from personal opinions of the author to knowledge management initiatives and customer relation tools (Ives & Watlington, 2005). Personal or public websites are used to host blogs and the posted messages can be distributed to other sites or readers via RSS. One of the most useful features of blogs is the functionality that allows readers to comment on each entry (Kolbitsch & Maurer, 2006; Rosenbloom, 2004). This feature enables readers to engage in an open discussion for every post (Zerfass & Boelter, 2005). The collective comments and links on blogs form a clustered network termed the blogosphere (Schmidt, 2007). A variety of public blogging services are available to individuals and firms. For example, Twitter is the most popular social networking and microblogging service which thrives on constant change and updates. Tweets are text-based posts of up to 140 characters displayed on the author's profile page and delivered to the author's subscribers who are known as followers. Authors can restrict delivery to those in their circle of friends or allow open access.

Firms can use public or private blog sites to establish a communication channel between themselves and customers. The publication of a blog enables the firm to interact directly with consumers. Leading firms like Boeing, IBM, and GE are all early adopters of corporate blogs. While the blog can be used for public relations, it can also be used to promote new products and receive consumer feedback to products and services. For example, GE makes public announcements on their blog sites, asks their employees to contribute articles/opinions on various topics, and invites other employees and customers (http://ge.geglobalresearch.com/blog). Senior management also utilizes internal and external blogs to make announcements and seek inputs from various stakeholders.

Internal corporate blog sites offer a communication channel for individual employees to express themselves and share information with each other. Internal bog sites can be used as a knowledge repository to store expert knowledge and experiences and a connection point among employees.

3) Collectively Arranged Metadata: Folksonomies and Tags

Collectively arranged metadata is the result of user participation in classification of digital objects. Collectively arranged metadata become more useful as more users participate in the creation. The process of individually assigning metadata about objects such as URLs, images, videos, and texts is called folksonomy or tagging. The process of assigning tags or labels to websites is also often referred to as social bookmarking. The primary benefit is that users will find information more easily and accurately. Folksonomies have become part of social software applications such as bookmarking and photograph annotation, and have become an important alternative to search engines or other instruments for navigating the Web. An empirical analysis of the complex dynamics of tagging systems has shown that consensus around stable distributions and shared vocabularies emerges, even in the absence of a centrally controlled vocabulary (Halpin et al., 2007). Some of popular tagging sites include del.icio.us - a social bookmarking system and Flickr - a photo publishing / sharing site.

4) Wikis

Wikis are easy-to-use, browser-operated platforms that enable collaborative publication on the Internet (Ebersbach & Glaser, 2005). Wikis also embody a specific mindset towards the accumulation of knowledge. They allow many individual participants to contribute to an online document or discussion, usually via centrally managed content management systems. In contrast to blogs, the content of wikis tends to be more unbiased, as the author allows the readers to co-edit the original document. Through multiple revisions of a document by a group of co-authors, the content becomes more credible (Kolbitsch & Maurer, 2006). One of the most successful applications of wikis is Wikipedia, a popular online encyclopedia for which any user can contribute and edit contents. However, the open collaborative nature of public wikis raises concern about the validity of information contributed by the public (Priedhorksy et al., 2007). Therefore, a number of validity checks have been implemented to the contributions made to a given topic. Wikis are designed to make it easy to correct mistakes and track changes.

For businesses, wikis serve as an excellent technological platform for knowledge management and can facilitate innovations (Tapscott & Williams, 2007). Corporate wikis can also be used as a collective intelligence tool to tap the expertise of a large group rather than an individual. Firms have the opportunity to derive value from the mass collaboration of the public that participates in wikis. By allowing consumers to contribute ideas revolving around the firm's products, the firm can not only develop the core consumer base, but also create values for any consumer that can benefit from the collaborative works. Internal wikis can be applied to a number of possibilities such as collaborative knowledge management (Wagner, 2004). Wikis are also an excellent project management tool due to their ease of use and update capability. Wikis can be created at any time of the project and updated throughout the project life. Wikis are increasingly used internally by firms such as Adobe Systems, Amazon.com, Intel, and Microsoft.

Web 2.0 Business Applications

Web 2.0 brought about a wide range of changes with respect to their influence on e-business (Fleck et al., 2010). Businesses can take advantage of a variety of Web 2.0 technologies in order to dynamically cooperate with customers and partners to generate new design innovations (Brown, 2008). Web 2.0 has contributed to an unprecedented growth of information volume, new forms of networking, many new shopping alternatives and customer empowerment (Constantinides & Fountain, 2008). A recent survey by Stelzner (2009) on the status of Social Media marketing reports that 81% indicated that it has generated exposure for their business, 61% that it has increased their traffic/subscribers and opt-in lists, 56% that it has resulted in new business partnerships, and 45% that it reduced their overall marketing expenses. Another recent survey published by the Aberdeen Group (2009) found that for 70% of the participating companies (what they call Best-in-Class and Industry Average performers) the use of Social Media as marketing strategy increased the return on marketing investment, improved the likelihood of customers recommending their products, and improved the customer acquisition rate (Constantinides, 2010).

Both practitioners and researchers are converging on the usefulness of Web 2.0 for organizations. Firms such as Procter & Gamble, Amazon, and others have gained a significant experience and benefits from the applications of Web 2.0 technologies. (Bughin & Manyika, 2007; Koplowitz & Young, 2007; McAfee, 2006a). The way for firms to capture benefits from Web 2.0 technologies differs substantially from the way they obtained benefits from other information technology (IT) projects (Bughin & Manyika, 2007; Koplowitz & Young, 2007; McAfee, 2006a; De Hertogh & Viaene, 2010). To stay competitive in the Web 2.0 environment, firms must understand how to navigate and capitalize on the changing Internet terrain (Dinger & Grover, 2010). Regarding the adoption of Web 2.0 technologies, evidence suggests that pioneers in this field are the large corporations rather than the SMEs (Constantinides, 2010). A review of the literature indicates that previous research focused mainly on the importance of online communities for corporations (Du and Wagner, 2006) and the effects of these new technologies on business (Karger and Quan, 2005; Deshpande and Jadad, 2006; Boll, 2007).

A TYPOLOGY OF WEB 2.0 BUSINESS APPLICATIONS

So far, the previous studies on Web 2.0 have mostly focused on the roles of Web 2.0 and the application of the technologies. However, as web technologies advance, the need for developing a framework of Web 2.0 applications that reflect the unique characteristics and capabilities has increased. In order to meet our specific research purposes, our study adopts a typology approach to the framework development. Typologies are specific rather than general classifications, otherwise known as taxonomies (Bailey, 1994). Typologies are mostly generated through qualitative classification rather than quantitative or statistical analysis.

In exploring the typology, three Web 2.0 support types are identified: social networking, information sharing, and collaboration. These three types are chosen based on the selection criteria of research purposes, significance of dimensions, and parsimony of the typology. Social networking Web 2.0 facilitates and expands the networks of businesses and customers on the Internet. Information sharing Web 2.0 facilitates creating, storing, refining and sharing information between users. Collaboration Web 2.0 supports and enhances the collaborative works on the Internet. Web 2.0 users' interaction space is classified into three spaces: business-to-employee-to-employee space, business-to-employee-to-consumer space, and business-to-employee-to-business space.

Business-to-Employee-to-Employee Space

Business-to-employee-to-employee space refers to a space created exclusively for a business organization and its employees. Business-to-employee-to-employee space enables businesses to complement existing e-commerce applications by integrating multiple Web 2.0 platforms. This space is intranet-based secure space. Unlike typical business-to-employee e-commerce, which is mostly for one-way communications, this space encourages employee-to-employee networking, information sharing, and collaboration. It is expected that employee-to-employee information sharing and collaboration contributes to the increase of the productivity. Businesses play a central role in this space by consciously designing Web 2.0 tools, creating and managing contents, supporting the active employee-to-employee interaction and involvement, and analyzing employee generated contents. Businesses should establish a Web 2.0 portal as a gateway to all corporate Web 2.0 tools, and set the strategic direction for future Web 2.0 investments. Internal blogs are used to announce corporate news and events and corporate wikis are used to conduct group works. Innovative use of Web 2.0 for consumers and business partners may be pilot-studied in this space. Knowledge management, training, ERP, SCM, CRM, research and development, and human resources are areas where potential value can be derived from this internal Web 2.0.

Business-to-Employee-to-Consumer Space

Business-to-employee-to-consumer space is formed for a business organization, its employees and consumers. This space is an extension of business-to-consumer e-commerce and can be designed as public and/or private. Business-to-employee-to-consumer space enables businesses to interact dynamically with their consumers via multiple Web 2.0 platforms. Firms initiate this space, and employees are engaged in dialogues with consumers in this space. Three major interactions occur in this space: business to consumer, and employee to customer, and business-to-employee-to-consumer. Firms have to invest in the content creation and in the design/implementation of tools to encourage the active customer interaction and involvement. Firms can keep their consumers informed of their products or services via tools such as RSS, Twitter, and blogs. In this space, employees are asked to write blog articles on certain subjects and consumers are invited to comments on them. Public and/or corporate social networking sites are used to create connections with consumers. An increasing number of companies use videos and pictures to enhance public relations. In this space, consumers' product reviews are solicited, analyzed regularly, and integrated into improvement programs. In addition, consumers may participate in the co-creation of products and services as a crowdsourcees. Marketing, sales, product development, and logistics are some of the areas to benefit from this space. This space serves as a business intelligence system with little money invested.

Business-to-Employee-to-Business Space

Business-to-employee-to-business space is a space for a business organization, its employees, and business partners such as suppliers and distributors. This space is an extension of business-to-business e-commerce and designed as private. The multiple Web 2.0 information sharing and collaboration plat-

Table 1. Typology of Web 2.0 applications

	Networking	Information Sharing	Collaboration	Value Creation
Business-to-Employee-to Employee Space	Human resources management, Employee relationship management	Company news, Knowledge dissemination	New product development, Prediction market, Collaborative Knowledge creation, Project development	Empowerment, Employee participation, Employee loyalty, Knowledge management, Increased productivity
Business-to-Employee-to-Consumer Space	Customer relationship management, Public relations	Company news, Product review, Complaints, Market research, Promotion, Public relations	Product innovation, Collaborative filtering	Consumer loyalty, Open innovation, Increased consumer satisfaction Targeted marketing, Leveraging custom-tailored experiences, Capturing consumer data
Business-to-Employee-to-Business Space	Partner relationship management	Company news, Product review, Complaints, New product announcements	Product innovation, Collaborative product development, Application development, Supply chain management	Relationship building, Business intelligence, Knowledge management, Increased productivity, Community of practices
Enabling Technologies	Private corporate networking sites, Public social networking sites (e.g., Facebook. MySpace, LinkedIn)	Podcast, RSS, AJAX, Mashup, Widget, Blog, Twitter, Forum, Bulletin, Social networking, Social bookmarking, Photo sharing, Video sharing	Wikis, AJAX, Widget, Open source software, Blog, Twitter, Social networking, Social bookmarking, Application sharing, Collective intelligence, Crowdsourcing	

forms are expected to strengthen the relationship between business partners. Unlike business-to-business e-commerce, employees' active participation in this space is encouraged. This space is extranet-based secure space. While business-to-employee-to-consumer space emphasizes the social networks, this space emphasizes information sharing and collaboration. On this space, business partners share experiences, problems, and ideas about products and services. By engaging employees in this space, rapid and proactive measures are taken to problems and opportunities arising from the business partner side. Purchasing, manufacturing, inventory, product development, and warehousing are some of the areas to benefit from this space.

Table 1 shows the typology of the Web 2.0 applications. By combining the Web 2.0 user space and Web 2.0 support types, Web 2.0 applications can be divided into nine categories with the three user spaces on a vertical axis and the three Web 2.0 support types on the horizontal axis. Each interaction cell represents the specific user space and support type for specific business processes/activities. Some business processes/activities may belong to more than one cell, and the same Web 2.0 tools may be utilized for more than one business process/activity. The bottom row shows the Web applications that support each Web 2.0 support type. The last column shows the benefits/values derived from the specific user spaces.

CONCLUSION

Web 2.0 represents a paradigm shift in the Web applications. With its promise of a more rich, participatory and interactive user experience, Web 2.0 has quickly emerged as a powerful method for both user participations and interactions. Web 2.0 technologies become less complicated and less costly due to its wide diffusion and technological advances. As consumers are rapidly adopting Web 2.0 applications such as social networks sites, blogs, wikis, and social bookmarks, Web 2.0 has opened new opportunities for customer relationship management, communication, and collaboration for businesses. Many firms have opened up social networking sites and built blogs to post new product news and innovations along with solicitations for comments. To stay competitive, firms need to quickly adopt Web 2.0 and develop related business models and marketing tools.

The choice of technology and management practices is a managerial decision on the part of the company, as there is a tradeoff between technology and cost. Given the current technological advances and the pace of environmental change, firms must proactively embrace Web 2.0 technologies and redesign their core business processes in order to maximize their values. Web 2.0 technologies are advancing quickly. The number of Web 2.0 tools is ever increasing. To help practitioners to better apply the dynamically changing Web 2.0 technologies to their businesses, we presented a typology of Web 2.0 business applications. We classified Web 2.0 into three application types: networking, information sharing, and collaboration. We also classified user space into three categories: business-to-employee-to-employee space, business-to-employee-to-consumer space, and business-to-employee-to-business space.

Web 2.0 has driven a paradigm shift in the business operations. As such, there are numerous research opportunities in Web 2.0. In light of the significant impact on marketing and sales, research is needed to develop a unified framework to understand how consumer perceptions, privacy, risk, trust, and attitudes affect the adoption of Web 2.0. Investigating the relationships between the organizational characteristics and the choices of Web 2.0 will be of significant practical value. An in-depth understanding of what data/information they ask for/contribute and how they use them can be another interesting avenue of research. Many other interesting questions remain to be answered: How firms can influence the customer decision-making process by means of Web 2.0 tools, generate values, and engage consumers in the value generation process?; How large is actual performance and ROI of those social technologies? (Bughin, 2010); To what extent do user generated reviews replace other means of information gathering about products and services that have traditionally been used for decision making by buyers? (van Iwaarden et al., 2010); Who own user generated contents, how trustworthy are user generated contents and who are allowed to benefit from it? (Fleck et al., 2010).

In Lee
Western Illinois University, USA

REFERENCES

Aberdeen Group. (2009). The ROI of social media marketing: Why it pays to drive word of mouth, www.adberdeen.com

Amit, R., & Zott, C. (2001). Value creation in e-business. *Strategic Management Journal,* 22(6-7), 493-520.

Bailey, K.D. (1994). *Typologies and Taxonomies: An Introduction to Classification Techniques.* Los Angeles, Sage Publications Inc.

Barney, J. (1991). Firm resources and sustained competitive advantage. *Journal of Management,* 17(1),

Boll, S. (2007), MultiTube-Where Web 2.0 and multimedia could meet. *IEEE Multimedia,* 14(1), 9-13.

Boyd, D.M., & Ellison, N.B. (2007). Social network sites: Definition, history, and scholarship. *Journal of Computer-Mediated Communication, 13,* 210-230.

Brown, T. (2008). Design thinking. *Harvard Business Review,* 86, 84-92.

Bughin, J. (2010). The power laws of enterprise 2.0. *Encyclopedia of E-Business Development and Management in the Global Economy (Lee I. Ed. Business Science Reference),* IGI Global, 55-67.

Bughin, J., & Manyika, J. (2007). *How businesses are using Web 2.0: A McKinsey global survey.* Retrieved March 18, 2009, from http://www.mckinsey.de/downloads/publikation/mck_on_bt/2007/mobt_12_How_Businesses_are_Using-Web_2_0.pdf

Cash, J.J.I., Earl, M.J., & Morison, R. (2008). Teaming up to crack innovation & enterprise integration. *Harvard Business Review,* 86, 90-100.

Constantinides, E. (2010). Connecting small and medium enterprises to the new consumer: The Web 2.0 as marketing tool. *Global Perspectives on Small and Medium Enterprises and Strategic Information Systems: International Approaches (Pratyush Bharati et al Eds. Business Science Reference),* 1-21.

Constantinides, E., & Fountain, S. (2008). Web 2.0: Conceptual foundations and marketing issues. *Journal of Direct, Data and Digital Marketing Practice,* 9(3).

De Hertogh, S., & Viaene, S. (2010). Grounding principles for governing Web 2.0 investments. *Encyclopedia of E-Business Development and Management in the Global Economy,* (Lee, I. Ed. Business Science Reference), 1225-1234. Hershey, PA: IGI Global.

Deshpande, A., & Jadad, A. (2006). Web 2.0: Could it help move the health system into the 21st century? *The Journal of Men's Health & Gender,* 3(4), 332-336.

Dinger, M., & Grover, V. (2010). The Web 2.0 trend: Implications for the modern business. *Encyclopedia of E-Business Development and Management in the Global Economy,* (Lee, I. Ed. Business Science Reference), 1199-1207. Hershey, PA: IGI Global.

Du, H., & Wagner, C. (2006). Weblog success: Exploring the role of technology. *International Journal Human-Computer studies,* 64, 789-798.

Ebersbach, A., & Glaser, M. (2005). Wiki. *Informatik-Spektrum, 28*(2), 131-135.

Fleck, M., von Kaenel, A., & Meckel, M. (2010). Web 2.0 Concepts, Social Software and Business Models, *Encyclopedia of E-Business Development and Management in the Global Economy*, (*Lee, I. Ed. Business Science Reference*), IGI Global, 1215-1224.

Forrester Research. (2009). *Can enterprise Web 2.0 survive the recession?,* G. Oliver Young et al., January 6.

Halpin, H., Robu, V., & Shepherd, H. (2007). The complex dynamics of collaborative tagging, *Proceedings of the 16th International Conference on the World Wide Web (WWW'07)*, 211-220.Banff, Canada: ACM Press.

Henricks, M. (2009). RECRUITING 2.0. *Entrepreneur, 37*(2), 55-57.

Ives, B., & Watlington, A. (2005). Using blogs for personal KM and community building. *Knowledge Management Review, 8*(3), 12-15.

Karger, D., & Quan, D. (2004). What would it mean to blog on the semantic web? *Lecture Notes in Computer Science*, Springer Berlin Heidelberd

Kolbitsch, J., & Maurer, H. (2006). The transformation of the Web: How emerging communities shape the information we consume. *Journal of Universal Computer Science, 12*(2), 187-213.

Koplowitz, R., & Young, G. (2007). *Web 2.0 social computing dresses up for business* (Enterprise Web 2.0 for I&KM Professionals Series Rep. No. 1. Cambridge

McAfee, A. (2006a). Mastering the three worlds of information technology. *Harvard Business Review*, 84(11), 141-149.

McAfee, A. (2006b). Enterprise 2.0: The dawn of emergent collaboration. *MIT Sloan Management Review*, 47(3), 21-28.

McKinsey (2008). Building the Web 2.0 Enterprise: McKinsey Global Survey Results. *The McKinsey Quarterly*, July 2008.

Middleton, C. (2008). The social side of business. *Computer Weekly*, 26-27.

O'Reilly, T. (2005). *What is Web 2.0? Design patterns and business models for the next generation of software.* Retrieved March 1, 2009, from http://www.oreillynet.com/pub/a/oreilly/tim/news/2005/09/30/what-is-web-20.html

O'Reilly, T. (2006). *Web 2.0 compact definition: Trying again.* Retrieved June 20, 2009 from http://radar.oreilly.com/archives/2006/12/web-20-compact.html

O'Reilly, T. (2007). What is Web 2.0: Design patterns and business models for the next generation of software. *Communications & Strategies*, 65, 17–37.

Parise, S., Guinan, P.J., & Weinberg, B.D. (2008). The secrets of marketing in a Web 2.0 world. *Wall Street Journal - Eastern Edition,* 252(141), R4.

Priedhorksy, R., Chen, J., Lam, S.K., Panciera, K., Terveen, L., & Riedl, J. (2007). Creating, destroying, and restoring value in Wikipedia. Paper presented at the *Conference on Supporting Group Work*, Sanibel Island, Florida, USA.

Rosenbloom, A. (2004). The Blogosphere. *Communications of the ACM*, 47(12), 32-33.

Schmidt, J. (2007). Blogging Practices: An Analytical Framework. *Journal of Computer-Mediated Communication*, 12(4), 1409-1427.

Stelzner, M. (2009). Social Media Marketing Industry Report, How marketers are using social media to grow their business, www.Whitepapersource.com

Tapscott, D., & Williams, A.D. (2007). *Wikinomics: How Mass Collaboration Changes Everything*. New York: Penguin.

van Iwaarden, J., van der Wiele, T., Williams, R., & Eldridge, S. (2010). Web 2.0: The era of user generated content on web sites. *Encyclopedia of E-Business Development and Management in the Global Economy (Lee I. Ed. Business Science Reference)*, IGI Global, 1208-1214.

Wagner, C. (2004). Wiki: A technology for conversational knowledge management and group collaboration. *CAIS*, (13), 265-289.

Zerfass, A., & Boelter, D. (2005). *Die neuen Meinungsmacher Weblogs als Herausforderung für Kampagnen, Marketing, PR und Medien*. Graz: Nausner & Nausner.

Chapter 1

The Internet as a Complementary Resource for SMEs:
The Interaction Effect of Strategic Assets and the Internet

Frank Schlemmer
Queen's University of Belfast, Northern Ireland

Brian Webb
Queen's University of Belfast, Northern Ireland

ABSTRACT

It has been suggested that the Internet can be used to leverage a firm's strategic assets. However, empirical research on complementarity is still rare and frequently inconclusive, especially in the context of small and medium-sized enterprises. We propose a theoretical framework with the independent variables business resources, dynamic capabilities and IT assets. Survey data of 146 small firms suggest that the Internet is complementary with business resources and dynamic capabilities but not with IT assets. Therefore, the framework may enable small firm managers to create competitive advantage by identifying strategic assets that are complementary with the Internet. Furthermore, our research our research highlights the threat of an over-investment in IT assets.

INTRODUCTION

The resource-based view of the firm (RBV) has become the dominant framework in strategic management research. Its basic assumption is that firms can exploit strategic assets in order to create competitive advantage and thus above average performance. Another core assumption of the RBV is that strategic assets can be complementary. This means their value increases when they are combined. "Complementarity represents an enhancement of resource value, and arises when a resource produces greater returns in the presence

DOI: 10.4018/978-1-60960-132-4.ch001

Copyright © 2011, IGI Global. Copying or distributing in print or electronic forms without written permission of IGI Global is prohibited.

of another resource than it does alone" (Powell and Dent-Micallef 1997, p.379). Teece (1986, p.301) suggests that complementary assets are especially important for small companies because, in contrast to their larger competitors, they "are less likely to have the relevant specialized and cospecialized assets within their boundaries and so will either have to incur the expense of trying to build them, or of trying to develop coalitions with competitors/owners of the specialized assets". However, the complementarity of strategic assets is typically taken for granted but has hardly been empirically scrutinised, and non-anecdotal studies analyzing the interaction effects of strategic assets within a firm are frequently inconclusive (Powell and Dent-Micallef 1997; Song, Droge, Hanvanich and Calantone 2005; Zhu and Kraemer 2002)[1]. Therefore, Song et al. (p.271) conclude "clearly, resource combinations do not always lead to synergistic performance impact."

This paper seeks to analyze whether strategic assets are complementary with the Internet. It contributes to the still underdeveloped research on complementarity by introducing the Internet as a complementary resource. We believe that the Internet can be extremely important for SMEs, and that it can be used to "level the playing field". With this research we want to give managers of SMEs some information about which strategic assets can be leveraged by the Internet. Based on the literature review and survey data we suggest that researchers should examine complementarity at research settings in which a clear distinction of strategic assets is feasible. The remainder of the paper is organized as follows. In the next section the literature on the resource-based view and complementarity is briefly reviewed and the hypotheses are presented. After that, the research methodology is described; followed by the results. And then the discussion, the conclusions, the limitations, and some suggestions for future research are offered.

COMPLEMENTARITY IN RESOURCE-BASED RESEARCH

According to the resource-based view of the firm (RBV), firms perform differently because they differ in terms of the strategic assets they control (Barney 1991; Penrose 1959; Wernerfelt 1984). The founding idea of viewing a firm as a bundle of strategic assets was pioneered in 1959 by Penrose in her theory of the growth of the firm. This paper focuses especially on the complementarity of strategic assets. Under the resource-based view, a complementary interaction typically enhances the value for both (or all) strategic assets, although the causality may be ambiguous (Barney, 1991). Yet, researchers have only started to analyze complementarity of strategic assets. Empirical work in that area can be divided in the following two research streams.

One stream of research focuses on complementarity at strategic alliances or at mergers and acquisitions. For example, Rothaermel (2001) found that firms focusing on complementarity outperform those firms that limit their focus on the exploration of new technologies. Stuart (2000) suggested that the reputation of a larger firm is a complementary resource for a smaller firm. In particular, an alliance with a larger firm can help a smaller firm build confidence and attract customers, which then drives financial performance for both partners. Chung, Singh, and Lee (2000) found out that banks tend to ally with other banks that can complement their weaknesses. Krishnan, Miller, and Judge (1997) suggest that complementary top management teams (defined as differences in functional backgrounds between acquiring and acquired firm managers) drive post-acquisition firm performance. Similarly, Capron and Pistre (2002) suggested that acquirers only earn abnormal returns when their strategic assets are complementary with the target and not if they only receive strategic assets from the target.

The second research stream focuses on complementarity within a company. Powell and Dent-Micallef (1997) examined complementarity of IT assets with business resources and human resources and came to inconclusive results. Similarly, Song et al. (2005) found complementarity between marketing-related capabilities and technology-related capabilities only in high, but not in low technology turbulent environments. Zhu and Kraemer (2002) examined the relationship of dynamic capabilities and firm performance and came to inconsistent results for traditional versus technology companies. In contrast, Zhu (2004) empirically demonstrated complementarity between IT infrastructure and e-Commerce capability.

In conclusion, research on complementarity can be divided into two research streams. The first one is about complementarity of both, internal strategic assets (those that are controlled by a firm) and external strategic assets (those that are controlled by other firms), and the second research stream is about complementarity of internal strategic assets (assets within a single firm). Whereas research of the first category yielded promising results (for example Rothaermel 2001; Capron and Pistre 2002) the inconclusiveness of research of the second category suggests that further work in this area is necessary (Powell and Dent-Micallef 1997; Song et al. 2005). A possible explanation for researchers' problems in evaluating the complementarity of internal strategic assets is that this would require a clear distinction between the different strategic assets (the independent variables). In other words it would be necessary to "unbundle" the performance-driving strategic assets, which appears to be impossible, considering that every firm's bundle of strategic assets is unique (Penrose, 1959). We therefore suggest searching for research settings in which an evaluation of separated strategic assets is more feasible, because this frequently yielded valuable insights, for example at strategic alliances (Rothaermel 2001; Stuart, 2000) or at mergers and acquisitions (Krishnan et al. 1997; Carpon and Pistre, 2002).

A notable exception of the research focusing on internal strategic assets is the study of Zhu (2004) which suggested complementarity between IT infrastructure and e-Commerce capability. It differs from other studies on internal strategic assets by including the Internet in the analysis. Therefore, the role of the Internet is explored in more detail in this research, and it is suggested that the Internet itself can be a complementary resource. In our research we analyze if the Internet can be used to enhance the relationship between strategic assets and financial performance. In particular, we analyze if there is an interaction effect between a construct we labelled Internet performance and the relationship between strategic assets and financial performance.

HYPOTHESES

We believe that the Internet can be seen as a complementary resource. For example it may enable a firm to enhance its supplier relationships, while the pre-existing supplier relationships maximize the Internet's inherent information-sharing capabilities. The ubiquitous Internet would be a commodity resource, yet it may combine with supplier trust to an embedded, mutually reinforcing, advantage producing resource bundle (Barua et al. 2004; Powell and Dent-Micallef 1997). Zhu (2004) demonstrated complementarity of IT infrastructure and e-Commerce capability. However, this research focuses especially on the attributes of the Internet as opposed to Zhu's e-Commerce capability. In particular, we argue that the Internet can be seen as an external strategic asset that can be used by any competing firm (further discussed below), and use the Powell and Dent-Micallef (1997) framework for examining complementarity of business resources, dynamic capabilities, and IT assets with the Internet (see figure 1).

Powell and Dent-Micallef's (1997) model for analyzing the relationships of business resources, human resources, and IT resources with perfor-

Figure 1. Complementarity of the Internet

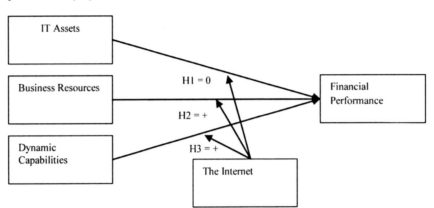

mance is based on the work of Walton (1989) and Keen (1993). It has been modified for this paper, in order to be applicable to small companies instead of larger retailers (details on the modifications are in the methodology section). Furthermore, Powell and Dent-Micallef used human resources as an independent variable. In this paper the newer concept of dynamic capabilities will be used instead. The influential paper about dynamic capabilities of Teece et al. (1997) was published in the same year and in the same journal as the Powell and Dent-Micallef (1997) paper (the Strategic Management Journal). Since then dynamic capabilities have become extremely influential in the strategic management and in the IS literature (see Newbert, 2007 for a review). Powell and Dent-Micallef's measures were especially designed for large enterprises with human resources departments and cross-sectional teams. These measures appeared to be inappropriate for small companies, which perform activities with less expertise, because they don't have functional specialists. In contrast to large firms, their capabilities are mainly determined by the owner manager and not by department managers (Verhees and Meulenberg 2004; Jones 2004). Compared to the construct of human resources (as used by Powell and Dent-Micallef), the dynamic capabilities framework appeared to be more appropriate for small firms, because it evaluates the skills

on an organizational rather than a department-level, and it puts a high emphasis on flexibility (in contrast to most human resources measures), and flexibility is a typical strength of small firms (Dean et al. 1998; Verdu-Jover et al. 2006). Furthermore, the theoretical concept of dynamic capabilities is deeply embedded in the resource-based view, whereas most theories on human resources appeared to have other theoretical groundings.

In contrast to Powell and Dent-Micallef's work the main focus of this paper is complementarity of the Internet rather than the direct relationships of strategic assets and performance. Definitions of resources, capabilities, and strategic assets are shown in table 1.[2] They are all taken out of the literature. A description of the independent variables (strategic assets) and the hypotheses follows.

IT Assets

IT assets can be defined as "the extent to which a firm is knowledgeable about and effectively utilizes IT to manage information within the firm." (Tippins and Sohi 2003, p.748). Tippins and Sohi's (2003) model was used for this study. It consists of IT knowledge, IT operations, and IT objects. *IT knowledge* is conceptualized as the extent to which a firm possesses a body of technical knowledge about objects such as computer based systems. *IT*

Table 1. Definitions

	Authors	Definition
Resources	Amit and Schoemaker, 1993	Stocks of available factors that are owned or controlled by the firm.
Dynamic capabilities	Teece et al., 1997	The firm's ability to integrate, build, and reconfigure internal and external strategic assets.
Strategic assets	Amit and Schoemaker, 1993	A set of difficult to trade and imitate, scarce, appropriable, and specialized resources and capabilities that bestow the firm's competitive advantage

operations are the extent to which a firm utilizes IT to manage market and customer information. *IT objects* represent computer-based hardware, software and support personnel.

Mata et al. (1995) examined IT assets as a possible source of competitive advantage. They focus especially on two underlying assertions of the RBV: (1) strategic assets differ between competing firms (resource heterogeneity) and (2) these differences are long lasting (resource immobility).[3] They conclude that those IT systems that are used by several competing firms can't be a source of competitive advantage because the assertion of resource heterogeneity is not met. Furthermore, IT could only be a source of sustainable competitive advantage if firms without it are at competitive disadvantage acquiring, developing, and using it (resource immobility). The majority of IT assets may be easily copied by competing firms, and subsequently research on the relationship of IT assets with financial performance is frequently inconclusive, and most studies fail to demonstrate IT's direct performance impacts (see Wade and Hulland 2004 for a review). However, Clemons and Row (1991) suggested that even if IT per se can't create sustainable competitive advantage, it can be used to leverage other strategic assets.

We argue that the same logic applies analogously to the Internet. The Internet does not fulfill any of the two criteria: It can be used by any company, and does therefore not fulfill the assertion of resource heterogeneity, and it is ubiquitous, and does therefore not fulfill the assertion of resource immobility. Thus, deploying the Internet can not be a source of competitive

advantage. However, it may be possible to deploy complementary strategic assets (like for example dynamic capabilities and business resources), and use the Internet for leveraging them (Fernandez and Nieto, 2006). In this section a set of hypotheses will be offered which suggest complementarity of strategic assets (business resources and dynamic capabilities) with the Internet. However, this does *not* apply to IT assets. We argue that both IT assets and the Internet don't fulfill the requirements of resource heterogeneity and resource immobility, and therefore can be used by any competing firm. Combining strategic assets that are ubiquitous can not be a source of competitive advantage. It is therefore suggested that:

Hypothesis 1: *IT assets are not complementary to the Internet. (Please note that this is the only hypothesis that does not imply complementarity.)*

Business Resources

In addition to the IT assets we also included a number of strategic assets that could be complementary with the Internet. Again we searched the literature for a construct that could be useful for our research. We decided to modify Powell and Dent-Micallef's (1997) set of variables because it appeared to be the most appropriate construct for our research. We define business resources as a set of strategic assets that can be used in combination with the Internet for creating competitive advantage. Business resources were divided into five sub-resources: relationships with customers and suppliers; external-driven e-business; benchmarking; strategic use of the Internet; and financial resources. We now consider each of these in turn.

Supplier relationships are becoming increasingly essential and strategic (Quayle, 2002, Cousins and Spekman 2003), and they play an important role for integrating processes via the Internet (Porter 2001). The capacity to craft and maintain trusting and economically viable supplier relationships, and then to leverage these relationships with the Internet, appears to require tacit, complex coordination and communication skills that competitors may find difficult to imitate (Hall 1993; Winter, 1987, Pollard and Diggles, 2006). This is especially important for SMEs that participate in supply chains. The marketplace now indicates competition between and among supply chains and industry-wide value chains. The use of the Internet is a necessity not just for remaining competitive, but for mere survival as well. An example of this is Walmart's mandate that top tier suppliers use radio frequency identification at the case and pallet levels. The use of the Internet, therefore, takes centre stage in the design of SMEs' strategic posture in the marketplace.[4]

Customer relationships are a critical success factor in e-business (Schroder and Madeja, 2004). Keller Johnson (2002) argued that companies that already excel in managing customer relationships seem best equipped to take advantage of the Internet's opportunities. Su, Chen and Sha (2007) highlight the importance of technology for managing customer knowledge in the digital economy, and Letaifa and Perrien (2007) suggest that successful implementation of e-CRM tools requires an innovative and customer-driven culture. Zhu et al. (2002) and Xu, Rohatgi and Duan (2007) found that a lack of trading partner readiness to adopt e-Business is a significant e-business adoption inhibitor. Within the RBV-logic, *supplier driven e-business* can be seen as a resource for companies that are deploying the Internet. Consumer readiness is an Internet adoption driver (Zhu et al. 2002), and like the above described supplier-driven

e-business *customer-driven e-business* can be seen as a resource for companies that are deploying the Internet. *Benchmarking* is important for small companies (Barclay, 2006; Chan, Bhargava, and Street 2006) and it is a widespread practice for the development of IT systems (Whitley 1992). Teo and Choo (2001) found out that using the Internet has a positive impact on the quality of competitive intelligence information. Furthermore they found a positive link between the quality of competitive intelligence and firm performance. Porter (2001) believed that strategies that integrate the Internet with traditional competitive advantages and ways for competing win in many industries. *Strategic use of the Internet* can lead to competitive advantage, because production and procurement can be more effective and buyers will value a combination of on- and off-line services. Small companies usually have fewer *financial resources* than larger ones, which often limits their opportunities (Caldeira and Ward 2003; Chow et al. 1997; Van Auken 2005).

We conclude that (in contrast to IT assets) business resources differ between competing firms and that these differences are long lasting. Therefore the assertions of resource heterogeneity and resource immobility are met. Thus business resources may be complementary with the Internet and it is suggested that:

Hypothesis 2: *Business resources are complementary to the Internet.*

Dynamic Capabilities

Dynamic capabilities have the following three characteristics (Teece et al. 1997): (1) coordination/integration, (2) learning, and (3) reconfiguration:

1. The effective and efficient internal **coordination or integration** of strategic assets determines a firm's performance. quality

performance is driven by special organizational routines for gathering and processing information, for linking customer experiences with engineering design choices and for coordinating factories and component suppliers (Garvin, 1988). Increasingly, competitive advantage also requires the integration of external activities and technologies, for example in the form of alliances and the virtual corporation. Internet technologies play an important role in the integration of collaborative activities and knowledge management in the product development process (Lee et al., 2006). Soo, Devinney and Midgley (2007) highlight the importance of integrating external knowledge into the organization.

2. **Learning** is the process by which repetition and experimentation enable tasks to be performed better and quicker. It also enables new production opportunities to be identified. In the context of the firm, learning has several key characteristics. It requires common codes of communication and coordinated search procedures. The organizational knowledge generated resides in new patterns of activity, in "routines", or a new logic of organization. Routines are patterns of interactions that represent successful solutions to particular problems. These patterns of interaction are resident in group behaviour; certain subroutines may be resident in individual behaviour. Collaborations and partnerships can be a source for new organizational learning, helping firms to recognize dysfunctional routines, and preventing strategic blind spots. Bierly and Daly (2007) highlight the importance of external learning sources and dynamic capabilities at SMEs. They suggest that learning from customers is a predictor of innovation speed, learning from suppliers is a predictor of operational efficiency, and learning from other industries is a predictor of superior process technolo-

gies. However, learning from competitors is negatively associated with the development of product technologies and basic research. Additionally, smaller firms learn more from suppliers and the scientific community than larger firms, while larger firms learn more from partnerships and consultants.

3. The capability to **reconfigure** and transform is itself a learned organizational skill. Fast changing markets require the ability to reconfigure the firm's asset structure, and to accomplish the necessary internal and external transformation (Amit and Schoemaker 1993). Change is costly and so firms must develop processes to minimize low pay-off change. The capability to change depends on the ability to scan the environment, to evaluate markets, and to quickly accomplish reconfiguration and transformation ahead of competition. This can be supported by decentralization and local autonomy (Teece et al., 1997).

Rindova and Kotha (2001) conducted case studies on Yahoo! and Excite and suggested that the fast changing virtual markets require dynamic capabilities. Ma and Loeh (2007) show that the dynamic capabilities approach can provide a holistic perspective to understand enterprise system driven process innovation at Chinese companies, which are facing a dynamic external environment. They believe that Chinese companies often lack the experience of enterprise system ERP-driven process innovation, however they could solve these challenges if they focus more on effectively building their dynamic capabilities. Wu, Lin and Hsu's (2007) survey of 100 Taiwan companies related to the electronic IT industries suggests that dynamic capabilities are related to innovative performance. They further found moderating effects between dynamic capabilities and relationship capital. Zhu and Kraemer (2002) found a positive relationship between e-commerce capability (a set of measures based on the dynamic capabilities framework) and some measures of financial performance. In his later work, Zhu (2004) then found complementarity between e-Commerce capability and IT-infrastructure and a positive relationship to financial performance. In this paper a more fine-grained approach is used by distinguishing between the Internet and dynamic capabilities. It is therefore suggested that:

Hypothesis 3: Dynamic capabilities are complementary to the Internet.

METHODOLOGY

The Sample

The Internet has the potential to affect entire organizations beyond the boundaries of their departments (Porter 2001). Therefore it may be difficult to identify respondents in large organizations because managers of large companies may have problems to completely understand the impact of the Internet. Even the CEOs of large companies may find it difficult to understand the usage of the Internet in different departments. In contrast, small firms tend to be structured more simply than larger enterprises (Hannan and Freeman 1984). We therefore focused on small firms because they are often governed by owner-managers, and the vast majority of strategic decisions is usually made by one person (Schlenker and Crocker 2003; Feindt, Jeffcoate and Chappel 2002), and they may be involved to a higher degree in the actual Internet usage of their organization.

In order to make sure that all companies of the sample use the Internet, only companies that have a website were examined. This study aimed at examining complementarity that is widely generalizable for small firms in different industries, and therefore does not focus on only one single industry. Thus it complies with the resource-based view, which is grounded in the assumption that

performance differences are mainly caused by firm and not by industry effects (Barney 1991; Hawawini et al. 2003). Yeoh and Roth (1999) argue that strategic assets are unique for each industry. In contrast, we believe that for example the quality of customer relationships, which has already been applied for retailers (Powell and Dent-Micallef 1997), or the capabilities of coordination, which has been used for manufacturing companies (Caloghirou et al., 2004), can be valuable for all profit-organizations. In the same vein, Chan et al. (2006) suggest that the key-organizational challenges of small firms are not influenced by the type of industry. Furthermore, the Internet blurs and shifts existing market boundaries (Amit and Zott 2001) and therefore the differentiation in different industries appears to be less important.

The "First Stop Shop" (an organization funded by the European Union and the Belfast City Council) database was used for this sample, because it was the only database that we are aware of that also included a large number of websites of local companies (Belfast/Northern Ireland/UK). We focused especially on local companies because this paper is part of a bigger research project, which also required interview data. Those companies that provided their Internet address in the database were selected and a paper-based questionnaire was sent to them. We only examined small firms with less than 250 employees.

The original database contained 7600 companies; 2377 of which provided their Internet address. After separating the non-profit organizations and companies with more than 250 employees, 1963 addresses remained. 50 companies were used for the pilot.[5] A questionnaire was sent to the remaining 1913 subjects. 44 questionnaires were returned because the companies have gone away or closed, and 11 answered that they would not complete the questionnaire because it was not appropriate for their organization. This led to a sample of 1858 companies. 228 questionnaires were returned therefore the response rate was 12.3 percent (228/1858). After eliminating the remaining non-profit organizations, non-independent and too large companies, 146 companies remained. The response rate of 12.3 percent is not great; however, it may be satisfactory considering the requirement of CEO's direct involvement (Lee, Lee, and Pennings 2001), and similar response rates are common in SME research (e.g. Voordeckers, Gils and Heuvel (2007) had 9.2% and Cooper, Upton and Seaman (2005) had 11.3%).

On average 14.4 percent of company revenues were generated online, 22.7 percent of products and services were procured on the Internet, and 22.9 staff were employed. Only four companies were pure dotcoms, creating 100 percent of their revenues online.

The Measures

All measures were taken out of the literature. The measures for IT assets are from Tippins and Sohi (2003), dynamic capabilities from Sher and Lee (2004), and business resources from Powell and Dent-Micallef (1997). However, some modifications were necessary because the original measures were actually designed for large rather than small companies. The following two variables were dropped: One of the set for business resources about cross sectional teams and one of the set for IT assets about a formal IT department. We believe that small companies typically neither have cross-sectional teams nor a formal MIS department, and they were therefore dropped. 10 new questions were included, the vast majority of them in the dynamic capabilities section according to the suggestions of Caloghirou et al. (2004). The reason for the modifications of the original dynamic capabilities construct was that they were used as a set of dependent variables and that section appeared therefore quite short. Details of the modifications can be obtained by the first author.

The financial performance measures consisted of revenues, sales growth and return on assets. Revenues indicate the company's success in its market transactions, sales growth indicates increasing customer acceptance, and return on assets indicates the management's effectiveness in deploying their assets. Managers were asked if their performance over the last three years was outstanding and if they have exceeded their competitors. We also measured Internet performance (a modification of Powell and Dent-Micallef's IT-performance), defined as the degree to which firm performance has been improved by the Internet. Similar to Zhuang and Lederer (2003), the Powell and Dent-Micallef measures were modified by replacing the impact of IT by the impact of the Internet. Therefore, managers were asked about the impact of the Internet on their productivity, competitive position, sales, profitability and overall performance. A 5-point Likert-type measurement scale was deployed.

By using Internet performance as a moderating variable we took Tanriverdi and Venkatraman's (2005) critique into consideration, which suggested that most studies on complementarity only capture potential complementarity, which is limited to a firm's potential for improving financial performance by synergy effects of strategic assets. Most researchers assume that the potential for the complementarity of strategic assets will automatically translate into actual complementarity and subsequently improved performance. In practice however, firms are not always able to exploit potential synergies of strategic assets. For example, many unsuccessful mergers, acquisitions, and joint ventures actually destroy value (Tanriverdi and Venkatraman, 2005). The interchangeable usage of potential complementarity and actual complementarity does not take into account that firms may not be able to create complementarity. In this study this problem was approached by asking the managers directly about the performance impacts of the complementary resource (the Internet).

It is broadly accepted that objective performance measures are highly correlated with the subjective ones, and can be used if subjective data is not available (Dess 1987; Dess and Robinson 1984; Powell and Dent-Micallef 1997). By using subjective measures it is assumed, given the senior executives involved, that respondents had sufficient perspective and information to assess their firm performance relative to competitors. Some researchers even prefer subjective measures, because it could reduce the problems of varying accounting conventions in areas such as inventory valuation, depreciation, and officers' salaries (Powell and Dent-Micallef 1997). We ideally would have preferred to triangulate the perceived performance with accounting-based data, but small firms are usually held privately and would not provide confidential information as a matter of policy. We have also been unable to find valid secondary data.[6] But even where secondary data is available, small firm organizational form (sole proprietorship, partnership, corporation, etc.) can cause artificial differences. Also, owner compensation can affect the performance of small, privately-held firms (Dess and Robinson 1984).

RESULTS

Strategic Assets and Financial Performance

Following Powell and Dent-Micallef (1997) the following linear regression model was estimated:

$$Z_Y = \alpha + \beta_B Z_B + \beta_D Z_D + \beta_I Z_I + \varepsilon$$

Z_Y stands for financial performance, α for the intercept B for the variable set of business resources, D for dynamic capabilities, and I for IT assets. β_X are the standardized partial regression coefficients for estimating performance Z_Y. We assume that β_B, and β_D will be positive and significant and β_I about zero (Powell and Dent-Micallef 1997). ε is the residual term that captures the net effect of all unspecified factors.

Table 2 shows the Cronbach alphas as a measure for scale reliability. The dependent variables were relatively high with 0.90 for financial performance and 0.95 for Internet performance. Cronbach alphas of all variables exceeded the recommended minimum of 0.6 (Bagozzi and Yi 1988), with a range from 0.66 to 0.88 for business resources (overall 0.74), 0.64 to 0.84 for dynamic capabilities (overall 0.87), and 0.61 to 0.92 for IT assets (overall 0.90). All variable sets correlate statistically significant with financial performance (see table 2).

Table 3 presents the results from multiple regression for the independent variable sets (business resources, dynamic capabilities, and IT assets), the control variable (firm size "ln emp" measured as the natural logarithm of employees), and for the dependent variables. The variables combined explain 22.4 percent of financial performance variance, and an estimated 20.2 percent of variance in population (using adjusted R^2, which estimates population effects based on sample degrees of freedom).

The significant intercorrelations between some of the sub-variables in the model led us to resolve multicollinearity problems by dropping variables (Gujarati 1995). Therefore, in addition to the analysis with the constructs, we dropped variables and the results after dropping variables were compared to the results of the construct. It was then checked if dropping variables changes the conclusions of the study. Variables were dropped if they had correlations higher than 0.5 with an included variable (benchmarking, integration, reconfiguration, IT knowledge, and IT objects). The regression analysis with the remaining variables yielded no significant results for the variables relationships, external driven e-Business, strategic Internet and IT operations. They were therefore also excluded. Thus, in this additional test, business resources were only measured by financial resources, dynamic capabilities by learning, and IT assets were excluded. The results of the regression analysis after dropping variables would not

Table 2. Descriptive statistics

N=146	Alpha	Mean	S.D.	Financial Performance
Relationships	0.69	3,97	0,67	0,07
Extern Driven e-Business	0.66	2,46	0,99	0,17*
Benchmarking	n.a.	2,72	1,22	0,14
Strategic Internet	0.88	3,43	1,14	0,04
Financial Resources	n.a.	3,00	1,11	0,51***
BUSINESS RESOURCES	0.74	3,12	0,65	0,31***
IT Knowledge	0.92	3,33	1,08	0,16*
IT Operations	0.87	2,55	0,93	0,25**
IT Objects	0.61	3,21	1,01	0,14
IT ASSETS	0.90	3,03	0,85	0,22**
Integration	0.64	3,69	0,59	0,27***
Learning	0.84	3,63	0,73	0,33***
Reconfiguration	0.68	3,38	0,63	0,38***
DYNAMIC CAPABILITIES	0.87	3,57	0,56	0,38***
Internet Performance	0.95	2,74	1,10	0,21**
Financial Performance	0.90	2,92	0,81	1

*** Correlation is significant at the 0.001 level (2-tailed).
** Correlation is significant at the 0.01 level (2-tailed).
* Correlation is significant at the 0.05 level (2-tailed).

Table 3. Regression results

	Internet Performance	Financial Performance
Business Resources	.424***	.190*
Dynamic Capabilities	-.059	.336***
IT Assets	.312***	-.114
ln emp	-.250***	.263***
R	.720***	.473***
R^2	.518	.224
Adjusted R^2	.505	.202

*** Correlation is significant at the 0.001 level (2-tailed).
** Correlation is significant at the 0.01 level (2-tailed).
* Correlation is significant at the 0.05 level (2-tailed).

have changed any of the conclusions. We therefore suggest that multicollinearity is not a problem.[7] Please note that this was just an additional test for ruling out multicollinearity issues; we used the constructs and not single variables for our regression. Furthermore, the assumptions of multiple regression (normality, linearity, homoscedasticity, and independence of residuals) were examined according to the suggestions of Pallant (2002) and the results suggest that the assumptions were not violated.

The results suggest a direct relationship of business resources, dynamic capabilities, and financial performance; and no affect of IT assets on financial performance. Furthermore, business resources and IT assets are related to Internet performance and dynamic capabilities are not.

Complementarity of the Internet and Strategic Assets

Powell and Dent-Micallef (1997) conducted a median split for analyzing complementarity of

Table 4. Internet-leading and Internet-lagging companies

	Internet-lagging (n=74)		Internet-leading (n=72)		Δ
	Mean	**Std. Deviation**	**Mean**	**Std. Deviation**	**T-Test**
Business Resources	2,8	0,5	3,4	0,6	6.49***
IT Assets	2,6	0,8	3,4	0,7	6.08***
Dynamic Capabilities	3,3	0,6	3,8	0,4	5,56***
Internet Performance	1,9	0,6	3,7	0,7	17,44***
Financial Performance	2,8	0,8	3,1	0,7	2,31*

*** T-Test is significant at the 0.001 level (2-tailed).
** T-Test is significant at the 0.01 level (2-tailed).
* T-Test is significant at the 0.05 level (2-tailed).

IT assets with other firm assets. They ranked all companies according to their IT assets and divided them into IT-leading and IT-lagging companies. We modified their methodology and ranked the companies according to their Internet performance. The median was at 2.8 with 74 companies that achieved 2.8 or less at Internet performance. They were labeled as Internet-lagging and 72 companies that achieved more than 2.8, and they were labeled as Internet-leading.

Powell and Dent-Micallef (1997) used three steps for examining complementarity. First, they compared the means of the independent variables (the strategic assets) between IT-leading and lagging companies. Second, they expected that the correlation between strategic assets and financial performance was stronger for IT-leading companies than for IT-lagging companies. And finally, they expected that financial performance would be better for IT-leading companies, compared to IT-lagging companies.

This study's results are shown in Table 4. As expected, the means of all independent variable sets (the strategic assets) are higher for the Internet-leading companies. Furthermore, financial performance of Internet-leading companies is better than financial performance of Internet-lagging performance. Independent samples t-test showed that the differences between Internet-leading and Internet lagging companies were statistically significant for all variables. Table 5

Table 5. Regression results

	Internet-lagging	Internet-leading
ln emp	.421***	.121
Business Resources	.012	.304*
Dynamic Capabilities	.206†	.460**
IT Assets	-.071	-.283*
R	.469**	.562***
R^2	.220	.316
Adjusted R^2	.175	.276

*** Correlation is significant at the 0.001 level (2-tailed).
** Correlation is significant at the 0.01 level (2-tailed).
* Correlation is significant at the 0.05 level (2-tailed).
† Correlation is significant at the 0.1 level (2-tailed).

suggests that the relationship between strategic assets and financial performance differs between Internet-leading and Internet-lagging companies. Whereas performance is strongly related to firm size (measured as the logarithm of employees) at Internet-lagging companies, strategic assets are strongly related to financial performance at Internet-leading companies. Furthermore, the explanatory power of the model is much higher for the Internet-leading companies (adjusted R^2= 0.276) than for Internet-lagging companies (adjusted R^2= 0.175).

Hypothesis 1 which suggested no complementarity of IT assets and the Internet was not supported. We would have expected that the relationship between IT assets and financial performance to be non-significant and about zero, like it is for the complete sample (including Internet-lagging and leading companies) and for Internet-lagging companies. Surprisingly, the relationship between IT assets and financial performance is *significantly negative* (-.283*) for Internet-leading companies. Possible reasons could be that Internet-leading companies over-invested in IT assets or that the investments have not paid off yet (further discussed in the next section). Hypotheses 2 and 3, which suggested complementarity between the Internet and business resources and the Internet and dynamic capabilities were supported.

In Appendix A we used hierarchical regression analysis for evaluating complementarity of the Inernet. The results strongly supported the findings above. However, we did not find a significant interaction effect between IT assets and the Internet. We believe that this could be a problem of the relatively small sample size.

DISCUSSION

This paper sought to examine complementarity between strategic assets and the Internet. The first step in the analysis was the examination of the main effect of strategic assets on financial performance. The analysis showed that business resources and dynamic capabilities are related to financial performance of small firms, and as expected IT assets didn't have a direct relationship to financial performance. In the next step complementarity of the Internet with strategic assets was examined. Therefore the sample was divided into Internet-leading and Internet-lagging companies, and the results suggest that the Internet is complementary with business resources and dynamic capabilities. Surprisingly the interaction effect between the Internet and IT assets was significantly negative at Internet-leading

companies. As already suggested in the literature review, research on the relationship between IT assets and financial performance is frequently inconclusive, however negative relationships are quite untypical (Wade and Hulland 2004), and according to the resource-based logic, we would have expected no direct relationship between IT assets and financial performance (Mata et al., 1995). However, these results are similar to the original study which suggested that financial performance of IT-leading companies was lower than financial performance of IT-lagging companies (Powell and Dent-Micallef 1997). We propose two possible reasons for this phenomenon: First, the Internet-leading companies may have over-invested in IT assets. Song et al. (2005, p.271) suggested "Clearly, resource combinations do not always lead to synergistic performance impact and managers should avoid over-investing in contexts where resources can not be leveraged through configuration, complementarity and/or integration. In terms of resource-based theory, synergistic rents cannot always be obtained". In the literature review we suggested that, according to the resource-based logic, IT assets and the Internet can not be complementary because they both don't fulfill the criteria of resource heterogeneity and resource immobility. However, this relatively sophisticated resource-based logic may be difficult to understand for managers of small firms, who perform some activities with less expertise because they do not have functional specialists, compared to larger companies (Verhees and Meulenberg 2004). Therefore, there appears to be a threat for managers of small firms to over-invest in IT assets. A second possible reason for the negative relationship could be that the IT investments haven't paid off yet. Performance was evaluated over the past three years. However, the Internet and e-Business are still relatively young areas, and many companies may be in an early stage, and it may take more time until the investments pay off.

CONCLUSIONS AND IMPLICATIONS

This research suggests that small firms can use the Internet to leverage their business resources and dynamic capabilities, but that IT-assets can not be leveraged by the Internet. The paper contributes to the still underdeveloped research on complementarity by discussing the role of the Internet as a complementary resource for small firms. Based on the literature review and the empirical findings we suggest that researchers should look out for research settings in which a clear distinction of the strategic assets, that are expected to be complementary, is feasible. We further believe that a strategic assets that neither meets the requirement of resource heterogeneity nor the requirement of resource immobility (like for example the Internet and IT assets) can still be used to leverage other strategic assets, if the other strategic assets fulfil those requirements. However, the improving price/performance ratios now emerging in the use of IT assets with the emergence of application service providers (ASPs) as outsourcing vendors and the use of web services, might be a promising development for SMEs. Therefore, it should be even more attractive to use the Internet and Internet-enabled technologies that enhance business resources and dynamic capabilities.[8]

This paper also has some managerial implications. In particular, the complementarity of the Internet with business resources and dynamic capabilities suggests that companies controlling those strategic assets should seriously consider conducting e-Business.

Furthermore, this research is a warning for mangers not to over-invest in strategic assets that have no rent-creating potential. If strategic assets are generic and mobile they can neither be a source of competitive advantage nor can they be complementary with other strategic assets that don't have rent-creating potential. In particular, this research poses the threat of an over-investment in IT assets to managers of small firms.[9]

LIMITATIONS AND FUTURE RESEARCH

Some limitations of this research should be noted. First, since the data was only collected from a single questionnaire, the results can be subject to common method bias. Second, the subjective measures for firm-performance have not been triangulated with secondary data. These limitations are a typical problem that arises when small firms are examined because they frequently don't publish their performance data as a matter of policy (Dess and Robinson 1984). However, we believe that analyzing small firms yields the advantage of relatively simple organizational structures. Furthermore, the owner manager of a small company may be more involved in the actual working processes and be better informed about the impact of the Internet on the processes than the CEO of a large company, who may never even have visited entire departments of his/her firm. In addition, the analysis represents only a snapshot in time, and there are no guarantees that the conditions under which the data is collected will remain the same, this applies especially to the fast changing virtual markets. And finally, we did not control for industry effects.

The limitations suggest avenues for additional research. Future research could aim at identifying research settings in which a separate evaluation of strategic assets is feasible, like for example at strategic alliances (Rothaermel 2001) and mergers and acquisitions (Carpon and Pistre 2002). Furthermore, little is known about complementarity of strategic assets that don't have rent-creating potential by themselves, like for example the Internet or generic IT assets. In addition, the findings could be supplemented by longitudinal research, for example using panel data or time series to examine the development of strategic assets and their complementarity. In addition, whereas the research on small companies yields some advantages, it would also be interesting to triangulate this study with research on large companies. And finally, our data does not yield an explanation for the negative interaction effect of the Internet on the relationship between IT assets and financial performance. We suggested that it could be due to the companies' early Internet adoption stage or due to over-investments in IT. However, these suggestions await empirical verification.

REFERENCES

Amit, R., & Schoemaker, P. J. H. (1993). Strategic assets and organizational rent. *Strategic Management Journal, 14*(1), 33–46. doi:10.1002/smj.4250140105

Amit, R., & Zott, C. (2001). Value creation in e-business. *Strategic Management Journal, 22*(6/7), 453–520.

Bagozzi, R. P., & Yi, Y. (1988). On the evaluation of structural equation models. *Journal of the Academy of Marketing Science, 16*(1), 74–94. doi:10.1007/BF02723327

Barclay, I. (2006). Benchmarking best practice in SMEs for growth. *International Journal of Technology Management, 33*(2-3), 234–254. doi:10.1504/IJTM.2006.008313

Barney, J. (1991). Firm resources and sustained competitive advantage. *Journal of Management, 17*(1), 99–120. doi:10.1177/014920639101700108

Barua, A., Konana, P., Whinston, A. B., & Yin, F. (2004). An empirical investigation of net-enabled business value. *Management Information Systems Quarterly, 28*(4), 585–620.

Bierly, P. E., & Daly, P. S. (2007). Sources of external organisational learning in small manufacturing firms. *International Journal of Technology Management, 38*(1/2), 45–68. doi:10.1504/IJTM.2007.012429

Caldeira, M. M., & Ward, J. M. (2003). Using resource-based theory to interpret the successful adoption and use of information systems and technology in manufacturing small and medium-sized enterprises. *European Journal of Information Systems, 12*(2), 127–141. doi:10.1057/palgrave.ejis.3000454

Caloghirou, Y., Protogerou, A., Spanos, Y., & Papagiannakis, L. (2004). Industry- versus firm-specific effects on performance: Contrasting SMEs and large-sized firms. *European Management Journal, 22*(2), 231–243. doi:10.1016/j.emj.2004.01.017

Capron, L., & Pistre, N. (2002). When do acquirers earn abnormal returns? *Strategic Management Journal, 23*(9), 781–794. doi:10.1002/smj.262

Chan, Y. E., Bhargava, N., & Street, C. T. (2006). Having arrived: The homogeneity of high-growth small firms. *Journal of Small Business Management, 44*(3), 426–440. doi:10.1111/j.1540-627X.2006.00180.x

Chow, C. W., Haddad, K. M., & Williamson, J. E. (1997). Applying the Balanced Scorecard to small companies. *Strategic Finance, 79*(2), 21–28.

Chung, S., Singh, H., & Lee, K. (2000). Complementarity, status similarity and social capital as drivers of alliance formation. *Strategic Management Journal, 21*(1), 1–22. doi:10.1002/(SICI)1097-0266(200001)21:1<1::AID-SMJ63>3.0.CO;2-P

Clemons, E. K., & Row, M. C. (1991). Sustaining IT advantage: The role of structural differences. *Management Information Systems Quarterly, 15*(3), 275–292. doi:10.2307/249639

Cooper, M. J., Upton, N., & Seaman, S. (2005). Customer relationship management: A comparative ananlysis of family and nonfamily business practices. *Journal of Small Business Management, 43*(3), 242–257. doi:10.1111/j.1540-627X.2005.00136.x

Cousins, P. D., & Spekman, R. (2003). Strategic supply and the management of inter- and intra-organisational relationships. *Journal of Purchasing and Supply Management*, *9*, 19–29. doi:10.1016/S1478-4092(02)00036-5

Dean, T. J., Brown, R. L., & Bamford, C. E. (1998). Differences in large and small firm responses to environmental context: Strategic implications from a comparative analysis of business formations. *Strategic Management Journal*, *19*(8), 709–728. doi:10.1002/(SICI)1097-0266(199808)19:8<709::AID-SMJ966>3.0.CO;2-9

Dess, G. G. (1987). Consensus on strategy formulation and organizational performance: Competitors in a fragmented industry. *Strategic Management Journal*, *8*(3), 259–277. doi:10.1002/smj.4250080305

Dess, G. G., & Davis, P. S. (1984). Porter's (1980) generic strategies as determinants of strategic group membership and organizational performance. *Academy of Management Journal*, *27*(3), 467–488. doi:10.2307/256040

Feindt, S., Jeffcoate, J., & Chappel, C. (2002). Identifying success factors for rapid growth in SME e-Commerce. *Small Business Economics*, *19*(1), 51–62. doi:10.1023/A:1016165825476

Fernandez, Z., & Nieto, A. J. (2006). The internet: competitive strategy and boundaries of the firm. *International Journal of Technology Management*, *35*(1-4), 182–195. doi:10.1504/IJTM.2006.009234

Garvin, D. (1988). *Managing Quality*. New York: Free Press.

Gujarati, D. N. (1995). *Basic Econometrics* (3rd ed.). New York: McGraw-Hill.

Hall, R. (1993). A framework linking intangible resources and capabilities to sustainable competitive advantage. *Strategic Management Journal*, *14*(8), 607–618. doi:10.1002/smj.4250140804

Hannan, M. T., & Freeman, J. H. (1984). Structural inertia and organizational change. *American Journal of Sociology*, *89*, 149–164.

Hawawini, G., Subramanian, V., & Verdin, P. (2003). Is performance driven by industry- or firm-specific factors? New look at the old evidence. *Strategic Management Journal*, *24*(1), 1–16. doi:10.1002/smj.278

Jones, C. (2004). An alternative view of small firm adoption. *Journal of Small Business and Enterprise Development*, *11*(3), 362–370. doi:10.1108/14626000410551618

Keen, P. (1993). Information technology and the management difference: A fusion map. *IBM Systems Journal*, *32*(1), 17–39. doi:10.1147/sj.321.0017

Keller Johnson, L. (2002). New views on digital CRM. *MIT Sloan Management Review*, *44*(1), 10–27.

Krishnan, H. A., Miller, A., & Judge, W. Q. (1997). Diversification and top management complementarity: Is performance improved by merging similar or dissimilar teams? *Strategic Management Journal*, *18*(5), 361–374. doi:10.1002/(SICI)1097-0266(199705)18:5<361::AID-SMJ866>3.0.CO;2-L

Lee, C., Lee, K., & Pennings, J. M. (2001). Internal capabilities, external networks, and performance: A study on technology-based ventures. *Strategic Management Journal*, *22*(6/7), 615–640. doi:10.1002/smj.181

Lee, H. J., Ahn, H. J., Kim, J. W., & Park, S. J. (2006). Capturing ans reusing knowledge in engineering change management: A case of automobile development. *Information Systems Frontiers*, *8*(5), 375–395. doi:10.1007/s10796-006-9009-0

Letaifa, S., & Perrien, J. (2007). The impact of E-CRM on organisational and individual bahavior: The effect of the remuneration and reward system. *International Journal of E-Business Research*, (3): 2–13.

Ma, X., & Loeh, H. (2007). Closing the gap: How should Chinese companies build the capabilities to implement ERP-driven process innovation? *International Journal of Technology Management*, *39*(3/4), 380–395. doi:10.1504/IJTM.2007.013501

Mata, F. J., Fuerst, W. L., & Barney, J. B. (1995). Information Technology and sustained competitive advantage: A resource-based analysis. *Management Information Systems Quarterly*, *19*(4), 487–495. doi:10.2307/249630

Newbert, S. L. (2007). Empirical research on the resource-based view of the firm: An assessment and suggestions for future research. *Strategic Management Journal*, *28*(2), 121–146. doi:10.1002/smj.573

Pallant, J. (2002). *SPSS Survival manual*. Buckingham: Open University Press.

Penrose, E. (1959). *The Theory of Growth of the Firm*. London: Basil Blackwell.

Pollard, C., & Diggles, A. (2006). The role of trust in Business-to-Business e-Commerce collaberation in a unique environment in Australia. *International Journal of E-Business Research*, *2*(3), 71–88.

Porter, M. E. (2001). Strategy and the internet. *Harvard Business Review*, (March): 63–78.

Powell, T. C., & Dent-Micallef, A. (1997). Information technology as competitive advantage: The role of human, business and technology resources. *Strategic Management Journal*, *18*(5), 375–405. doi:10.1002/(SICI)1097-0266(199705)18:5<375::AID-SMJ876>3.0.CO;2-7

Quayle, M. (2002). Supplier development and supply chain management in small and medium size enterprises. *International Journal of Technology Management*, *23*(1-3), 172–188. doi:10.1504/IJTM.2002.003004

Rindova, V. P., & Kotha, S. (2001). Continuous "morphing": competing through dynamic capabilities form and function. *Academy of Management Journal*, *44*(6), 1263–1280. doi:10.2307/3069400

Rothaermel, F. T. (2001). Incumbent's advantage through exploiting complementary assets via interfirm cooperation. *Strategic Management Journal*, *22*(6/7), 687–699. doi:10.1002/smj.180

Schlenker, L., & Crocker, N. (2003). Building an e-Business scenario for small businesses: The IBM SME Gateway project. *Qualitative Market Research: An International Journal*, *6*(1), 7–17. doi:10.1108/13522750310457339

Schroder, D., & Madeja, N. (2004). Is customer relationship management a success factor in electronic commerce? *Journal of Electronic Commerce Research*, *5*(1), 38–52.

Sher, P. J., & Lee, V. C. (2004). Information technology as a facilitator for enhancing dynamic capabilities through knowledge management. *Information & Management*, *41*(8), 933–945. doi:10.1016/j.im.2003.06.004

Song, M., Droge, C., Hanvanich, S., & Calantone, R. (2005). Marketing and technology resource complementarity: An analysis of their interaction effect in two environmental contexts. *Strategic Management Journal*, *26*(3), 259–276. doi:10.1002/smj.450

Soo, C. W., Devinney, T. M., & Midgley, D. F. (2007). External knowledge acquisition, creativity and learning in organisational problem solving. *International Journal of Technology Management*, *38*(1/2), 137–159. doi:10.1504/ IJTM.2007.012433

Stuart, T. E. (2000). Interorganizational alliances and the performance of firms: A study of growth and innovation rates in a high-technology industry. *Strategic Management Journal*, *21*(8), 791–811. doi:10.1002/1097-0266(200008)21:8<791::AID-SMJ121>3.0.CO;2-K

Su, C., Chen, Y., & Sha, D. Y. (2007). Managing product and customer knowledge in innovative new product development. *International Journal of Technology Management*, *39*(1/2), 105–130. doi:10.1504/IJTM.2007.013443

Tanriverdi, H., & Venkatraman, N. (2005). Knowledge relatedness and the performance of multi-business firms. *Strategic Management Journal*, *26*(1), 97–119. doi:10.1002/smj.435

Teece, D. J. (1986). Profiting from technological innovation: Implications for integration, collaboration, licensing and public policy. *Research Policy*, *15*(6), 285–305. doi:10.1016/0048-7333(86)90027-2

Teece, D. J., Pisano, G., & Shuen, A. (1997). Dynamic capabilities and strategic management. *Strategic Management Journal*, *18*(7), 509–533. doi:10.1002/ (SICI)1097-0266(199708)18:7<509::AID-SMJ882>3.0.CO;2-Z

Teo, T. S. H., & Choo, W. Y. (2001). Assessing the impact of using the internet for competitive intelligence. *Information & Management*, *39*(1), 67–83. doi:10.1016/S0378-7206(01)00080-5

Tippins, M. J., & Sohi, R. (2003). IT competency and firm performance: Is organizational learning the missing link? *Strategic Management Journal*, *24*(8), 745–761. doi:10.1002/smj.337

Van Auken, H. (2005). Differences in the usage of bootstrap financing among technology-based versus nontechnology-based firms. *Journal of Small Business Management*, *43*(1), 93–103. doi:10.1111/j.1540-627X.2004.00127.x

Verdu-Jover, A., Llorens-Montes, F. J., & Garcia-Morales, V. J. (2006). Environment-flexibility coalignment and performance: An analysis in large versus small firms. *Journal of Small Business Management*, *44*(3), 334–349. doi:10.1111/ j.1540-627X.2006.00175.x

Verhees, F. J. H. M., & Meulenberg, M. T. G. (2004). Market orientation, innovativeness, product innovation, and performance in small firms. *Journal of Small Business Management*, *42*(2), 134–154. doi:10.1111/j.1540-627X.2004.00102.x

Voordeckers, W., & Gils, A. V. and Heuvel, Jeron Van Den. (2007). Board Composition in small and medium-sized family firms. *Journal of Small Business Management*, *45*(1), 137–157. doi:10.1111/j.1540-627X.2007.00204.x

Wade, M., & Hulland, J. (2004). Review: The resource-based view and information systems research: Review, extension, and suggestions for future research. *Management Information Systems Quarterly*, *28*(1), 107–142.

Walton, R. (1989). *Up and Running: Integrating Information Technology and the Organization*. Boston, MA: Harvard Business School Press.

Wernerfelt, B. (1984). A resource-based view of the firm. *Strategic Management Journal*, *5*(2), 171–180. doi:10.1002/smj.4250050207

Whitley, R. (1992). *The Customer Driven Company*. Reading, MA: Addison-Wesley.

Winter, S. G. (1987). Knowledge and competence as strategic assets. In Teece, D. (Ed.), *The Competitive Challenge* (pp. 159–184). Berkeley, CA: Center for Research in Management.

Wu, S., Lin, L., & Hsu, M. (2007). Intellectual capital, dynamic capabilities and innovative performance of organisations. *International Journal of Technology Management, 39*(3/4), 279–296. doi:10.1504/IJTM.2007.013496

Xu, M., Rohatgi, R., & Duan, Y. (2007). E-Business adoption in SMEs: Some preliminary findings from electronic components industry. *International Journal of E-Business Research, 3*(1), 74–90.

Yeoh, P., & Roth, K. (1999). An empirical analysis of sustained advantage in the U.S. pharmaceutical industry: Impact of firm resources and capabilities. *Strategic Management Journal, 20*(7), 637–653. doi:10.1002/(SICI)1097-0266(199907)20:7<637::AID-SMJ42>3.0.CO;2-Z

Zhu, K. (2004). The complementarity of information technology infrastructure and e-Commerce capability: A resource-based assessment of their business value. *Journal of Management Information Systems, 21*(1), 167–202.

Zhu, K., & Kraemer, K. L. (2002). e-commerce metrics for Net-enhanced organizations: Assessing the value of e-commerce to firm-performance in the manufacturing sector. *Information Systems Research, 13*(3), 275–295. doi:10.1287/isre.13.3.275.82

Zhu, K., Kraemer, K. L., & Xu, S. (2002) A cross-country study of electronic business adoption using the Technology-Organization-Environment Framework, *Twenty Third International Conference on Information Systems,* 2002, 337-348.

Zhuang, Y., & Lederer, A. L. (2003). An instrument for measuring the business benefits of e-commerce retailing. *International Journal of Electronic Commerce, 7*(3), 65–99.

ENDNOTES

[1] There were also studies that examined complementarity at strategic alliances (Rothaermel, 2001; Stuart, 2000) and mergers and acquisitions (Krishnan, Miller and Judge, 1997; Capron and Pistre, 2002. However, it may be difficult to apply the findings to this research setting (further discussed in the literature review).

[2] For a more detailed discussion of different definitions see McGrath et al. (1995) and Caldeira and Ward (2003).

[3] This is based on Barney's (1991) earlier work, which suggests that resources can only lead to competitive advantage if they are valuable, rare, imperfectly imitable, and not strategically substitutable by other resources (the VRIN-attributes).

[4] The authors thank an anonymous reviewer for this thoughtful comment.

[5] Following the suggestions of Dillman (1978) we used a pilot test to identify possible problems with the questionnaire. Therefore managers were asked to complete the questionnaire and then they were asked to identify problems, like for example unclear questions or questions that were difficult to answer. They were furthermore asked, if they believe that any important variables are missing. However, only some minor points were raised, and subsequently the result of the pilot was only some minor changes in the wording of a few questions.

[6] The following two attempts were made for triangulating the survey's performance data. First, this research was part of a bigger research project, which also required the collection of qualitative data. We therefore visited 17 companies and conducted interviews with the owner managers, and they were asked about their performance. 9 of the 17 managers refused to offer any performance information as a matter of firm

policy, and only 8 managers gave us some performance information. It is of course not possible to triangulate this information with the survey data and to get statistically significant results with a sample size of 8. However, the qualitative analysis of the interviews and of the information that was offered on the firms' websites strongly supported the survey data. Second, a literature review of the leading strategic management journals was conducted to identify suitable databases for this research. Databases that were frequently used in strategic management research were, for example, Dun & Bradstreet, Standard and Poor and Kompass. In addition, we went to the local city council, which provides some basic performance data. However, this data did not appear to be valid. First, we would have expected to find relatively "irregular" numbers with a variety of digits, like for example £123,456. However, we only found numbers that were suspiciously regular, which typically started with the digit 1 and ended with zeros, like for example £100,000. Therefore, the data ap-

peared to be very imprecise. In addition, the performance data appeared to be completely outdated. For example, we couldn't find data on young companies at all, and when we triangulated the data from secondary sources, with current information from our survey, the interviews and the companies' websites the data appeared too old. Similar problems are frequently reported in small firm research, because they frequently don't publish and performance data (Dess and Robinson, 1984).

[7] The VIF values for the construct were between 1.1 and 1.7. The VIF values for the single variables (after dropping variables) were between 1.1 and 1.4 which also suggests that multicollinearity is not a problem.

[8] The authors thank an anonymous reviewer for this thoughtful comment.

[9] Please note that we don't suggest that managers should stop all investments in IT, we just suggest that managers should monitor their IT budgets carefully and try to increase value for money in terms of IT spending.

APPENDIX A

Business Resources	strongly disagree ←			strongly agree →	
1. We have very open, trusting relationships with our suppliers	1	2	3	4	5
2. We have very open, trusting relationships with our customers	1	2	3	4	5
3. Our suppliers strongly urged us to adopt e-business	1	2	3	4	5
4. Our customers strongly urged us to adopt e-business	1	2	3	4	5
5. We actively research the best e-business practices of our competitors	1	2	3	4	5
6. The internet has a strategic meaning for our company	1	2	3	4	5
7. We use the internet actively to reach strategic aims	1	2	3	4	5
8. Overall, we have enough financial resources	1	2	3	4	5

IT Assets	strongly disagree ←			strongly agree →	
IT knowledge					
9. Overall, our technical support staff is knowledgeable, when it comes to computer-based systems	1	2	3	4	5
10. Our firm possesses a high degree of computer-based technical expertise	1	2	3	4	5
11. We are very knowledgeable about new computer-based innovations	1	2	3	4	5
12. We have the knowledge to develop and maintain computer-based communication links with our customers	1	2	3	4	5
13. Our firm is skilled at collecting and analyzing market information about our customers via computer-based systems	1	2	3	4	5
14. We routinely utilize computer-based systems to access market information from outside databases	1	2	3	4	5
15. We have set procedures for collecting customer information from online sources	1	2	3	4	5
16. We use computer-based systems to analyze customer and market information	1	2	3	4	5
17. We utilize decision-support systems frequently when it comes to managing customer information	1	2	3	4	5
18. We rely on computer-based systems to acquire, store, and process information about our customers	1	2	3	4	5
19. Every year we budget a significant amount of funds for new information technology hardware and software	1	2	3	4	5
20. Our firm creates customized software applications when the need arises	1	2	3	4	5
21. Our firm's members are linked by a computer network	1	2	3	4	5

Dynamic Capabilities	strongly disagree ←				strongly agree →
Integration					
22. Overall, our management has expertise to conduct the major strategic moves	1	2	3	4	5
23. Overall, our employees have very good communication skills	1	2	3	4	5
24. Our management has expertise in coordinating internal processes and operations	1	2	3	4	5
25. The feedback of our customers helps us to improve our products and/or services	1	2	3	4	5
26. The internet has changed our processes significantly	1	2	3	4	5
27. We have had problems integrating e-business applications in previous IT (reversed)	1	2	3	4	5
Learning					
28. Overall, our company acquires new knowledge effectively	1	2	3	4	5
29. Overall, our company reacts quickly to market changes	1	2	3	4	5
30. Overall, our company accumulates knowledge effectively	1	2	3	4	5
31. Our company recognizes how customers can benefit from new technologies	1	2	3	4	5
Reconfiguration					
32. We continuously adapt to customers shifting needs.	1	2	3	4	5
33. We quickly respond to competitive strategic moves	1	2	3	4	5
34. We easily get rid of assets that have no more value	1	2	3	4	5

Performance	strongly disagree ←				strongly agree →
Internet Performance					
35. The internet has dramatically increased our productivity	1	2	3	4	5
36. The internet has improved our competitive position	1	2	3	4	5
37. The internet has dramatically increased our sales	1	2	3	4	5
38. The internet has dramatically increased our profitability	1	2	3	4	5
39. The internet has dramatically improved our overall performance	1	2	3	4	5
Financial Performance					
40. Over the past 3 years, our revenues have been outstanding	1	2	3	4	5
41. Over the past 3 years, our revenues have exceeded our competitors	1	2	3	4	5
42. Over the past 3 years, our sales growth has been outstanding	1	2	3	4	5
43. Over the past 3 years, our sales growth has exceeded our competitors	1	2	3	4	5
44. Over the past three years, our return on assets has been outstanding	1	2	3	4	5
45. Over the past 3 years, our return on assets has exceeded our competitors	1	2	3	4	5

General Questions		
46. How many full-time employees work in your company?		
47. What percentage of your revenue is created by e-commerce?		
48. What percentage of the goods and services you buy are ordered via the internet?		
49. What is your SIC-code?		
50. Are you a for-profit or a non-profit organization?	For-profit	Non-profit
51. Is your company independent? (This means you have e.g. no parent company or you are not part of a franchising system).	Yes	No

APPENDIX B

There are two dominant methods for analysing the interaction effect (in this case, the complementarity of strategic assets with the Internet) in social sciences (Jaccard, Turrisi and Wan, 1990). First, in the dichotomising is based on median splits. This procedure was used by Powell and Dent-Micallef (1997), when they ranked all companies according to their IT assets and divided them into IT-leading and IT-lagging companies. We used this approach in the paper. Second, complementarity can be evaluated by deploying hierarchical regression. This approach was chosen by Zhu (2004) and Song et al. (2005). In the appendix we also deploy this approach for demonstrating the validity of our method.

The term without the interaction effect is compared with a term including the interaction effect (the interaction effect is the statistical term for complementarity). At term 1:

$$Z_Y = \alpha + \beta_I Z_I + \beta_B Z_B + \beta_D Z_D + \beta_{IP} Z_{IP} + \varepsilon$$

Z_Y stands again for financial performance, α for the intercept I for the variable set of IT assets, B for business resources, and D for dynamic capabilities. We now also introduce IP for Internet performance. β_X are the standardized partial regression coefficients for estimating performance Z_Y. ε is the residual term that captures the net effect of all unspecified factors. Term 1 is supplemented by an interaction effect (term 2):

Whereas term 2a is the interaction effect of IT and the Internet:

$$Z_Y = \alpha + \beta_B Z_B + \beta_D Z_D + \beta_I Z_I + \beta_{IT} Z_{IP} + \beta_{ITIP} Z_{IT*} Z_{IP} + \varepsilon$$

And term 2b is the interaction effect of business resources and the Internet:

$$Z_Y = \alpha + \beta_B Z_B + \beta_D Z_D + \beta_I Z_I + \beta_{BRIP} Z_{BR*} Z_{IP} + \varepsilon$$

And term 2c is the interaction effect of dynamic capabilities and the Internet:

$$Z_Y = \alpha + \beta_B Z_B + \beta_D Z_D + \beta_I Z_I + \beta_{DCIP} Z_{DC*} Z_{IP} + \varepsilon$$

ITIP stands for the interaction effect of IT assets and the Internet, BRIP for the interaction of business resources and the Internet and DCIP for dynamic capabilities and the Internet (Jaccard et al., 1990; Zhu, 2004; Song et al., 2005). If an interaction effect is present, then the R^2 of term 2 must be higher than at term 1. A hierarchical regression analysis was conducted. The first level were the control variable (ln emp), the second level was term 1, and the third level term 2. The results are shown in the table below.

As described above, complementarity can be demonstrated by comparing the term without the interaction effect (term 1) with the term with the interaction effect (term 2). A higher adjusted R^2 of term 2

	Adjusted R^2		
Term 1	0.203***		
Term 2	Term 2a	Term 2b	Term 2c
	IT-IP	BR-IP	DC-IT
	0.201***	0.226***	0.225***

would indicate complementarity. As expected adjusted R^2 was lower at term 2a, because the Internet is not complementary with IT assets. However, terms 2b and 2c were higher than term 1, which suggests that the Internet is complementary with business resources and dynamic capabilities. This suggests that hypotheses 2 and 3 were also supported with this method.

The dichotomising approach showed a negative interaction effect of the Internet on the relationship between IT assets and financial performance. At the hierarchical regression analysis the interaction effect was not statistically significant. We believe that this could be due to the relatively small sample size (n=146). The hierarchical regression approach appears to be difficult at small sample sizes because it requires the consideration of additional constructs; which would require larger samples (Jaccard, Turrisi, and Wan, 1990).

This work was previously published in International Journal of E-Business Research (IJEBR), edited by In Lee, pp. 1-24, copyright 2009 by IGI Publishing (an imprint of IGI Global).

Chapter 2
Organizational Slack and Information Technology Innovation Adoption in SMEs

Jaume Franquesa
Kent State University, USA

Alan Brandyberry
Kent State University, USA

ABSTRACT

This study explores the relevant dimensions of organizational slack in small and medium enterprises (SMEs) and investigates their impact on adoption of different types of information technology (IT) innovations. Using recent data from a representative sample of 2,296 U.S. SMEs, we find that the slack-innovation relationships previously described in larger firms do not hold well for SMEs. Our results show potential slack (measured as access to external credit) to be a strong predictor of technology adoption in SMEs. By contrast, available slack appeared not to be a significant factor in SME innovation adoption. Moreover, the direction of the effects of potential slack was moderated by the capital-intensity of the innovation. In particular, e-commerce, which required lesser financial resources for SME adoption, was found to be pursued by those with lesser potential slack. We argue that, in some cases, innovation adoption may represent a form of "bricolage" by resource constrained SMEs.

INTRODUCTION

Organizations must strike a balance between stability and innovation –i.e., between exploitation of their current business model and processes and exploration and adoption of alternative solutions (March, 1991). Accordingly, understanding the processes by which organizations adjust their propensity to innovate, as well as the condi-

tions most likely to foster innovation in a firm, is an important endeavor that has motivated a large innovation literature in management (see Daniel et al., 2004; Damanpour, 1991; Drazin & Schoonhoven, 1996; and Fiol, 1996, for reviews of this literature).

Prior theory predicting innovation rates highlights the role of organizational slack as an important condition that facilitates exploration and, thus, contributes to a firm's innovativeness (Cyert & March, 1963; Greeve, 2003). On the

DOI: 10.4018/978-1-60960-132-4.ch002

Copyright © 2011, IGI Global. Copying or distributing in print or electronic forms without written permission of IGI Global is prohibited.

other hand, slack is also argued to be related to inefficiencies in the use of resources (Bourgeois, 1981) and to less disciplined investment (Jensen, 1986), which may be detrimental to innovation. Given these competing arguments, Nohria and Gulati (1996) argued and found support for an inverted U-shaped relationship between slack and innovation. Their findings suggest that greater levels of slack increase the rate of adoption of technical and administrative innovations, but only up to a point. Beyond this point, excess slack appears to be counterproductive and results in reduced innovation rates.

Subsequent research by Geiger and Cashen (2002) extended Nohria & Gulati's (1996) work by examining the shape of the slack-innovation relationship for different dimensions of slack. Prior studies had distinguished among available slack, recoverable slack, and potential slack (Bourgeois & Singh, 1983; Bromiley, 1991). Geiger & Cashen (2002) found available and recoverable slack to have a curvilinear, inverted-U shaped, relationship with innovation, while potential slack had a linear positive relationship to innovation.

An important limitation of the prior organizational slack literature is that it has overwhelmingly focused on large, publicly traded firms[1]. With regard to the slack-innovation relationship, the technology adoption literature in information systems (IS) has shown a greater interest in small and medium enterprises (SMEs) and, thus, can be seen as filling some of the void left by the broader literature. In particular, a number of studies have explored the role of financial resources as an antecedent to SME adoption of specific IT innovations (e.g., Iacovou, Benbasat, & Dexter, 1995; Kuan & Chau, 2001; Mirchandani & Motwani, 2001). To date, however, this literature can offer only limited and tentative insights regarding slack-innovation relationships: First, most prior SME technology adoption studies undertake a superficial treatment (at best) of financial resource considerations as one of the many factors in the typical technology adoption model. Also, the definition and mea-

surement of financial resource variables differs widely across studies and often deviates form the concept of financial slack. Moreover, in the few cases where financial drivers are operationalized as financial slack (i.e., Grandon & Pearson, 2004; Wang & Cheung, 2004), the reliance on relatively small samples and the focus on a single technological innovation limits the generalizability of findings and prohibits a comparative analysis of the characteristics of the innovation as a possible moderator of the slack-adoption relationship. In sum, there is limited evidence regarding the role of organizational slack on SME innovation adoption. Also, no prior study has investigated how different dimensions of organizational slack may influence innovation in SMEs. Furthermore, the presence of curvilinear relationships between slack and SME adoption has yet to be explored.

Given the importance of SMEs to the U.S. economy (e.g., Bharati & Choudhury, 2006; Small Business Administration, 2006), as well as the expectation that prior findings using samples of large firms will not generalize to the SME context (Dandridge, 1979; Thong, 1999), the lack of in-depth study of the role of organizational slack in the context of small firms represents an important gap in our understanding of slack-innovation relationships. SMEs represent 99.7 percent of all U.S. employers, are responsible for about half of the private sector jobs, and generate about half of the private GDP (Small Business Administration, 2006). Moreover, SMEs play a critical role in industrial innovation and renewal of economic sectors (Baumol, 2002; Small Business Administration, 2003) and, thus, are major contributors to the competitiveness of the economy. At the same time, there are fundamental differences between SMEs and large businesses (Dandridge, 1979; Welsh & White, 1981; Thong, 1999) which suggest that both the levels and types of slack, as well as the mechanisms by which slack influences innovation, may vary across contexts. In particular, SMEs are usually severely resource constrained (Oviatt & NcDougall, 1994; Baker & Nelson, 2005). Also, they exhibit high mortality rates that result from their double *liabilities of smallness and newness* (Freeman, Caroll, & Hannan, 1983), which affects their willingness to take risks.

The purpose of the present research is to extend prior slack-innovation studies (i.e., Geiger & Cashen, 2002; Nohria & Gulati, 1996) by developing the concept and dimensions of organizational slack in the context of SMEs, and investigating how different types of slack relate to innovation adoption in these firms. Our study is based on a representative sample of 2,296 U.S. SMEs. In an attempt to explore how characteristics of the innovation itself may moderate the slack-innovation relationship, we study SMEs' adoption of two specific information technologies that represent opposite minimum requirements in terms of their capital intensity and complexity: e-commerce and computerized core process technologies.

The remainder of the paper is organized as follows. First we define and discuss organizational innovation and present previous research on IT innovation adoption in SMEs. We then discuss organizational slack as well as the multidimensional aspects of slack and its relationship with innovation. This is followed by a discussion of how the distinctive environment of SMEs is likely to affect both the relevant dimensions of organizational slack and their relationship to innovation adoption. This section concludes with our hypotheses. Next, data and measures are presented followed by methods and results. Finally, we offer a discussion of results, directions for future research, and limitations of the present study.

ORGANIZATIONAL INNOVATION

Organizational innovation research has been approached from many diverse perspectives and has been extensively researched over the past half century. If Rogers (1962) did not originate the field, his work is often given credit for popularizing it. Several distinctions can be made concerning the different research streams in this area. One important distinction (Damanpour & Wischnevsky, 2006) is whether the focus is on internal innovation concerning the development of innovations within an organization (e.g., Cormican & O'Sullivan, 2004; Dougherty & Hardy, 1996; Kivimaki & Lansisalmi, 2000; Wong & Chin, 2007) or on the adoption of innovations within an organization regardless of the origin of the innovation (e.g., Brancheau & Wetherbe, 1990; Compeau, Higgins, & Huff, 1999; Davis, 1989; Kishore & McLean, 2007; Moch & Morse, 1977; Moore & Benbasat, 1991; Venkatesh, Morris, Davis, & Davis, 2003; Yang, Lee, & Lee, 2007). In this research we focus on the later form of adoption of external innovations.

In this context, it is important to define specifically what is meant by an innovation. Although competing definitions exist, most research has adopted a definition similar to that of Damanpour (1991, p. 556), "innovation is defined as adoption of an internally generated or purchased device, system, policy, program, process, product, or service that is new to the adopting organization." This definition provides sufficient specificity as to what is considered an innovation and removes the problem of subjectively determining the level of innovativeness represented by the technology. It simply requires that the technology be new to the adopting organization. Many other distinctions may be made to differentiate between types of innovations. Innovations may be considered technical or administrative, radical or incremental, and product or process. These and other distinctions are discussed in detail in the extant literature (Damanpour, Szabat, & Evan, 1989; Damanpour, 1991; Swanson, 1994).

The two specific innovations chosen for this research are *electronic commerce* adoption and what we will term *computerized core* adoption. E-commerce adoption is present when a firm engages in any level of sales of products and/or services via the Internet. In the general population such adoption can vary immensely in scope. As we discuss more fully in our measurement section, the type of adoption we expect our sample to engage in is supplementary rather than primary. Computerized core adoption relates to the adoption of computer systems that contribute directly to the firm's primary business activity. As explained below, the differences represented in these two innovations will allow us to explore the extent to which slack-innovation relationships may be moderated by characteristics of the innovation itself.

IT INNOVATION ADOPTION IN SMES

A substantial amount of research in the information systems literature has been devoted to studying predictors of adoption of new information technologies by SMEs (see Premkumar, 2003; Parker & Castleman, 2007 for reviews of some of this literature). However, organizational slack has received relatively little attention in this research.

The Technology Acceptance Model (TAM) introduced by Davis (1989) is adapted in a number of SME technology adoption studies (e.g., Igbaria et al., 1997; Riemenschneider, Harrison, & Mykytyn, 2003). Others (e.g., Riemenschneider & McKinney, 2001) employ the Theory of Planned Behavior (TPB) which Ajzen (1991) adapted from the Theory of Reasoned Action (Fishbein & Ajzen, 1975). Both of these approaches focus on the perceived characteristics of the particular technology as the key driver of adoption. Hence, this has been termed the "technological" perspective. Others extend this perspective to include characteristics of the organization and of its external environment as further predictors of adoption. This is commonly referred to as the Technology-Organization-Environment (TOE) framework (Tornatzky and Fleischer, 1990; Premkumar and Roberts, 1999; Kuan and Chau, 2001).

The TOE model has been applied to SME adoption of specific technological innovations. Iacovou et al. (1995) developed a model of adoption of Electronic Data Interchange (EDI) by SMEs that proposes *perceived benefits* of the innovation (i.e., the technological context), *organizational readiness* (organizational context) and *external pressure* (environmental context) as the key determinants of the decision to adopt. Of particular interest to the present study is the organizational readiness factor, which is composed of two sub-dimensions: the extent to which the SME possesses the (i) technological resources and (ii) the financial resources necessary to adopt e-commerce. The later may be understood as (or including) financial slack. Iacovou et al.'s (1995) model was subsequently tested by Chwelos et al. (2001) using a sample of 268 Canadian SMEs, and by Kuan & Chau (2001) using a sample of 575 small trading companies based in Hong Kong. In both cases, the financial dimension of organizational readiness (measured as financial resources in one case and as perceived financial costs of adoption in the other) was found to be an important contributor to the intent to adopt EDI.

The TOE model has also been applied to adoption of internet-based technologies in SMEs. Interestingly, financial considerations have been found to play a lesser role in this context[2]. Mehrtens, Cragg, & Mills (2001) developed a model of internet adoption by SMEs through a multi-case inductive study. Their final model was very similar to Iacovou et al.'s (1995), except that it did not include financial resources as a subcomponent of the organizational readiness factor. Subsequently, survey-based studies of internet adoption in SMEs using the TOE framework have often de-emphasized financial resources (e.g., Premkumar & Roberts, 1999; Beckinsale, Levy & Powell, 2006). Others have included this element but have found it not to be an influencing factor. In particular, in the specific context of e-commerce adoption in SMEs, both Mirchandani & Motwani (2001) and Grandon & Pearson (2004) found financial considerations not to be an important factor.

Overall, most prior SME innovation adoption studies have either paid no attention to financial resources or have modeled this as a sub-dimension of the broader construct of organizational readiness. Most important, when included, the financial component of readiness has been operationalized as something other than financial slack. For example, Chwelos et al. (2001) used a 3-item scale that includes number of employees and annual sales, so that their measure is actually capturing firm size. Similarly, others have used profit levels to proxy for financial resources (e.g., Dembla, Palvia, & Brooks, 2007). Still others have focused on the perceived financial cost of the innovation as opposed to financial resources (Kuan & Chau, 2001; Mirchandani & Motwani, 2001).

The studies by Grandon & Pearson (2004) and by Wang & Cheung (2004) provide exceptions to this and, as such, represent important precedents to the present study. Grandon & Pearson's (2004) single-item measure of financial resources was constructed by asking respondents if they thought they had the "Financial resources to adopt e-commerce" (p. 213). This appears to capture financial slack conditional on perceived costs of adoption (we also suspect this measure is rather capturing *available slack*, as defined below). As noted above, this measure was found not to be an important factor in e-commerce adoption. Wang & Cheung (2004) used a 4-item measure that captures overall (perceived) financial slack of the firm. In a sample of 137 small travel agencies in Taiwan, this measure was found to be negatively related to the intention to adopt e-commerce, but positively related to the degree of e-commerce implementation. The authors argued that the availability of funds facilitates implementation; however, greater levels of financial slack may result from better past performance and, thus, may be related to resistance to change in the first place.

In sum, taken as a whole, the prior IT innovation adoption literature provides some, but limited, insight into the role of slack on innovation adoption in SMEs. We believe that further understanding of SME adoption issues will benefit from greater attention to, as well as more precise definition of, financial slack.

ORGANIZATIONAL SLACK

Organizational slack is defined as resources in excess of what an organization requires to maintain its standard operations (Cyert & March, 1963). Cyert and March (1963) argued that slack is crucial to resolving political conflicts aligned with goal expectations of different coalitions within organizations. Slack has long been held to have a positive effect on various aspects of performance within a firm. Bourgeois (1981) discusses four often cited functions of slack within an organization: as motivation for organizational participants to remain; as a source of resolving conflicts; as workflow buffers; and to aid in the facilitation of creative or innovative processes within the organization. With regard to the latter, it has been suggested that slack allows (i) the exploration of new ideas before they are actually needed, (ii) the purchase of innovations, (iii) the funding of innovation implementation costs, and (iv) the absorption of failure (Rosner, 1968).

Types of Organizational Slack

Singh (1986) suggested two different types of organizational slack. *Absorbed* (or recoverable) slack relates to administrative resources beyond what is necessary for the normal operation of the organization –i.e., excessive organizational overhead. This creates a "cushion" of resources that can be made available either by eliminating costs that are not required or by deploying underutilized staff, facilities, or other assets. By contrast, *unabsorbed* slack is resources that are liquid and uncommitted in the organization, like cash reserves (Singh, 1986). Singh empirically demonstrated that absorbed and unabsorbed slack have different effects on risk-taking behavior. Subsequently, Bourgeois and Singh (1983) suggested further dividing slack into three categories: available (unabsorbed) slack, recoverable (absorbed) slack, and potential slack. *Potential* slack refers to additional financial resources that may be obtained through credit, as indicated by the firm's unused borrowing capacity. Bourgeois and Singh's (1983) typology has been broadly adopted in the prior literature, which has focused on the study of large organizations (Geiger & Cashen, 2002; Greeve, 2003; Herold, Jayaraman, & Narayanaswamy, 2006).

Slack and Innovation

Slack has been argued to allow and, to some extent, promote expenditures associated with creativity and experimentation which, in turn, leads to greater organizational performance (Cyert & March, 1963; Bourgeois, 1981). Other researchers, however, argue that slack promotes wasteful use of resources and, thus, is negatively associated with firm innovation and performance (Simon, 1957; Jensen & Meckling, 1976). Hence, the divergence of opinion appears to revolve around how wisely slack resources will be allocated (Herold et al., 2006; Nohria & Gulati, 1996). Consistent with this ambiguity, a meta-analysis of organizational innovation research by Damanpour (1991) produced only a weak positive relationship between slack and innovation.

Bourgeois (1981) synthesized the competing arguments regarding the role of slack by hypothesizing "that the correlation between 'success' and slack is positive, up to a point, then negative; in other words, the relationship is curvilinear" (p. 31). There are several reasons why excessive slack may lead to inefficiencies: If the number of investment projects increases with additional slack and if projects are funded rationally, it makes sense that the most promising will be funded first and additional projects may have diminishing returns (Herold et al., 2006; Nohria & Gulati, 1996). Moreover, additional slack may lead to less disciplined management of projects in terms of their selection, support, and termination (Herold et al., 2006; Nohria & Gulati, 1996).

Nohria and Gulati (1996) extended this argument to the relationship of organizational slack and innovation (arguably a subset of Bourgeois' (1981) concept of "success"). The authors argued that the relationship between slack and innovation (measured either as total economic impact or as total number of innovations) would be inverse U-shaped, and provided empirical support for this hypothesized relationship. Subsequently, Geiger and Cashen (2002) extended Nohria and Gulati (1996) by taking a multidimensional view of slack. Specifically, they studied possible curvilinear relationships of available, recoverable, and potential slack with innovation. There are few other empirical studies utilizing a multidimensional view of slack and considering non-linear relationships but, apart from Geiger and Cashen (2002), no other study of this sort investigates slack-innovation effects[3].

ORGANIZATIONAL SLACK IN SMES

As discussed above, the previous slack-innovation literature has focused almost exclusively on the study of larger publicly-traded firms. Only a few studies in the I.S. literature have investigated the role of organizational slack on innovation adoption by SMEs (Grandon & Pearson, 2004; Wang & Cheung, 2004). Moreover, no prior study has pursued a multidimensional view of slack within the SME context. Also, no study has explored the existence of a curvilinear relationship of slack (or dimensions of slack) with innovation in SMEs. Consequently, there is no evidence that current arguments and findings in the slack-innovation literature will hold for small firms. Indeed, there is little reason to expect that they would (Dandridge, 1979; Welsh & White, 1981).

There are fundamental differences between SMEs (defined as firms with fewer than 500 employees) and large firms. The U.S. Small Business Administration reports that the average SME has one location and 10 employees, while the average large employer had 61 locations and 3,300 employees in 2003 (SBA, 2006). Similarly, population estimates with the database used in the present study suggest that more than 80 percent of U.S. SMEs employed fewer than 10 workers in 2004, and more than 70 percent had annual sales of less than $500,000 in 2003 (Mach & Wolken, 2006). Also 59 percent of SMEs were less than 15 years old, and 94 percent were owner-managed (Mach & Wolken, 2006). In short, the large majority of SMEs are very small, rather young, owner-managed firms. There are several important implications that derive from this. First, SMEs are severely undercapitalized (Holtz-Eakin, Joulfaian, & Rosen, 1994a, 1994b) and resource constrained (Baker & Nelson, 2005; George, 2005; Oviatt & NcDougall, 1994). Second, they tend to have highly centralized structures, where the owner-manager (or owner-manager group) makes most of the firm's decisions. Third, they are afflicted by rather volatile performance (Ekanem, 2005) and high mortality rates that result from their double *liabilities of smallness and newness* (Freeman, Caroll, & Hannan, 1983), which may impact their willingness to take risks. Given these characteristics, it is reasonable to expect that the levels and types of slack, as well as the mechanisms by which slack influences innovation, will differ in the context of SMEs as compared to the context of large and well-established firms.

Dimensions of slack that are relevant for larger firms may be immaterial in the case of SMEs (George, 2005). In particular, the concept of *absorbed* slack seems a contradiction of terms with the size, resource scarcity, and volatility and precariousness that characterize these firms. Even in the case of firms that beat the odds and have protracted periods of above-average returns, the highly centralized ownership structure characteristic of these firms makes it unlikely that surpluses will be "absorbed" throughout the organization in the form of idle or underutilized personnel and facilities. Hence, we do not believe absorbed (or recoverable) slack to be a consequential phenomenon, and thus a meaningful driver of innovativeness, in the context of SMEs.

With regard to *available* slack, it is important to understand that the financial reserves of SMEs will tend to be very limited. SMEs are often "running on fumes" and need to rely on several forms of financial bootstrapping to continue their operations (Winborg & Landstrom, 2000). Given this, the typical SME will not have funds to develop breakthrough innovations internally, and will rather adopt innovations already in existence (Baumol, 2002). Their limited funds also mean that SMEs will tend to seek the lowest cost adoption of IT innovations (Thong, 1999).

Finally, in terms of *potential* slack, which refers to an organization's ability to raise external capital, it is important to recognize that since they may have little financial records or collateral, many SMEs represent high-risk borrowers and may not have access to commercial credit at all (i.e., have very little chance to obtain a bank loan), or may be credit constrained by their lenders (i.e., may receive lesser amounts of credit than their business can responsibly carry). Thus, in contrast to the prior literature which has emphasized financial leverage (i.e., debt-to-equity ratio) as the key indicator of potential slack, we believe that the most salient indicator of potential slack for SMEs is access to credit in the first place.

ORGANIZATIONAL SLACK AND INNOVATION ADOPTION IN SMES

Available Slack

As previously discussed, past studies of larger firms have argued and found support for an inverted U-shaped relationship between available slack and innovation (Geiger & Cashen, 2002; Nohria & Gulati, 1996). Despite a tighter resource environment as well as differences in management processes and the types of innovations that will be pursued, we expect this type of slack to influence innovation in a similar way in SMEs. At low levels of available slack it is unlikely that there are resources for innovation adoption. As financial reserves increase, we expect adoption of e-commerce and computerized core processes to increase. However, for very high levels of cash reserves, which may signal a very successful business model, we expect greater inertial pressure and a lesser willingness to innovate (Wang & Cheung, 2004). Stated formally:

H1: *The relationship between available slack and SME adoption of e-commerce will be inverted U-shaped (i.e., positive but declining in strength, and becoming negative beyond an intermediate optimal level).*

H2: *The relationship between available slack and SME adoption of computerized core will be inverted U-shaped (i.e., positive but declining in strength, and becoming negative beyond an intermediate optimal level).*

Potential Slack

Geiger and Cashen (2002) argue that, unlike available and (for larger firms) recoverable slack, potential slack is unlikely to display an inverse U-shaped relationship with innovation. A high level of potential slack simply represents little or no debt rather than current resources. Since greater use of debt generates new (interest) expenses and may prompt increases in other (capital) costs, it is unlikely that greater access to external credit will lead to lesser managerial attention and a laxer use of such resources. Regardless of the level of potential slack, decisions concerning new debt cannot be made carelessly. Consistent with this, Geiger & Cashen (2002) hypothesize and empirically confirm a positive linear relationship between potential slack and innovation.

We believe that discipline in the use of debt may be even more intense in the SME context. SMEs seeking new debt are likely to receive rigorous external scrutiny by would-be creditors at any level of potential slack. Hence, we similarly expect the relationship between potential slack and SME adoption to be linear (i.e., invariant over the range of potential slack values).

In terms of direction, however, specific characteristics of the innovation being considered may moderate how adoption is affected by potential slack (Herold et al., 2006). In particular, the capital-intensity of minimum requirements to adopt a given IT innovation relative to the minimum investment required for alternative processes may determine the role of potential slack in SME contexts. In the case of e-commerce, this innovation offers a low-investment alternative to SME expansion via traditional means such as opening new locations[4]. Hence, SMEs may adopt e-commerce as a way to develop a cost-minimizing marketing channel (Santarelli & D'Altri, 2003). Indeed, for SMEs, e-commerce might be regarded as a form of *bricolage*, or utilizing 'what is at hand' (Baker & Nelson, 2005), in order to be able to grow the business. Consistent with this, we expect firms that are more credit constrained (i.e., with lower potential slack) to be more likely to adopt this innovation. Formally:

H3: *Potential slack will exhibit a linear and negative relationship with SME adoption of e-commerce.*

Conversely, process-enhancing technological innovations such as computerizing core activities are likely to require substantial capital investment over and above the no-adoption alternative. Some of this investment may be derived from available slack but this type of innovation is likely to require additional financial resources. Hence, adoption of computerized core innovations is more likely to be pursued by financially healthier SMEs with greater potential slack. This leads to our final hypothesis:

H4: *Potential slack will exhibit a linear and positive relationship with SME adoption of computerized core.*

DATA AND MEASURES

Sample

The data used for this study were obtained from the *2003 Survey of Small Business Finances* (SSBF). The SSBF is a survey conducted every five years by the Federal Reserve Board to gather information about the use of credit and other financial services by SMEs[5]. The newest survey was administered between June 2004 and January 2005 and gathered data from a nationally representative sample of 4,240 private, nonfinancial, nonfarm firms with fewer than 500 employees. Besides credit use, it contains 2003 financial statement information, as well as other details on the characteristics of these firms and their owners. Both the 1998 and 2003 editions of the SSBF included information about computer use by SMEs. However, the 2003 survey offers greater level of detail regarding firms' adoption of different IT applications.

The sampling frame for 2003 SSBF was about 6.3 million firms listed in the Dun's Market Identifier (DMI) file as of May 2004, and which met the target population definition. The DMI file is thought to be an almost complete listing of all U.S. business establishments (Reynolds, 1994) –although it is likely to under-represent the smallest and newest firms (March & Wolken, 2006). The survey design was a stratified random sample by (i) employment size categories, (ii) broad U.S. Census regions, and (iii) metropolitan versus rural locations. Also, since mid-size firms represent a small percentage of the U.S. population of SMEs, the survey over-sampled larger firms (20-499 employees) –to ensure reliable estimators for this sub-group. As a result, in order to obtain unbiased population estimates from these data, researchers must use techniques that account for the complex structure of the survey (2003 SSBF Technical Codebook: 10-11). Response rate was about 32%.

Prior SSBF editions were released as a complete data set where all missing values (about 2% of data values sought) had been imputed. Imputation of missing data is performed by the Federal Reserve using randomized regressions that model a variable as a function of other survey variables. This practice was often regarded as problematic by prior management authors, and has been cited as a detriment to the use of SSBF data (Cox, Camp & Sexton, 2000)[6]. Interestingly, the 2003 SSBF release provides greater information regarding imputation, and thus greater flexibility in its treatment. The newest data set contains five separate versions of the fully imputed data, referred to as "implicates". This allows researchers to employ statistical techniques that combine estimates from the separate implicates to obtain adjusted standard errors that account for the additional variation due to imputation (Rubin, 1996). The 2003 release also "flags" values that have been imputed. Therefore, researchers have the option to identify and delete observations with imputed values. We conducted analyses under both alternatives and obtained similar results. For simplicity, only results with the reduced sample that contains no imputed values are presented here.

In order to provide a clear demarcation among the two types of IT application of interest, our study was limited to non-retail and non-wholesale firms (i.e., SIC codes 50, 51, 52, 53, 54, 55, 56, 57 & 59). Retailers and wholesalers may regard selling as their primary activity, so that adoption of e-commerce in these firms might be inextricable from adoption of a computerized core. There were 3,101 observations in the 2003 SSBF with non-missing values in the variables used in the present study. Of these, 2,464 observations corresponded to non-distribution firms. We also required that businesses that (i) were not corporate subsidiaries, (ii) had positive sales and positive assets, and (iii) had their three primary owners control more than 50% of the firm's ownership[7]. This resulted in a total of 2, 313 firms that could be used for our analyses. After deleting 17 observations with outlier values of accounting-based available slack (defined below), we were left with a study sample of 2,296 firms.

Dependent Variables

E-Commerce Adoption

Respondents were asked if their firm used the computer "to sell business products and services via the internet". We coded affirmative responses as 1 and negative responses as zero. There were 711 study firms that had adopted this innovation by the end of 2004. Given their analytical survey weights, adopters are estimated to represent 27.9 percent of the U.S. population of non-retail & non-wholesale SMEs. The survey also asked where did the business primarily sell its products or services, and only two respondents (four respondents for the overall 2003 SSBF), or .08 percent of the population, reported conducting business primarily through the internet or phone. This suggests that practically all adopters used e-commerce as a way to complement their primary sales channel.

There is reason to believe that the vast majority of e-commerce users in our sample are recent adopters. Unfortunately, a precise estimate of the growth of e-commerce adoption in this population is not available. While the 2004 questionnaire distinguished between participation in internet purchases (i.e., e-procurement) and internet sales (i.e., e-commerce), the 1999 SSBF questionnaire merely inquired if the firm used "the computer to purchase or sell business products and services via the Internet". Nevertheless, we can derive useful information from the available data. First, a comparison of the *1998 SSBF* data (collected in 1999) with the data used in the present study, shows that adoption of the internet for business transactions (either purchases or sales) exploded from 26.9% in 1999 to 66.0% of the population of non-distribution SMEs in 2004. Second, the data shows that almost all SMEs that had adopted the internet for business transactions by 2004 were using it to purchase products/services (94%). By contrast, a minority of those transacting via the

internet in 2004 used it to sell their own products/services (41%). Thus, similarly, we would expect that a minority of those reporting to have adopted electronic transactions in 1999 would have been e-commerce firms. Moreover, prior research, as well as the lesser prevalence of e-commerce observed here, suggest a staged adoption of electronic processes, so that it is reasonable to assume an even lesser relative incidence of e-commerce *vis-a-vis* e-procurement in 1999 than in 2004. Prior studies have found SMEs to pass through a set of sequential adoption stages from e-mail use, to a web presence, to e-procurement, and culminating with e-commerce adoption (e.g., Daniel, Wilson, & Myers, 2002; Rao, Metts, & Monge, 2003). E-procurement may precede e-commerce adoption due to the greater involvement and greater commitment of resources needed for the latter. Also, by becoming an on-line purchaser of goods and services first, the business owner gains familiarity and experience with the internet, which may be instrumental to his/her motivation and ability to adopt an on-line store-front later on[8]. In short, we believe that e-commerce adoption among SMEs occurred primarily and progressively in the years after 1999. Since our independent variables are measured at the end of the 2003 fiscal year, we believe to be capturing the relationships of interest at around the time of innovation adoption. Also, as discussed below, our study focuses on dimensions of financial slack that would be more static or slow to adjust after adoption, so that, even if captured several months later, they would still be reflective of conditions present at the time of adoption.

Computerized Core

Respondents were asked if their firm used computers "to directly contribute to the firm's primary business activity". We coded affirmative responses as 1 and negative responses as zero. There were 258 firms in our sample that had adopted this innovation. Given their survey weights, we estimate that 9.06 percent of the U.S. population of non-retail & non-wholesale SMEs had computerized their core processes by the end of 2004.

Independent Variables

Available Slack

In prior studies using samples of larger firms, available slack is normally measured using either the quick ratio (Herold et al., 2006; Geiger & Cashen, 2002) or current ratio (Bromiley, 1991; Cheng & Kesner, 1997). These are measures of liquidity or solvency, defined as current assets divided by current liabilities. However, using a measure of this sort proved to be problematic with the present sample of SMEs, as 32 percent of firms in our sample had zero current liabilities. Thus, we opted for using working capital instead, defined as current assets (cash, inventory, account receivables, and other assets that can be converted to cash within one year) minus current liabilities (accounts payable and other debts due within one year). Since this measure was denominated in absolute dollar values, it was important to adjust it for the different operational resource requirements of firms (George, 2005; Greve, 2003). We decided to use working capital over sales as our final measure, as firms with greater sales need greater amounts of working capital[9]. As opposed to measures used in the prior literature that focus on more ephemeral or high-discretion dimensions of available slack (e.g., George, 2005), our measure captures aspects that are more static or slow to adjust after adoption. In particular, cash reserves, which is the more ephemeral component of current assets, are rather small for firms in our study (31% of non-retail SMEs had $2,000 or less in cash, and the median cash amount was $6,000).

Potential Slack

As discussed above, we believe that the most relevant measure of potential slack for SMEs is access to commercial credit. Given recent technological developments in banking leading to broad adoption of automated underwriting technologies (i.e.,

credit scoring) for small business loans (Frame, Srinivasan & Woosley, 2001; Berger, Frame, & Miller, 2005), we used the firm's credit score as an indicator of its access to credit. Our measure is derived from the Dun & Bradstreet Commercial Credit Score Percentile, as provided in SSBF. The credit score percentile is a measure of credit quality. For example, as of the time of this writing, the D&B customer service website reported that firms that fall in between the 1 and 10 percentiles have an incidence of delinquency of 58.8%; by contrast, firms in the 91 to 100 percentiles have an incidence of delinquency of only 2.5%. The measure available in the SSBF database, is an ordinal index ranging from 1 (worst credit) to 6 (best credit): Firms with a credit score percentile between 1-10 are coded as 1, 11-25 percentiles are coded as 2, 26-50 percentiles are coded as 3, 51-75 percentiles are coded as 4, 76-90 are coded as 5, and firms in the 91-100 percentile are coded as 6. Firms with a high credit score have greater access to credit (i.e., are more likely to be approved for greater amounts of credit) and, thus, have greater potential slack. By contrast, firms with a low credit score will be credit constrained and, thus, have lower potential slack.

Control Variables

Owner(s)' Characteristics

Since it is often difficult to separate small business owners from their firms, we sought to control for characteristics of the owner (or owner-group) that might be related to his/her/their willingness to take risks and/or to their propensity to adopt IT applications. We controlled for *age* and *education* of the owner(s), which prior studies found to be related to computer adoption (e.g., Dickerson & Gentry, 1983). The 2003 SSBF includes demographic information for up to three (largest) owners, and our study selected only firms where three or less owners would represent a majority of ownership. Given this, our measure of owner age is the weighted average age of the dominant owner group in years, using ownership shares as weights. Our measure of owner education is also a weighted average across the dominant owner group. Education was an ordinal variable coded 1 if the person had "less than a high school degree"; 2 for "high school graduate", 3 for "some college but no degree granted", 4 for "associate degree", 5 for "trade school/vocational program", 6 for "college degree (BA, BS, AB, etc.)", and 7 for "post graduate degree". In our analyses we also controlled for the *managerial experience* of owners, which may be related to the level of understanding of business processes as well as to familiarity with business IT applications (Damanpour, 1991). This variable, however, was never significant and it was very strongly correlated with other control variables (owners' age and firm age, in particular). Thus, we decided to drop it from the regression models presented here.

Firm's Characteristics

We controlled for *firm age*, which may be related to adoption and which has been found to be related to the effective use of financial slack in private firms (George, 2005). We also controlled for *firm size*, which has been related to IT adoption in SMEs (Bharati & Chaudhury, 2006; Wang & Cheung, 2004), as well as in larger firms (e.g., Tsikriktsis, Lanzolla & Frohlich, 2004). We used the natural log of the number of employees, as well as the number of different sites or locations as proxies for firm size. Albeit related, these measures capture two slightly different aspects of size that may drive adoption. Prior studies have found *centralization* and *professionalism* to be related to innovation (e.g., Damanpour, 1991). We used the ownership share of the primary owner as our proxy for centralization. We added a dummy variable to control for *professionally managed firms* (1=yes). The firm's *legal form* has been related to risk-taking. In particular, because of limited liability, corporations and S-corporations are regarded as more inclined to take risks (e.g., Petersen & Rajan, 1994). Given this, we included

a dummy variable coded 1 for corporations and S-corporations. We also added a control for prior performance, which has similarly been found to be related to risk-taking (e.g., Wiseman & Bromiley, 1996) and to innovation adoption (e.g., Greve, 2003). We used *sales growth* during the past 3 years as our measure for prior performance. This variable was coded 1 if sales had increased in comparison to the fiscal-year ended in 2000; 0 if sales were the same; and -1 if sales had declined in comparison to fiscal-year 2000. Finally, to account for possible differences in the propensity to adopt the two technical innovations of interest –over and above industry effects (see below), we controlled for different levels of *fixed asset intensity* across firms. The latter was measured as net fixed assets (i.e., book value of land plus net book value of depreciable assets) divided by sales (Kracaw, Lewellen & Woo, 1992).

Environmental Drivers

We controlled for *industry* effects, using dummy variables for each two-digit SIC code that was represented by at least 1 percent of firms in the sample (e.g., Ang, Cole & Lin, 2000). Hence, the reference group for industry effects is the set of minority industries in the U.S. population of non-distribution SMEs (small firms are a lesser presence in industries that are more capital intensive). We also controlled for the firm's *urban versus rural* location of the firm's headquarters office, as this may be related to the need to seek business beyond the local market. Our variable took the value 1 if the firm was located in a Metropolitan Statistical Area (MSA) as designated by the Bureau of the Census, and 0 otherwise. Finally, since our arguments regarding potential slack are based on a firm's access to commercial credit, we decided to control for the level of *concentration in the local banking market*, as prior research with SSBF data has found firms in more concentrated markets to have less access to credit (e.g., Cavalluzzo & Wolken, 2005). The SSBF measure used is an ordinal variable, ranging

Figure 1. Descriptive statistics and Pearson correlation coefficients[a]

Variables	Mean	S.D.	1	2	3	4	5	6	7	8	9	10	11	12	13	14	15
1 . e-Commerce adoption	0.28	0.46															
2 . Computerized-core adoption	0.09	0.32	0.06														
3 . Average age of owner group	50.56	10.52	-0.03	0.01													
4 . Average education of owner group	4.68	1.88	0.05	0.06	0.09												
5 . Firm age	13.93	11.23	-0.06	0.01	0.53	-0.04											
6 . Number of employees (ln)	1.32	1.60	0.08	0.01	0.02	-0.02	0.08										
7 . Number of sites	1.21	0.98	0.07	0.03	-0.01	0.03	0.01	0.29									
8 . Ownership share of primary owner	83.07	26.09	-0.08	-0.02	-0.01	0.00	0.05	-0.30	-0.15								
9 . Professionally managed firm	0.04	0.26	0.01	-0.02	0.09	-0.04	0.05	0.17	0.03	-0.06							
10 . Legal form (incorporated)	0.46	0.49	0.11	0.07	0.00	0.04	-0.04	0.42	0.12	-0.21	0.06						
11 . Sales growth	0.36	0.86	-0.01	-0.01	-0.18	0.04	-0.26	0.08	0.07	-0.06	0.06	0.02					
12 . Fixed asset intensity	0.47	0.95	-0.02	0.02	0.02	-0.08	-0.03	-0.07	0.01	-0.08	-0.02	-0.17	-0.06				
13 . Urban location	0.79	0.41	0.07	0.05	-0.02	0.14	-0.06	0.01	-0.01	0.02	0.04	0.09	0.05	-0.06			
14 . Local banking market concentration	2.43	0.61	-0.04	-0.02	0.01	-0.06	0.02	-0.03	-0.01	-0.01	-0.02	-0.06	-0.02	0.01	-0.36		
15 . Available slack (working capital/sales)	0.25	0.51	0.04	-0.01	0.05	0.04	0.03	-0.06	-0.02	0.01	0.01	-0.06	-0.06	0.14	0.02	-0.01	
16 . Potential slack (credit rating)	3.62	1.44	-0.05	0.06	0.17	0.07	0.23	0.05	-0.02	-0.01	-0.04	0.09	-0.07	-0.04	-0.03	0.04	0.02

[a]n = 2,296. Population estimates (i.e., statistics are adjusted for sampling weights). Correlations greater than |.07| are significant at p<.001.

from 1 to 3, based on the Herfindahl index (HI) of commercial bank deposits at the end of 2003 for the MSA or county where the firm is located. The measure takes value 1 if the local HI is between 0 and 1000; 2 if the HI is between 1000 and 1800; and 3 if the HI is above 1800, indicating high levels of concentration.

METHODS AND RESULTS

Statistical Analysis

To test our hypotheses regarding the effects of different types of financial slack on adoption of different IT applications we ran maximum-likelihood logistic regression analyses of our dependent variables. In each case, we fitted a reduced model first, with control variables only, followed by the full model that added the financial slack variables of interest and their quadratic terms. Although we did not hypothesize quadratic effects for potential slack, we included the quadratic term for this variable as well, so as to provide a thorough test of our hypothesis. In order to facilitate interpretation of the quadratic equations, slack variables were mean-centered

–i.e., expressed as deviations from their means (Aiken & West, 1991). To produce appropriate population estimates of regression parameters we used the SURVEYLOGISTIC procedure in SAS 9.1, which takes into account the stratified sample design and corrects for the sampling weight of each observation. Therefore, our regression coefficient estimates provide evidence regarding the effect of a change in independent variables on the likelihood of e-commerce (or computerized core processes) adoption by non-retail, non-wholesale U.S.-based SMEs.

Results

Figure 1 shows descriptive statistics and correlations among the variables included in the study.

Figure 2 provides the results of the logistic regression analyses. The columns labeled Model 1 and Model 3 present results for the reduced regression equations that include only control variables, for e-commerce and computerized-core adoption respectively. Both regression equations are strongly significant, due in large part to very strong industry effects. A brief comment on the contrast of these two equations seems warranted. First, in terms of industry effects, the likelihood

Figure 2. Results of logistic regression models predicting the likelihood of innovation adoption[a]

Variables	E-commerce adoption				Computerized -core adoption			
	Model 1		Model 2		Model 3		Model 4	
Owners' characteristics:								
Average age of owner group	-0.009	(0.007)	-0.008	(0.007)	-0.010	(0.011)	-0.011	(0.011)
Average education of owner group	0.027	(0.039)	0.027	(0.039)	0.112 †	(0.064)	0.108 †	(0.063)
Firm's characteristics:								
Firm age	-0.013 †	(0.008)	-0.009	(0.008)	0.018 †	(0.011)	0.014	(0.011)
Number of employees (ln)	0.173 **	(0.066)	0.192 **	(0.067)	0.118	(0.097)	0.090	(0.100)
Number of sites	0.082	(0.099)	0.082	(0.099)	0.081	(0.185)	0.086	(0.180)
Ownership share of primary owner	-0.002	(0.003)	-0.002	(0.003)	0.000	(0.004)	-0.001	(0.004)
Professionally managed firm	-0.006	(0.347)	-0.055	(0.343)	-0.347	(0.476)	-0.343	(0.493)
Legal form (incorporated)	0.248 †	(0.149)	0.303 *	(0.152)	0.354	(0.238)	0.304	(0.237)
Sales growth	-0.136 †	(0.082)	-0.150 †	(0.083)	-0.006	(0.111)	0.008	(0.112)
Fixed asset intensity	-0.121	(0.075)	-0.133 †	(0.076)	0.332 ***	(0.096)	0.352 ***	(0.099)
Environmental factors:								
Urban location	0.170	(0.177)	0.164	(0.178)	0.178	(0.288)	0.175	(0.290)
Local banking market concentration	-0.088	(0.113)	-0.072	(0.115)	0.103	(0.177)	0.089	(0.179)
Industry: 2-digit SIC code dummies	included ***		included ***		included ***		included ***	
Financial Slack:								
Available slack (working capital/sales)			0.328	(0.235)			-0.295	(0.299)
Available slack squared			-0.059	(0.077)			0.046	(0.080)
Potential slack (credit rating)			-0.164 **	(0.051)			0.177 **	(0.068)
Potential slack squared			-0.050	(0.031)			0.068	(0.042)
Intercept	0.406	(0.575)	0.293	(0.586)	-3.373 **	(1.143)	-3.243 **	(1.188)
Wald χ^2	222.29 ***		236.2829 ***		20,955.01 ***		20,652.43 ***	
d.f.	34		38		34		38	

[a] n= 2,296. Coefficient estimates and their standard errors are adjusted for sampling weights and stratification of the survey design. Standard errors are in parentheses.

Detailed industry dummy estimates not reported. † p < .10, * p < .05, ** p < .01, *** p < .001

of e-commerce adoption was found to be greater in some of the capital-intensive industries that SMEs tend to shy away from (e.g., SIC 37-Transportation Equipment; or SIC 38-Measurement and Control Instruments), as well as in hotels (SIC 70) and insurance and brokerage services (SIC 64). By contrast, computerized-core adoption was most likely among SMEs in printing and publishing (SIC 27), machinery and computer equipment (SIC 35), and engineering, accounting, research, and management services (SIC 87). Beyond industry differences, the likelihood of e-commerce adoption was found to increase for larger firms, as well as for younger firms, firms that are incorporated, and firms which have suffered performance declines in the recent past (although the latter effects were only marginally significant). In turn, the likelihood of adoption of computerized core processes was greater for more asset-intensive firms, as well as for older firms with more educated owners (tentatively).

Hypothesis 1 predicts an inverted U-shaped relationship between available slack and the likelihood of e-commerce adoption. Consistent with this, we expected to find a negative coefficient for the quadratic available slack term. As shown in Figure 2 (Model 2) this coefficient was negative, as expected, but was not statistically significant (β = -.059; p=.439). Hence, Hypothesis 1 was not supported. Indeed, we found no evidence that available slack is related to e-commerce adoption among the population of U.S. SMEs, as the linear available slack term was also non-significant.

Hypothesis 2 predicts an inverted U-shaped relationship between available slack and the likelihood of computerized-core adoption. However, the estimated regression coefficient for the quadratic available slack term in Figure 2 (Model 4) was positive (against prediction) and non-significant. Hence, Hypothesis 2 was not supported. As in the case of e-commerce, computerized-core adoption by U.S. SMEs appears not to be related to available slack as the linear effect failed to reach statistical significance as well.

Hypothesis 3 predicts an inverse relationship between potential slack and the likelihood of e-commerce adoption. Consistent with this, the regression coefficient for potential slack in Figure 2 (Model 2) was negative and significant ($\beta = -.164$; $p=.001$). Hence, Hypothesis 3 is strongly supported.

Hypothesis 4 predicts a direct relationship between potential slack and the likelihood of adoption of computerized core processes. As expected, the regression coefficient for potential slack in Figure 2 (Model 4) was positive and significant ($\beta = .177$; $p=.009$). This result provides strong support for Hypothesis 4.

DISCUSSION

This study sheds light on the relevance of different types of financial slack in SMEs, as well as on the relationships between slack and adoption of different types of IT applications. Our first contribution relates to our characterization of organizational slack in the context of SMEs. We argue that available and potential slack will be the most salient sources of financial slack in the case of SMEs, while absorbed or recoverable slack will tend to be immaterial and, thus, play a negligible role as a driver of innovation. In contrast to larger and well-established firms, SMEs are unlikely to experience lengthy surpluses in returns and cashflows, and are unlikely to absorb those surpluses in the form of redundant or underutilized firm assets. Rather, SMEs tend to be characterized as operating under severe resource constraints (e.g., Storey, 1994). Furthermore, we argue that the salient dimension of potential slack for SMEs is not the financial leverage capacity implicit in their capital structure (and measured by the debt-to-equity ratio) as professed for larger firms, but rather their ability to access external debt in the

first place. Access to commercial credit or other sources of external financing (like venture capital) are not a given and, rather, tend to be the exception for these firms (e.g, Baker & Nelson, 2005).

Second, this is the first study to investigate relationships between different types of slack and innovation adoption in SMEs. Drawing from the prior literature, we argued for an inverted U-shaped relationship between available slack and innovation adoption in SMEs. Conforming to prior studies of larger firms, we posited that available slack would increase innovation adoption in SMEs up to an optimal point, beyond which greater amounts of slack would provide disincentives to innovation. By contrast, and also based on the prior literature, we argued for a linear relationship between potential slack and adoption. However, as an extension to prior theory, we further espoused that in the SME context this relationship would be moderated by the capital requirements associated with implementing the innovation relative to the no-innovation scenario. We hypothesized that e-commerce would tend to be pursued by SMEs with lesser potential slack, as this innovation may allow the development of a sales channel for considerably less investment than alternative forms of distribution (Santarelli & D'Altri, 2004). By contrast, we argued that computerized-core applications will tend to be more capital intensive than alternative processes and, thus, will tend to be pursued by those with greater potential slack (i.e., greater access to credit). Our test of these hypotheses using a representative sample of non-retail and non-wholesale SMEs in the U.S. produced mixed support for our theoretical model: Hypotheses regarding potential slack were strongly supported. However, we found no support for the hypothesized inverted U-shape relationship between available slack and innovation adoption. Indeed, our findings suggest that available slack plays no meaningful role as a driver of innovation adoption in the SME context. This is in stark contrast to its role as a driver of innovation in the case of larger and better established organizations (Geiger & Cashen, 2002).

The third contribution of the study stems from its characterization of some forms of innovation as "bricolage" –i.e., "make do with what's at hand" (Baker & Nelson, 2005) or, at the very least, as alternative business models that are adopted in an attempt to economize resources when organizational slack is limited. In this view, innovation adoption may be born out of necessity, or may be motivated by a desire to preserve (as opposed to spend) resources. This contrasts with virtually all prior research investigating the relationship between slack and innovation, which has been built on the premise that the latter is germane to greater marginal resource expenditures. As such our work extends emerging research on the positive or 'enabling' aspects of resource constraints with regard to innovation (Katila & Shane, 2005). I also answers a recent call for research that explores how the nature of innovations themselves, and in particular their relative dependency on funding from slack resources, moderates their relationship to organizational slack (Herold et al., 2006).

Consistent with our proposition that e-commerce adoption represents a form of "bricolage" by resource-constrained SMEs, we found adopters to be lesser asset-intensive firms; firms that had experienced performance declines in the recent past; and, most important, firms with lesser potential slack. By contrast, adopters of computerized-core applications were firms with greater levels of asset intensity and with greater potential slack.

Implications for Research

Our study has important implications for organizational slack research. We have filled a gap in the prior literature by investigating slack-innovation relationships in SMEs. We discuss the relevant dimensions of organizational slack in the context of SMEs, document the challenges of using established measures of financial slack in this context, and advance what we believe

are sensible alternative measures for available and potential slack of small firms. We also show that available slack and potential slack play very different roles as drivers of innovation in SMEs as opposed to their roles in larger organizations (Geiger & Cashen, 2002; Nohria & Gulati, 1996). All of this, then, challenges the generalizability of received slack-innovation theory, and underscores the need for further organizational slack research using SME populations.

Indeed the present research raises many new questions that may be answered by future research. In particular, future studies might further investigate the role of available slack in SMEs. After modeling both linear and quadratic effects, the present study suggests that available slack has no influence on innovation adoption by SMEs. Given the observed low levels of working capital among U.S. SMEs, it is possible that business owners don't perceive the latter to be resources "in excess of what an organization requires to maintain its standard operations" (Cyert & March, 1963). Population frequency estimates from the 2003 SSBF indicate that 13 percent of non-distribution SMEs have zero or negative working capital, 36 percent have $5,000 or less of working capital, and the median working capital is $13,928. These marginal amounts may not be regarded as "available" resources to fund investment projects, but rather as necessary buffer to protect operations against cash-flow fluctuations during the normal course of business. Alternatively, our results might be due to a limitation of our research design whereby our measure of available slack may be captured several months after adoption (this limitation is further discussed below). Although we believe that adoption for most firms occurred around the time of the 2003 SSBF survey, and that the aspects of available slack that are more salient in this population (i.e., inventories) are slow to change, if levels of working capital were to decrease significantly after adoption (either because "excess" cash reserves were deployed with adoption, or because the innovation increased the efficiency of internal processes and, thus, reduced inventories) our study would fail to capture the true effects of available slack. Hence, further research is needed to confirm the findings of the present study.

Future research may also explore the relationship between types of slack developed here and performance of SMEs. Also, how are these relationships mediated by innovation adoption? For example, is a firm with low levels of potential slack who adopts e-commerce as a form of bricolage more or less likely to survive and increase performance?

Our study also has implications for research on adoption of new IT innovations by SMEs. First, as far as adoption of e-commerce is concerned, our findings may explain prior mixed results regarding organizational slack. Consistent with our findings, Grandon & Pearson (2004) found a single-item measure that appears to capture available slack not to be a determinant of adoption. By contrast, Wang & Cheung (2004) found a broader measure of organization slack to be marginally significant ($p<0.10$) and negatively related to the intention to adopt e-commerce. Interestingly, Wang & Cheung's measure includes items that seem related to available slack (e.g., "sufficient slack capital"), as well as others that capture potential slack (e.g., "able to secure necessary funds"). Based on findings from the present study, we would venture that the effect observed in Wang & Cheung's study resulted from the potential slack component of their measure. Second, our study suggests that (potential) slack is an important determinant of adoption. This contrasts with the little attention given to financial slack in the prior SME innovation adoption literature. Interestingly, Wang & Cheung (2004) also found their organizational slack measure to be positively related to the degree of e-commerce implementation after adoption. Their broad measure, however, does not allow concluding if this effect was due to available or potential slack, or both. Others have also applied the TOE framework to explore the

extent of implementation of new technologies as opposed to adoption (e.g., Xu, Zhu, & Gibbs, 2004). Hence, this opens an interesting avenue for future investigation as researchers may seek to explore the role of different dimensions of slack on innovation adoption as well as on subsequent implementation. In short, future studies need to include financial slack among organizational drivers of SME innovation and, most importantly, need to discriminate between available and potential slack. This can be done within the confines of the TOE framework or as part of other theoretical schemes. Finally, our review of this literature suggests that it is important to develop more consistent measurement across innovation adoption studies, and to distinguish organizational slack from other concepts like firm size, firm profitability, or perceived cost of adoption.

Implication for Practice and Policy

Using a representative sample of the U.S. population of SMEs, our study shows that the ability to obtain external credit is a strong driver of innovation adoption in this population. Indeed this is the only dimension of organizational slack that is related to SME adoption. In terms of the practical significance of our results, it is important to note the substantial magnitude of the estimated population effects. The odds ratio estimate for the effect of potential slack on e-commerce adoption is 0.849 ($p=.0014$), indicating that improving the firm's potential slack score from the sample mean of 3.6 to one unit above the mean (which corresponds, approximately, to an increase from the 53rd to the 75th percentiles of the Dun &Bradstreet Commercial Credit Score) decreases the likelihood of e-commerce adoption by 15.1 percent.[10] In turn, the odds ratio estimate for the effect of credit rating on computerized-core adoption is 1.194 (p=.009), which suggests that improving the firm's potential slack by one unit from the mean (i.e., increasing the firm's Credit Score from the 53rd to the 75th percentile) increases the likelihood of computerized-core adoption by 19.4 percent. Hence our results show that improving SMEs access to credit can indeed have meaningful effects in their ability to adopt capital-intensive technological innovations.

Although a firm's credit rating was used here as only a proxy for its access to external credit, credit ratings have become increasingly important for U.S. SMEs in obtaining external funding so that they may constitute an end in themselves. During the second half of the 1990's most banks (especially large banks) substituted traditional "relationship" lending (based on direct, long-term relationships between local loan officers and business owners) for automated underwriting of small business loans based on business credit scores (Frame et al., 2001; Berger et al., 2005). As credit-scored loans become the norm, the implication for practitioners is that maintenance of a good credit score may become instrumental to be able to adopt new technological innovations.

A related implication is that the recent changes in the banking industry may make it more difficult for young firms to become adopters of capital-intensive innovations. Younger firms have less of a credit record and, as a result, tend to have lower business credit scores. For example, as shown in Figure 1, the correlation between firm age and business credit rating was $r=.23$ in the present study. Also, as shown in Figure 2, prior to adding credit rating to our regression model, firm age was negatively related to e-commerce adoption (Model 1) and positively related to computerized-core adoption (Model 3). As a result, capital-intensive innovation adoption by young firms may depend on the availability of relationship-based loans (Ang, 1992; Petersen & Rajan, 1994). The implication for policy makers is that support of small, independent local banks operating under the traditional relationship lending model may contribute to a healthier rate of business innovation.

Limitations

The use of the 2003 SSBF for the purpose of the present study affords the opportunity to draw from a large, representative data set and to derive population estimates of the effects of interest. This benefit, however, comes at the expense of imposing other shortcomings on our analysis.

Results from the present study must be considered in the context of the following limitations: First and foremost, we do not know the time of innovation adoption and, thus, the extent to which our independent variables reflect the organizational context at that time. This concern is most important with regard to available slack, as endogeneity could be more acute in this case. By contrast, our measure of potential slack (i.e., credit score) is both more unchanging and less likely to be affected by technology adoption. Second, while measures of financial slack derived from the SSBF data compare favorably with those used in the prior literature on technology adoption in SMEs, SSBF measures of computer adoption were rather coarse. In particular, as far as our computerized-core variable is concerned, it is not known what specific IT innovations are being adopted. Finally, another aspect that may limit comparison with prior studies is that, as the population of U.S. SMEs is overwhelmingly dominated by micro firms (<10 employees), the population statistics produced in the present study will largely reflect conditions and relationships characteristic of these firms. Our results need to be interpreted in this context.

CONCLUSION

The present study fills a gap in the prior literature by investigating how different dimensions of slack relate to innovation adoption in the SME context. It is found that both the dimensions of slack and their relationships to innovation differ in this context as compared to the case of larger and better established firms. This challenges the generalizability of extant slack-innovation theory and underscores the need for further organization-slack research using SME populations. Our study provides a valuable contribution toward this endeavor. Nevertheless, as a first multidimensional examination of slack and its effects within SMEs we leave other questions to be answered.

REFERENCES

Aiken, L. S., & West, S. G. (1991). *Multiple Regression: Testing and Interpreting Interactions*. Thousand Oaks, CA: Sage Publications.

Ajzen, I. (1991). The theory of planned behavior. *Organizational Behavior and Human Decision Processes*, *50*(2), 179–211. doi:10.1016/0749-5978(91)90020-T

Ang, J. S. (1992). On the theory of finance for privately held firms. *Journal of Small Business Finance*, *1*(3), 185–203.

Ang, J. S., Cole, R. A., & Lin, J. W. (2000). Agency costs and ownership structure. *The Journal of Finance*, *55*(1), 81–106. doi:10.1111/0022-1082.00201

Baker, T., & Nelson, R. E. (2005). Creating something from nothing: Resource construction through entrepreneurial bricolage. *Administrative Science Quarterly*, *50*(3), 329–366. doi:10.2189/asqu.2005.50.3.329

Baumol, W. J. (2002). Entrepreneruship, innovation and growth: The David-Goliath Symbiosis. *Journal of Entrepreneurial Finance and Business Ventures*, *7*(2), 1–10.

Beckinsale, M., Levy, M., & Powell, P. (2006). Exploring internet adoption drivers in SMEs. *Electronic Markets*, *16*(4), 361–370. doi:10.1080/10196780600999841

Berger, A. N., Frame, W. S., & Miller, N. H. (2005). Credit scoring and the availability, price, and risk of small business credit. *Journal of Money, Credit and Banking*, *37*(2), 191–222. doi:10.1353/mcb.2005.0019

Bharati, P., & Chaudhury, A. (2006). Studying the current status of technology adoption. *Communications of the ACM*, *49*(10), 88–93. doi:10.1145/1164394.1164400

Bourgeois, L. J. (1981). On the measurement of organizational slack. *Academy of Management Review*, *6*, 29–39. doi:10.2307/257138

Bourgeois, L. J., & Singh, J. V. (1983). Organizational slack and political behavior within top management teams. *Academy of Management Proceedings*, 43-47.

Brancheau, J. C., & Wetherbe, J. C. (1990). The adoption of spreadsheet software: Testing innovation diffusion theory in the context of end-user computing. *Information Systems Research*, *1*(2), 115–143. doi:10.1287/isre.1.2.115

Bromiley, P. (1991). Testing a causal model of corporate risk taking and performance. *Academy of Management Journal*, *34*(1), 37–59. doi:10.2307/256301

Cavalluzzo, K., & Wolken, J. (2005). Small business loan turndowns, personal wealth, and discrimination. *The Journal of Business*, *78*(6), 2153–2177. doi:10.1086/497045

Cheng, J., & Kesner, I. (1997). Organizational slack and response to environmental shifts: The impact of resource allocation patterns. *Journal of Management*, *23*, 1–18. doi:10.1177/014920639702300101

Chwelos, P., Benbasat, I., & Dexter, A. S. (2001). Research report: Empirical test of an EDI adoption model. *Information Systems Research*, *12*(3), 304–321. doi:10.1287/isre.12.3.304.9708

Compeau, D. R., Higgins, C. A., & Huff, S. (1999). Social cognitive theory and individual reactions to computing technology: A longitudinal study. *Management Information Systems Quarterly, 23*(2), 145–158. doi:10.2307/249749

Cormican, K., & O'Sullivan, D. (2004). Auditing best practice for effective product innovation management. *Technovation, 24*, 819–829. doi:10.1016/S0166-4972(03)00013-0

Cox, L. W., Camp, S. M., & Sexton, D. L. (2000). The Kauffman Financial Statements Database. In Katz, J.A.(ed): Databases for the Study of Entrepreneurship. *Advances in Entrepreneurship Research, 4*, 305-334.

Cyert, R. M., & March, J. G. (1963). *A behavioral theory of the firm*. Engelwood Cliffs, NJ: Prentice-Hall, Inc.

Damanpour, F. (1991). Organizational innovation: A meta-analysis of effects of determinants and moderators. *Academy of Management Journal, 34*(3), 555–590. doi:10.2307/256406

Damanpour, F., Szabat, K. A., & Evan, W. M. (1989). The relationship between types of innovation and organizational performance. *Journal of Management Studies, 26*(6), 587–601. doi:10.1111/j.1467-6486.1989.tb00746.x

Damanpour, F., & Wischnevsky, J. D. (2006). Research on innovation in organizations: Distinguishing innovation-generating from innovation-adopting organizations. *Journal of Engineering and Technology Management, 23*(4), 269–291. doi:10.1016/j.jengtecman.2006.08.002

Dandridge, T. C. (1979). Children are not little grown-ups: Small business needs its own organizational theory. *Journal of Small Business Management, 17*(2), 53–57.

Daniel, E., Wilson, H., & Myers, A. (2002). Adoption of e-commerce by SMEs in the UK. *International Small Business Journal, 20*(3), 253–270. doi:10.1177/0266242602203002

Daniel, F., Lohrke, F. T., Fornaciari, C. J., & Turner, R. A. (2004). Slack resources and firm performance: a meta-analysis. *Journal of Business Research, 57*, 565–574. doi:10.1016/S0148-2963(02)00439-3

Davis, F. D. (1989). Perceived usefulness, perceived ease of use, and user acceptance of information technology. *Management Information Systems Quarterly, 13*, 319–339. doi:10.2307/249008

Dembla, P., Palvia, P., & Brooks, L. (2007). Organizational adoption of web-enabled services for information dissemination. *Journal of Information Science and Technology, 3*(3), 24–49.

Dickerson, M. D., & Gentry, J. W. (1983). Characteristics of adopters and non-adopters of home computers. *The Journal of Consumer Research, 10*, 225–235. doi:10.1086/208961

Dougherty, D., & Hardy, C. (1996). Sustained product innovation in large, mature organizations: Overcoming innovation-to-organization problems. *Academy of Management Journal, 39*(5), 1120–1153. doi:10.2307/256994

Drazin, R., & Schoonhoven, C. B. (1996). Community, population, and organization effects on innovation: A multilevel perspective. *Academy of Management Journal, 39*(5), 1065–1083. doi:10.2307/256992

Ekanem, I. (2005). 'Bootstrapping': The investment decision-making process in small firms. *The British Accounting Review, 37*(3), 299–318. doi:10.1016/j.bar.2005.04.004

Fiol, C. M. (1996). Squeezing harder doesn't always work: Continuing the search for consistency in innovation research. *Academy of Management Review, 21*(4), 1012–1021.

Fishbein, M., & Ajzen, I. (1975). *Belief, attitude, intention, and behavior: An introduction to theory and research*. Reading, MA: Addison-Wesley.

Frame, W. S., Srinivasan, A., & Woosley, L. (2001). The effect of credit scoring on small-business lending. *Journal of Money, Credit and Banking, 33*(3), 813–825. doi:10.2307/2673896

Freeman, J., Caroll, G. R., & Hannan, M. T. (1983). The liability of newness: Age dependence in organizational death rates. *American Sociological Review, 48*, 692–710. doi:10.2307/2094928

Geiger, S. W., & Cashen, L. H. (2002). A multi-dimensional examination of slack and its impact on innovation. *Journal of Managerial Issues, 14*(1), 68–85.

George, G. (2005). Slack resources and the performance of privately held firms. *Academy of Management Journal, 48*(4), 661–676.

Grandon, E. E., & Pearson, J. M. (2004). Electronic commerce adoption: an empirical study of small and medium US businesses. *Information & Management, 42*(1), 197–216.

Greve, H. R. (2003). A behavioral theory of R&D expenditures and innovations: Evidence from shipbuilding. *Academy of Management Journal, 46*(6), 685–702. doi:10.2307/30040661

Herold, D. M., Jayaraman, N., & Narayanaswamy, C. R. (2006). What is the relationship between organizational slack and innovation? *Journal of Managerial Issues, 18*(3), 372–392.

Hillman, A. J., Shropshire, C., & Cannella, A. A. (2007). Organizational predictors of women on corporate boards. *Academy of Management Journal, 50*(4), 941–952.

Holtz-Eakin, D., Joulfaian, D., & Rosen, H. S. (1994a). Entrepreneurial decisions and liquidity constraints. *The Rand Journal of Economics, 25*(2), 334–347. doi:10.2307/2555834

Holtz-Eakin, D., Joulfaian, D., & Rosen, H. S. (1994b). Sticking it out: Entrepreneurial survival and liquidity constraints. *The Journal of Political Economy, 102*(1), 53–75. doi:10.1086/261921

Iacovou, A. L., Benbasat, I., & Dexter, A. (1995). Electronic data interchange and small organizations: adoption and impact of technology. *Management Information Systems Quarterly, 19*(4), 465–485. doi:10.2307/249629

Igbaria, M., Zinatelli, N., Cragg, P., & Cavaye, A. (1997). Personal computing acceptance factors in small firms: a structural equation model. *Management Information Systems Quarterly, 21*(3), 279–302. doi:10.2307/249498

Jensen, M. C. (1986). Agency costs of free cash flow, corporate finance, and takeovers. *The American Economic Review, 76*, 323–329.

Jensen, M. C., & Meckling, W. H. (1976). Theory of the firm: Managerial behavior, agency costs, and ownership structure. *Journal of Financial Economics, 3*, 305–360. doi:10.1016/0304-405X(76)90026-X

Katila, R., & Shane, S. (2005). When does lack of resources make new firms innovative? *Academy of Management Journal, 48*(5), 814–829.

Kishore, R., & McLean, E. R. (2007). Reconceptualizing innovation compatibility as organizational alignment in secondary IT adoption contexts: An investigation of software reuse infusion. *IEEE Transactions on Engineering Management, 54*(4), 756–775. doi:10.1109/TEM.2007.906849

Kivimaki, M., & Lansisalmi, H. (2000). Communication as a determinant of organizational innovation. *R & D Management, 30*(1), 33–42. doi:10.1111/1467-9310.00155

Kracaw, W. A., Lewellen, W. G., & Woo, C. Y. (1992). Corporate growth, corporate strategy, and the choice of capital structure. *Managerial and Decision Economics, 13*, 515–526. doi:10.1002/mde.4090130607

Kuan, K. K. Y., & Chau, P. Y. K. (2001). A perception-based model for EDI adoption in small businesses using a technology-organization-environment framework. *Information & Management, 38*, 507–521. doi:10.1016/S0378-7206(01)00073-8

Lee, R. P., & Grewal, R. (2004). Strategic responses to new technologies and their impact on firm performance. *Journal of Marketing, 68*, 157–171. doi:10.1509/jmkg.68.4.157.42730

Mach, T.L. & Wolken, J.D. (2006). Financial services used by small businesses: Evidence from the 2003 Survey of Small Business Finances. *Federal Reserve Bulletin*, October, A167-A195.

March, J. G. (1991). Exploration and exploitation in organizational learning. *Organization Science, 2*, 71–87. doi:10.1287/orsc.2.1.71

Mehrtens, J., Cragg, P. B., & Mills, A. M. (2001). A model of internet adoption by SMEs. *Information & Management, 39*, 165–176. doi:10.1016/S0378-7206(01)00086-6

Mirchandani, A. A., & Motwani, J. (2001). Understanding small business electronic commerce adoption: an empirical analysis. *Journal of Computer Information Systems, 41*(3), 70–73.

Moch, M. K., & Morse, E. V. (1977). Size, centralization, and organizational adoption of innovations. *American Sociological Review, 42*(5), 716–725. doi:10.2307/2094861

Moore, G. C., & Benbasat, I. (1991). Development of an instrument to measure the perceptions of adopting an information technology innovation. *Information Systems Research, 2*(2), 192–222. doi:10.1287/isre.2.3.192

Nohria, N., & Gulati, R. (1996). Is slack good or bad for innovation? *Academy of Management Journal, 39*(5), 1245–1264. doi:10.2307/256998

Oviatt, B. M., & McDougall, P. P. (1994). Toward a theory of international new ventures. *Journal of International Business Studies, 25*(1), 45–64. doi:10.1057/palgrave.jibs.8490193

Parker, C. M., & Castleman, T. (2007). New directions for research on SME-eBusiness: insights from an analysis of journal articles from 2003 to 2006. *Journal of Information Systems and Small Business, 1*(1-2), 21–40.

Petersen, M. A., & Rajan, R. G. (1994). The benefits of lending relationships: Evidence from small business data. *The Journal of Finance, 49*(1), 3–37. doi:10.2307/2329133

Premkumar, G. (2003). A meta-analysis of research on information technology implementation in small business. *Journal of Organizational Computing and Electronic Commerce, 13*(2), 91–121. doi:10.1207/S15327744JOCE1302_2

Premkumar, G., & Roberts, M. (1999). Adoption of new information technologies in rural small businesses. *OMEGA. The International Journal of Management Science, 27*(4), 467–484.

Rao, S. S., Metts, G., & Monge, C. A. M. (2003). Electronic commerce development in small and medium sized enterprises: A stage model and its implications. *Business Process Management Journal, 9*(1), 11–32. doi:10.1108/14637150310461378

Reynolds, P. (1994). Autonomous firm dynamics and economic growth in the United States, 1986-1990. *Regional Studies, 28*(4), 429–442. doi:10.1080/00343409412331348376

Riemenschneider, C. K., Harrison, D. A., & Mykytyn, P. P. (2003). Understanding IT adoption decisions in small business: integrating current theories. *Information & Management, 40*(4), 269–285. doi:10.1016/S0378-7206(02)00010-1

Riemenschneider, C. K., & McKinney, V. R. (2001). Assessing belief differences in small business adopters and non-adopters of web-based e-commerce. *Journal of Computer Information Systems, 42*(2), 101–107.

Rogers, E. M. (1962). *Diffusion of innovations.* New York: The Free Press.

Rosner, M. (1968). Economic determinants of organizational innovation. *Administrative Science Quarterly, 12,* 614–625. doi:10.2307/2391536

Rubin, D. B. (1996). Multiple imputation after 18+ years. *Journal of the American Statistical Association, 91,* 473–489. doi:10.2307/2291635

Santarelli, E., & D'Altri, S. (2003). The diffusion of e-commerce among SMEs: Theoretical implications and empirical evidence. *Small Business Economics, 21,* 273–283. doi:10.1023/A:1025757601345

Simon, H. A. (1957). *Administrative Behavior.* New York: Free Press.

Singh, J. V. (1986). Performance, slack, and risk taking in organizational decision making. *Academy of Management Journal, 29*(3), 562–585. doi:10.2307/256224

Small Business Administration. (2003). Small Serial innovators: The small firm contribution to technical change. *Small Business Research Summary, #225.* Washington, D.C.: www.sba.gov/advo/.

Small Business Administration. (2006). *The Small Business Economy: For Data Year 2005.* Washington, D.C.: www.sba.gov/advo/.

Stotey, D. (1994). *Understanding the Small Business Sector.* New York: Routledge.

Swanson, E. B. (1994). Information systems innovation among organizations. *Management Science, 40*(9), 1069–1092. doi:10.1287/mnsc.40.9.1069

Tan, J. (2003). Curvilinear relationship between organizational slack and firm performance: Evidence from Chinese state enterprises. *European Management Journal, 21*(6), 740–749. doi:10.1016/j.emj.2003.09.010

Tan, J., & Peng, M. W. (2003). Organizational slack and firm performance during economic transitions: Two studies from an emerging economy. *Strategic Management Journal, 24*(13), 1249–1263. doi:10.1002/smj.351

Thong, J. Y. L. (1999). An integrated model of information systems adoption in small businesses. *Journal of Management Information Systems, 15*(4), 187–214.

Tornatzky, L. G., & Fleischer, M. (1990). *The Processes of Technological Innovation.* Lexington, MA: Lexington Books.

Tsikriktsis, N., Lanzolla, G., & Frohlich, M. (2004). Adoption of e-processes by service firms: An empirical study of antecedents. *Production and Operations Management, 13*(3), 216–229. doi:10.1111/j.1937-5956.2004.tb00507.x

Venkatesh, V., Morris, M. G., Davis, G. B., & Davis, F. D. (2003). User acceptance of information technology: Toward a unified view. *Management Information Systems Quarterly, 27*(3), 425–478.

Wang, S., & Cheung, W. (2004). E-business adoption by travel agencies: Prime candidates for mobile e-business. *International Journal of Electronic Commerce, 8*(3), 43–63.

Welsh, J. A., & White, J. F. (1981). A small business is not a little big business. *Harvard Business Review, 59*(4), 18–32.

Winborg, J., & Landstrom, H. (2000). Financial bootstrapping in small businesses: Examining small business managers' resource acquisition behaviors. *Journal of Business Venturing, 16,* 235–254. doi:10.1016/S0883-9026(99)00055-5

Wiseman, R. M., & Bromiley, P. (1996). Toward a model of risk in declining organizations: An empirical examination of risk, performance and decline. *Organization Science*, *7*(5), 524–543. doi:10.1287/orsc.7.5.524

Wong, S., & Chin, K. (2007). Organizational innovation management: An organization-wide perspective. *Industrial Management & Data Systems*, *107*(9), 1290–1315. doi:10.1108/02635570710833974

Xu, S., Zhu, K., & Gibbs, J. (2004). Global technology, local adoption: A cross-country investigation of internet adoption by companies in the United States and China. *Electronic Markets*, *14*(1), 13–24. doi:10.1080/1019678042000175261

Yang, K. H., Lee, S. M., & Lee, S. (2007). Adoption of information and communication technology: Impact of technology types, organization resources and management style. *Industrial Management & Data Systems*, *107*(9), 1257–1275. doi:10.1108/02635570710833956

ENDNOTES

[1] A notable exception is George (2005) which investigates the relationship between slack and performance in privately held firms.

[2] This is consistent with arguments presented later on in this paper that e-commerce is a form of innovation that allows an SME to economize in the use of financial resources as compared to other alternatives.

[3] Tan (2003) explores curvilinear effects of slack dimensions on the performance of medium to large Chinese state-operated firms, and finds that both absorbed and unabsorbed slack have an inverse U-shaped relationship with firm performance. Another study using the same population of firms found similar results (Tan & Peng, 2003).

[4] Our data shows that most SMEs adopt e-commerce as supplemental sales channels, which suggests that they invest in this innovation at the lower end of the spectrum.

[5] The 1987 and 1993 surveys were called the National Survey of Small Business Finances.

[6] Although the overall SSBF rate of missing values is rather low, missing data problems are widely divergent across variables, and are most acute for items that are financial in nature. Since the present study draws on several of these financial indicators, careful attention to this issue was important.

[7] Since the 2003 SSBF provides demographic information on up to three owners only, this screen was needed to guarantee that our owner-characteristic variables would properly depict the dominant owner group.

[8] Consistent with this, Bharati & Chaudhury (2006) found that simpler technologies are more broadly adopted by SMEs.

[9] Standardizing on the basis of sales volume was preferable here to standardizing on the basis of assets (e.g., Lee & Grewal, 2004), as the latter may change substantially for SMEs upon technology adoption –especially in the case of computerized-core adoption. It is important to note also that we ran additional analyses on the reduced sample for which current ratio could be defined (n=1534, after deleting outliers), and that regression results using either current ratio or working capital over sales were essentially the same. Results for current ratio were also essentially the same as those presented here for working capital over sales using all available data.

[10] Since variables are log-transformed for the logistic regression analysis, the magnitude of effects is nonlinear so that, here, the straightforward interpretation of odds ratios informs about effect sizes for one-unit changes around the sample mean only (Hillman, Shropshire & Cannella, 2007). Odds ratios are not reported in our results table.

This work was previously published in International Journal of E-Business Research (IJEBR), edited by In Lee, pp. 25-48, copyright 2009 by IGI Publishing (an imprint of IGI Global).

Chapter 3

Business Process Digitalization and New Product Development:
An Empirical Study of Small and Medium-Sized Manufacturers

Jun Li
University of New Hampshire, USA

Michael Merenda
University of New Hampshire, USA

A.R. (Venky) Venkatachalam
University of New Hampshire, USA

ABSTRACT

Previous research has largely ignored how business process digitalization across the value chain enhances firm innovation. This chapter examines the relationship between the extensiveness of business process digitalization (BPD) and new product development (NPD) in a sample of 85 small U.S. manufacturers. Scores of extensiveness were derived from the number of adopted e-business practices regarding inter and intra-firm activities such as: customer and supplier services (computer-aided design and manufacturing), employee services (education/training), and industry scanning (technology sourcing). The authors found that (1) NPD is positively related to the extensive use of BPD, and (2) the relationship between NPD and the extensiveness of BPD is stronger in more mature firms than that in younger firms. The authors conclude that small and medium-sized enterprise (SME) production innovation strategies are positively associated with the strategic use of BPD and span spatial, temporal, organizational, and industry boundaries thus aiding SME global competitiveness.

INTRODUCTION

Over the past decades, the rapid developments of the Internet and the information technologies have profoundly impacted every aspect of organizational and social activities. Many business organizations, including small and medium-sized enterprises (SMEs), have started to adopt business process digitalization (hereafter "BPD") as a tool to gain market and operational efficiency (e.g.,

DOI: 10.4018/978-1-60960-132-4.ch003

Copyright © 2011, IGI Global. Copying or distributing in print or electronic forms without written permission of IGI Global is prohibited.

BarNir, Gallaugher & Auger, 2003; Bharadwaj & Soni, 2007; Johnston, Wade & McClean, 2007). Business process digitalization, in this study, is defined as an enterprise-wide information system based on the technological foundation of the Internet. To date, the majority of research on SME's BPD has focused on the antecedents of SMEs engaging in one or few specific types of e-business practice or process (Wymer & Regan, 2005). For example, scholars have examined factors at the organizational level (e.g., Burke, 2005; Dholakia & Kshetri, 2004; Nielson, Host & Mols, 2005; Xu, Rohatgi & Duan, 2007); the industrial level (e.g., Dholakia & Kshetri, 2004; Lee, 2004); and the institutional level (e.g., Kshetri, 2007) that influence the SME's decision to adopt BPD. Less in quantities, studies also have looked at the role of BPD in influencing SMEs' market and operational performance (e.g., Johnston et al., 2007; Merono-Cerdan & Soto-Acosta, 2006; Rajendran & Vivekanandan, 2008; Zhu, Kraemer, Xu & Dedrick, 2004).

While these studies provide good understanding of the antecedents and the financial consequences of BPD, how BPD affects SME's new product development is still unclear. As a key indicator of firm innovation, new product development is crucial to the survival and success of business and enterprise, including SMEs (Huang, Soutar & Brown, 2002). This study aims to understand how SMEs can enhance new product development through use of BPD. Building upon insights from the knowledge-based view (Conner, 1991; Grant, 1996; Kogut & Zander, 1992) and the organizational learning theory (Argyris & Schon, 1978; Cyert & March, 1963), the central thesis of this study is that the extensive use of BPD enhances the firm's knowledge-base resources and improves its organizational learning, therefore contributing to SME's new product development.

This study has several contributions. First, it complements current research on the consequences of SME e-business practices and processes. The existing studies on the impact of SME BPD have largely focused on operational outcomes such as financial or market performance (e.g., Johnston et al., 2007; Servais, Madsen & Rasmussen, 2007). Our study enriches this research stream by looking at the impact of BPD on new product development, one of the important measures for firm competitiveness. Second, we attempt to conceptualize BPD as a strategic process employed by SMEs to leverage information technologies as rent seeking and value creation initiatives. We posit that BPD not only enhances operational effectiveness of the firm (Porter, 1991), but also is conducive to entrepreneurial decision-making and innovation (von Hippel, 2005). Third, the existing studies typically examine BPD independent of other possible moderating variables. The contingency theory (Donaldson, 2001) suggests that the impacts of BPD may vary, depending on certain types of organizational characteristics. We explored the potential moderating effects of organizational characteristics (firm age and type of products) on the effect of BPD on new product development.

THEORY AND HYPOTHESES

The Knowledge-Based View

Extending from the resource-based view of the firm (Barney, 1991; Wernerfelt, 1984), the knowledge-based view (Conner, 1991; Grant, 1996; Kogut & Zander, 1992) considers knowledge as the most strategically significant resource of the firm. Organizational knowledge is embedded and carried through multiple entities including organizational culture and identity, policies, routines, documents, systems, and employees (Nonaka, 1994). Because knowledge-based resources are heterogeneous and difficult to imitate and transfer across organizations, the knowledge bases and capabilities among firms are the major determinants of sustained competitive advantage and superior firm performance (Barney, 1991).

Scholars have argued that information technologies[1] can play an important role in the knowledge-base of the firm in that information systems can be used to synthesize, enhance, and expedite large-scale intra- and inter-firm knowledge management (Alavi & Leidner, 2001). Furthermore, scholars have argued that information technology *capability* is one of the critical firm capabilities that may contribute to firm superior performance (e.g., Mata, Fuerst & Barney, 1995; Wade & Hulland, 2004). Bharadwaj (2000) proposed and empirically tested three types of IT-based resources that generally contribute to firm superior performance. They are (1) tangible IT infrastructure, which includes physical IT assets and systems; (2) human IT resources, the IT employees and managers; and (3) IT enabled intangible resources, which includes customer orientation, knowledge-base assets and synergy. Bharadwaj further argued that IT *capability* as an important organizational capability, does not come from any specific set of IT functionalities, rather it comes from the *integration* of the three IT-based resources. This capability can serve as a form of isolation mechanism, which is hard for rivals to imitate due to its social complexity, path dependence, and causal ambiguity (Bharadwaj, 2000).

Organizational Learning

Early theorists in organization learning (e.g., Argyris & Schon, 1978; Cyert & March, 1963; Daft & Weick, 1984) view organizations as open systems in which insights and knowledge can be developed though the interaction between the organization and its environment. Although different models/terms have been used to describe the process of organization learning, scholars tend to agree that an organizational learning process consists of four basic components: information acquisition, information dissemination, shared interpretation, and development of organizational memory (c.f., Tippins & Sohi, 2003). According to Tippins and

Sohi's summary, information acquisition refers to the process in which firms seek and gather useful information. Dissemination of information refers to the distribution of information among organizational units and people. Shared interpretation is organization's consensus among organization members with regard to the meaning of information. And organizational memory refers to the stored information or experience the organization has about a particular phenomenon.

A general finding of research on the relationship between information technologies and organizational learning is that information systems facilitate the process of organizational learning by enabling and supporting knowledge acquisition, information distribution, information interpretation, and organizational memory (e.g., Kane & Alavi, 2007). The information system flattens the structure of the organization and promotes greater dissemination of information throughout the organization. This makes the organization more open, informed, flexible, and organic. Increased availability of information helps members share information thereby increasing learning. For example, market intelligence systems help the firm acquire critical competitive and market information; and the internal IT system (E-mails, forums, and bulletin boards, etc.) facilitates internal information distribution and interpretation process. Furthermore, information technology helps expand the scale and/scope of organization learning in that the firm can access, acquire, absorb, and utilize external information and/or knowledge by overcoming spatial and temporal distances (Boudreau, Loch, Robey & Straud, 1998).

The Extensiveness of BPD and New Product Development

As mentioned earlier, we define business process digitalization as an enterprise-wide information system based on the technological foundation of the Internet. Specifically, we refer to enterprise-wide Internet/Intranet applications which compass various aspects of organizational activities and processes. This includes B2C (business to customers), B2S (business to suppliers), B2E (business to employees) and B2O (business to others) IT applications that cover various inter and intra-firm activities, such as customer and supplier services (computer-aided design and manufacturing), employee services (education/training), and industry scanning (technology sourcing) and so on[2]. The focus of this study is not the *intensity* of BPD in any specific category. Instead, we are interested in how *extensive* use of BPD, i.e., the *scope* of Internet and Intranet applications applied across both horizontal and vertical value chains influences SME product innovation.

The scope of BPD and its relationship with firm innovation has received increasing attention among scholars in this field recently. Zwass (2003) identified five domains of e-business and proposed a "5-C framework", which includes (1) commerce (for example marketplace and universal supply chain linkage), (2) collaboration (the network and collaborative relationships between the firm and external parties); (3) communication (such as forum, interactive medium, and delivery vehicle); (4) connection (the connectivity, development platform, as well as universal telecommunication network), and (5) computation (computing utility). In each of these domains, e-business practices lead to specific innovational opportunities. For example, e-marketplace allows for the opportunities for customization, price discovery, and new business models. e-collaboration helps expand the boundary of organizational knowledge and enhance the firm's overall innovation ability. Zwass finally emphasizes that it is the combination of these aspects, not isolation, leads the firm to be more innovative in terms of opportunity seeking and capturing. In an empirical study, Beck and his colleagues found that firms with an all-embracing approach utilizing e-commerce applications are often more efficient than others with lower e-commerce diffusions (Beck, Wigand & Konig, 2005).

We argue that the scope of BPD (i.e., the extensiveness of Internet use through B2C, B2S, B2E and B2O models) will have positive impact on SME new product development. A fully-embraced approach of BPD not only enhances the knowledge base for the firm, but also enhances the firm's competency in learning through the systems. From the knowledge-based view, applying Internet technology in various business practices and processes enhances the firm's IT infrastructure as well as human IT resources (Bharadwaj, 2000). The extensive use of BPD enables the firm to collect and analyze large amount of information at relatively lower cost. Further, firms with a full spectrum of e-business system are able to build up a set of complementary resources (technological and/or organizational) that are unique to the venture (Bharadwaj, 2000). In a recent study, Devaraj, Krajewski, and Wei found that while firms using e-business for customer integration does not have direct impact on firm performance, firms using e-business for *both* customer integration *and* supplier integration significantly outperform the others (Devaraj, Krajewski & Wei, 2007). It is the enterprise-wide information system, rather than any particular IT system, leads to competitive advantage of the firm (Henderson & Venkatraman, 1993).

Taking an organization learning perspective, extensive BPD enhances firm's ability to generate product innovations as well. First, as discussed earlier, extensive Internet and Intranet applications enhance the firm's ability to acquire information; Second, the wide use of Internet improves communication efficiently and effectiveness within the organization which will enhance the process of knowledge dissimilation and sharing within the organization. For example, Ortega, Marinez, and Hoyos found that for firms using different information technologies (Internet, EDI, etc.) on e-customer relationship management (E-CRM), there is a direct and positive transmission of knowledge from E-CRM to B2B development (Ortega, Marinez & Hoyos, 2008). Third, extensive use of BPD expands organization boundary in terms of technology transfer and knowledge creation. Research has demonstrated that firms' ability to generate product innovations increasingly relies on the effective acquisition of new product knowledge through external linkages (Bierly & Chakrabarti, 1996; Rothwell & Dodgson, 1991). The more extensive a SME uses BPD for its business and organizational activities, the more the firm builds up links with external entities (such as suppliers, customers, trade associations, industry research institutes and/or universities), which increases the firm's learning base for knowledge creation (Nonaka, 1994).

Therefore we predict,

Hypothesis 1: *The extensiveness (the scope) of business process digitalization is positively associated with SME new product development.*

Moderating Effects of Firm Age and Product Type

Contingency theory posits that the effects of organizational characteristics on effectiveness and/or performance are often influenced by third variable such as organization size and environmental uncertainty (Donaldson, 2001). In this study we considered two important contingencies: firm age and type of products. Firm age is one of the central constructs studied by organizational ecologists and has been demonstrated to have important implications to venture success (Freeman, Carroll & Hannan, 1983; Henderson, 1999). Research has shown that compared to older firms, younger (or newer) firms have higher liabilities of newness (Stinchcombe, 1965), less financial and personal resources, and have not yet developed organizational routines or systems (Nelson & Winter, 1982). We argue that these limitations will weaken the impact of BPD on new product development. From a knowledge-based view, the lack of IT infrastructure, less developed human IT resources, and immature organizational systems

makes it difficult for younger firms to fully exploit the values of BPD. Indeed, younger firms may not have strong incentives to apply a fully integrated information system, as there is less need for it until the business is growing. Researchers have found that younger firms tend to have less formal market research an environmental scanning behaviors (Mohan-Neill, 1995). Also, with limited linkages to external partners, younger firms will have less chance to expand their knowledge bases across organization boundaries. Therefore we predict,

Hypothesis 2.1: *Firm age positively moderates the relationship between the extensiveness (the scope) of business process digitalization and SME new product development.*

Another moderator we examined is the firm's type of products. Specifically we categorized the products of the sample firms into two categories, one is the *"off-the-shelf"* products which are standardized products targeting the mass market, the other is customer-collaborated products, which involves customer designing, testing, and collaborations. We argue that in firms that have higher percentage of customer-collaborated products in their product lines, the relationship between the extensiveness of BPD and new product development would be stronger than that in firms that have higher percentage of *"off-the-shelf"* products. Firms producing higher percentage of customer-collaborated products have both incentives and the needs to have more frequent interactions with customers, suppliers, designers as well as producers than those producing lower percentage of such products. In many cases, small and medium-sized firms produce customer-collaborated products required by large corporations outsourcing programs through increased collaboration and development of advanced information technologies (Chan & Chung, 2002). From the knowledge-based view and organizational learning perspectives, a higher percentage of customer-collaborated products suggests a higher level of information exchange, knowledge sharing and integration, which ultimately lead to a higher level of product innovation. Therefore we predict,

Hypothesis 2.2. *The percentage of customer-collaborated products in total sales positively moderates the relationship between business process digitalization and SME new product development.*

METHODOLOGY

Sample and Data Collection

The initial sample consists of 414 small and medium-sized manufacturers in engineering, electronics, computer and software industries that were identified from Reference USA and Mass High Tech Databases. We selected small manufacturers in these industries of their capacity for innovation and intensive and extensive use of electronic and non-electronic environments to link with customers, suppliers, employees and others in the value chain. To be qualified to be included in the sample, a firm must (1) have less than 500 employees, and (2) annual sales are between $5 million and $1 billion. These criteria are consistent with previous research (BarNir et al., 2003).

Telephone survey was made to the CEO or the President of the company to collect data about the firm and their e-business strategies. In addition to providing background information on the company and themselves, respondents were asked to evaluate their use of the Internet with customers, suppliers, employees and others. Out of 414 firms, 50 firms didn't have correct contact information, giving a pool of 364 firms to contact. 85 firms responded the telephone survey for a response rate of 23.3%. The telephone survey was administered by the University's survey center during 2005.

Measures

New product development. In the questionnaire, we asked the respondent what percentage of the company's sales was generated from new products introduced in the past 3 years, compared to its top 3 competitors. Answers range from (1) "Substantially below top 3 competitors"; (2) " Somewhat below top 3 competitors"; (3) "Average of top 3 competitors"; (4) "Somewhat above top 3 competitors"; to (5) "Substantially above top 3 competitors". Therefore this variable was measured by an index, with 1 as the lowest level and 5 as the highest.

Extensiveness of BPD. Adopting the measures used by Theyel, Merenda and Venkatachalam (2001), we identified and categorized 19 distinct e-business practices encompassing areas of B2C, B2S, B2E and B2O to measure the firm's extensiveness (the scope) of business process digitalization. A detailed list of these 19 activities is listed in Appendix A. For each activity, if the SME has implemented in its organization, the firm will be scored 1. If the firm has never conducted the specific e-business practice, the firm will be scored 0. The extensiveness of business process digitalization then is operationalized as: [(the firm's total score)/19].

Firm age. Firm age is measured by the difference between the founding year of the firm and the year when the survey was completed (2005).

Customer-collaborated products. This is a ratio variable, measuring the percentage of products that were manufactured through customer cooperation in total sales.

The following variables were included as controls. The first one is *IT expenditure.* We asked the respondent to evaluate their annual spending on information technology compared to their top 3 competitors in choosing one of the followings: (1) Substantially below top 3 competitors; (2) Somewhat below top 3 competitors; (3). Average of top 3 competitors; (4) Somewhat above top 3 competitors; and (5) Substantially above top 3 competitors. Therefore IT expenditure was scaled from 1 (the lowest) to 5 (the highest). *IT manager* was included to control whether or not a senior manager was assigned to be in charge of IT system in the firm. Finally we included a dummy variable, *Using Internet as management tool,* to control how important the management team utilizes the Internet as an administrative or management tool for firm activities (with lowest as 0, and highest as 5).

Analysis and Results

We employed a hierarchical approach in analyzing both the main and interaction effects. First we created a base model of OLS regression, which includes all our control variables. We subsequently added independent variables and moderating variables in full models. We then tested for the significance of the difference between the full models and the nested base model by using Chi-square tests. A significant Chi-square test means additional variance of probability of persistence explained by the added-on predictors.

Despite overall statistical significance, the original model (the normal model) suffered from reduced sample caused by missing values. To address this, we employed multiple imputation method (Robin, 1977; Rubin, 1987). Multiple imputation involves three steps. First, the missing data are filled in m times to generate m complete data sets; second, the m complete data sets are analyzed using standard procedures; third, the results from the m complete data sets are combined for the inference. It is noted that the imputed values produced from an imputation model are not intended to be "guesses" as to what a particular missing value might be; rather, this procedure is intended to create an imputed data set which maintains the overall variability in the population while preserving relationships with other variables. For this paper we reported results from both the normal model and the imputed model.

Means, standard deviations, and correlation matrix are reported in Table 1. Table 2 and Table 3 report the results obtained from the hierarchical OLS regressions for the normal model and the imputed model respectively. In Table 2, Model 1 only included control variables. Model 2 test the impact of extensiveness of business process digitalization on new product development. Models 3-4 included moderating variables (firm age and product type). Since including different interaction variable requires different imputed data sets, we did two sets of hierarchical regressions for imputed model in Table 3. Similar with Table 1, in Table 3, Model 1 and Model 4 only included control variables. Model 2 and Model 5 included independent variable. Model 3 and Model 6 included the interaction term of firm age and the interaction term of product type respectively. In most cases, positive change of Chi-square values and their significance levels confirm that adding the independent variables as well as the moderating variables help improve the overall explanatory power of the model of new product development.

Hypothesis 1 predicts that the extensiveness of business process digitalization is positively related with new product development. Results from the normal model (Table 2) support this hypothesis. The coefficients for this independent variable are consistently positive and significant (b=1.769, p<.05; b=2.649, p<.01; and b=2.178, p<.05 in Model 2, 3 and 4 respectively). Results from the imputed model (Table 3) reported partial support (b=.775, p<.05 in Model 5). Overall the results from both models suggest that the extensiveness of business process digitalization has a positive influence on new product development. Therefore Hypothesis 1 is supported.

Hypothesis 2.1 predicts that firm age has a positive moderating effect on the relationship between the extensiveness of business process digitalization and new product development. Results from both the normal model (Table 2) and the imputed model (Table 3) provide strong evidence for this hypothesis. The coefficients for this variable are

Table 1. Means, standard deviations and correlation matrix (normal model)

Variable	N	Mean	S.D.	1	2	3	4	5	6
1. New product development	62	3.58	.86						
2. IT expenditure	55	2.85	1.13	.62 ***					
3. IT manager	84	.44	.50	.26 *	.44 ***				
4. Internet as management tool	73	1.82	1.05	.21	.20	.09			
5. Customer-collaborated products (%)	71	25.86	30.45	-.14	-.11	-.07	-.09		
6. Firm age	81	34.84	22.67	.09	-.15	.11	-.23†	-.05	
7. Extensiveness of BPD	85	.85	.23	.30 *	.31 *	.18†	.09	-.12	.27 *

*** $p<.001$, **$p<.01$, *$p<.05$, †$p<.1$;

Table 2. Results of hierarchical regressions on new product development (normal model) *

Variable	Model 1	Model 2	Model 3	Model 4
IT expenditure	.434 **	.402 **	.374 **	.399 **
IT manager	.423	.450	.475	.506
Internet as management tool	.201	.123	.109	.078
Customer-collaborated products	.002	.007 †	.007 †	.006
Firm age	.006	.003	-.011	.002
Extensiveness of BPD		1.769 *	2.649 **	2.178 *
Extensiveness of BPD × Firm age			.135 *	
Extensiveness of BPD ×				
Customer-collaborated products				-.027
F-value	5.75 **	7.19 **	9.71 ***	7.02 ***
R-Squared	.43	.51	.60	.53
Δ F		4.56 *	5.76 *	.90
Δ R-Squared		.09 *	.09 *	.02
N	33	33	33	33

***$p<.001$, **$p<.01$, *$p<.05$, †$p<.1$
* OLS regression with robust errors on centered variables.

positive and significant (b=.135, p<.05 in Model 3 of Table 2, b=.077, p<.001 in Model 3 of Table 3). To facilitate interpretation, we conducted the following analysis to plot this interaction effect. First, variable means in Model 3 of Table 3 were substituted for all predictors except firm age and extensiveness of business process digitalization. The result was a reduced equation with two predictors and their cross product. Second, we followed the procedure of Cohen and Levinthal (1990). The values for firm age were taken one standard deviation above zero point and one standard deviation below zero point respectively. Substituting each of these values into the reduced equation yielded two linear equations, which are depicted in Figure 1. As shown in Figure 1, when firm age is higher (+1 standard deviation), the effect of extensiveness of business process digitalization on new product development is stronger than when firm

Table 3. Results of hierarchical regressions on new product development (imputed model) *

Variable	Model 1	Model 2	Model 3	Model 4	Model 5	Model 6
IT expenditure	.518 ***	.508 ***	.502 ***	.558 **	.506 ***	.511 ***
IT manager	.164	.164	.138	.115	.111	.090
Internet as management tool	.078	.073	.081	.104	.066	.085
Customer-collaborated products	.005 *	.005 *	.005 *	.003	.003	.003 †
Firm age	.007	.006	-.000	.009 **	.007 †	.007 †
Extensiveness of BPD		.169	1.139		.775 *	.694
Extensiveness of BPD × Firm age			.077 **			
Extensiveness of BPD × Customer-collaborated products						.008
F-value	15.64 ***	13.46 ***	12.78 ***	19.50 ***	15.50 ***	21.49 ***
R-Squared	.44	.45	.54	.50	.53	.54
Δ F		.26	15.28 ***		5.90 *	.51
Δ R-Squared		.01	.09 ***		.04 *	.01
N	85	85	85	85	85	85

***p<.001, **p<.01, *p<.05, †p<.1

* OLS regression with robust errors on centered variables.

age is lower (-1 standard deviation). Therefore, Hypothesis 2.1 is supported.

Hypothesis 2.2 predicts that customer-collaborated products moderate the relationship between business process digitalization and new product development. We predict that business process digitalization has greater impact on new product development in firms with higher percentage of customer-collaborated products in sales than that in firms with lower percentage of customer-collaborated products in sales (higher percentage of "off-the-shelf" type products in sales). Results from Table 2 and Table 3 didn't provide supportive evidences (b=-.027 n.s. in Model 4 of Table 2; b=.008, n.s. in Model 6 of Table 3). Therefore we didn't find evidence supporting Hypothesis 2.2.

DISCUSSION, LIMITATIONS, AND CONCLUSION

This study investigates the relationship between the extensiveness of business process digitalization (the extensive use of e-business practices across value chains) and SME new product development. Driven by the interest of how small and medium-sized firms achieve enhanced innovation capability, we performed a quantitative study on 85 SMEs. We found that the extensiveness of business process digitalization has a significantly positive impact on SME new product development. Furthermore, this impact is greater in more mature firms than in younger firms. We did not find evidence that firms with higher percentage of customer-collaborated products in total sales

Figure 1. Moderating effect of firm age

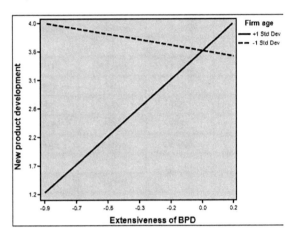

benefited more from business process digitalization with regard new product development.

We believe our study is one of the first empirical studies examining the impact of extensiveness of business process digitalization on SME new product development. Previous literature has mostly focused on either the antecedents of BPD or the financial consequences of using one or more specific types of e-business practice or process, leaving the impact of using an enterprise-wide BPD on firm product innovation largely unexplored (e.g., Nielson et al., 2005; Xu et al., 2007). By adopting insights from the knowledge-based view of the firm and organization learning theory, this study found a linkage between BPD and new product development. This is a critical finding for small and medium-sized enterprise competitiveness. The positive relationship between BPD and new product development suggests that SMEs can achieve competitive advantages by embracing and exploiting an enterprise-wide information system. The advantages are created through the enhanced efficiency and effectiveness in information and/or knowledge acquisition, absorption, interpretation, and dissemination process. The extensiveness of BPD also allows the firm to develop unique, hard-to-imitate IT capability and IT enabled knowledge base through synergy and learning effects. More importantly, our study echoes recent research on

strategic use of Internet (e.g., Lumpkin & Dess, 2004; Sadowski, Maitland & van Dongen, 2002). Most organizations and their CEOs have failed to comprehend that the Internet is both a new technology and a strategic innovation, particularly when SMEs are constrained by technological, financial and human resources. The results from this study imply that despite these constraints and limitations, SMEs have the opportunity to enhance its firm competency by applying BPD throughout the organization.

The moderating effect of firm age on the relationship between BPD and new product development is interesting. Organizational ecologists argue that age is a critical factor in determining organizational survival and performance (Freeman et al., 1983; Henderson, 1999). Age is often been considered as one of the factors inhibiting innovation due to organizational inertia (Hannan & Freeman, 1984) and path dependence in firm strategy (Henderson, 1999). Previous research tends to relate firm age negatively with innovation (e.g., Hansen, 1992). In this study, although we did not find a direct relationship between age and new product development, the moderating effect of firm age on the relationship between BPD and new product development is positive and significant, suggesting an indirect impact of firm age on innovation in SMEs. This is consistent with the structural view of the organization (Churchill & Lewis, 1983; Miller, 1982). Mature small firms are more stable than younger firms so that the enterprise-wide information system can be fully exploited and integrated with business and organization processes. Further, the strategic use of the Internet across the organization requires adoption and implementation of Internet/IT systems, and leadership and an organizational culture for support and reinforcement (Claver, Llopis, Garcia & Molina, 1998). Mature small businesses have advantages in this regard because they are more stable than younger firms.

The failure to observe a positive moderating effect of customer-collaborated products deserves our explanation. One plausible explanation might be that for many small and medium-sized manufacturers, customer-collaborated products are often designed and manufactured collaboratively with larger OEMs (Wood, Kaufman & Merenda, 1996). As a major platform, the business to customer system in SME serves to strengthen the relationships between the focal SME and providing innovative products and services to the OEMs. Although the e-system enhances the efficiencies and effectiveness in knowledge sharing between the SME and their larger customers, there are limitations. Research has shown that customer concentration may impede the firm's ability to conduct radical innovation as the firm may become focused on trivial improvements and become insulated from the fast-changing environment and/or technology (c.f., Zhou, Yim & Tse, 2005). Therefore under such conditions, the impact of BPD on new product development may become limited.

This study contains some limitations. Like most survey research, our results primarily relied on subjective measures of business process digitalization and new product development therefore common method bias is a concern. Future studies should aim to incorporate both subjective and objective measures, and/or multiple respondents to alleviate this potential problem. The study's cross-sectional design is also a limitation. The current model does not allow for causal interpretations among the variables. Future research could investigate the dynamic relationship between changes in the firm's extensive use of new product development and innovation by using longitudinal data. Finally, although the results from the imputed model are mostly consistent with that of the normal model and has legitimate statistical significance, this method has its own limitations. Future studies should aim to enhance the dataset to deal with the missing values, for example, expanding the sample size.

In summary, with a sample of 85 small and medium-sized U.S. manufacturers, this paper examines the role of business process digitalization in new product development. We found that it is the *extensiveness* of business process digitalization that contributes to new product development in SMEs. We demonstrated that this positive relationship was moderated by firm age. It is our hope that this study will facilitate further discussion and provide meaningful implications for SMEs on the value of business process digitalization in fostering new product development and long-term competitiveness.

REFERENCES

Alavi, M., & Leidner, D. E. (2001). Review: Knowledge management and knowledge management systems: Conceptual foundations and research issues. *MIS Quarterly*, *25*(1), 107–136. doi:10.2307/3250961

Argyris, C., & Schon, D. (1978). *Organizational learning: A theory of action perspective*. Reading, MA: Addison-Wesley.

Barney, J. (1991). Firm resources and sustained competitive advantage. *Journal of Management*, *17*(1), 99–120. doi:10.1177/014920639101700108

BarNir, A., Gallaugher, J. M., & Auger, P. (2003). Business process digitization, strategy, and the impact of firm age and size: The case of the magazine publishing industry. *Journal of Business Venturing*, *18*(6), 789–814. doi:10.1016/S0883-9026(03)00030-2

Beck, R., Wigand, R. T., & Konig, W. (2005). The diffusion and efficient use of electronic commerce among small and medium sized enterprises: An international three industry survey. *Electronic Markets*, *15*(1), 38–52. doi:10.1080/10196780500035282

Bharadwaj, A. S. (2000). A resource-based perspective on information technology capability and firm performance: An empirical investigation. *MIS Quarterly*, *24*(1), 169–196. doi:10.2307/3250983

Bharadwaj, P. N., & Soni, R. G. (2007). E-commerce usage and perception of e-commerce issues among small firms: Results and implications from an empirical study. *Journal of Small Business Management, 45*(4), 501–521. doi:10.1111/j.1540-627X.2007.00225.x

Bierly, P., & Chakrabarti, A. (1996). Generic knowledge strategies in the us pharmaceutical industry. *Strategic Management Journal, 17*, 123–135.

Boudreau, M.-C., Loch, K. D., Robey, D., & Straud, D. (1998). Going global: Using information technology to advance the competitiveness of the virtual transnational organization. *The Academy of Management Executive, 12*(4), 120–128.

Burke, K. (2005). The impact of firm size on Internet use in small businesses. *Electronic Markets, 15*(2), 79–93. doi:10.1080/10196780500083738

Chan, M. F. S., & Chung, W. W. C. (2002). A framework to development an enterprise information portal for contract manufacturing. *International Journal of Production Economics, 75*(1/2), 113–126. doi:10.1016/S0925-5273(01)00185-2

Churchill, N. C., & Lewis, V. L. (1983). The five stages of small business growth. *Harvard Business Review, 61*(3), 30–39.

Claver, E., Llopis, J., Garcia, D., & Molina, H. (1998). Organizational culture for innovation and new technological behavior. *The Journal of High Technology Management Research, 9*(1), 55. doi:10.1016/1047-8310(88)90005-3

Cohen, W. M., & Levinthal, D. A. (1990). Absorptive-capacity - a new perspective on learning and innovation. *Administrative Science Quarterly, 35*(1), 128–152. doi:10.2307/2393553

Conner, K. R. (1991). A historical comparison of resource-based theory and 5 schools of thought within industrial-organization economics - do we have a new theory of the firm. *Journal of Management, 17*(1), 121–154. doi:10.1177/014920639101700109

Cyert, R. M., & March, J. G. (1963). *A behavioral theory of the firm.* Englewood Cliffs, NJ: Prentice-Hall.

Daft, R. L., & Weick, K. E. (1984). Toward a model of organizations as interpretation systems. *Academy of Management Review, 9*(2), 284–295. doi:10.2307/258441

Devaraj, S., Krajewski, L., & Wei, J. C. (2007). Impact of e-business technologies on operational performance: The role of production information integration in the supply chain. *Journal of Operations Management, 25*(6), 1199–1216. doi:10.1016/j.jom.2007.01.002

Dholakia, R. R., & Kshetri, N. (2004). Factors impacting the adoption of the Internet among SMEs. *Small Business Economics, 23*(4), 311–322. doi:10.1023/B:SBEJ.0000032036.90353.1f

Donaldson, L. (2001). *The contingency theory of organizations.* Thousand Oaks, CA: Sage Publications.

Freeman, J., Carroll, G. R., & Hannan, M. T. (1983). The liability of newness: Age dependence in organizational death rates. *American Sociological Review, 48*(5), 692–710. doi:10.2307/2094928

Grant, R. M. (1996). Toward a knowledge-based theory of the firm. *Strategic Management Journal, 17*, 109–122. doi:10.1002/(SICI)1097-0266(199602)17:2<109::AID-SMJ796>3.0.CO;2-P

Hannan, M. T., & Freeman, J. (1984). Structural inertia and organizational change. *American Sociological Review, 49*(2), 149–164. doi:10.2307/2095567

Hansen, J. A. (1992). Innovation, firm size, and firm age. *Small Business Economics*, *4*(1), 37–44.

Henderson, A. D. (1999). Firm strategy and age dependence: A contingent view of the liabilities of newness, adolescence, and obsolescence. *Administrative Science Quarterly*, *44*(2), 281–314. doi:10.2307/2666997

Henderson, J. C., & Venkatraman, N. (1993). Strategic alignment: Leveraging information technology for transforming organizations. *IBM Systems Journal*, *32*(1), 4–16.

Huang, X., Soutar, G. N., & Brown, A. (2002). New product development processes in small and medium-sized enterprises: Some Australian evidence. *Journal of Small Business Management*, *40*(1), 27–42. doi:10.1111/1540-627X.00036

Johnston, D. A., Wade, M., & McClean, R. (2007). Does e-business matter to SMEs? A comparison of the financial impacts of Internet business solutions on European and North American SMEs. *Journal of Small Business Management*, *45*(3), 354–361. doi:10.1111/j.1540-627X.2007.00217.x

Kane, G. C., & Alavi, M. (2007). Information technology and organizational learning: An investigation of exploration and exploitation processes. *Organization Science*, *18*(5), 796–812. doi:10.1287/orsc.1070.0286

Kogut, B., & Zander, U. (1992). Knowledge of the firm, combinative capabilities, and the replication of technology. *Organization Science*, *3*(3), 383–397. doi:10.1287/orsc.3.3.383

Kshetri, N. (2007). The adoption of e-business by organizations in china: An institutional perspective. *Electronic Markets*, *17*(2), 113–125. doi:10.1080/10196780701296022

Lee, J. (2004). Discriminant analysis of technology adoption behavior: A case of Internet technologies in small businesses. *Journal of Computer Information Systems*, *44*(4), 57–66.

Lumpkin, G. T., & Dess, G. G. (2004). E-business strategies and Internet business models: How the Internet adds value. *Organizational Dynamics*, *33*(2), 161–173. doi:10.1016/j.orgdyn.2004.01.004

Mata, F. J., Fuerst, W. L., & Barney, J. B. (1995). Information technology and sustained competitive advantage: A resource-based analysis. *MIS Quarterly*, *19*(4), 487–505. doi:10.2307/249630

Merono-Cerdan, A. L., & Soto-Acosta, P. (2006). Examining e-business impact on firm performance through website analysis. *International Journal of Electronic Business*, *3*(6), 1–1.

Miller, D. (1982). Evolution and revolution - a quantum view of structural-change in organizations. *Journal of Management Studies*, *19*(2), 131–151. doi:10.1111/j.1467-6486.1982.tb00064.x

Mohan-Neill, S. I. (1995). The influence of firm's age and size on its environmental scanning activities. *Journal of Small Business Management*, *33*(4), 10–21.

Nelson, R. R., & Winter, S. G. (1982). *An evolutionary theory of economic change*. Cambridge, MA: Harvard University Press.

Nielson, J. F., Host, V., & Mols, N. P. (2005). Adoption of internet-based marketing channels by small- and medium-sized manufacturers. *International Journal of E-Business Research*, *1*(2), 1–23.

Nonaka, I. (1994). A dynamic theory of organizational knowledge creation. *Organization Science*, *5*(1), 14–37. doi:10.1287/orsc.5.1.14

Ortega, B. H., Marinez, J. J., & Hoyos, M. (2008). The role of information technology knowledge in b2b development. *International Journal of E-Business Research*, *4*(1), 40–54.

Porter, M. E. (1991). Towards a dynamic theory of strategy. *Strategic Management Journal*, *12*, 95–117. doi:10.1002/smj.4250121008

Rajendran, R., & Vivekanandan, K. (2008). Exploring relationship between information systems strategic orientation and small business performance. *International Journal of E-Business Research*, *4*(2), 14–28.

Robin, D. B. (1977). Formalizing subjective notions about the effect of nonrespondents in sample surveys. *Journal of the American Statistical Association*, *72*, 538–543. doi:10.2307/2286214

Rothwell, R., & Dodgson, M. (1991). External linkages and innovation in small and medium-sized enterprises. *R & D Management*, *21*(2), 125–138. doi:10.1111/j.1467-9310.1991.tb00742.x

Rubin, D. B. (1987). *Multiple imputation for nonresponse in surveys*. New York: John Wiley.

Sadowski, B. M., Maitland, C., & van Dongen, J. (2002). Strategic use of the internet by small- and medium-sized companies: An exploratory study. *Information Economics and Policy*, *14*(1), 75–93. doi:10.1016/S0167-6245(01)00054-3

Servais, P., Madsen, T. K., & Rasmussen, E. S. (2007). Small manufacturing firms' involvement in international e-business activities. *Advances in International Marketing(17)*, 297-317.

Stinchcombe, A. L. (1965). Social structure and organizations. In J. G. March (Ed.), *Handbook of organizations* (pp. 142-193). Chicago: Rand McNally & Company.

Theyel, G., Merenda, M., & Venkatachalam, A. R. (2001 October). How small and medium size manufacturers use the internet for technology development. *Journal of Business and Entrepreneurship*, 83-106.

Tippins, M. J., & Sohi, R. S. (2003). It competency and firm performance: Is organizational learning a missing link? *Strategic Management Journal*, *24*(8), 745–761. doi:10.1002/smj.337

von Hippel, E. (2005). *Democritizing innovation*. Cambridge, MA: MIT Press.

Wade, M., & Hulland, J. (2004). Review: The resource-based view and information systems research: Review, extension, and suggestions for future research [1]. *MIS Quarterly*, *28*(1), 107–142.

Wernerfelt, B. (1984). A resource-based view of the firm. *Strategic Management Journal*, *5*(2), 171–180. doi:10.1002/smj.4250050207

Wood, C. H., Kaufman, A., & Merenda, M. (1996). How Hadco became a problem solving supplier. *Sloan Management Review*, *37*(2), 77–88.

Wymer, S., & Regan, E. (2005). Factors influencing e-commerce adoption and use by small and medium businesses. *Electronic Markets*, *15*(4), 438–453. doi:10.1080/10196780500303151

Xu, M., Rohatgi, R., & Duan, Y. (2007). E-business adoption in SMEs: Some preliminary findings from electronic components industry. *International Journal of E-Business Research*, *3*(1), 74–90.

Zhou, K., Yim, C. K., & Tse, D. K. (2005). The effects of strategic orientations on technology- and market-based breakthrough innovations. *Journal of Marketing*, *69*(2), 42–60. doi:10.1509/jmkg.69.2.42.60756

Zhu, K., Kraemer, K. L., Xu, S., & Dedrick, J. (2004). Information technology payoff in e-business environments: An international perspective on value creation of e-business in the financial services industry. *Journal of Management Information Systems*, *21*(1), 17–54.

Zwass, V. (2003). Electronic commerce and organizational innovation: Aspects and opportunities. *International Journal of Electronic Commerce*, *7*(3), 7–37.

ENDNOTES

[1]   Although in theory part we use information technologies in general sense, we used it as a synonym of BPD in the hypothesis development section.

[2]   For a detailed list of applications, see Appendix A.

APPENDIX A

Survey questions on the extensiveness of BPD:

1. Please indicate the extent of use the following Internet applications when dealing with your major customers (B2C):
   (1) Storefronts
   (2) Customer services
   (3) E-payments
   (4) E-collaboration in product design and development
   (5) E-collaboration in manufacturing
2. Please indicate the extent of use the following Internet applications when dealing with your major suppliers (B2S):
   (1) Storefronts
   (2) Customer services
   (3) E-payments
   (4) E-collaboration in product design and development
   (5) E-collaboration in manufacturing
3. Please indicate the extent of use the following Internet applications when dealing with your major employees (B2E):
   (1) Training and education
   (2) Human resource applications (benefits, job postings)
   (3) Product design and development
   (4) Product manufacturing
4. Please indicate the extent to use the following Internet applications when dealing with other external entities (i.e., Government, Consultants, Industry Associations, Educational Institutions) (B2O):
   (1) Technology sourcing
   (2) Competitive intelligence
   (3) Market research/ industry analysis
   (4) Government compliance
   (5) New business development

This work was previously published in International Journal of E-Business Research (IJEBR), edited by In Lee, pp. 49-64, copyright 2009 by IGI Publishing (an imprint of IGI Global).

Chapter 4
Beyond Efficiency and Productivity:
ICT Business Value, Competitive Growth and the Construction of Corporate Image

Susan J. Winter
National Science Foundation, USA

Connie Marie Gaglio
San Francisco State University, USA

Hari K. Rajagopalan
Francis Marion University, USA

ABSTRACT

Firms employ information and communication technology (ICT) in their pursuit of competitive growth and the productivity-related business value that accrues from its use is widely acknowledged. However, the organizational literature has long recognized that operational efficiency and productivity are not the only factors required for corporate success. One of the primary tasks facing firm leaders is the management of external stakeholders' impressions of the firm that enable it to gain access to external resources. This chapter explores this additional symbolic dimension of ICT business value by investigating how and when the simple possession and use of ICT itself might create favorable impressions of the firm, yielding business value and competitive growth over and above its effects on operational efficiency and productivity. Using qualitative and inductive methods, the authors identify established and emerging ICTs' additional symbolic meanings for potential customers and develop a model of the judgment process through which ICT affects corporate images. When assessing the business value of ICT savvy managers should consider both efficiency and organizational image. Implications for theory, practice, and future research are discussed.

DOI: 10.4018/978-1-60960-132-4.ch004

Copyright © 2011, IGI Global. Copying or distributing in print or electronic forms without written permission of IGI Global is prohibited.

INTRODUCTION

Firms employ established and emerging information and communication technologies (ICT) in their pursuit of competitive growth and the productivity-related business value that accrues from their use is widely acknowledged. Advice for increasing the positive impacts of ICT has focused on developing planning and implementation processes that are most likely to result in operational productivity benefits (e.g., Peppard, et al. 2007). The literature on justifying ICT investments often rests on demonstrating the business value of ICT as a complementary asset in the efficient and effective handling of information. It is believed that the value of ICT lies in its potential to improve the efficiency of transactions and other routine operations, enabling better analysis and strategy, etc. These, in turn, will enable firms to efficiently manage internal operations and supply chain activities to enhance productivity and profitability (Gregor, et al., 2006; Melville et al., 2004; Murphy & Simon, 2007) and achieve competitive growth. Rarely do researchers consider the business value of ICT from a perspective other than that of the operational efficiency/productivity paradigm (Kwon & Watts, 2006).

However, reliance on a single paradigm or method may seriously limit our understanding of any IS phenomenon (Orlikowski & Iacono, 2001). This paper steps back from the dominant paradigm and explores the business value of ICT using a comparatively nontraditional approach that draws upon commonly accepted traditions in non-IS business research. The organizational literature has long recognized that operational efficiency and productivity are not the only prerequisites for organizational success and competitive growth (Meyer & Rowan, 1977). One important task facing firm leaders is the management of internal and external stakeholders' impressions of the firm (Elsbach, et al., 1998; Pfeffer & Salancik, 1978). Creating desired impressions enables firms to gain access to external resources that are crucial to their survival and growth such as labor, financing, and most importantly, a stream of income from sales (Starr & MacMillan, 1990; Stinchcombe, 1968).

Theoretical analysis by Feldman and March (1981) and subsequent empirical study by Feldman (1989) demonstrated that the simple possession of information in organizations can produce benefits irrespective of the actual use of such information. In their work, information proved to play a powerful role as a signal and symbol of desirable organizational qualities. By transitivity, it is reasonable to assume that the long-recognized, socially interpreted properties of ICT (cf., Robey & Azevedo 1994) might generate business value through such signaling and symbolic mechanisms. This assumption has been supported by recent research on the link between ICT and perceptions of legitimacy (Noir & Walsham, 2007; Gaglio, et al., 1998; Winter, et al., 2009), demonstrating that the business value of ICT extends beyond efficiency improvements to include a symbolic dimension. This paper while confirming the value of ICT in creating legitimacy explores this additional symbolic dimension of ICT business value by investigating how and when the simple possession and use of established and emerging ICT itself might create favorable impressions of the firm, providing business value over and above its effects on operational efficiency, productivity and legitimacy.

Research on the computerization of work has explored what ICT symbolizes to internal stakeholders (employees) and the effects of these meanings on implementation (e.g. Fichman, 2000; Jackson, et al., 2002; Moore & Benbasat, 1991; Prasad, 1993, Robey & Azevedo, 1994; Robey & Boudreau, 1999; Saga & Zmud, 1994). It has also considered what ICT signals to external stakeholders such as shareholders, regulators and funders (Noir & Walsham, 2007; Ranganathan 7 Brown, 2006) and to developers and special interest groups who create an emerging ICT's symbolic meaning (e.g. Garud 7 Rappa, 1994; Swanson and Ramiller, 1997).

Indeed, a sizable body of research has investigated symbolism and ICT suggesting that the paradigm is maturing. However, a maturing paradigm risks developing rigid beliefs and methodological assumptions that obstruct progress in fully understanding a phenomenon. Despite a tradition of investigating the symbolic value of ICT, only sketchy information is available about the influence of the external stakeholder group that is most directly involved in the firm: the customers themselves. Consistent with new institutional theory (Meyer and Rowan, 1977), research on customer views has discovered that ICT is a valuable signal of firm legitimacy and affects purchase behavior (Gaglio, et al., 1998), but it is not know what other corporate image dimensions it may signal. This paper systematically explores the link between a firm's ICT choices and additional important corporate image dimensions as experienced and expressed through the customer's own voice, an important concern for both managers and researchers.

If ICT is linked to impressions of an organization, managers should take into account this signaling value when assessing the total business value of established and emerging ICT. Managers may highlight or hide the presence and use of ICTs, depending on whether the impressions created are positively or negatively related to support behavior. Thus, the symbolic value of ICT represents a previously under-researched portion of its total business value, which may include improvements in efficiency, its ability to act as a signal of legitimacy and other corporate images that are important to external stakeholders such as customers.

This study seeks to address this gap in our understanding of ICT by answering three research questions. The first two related research questions addressed here are: What organizational image—related meanings do prospective customers infer from the presence of established and emerging ICT? What factors moderate customer expectations and how does this affect ICT's symbolic

value? The third research question addressed is: What is the decision process that prospective customers engage in when forming ICT-based organizational images? Answering this question will clarify how ICT acts as a symbol.

IS researchers have been advised that the nature of the subject should drive the choice of research methods (Lee, 1991). The phenomenological view assumes that informants' meanings and subjective experiences are important targets of study. Adopting a phenomenological perspective, this paper identifies the symbolic meanings of established and emerging ICT from a customer perspective and how these meanings are related to corporate image, but is not an in-depth ethnography (Boland, 1986). Inductive methods are used to identify these subjective understandings (Bryman, 2001) and answer the first two research questions. An interpretivist analysis allows us to improve our understanding of the phenomena and answer the third research question (Walsham, 1993).

We begin by briefly describing the existing corporate image literature with particular attention to its relationship to institutional theory and the potential symbolic role of ICT. This is followed by an in-depth presentation of an inductive investigation of the causal links between ICT and corporate image, and the judgment process that explains these causal links. Although it is generated from our more specific results, our findings begin with the presentation of the abstract theoretical frame or paradigm model (as recommended by Strauss and Corbin, 1998), highlighting factors that affect customer's expectations in the process by which corporate image is created and the symbolic role of ICT in this process and addressing the third research question. Addressing the first two research questions, each element of the model is then described with supporting evidence and comparisons between the findings and existing theory to identify areas of confirmation or contradiction. The result is an integrative, general and particularistic theory of the symbolic role of ICT in corporate image (Martin and Turner, 1986).

Finally, implications of this model for managers and directions for future theory and research are discussed.

BACKGROUND

Existing theory does not specifically predict the symbolic value of a firm's ICT in forming a corporate image, but several tangential areas of research are relevant. A fairly extensive organizational literature explores stakeholders' firm perceptions and their effects on organizational members (Gioia, et al., 2000). Drawing on this tradition, the ICT literature has considered employees' and managers' interpretations of ICT highlighting the role of metaphors and their symbolic effects on the adoption and implementation of technologies (e.g. Fichman, 2000; Jackson, et al., 2002; Orlikowski & Iacono, 2000), but the role of ICT and the customer perspective has not been considered.

Institutional theory emphasizes matching audience expectations and the importance of symbols in managing perceptions, particularly of legitimacy (Meyer and Rowan, 1977). ICT and perceptions of legitimacy have been explored from the perspective of regulators, employees and customers (e.g. Noir & Walsham, 2007; Prasad, 1993; Gaglio, et al., 1998), but other possible image dimensions have not been explored. Institutional theorists agree that schema theory and mental models provide a link between shared social meaning and individual-level perceptions of appropriate behaviors (Powell & DiMaggio, 1991). The study of social cognition assumes that information is stored in memory in structured symbolic networks called schemas (Lord & Foti, 1986), integrated knowledge bases that guide the information perceived and retrieved from memory, the inferences drawn and the actions taken (Fiske & Taylor, 1991; Markus & Zajonc, 1985). Neither institutional theorists nor schema theorists have addressed ICT- related behaviors.

The literature on marketing and public relations addresses symbolism and customer perceptions of a firm in research on corporate identify and image. Though this perspective has not investigated the signaling function of ICT, it provides a useful research tradition we can draw upon and integrate with institutional theory and mental models to better understand the symbolic dimension of ICT's business value and role in competitive growth.

Corporate Image

The term "corporate image" is widely accepted in the marketing literature, but is not meant to exclude not-for-profit, volunteer, or governmental organizations. Specific definitions of corporate identity and image are hotly debated in the literature, but they are generally accepted terms for how a firm is perceived. Corporate identity has been described as a firm's personality, what it stands for, what is central and distinctive about it, or the essence of what the firm is (Albert & Whetten, 1985; Balmer, 1998). It is considered to reflect the corporate-level mission, values, vision, history, philosophy, culture, and behavior (Ind, 1992; Van Riel, 1997). Within the field of corporate identity, corporate image refers to stakeholder impressions and definitions of this construct vary depending upon which stakeholder group's view of the firm is emphasized. Our interest is in the views of customers, which is consistent with the work of Berg (1985) and with the concerns of the public relations field (Melewar & Karaosmanoglu, 2006). The importance of establishing a corporate image has long been accepted in both marketing and organizational theory (Christian, 1959; Easton, 1966; Hatch & Schultz, 1997; Meyer & Rowan, 1977; Pfeffer & Salancik, 1978; Spector, 1961).

Recent work argues that corporate image comprises seven elements: (1) corporate culture; (2) brand and organizational structure; (3) industry identity; (4) strategic positioning; (5) the behavior of the corporation, its employees, and managers; (6) corporate communication; and (7) corporate design. This last element includes components of what is called the corporate visual identity system such as buildings, clothes, graphics, and slogans (Melewar and Karaosmanoglu, 2006). Within public relations, corporate brand management argues that corporate identity is represented to the public through behavior, communication and visual design (the last three elements of the construct), which express the corporation's culture, structure, industry, and strategic positioning (the first four elements). Thus, the corporate identity literature provides broad guidance on the dimensions of an organization that affect corporate image, but does not provide information about the detailed particularistic meanings of specific cues such as ICT or about the process by which ICT communicates symbolic information.

Corporate Image, Institutional Theory, and Symbols

In pursuing competitive growth, each organization may differentiate itself in the marketplace by creating a distinct identity and managing its image. Doing so requires managers to leverage the symbolic and physical resources institutionalized in their business environment. A focus on managerial action in pursuit of firm goals has been termed the strategic perspective (Oliver, 1991). The strategic perspective in the corporate image literature emphasizes the actions managers can take in manipulating symbols to convey impressions that their firms adhere to accepted codes of conduct, which have been identified as central to corporate identity (Melewar & Karaosmanoglu, 2006). Institutional theory emphasizes the social constraints that shape and influence managerial actions. These constraints are created by the need to appear to conform to shared social norms (Meyer & Rowan, 1977). It has illuminated the role of social structure in the creation of symbolic meaning and reciprocal effects on individual behavior (Scott, 2001). Institutional researchers have argued that group-level norms are linked to individual

judgments through mental models, schemas, and scripts (DiMaggio & Powell, 1983). From this perspective, organizational decision-makers' actions (such as adopting and using established and emerging ICT) represent attempts to leverage socially constructed symbols to manage the firm's valuable image by appearing to conform to the schema-informed stakeholder expectations about appropriate behavior (Meyer & Rowan, 1977; Pfeffer & Salancik, 1978).

Thus, creating and maintaining a corporate image represents the intersection between strategy, institutional theory, schema theory (Oliver, 1991; Suchman, 1995) and the enactment of ICT (Orlikowski & Iacono, 2000). In addition to efficiency concerns, competitive growth depends on adoption of ICT that conveys the "right" impression, which requires an understanding of customer expectations (Feldman & March, 1981). Previous IS research has not investigated the role of customer expectations or the effects of ICT on customer's images of the firm aside from its legitimacy. An awareness of customer assumptions enables organizational decision-makers to be more effective in choosing which established and emerging ICTs to adopt to create their preferred corporate image, attract a particular target market and enable competitive growth. This symbolic power forms part of the total business value of ICT (Dutton & Dukerich, 1991; Gaglio, et al., 1998).

Much of the empirical research informed by institutional theory emphasizes perceptions of legitimacy. Legitimacy has been consistently linked to survival and is universally desirable (Suchman, 1995; Zimmerman & Zeitz, 2002), and matching ICT to customer expectations has been linked to perceptions of legitimacy (Gaglio, et al., 1998). However, firms focus on different market niches so there are a variety of additional images they may wish to convey. What is not known is whether ICT symbolizes additional corporate image dimensions of interest or how customers use established and emerging ICT as a signal of these qualities. To better understand the process underlying this phenomenon, we explore the attributions about firms that are drawn from their use of ICT and how ICT affects the corporate images that are created. We are particularly interested in the role of customer expectations and accepted standards for ICT adoption and use, issues that have previously been linked to successful symbolic management (DiMaggio & Powell, 1983; Feldman and March, 1981; Suchman, 1995).

The importance of expectations suggests that each actor must have an internal mental model or schema of various types of firms, the rules of the business including those guiding ICT use and how to evaluate compliance. Presumably, managers recall this mental model as they choose which ICT symbols to display in creating a corporate image; potential customers recall their mental models as they judge the meaning of these symbols. Creating an image, then, involves matching the ICT use of an organization to those of an ideal type (Powell & DiMaggio, 1991). This study identifies the detailed contents of these mental models linking ICT use on the one hand and corporate image and symbolic meaning on the other.

ICT and Corporate Image

When examining the role of ICT in creating corporate images then, one is asking how managers can use ICT in ways that meet customer expectations. This study extends our understanding by identifying the language, behavior, and symbols that ordinary people use to convey and evaluate these images and by developing a particularistic account of the role of ICTs as a symbol and how it carries meaning. To understand the role of ICT in creating corporate image we explore the interaction between firms and their customers in greater depth to clarify when creating a valuable corporate image requires using ICT and what factors affect stakeholders' expectations about ICT. This research provides particularistic details to elaborate abstract substantive theories. It adopts the process view inherent in any model of decision--making

(Eisenhardt, 1989; Martin & Turner, 1986) and relates the results obtained to existing theories regarding symbolic meanings that may underlie ICT, identifying areas in which our data confirm or contradict existing explanations (Martin & Turner, 1986). In addition it combines the particularistic results into a more abstract model examining the mechanism underlying the communication of image and determines if it resembles the use of mental models and schema theory.

METHOD

Given space limitations, it is not our intent to rehearse well known epistemological and methodological debates already extant in the IS literature. This research engages in theory development and focuses on the relationships among context (including external stakeholder groups such as customers) and actors (firm decision makers), for which grounded inductive techniques are considered particularly appropriate (Eisenhardt, 1989; Martin & Turner, 1986). Integrating our inductively derived concepts with abstract theory provides analytic generalization (Yin, 1989). Empirical qualitative data about the role of ICT in communicating image was collected and analyzed using a mix of qualitative and quantitative methods (Glaser & Strauss, 1967; Strauss & Corbin, 1998). In-depth, semi-structured interviews employing focus group techniques commonly used in marketing research allowed a greater depth of understanding. Consistent with a phenomenological perspective, inductive methods allowed us to identify the dimensions and language that are meaningful to our informants with corporate image and customer expectations acting as sensitizing concepts (van den Hoonaard, 1997). This section describes the sample, explains the procedures used to collect the data, outlines the steps taken in developing the data classification scheme used to code the data, and describes the quantitative measures used to summarize the data.

Sample

We focused on sales pitches of new firms to control for issues that could affect a corporation's image (such as previous experience with advertisements), but are unrelated to the use of ICT. The sales pitches of new firms are particularly appropriate for studying the process of creating corporate images because founders often recount how they managed firm impressions when making their first sales (Darwell, et al., 1998), so establishing a corporate image should be salient to the informants (Singh, et al., 1991). In addition, the sales pitch is a bounded interaction between two parties and is a readily recognizable form of communication. Each participant in the sales pitch event brings a set of general expectations and assumptions, which should make it easier to identify participants' ICT expectations. However, the age of the firm is not expected to affect the meaning of ICT and the corporate images created.

Two kinds of samples were drawn, one comprised founders of young companies and the other prospective customers (experienced buyers who had purchased from new firms). This provided multiple perspectives on the issue, more information on the emerging concepts and allowed cross-checking, and so yielded stronger substantiation of the resulting constructs (Martin and Turner, 1986; Strauss & Corbin, 1998). The sampling strategy was developed to maximize the applicability of the resulting theory to a variety of contexts. To elicit a wide range of ICT expectations, a purposive sample that included variety rather than statistical representation was developed, a common practice in qualitative research called theoretical sampling (Denzin, 1989). The final sample size was influenced by the redundancy of the data. When new interviews failed to yield novel responses, new properties, dimensions or relationships, we inferred that the likely range of responses had been mapped and data collection ended.

The Dun and Bradstreet database was used to draw a sample of 15 vendor firms between 2 and 5 years old and in South Florida (a 27% participation rate). As expected, many founders were too busy to participate. A list of potential customers was developed through referrals from founders of new firms and through the local telephone book. Many who were contacted were ineligible for inclusion in the study because they would not knowingly support a new firm. The remainder said that they were unwilling to make the time commitment. Purchase decision-makers of 14 businesses in South Florida (a response rate of 15%) agreed to participate. Each had used a new firm in the past and received sales pitches from a variety of vendors. To avoid inflating the degree of agreement between vendors and customers, we included three customers who had done business with a new firm in our sample and eleven who had not. As shown in Appendix A, the firms in our samples included a variety of sectors, scopes and sizes. Purchase decisions also were diverse and ranged from purchasing office supplies, business services, raw materials and finished goods for resale through sub-contracting entire portions of the firm's activities. Founders reported that they had little power over prospective customers when negotiating their first sales.

Procedures

Interviews were conducted by one of the authors at the participant's place of business, lasted between 45 and 90 minutes, were tape-recorded and later transcribed verbatim. Early open-ended questions encouraged respondents to talk about the issues that they considered important in convincing customers to place an order. Loosely structured questions asked informants to describe the work their organization performs, their products, customers and competitors. Vendors were asked about their first sales pitches. Follow-up probes asked about the most effective cues or tactics for convincing a potential customer to place an order, including probes about the role of ICT.

Consistent with organizational research on symbolism, the role of ICT in creating perceptions of firm legitimacy has been found to be tacit representing a taken-for-granted assumption that is unlikely to be elicited through direct questioning (Feldman, 1995; Winter, et al., 2009). To illuminate meaning in these instances, Garfinkel (1967) recommends engaging in "breaking experiments" that disrupt institutional realities and looking for the explanations provided for these transgressions. Strauss and Corbin (1998) suggest a similar practice they call the flip-flop technique in which researchers look at opposites and extremes, and ask participants about theoretical variations. Specifically, they recommend asking questions in the form: "What would happen if …?" Based on these recommendations, we created appropriate interview questions informed by the traditional marketing research structured focus group paradigm to elicit assumptions. However, the nature of our sample precluded the use of traditional focus groups because it was diverse, composed of professionals (who are very hard to recruit) and involved potential competitors divulging their business techniques (Greenbaum, 1998; Stewart and Shamdasani, 1990). Consequently, as recommended by Greenbaum (1998) one-on-one in-depth interviews using focus group techniques were conducted.

Three common focus group techniques were adopted. First, to surface less salient issues (symbolic value of ICT), we bounded and cued the questions, but left them open-ended so that the answer was not implied (Greenbaum, 1998; Krueger, 1998) and provided background information to the participants (Krueger, 1998). Second, a projective technique involving analogies was included to evoke participants' feelings about a familiar stimulus and help them articulate their reactions to ICT. Consistent with marketing research focus group techniques, we drew an analogy between the symbolic value of a Ferrari and a Honda Civic (while explicitly recognizing that both provide adequate transportation) and

the symbolic value of ICT (Greenbaum, 1998; Krueger, 1998; Sudman, et al., 1996).

Finally, we asked founders to answer as though they were customers and used sentence completion, and breaking experiments that describe actions that violate common expectations (Greenbaum, 1998; Krueger, 1998). A set of customer-firm interaction scenarios involving ICT (like receiving a fax from Kinko's vs. a proprietary machine owned by the sender) were developed and respondents were asked what inferences they would draw from each if they were the customer and why. Founders were then asked what their customers would think if their firm did something similar and what customers thought of their firm's use of these technologies. Customers were asked what they would think if a vendor did something similar and many spontaneously commented on their firms' use of these technologies and speculated on the inferences that their customers drew. Informants responded readily when asked if a scenario would "raise a red flag" or "raise a yellow flag", indicating that this metaphorical language is broadly understood. These questions are shown in Appendix B (for the complete interview schedule, please see Winter, et al., 2009).

Analysis

Our analytical approach was driven by the study's objectives and followed Martin and Turner's (1986) recommendation that qualitative data be used both to challenge existing theory and to develop new theory. Data were coded and interpreted according to the extant institutionalism literature leading to the identification of extensions and anomalies. For building our model of the judgment process, we adhered to the recommendations of Glaser and Strauss (1967), focusing particularly on negative cases – those that did not clearly fit a priori theory. These served as springboards for the modification of existing or instantiation of new paradigms and models. Our analysis proceeded iteratively, taking place both during data collection and afterward. This provided opportunities to pursue emergent ideas, modify the interviewer's language to more closely reflect that of the informants, and later to view the entire set of data for insights (Eisenhardt, 1989; Glaser & Strauss, 1967). This allowed us to reconcile discrepancies between theory and data during the data collection process and determine when closure had been achieved (Denzin, 1989).

Coding Scheme Development

Analysis began with one author coding the customer transcripts and the other coding the vendor transcripts using a priori categories as sensitizing constructs (e.g. expectations) and identifying emergent categories (e.g. historical period) that were negotiated between the authors. In open coding, each coder created a preliminary coding framework that represented the features of the data and the distinctions made by the informants (Martin & Turner, 1986; Strauss & Corbin, 1998). We sought an inclusive framework that could be refined in later studies. As suggested by Strauss and Corbin (1998), we performed a microscopic examination of the data to generate initial categories, recognize taken-for-granted assumptions, and identify other cases for theoretical sampling. This involved comparing across participants to find similarities and differences and within participants to find contradictions. We also made theoretical comparisons between the images created by visual identity symbols such as furnishings, and wardrobe and those created by ICT. Data were also coded for evidence of the importance of violations of expectations, a sensitizing construct drawn from institutional theory.

Data Coding

Often participants' responses were multidimensional with informants describing multiple corporate images in a single sentence. Meaningful phrases from each of the responses were first parsed before they were mapped to the coding scheme. Comments were coded based on apparent category membership and coders discussed categories into which the data fell based on the issues identified by our informants. Comparing the data to the emerging model, we continued to refine our categories. Disagreements about the elements and their relationships were discussed and resolved, often by refining the typology.

All transcripts were then coded for each element one final time by the third author. Summary information was created by counting the number of informants who mentioned a category and the number of times a category was mentioned. Fisher's Exact tests were performed and determined that the responses of founders did not differ from those of customers.

Concepts were then organized by recurring themes, forming a set of stable and common categories during axial coding (Martin & Turner, 1986; Strauss & Corbin, 1998). This yielded a network of broad categories and associated maps of causal elements that described the participants' understanding of the symbolic information transmitted by ICT and its role in the purchase decision. Memos reflecting the narrative interpretation of the corporate image formation process evinced by the data were then written (Martin & Turner, 1986). Responses of various informants were compared to each other (Strauss & Corbin, 1998) and an integrative framework was developed. After moving back and forth between memos, pertinent case data and relevant literature, an agreed upon final "story line" and a model of the important corporate images, their cues and interrelationships was created. Finally, models of judgment and decision-making were reviewed to identify any that provided a useful account of the data. The resulting framework derives empirical validity from the fact that it accounts for the data from each source and provides a general pattern across the data sources (Martin and Turner, 1986).

Figure 1. Model of information and communications technology, corporate image and support

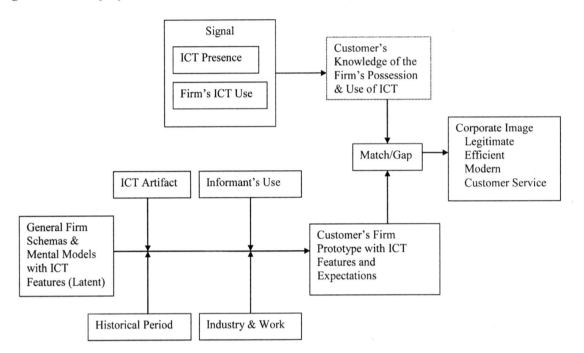

RESULTS

Theoretical Frame

Addressing the third research question, the more abstract theoretical frame also called a paradigm model is presented first. This model shows the judgment process and factors affecting it. It summarizes the theory that emerged from our data (Strauss & Corbin, 1998). This model shows connections between the elements that were identified during open coding and helps provide a guide to the detailed results (addressing the first two research questions), which are presented after the model, although the latter is actually an aggregate of the former.

Consistent with institutional theory and previous research on ICT and customer perceptions of legitimacy, the image-creation process (shown in Figure 1) resembles that of schema theory, in which mental models play a central role (Fiske & Taylor, 1991; Gaglio, et al., 1998; Powell and DiMaggio, 1991; Winter, et al., 2009). Some el-

ements of the model cannot be signaled by ICT (industry, historical time frame, respondent's use of ICT), but play an important role in forming the expectations against which a firm will be judged. Other elements provide information about the ICT artifacts used by a firm. In addition to legitimacy, three corporate images can be signaled by ICT (modernity, efficiency and customer service). The purchase decision process is influenced by the schemas held by the prospective customer who infers firm characteristics from the symbolic information provided by ICT.

An individual's knowledge and beliefs are stored in memory as schemas, which are mental models about how a portion of the world works that guide understanding, judgment and action (Gioia, 1986). Mental models represent an actor's understanding and feelings about what kinds of elements (events, people and objects) are relevant to a given situation, the types of relationships among these elements, how they are formed, what causal sequences of events are possible and what actions are permissible, sanctioned, and previously successful or misguided (Fiske & Taylor, 1991; Markus & Zajonc, 1985). They are developed and modified over time through personal experience and secondhand information and include prototypes which represent sets of elements associated with typical instances of a category.

The process of signaling a corporate image with ICT begins with actors' general mental models -about various kinds of firms and about ICT. This mental model includes several possible firm categories represented as prototypes. The firm may be a large national or multi-national chain, a small custom firm, a rapidly growing start-up, a mom-and-pop operation, a hobbyist trying to become a professional, or a company of shaky legitimacy sometimes called fly-by-night. Each of these includes a set of ICT elements. Drawing upon their general mental models of organizations and contextual information, actors retrieve a set of possible prototype firms and their collection of elements. A firm that shares a set of elements with a given prototype will be judged to be a member of that category and assumed to have other characteristics of the category.

These mental models and prototypes start with general assumptions about businesses and the meaning of ICT (e.g. cool, neat, nerdy, lame) and are updated dynamically as new information is encountered, so they vary based on the historical time period (work in the 1930s vs. today), the nature of the vendor's industry (MRI lab vs. landscapers) and the work that is performed (sales vs. mechanics). These models comprise the complex constellation of diverse elements of corporate image including the firm's location, production facilities, employee appearance, sales brochures, etc. When some of these elements are ICTs, the customer forms expectations that these elements will be present in a firm of a given type.

Firms possess and use various kinds of office and production technologies in providing their products or services. During the sales pitch, a firm's representative describes the company and its products or services and may display or describe the ICTs they have, or provide indirect evidence of them.

During a sales pitch, the potential customer tries to categorize the firm accurately. He or she collects information about the kind of firm to determine whether placing an order would result in a positive transaction. The mental model accessed by the potential customer reflects the general meaning of ICT, but this is moderated by the historical time period, the industry and work performed and the potential customer's own use of an ICT. This mental model includes prototypes and their associated ICTs and the potential customer attempts to determine which category this firm belongs to by comparing its characteristics to those of each prototype. It is here that information about the vendor's ICT carries symbolic information. Based on these mental models, the potential customer forms a set of expectations regarding which specific ICT artifacts firms of each kind are expected to have.

During the sales pitch, the potential customer learns which ICTs a firm has and compares this to what they expected based upon their mental model and prototypes. Matches or gaps between expectations of the firm's ICT and the firm's actual ICT are then used to infer other characteristics of the firm based on the interconnected information elements in the mental model. In addition to legitimacy, the corporate images inferred include how modern and up-to-date the firm is, how efficient and well organized it is, and what level of customer service it is likely to provide.

Addressing the first research question, In the following section, these concepts and their interactions are discussed in detail.

Model Elements

Four sets of firm characteristics related to corporate images are inferred from ICT, but informants discussed complex contingencies affecting their ICT-related expectations. Each of these areas is described in more detail below.

Corporate Image Inferred From ICT

As mentioned previously, ICT acts as a cue from which four dimensions related to corporate image are inferred: (a) whether the firm is a legitimate organization, (b) how efficient and well organized it is; (c) whether it is modern or up-to-date; and (d) the level of customer service (related to success). Participants agree that these characteristics influence the firm's ability to attract customers, and often mention images and support together. However, not all firms strive to create the same image and not all customers choose to place orders with firms of the same type.

Although conceptually distinct, many of the firm characteristics are mentioned together and cued by the same symbol, suggesting that they form a constellation of interrelated elements stored in participants' mental models of firms. This kind of overlap is consistent with the retrieval of prototype characteristics from mental models as outlined in the paradigm model presented earlier (Fiske and Taylor, 1991). The purpose of this paper is to build a particularistic and general model that accurately represents the richness of the participants' view of the phenomenon. To preserve the structure of these mental models, we chose not to orthogonalized categories that were conflated by our informants. Instead, they are presented as the intact, compound, multidimensional constructs that were described by the participants.

First, ICT as a signal of legitimacy, as shown in Table 1. ICT acts as a cue symbolizing dimensions of legitimacy (Suchman, 1995), which was mentioned by the overwhelming majority (90%) of the participants a total of 92 times. Participants agree that legitimacy influences the firm's ability to attract customers, and often mention legitimacy elements (size, seriousness, professionalism, capitalization) and support together.

Apparel Catalog: *It's the little things that make you aware of what type of company you're dealing with. Again, if they don't have voice mail, if*

Table 1. Percent of informants discussing a category and number of times mentioned

Element	%	No. of Times Mentioned
Corporate Image		
Legitimacy	90	92
Efficient	66	38
Modern	83	57
Customer Service	83	71
Moderators		
Industry and Work Personal Use	72 / 45	62 / 23
Company Use	79	44
Historical Period	90	62
Knowledge of Firm's ICT	93	99
General ICT Meaning	48	29

they don't have a cell phone, if they don't have fax capabilities, e-mail capabilities, these are the signs. This is what you sense. This is how you know that this isn't a real big company. If they make the commitment to have a fax machine, to have everything in place before they start up then they are a little more serious and maybe you'll take the chance and take the risk of putting the product in the book... You know that they're not financed if they don't even have a fax machine

Although conceptually distinct, the elements of legitimacy are mentioned together and cued by the same symbol, suggesting that they co-occur in participants' mental models of legitimate and illegitimate firms. This is consistent with the retrieval of prototype characteristics as outlined in the earlier paradigm model (Fiske & Taylor, 1991). Large, serious, professional firms are often contrasted with "hobbyists" or "fly-by-night" firms, suggesting that these represent common firm prototypes. Consistent with previous research on legitimacy, no participants wanted to work with "hobbyists" or "fly-by-night" firms.

Our results suggest that the adoption and use of ICT is a form of behavior linked to judgments that a firm is legitimate, an image that is universally desirable and is central to a firm's success and competitive growth (Zimmerman & Zeitz, 2002). Customers' assumptions about the appropriate adoption and use of ICT affect their judgment of the firm as legitimate. If decision-makers adopt and use ICT in ways that are consistent with customers' assumptions about what is appropriate, they can create an image of legitimacy, avoid being labeled "fly-by-night", and improve the likelihood that they will receive customer orders (Dutton & Dukerich, 1991).

Second, ICT acts as a signal about how well organized and efficient a firm is. As shown in Table 1, they were mentioned 38 times and by about 2/3 of participants (66%). A corporate image of organization and efficiency are often inferred from ordering, billing, or inventory control software. Most believe that well-organized and efficient firms have greater capacity, thus they are able to fulfill their contracts.

Pager: [laptop ordering is] a form of communication that they're much more organized all around it's a plus. I would probably say that their production is probably a lot more efficient and they're probably able to produce their product you know in a larger quantity than someone who's not as organized.

Environmental Clean-up Consulting: [laptop ordering shows] that they're more organized. More efficient. They should be more efficient.

An important task of executive officers is to create and maintain an image that attracts resources such as customers (Elsbach, et al., 1998; Meyer & Rowan, 1977; Starr & MacMillan, 1990; Stinchcombe, 1968). To do so, executives make symbolic choices about the artifacts displayed in work areas and about corporate appearance and behavior in general. These decisions include the location, furnishing and decor of office space, the design of letterhead and business cards and the number, appearance and behavior of employees, etc. (Schmitt & Simonson, 1997). Corporate impression management has been studied in a wide variety of public work settings (Futrell, 1998; Gaglio, et al., 1998; Gardner, 1992; Gardner & Avolio, 1998; Grayson & Shulman, 2000; Grove & Fisk, 1989; Ornstein, 1989). Areas that are viewed by customers are of particular interest because firms are dependent upon customers for a revenue stream; therefore, the images portrayed in these areas are central to a firm's success. Today's firms pursuing a strong corporate identity must make choices about ICT artifacts including cell phones, pagers, Web sites, voice mail, e-mail, etc. (Winter, et al., 2009). In general, firms that appear to be well-organized and efficient are more likely to receive orders, so the use of ordering, billing, or inventory control software could provide image-based business value because of their symbolic meaning in addition to any actual improvements in organization and efficiency.

Third, an overwhelming majority of participants (83%) said 57 times that the use of ICT symbolizes that a firm is modern, up-to-date, advanced, on the cutting edge, proactive, and understands industry trends, which was linked to long term success.

Custom Linens (retail): But I'm sure that they're advanced if they have [e-mail].

Promotional Products Distributor: [Having a webpage says] They're a little more progressive; they're on the ball. They're progressive; they're proactive.

General Contractor: [Vendors who bring in results of computer runs] seem to be on top of their industry and staying in the lead. Gives us a comfort level as opposed to the one that's scratched out on a piece of paper.

Firms that lacked some expected forms of ICT were judged to be outdated and less likely to survive.

Flowers and Gifts Retailer: *If you manage your business on a sheet of paper versus a computer, or versus this whiz-bang system, my perception is, well you haven't gotten from the '60s to here, what makes you think you're going to get from here forward with us?*

Customers were less comfortable placing orders with less modern firms, suggesting that these firms will have difficulty attracting resources and achieving competitive growth. For firms that want to appear modern, adopting emerging forms of ICT could provide business value because they create a corporate image that fits the firm's market position in addition to any improvements in efficiency or productivity.

Finally, 83% of participants mentioned 71 times that they infer the firm's orientation toward customer service from the presence or absence of various forms of ICT, especially communications ICT such as cell phones and pagers.

Wireless Services Provider: *[A web site with downloadable manuals] says to me that ... they're willing to do whatever it takes to get your business.*

Kidney Dialysis Lab: *[what does having voice mail symbolize to your customer]: Impersonal, I don't care, and this is done to suit our needs rather than yours.*

However, they acknowledge that the availability of the ICT does not always mean it would be used appropriately (a moderator that is described in more detail later).

General Contractor: *[cell phone or pager symbolizes] that he's [the customer's] the most important person and, when he calls, he's going to get service... If you have to continue to call back*

and talk to voicemail, talk to voicemail, that's a negative." ... *It says that ... they don't care.*

Poor voice mail use over time can actually indicate a lack of customer service, but, in the absence of a track record of performance, most participants inferred from its presence that a new firm would value the customer and provide excellent service.

In sum, ICT acts as a cue from which customers infer a firm's legitimacy, efficiency, modernity and level of customer service. A firm must compete for a market segment and so must establish a corporate image that appeals to its target customers. Creating and maintaining a valuable corporate image represents the intersection between strategy and institutional theory (Oliver, 1991; Suchman, 1995). The strategic perspective emphasizes managerial action in manipulating the firm's behavioral, verbal and non-verbal symbols to convey the impression that the firm adheres to the stakeholders' expectations and codes of conduct identified by institutional theory (Pfeffer & Salancik, 1978).

These codes of conduct reflect the system of meaning that underlies the social construction of reality (Berger & Luckmann, 1967; Feldman & March, 1981; Schein, 1985). Actors use these meanings to make sense of their world by interpreting verbal, behavioral and graphic symbols (Gioia, 1986). Creation of the desired corporate image depends on the degree to which the manager understands stakeholders' expectations and knows which symbols would convey the "right" impression. This paper provides evidence that ICT is one of those symbols and that these expectations form accepted standards for established and emerging ICT use (DiMaggio and Powell, 1983) informed by customers' mental models and firm's prototypes. Corporate images influence the likelihood that customers will place an order, a crucial determinant of firm's competitive growth and an important component of ICT's business value.

Contingencies Affecting ICT Expectations

The data indicate that not all firms are held to the same standards and expectations are not uniform. Participants differentiate among firms based on four contingencies. First, for firms in some industries the bar is considerably lower than it is for others. A large majority of informants (72%) described on 62 occasions that there were two dimensions that influenced their expectations: how sophisticated the firm or industry is, and the nature of the work itself.

Architecture and Interior Design: Depends on what they do. If it's a labor-oriented business, you wouldn't necessarily expect that they would be running a business from a computer. Depends on how sophisticated the business is.

Facilities Manager: So the snack guy might not be as technologically advanced as the air conditioning and the alarm people. You know what I'm saying? So different fields are going to have different levels of technology.

Organizational theorists have noted remarkable similarities in the structures and practices of diverse firms within an industry sector and have applied concepts of organizational mimicry and institutional isomorphism to account for them (DiMaggio & Powell, 1983; Meyer & Rowan, 1977). The institutional perspective focuses on the social structure of the environment and investigates its effects on individual behavior (Scott, 2001). Central to this work is the finding that organizations, their actions, structure and survival are affected by institutions in the environment and may not reflect the most efficient means of production. These institutions are seen as socially constructed systems of widely accepted rules, norms and beliefs that may be set down as laws and customs (Scott, 2001) and conformity with these norms provide explanations and justifica-

tions for patterns of action (Feldman & March, 1981). The fact that expectations regarding ICT differ depending on the nature of the industry and work performed reflects the influence of institutionalized norms and beliefs that vary by institutional field. A couple of respondents even reported hiding their use of advanced ICT that was crucial to their business strategy, but inconsistent with the norms of their field.

Second, 45% of participants judge the appropriateness of an ICT based on a comparison with their own adoption and use and mentioned this link 23 times.

Community Association Manager: I consider it to be a positive image if you have e-mail. Of course, I have e-mail so that's probably why.

The importance of personal experience is consistent with previous research on the development of mental models and social cognition. The study of social cognition assumes that people make sense of their environments by actively perceiving, organizing and drawing inferences about the objects and events that they encounter either directly, through personal experience, or indirectly, through stories told to them by others (Fiske & Taylor, 1991; Markus & Zajonc, 1985). Consequently, personal experience with an ICT affects participants' mental models, which influence their expectations.

Third, how ICT is used as one interacts with the firm over time is also important to its image, with 79% of participants discussing this issue 44 times. For example, many respondents inferred that firms that did not return voice mail messages did not value their customers.

General Engineering Contractor: They all have voice mail. Like I said, some hide behind it. Like the person I just called, I left a message for him to call me. It's been almost a week now. I faxed him; I paged him; I left a message on voice mail.

Firm behavior has been identified as one dimension of corporate identity and as a means by which corporate identity is represented to the public to form a corporate image (Melewar & Karaosmanoglu, 2006). Our data suggest that the use of ICT is one kind of behavior that affects corporate images perceived by customers.

Fourth, 90% of participants indicated 62 times that the symbolic meaning of ICT use has changed over time.

Legal Copying Service: *[having a Web page] I think a couple years ago, it would've said more. They must be a bigger company, they must think they're more organized or something because they can put something like this together. But now, we get calls I would say weekly from somebody trying to sell us a Web page for $99 or whatever.*

This is consistent with Saga and Zmud's (1994) stage model of ICT implementation which predicts that emerging ICTs diffuse into an industry over time and eventually become fully integrated into firms within the industry. Schema theory has shown that mental models can change over time to accommodate new information (Fiske & Taylor, 1991). Similarly, institutionalism has investigated the structure of institutions, their functions, development and change (Meyer & Rowan, 1977). These institutions encapsulate social norms and expectations.

Customers hold generalized attitudes and beliefs about ICT. They have stored information about firms in the form of mental models, which include many different elements. Pre-existing categories of firms form prototypes that reflect constellations of elements. These four contingencies guide customers in identifying which set of prototypes to retrieve from memory and use to classify a firm. Thus, they act as moderators affecting what established and emerging ICT customers expect and influence the likelihood that these expectations would be violated.

In addition, mismatches between expectations and ICT use could enhance or tarnish a firm's image, depending on the inferences drawn (Winter, et al. 2009). When ICT is taken-for-granted or assumed, its absence has a negative effect on the firm's image. When ICT is novel or optional, its presence can be positive when its symbolic meaning indicates conformity to desirable values and behaviors, but negative when it indicates characteristics or values that are undesirable. However, regardless of these moderators, ICT artifacts are clearly used as cues from which a firm's characteristics such as efficiency, modernity, and level of customer service are inferred. Our attention now turns to the process by which an observed ICT artifact is linked to its symbolic meaning.

How ICT Acts as a Symbol

Participants use ICT as a cue from which firm characteristics can be inferred and a corporate image is created during the sales process. These characteristics are not separate and distinct, but bundled together, along with many missing details that are filled in liberally. As the founder tells the story of the firm, the customers glean information about the firm's ICT. Over 90% of participants (93%) reported knowing or inferring the presence of ICT either by being told directly or by inference during the course of doing business, mentioning this 99 times.

Environmental Clean-up Consulting: *[So you're telling your customers about this website?] Yes. Oh yeah. Definitely.*

Catalog Apparel: *[Do your suppliers have laptops?] Some do, because they can tell you right there the quantity on hand, what they have available, deliveries, things like that.*

Customers compare this information to their standards and expectations regarding each mental model element. The observed and inferred characteristics are then used to categorize firms by comparison with existing firm prototypes (e.g. professionals or hobbyists). Based on the image created, firms that share a large number of characteristics with a particular prototype will be considered a member of that group. Customers prefer to work with vendors that fit particular prototypes (e.g. large, modern, efficient vs. small, personal, customer-oriented).

The entire process rests on the customers' understanding of the meaning of ICT, and 48% of participants mentioned generalized impressions of ICT a total of 29 times.

Environmental Clean-up Consulting: *They have caller ID and they know when you call what you're looking for already, which is really cool.*

To the extent that customers and vendors or organizational decision-makers have similar meanings of ICT, the latter are more likely to be able to control the corporate image communicated to customers.

Consequently, the symbolic meaning of ICT is used to categorize firms; this determines whether or not the firm receives purchase orders. This process resembles the cognitive dynamics of schema theory, which has been found to underlie many areas of social judgment. Information processing begins with the classification of stimuli based on matching attributes with those of pre-existing categories stored in schemas. Once categorized, missing pieces are filled in with category-consistent information. Schematic processing of symbols appears to be very efficient for handling large amounts of information (Bargh, 1984; Gioia, 1986).

Symbols can include artifacts such as established and emerging ICT and actions such as their use (Morgan, et al., 1983). However, their communicative power lies in the meaning attached to them, which, like schemas, may vary in different situations or social groups. When a potential symbol is encountered, it is compared

to existing knowledge stored as schemas to generate meaning (Gioia, 1986). When a symbol is associated with a schema, understanding occurs that guides interpretation and action in ambiguous or uncertain situations.

In the absence of a track record, customers of new firms will generate meaning by scrutinizing available signals, such as the use of ICT (Synder & Stukas, 1999), compare this information to their existing schemas for various types of firms and their use of ICT, classify the firm into an appropriate category, fill in missing information, and make inferences about the desirability of choosing a firm as an exchange partner.

Quite simply, a corporate image is judged based partly upon ICT whose meaning has been stored in schemas reflecting social institutions (Barley & Tolbert, 1997). The ICT acts as a symbol of conformity to the expectations and values of the perceiver for firms of a particular type. Customers compare the characteristics of a new firm, including its use of ICT, to a cognitive prototype of desirable firms. To be judged desirable, a founder should match customers' schemas for desirable firms or violate them in a manner that indicates pursuit of goals that conform to societal or market segment values. Thus, an ICT's symbolic meaning forms part of its business value because it affects a firm's image and influences purchase decisions that determine survival and enable competitive growth.

In order to assess a new firm, it appears that customers activate schemas about doing business in general, businesses in a specific industry at a particular period in time and about new businesses. The schemas activated by the customer bring to mind a set of prototypes and expectations about good and bad business transactions, and the use of ICT against which customers then evaluate the firm in order to determine whether they should place an order. New firms should consider matching their ICT signals to the meanings inferred by potential customers to project an image of a desirable firm. Thus, the mere presence of ICT itself can create a valuable corporate image in addition to any improvements in information handling efficiency or productivity, suggesting multiple dimensions of ICT business value.

DISCUSSION

These results show that ICT does provide a signal and creates a corporate image. The ultimate purpose of a customer interaction such as a sales pitch or store visit is to develop active support in the form of a sale, but a proximal purpose is the display of symbols such as established and emerging ICT that create a positive image of the firm. Potential customers clearly use ICT to infer firm characteristics such as legitimacy, efficiency modernity, and customer service in light of important contingency factors such as industry norms. Interestingly, customers fill in unknown details that allow them to locate the firm in an accepted model of economic activity. They seek to categorize the firm in terms of its type, based in part on a comparison of its ICT capabilities with those that were expected, not necessarily on the basis of objective productivity information. Assessments of the business value of ICT should include its effects on efficiency, firm legitimacy, and corporate image.

Contributions

Using inductive, qualitative and quantitative methods adapted from non-IS business research paradigms, a general and particularistic model of the subjective understandings of ICT that drive customers' purchase behavior was developed. This extends our understanding of the business value of ICT, the creation of corporate images, mental models, and schemas. This paper identifies the language, behavior and symbols that ordinary people use to convey and evaluate images, focusing specifically on the role of ICT as a signal, the firm characteristics that are judged, and how

ICTs carry meaning. In addition, this research clarifies if and when creating a corporate image will require the use of ICT and how stakeholders will know about such use.

We have extended the literature on the symbolic meaning of ICT by considering the interpretations of customers, an understudied external stakeholder group. In addition, we have extended the literature on corporate image, which has previously considered the effects of public communications and visual design strategies such as letterhead and uniforms (e.g. Grayson and Shulman, 2000), to include the effects of ICT. Finally, our understanding of the business value of ICT has been expanded by identifying an underrepresented symbolic dimension.

Implications for Managers

Support decisions are influenced by external stakeholders' images of the firm. In addition to productivity concerns, decisions about the use of ICT should consider image issues and symbolic meaning as part of business value. To be successful, executives must be familiar with the norms in their industry and with their stakeholders' expectations regarding an ICT to ensure that they draw positive inferences about the firm from its ICT use. As schema theory predicts, executives must also understand the symbolic meaning underlying their use. For example, voice mail call routing may enhance one firm's image of efficiency, but may be incompatible with another's efforts to be seen as providing excellent, personalized customer service.

Of course, the task of managing corporate image through the judicial use of ICT increases in importance for founders of new firms because they are creating an image before they have established a reputation based on performance, so they must rely most heavily on signals and symbols. Some may choose to obscure their use of ICTs that are incompatible with their preferred images or mimic the use of ICTs they do not actually posses. Others may make targeted purchases of only those ICTs that are central to creating their desired images. Recent advances in cloud computing and web services are increasingly allowing firms to pick and choose a customized suite of IT services. The resulting flexibility and changing cost structures may alter the symbolic value of ICT over time.

Implications for Theory

Meanings and symbolism represent an important component of the business value of ICT. Our study of potential customers in business-to-business transactions found a strong relationship between the symbolic meaning of an ICT and corporate image, which has previously been linked to customer support, competitive growth, and firm survival. Organizations that wish to attract customers should consider the benefits of choosing ICT that is consistent with their corporate image, in addition to any improvement in productivity. To be most effective, a firm must make these choices in the light of customer expectations and the norms for its location, industry and products or services.

These results also contribute to our understanding of the relationship between symbolic meaning and action. Organizational cognition synthesizes the literatures on schema theory and symbols while suggesting that the symbolic meaning of ICT will drive behavior. Symbolic issues may dominate diffusion of an emerging ICT before its objective productivity effects have been documented and may continue thereafter as the presence of an ICT becomes an institutionalized norm. Corporate image forms a potentially important link between the symbolic meaning of ICT and its business value. Integrating these fields clarifies how an ICT acquires symbolic meaning which can be used by firms to create and maintain valuable corporate images. Social cognition and the role of schemas in interpreting an ICT as a cue are central to the creation of perceptions that the new firm is legitimate, organized, efficient, customer-oriented, modern and likely to succeed.

When these characteristics are valued, the firm is considered a desirable exchange partner and is more likely to be supported. Firms that evaluate the business value of an ICT based solely on improvements in operational or supply chain efficiencies may risk their corporate images, sales, competitive growth potential, and future survival (Melewar & Karaosmanoglu, 2006).

CONCLUSION

Justifying ICT investments often rests on demonstrating the business value of ICT as a complementary asset in the efficient and effective handling of information to manage internal operations and supply chain activities (Gregor, et al. 2006; Kwon & Watts, 2006; Melville et al. 2004; Murphy & Simon 2002). However, the organizational literature has long recognized that operational efficiency and productivity are not the only factors required for corporate success. To accurately understand the total business value of ICT both image-related and productivity-related value must be assessed and planning and implementation processes should be developed for optimizing both. Our research has extended the literature on the business value of ICT by including its symbolic meaning and has extended the literature on its symbolic meaning by focusing on customers. We have shown that customers believe that ICT signals a firm's legitimacy, efficiency, modernity, and customer service. Savvy managers should consider aligning their ICT with desired corporate images even if productivity benefits are elusive.

We have begun mapping the nature of the ICT symbols, their meanings and the processes by which ICT affects corporate images among customers, an external stakeholder group whose influence has not previously been examined. Future research should consider other valued organizational outcomes related to the symbolic meaning of ICT for external stakeholders, such as attracting high quality employees, financing and accreditation or licensure. In addition, the meanings of ICT and mediating concepts of corporate image will likely differ in other cultures. To provide additional value in guiding global practice, considerably more work is needed to map the meanings to different contexts and track their evolution over time. Understanding the complex multidimensional costs and benefits of ICT will allow us to develop a more complete view of its business value.

REFERENCES

Albert, S., & Whetten, D. (1985). Organizational Identity. In Cummings, L. L., & Staw, B. (Eds.), *Research in Organizational Behavior, (7)* (pp. 263–295). Greenwich, CT: JAI Press.

Balmer, J.M.T. (1998) Corporate Identity and Advent of Corporate Marketing. *Journal of Marketing Management, (14)*, 963-996.

Bargh, J. A. (1984). Automatic and Conscious Processing of Social Information. In Wyer, R. S. Jr., & Srull, T. K. (Eds.), *Handbook of Social Cognition* (pp. 1–43). Hillsdale, NJ: Erlbaum.

Barley, S. R., & Tolbert, P. S. (1997). Institutionalization and Structuration: Studying the Links between Action and Institution. *Organization Studies, 18*(1), 93–117. doi:10.1177/017084069701800106

Berg, P. O. (1985). Organization Change as a Symbolic Transformation Process. In Frost, P., Moore, L., Louis, M. R., Lundberg, C., & Martin, J. (Eds.), *Reframing Organizational Culture* (pp. 281–300). Beverly Hills, CA: Sage.

Berger, P. L., & Luckmann, T. (1967). *The Social Construction of Reality.* New York: Anchor Books.

Boland, R. (1986). Phenomenology: A Preferred Approach to Research in Information Systems. In E. Mumford, R. Hirschheim, G. Fitzgerald, and T. Wood-Harper (eds.), *Proceedings of the IFIP WG8.2 Colloquium,* Manchester Business School, Manchester: Elsevier Science.

Bryman, A. (2001). *Social Research Methods.* Oxford: Oxford University Press.

Christian, R. C. (1959). Industrial Marketing. *Journal of Marketing*, 79–80. doi:10.2307/1248856

Darwell, C., Sahlman, W. A., & Roberts, M. J. (1998) *DigitalThink: Startup (Case # 9-898-186).* Cambridge, MA: Harvard Business School Publishing.

Denzin, N. K. (1989). *The Research Act: A Theoretical Introduction to Sociological Methods.* Englewood Cliffs, NJ: Prentice Hall.

DiMaggio, P. J., & Powell, W. W. (1983). The Iron Cage Revisited: Institutional Isomorphism and Collective Rationality in Organizational Fields. *American Sociological Review, 48,* 147–160. doi:10.2307/2095101

Dutton, J., & Dukerich, J. (1991). Keeping an Eye on the Mirror: Image and Identity in Organizational Adaptation. *Academy of Management Review, (34):* 517–554.

Easton, A. (1966). Corporate Style versus Corporate Image. *JMR, Journal of Marketing Research, 3,* 168–174. doi:10.2307/3150206

Eisenhardt, K. M. (1989). Building Theories from Case Study Research. *Academy of Management Review, 14*(4), 532–550. doi:10.2307/258557

Elsbach, K. D., Sutton, R. I., & Principe, K. E. (1998). Averting Expected Challenges Through Anticipatory Impression Management: A Study of Hospital Billing. *Organization Science, 9*(1), 68–86. doi:10.1287/orsc.9.1.68

Feldman, M. S. (1989). *Order without design: Information production and policymaking*. Stanford, CA: Stanford University Press.

Feldman, M. S. (1995). *Strategies for Interpreting Qualitative Data*. Thousand Oaks, CA: Sage Publications.

Feldman, M. S., & March, J. G. (1981). Information in Organizations as Signal and Symbol. *Administrative Science Quarterly, 26*(2), 171–186. doi:10.2307/2392467

Fichman, R. (2000) The Diffusion and Assimilation of Information Technology Innovations. In R. Zmud (ed.) *Framing the Domains of IT Management: Projecting the Future Through the Past*.pp. 105-104. Cincinnati, OH: Pinnaflex Educational Resources.

Fiske, S.T. & Taylor, S.E. (1991) *Social Cognition (2nd ed.)*. NY: McGraw Hill.

Futrell, R. (1998). Performance Governance: Impression Management, Teamwork, and Conflict Containment in City Commission Proceedings. *Journal of Contemporary Ethnography, 27*(4), 494–529. doi:10.1177/089124199129023316

Gaglio, C. M., Cechini, M., & Winter, S. J. (1998). *Gaining Legitimacy: The Symbolic Use of Technology by New Ventures* (pp. 203–215). Frontiers of Entrepreneurship Research.

Gardner, W. L. (1992). Lessons in Organizational Dramaturgy: The Art of Impression Management. *Organizational Dynamics, 21*(1), 33–46. doi:10.1016/0090-2616(92)90084-Z

Gardner, W. L., & Avolio, B. J. (1998). The Charismatic Relationship: A Dramaturgical Perspective. *Academy of Management Review, 23*(1), 32–58. doi:10.2307/259098

Garfinkel, H. (1967). *Studies in Ethnomethodology*. Cambridge, MA: Polity.

Garud, R., & Rappa, M. A. (1994). A Sociocognitive Model of Technology Evolution: The Case of Cochlear Implants. *Organization Science, 5*(3), 344–362. doi:10.1287/orsc.5.3.344

Gioia, D. A. (1986). Symbols, Scripts, and Sensemaking: Creating Meaning in the Organizational Experience. In Sims, H. P. Jr, & Gioia, D. A. (Eds.), *The Thinking Organization: Dynamics of Organization Cognition* (pp. 49–74). San Francisco: Jossey Bass.

Gioia, D. A., Shultz, M., & Corley, K. G. (2000). Organizational Identity, Image, and Adaptive Instability. *Academy of Management Review, 25*(1), 63–81. doi:10.2307/259263

Glaser, B. G., & Strauss, A. L. (1967). *The Discovery of Grounded Theory*. Chicago, IL: Aldine.

Grayson, K., & Shulman, D. (2000). Impression Management in Services Marketing. In Swatz, T., & Iacobucci, D. (Eds.), *Handbook of Services Marketing and Management* (pp. 51–67). Thousand Oaks, CA: Sage.

Greenbaum, T. L. (1998). *Handbook of Focus Group Research*. Thousand Oaks, CA: Sage.

Gregor, S., Martin, M., Fernandez, W., Stern, S., & Vitale, M. (2006). The Transformational Dimension in the Realization of Business Value from Information Technology. *The Journal of Strategic Information Systems, 15*, 249–270. doi:10.1016/j.jsis.2006.04.001

Grove, S. J., & Fisk, R. P. (1989). Impression Management in Services Marketing: A Dramaturgical Perspective. In Giacalone, R. A., & Rosenfeld, P. (Eds.), *Impression Management in the Organization* (pp. 427–438). Hillsdale, NJ: Lawrence Erlbaum.

Hatch, M. J., & Schultz, M. (1997). Relations between Organizational Culture, Identity, and Image. *European Journal of Marketing, 5*(6), 356–365.

Ind, N. (1992). *The Corporate Image*. London: Kogan Page.

Jackson, M. H., Poole, M. S., & Kuhn, T. (2002). The Social Construction of Technology in Studies of the Workplace. In Lievrouw, L., & Livingstone, S. (Eds.), *Handbook of New Media: Social Shaping and Consequences of ICTs* (pp. 236–253). Thousand Oaks, CA: Sage.

Krueger, R. A. (1998). *Developing Questions for Focus Groups*. Thousand Oaks, CA: Sage.

Kwon, D., & Watts, S. (2006). IT Valuation in Turbulent Times. *The Journal of Strategic Information Systems*, 15(4), 327–354. doi:10.1016/j.jsis.2006.07.003

Lee, A. S. (1991). Integrating Positivist and Interpretive Approaches to Organizational Research. *Organization Science*, 2, 342–365. doi:10.1287/orsc.2.4.342

Lord, R. G., & Foti, R. J. (1986). Schema Theories, Information Processing and Organizational Behavior. In Sims, H. P. Jr, & Gioia, D. A. (Eds.), *The Thinking Organization: Dynamics of Organization Cognition* (pp. 20–48). San Francisco, CA: Jossey Bass.

Markus, H., & Zajonc, R. B. (1985). The Cognitive Perspective in Social Psychology. In Lindzey, G., & Aronson, E. (Eds.), *Handbook of Social Psychology* (pp. 137–230). NY: Random House.

Martin, P. Y., & Turner, B. A. (1986). Grounded Theory and Organizational Research. *The Journal of Applied Behavioral Science*, 22(2), 141–157. doi:10.1177/002188638602200207

Melewar, T. C., & Karaosmanoglu, E. (2006). Seven Dimensions of Corporate Identity: A Categorisation from the Practitioners' Perspectives. *European Journal of Marketing*, 40(7/8), 846–869. doi:10.1108/03090560610670025

Melville, N., Kraemer, K. L., & Gurbaxani, V. (2004). Information Technology and Organizational Performance: An Integrative Model of IT Business Value. *Management Information Systems Quarterly*, 28(2), 283–322.

Meyer, J., & Rowan, B. (1977). Institutionalized Organizations: Formal Structure as Myth and Ceremony. *American Journal of Sociology*, 83, 340–363. doi:10.1086/226550

Moore, G. C., & Benbasat, I. (1991). Development of an Instrument to Measure the Perceptions of Adopting an Information Technology Innovation. *Information Systems Research*, 2(3), 192–222. doi:10.1287/isre.2.3.192

Morgan, G., Frost, P. J., & Pondy, L. R. (1983). Organizational Symbolism. In Pondy, L. R., Frost, P. G., Morgan, G., & Dandridge, T. C. (Eds.), *Organizational Symbolism*. Greenwich, CT: JAI Press.

Murphy, K. E., & Simon, S. J. (2007). Intangible Benefits Valuation in ERP Projects. *Information Systems Journal*, 12, 301–320. doi:10.1046/j.1365-2575.2002.00131.x

Noir, C., & Walsham, G. (2007). The Great Legitimizer: ICT as Myth and Ceremony in the Indian Healthcare Sector. *Information Technology & People*, 20(4), 313–333. doi:10.1108/09593840710839770

Oliver, C. (1991). Strategic Responses to Institutional Processes. *Academy of Management Review*, 16, 145–179. doi:10.2307/258610

Orlikowski, W. J., & Iacono, C. S. (2000). The Truth is Not Out There: An Enacted View of the 'Digital Economy. In Brynjolfsson, E., & Kahin, B. (Eds.), *Understanding the Digital Economy: Data, Tools, and Research Cambridge*. Cambridge, MA: EMIT Press.

Orlikowski, W. J., & Iacono, C. S. (2001). Research Commentary: Desperately Seeking the "IT" in IT Research – A Call to Theorizing the IT Artifact. *Information Systems Research, 12*(2), 121–134. doi:10.1287/isre.12.2.121.9700

Ornstein, S. (1989). Impression Management Through Office Design. In Giacalone, R. A., & Rosenfeld, P. (Eds.), *Impression Management in The Organization*. Hillsdale, NJ: Erlbaum.

Peppard, J., Ward, J., & Daniel, E. (2007). Managing the Realization of Business Benefits from IT Investments. *MISQ Executive, 6*(1), 1–11.

Pfeffer, J., & Salancik, G. R. (1978). *The External Control of Organizations: A Resource Dependence Perspective*. New York: Harper and Row.

Powell, W. W., & DiMaggio, P. J. (1991). Introduction. In W.W. Powell a& P.J. DiMaggio (eds.), *The New Institutionalism in Organizational Analysis*. London: University of Chicago Press.

Prasad, P. (1993). Symbolic Processes in the Implementation of Technological Change: A Symbolic Interactionist Study of Work Computerization. *Academy of Management Journal, 36*, 1400–1429. doi:10.2307/256817

Ranganathan, C., & Brown, C. V. (2006). ERP Investments and the Market Value of Firms: Toward an Understanding of Influential ERP Project Variables. *Information Systems Research, 17*(2), 145–161. doi:10.1287/isre.1060.0084

Robey, D., & Azevedo, A. (1994). Cultural Analysis of the Organizational Consequences of Information Technology. *Accounting, Management, and Information Technologies, 4*, 23–37. doi:10.1016/0959-8022(94)90011-6

Robey, D., & Boudreau, M. C. (1999). Accounting for the Contradictory Organizational Consequences of Information Technology: Theoretical Directions and Methodological Implications. *Information Systems Research, 10*(2), 167–185. doi:10.1287/isre.10.2.167

Saga, V. L., & Zmud, R. W. (1994). The Nature and Determinants of IT Acceptance, Routinization and Infusion. In L. Levine (Ed.) *Diffusion, Transfer and Implementation of Information Technology*, pp. 67-86. North Holland: Elsevier Science.

Schein, E. H. (1985). *Organizational Culture and Leadership*. San Francisco: Jossey-Bass.

Schmitt, B., & Simonson, A. (1997). *Marketing Aesthetics -- The Strategic Management of Brands, Identity, and Image*. New York: The Free Press.

Scott, W. R. (2001). *Institutions and Organizations* (2nd ed.). Thousand Oaks, CA: Sage.

Singh, J. V., Tucker, D., & Meinhard, A. G. (1991). Institutional Change and Ecological Dynamics. In Powell, W. W., & DiMaggio, P. J. (Eds.), *The New Institutionalism in Organizational Analysis* (pp. 390–422). Chicago, IL: University of Chicago Press.

Spector, A. (1961). Basic Dimensions of the Corporate Image. *Journal of Marketing, 47*–51. doi:10.2307/1248513

Starr, J. A., & MacMillan, I. C. (1990). Resource Co-optation via Social Contracting: Resource Acquisition Strategies for New Ventures. *Strategic Management Journal, 11*, 79–92.

Stewart, D. W., & Shamdasani, P. N. (1990). *Focus Groups: Theory and Practice*. Newbury Park, CA: Sage Publications.

Stinchcombe, A. (1968). *Constructing Social Theories*. New York: Harcourt Brace.

Strauss, A. L., & Corbin, J. (1998). *Basics of Qualitative Research: Technique and Procedure for Developing Grounded Theory*. Thousand Oaks, CA: Sage.

Suchman, M. C. (1995). Managing Legitimacy: Strategic and Institutional Approaches. *Academy of Management Review, 20*(3), 571–610. doi:10.2307/258788

Sudman, S., Bradburn, N. M., & Schwarz, N. (1996). *Thinking About Answers: The Application of Cognitive Processes to Survey Methodology.* San Francisco: Jossey-Bass.

Swanson, E. B., & Ramiller, N. C. (1997). The Organizing Vision in Information Systems Innovation. *Organization Science, 8*(5), 458–474. doi:10.1287/orsc.8.5.458

Synder, M., & Stukas, A. (1999). Interpersonal Processes: The Interplay of Cognitive, Motivational and Behavioral Activities in Social Interaction. *Annual Review of Psychology, 50,* 273–303. doi:10.1146/annurev.psych.50.1.273

van den Hoonaard, W. C. (1997). *Working with Sensitizing Concepts: Analytical Field Research.* Thousand Oaks, CA: Sage.

Van Riel, C. B. M. (1997). Research in Corporate Communications: An Overview of An Emerging Field. *Management Communication Quarterly, 11*(2), 340–355. doi:10.1177/0893318997112005

Walsham, G. (1993). *Interpreting Information Systems.* Chichester, UK: John Wiley.

Winter, S. J., Gaglio, C. M., & Rajagopalan, H. K. (2009). The Value of Information Systems to Small and Medium-sized Enterprises: Information and Communications Technologies as Signal and Symbol of Legitimacy and Competitiveness. *International Journal of Electronic Business Research, 5*(1), 65–91.

Yin, R. K. (1989). *Case Study Research: Design and Methods.* Beverly Hills, CA: Sage.

Zimmerman, M. A., & Zeitz, G. J. (2002). Beyond Survival: Achieving New Venture Growth by Building Legitimacy. *Academy of Management Review, 27*(3), 414–431. doi:10.2307/4134387

APPENDIX A: INFORMANT CHARACTERISTICS

New Firm	Products/Services	Market	Scope
General Engineering Contractor	Environmental Clean-up & Construction	Large Primary Contractors	Local
Building Supply	Construction Supplies	Contractors	Local
Moving Company	Packing, Storage and Delivery Services	Consumers, Government, Businesses	Regional
Kidney Dialysis Lab	Renal Testing	Clinics	National
MRI Lab	Radiography Services	Doctors & Patients	Local
Dietary Supplements Wholesaler	Herbal Supplements	Grocery & Health Stores	National
Pager	Pagers & Services	Paging Services Providers	National
Systems Integrator	Systems Development & Maintenance	Mid-size Businesses	Local
Software Development	Groupware	Software Consultants	National
Temporary Agency	Temporary Workers	Businesses	Local
Legal Copying Service	Duplication	Legal Firms	Local
Community Association Manager	Groundskeeping & Maintenance	Businesses	Local
TV & Web Production	Program Production	Businesses	National
Fiberglass Parts Manufacturing	Custom Auto Parts	Auto Purchasers	Regional
Medical Supplies Retailer	Diabetes Management Supplies	Diabetes Patients	National

Customers	Products	Market	Scope	# Vendors
Flowers/Gifts Retailer	Fresh Flowers & Related Gift Items	Consumers	National	200-300
Promotional Products Distributor	Custom Promotional Products	Businesses & Resellers	Regional	1000
Food Import/Export	Processed Foods	Retail Groceries & Restaurants	Inter-national	200
Wireless Services Provider	Paging and Cell Phone Services	Consumers & Businesses	National	1000
Facilities Manager	Supervise Maintenance, Grounds Keeping & Supplies	Consumers	Local	10-15
General Contractor	Construction Management	Developers Owners & Public Agencies	National	800-1200
Environmental Clean-up Consulting	Engineering, Design, Consulting & Contracting	Major Oil Cos.& Firms w/ Underground Tanks	Southeast U.S.	200
Health Spa	Beauty, Spa, Fitness & Nutrition Services	Consumers	Local	50
Architecture/Interior Design	Architectural Plans, Interior Designs & Decoration Services	Consumers & Designers	Local	20-25
Catalog Apparel	High-end Apparel	Consumers	National	100
Custom Linens	Bedroom, Bath, Table Linens, Upholstery, Drapes & Accessories	Designers & Consumers	Local	1000
Book Exporter	Foreign Language Lit.	Distributors	Inter-national	30-40
Fitness Center	Fitness Services	Consumers	Local	6-10
Metal Framing Contractor	Management of Residential & Commercial Framing & Finishing	Owners & General Contractors	Local	500

APPENDIX B: INTERVIEW QUESTIONS USING FOCUS GROUP TECHNIQUES

Customer

We know that the technology a supplier has performs many important business-related functions. However, lots of things that we interact with are functional, but also act as symbols. For example, a Ferrari and a Honda Civic both provide transportation. You can get from point A to point B in either one, but doing it in a Ferrari symbolizes wealth and a certain style. Designer clothing keeps us warm, but also acts as a symbol.

1. Do you think that a supplier's technological capabilities helps convince you to choose them over their equally qualified competitors? Does it help you to believe that a new venture is better than its competitors? Why do you say that? What would you think of a new supplier if its representative talked a lot about technology-related subjects in their sales pitch?
2. What do you know or assume about a new suppliers' technological capabilities? How do you know about it? Did they provide any cues? If not, why not? What would it have meant to you if the supplier had highlighted their technological capabilities?
3. In your opinion, what is the difference between a Mac user and an IBM user?
4. In your opinion, what is the difference between a company that has _____ and one that does not? Cell phones, Pagers, Voice mail, E-mail. Do your suppliers give you their cell phone #, pager #, voicemail access, or e-mail address? Why do they do this? What would it mean to you if you did not get this information?
5. How important is it to you that the new venture have the ability to check things like inventory, order status, and prices immediately (on a laptop or palm top), or is it okay to get back to you later about this (within an hour or two)? How would your impression differ if they checked paper files versus doing it on a laptop or palm?
6. In your opinion, what is the difference between a company that uses Kinko's to send and receive faxes and one that has its own private fax? Do you send faxes from a private number? What would it mean to you if you received a fax from a potential supplier and saw that it was sent from, say, Kinko's instead of a private fax #? Would it mean different things for different suppliers? Why?
7. In your opinion, what is the difference between a company that has a Web page and one that does not? Do your suppliers have Web page addresses? What would it mean to you if you did not receive a Web page address from a supplier?
8. Would you consider contacting a potential supplier based solely on its Web page? Why do you say that?
9. What would you think if you called this supplier early in the day planning to leave a message that they would get at the start of business, but instead woke up the company's sole employee because the business was run out of his private home? Why do you say that?
10. I'm going to read you a list of technologies that may perform important functions that allow your suppliers to provide excellent products or services. Over and above their functional use, these items may also provide cues that would give you permission to believe that a supplier has the qualities that would be required to provide a better product or service than their competitors. For each one, please tell me if you would expect a supplier to have it, if it could act as a cue to allow you to believe in their abilities, and, finally, if you would just assume that they had it, or if you would

ask your suppliers about them or hear about them during the marketing or sales pitch: Cellular Phones for Work, Pagers/Beepers for Work, Voice Mail, Answering Machine, Fax Machines, Photocopiers, Color Copier, Personal Computers, Laptop Computers, Palmtop Computers, Data/ Graphics Scanners, Graphics Capabilities, Desktop Publishing, Modem, Fax Modem, Modem Links to Clients, Ability to e-mail clients, Internal e-mail, Connections to Internet, Presence on Internet (Web Page), Intranet, Electronic Data Interchange, Database Systems, Groupware (e.g., Lotus Notes), Workflow Software, Wireless Data Communications, Machines for Manufacture of Products or Services

Founder

We know that the technology you have performs many important business-related functions. However, lots of things that we interact with are functional, but also act as symbols. For example, a Ferrari and a Honda Civic both provide transportation. You can get from point A to point B in either one, but doing it in a Ferrari symbolizes wealth and a certain style. Designer clothing keeps us warm, but also acts as a symbol.

1. Do you think that your technological capabilities helped convince your customers to choose you over your equally qualified competitors? Did it help your customer to believe that your company was better than your competitors? Why do you say that? Did you avoid any technology-related subjects in your sales pitch so that clients would not get the wrong impression of you or of your firm?
2. What do you think your customers knew or assumed about your technological capabilities as you made your sales pitch? How did they know about it? Did you provide any cues? If not, why not? What would it have meant to your customer if you had highlighted your technology?
3. In your opinion, what is the difference between a Mac user and an IBM user?
4. In your opinion, what is the difference between a company that has _____ and one that does not? Cell phones, Pagers, Voice mail, E-mail. Do you give your customers your cell phone #, e-mail address, voicemail #, or pager #? Why do you do this? What would it mean to them if they did not get this information?
5. In your opinion, what is the difference between a company that uses Kinko's to send and receive faxes and one that has its own private fax? Do you send faxes from a private number? What would it mean to your customers if they received a fax from you and saw that it was sent from, say, Kinko's instead of a private fax #? Would it mean different things to different customers? Why?
6. In your opinion, what is the difference between a company that has a Web page and one that does not? Do you give prospective customers your Web page address? What would it mean to your customers if they did not receive a Web page address from you?
7. I'm going to read you a list of technologies that may perform important functions that allow your suppliers to provide excellent products or services. Over and above their functional use, these items may also provide cues that would give you permission to believe that a supplier has the qualities that would be required to provide a better product or service than their competitors. For each one, please tell me if you would expect a supplier to have it, if it could act as a cue to allow you to believe in their abilities, and, finally, if you would just assume that they had it, or if you would ask your suppliers about them or hear about them during the marketing or sales pitch. Cellular

Phones for Work, Pagers/Beepers for Work, Voice Mail, Answering Machine, Fax Machines, Photocopiers, Color Copier, Personal Computers, Laptop Computers, Palmtop Computers, Data/ Graphics Scanners, Graphics Capabilities, Desktop Publishing, Modem, Fax Modem, Modem Links to Clients, Ability to e-mail clients, Internal e-mail, Connections to Internet, Presence on Internet (Web Page), Intranet, Electronic Data Interchange, Database Systems, Groupware (e.g., Lotus Notes), Workflow Software, Wireless Data Communications, Machines for Manufacture of Products or Services

Chapter 5

Training, Competence, and Business Performance:
Evidence from E-Business in European Small and Medium-Sized Enterprises

Dag H. Olsen
University of Agder, Norway

Tom R. Eikebrokk
University of Agder, Norway

ABSTRACT

This article examines the relationship between training, competence and performance of small and medium-sized enterprises (SMEs) in the context of e-business. Literature review combined with a triangulation of qualitative and quantitative methods were used to investigate these relationships. Data about e-business competences and performance in 339 SMEs in three European countries was combined with data about training supply from 116 providers of e-business related training. The empirical findings document a positive relationship between training, competence and performance and show that training explains variances in e-business competences and performance in terms of efficiency, complementarities, lock-in and novelty. The research has both theoretical and practical implications. It contributes to theoretical development by lending support to the idea that methodological issues are an important reason behind the lack of empirical support frequently reported in the literature. The study has practical implications for public policy makers, training suppliers and SME managers.

INTRODUCTION

This exploratory study investigates the relationships between training supply, e-business competence and e-business performance in SMEs. More specifically, we investigate whether the provision of training lead to more competence, and eventually, to better performance in the context of e-business. This issue has received interest from researchers in the general field of SME research, but few studies have focused on the context of e-business. There is scarce and ambiguous evidence that training leads to better performance in SMEs (Bryan, 2006; Devins & Johanson, 2003; Patton, Marlow, & Hannon, 2000; Westhead & Storey,

DOI: 10.4018/978-1-60960-132-4.ch005

Copyright © 2011, IGI Global. Copying or distributing in print or electronic forms without written permission of IGI Global is prohibited.

1996, 1997). Small and medium sized enterprises (SMEs) generate a substantial share of the GDP in industrial economies. The more than 20 million SMEs in Europe are an important source of new jobs and entrepreneurial activity (European Commission, 2002a, 2002b). Considerable funding has been granted to research programs targeting the development of SMEs in general and in specific areas as the diffusion of e-business. It is assumed that success with e-business in the SME segment will increase a country's competitiveness in the long run, and that successful adoption and use of e-business technology is crucial for survival in the new economy (see Debreceny, Putterill, Tung, & Gilbert, 2002 for an overview).

Several studies indicate that development of the SME segment is challenging and that SMEs for the most part are unable to successfully adopt and use e-business technology (Debreceny et al., 2002). A number of studies has emphasized the lack of e-business competence and lack of training (Fillis, Johannson, & Wagner, 2003; Ihlström & Nilsson, 2003; Ivis, 2001; Johnston, Shi, Dann, & Barcay, 2006; Kinkaide, 2000; Lewis & Cockrill, 2002) as the major cause for this problem. Such competence is seen as important for understanding the implications of e-business for the business domain, and for developing the distinctive capabilities needed to perform well in the e-business era (Grandon & Pearson, 2004). Governments in most industrialized countries have implemented various stimulation programs including training to increase e-business competence. Despite these efforts, there is only scarce knowledge of how training programs influence the creation of competence and e-business performance. SMEs are reluctant to engage in training initiatives despite the existence of incentives (Maton, 1999). Organizational constraints seem to create barriers to SMEs. Lack of time and financial resources, along with ignorance to the supply of training have been found to represent such barriers (Marlow, 1998; Westhead & Storey, 1997). With better understanding of the relationship between train-

ing, e-business competence and performance in the SME segment, governments would be able to better tailor stimulation programs to target SME competence needs.

THEORY

E-Business and SMEs

We have adopted a relatively broad definition of e-business as the conduct of business generally with the assistance of telecommunication and telecommunications-based tools (Clarke, 2003). E-business and the internet have opened new arenas for competing and collaborating for SMEs, but most of them are in an early stage of their e-business. There is not a common definition of Small and Medium sized organizations. The term Small Business is commonly used in the United States where measures as number of employees, total turnover, and industry are used to define a Small Business. The European Union (EU) uses a uniform definition of SMEs as independent companies with fewer than 250 employees, with either a turnover of less than 40 million € or total assets of less than 27 million € (European Commission, 2004). Independent companies are those that are not owned as to 25% or more of the capital or the voting rights by one enterprise, or jointly by several enterprises. We have adopted the EU definition.

Training and Performance in the Context of E-Business in SMEs

Governments invest substantial resources in stimulating training suppliers to develop competence programs to the SME sector. Such programs are based on the assumption that the provision of training in terms of developing existing or introducing new skills and/or knowledge to SMEs, will increase their business performance. This assumption is general and includes the context of e-business. The demand side is also stimulated. Financial incentives encourage organizations, including SMEs, to develop training programs for their employees. Yet, there is an ongoing debate about whether a positive relationship exists between training and small business performance. We can split the debate into three components. Some studies investigate the effect of training on small business performance. Other studies divide the link into two parts: the impact of training on competence, and the impact competence on performance.

Patton, Marlow and Hannon (2000) reviewed the status of the research on training and performance in small firms. They conclude that despite the almost axiomatic proposition that training increases business performance, very few empirical studies have been able to demonstrate the significance of this relationship. A similar review by Westhead and Storey (1996, 1997) concluded in a similar vein that there was no substantial evidence for the causal link between training and performance in SMEs. A more recent study (Fuller-Love, 2006) reviewed the literature on management development in small firms and concluded that management development programs in general are effective for small firms through the development of competence. By focusing on developing new skills in management, capabilities of management systems and techniques, team building, planning, delegation and financial management, the training programs led to reduction in failure and improvement in performance.

Troshano and Rao (2007) focused on the enabling factors behind e-business competitive advantage in the Australian financial services industry. After interviewing 12 companies in an exploratory study they argue that e-business technologies enable or stimulate organizational competences which, in turn, explain higher levels of performance. The authors do not present any empirical evidence that demonstrate the existence of the link between e-business technologies and organizational performance. Bryan (2006) con-ducted a study of the relationship between training and performance, taking the effect of time into consideration. By studying a random sample of 114 manufacturing SMEs in 1996 and then in 2003, Bryan concludes that external management training has a greater impact on sales growth than in-house training programs.

Patton et al (2000) propose three possible explanations for the mixed and inconclusive results and the problems of finding a casual link between training and performance: Firstly, it is possible that a causal relationship does not exist. Secondly, methodological problems associated with measuring and isolating the effects could explain the lack of evidence. Thirdly, the lack of evidence could be a result of not taking into account other possible variables that influence the relationship between training and business performance. Patton et al (2000) argue that since studies already have demonstrated that it is possible to find a significant link between training and business performance, it is less likely that a causal relationship does not exist. They find it much more likely that there are methodological explanations behind to the inability to explain the lack of clear empirical findings and to identify and separate the effects of training. They suggest that improvements in research methodology could improve the ability to detect contextual factors. In addition, improved research methodology could improve the ability to generalize the results. They advise that future studies should explore the differences in business context and utilize research methods that triangulate qualitative field research with quantitative surveys. Future studies should also focus on characteristics of the providers of training along with the characteristics, needs and available resources of the small businesses themselves. Studies from UK (e.g. Westhead & Storey, 1996) have analyzed the training supply and found that the supply rarely is based on what is demanded, thereby creating a gap between the content of the supply and the needs of the business sector.

Training and Competence Development in SMEs

It is generally assumed that training leads to improved competence, and the development of appropriate competence and investments in staff training has been identified as central barriers to successful e-business implementation and use (Fillis et al., 2003). Several EU programs have targeted the provision of e-business training for SMEs. However obvious the assumption about the relation between training and competence may be, there is scarce empirical support. In their review, Fuller-Love (2006) identified five studies from 1992-1997 that empirically identified a link between training and performance through the development of competence. These improved competences led to reduction in failure and improvement in performance. Still, Fuller-Love concludes that the empirical evidence is limited and should be complemented by more studies focusing on both single cases and on cross-sectional data from different industries and geographical areas.

Several government initiatives in Europe have targeted the need for training and management development in small firms. The EU Commision initiated a benchmarking study in order to describe and benchmark the national and regional policies and instruments promoting e-business in SMEs (European Commission, 2002b). Based on the experiences from more than 150 initiatives in 16 countries the benchmarking study concludes that the training initiatives had varying impact on awareness and competence development. The best training initiatives were characterized by being based on solid research and data, flexible, coordinated, and tailored to the needs of the SMEs in different regions and sectors.

Competence and E-Business Performance in SMEs

Several studies document the existence of a link between e-business competence and e-business performance. With data from 73 companies listed among the top 500 US Internet companies, Saeed, Grover and Hwang (2005) identified a positive relationship between e-business competence and subsequent e-business performance. Eikebrokk and Olsen (2007) found empirical evidence in support of this link for small and medium-sized companies. We base our identification of competence dimensions on a review of several sources including the IS field and organization science.

First, there is the dimension of strategy competence. Bharadwaj et al. (2000) and Feeny and Willcocks (1998) conceptualized this dimension as "Business IT strategic thinking". Elements of this dimension are also implicitly contained in two of the dimensions of both Peppard et al. (2000) and Basselier et al. (2001), and one of the dimensions of Sambamurthy and Zmud (1994) and Feeny and Willcocks (1998). Several empirical studies have documented the important role of strategic vision for SMEs' adoption of e-business (Grandon & Pearson, 2004; Love & Irani, 2004). This dimension can be divided into two sub-dimensions. A significant part of this dimension is the company's ability to envision the strategic potential of new e-business technology in its marketplace (Bharadwaj et al., 2000; Feeny & Willcocks, 1998). It involves understanding the concept of e-business, and it will reflect the maturity of the enterprises' understanding of the e-business domain and what new possibilities and threats e-business creates in the business domain. On the other hand, this dimension also includes the ability to understand and use strategic planning methods needed to develop an e-business strategy, which describes how e-business will be put into action (Bharadwaj et al., 2000).

Second, we have the issue of competence in IT-business process integration. The IS literature offers broad support for the notion that a company's ability to realize potential benefits of new technology is influenced by the ability to organize business processes that leverage this potential (e.g. Hammer, 1990; Keen, 1991). More specifically, empirical studies in the area of IS economics have documented that among Fortune 500 companies productivity gains from utilizing new technologies are higher in companies that organize themselves in ways that leverage the potential of the new technology (e.g. Brynjolfsson & Hitt, 1998). In a European study of 441 Spanish SMEs, Dans (2001) found a similar correlation between IT-investments and productivity for SMEs that can partly be attributed to organizational redesign. The most fundamental challenge to SMEs may lie in changing the mindset of the organization. Several authors (Lawrence, 1997; C. S. Lee, 2001; Tetteh & Burn, 2001) have argued that the adoption of e-business fundamentally alters internal procedures within SMEs. This dimension is explicitly recognized in recent articles on IT/IS competence (Bharadwaj et al., 2000; Peppard et al., 2000), and implicitly present in the other sources. New business or IT work processes can be designed or old processes can be restructured in order to leverage the opportunities of new technology (Davenport, 1993). Regardless of which strategy is chosen, the company must have the ability to identify and implement changes in business processes in order to increase process efficiency to the level required by the business and the potential of the technology (Bharadwaj et al., 2000; Davenport, 1993). Companies need competence to organize and manage work processes in new and powerful ways. Competence is needed both in developing the new business model and in the subsequent implementation of this model in the organization.

Third, there is the dimension of IT management. It is defined as activities related to the management of the IT function, such as IS planning and design, IS application delivery, IT project management, and planning for control and standards (Bharadwaj et al., 2000; DeLone, 1988). Bharadwaj et al. (2000) demonstrates the empirical significance of IT management. SMEs generally have an ad-hoc approach to IT management, and therefore seldom have a defined IT budget or an explicit IT plan or strategy, and

investments in technology are often driven by the owner, rather than by any formal cost-benefit or strategic analysis (Ballantine, Levy, & Powell, 1998; Dans, 2001).

Fourth, competence in systems and infrastructure was covered in several literature sources, including the empirical study of Bharadwaj et al. (2000). We define competence in systems and infrastructure as the knowledge of the data, network, and processing architectures that support the enterprise applications and services. Systems and infrastructure influence the gamut of business opportunities available to firms applying IT in their business strategies (Keen, 1991). Successful use of e-business technologies involves both finding technology with a strategic potential and having a technological and managerial infrastructure that can implement and support it. As a result, companies need competence on available e-business solutions as well as on the importance of having or creating internal structures that can utilize the new solutions.

Fifth, there is the issue of relationship competence. A core premise of the network economy is that business networks that effectively source and coordinate resources and capabilities will be highly competitive (Mowshowitz, 1997; Rayport & Sviokla, 1995; Timmers, 1999). Therefore effective communication and interaction internally as well as with business partners will be important to e-business performance. Our literature review identified two sub-dimensions of relationship competence, sourcing and alignment. These dimensions are present in Bharadwaj et al. (2000) where they are termed "IT-business partnerships" and "External linkages", and implicitly contained in other competence terms in all our other sources.

We define the first sub-dimension, competence in *sourcing,* as the ability to secure access to relevant competences either inside or outside of the company. MacGregor (2004) argues that electronic business has forced organizations to reassess their boundaries and focus their attention on inter-organizational issues. A study of small manufacturing firms found that inter-organizational relationships are important for performance (Golden & Dollinger, 1993). Networks, whether in the form of strategic alliances or informal linkages, are important to pool resources and talents for mutual benefit of participants (Dean, Holmes, & Smith, 1997; Premaratne, 2001; Rosenfeld, 1996). Jarrat (1998) found that competence derived through participation in networks overcame other business weaknesses. Studies on EDI adoption and Internet adoption have also highlighted the role of relationship competence (S. Lee & Lim, 2005; Mehrtens, Cragg, & Mills, 2001). Also, studies of IS outsourcing success have documented the importance of the ability to form high quality partner relationships and having the capability to learn or to acquire the needed knowledge (J.-N. Lee, 2001; Shi, Kunnathur, & Ragu-Nathan, 2005).

We define the other sub-dimension, competence in *alignment,* as the ability to combine and use available competences. For example, sourcing could take place through two different activities that either create access to competences through recruitment, training, or contractual arrangements, or outsource activities where competences are needed. When the need for and access to competences are defined by sourcing arrangements, competences in alignment will influence how well accessible competences are combined and activated in the use process. Normally, alignment is regarded in the literature as an intra-organizational activity (e.g. "IT-Business partnership" in (Bharadwaj et al., 2000)); but when companies cooperate and form alliances, alignment takes on an inter-organizational dimension. As a result, competence in alignment will have both an internal and an external perspective. Most studies point to the importance of flexible systems and IT infrastructure with key business partners without explicitly recognizing the importance of competences in managing these inter-organizational relationships (e.g Bharadwaj et al., 2000). In the network economy, businesses that are able to form effective partnerships will be more agile

(Sambamurthy, Bharadwaj, & Grover, 2003) and competitive. This ability is particularly important for small and medium-sized enterprises, which typically have scarce resources and limited ability to exploit business opportunities on their own. Sourcing and alignment competences will enable small businesses to take advantage of e-business opportunities and take part in business network partnerships.

E-Business Performance Dimensions

Amit and Zott (2001) conducted one of the most cited studies on e-business performance. They perform a thorough review of the entrepreneurship and strategic management literature. They conclude that no single economic theory can fully explain the sources of value creation of e-business. Johansson and Mollstedt (2006) argue that Amit and Zott's four dimensions of e-business success are not only relevant for understanding the drivers of value but could also be used as performance dimensions when evaluating the success of e-business.

Wade and Hulland (2004) argue that the researcher need to conceptualize resources as well as performance with a certain level of specificity, to identify the effects of resources on performance. They suggest that in choosing a dependent variable for understanding the importance of resources, the researcher needs to address three key attributes regarding the constructs ability to address: 1) performance, 2) competitive aspects, and 3) performance over time. The performance dimensions of Amit and Zott (2001) used as evaluative dimensions of e-business performance as suggested by Johansson and Mollstedt (2006), exhibit all three of these criteria. Consequently, we base our definition of e-business performance on the work of Amit and Zott (2001) who describe the potential of value creation in e-business in four interrelated dimensions: efficiency, complementarities, lock-in, and novelty. Efficiency describes possible reductions

Figure 1. Research model

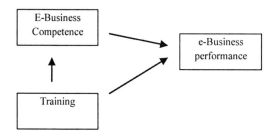

in transaction costs, whereas complementarities describe the value potential from combining products and services, technologies and activities in new and innovative ways. Lock-in describes the potential value in creating switching costs from arrangements that motivate customers and business partners to repeat and improve transactions and relationships. Novelty describes value creation resulting from innovations in the way business is conducted (e.g. web-based auctions, etc.).

RESEARCH MODEL AND HYPOTHESES

Our research model and hypotheses will test the influence of training and competence on performance in small and medium-sized enterprises by focusing on how these influences work in the context of e-business. We follow the advice put forward by Patton et al. (2000), Fuller-Love (2006) and Wade and Hulland (2004). They argue that further studies should narrow their focus on a specific setting involving a limited set of competences, industries or geographical regions. Moreover, following the advices from the benchmarking report of European training initiatives (European Commission, 2002a), we will base our inclusion of competence on previous research and focus on the relevance of competence supplied through the training offered.

We define e-business competence as the knowledge, skills and capability of SMEs to utilize the concept of e-business and e-business related tech-

Figure 2. Structural model with significant paths and path coefficients

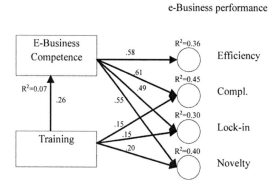

nologies. The concept of training is included as a potential predictor of both e-business competence and e-business performance. Training is defined as the relevant training supply in the context of e-business and SMEs. Training will be measured by collecting information from the different training providers in the chosen industries and countries. The providers' interest in the SME segment and the content of the training supply are important factors in defining the training supply as it appears to the SMEs. The demand for training is formed by the SMEs' awareness of the training supply and the ability to invest in the training offered.

We propose that e-business performance is influenced by both e-business competence and relevant training supply in this context. E-business performance is defined as the results of the e-business efforts in terms of the effects created in the four dimensions of efficiency, complementarities, lock-in and novelty. The research model is illustrated in figure 2. We propose the following research hypotheses:

H1: There is a positive association between training and e-business performance in terms of a) efficiency, b) complementarities, c) lock-in and d) novelty.

H2: There is a positive association between training and e-business related competence.

H3: There is a positive association between e-business related competence and e-business performance in terms of a) efficiency, b) complementarities, c) lock-in and d) novelty.

METHODOLOGY

We conducted a cross sectional study with a sample of 339 SMEs from three industries (tourism, transportation, and food and beverages) in three European countries (Norway, Finland and Spain). A sample of 116 training providers was also drawn randomly from the same countries.

Based on a random sample of SMEs, executives were phoned, and if their company used web pages, e-mail or e-commerce systems for business purposes, they were invited to take part in the survey. 339 executives accepted and were subsequently interviewed. A total sample of 130 training providers, equally shared between the countries, were phoned and invited to take part in a sample. 116 providers accepted and were then interviewed.

We based the operationalizations of e-business competence on instruments and operationalizations previously documented (Bassellier et al., 2001; Bharadwaj et al., 2000; Feeny & Willcocks, 1998; Heijden, 2000; D. M. S. Lee, Trauth, & Farwell, 1995; Sambamurthy & Zmud, 1994). The operationalization of e-business training was based on the work of Patton et al. (2000) who identified characteristics of both the supply side and demand side as important to understand the relevance of the training supply. As a result, training supply was operationalized in four dimensions: the attractiveness of the different SME size segments to the training provider, the financial ability of SMEs of different sizes to invest in training programs, the SMEs' awareness of existing training programs, and the content of the training offered in terms of the types of competence offered. The competence dimensions characterizing the training supply were the same as in the e-business competence

variable targeting the SMEs. The final measure of training was constructed as a summed index for each country.

The supply and demand of training as a function of SME size, were added to the data set of each country. The average awareness of SMEs about the training supply in each country was coded with the average value for each SME in the respective countries. The index representing the training content in each country was coded in a similar fashion.

We constructed the final measure of training as a formative measure where training emerged as a result of the external supply and internal demand described above. The data about training represents a pooling of information from the supply side (providers) and the demand side (SMEs as customers). Training suppliers were asked to report which competences they cover for the different SME size segments. The suppliers were also used as informants on how SMEs of different size have varying demand of training as a function of their awareness and financial ability to pay for the training supply. By combining data from the SMEs and their training providers we get richer information about how the training supply appears to the SMEs in terms of content, availability and relevance, as suggested by Patton et al. (2000).

'E-business performance' was operationalized according to the dimensions described by Amit and Zott (2001). The indicators for all constructs were measured on a seven point Likert-type scale between 'totally disagree'/'not at all' and 'totally agree'/'very large extent'. The independent variables were measured as formative indicators (for a review of construct indicators and measurement model specification, see (Burke Jarvis, Mackenzie, & Podsakoff, 2003)). The dependent variable e-business performance was measured with reflective indicators of each of the four dimension of performance: efficiency, complementarities, lock-in and novelty. We then conducted open-ended interviews with eight SME managers and two related consultants as an additional reality check of our model and as a test of the relevance, wording and response format of the indicators. The outcome of this process led to the resulting questionnaires. The survey instruments are shown in appendix 2 and 3.

DATA ANALYSIS

We determined that partial least squares analysis (PLS) would be the most appropriate technique in the testing of our hypotheses along with the measurement quality of our formative and reflective indicators. PLS is a confirmatory, second-generation multivariate analysis technique (Fornell, 1982) that is well suited for highly complex predictive models (Jöreskog & Wold, 1982). PLS has several advantages that makes it well suited for this study, including the ability to handle reflective and formative indicators and robustness in relation to departure from multivariate normality, as occurred in our data. Moreover, as with multiple regression, PLS focuses on the model's ability to predict rather than explain the variability of the dependent variables. PLS is therefore most useful in situations where the theory is still being developed (W. W. Chin, 1998) and can suggest refinements in theory by showing how substantially indicators are related to constructs and how assumed predictors are related to one or more dependent variables. In PLS, the predictive ability of constructs is optimized and the performance of the individual scale items is reported.

Descriptive Statistics

We show descriptive statistics for the two samples in appendix 1. All 339 SMEs in our sample used at least one of the eight e-business systems surveyed (Q4) in addition to e-mail. Each company had at least a web presence where individual customers or companies could find information about products and services. Appendix 1 shows the distribution of the different e-business systems (Q4a-h) in the

Table 1. Descriptive statistics, weights and t-statistics for formative indicators measuring competence

	Mean	Std. dev.	Weight	t-stat.
Competence (Formative)				
Q10	4.11	1.73	0.16	1.82
Q11	4.25	1.71	0.04	0.34
Q14	3.65	1.64	0.11	1.10
Q16	4.38	1.74	0.13	1.80
Q22	4.08	1.53	0.55	6.39
Q25	4.31	1.61	0.10	1.09
Q26	4.55	1.60	0.11	1.41
Q27	3.63	1.83	0.13	1.40
Training (Formative)				
V8	3.98	1.06	0.18	2.02
V9-28	4.80	0.33	0.14	5.62

SME sample. The second sample consisted of 116 training providers, where Norway and Finland were represented by 40 providers each and Spain by 36 suppliers. The size of the training providers varied substantially, ranging from 1 to almost 800 employees. The median size of the training providers in the sample was 37.4 employees.

Measurement and Measurement Quality

Formative items represent measures that cause the construct under study (Bollen, 1989). Changes in the construct are therefore not expected to cause any changes in the indicators (for an overview of indicator specification, see (Jarvis, Mackenzie, & Podsakoff, 2003)). As a result, items within a formative scale are not expected to correlate. Tests of convergent and discriminant validity based on the inter-correlations between items are therefore not relevant for evaluating the psychometric properties of formative items. Instead, item weights and their significance are used to indicate how relevant each item is in measuring its latent construct. These results are reported in table 3. After examining the indicator weights and t-statistics, several indicators in the e-business competence scale were deleted because of negative weights indicating problems with multicollinearity. A new analysis of the reduced model showed no further problems. Of the eight remaining indicators three were found to have significant t-values (p≤ .05). These indicators were related to competences in e-business strategy and vision, sourcing of competence, and IT business process integration. This empirically suggests that the overall e-business related competence is primarily formed by competence in IT business process integration (Q22), knowledge of the value of e-business technologies in relation to business (Q10), and knowledge of outsourcing (Q16).

We found that the two indicators measuring training, V8 (financial resources of SMEs of different size to invest in training) and the index of V9-28 (competence areas represented in the training content offered) had both both positive and significant weights (p≤.05). The other two indicators included in the measurement model of training had negative weights, indicating a problem with multicollinearity and were therefore removed. The resulting measure of training consists of the SMEs' ability to invest in training, and the content of the training offered by the provider.

We assessed the reliability of the dependent variable constructs using Cronbach's alpha. Hair et al. (Hair, Anderson, Tatham, & Black, 1992) suggest that an alpha of 0.60 is acceptable for exploratory research and 0.80 for confirmatory research. Reliability analysis for the multi-item scales showed the following coefficient alphas: e-business efficiency 0.86, e-business complementarities 0.88, e-business lock-in 0.70, and e-business novelty 0.72. These results show that all concepts had sufficient reliability for exploratory research.

The reflective items are believed to be caused by the latent constructs they intend to measure

Table 2. Results of the reliability test

Variable	Reliability of scale
E-business performance: efficiency (v11-13)	0.86
E-bus. performance: complementarities (v14-16)	0.88
E-business performance: lock-in (v17-18)	0.70
E-business performance: novelty (v19-20)	0.72

(Bollen, 1989). Inter-correlations between the items are therefore expected. The psychometric properties of the reflective items were examined by analyzing their internal consistency in terms of their convergent and discriminant validity. Convergent validity was estimated based on the item loadings, and a loading of above .70 is recommended, which indicates that at least half of the variance in each item is accounted for by the latent construct (Nunnally, 1978). For all dimensions of e-business performance the items had sufficient convergent validity in terms of their squared loadings (see table 2). In addition, average variance extracted (AVE) was calculated. AVE indicated that the set of indicators as a whole was sufficient of explaining the latent construct. All constructs with reflective items had AVE above the recommended level of 0.5 (Fornell & Larcker, 1981), as shown in table 3.

Test of Hypotheses

We tested the structural model with the estimated path coefficients and their standard errors, along with the R^2 value, which reflects the predictive ability of the model including the dependent variables' ability to explain the dependent variable. We used PLS-graph version 3.0 (W.W. Chin, 2001) for the structural analyses and hypotheses tests. The significance of each path in the structural model was estimated using the bootstrap re-sampling method with 200 re-samples. Our sample size of 339 exceeds the minimum recommended sample size of the greater of either 1) ten times the number

Table 3. Descriptive statistics: E-business performance, reflective indicators

E-business efficiency (Reflective)				
Composite Reliability 0.86; AVE 0.67	Mean	Std. dev.	Loading	t-stat.
Q28	3.66	1.90	0.84	49.20
Q29	3.84	1.91	0.85	62.36
Q30	4.20	1.76	0.76	22.77
E-business complementarities (Reflective)				
Composite Reliability 0.90; AVE 0.75				
Q31	3.78	1.76	0.84	35.37
Q32	3.98	1.75	0.90	81.06
Q33	3.60	1.78	0.86	59.06
E-business Lock-in (Reflective)				
Composite Reliability 0.85; AVE 0.74				
Q34	2.97	1.73	0.84	33.26
Q35	3.76	1.81	0.88	47.79
E-business Novelty (Reflective)				
Composite Reliability 0.87; AVE 0.77				
Q36	2.93	1.85	0.88	46.59
Q37	3.75	1.76	0.87	45.12

of indicators in the scale with the largest number of formative indicators, or 2) ten times the largest number of structural paths directed at a particular dependent construct in the structural model (W. W. Chin, Marcolin, & Newsted, 1996).

Hypotheses H1a states a positive association between training and e-business performance in terms of efficiency, and this was not supported. Hypothesis H1b holds that training will be positively related to e-business performance in terms of complementarities, which was supported (.15, $p \leq .01$). Hypothesis H1c states a positive relationship between training and lock-in, which was supported (.15; $p \leq .01$), and finally hypothesis H1d states that training will be positively related to e-business performance in terms of novelty, which was also supported (.20, $p \leq .01$). Hypothesis H2 states a positive relationship between training and the e-business related competence in the SMEs, which was supported (.26, $p \leq .01$, $R^2 = .07$). Finally, hypothesis H3a states a positive

relationship between e-business competence and e-business performance in terms of efficiency, which received strong support (.58, $p \leq .01$). Hypothesis H3b suggest that e-business competence is positively related to e-business performance in terms of complementarities, which was strongly supported (.61, $p \leq .01$). Hypothesis H3c states that e-business competence is positively related to e-business performance in terms of lock-in, which received strong support (.49, $p \leq .01$). The last hypothesis, H3d, holds that e-business competence will be positively related to e-business performance in terms of novelty, which was also strongly supported (.55, $p \leq .01$). As a whole the structural model explained a substantial amount of variance in e-business performance. Competence and training explained 36%, 45%, 30% and 40% of the variance in e-business efficiency, complementarities, lock-in, and novelty, respectively. Figure 2 summarizes the significant findings of the structural model.

DISCUSSION

The literature on the relationship between training and performance in SMEs is ambiguous. The same is true for the relationships between e-business related training, e-business competence and business performance, and between e-business training and competence. This confusion is most likely a result of the partial focus in most of these studies where few have included both the effect of training and competence in understanding how e-business applications can influence e-business performance. This exploratory study examined the factors that affect e-business performance in SMEs by combining a research model developed from a review of the IT competence literature and the small business literature, with interviews and survey data from both SMEs and training providers. We have three contributions.

First, we have developed a conceptualization of e-business related training that both include the supply side as well as the demand side of training as suggested by Patton et al (2000). This conceptualization combines factors identified in the IS literature with factors identified in the small business literature.

Second, our empirical results from the context of e-business demonstrate a relationship between training, competence, and performance in SMEs. In addition to the direct relationship between e-business competence and performance, training was found both to influence competence levels and performance both direct and indirectly. These findings add to and support the small business literature which suggests that a positive relationship exists between SME training and performance (e.g. Cosh, Duncan, & Hughes, 1998). The findings also support the proposition of Patton et al.(2000) that empirical studies should focus more on specific contexts when investigating the relationship between training and performance. Indeed, after implementing methodological improvements suggested by several authors our findings support the views that the ambiguities in the literature to a large extent are caused by methodological weaknesses in many empirical studies, thus hindering or obscuring the documentation of these relationships (e.g. Fuller-Love, 2006; Patton et al., 2000; Wade & Hulland, 2004).

Third, we have demonstrated that value creation in e-business can be explained by a limited set of e-business related competences as well as the demand and supply side of training. The competences which explained a substantial amount of e-business performance were competence in e-business strategy and vision, competence in sourcing, and competence in process integration between IT and business. These competences explain a substantial amount of the variance in performance and should be considered by the SMEs in evaluating their e-business related competence level.

Public stimulation programs targeting SMEs would benefit from these results. Training providers should evaluate whether the content of their training programs sufficiently cover the competences identified in this study. Both public programs and training suppliers should be aware of the fact that the SMEs' lack of awareness and inability to invest in these training programs could represent significant barriers to developing e-business related competence and hence e-business performance.

Lacking financial ability can be a significant factor in explaining difference in survival rates between SMEs of different size. Our data includes training supply and ability to invest in training in three countries in Europe. Of these countries, Spain had public arrangements that helped the smallest SMEs in particular, since they have the lowest ability to pay for training and the greatest need for competence. Our data suggest that such public arrangements that increase the ability to pay for training for the smallest of the SMEs, could increase e-business performance as well as survival of these SMEs. The impact of this policy could be positive for the economy, since small SMEs dominate the SME segment through their numbers as well as are the ones with the lowest survival rates.

There is need for more studies on the issue of training and e-business competence, particularly in the context of SMEs. The lack of theoretical and empirical work on this topic and the results from our exploratory study, suggest that future research should devote more resources to further explore the importance of training, competence and performance in SMEs and investigate how improvements could influence the economy. Our findings suggest that specificity regarding context is necessary to document effects of training and competence. Future studies should explore other contexts and investigate whether it is possible to generalize findings to other contexts or to SMEs in general.

This exploratory study has several limitations. Our data consist of subjective evaluations of e-business managers and training providers and are not necessarily reflecting objective facts. Future studies should include less subjective information about e-business performance and its antecedents. An interesting approach would be to follow e-business training programs over time with more in depth research methods focusing on how several characteristics of the training offered could influence the competence build up and the SME performance over time. Such studies should be followed by quantitative research methods that could test the hypotheses developed with the ability to generalize the results.

REFERENCES

Amit, R., & Zott, C. (2001). Value creation in e-business. *Strategic Management Journal*, *22*(6-7), 493–520. doi:10.1002/smj.187

Ballantine, J., Levy, M., & Powell, P. (1998). Evaluating information systems in small and medium-sized enterprises: issues and evidence. *European Journal of Information Systems*, *7*(4), 241–251. doi:10.1057/palgrave.ejis.3000307

Bassellier, G., Reich, B. H., & Benbasat, I. (2001). Information technology competence of business managers: A definition and research model. *Journal of Management Information Systems*, *17*(4), 159–182.

Bharadwaj, A. S., Sambamurthy, V., & Zmud, R. W. (2000). *IT capabilities: theoretical perspectives and empirical operalization.* Paper presented at the 21st International Conference on Information Systems, Brisbane, Australia.

Bollen, K. A. (1989). *Structural equations with latent variables.* Wiley-Interscience.

Bryan, J. (2006). Training and Performance in Small Firms. *International Small Business Journal*, *24*(6), 635–660. doi:10.1177/0266242606069270

Brynjolfsson, E., & Hitt, L. M. (1998). Beyond the productivity paradox. *Communications of the ACM*, *41*(8), 49–55. doi:10.1145/280324.280332

Burke Jarvis, C., Mackenzie, S. B., & Podsakoff, P. M. (2003). A Critical Review of Construct Indicators and Measurement Model Misspecification in Marketing and Consumer Research. *The Journal of Consumer Research*, *30*(September), 199–218. doi:10.1086/376806

Chin, W. W. (1998). The Partial Least Squares Approach for Structural Equation Modelling. In Marcoulides, G. A. (Ed.), *Modern Methods for Business Research*. Hillsdale, NJ: Lawrence Erlbaum Associates.

Chin, W. W. (2001). PLS-Graph User's Guide, Version 3.0: Unpublished.

Chin, W. W., Marcolin, B. L., & Newsted, P. R. (1996). *A Partial Least Squares Latent Variable Modeling Approach for Measuring Interaction Effects: Results from a Monte Carlo Simulation Study and Voice Mail Emotion/Adoption Study.* Paper presented at the Seventeenth International Conference on Information Systems.

Clarke, R. (2003). If e-business is different, then so is reseach in e-business. In Viborg Andersen, K., Elliott, S., Swatman, P., Trauth, E. M., & Bjørn-Andersen, N. (Eds.), *Seeking success in e-business*. Boston, Massachusetts: Kluwer Academic Publishers.

Cosh, A., Duncan, J., & Hughes, A. (1998). *Investment in Training and Small Firm Growth and Survival: An Empirical Analysis for the UK 1987-95*: Dfee Publivations Research Report No. 36.

Dans, E. (2001). IT investment in small and medium enterprises: paradoxically productive? *The Electronic Journal of Information Systems Evaluation, 4*(1).

Davenport, T. H. (1993). *Process Innovation: Reengineering Work Through Information Technology*. Boston: Harvard Business School Press.

Dean, J., Holmes, S., & Smith, S. (1997). Understanding Business Networks: Evidence from Manufacturing and Service Sectors in Australia. *Journal of Small Business Management, 35*(1), 79–84.

Debreceny, R., Putterill, M., Tung, L. L., & Gilbert, A. L. (2002). New tools for the determination of e-commerce inhibitors. *Decision Support Systems, 34*(2), 177–195. doi:10.1016/S0167-9236(02)00080-5

DeLone, W. H. (1988). Determinants of Success for Computer Usage in Small Business. *Management Information Systems Quarterly, 12*(1), 51–61. doi:10.2307/248803

Devins, J., & Johanson, S. (2003). Training and Development Activities in SMEs: Some Findings from an Evaluation of the OSF Objective 4 Programme in Britain. *International Small Business Journal, 22*(2), 205–218.

Eikebrokk, T. R., & Olsen, D. H. (2007). An empirical investigation of competency factors affecting e-business success in European SMEs. *Information & Management, 44*(4). doi:10.1016/j.im.2007.02.004

European Commission. (2002a). *eEurope Go Digital - Benchmarking national and regional e-business policies for SMEs*.

European Commission. (2002b). *Synthesis Report - Bechmarking National and Regional e-Business Policies*.

European Commission. (2004). *SME definitions*. Retrieved 23.03.2004, 2004, from http://europa.eu.int/comm/enterprise/enterprise_policy/sme_definition/index_en.htm

Feeny, D. F., & Willcocks, L. P. (1998). Core IS capabilities for exploiting information technology. *Sloan Management Review, 39*(3), 9–21.

Fillis, I., Johannson, U., & Wagner, B. (2003). A conceptualisation of the opportunities and barriers to e-business developemnt in the smaller firm. *Journal of Small Business and Enterprise Development, 10*(3), 336–341. doi:10.1108/14626000310489808

Fornell, C. (1982). *A Second generation of multivariate analysis*. New York: Praeger.

Fornell, C., & Larcker, D. F. (1981). Evaluating Structural Equation Models with Unobservable Variables and Measurement Error. *JMR, Journal of Marketing Research, 28*, 39–50. doi:10.2307/3151312

Fuller-Love, N. (2006). Management development in small firms. *International Journal of Management Reviews, 8*(3), 175–190. doi:10.1111/j.1468-2370.2006.00125.x

Golden, P. A., & Dollinger, M. (1993). Cooperative Alliances and Competitive Strategies in Small Manufacturing Firms. *Entrepreneurship Theory and Practice*, 43-56.

Grandon, E. E., & Pearson, J. M. (2004). Electronic commerce adoption: an empirical study of small and medium US businesses. *Information & Management, 42*, 197–216.

Hair, J. F., Anderson, R. E., Tatham, R. L., & Black, W. C. (1992). *Multivariate Data Analysis*. New York: Macmillan Publishing Company.

Hammer, M. (1990). Reengineering work: Don't Automate, Obliterate. *Harvard Business Review, 68*(4).

Heijden, H. d. (2000). *Measuring IT core capabilities for electronic commerce: results from a confirmatory analysis.* Paper presented at the 21st International Conference on Information Systems, Brisbane, Australia.

Ihlström, C., & Nilsson, M. (2003). E-business adoption by SMEs - Prerequisites and attitudes of SMEs in a Swedish network. *Journal of Organizational Computing and Electronic Commerce, 13*(3-4), 211–223. doi:10.1207/S15327744JOCE133&4_04

Ivis, M. (2001). *Analysis of barriers impeding e-business adoption among Canadian SMEs.* Canadian E-Business Opportunities Roundtable.

Jarratt, D. G. (1998). A Strategic Classification of Business Alliances: A Qualitative Perspective Built from a Study of Small and Medium-sized Enterprises. *Qualitative Market Research: An International Journal, 11*(1), 39–49. doi:10.1108/13522759810368442

Jarvis, C. B., Mackenzie, S. B., & Podsakoff, P. M. (2003). A critical review of construct indicators and measurement model misspecification in marketing and consumer research. *The Journal of Consumer Research, 30*(september), 199–218. doi:10.1086/376806

Johansson, N., & Mollstedt, U. (2006). Revisiting Amit and Zott's model of value creation sources: The SymBelt Customer Center case. *Journal of Theoretical and Applied Electronic Commerce Research, 1*(3), 16–27.

Johnston, K., Shi, J., Dann, Z., & Barcay, I. (2006). Knowledge, power and trust in SME e-based virtual organisations. *International Journal of Networking & Virtual Organizations, 3*(1), 42–59. doi:10.1504/IJNVO.2006.008784

Jöreskog, K. G., & Wold, H. (1982). *Systems under indirect observation: Causality, structure, prediction.* North-Holland.

Keen, P. G. W. (1991). Redesigning the organization through Information Technology. *Planning Review, 19*(3).

Kinkaide, P. (2000). *The New Frontier: SME's Enterprise and E-Business in Western Canada.* Unpublished manuscript, Edmonton.

Lawrence, K. L. (1997). *Factors Inhibiting the Utilisation of Electronic Commerce Facilities in Tasmanian Small-to-Mediun Sized Enterprises.* Paper presented at the 8th Australasian Conference on Information Systems.

Lee, C. S. (2001). An analytical Framework for Evaluting E-commerce Business Models and Strategies. *Internet Research: Electronic Network Applications and Policy, 11*(4), 349–359. doi:10.1108/10662240110402803

Lee, D. M. S., Trauth, E. M., & Farwell, D. (1995). Critical Skills and Knowledge Requirements of Is Professionals - a Joint Academic-Industry Investigation. *Management Information Systems Quarterly, 19*(3), 313–340. doi:10.2307/249598

Lee, J.-N. (2001). The impact of knowledge sharing, organizational capability and partnership quality on IS outsourcing success. *Information & Management, 38*, 323–335. doi:10.1016/S0378-7206(00)00074-4

Lee, S., & Lim, G. G. (2005). The impact of partnership attributes on EDI implementation success. *Information & Management, 42*, 503–516. doi:10.1016/S0378-7206(03)00153-8

Lewis, R., & Cockrill, A. (2002). Going global-remaining local: the impact of e-commerce on small retail firms in Wales. *International Journal of Information Management, 22*(3), 195–209. doi:10.1016/S0268-4012(02)00005-1

Love, P. E. D., & Irani, Z. (2004). An exploratory study of information technology evaluation and benefits management practices of SMEs in the construction industry. *Information & Management, 42*, 227–242.

MacGregor, R. C. (2004). The Role of Strategic Alliances in the Ongoing Use of Electronic Commerce Technology in Regional Small Business. *Journal of Electronic Commerce in Organizations, 2*(1), 1–14.

Marlow, S. (1998). So Much Opportunity -- So Little Take-up: The Case of Training in Small Firms. *Small Business and Enterprise Development, 5*(1), 38–47. doi:10.1108/EUM0000000006729

Maton, K. (1999). *Evaluation of Small Firms Training Loans*. UK Research Partnerships Ltd., Dfee Publications.

Mehrtens, J., Cragg, P. B., & Mills, A. B. (2001). A model of Internet adoption by SMEs. *Information & Management, 39*, 165–176. doi:10.1016/S0378-7206(01)00086-6

Mowshowitz, A. (1997). Virtual Organization. *Communications of the ACM, 40*(9). doi:10.1145/260750.260759

Nunnally, J. C. (1978). *Psychometric theory* (2nd ed.). New York: McGraw-Hill.

Patton, D., Marlow, S., & Hannon, P. (2000). The Relationship Between Training and Small Firm Performance, Research Frameworks and Lost Quests. *International Small Business Journal, 19*(1), 11–27. doi:10.1177/0266242600191001

Peppard, J., Lambert, R., & Edwards, C. (2000). Whose job is it anyway? organizational information competencies for value creation. *Information Systems Journal, 10*, 291–322. doi:10.1046/j.1365-2575.2000.00089.x

Premaratne, S. P. (2001). Networks, Resources and Small Business Growth: The Experience in Sri Lanka. *Journal of Small Business Management, 39*(4), 363–371. doi:10.1111/0447-2778.00033

Rayport, J. F., & Sviokla, J. J. (1995). Exploiting the Virtual Value Chain. *Harvard Business Review*, (November-December): 75–85.

Rosenfeld, S. (1996). Does Cooperation Enhance Competitiveness? Assessing the Impacts of Inter-firm Collaboration. *Research Policy, 25*(2), 247–263. doi:10.1016/0048-7333(95)00835-7

Saeed, K. A., Grover, V., & Hwang, Y. (2005). The relationship of e-commerce to customer value and firm performance: an empirical investigation. *Journal of Management Information Systems, 22*(1), 223–256.

Sambamurthy, V., Bharadwaj, A., & Grover, V. (2003). Shaping agility through digital options: Reconceptualizing the role of information technology in contemporary firms. *Management Information Systems Quarterly, 27*(2), 237–263.

Sambamurthy, V., & Zmud, R. W. (1994). *IT management competency assessment: a tool for creating business value through IT*. Morristown, New Jersey: Financial Executives Research Foundation.

Shi, Z., Kunnathur, A. S., & Ragu-Nathan, T. S. (2005). IS outsourcing management competence dimensions: instrument development and relationship exploration. *To be published in Information & Management*.

Tetteh, E., & Burn, J. (2001). Global Strategies for SME-business: Applying the SMALL Framework. *Logistics Information Management*, *14*(1-2), 171–180. doi:10.1108/09576050110363202

Timmers, P. (1999). *Electronic commerce: strategies and models for business-to-business trading*. West Sussex, England: John Wiley & Sons Ltd.

Troshani, I., & Rao, S. (2007). Enabling e-business competitive advantage: perspectives from the Australian Financial Services Industry. *International Journal of Business and Information*, *2*(1), 80–103.

Wade, M. R., & Hulland, J. (2004). Review: The resource-based view and information systems research: review, extension, and suggestions for future research. *Management Information Systems Quarterly*, *28*(1), 107–142.

Westhead, P., & Storey, D. (1996). Management Training and Small Firm Performance: Why is the Link so Weak? *International Small Business Journal*, *14*(4), 3–25. doi:10.1177/0266242696144001

Westhead, P., & Storey, D. (1997). *Training Provision and the Development of Small and Medium-sized Enterprises*. London: Dfee.

APPENDIX A. DESCRIPTIVE STATISTICS

Table 4. SME sample

Item	n	Mean	Std. Deviation
Q1	339	29,52	34,84
Q2	339	1,00	,00
Q3	339	2,06	,80
Q5	321	4,38	1,74
Q6	327	4,43	1,42
Q7	309	4,72	1,55
Q8	299	4,34	1,72
Q9	330	4,74	1,45
Q10	325	4,32	1,42
Q11	261	3,66	1,90
Q12	258	3,84	1,91
Q13	303	4,20	1,76
Q14	274	3,78	1,76
Q15	283	3,98	1,75
Q16	286	3,60	1,78
Q17	287	2,97	1,73
Q18	299	3,76	1,81
Q19	309	2,93	1,85
Q20	307	3,75	1,76
E-bus. Efficiency	234	3,89	1,64
E-bus. Complem.	255	3,79	1,59
E-bus. Lock-in	276	3,34	1,55
E-bus. Novelty	299	3,36	1,59
Valid N (listwise)	172		

Table 5. E-business systems used in the SME sample

E-business systems	# SMEs	Percent
Web pages with information to individual customers about products and services (V4a)	256	75,5
Web pages where individual customers can make orders (V4b)	134	39,5
Web pages where companies can find information about products and services (V4c)	270	79,6
Systems for electronic sales of products and services to other companies (V4d)	51	15
EDI solutions on the Internet (V4e)	73	21,5
Systems where suppliers can find information about our demand and supply (V4f)	62	18,3
Systems that integrate supply chains (V4g)	36	10,6
Other (V4h)	102	30,1

APPENDIX B. THE SURVEY INSTRUMENT FOR SMES

Country: ☐ Finland ☐ Norway ☐ Spain

Introduction to Respondent

This interview is part of a project that investigates the use of e-commerce or e-business in small and medium-sized companies in Europe. In this interview you will be presented with questions about e-business, which can be defined as utilizing technologies for conducting business over the Internet. This implies all types of business interactions over the Internet with suppliers, customers and other business partners.

We ask you to answer as correct as possible based on the knowledge you have of your company. This survey is anonymous and we guarantee that it will not be possible to trace any of the answers back to you and your company.

Background Information

Q1. Approximately, how many employees are there in your company? _____ **employees**

Q2. In what type of industry is your company?
☐ **Tourism**
☐ **Transport**
☐ **Food & Beverages**

Q3. Does your company use web pages, e-mail or e-commerce systems for business purposes?
☐ **Yes**
☐ **No**

Q4. What types of e-business systems does your company use? (multiple responses possible)
☐ web pages whith information to individual customers about products or services
☐ web pages where individual customers can make orders
☐ web pages where companies can find information about products or services
☐ systems for electronic sales of products and services to other companies
☐ EDI solutions on the Internet
☐ systems that enables your suppliers to see information about your demand or production
☐ systems that integrates supply chains
☐ other

	a very low extent	1	2	3	4	5	6	7	*a very high extent*
Q5. To what extent are IT activities in your company outsourced to external providers?		☐	☐	☐	☐	☐	☐	☐	
Q6. To what extent is your company informed about commercially available e-business systems?		☐	☐	☐	☐	☐	☐	☐	
Q7. To what extent is your company informed about providers of e-business related training?		☐	☐	☐	☐	☐	☐	☐	
Q8. To what extent has your company implemented its e-business intentions?		☐	☐	☐	☐	☐	☐	☐	

In the next section we would like you to assess your company's level of competence in various topics related to e-business. The questions are in the form of propositions. We ask you to give your evaluation of how accurately you feel that these propositions describe the situation in your company. If you find that any of the propositions are irrelevant, please indicate so by answering "not applicable". Please indicate how well you agree with the proposition by answering a number between 1: totally disagree and up to 7: totally agree.

Strategy and Vision

The Concept of E-Business

		totally disagree	1	2	3	4	5	6	7	*totally agree*	*N/A*
Q10.	Our company has a high level of knowledge how e-business technologies can be of value to our business		□	□	□	□	□	□	□		□
Q11.	Our company has a high level of knowledge of how our main competitor(s) use IT to support similar business areas		□	□	□	□	□	□	□		□
Q12.	In general, e-business is well understood by my company		□	□	□	□	□	□	□		□

Strategic Planning

		totally disagree	1	2	3	4	5	6	7	*totally agree*	*N/A*
Q13.	Our company has a high level of knowledge of strategic planning		□	□	□	□	□	□	□		□
Q14.	Our company has a well developed set of strategic planning techniques		□	□	□	□	□	□	□		□
Q15.	In general, strategic planning is well understood by our company		□	□	□	□	□	□	□		□

Sourcing and Alignment

Sourcing Competencies

		totally disagree	1	2	3	4	5	6	7	*totally agree*	*N/A*
Q16.	Our company has a high level of knowledge on outsourcing of activities to other companies		□	□	□	□	□	□	□		□
Q17.	Our company has a high level of knowledge on how to use competencies in our business partners		□	□	□	□	□	□	□		□

Alignment competencies

		totally disagree	1	2	3	4	5	6	7	*totally agree*	*N/A*
Q18.	In my company business and IT managers very much agree on how IT contributes to business value		□	□	□	□	□	□	□		□

		1	2	3	4	5	6	7	N/A
Q19.	In my company there is effective exchange of ideas between business people and IT people	☐	☐	☐	☐	☐	☐	☐	☐
Q20.	In general, my company is good at using the competencies it already has	☐	☐	☐	☐	☐	☐	☐	☐
Q21.	In general, my company is good at using competencies represented in our business partners	☐	☐	☐	☐	☐	☐	☐	☐

IT-Business Process Integration

Competence in Process Integration

		totally disagree	1	2	3	4	5	6	7	*totally agree*	N/A
Q22.	My company is actively working with the impact of e-business on its business processes		☐	☐	☐	☐	☐	☐	☐		☐
Q23.	In general, my company is good at reorganizing work to utilize new information technology		☐	☐	☐	☐	☐	☐	☐		☐

Management of IT

		totally disagree	1	2	3	4	5	6	7	*totally agree*	N/A
Q24.	My company's IT resources are effectively managed		☐	☐	☐	☐	☐	☐	☐		☐
Q25.	My company is good at achieving the anticipated benefits from IT investments		☐	☐	☐	☐	☐	☐	☐		☐

Systems and Infrastructure

		totally disagree	1	2	3	4	5	6	7	*totally agree*	N/A
Q26.	The systems infrastructure is very flexible in relation to my company's future needs		☐	☐	☐	☐	☐	☐	☐		☐
Q27.	The IT systems make it possible for my company to effectively cooperate electronically with business partners		☐	☐	☐	☐	☐	☐	☐		☐

In the last section we would like you to assess your company's experiences with the effects of its e-business efforts. We ask you to give your evaluation of what you feel has come out of your company's e-business efforts.

E-Business Success

		totally disagree	1	2	3	4	5	6	7	*totally agree*	N/A
Q28.	Our e-business efforts have reduced costs by electronic order taking over the Internet		☐	☐	☐	☐	☐	☐	☐		☐
Q29.	Our e-business efforts have made us able to deliver faster		☐	☐	☐	☐	☐	☐	☐		☐

| Q30. | Our e-business efforts have reduced costs in communication with suppliers and customers | ☐ | ☐ | ☐ | ☐ | ☐ | ☐ | ☐ | ☐ |

Complementarities

		totally disagree	1	2	3	4	5	6	7	*totally agree*	*N/A*
Q31.	As a result of our e-business efforts our products or services complement products or services from other suppliers		☐	☐	☐	☐	☐	☐	☐		☐
Q32.	Our business efforts make it possible for other suppliers to complement our products or services		☐	☐	☐	☐	☐	☐	☐		☐
Q33.	Our e-business efforts have made our supply chain strongly integrated to our partners' supply chains		☐	☐	☐	☐	☐	☐	☐		☐
Lock-in	Our e-business efforts make it more expensive for our customers or suppliers to replace us. Our e-business efforts have made our products and services more tailored to our customers' needs		☐	☐	☐	☐	☐	☐	☐		☐

Novelty

		totally disagree	1	2	3	4	5	6	7	*totally agree*	*N/A*
Q34.	Our e-business efforts have made our company a pioneer in utilizing e-commerce solutions		☐	☐	☐	☐	☐	☐	☐		☐
Q35.	Our e-business efforts have made us cooperating with our customers or suppliers in new and innovative ways		☐	☐	☐	☐	☐	☐	☐		☐

General

		totally disagree	1	2	3	4	5	6	7	*totally agree*	*N/A*
Q36.	In general, my company has experienced very positive effects from its e-business efforts		☐	☐	☐	☐	☐	☐	☐		☐

Other/Control

Leader vs. Follower

		totally disagree	1	2	3	4	5	6	7	*totally agree*	*N/A*
Q37.	There is a dominating customer or supplier who dictates our e-business efforts		☐	☐	☐	☐	☐	☐	☐		☐
Q38.	Our company is good at implementing changes in its organization		☐	☐	☐	☐	☐	☐	☐		☐

Q39. Overall, my company has a high level of competence for utilizing e-business technology □ □ □ □ □ □ □ □

APPENDIX C. THE SURVEY INSTRUMENT FOR TRAINING SUPPLIERS

V1. Approximately, how many employees are there in your company? _____ employees
V2. Does your company off e-business-related training and courses? □ Yes, □ No
V3. Does your company off software related to e-business solutions to SMEs? □ Yes, □ No
V4. Does your company offer training and courses, which assist SMEs in utilizing web pages or e-commerce systems? □ Yes, □ No
V5. To what extent do you supply training and courses to these categories of SMEs

	Not at all	1	2	3	4	5	6	7	very large extent
1-5 employees		□	□	□	□	□	□	□	
6-10 employees		□	□	□	□	□	□	□	
11-30 employees		□	□	□	□	□	□	□	
31-100 employees		□	□	□	□	□	□	□	
101-250 employees		□	□	□	□	□	□	□	

V6. To what extent are SMEs informed about providers of e-business related training?

a very low extent	1	2	3	4	5	6	7	a very high extent
	□	□	□	□	□	□	□	

V7. In your view, to what extent are SMEs successfully implementing e-business efforts?

a very low extent	1	2	3	4	5	6	7	a very high extent
	□	□	□	□	□	□	□	

V8. In your view, to what extent do the following types of SMEs have sufficient financial resources to invest in training programs?

	Not at all	1	2	3	4	5	6	7	very large extent
1-5 employees		□	□	□	□	□	□	□	
6-10 employees		□	□	□	□	□	□	□	
11-30 employees		□	□	□	□	□	□	□	
31-100 employees		□	□	□	□	□	□	□	
101-250 employees		□	□	□	□	□	□	□	

In this section we would like you to focus on the building of competencies in SMEs. As a provider of training and courses, to what extent do you stimulate building of competence in the following areas?

		Not at all	1	2	3	4	5	6	7	Very large extent
V9.	The value of e-business solutions for SMEs		□	□	□	□	□	□	□	
V10.	The utilization of e-business solutions in the customer's industry		□	□	□	□	□	□	□	
V11.	General understanding of e-business		□	□	□	□	□	□	□	
V12.	Strategic planning in general		□	□	□	□	□	□	□	
V13.	The use of strategic planning techniques		□	□	□	□	□	□	□	
V14.	Outsourcing in general		□	□	□	□	□	□	□	
V15.	Sourcing of e-business related competencies		□	□	□	□	□	□	□	

		Not at all	1	2	3	4	5	6	7	Very large extent
V16.	Alignment of IT and business		□	□	□	□	□	□	□	
V17.	Consensus building between IT and business people		□	□	□	□	□	□	□	
V18.	Utilizing competencies in the organization		□	□	□	□	□	□	□	
V19.	Utilizing competencies in business partners		□	□	□	□	□	□	□	
V20.	The improvement of business processes		□	□	□	□	□	□	□	
V21.	Process integration between IT and business		□	□	□	□	□	□	□	
V22.	Reengineering work to utilize new information technology		□	□	□	□	□	□	□	
V23.	Change management in general		□	□	□	□	□	□	□	
V24.	Change management in relation to IT-investments		□	□	□	□	□	□	□	
V25.	IT management		□	□	□	□	□	□	□	
V26.	The ability to realize benefits of IT-investments		□	□	□	□	□	□	□	
V27.	IT systems infrastructure		□	□	□	□	□	□	□	
V28.	Effective electronic cooperation between business partners		□	□	□	□	□	□	□	

This work was previously published in International Journal of E-Business Research (IJEBR), edited by In Lee, pp. 92-116, copyright 2009 by IGI Publishing (an imprint of IGI Global).

Chapter 6
Promoting Competitive Advantage in Micro-Enterprises through Information Technology Interventions

Mehruz Kamal
The College at Brockport, State University of New York, USA

Sajda Qureshil
University of Nebraska at Omaha, USA

Peter Wolcott
University of Nebraska at Omaha, USA

ABSTRACT

The use of Information and Communication Technologies (ICTs) by Small and Medium Sized Enterprises (SMEs) have the potential to enable these businesses to grow through access to new markets and administrative efficiencies. However, the growth of the smallest of these SMEs which are micro-enterprises is hindered by their inability to adopt ICTs effectively to achieve competitive advantage. This chapter investigates how micro-enterprises can adopt ICTs to grow and achieve competitiveness. This investigation of a set of seven micro-enterprises took place through an interpretive field study in which action research was used to diagnose and treat the micro-enterprises with interventions through a process of "Information Technology (IT) Therapy". This process involved providing individualized IT solutions to pressing problems and opportunities and the development of a longer-term IT project plan, customized for each of the businesses. The increase in competitiveness of these micro-enterprises was assessed using the Focus Dominance Model and their growth through a modified model of micro-enterprise growth based on the resource based view of the firm. This research also contributes with a unique set of skills and experiences that ITD innovators can bring in helping micro-enterprises achieve sustained growth and competitive advantage.

DOI: 10.4018/978-1-60960-132-4.ch006

Copyright © 2011, IGI Global. Copying or distributing in print or electronic forms without written permission of IGI Global is prohibited.

INTRODUCTION

There is evidence to suggest that use of Information and Communications Technology (ICT) can play an important role on the growth of small businesses (Matthews 2007, Sullivan 1985, Qiang et al 2006, Raymond et al 2005). In this sense, IT can be employed to bring about increased competitiveness if it enables businesses to create new jobs, increase productivity and sales through access to new markets and administrative efficiencies (Qureshi 2005, Matthews 2007). These outcomes can be achieved through measurable improvements in the lives of people living with limited resources to sustain themselves. Duncombe and Heeks (2003) suggest that there is a role for the ICT intermediary in providing the needed information on markets, customers and suppliers. In their study of 1000 small business enterprises in the US, Riemenschneider et al (2003) found that businesses were prepared to overcome obstacles to IT adoption to achieve web presence. This is because pressures to keep with the competition and promote services to customers are greater than the obstacles to setting up websites. There is a sense that small and medium enterprises hold the promise of growing incrementally on existing capabilities, and providing a seedbed for the emergence of dynamic and efficient larger national firms (Levy 2001, Mathews 2007, Servon and Doshna 2000).

It also appears that the promise of eBusiness adoption by micro-enterprises can potentially provide these businesses with the ability to access new markets and reduce costs through administrative efficiencies (Brown and Lockett 2004, Pateli and Giaglis 2004). However, the use of ICT by Small and medium Sized Enterprises (SMEs) remains a challenge in both developed as well as developing countries (Schreiner and Woller 2003, Sanders 2002, Lichtenstein and Lyons 2001, Hyman and Dearden 1998, Honig 1998, Piscitello and Sgobbi 2004). In particular the opportunities opened up by the internet are limited in SMEs especially due to the challenges faced by globalization (Piscitello and Sgobbi 2004). Small and medium sized businesses are seen to be organizations that employ less than 500 people and typically have problems adopting IT due to competitive pressures and underestimation of time taken to implement IT (Riemenschneider et al 2003). A form of small business being investigated in this paper is the micro-enterprise. Micro-enterprises are tiny businesses with fewer than 10 employees - often just one. The micro-enterprises studied in this paper are part of a Micro-enterprise development program. Such programs make loans and or provide classes to poor people to help them start or strengthen their businesses (Schreiner and Woller 2003).

The challenges faced by micro-enterprises make it even more difficult for them to adopt ICTs for competitiveness. In particular, Piscitello and Sgobbi (2004) suggest that the key barrier to the adoption of ICTs is not size but the learning processes followed by the firms and access to networks of similar internet enabled business services. While a great deal has been written about the challenges faced by micro-enterprise adoption of ICTs, little has been done to provide business models that enable micro-enterprises to use ICTs competitively. According to Grosh and Somolekae (1996), barriers to growth of micro-enterprises are access to capital, educational level of the entrepreneur, legal barriers and start-up financing. In their study of information systems for rural micro-enterprise in Botswana, Duncombe and Heeks (2003) suggest that the role of ICT in enabling information and knowledge is important for both social and economic development. They found that there was a reliance on localized, informal social networks for their information for rural micro-enterprise. Information from these networks was of poor quality and not readily available; it appeared to fail the poorest and most disadvantaged entrepreneurs. In this sense, ICTs can represent an unaffordable addition to costs and the benefits of using them are not always apparent (Duncombe and Heeks 2003, Matthews 2007, Southwood 2004).

This paper investigates how micro-enterprises can adopt ICTs to grow and achieve competitiveness. The question investigated in this paper is: How can micro-enterprises adopt ICTs to achieve competitiveness? In order to answer this question, this paper investigates a set of seven micro-enterprises in the underserved communities of Omaha, Nebraska. The micro-enterprises had received hardware and software through a grant from the eBay Foundation administered by a micro-enterprise development program called the New Community Development Corporation. Through a series of action research steps carried out by the researchers, the ICT challenges faced by the micro-enterprises were diagnosed and treated with interventions through a process of "Information Technology (IT) Therapy" (Wolcott et al, 2007; Qureshi et al, 2008). This process involved providing individualized IT solutions to pressing problems and opportunities and the development of a longer-term IT project plan, customized for each of the businesses. In addition to the IT therapy process, the researchers were able to analyze the potential use of the awarded technology to help achieve operational efficiency and competitive advantage. This was done by mapping each of the micro-enterprises' current IT use combined with increase in IT awareness (on the part of the micro-entrepreneur) and transferred IT skills (to the micro-entrepreneur) – both as a result of the IT therapy process - to a theoretical model.

THEORETICAL BACKGROUND

Small Businesses and Information Technology

Past studies have shown that the use of ICT can play an important role on the growth of small businesses (Matthews 2007, Sullivan 1985, Qiang et al 2006, Raymond et al 2005). Cragg and King

(1993) have shown that there is a gradual increase in the number of small firms that either adopt various new technologies or take steps to upgrade what they currently possess. The studies suggest that IT can be employed to bring about increased competitiveness if it enables businesses to create new jobs, increase productivity and sales through access to new markets and administrative efficiencies (Qureshi 2005, Matthews 2007). Small and medium sized businesses that have adopted and used ICTs have seen positive outcomes related to operational efficiencies, increased revenues, and are able to better position themselves within their market niche. Qiang et al. (2006) observed that businesses that utilized e-mail to communicate with their customers experienced sales growth 3.4 per cent greater than those which did not. Similar outcomes were also observed for productivity and reinvestment. Both these components were found to be greater for more intensive users of IT (Qiang et al., 2006). Other research in this area also highlights the positive impact of IT use within small businesses. A 4% increase in sales as well as 5% increase in export performance was obtained when e-business techniques were adopted by SMEs in the manufacturing sector in Canada (Raymond *et al.,* 2005). Specifically, Raymond et al. (2005) mention that by using technologies such as websites, email and telephones to communicate with customers, SMEs can provide better customer service as well as expand their customer base to help reach out to both local as well as international consumers for their products. In another study Southwood (2004) found that ICT investments by SMEs in South Africa resulted in profitability gains from cost savings rather than from increase in sales.

In addition, studies have established that Information Systems play a significant role in small firms (Harrison et al. 1997, Igbaria et al. 1997). In particular, Street and Meister (2004) conducted a study that showed that improved internal transparency is a key component for small business development. The study concluded that Information Systems play a major role in enhancing communication and that the need for an appropriate IS occurs at a very early stage, even before many of the other structural or organizational changes are required. There also exist a number of studies that take the focus away from the direct impacts of IT in small businesses and instead look into various other angles of IT adoption and use in such types of businesses: Raymond (1988) studied the effect of computer training on attitudes and usage behavior; Montazemi (1988) investigated the relationship between computing issues and satisfaction of end-users; DeLone (1988) examined the link between CEO involvement and computer use effectiveness. While developing upon current research, this paper focuses on the adoption of ICTs by micro-enterprises to achieve competitiveness.

Although current literature supporting adoption of technology by small businesses exists, in practice, this is not the scenario – particularly in the case of micro enterprises. In a study of a set of micro enterprises in North Omaha, many entrepreneurs who had received state-of-the-art technology to assist them with their businesses had not even opened the packaging within which these technologies were contained six months after they had received them (Wolcott *et al.* 2007)! In another study by Qiang *et al* (2006), among the *micro firms*, only 27 percent use e-mail and 22 percent use Web sites to interact with clients and suppliers. The study suggests that if computer use affects firm productivity and ICT expands networking within sectors and industries, the micro firms may not be benefiting from these externalities – benefits from ICTs. In addition, Bharati and Chaudhury (2006) surveyed micro, small and medium manufacturing firms within the Boston metropolitan area and found that most of the micro firms were using simple technologies such as basic e-mail, and simple software packages as compared to more complex technologies that were being used by the medium sized firms. Their survey results showed that the micro firms

were not aware of most technologies that could be used for improving their business performance.

Challenges Facing Small Businesses

In order for micro-enterprises to benefit from ICTs and reach a level where they may be competitive, they need to overcome some of the barriers that are holding them back. Relevant literature in this area has identified a number of different challenges facing these small businesses.

- *Affordability* (Mansell & When, 1998; Hazan, 2002): This is a major issue with small businesses as they operate on very restricted budgets and do not have sufficient capital to invest towards state-of-the-art technologies.
- *Awareness about IT* (Owen & Darkwa, 1999): Most micro-entrepreneurs do not possess any technical skills and are oblivious to the capabilities that ICT has to offer. As a result, their ignorance on the power of IT may inhibit small businesses from growing and flourishing.
- *Infrastructure* (Baark & Heeks, 1998; Latchem & Walker, 2001; O'Farrell, Norrish, & Scott, 1999; Barton & Bear, 1999): A core requirements for any form of ICT implementation is to have a basic infrastructure in place that will support the new form of technology that is being introduced into that environment. Lack of such infrastructure will be a major barrier to the adoption and use of ICT.
- *Private/Government sectors* (Lefebvre and Lefebvre, 1996): These two agencies in any community play an important role in either facilitating or inhibiting the development of IT infrastructures to promote increased ICT adoption and use.
- *Management's capacity* (Lefebvre and Lefebvre, 1996): Management's capacity to incorporate IT into small business

environments are also a crucial aspect in successful IT adoption and use; and lack of such capacity could become a major hindrance.

In other studies by Duncombe & Heeks (2002) as well as Moyi (2003), obstacles faced by rural micro-enterprises were highlighted. The challenges related to issues of remote locations, lack of education and literacy on the part of the business owner, poor business skills, poverty and lack of affordability, and lack of transportation.

Information Technology and Competitiveness

Despite these limitations, the competitive advantages of using ICT by the micro-enterprises outweigh the challenges. The relationship between IT and competitive advantage was first researched by McFarlan and McKenney (1983) who came up with a grid to place organizations based on the strategic impact of existing IT applications and the strategic impact of current IT applications development within the firm. The grid was helpful to the extent that management could utilize it to consider the right alternatives to pursue for improved competitiveness. Information technology can add economic value to an organization through 1) the reduction in the costs incurred by the organization, and 2) by differentiating the organization's products or services (Bakos and Treacy, 1986; McFarlan, 1984; Wiseman, 1988). Taking this notion that IT can add value to a firm, Porter and Millar (1985) moves the discussion further by analyzing how advances in information technology have changed the way organizations conduct business and how it may serve to provide a competitive advantage. They explain three core ways in which IT may impact competitiveness: 1. by changing the industry structure, 2. by supporting cost and differentiation strategies, and 3. by creating opportunities to generate new businesses from within existing businesses. Ives and

Learmonth (1984) narrow down the focus of a firm to emphasize customer relationships, and they show how information system technology can enhance relationships with the company's customers. They outline a 13-step customer resource lifecycle highlighting potential uses of IT at the various stages to enable competitive advantage for the firm providing the product or service to the customer (Ives and Learmonth,1984).

Sethi and King (1994) have attempted to measure the extent to which IT applications may provide competitive advantage. They referred to the construct measuring this notion as "CAPITA" (competitive advantage provided by an information technology application) and operationalized it through five main dimensions – efficiency (degree to which an IT application enables a company to produce lower priced products than competing products), functionality (degree to which an IT application provides users with the functionality they desire), threat (impact of the IT application on the bargaining power of customers and suppliers), preemptiveness (early and successful penetration of the IT application into the market), and synergy (the degree to which the IT application is tightly integrated with the business goals, and strategies of the organization). In summarizing the early notions of how IT may impact an organization's competitive advantage, see four distinct strategies emerge: 1) Low-cost leadership – using information systems and technology to produce products and services at a lower price than competitors while enhancing quality and level of service; 2) Product differentiation – using information systems and technology to differentiate products, and enable new services and products; 3) Focus on market niche – using information systems and technology to enable a focused strategy on a single market niche; and 4) Customer and supplier intimacy – using information systems to develop strong ties and loyalty with customers and suppliers.

Due to rapid changes in markets, customer expectations, as well as technologies and most importantly globalization, has made competi-

Figure 1. Resource-based view of the firm

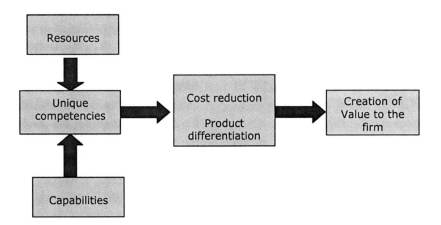

tive advantages short lived. Along those lines, Mata, Fuerst, and Barney (1995) talk about how IT may provide not only competitive advantage but also *sustained* competitive advantage using a resource-based analysis. They emphasize that the "create-capture-keep" paradigm (Clemons and Kimbrough, 1986; Clemons and Row, 1987, 1991b; Feeny and Ives, 1990) whereby customers make certain investments (switching costs) specific to a particular supplier of IT, enabling those suppliers of IT to achieve competitive advantage does not truly hold when it comes to the sustainability of the competitive advantage. Instead, Mata et al (1995) takes the resource-based view of the firm (Clemons, 1991; Barney, 1991; Conner, 1991). In the resource-based view of the firm, resources and capabilities may provide a unique set of competencies that may serve to address either cost reduction or product differentiation strategies to eventually create value for the organization. This is summarized in figure 1.

Using the resource-based perspective, Mata et al (1995) put forward two major notions to explain sustained competitive advantage. The first concept is that of resource heterogeneity which states that competing firms may vary in their resources and capabilities. The second concept is that of resource immobility which says that the

differences in resources and capabilities between competing firms may be long lasting. Their argument is that if a firm's IT resources are distributed heterogeneously among competing firms and if the firms without the resources find it more costly to develop, acquire and implement the same strategy as the firms that already have the resources, then those resources can serve to be a source of sustained competitive advantage. Mata et al (1995) develop a framework using the concepts of resource heterogeneity and resource immobility to depict how these two notions relate to competitive advantage. They then apply this model to four characteristics of IT – access to capital (McFarlan, 1984), proprietary technology, technical IT skills (Copeland and McKenney, 1988), and managerial IT skills (Capon and Glazer, 1987) – that prior literature has suggested to be sources of sustained competitive advantage. Their findings imply that organizing and managing IT within a firm, or in other words, managerial IT skills are the only source of sustained IT competitive advantage and that less focus should be made on the information technology itself.

In order to be able to achieve competitive advantage through its adoption of ICTs, what should a micro-enterprise facing multiple challenges do? Prior research has shown that there are two distinct routes by which small businesses incorporate ICTs. One route is to enhance day-to-day operational support and transaction processing activities (Blili and Raymond, 1993; Foong, 1999; Levy and Powell, 1998; Poon and Swatman, 1999). These studies have shown that small businesses adopt and use simple ICTs without any form of planned strategy to integrate other aspects of the business. And so any form of IT-based competitive advantage is accidental rather than planned (Hashmi and Cuddy, 1990). The second route that is typically taken is to use ICTs to improve interaction and relationships with customers. SMEs, and in particular micro-enterprises are strongly influenced by customer needs. Porter (1980) states, that in many small businesses, customer power is very high. It has been seen that a majority of SMEs depend on a small number of customers who purchase large amounts of goods and services. These major customers are then in a position to influence the price of goods and services that are being produced by the small businesses (Reid and Jacobsen, 1988). Close relationships among SMEs and their customers enable these businesses to respond quickly to customers' changed requirements. Lefebvre and Lefebvre (1993) have shown that there is a link between the innovative efforts of an SME and its competitive position.

Levy et al. (2001) formulated an analytical framework (focus-dominance model), that incorporates both forms of strategic focus - the issue of cost reduction versus value added and the second one being customer dominance i.e. few versus many customers - that emerged from prior research described above. The model examines the potential for SMEs to realize value from IS capabilities. The framework shows where SMEs would fit in terms of the trend they show in IT investments and market strategies. The model is shown below in figure 1. The framework may be viewed as providing four different approaches to ICT adoption as a result of integrating the two dimensions of strategic focus. The *efficiency* quadrant may comprise SMEs that exploit simple

systems such as word processing and trivial accounting processes (Naylor and Williams, 1994). The *co-ordination* quadrant is composed of those SMEs that have a need to increase market share and their customer base. The *collaboration* segment then attracts SMEs that attempt to incorporate emerging technologies to manage relationships with the businesses' major customers. And finally the *innovation* quadrant comprises of those SMEs that actively seek to adopt new information and communication technologies to help achieve competitive advantage. In a follow-up study, Levy *et al.* (2002) investigated 43 SMEs to observe their positions in the focus-dominance model. The results revealed that most of the 43 SMEs make only one move, from *efficiency* to *co-ordination*, or from *efficiency* to *collaboration*. SMEs taking either one these routes tend to avoid losing control and so opt to stay within their current markets. It was also seen that only 17 of the 43 SMEs wanted to move to the *innovation* quadrant possibly due to an environment scan whereby they become aware of "best practices" and strategies that would assist them to manage business growth.

This focus-dominance model was chosen to investigate how micro-enterprises can adopt ICTs to achieve competitiveness. This model is seen to be a valuable means for the analysis of each of the micro-enterprises in the study because it enables us to: 1) Identify the strategic position of each micro-enterprise at the time the study was conducted; 2) Predict the strategic position the micro-enterprise will be in a few years based on the context-specific business goals of each micro-enterprise; 3) Identify the information systems that will support the micro-enterprise in its current strategic position and 4) Map what information systems will be needed to support the micro-enterprise in its projected strategic position.

Moreover, the four quadrants of the focus-dominance model is an outcome of the true conditions encountered by SMEs highlighted through prior research. The unique contribution of the research taken up by the authors of this paper is to apply

Figure 2. The Focus-Dominance Model (Source: Levy et al., 2001)

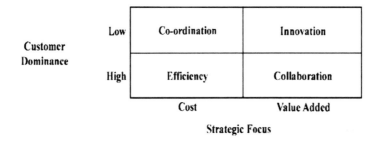

this model to the context of micro-enterprises (as noted earlier, these are the smallest form of businesses) – which has not yet been studied in the realm of this or any other theoretical model. The results will show that micro-enterprises do indeed fall into distinct categories and we provide support for our results by using the established notion of resource-based view of the firm to illustrate competitive advantage (Clemons, 1991; Barney, 1991; Conner, 1991; Mata et al., 1995). Our analysis reveals that through the micro-enterprises' current IT resources – combined with capabilities provided through the IT therapy process, produce unique competencies to position these small businesses to be competitive.

METHODOLOGY

In order to investigate how the micro-enterprises can use ICTs to increase their competitiveness, an interpretive field study was carried out. According to Klein and Myers (1999), Information Systems research can be classified as interpretive if it is assumed that our knowledge of reality is gained only through social constructions. Interpretive methods in IS are aimed at producing an understanding of the context of the information system and the process by which the information system influences and is influenced by the context (Walsham 1993). This research follows an interpretive field study approach in which seven case studies are

carried out. These case studies are carried out using Klein and Myers (1999) principles of the hermeneutic circle, contextualization, interaction between researchers and subjects, abstraction and generalization, dialogical reasoning, the principle of multiple interpretations, and the principle of suspicion. Within each case study, the data was collected and analyzed in iterative cycles of action research. Action research involves the application of tools and methods from the social and behavioral sciences to practical problems with the intention both of improving the practice and of contributing to theory and knowledge in the area studied. Action researchers participate directly or intervene in a situation or phenomenon in order to apply a theory and evaluate the value and usefulness of that theory (Checkland, 1981, 1991; Galliers, 1991). This conforms to Klein and Myers (1999) third principle which requires that there is critical reflection on how the data are socially constructed through interaction between researchers and participants. Action research is a change oriented research methodology that seeks to introduce changes with positive social values, the key focus being on a problem and its solution (Elden and Chisholm 1993). Action research is typically carried out as part of an attempt to solve problems by allowing the researcher to become a participant in the action, the process of change itself becoming the subject of research (Checkland 1981).

Research Setting

This study investigated seven micro-enterprises undergoing change through the adoption of ICTs for competitiveness. Each business has been given an arbitrary name for the purpose of this study and to maintain confidentiality of the businesses. All of the businesses are located in Omaha, Nebraska. Following are brief descriptions of each of the micro-enterprises studied:

1. LD specializes in high quality soups and sandwiches. During the period of this study LD moved its deli from its original location to a better one that could serve local businesses and students.
2. FD specializes in the design of elegant, conservative women's clothing. The owner has aspirations of being a player in the global fashion market.
3. CZ is a franchise that pairs individuals of all ages who need tutoring in any subject with tutors who can provide the service.
4. HH offers a structured residence with treatment and support services to individuals who are transitioning from a treatment program back to society.
5. HE offers massage therapy services. The owner is seeking to diversify into the retail sale of a variety of natural health products.
6. EP is a modeling agency that provides models who reflect the diversity of "normal" (non-glamorous) Americans.
7. HC This on-line business sells wedding cake toppers that reflect the ethnic diversity of customers.

The micro-enterprise owners were all recipients of small technology grants from eBay Foundation's Techquity Grant Program. The Techquity Grant Program offers small grants, typically around $2000, to be used for purchasing hardware, software, and training that would promote the development of micro-enterprises.

The grant program was locally administered by the New Community Development Corporation (NCDC), a non-profit that provides affordable housing and business development services in the greater Omaha area. The anticipated benefit to the micro-enterprises would be more effective utilization of technology, improved thinking about technology and the role of information, and, in general, economic and human development.

Research Design

The design of the research involved seven case studies in which action research was carried out to diagnose the problem in each case, intervene to solve the problem, collect data through interviews and observations of the effects of the interventions and analyze the results in preparation for the next cycle. Action research used in this way was an iterative cycle in which the researcher begins with a plan of how to carry out the activity, then act to intervene to solve the immediate problem, observe the results of the intervention and reflect on the impact and next steps (Zuber-Skerrit, 1991, Avison et al. 1999). Carried out as part of an academic service-learning course – Information Technology for Development (IT4D), the action research was supplemented by the absorbing of knowledge through classroom lectures and discussion. The participative learning process took place in the form of group discussions in which problems were discussed and solutions arrived at collectively.

In this study, the plan was to assist the micro-enterprises through partnership with New Community Development Corporation (NCDC). The cycle continued to action or intervention, to solve the problem or manage the change process; this is where the researcher collected the data. On location at the micro-businesses, the ITD innovators worked with business owners to understand the business and existing technology, implement technology-based projects, and train business owners as appropriate. This process was referred to

Table 1. Data collection steps

Action Research	Case 1: LD	Case 2: FD	Case 3: CZ	Case 4: HH	Case 5: HE	Case 6: EP	Case 7: HC
Plan	Researchers' and the micro-entrepreneurs share initial understandings in Hermeneutic dialogue. Contextualization of the social and historical background of the micro-enterprise and diagnosis of the problem to arrive at the current state of the micro-enterprise on the focus-dominance model.						
Act	IT Therapy interventions through interactions between the researchers and participants to solve the problem. Principle of abstraction and generalization adhered to through the use of two theoretical models to frame and interpret findings from this study.						
Observe	Collection of data through interviews and observations. The principle of multiple interpretations was achieved through class discussions when the ITD innovators implementing the IT interventions discussed the results in class and the second form of interpretation came from the subjects, or in other words, the micro-entrepreneurs						
Reflect	Analysis of the data and interpretation to reveal future state on the focus-dominance model.. Principle of dialogical reasoning used to analyze how context-sensitive assistance (IT therapy) may enable micro-entrepreneur to overcome some of the technical and social barriers that they face.						

as "IT therapy" in which assistance was given to the micro-business owner to solve their immediate IT needs. The process of IT therapy involves the diagnosis of business problems, investigation of alternative technology solutions, selection of the most appropriate solution to fit the business problem and implementation of the technology and training solution. The final implementation involves training of microbusiness owners to ensure that they are able to continue to develop upon the solution.

These steps were carried out within each case study using Klein and Myers (1999) principles. These principles guide our assessment of the action research steps taken to understand the current situation and map it on to Levy et al's (2001) focus-dominance model. Then diagnose the problem, carry out the IT therapy interventions, collect the data and map the future state of each micro-enterprise using Levy et al (2001)'s model. This iterative data collection and analysis process was designed to enable each micro-enterprise's ability to adopt ICTs to achieve competitiveness to be investigated. This is illustrated in Table 1.

The design of this field study conforms to the principles that guide the evaluation of interpretive field studies model by Klein and Myers (1999). The *Principle of the Hermeneutic Circle* states

that an understanding of a complex whole is obtained from preconceptions regarding the meanings of its parts and their interrelationships. Applying this principle to the current study, the *parts* are the researchers' and the micro-entrepreneurs initial understandings and the *whole* are the shared meanings (e.g. increased awareness and acceptance of the utility that the awarded technology can help the micro-entrepreneurs in their business) that arise from the close interactions between them. The multiple interventions in the IT therapy process is supported by the view that in a number of iterations of the hermeneutic circle, a complex whole of shared meanings emerges. *The Principle of Contextualization*: is addressed by treating the micro-entrepreneurs as active actors (e.g. learning new IT skills, gaining trust over technology, working together with the ITD innovators to develop technology plans, etc.) and through the action research steps that were used to collect data for this research, they served as producers of history. *The Principle of Interaction between the Researcher and the Subjects was* addressed by the close and continuous interaction of the researchers with the microentrepreneurs as described in the action research steps utilized for the data collection phase of the study (Klein and Myers, 1999).

Figure 3. Focus-Dominance model mapping for LD

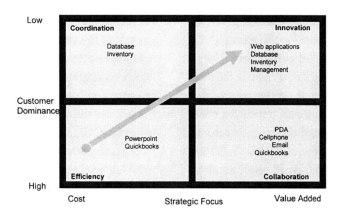

In developing the theoretical contributions of this research, *the Principle of Abstraction and Generalization* guided our use of the focus-dominance model (Levy et al., 2001) which was used to provide a systematic means for understanding the historical, current as well as the future predicted IS-based positions of each of the micro-enterprises. The resource-based view of the firm helped us tie in the concept of IT therapy as a *capability* that when integrated with IT resources within each of the micro-enterprises may help bring about competitiveness. *The Principle of Dialogical Reasoning* formed the basis of the context-sensitive assistance (IT therapy) may assist small businesses to overcome some of the technical and social barriers that they face (Klein and Myers, 1999).

Data on each case being studied was gathered through observation while implementing the IT therapy. The reflection entailed interpretation of the data, and consequences of action that then fed into the planning stage to modify the methodology or model that then determine what action would be taken in the next cycle. On their own time, the ITD innovators maintained a reflective journal, worked on assigned class exercises and readings, and prepared a technology plan for the micro-businesses. Using the techniques provided to them, the ITD innovators implemented the IT interventions by

interacting closely with the micro-entrepreneurs. In this way they interacted as *IT for Development (ITD) innovators* as they implemented the IT and training interventions that enabled the technology to be adopted in innovative ways. The IT4D class sessions served as a sounding board for issues and proposed solutions, offered advice or relevant information, and offered constructive criticism of proposed courses of action to address any IS/ICT adoption/implementation issues specific to any of the micro-businesses. Further cycles of activities continued until a desired end-state is achieved (Zuber-Skerrit, 1991, Avison et al. (1999, p.96).

RESULTS

The current and the future trends in how each of the micro-enterprises use their IS have been mapped onto the focus-dominance model (Levy et al., 2001) after the researchers in the study had an opportunity to discuss and observe the manner in which these small businesses carry out their activities following the action research steps outlined in the methodology section. The IT therapy phase involved the ITD innovators working with business owners to understand the business and existing technology, implementing technology-based projects, and training business owners is also mentioned. This process of "IT therapy", or in other words, assistance given to the micro-business owner to solve their immediate IT needs, is important to the extent that it supports a major resource capability that is lacking and in much needed demand on the part of the micro-enterprises. The future IS trends for each of the businesses were based on the researchers' understanding of the micro-enterprise's future strategic growth plans and their IS requirements. The results were discussed with the business partners (the micro-enterprises) in the study. Following are the individual mappings for each of the micro-enterprises in the study.

LD: LD specializes in high quality soups and sandwiches. During the period of this study LD moved its deli from its original location to a better one that could serve local businesses and students.

Current state: LD has high customer dominance because it is currently dependent on a specific client group. The owner of LD typically uses a PDA, Cell phone, email and a simple software package such as, QuickBookas for the business operations. The old register system is merely a calculator. It does not provide any data to the owner on trends, sandwich purchases, inventory usage, or payroll. Although, the owner is aware of the benefits of the technology the business currently possesses might bring, due to lack of skills and IT knowledge, the business is yet to exploit the technology for competitive advantage. LD's current state of affairs makes it position itself in the *efficiency* quadrant of the focus-dominance model since according to Levy et al. (2001), the main focus of IS use in the *efficiency* quadrant is for control of the business, primarily financial control. The information systems in this context are concerned with improving the efficiency of internal processes.

IT therapy: The ITD innovators helped the owner select a register system that will not only handle ideal usage issues (ideal usage is the total amount of use of a particular item that is an ingredient for various menu items) but also maintain payroll information – thus eliminating the problems of previously manually calculating payroll at the end of each pay period. The Internet café implementation is a work in progress. A wireless communication network through a local Internet Service provider was set up. For a small fee per month, LD will have enough bandwidth to operate 20-25 computers on the same network.

Future state: LD's biggest struggle is going to be integrating a logical inventory and database system into the business. The owner is really working hard to be innovative with the move to the new location. The owner knows what it will take for the business to be successful at this new location and part of that will be incorporating a better inventory system and a customer database. The new location will have free wireless access for customers. Eventually, the business web site will have a customer information database that will be used as an advertising and marketing tool for LD for improved customer service. Since LD is looking to grow and build its customer base, it will eventually have low customer dominance (many customers i.e. few customers will not be able to dominate the business) and moreover the owner's intention of integrating the heart of the business which is the inventory management system with the other aspects of the business makes it position itself distinctly within the *innovation* quadrant. Levy et al. (2001) state that in this quadrant, the IS are a tightly woven part of the business strategy.

CZ: CZ is a franchise that pairs individuals of all ages who need tutoring in any subject with tutors who can provide the service.

Current state: The current state of CZ can be classified as residing in both the *coordination* as well as in the *collaboration* quadrants. CZ's presence in the coordination quadrant arises from the fact that CZ has to deal with a large number of students and tutors and so customer dominance is low. CZ already has its own coordination components such as infrastructure, database, accounting system and marketing means from the franchiser to help it maintain its relationships with its

Figure 4. Focus-Dominance model mapping for CZ

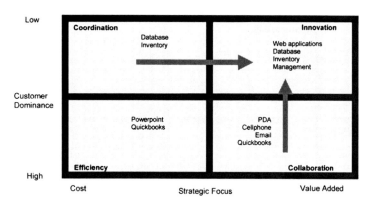

customers (Levy et al., 2001). Additionally, CZ is viewed to reside in the collaboration quadrant since they have collaborative systems such as internal work processes using manual and automatic tools.

IT therapy: The owners of CZ would like to have the process of matching tutors with students automated through online means. In addition they would like to have a software package that can take care of scheduling issues. In response to the needs of CZ, the following IT therapy interventions were carried out: creation of a decision-making framework to resolve whether it would make more sense to build the matching and scheduling system in-house versus purchasing an off-the-shelf application and customizing it to fit the needs of the micro-enterprise.

Future state: CZ is heading to a possible *innovation* state from both the *coordination* and *collaboration* quadrants for its business. Once the owner invests money to develop their own application or purchase an existing off-the-shelf one, the business will generate exponential growth based on their current footing. Once they confirm their decision in investing capital on IT development, they will get more customers and tutors online. It will bring them financial freedom exponentially. The owner is clear as to what needs to be done to align the business strategy with the needed

IS requirements to be a competitive force in the market (Levy et al., 2001).

HH: HH offers a structured residence with treatment and support services to individuals who are transitioning from a treatment program back to society.

Current state: HH had an office management system which included a desktop and a laptop computer. Both computers were used for normal operations such as writing assessment reports, working on Power Point, internet research and e-mail communications. The desktop was the main repository for historical records including past guest records and financial information. The desktop was used for writing standard forms used in operations such as rules violation notices. The laptop was mainly used by the owner and is used in the same way as the desktop except in the case of the financial information. This redundancy in operations increased the ability for all employees to work on separate assignments simultaneously. Some of the functions of the laptop system were that the owner is managing progress and evaluative data in an Excel spreadsheet and used offsite for presentations and guest evaluations. In addition HH had a guest computer lab consisting of one desktop computer located in a common area. The intent of this system was to give guests a resource for looking for jobs and staying in contact with family and friends. The computers could

Figure 5. Focus-Dominance model mapping for HH

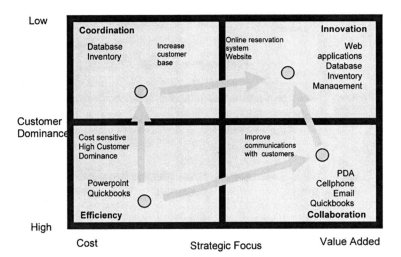

be used for resume writing and for enhancing computer skills as well computer based training. The computer lab accessed the internet from the same wireless connection as the management system. WiFi capability in the house made the guest computer systems expandable with relative ease and low cost. The state of HH was purely in the *efficiency* quadrant of the focus-dominance chart since the focus was on low-cost IS to maintain operational effectiveness (Levy et al., 2001).

IT therapy: In responding to the immediate IT needs of HH, the following IT therapy interventions were carried out: Streamlined business practices including system maintenance and backup of standard procedures; financial data updated and used for making proposals to prospective lenders; business input, output and outcome data updated for display to potential donors and stake holders as well as referral services; data prepared for a database on resident statistics.

Future state: HH is looking to take a phased incremental approach via *coordination* and *collaboration* to reach its desired spot in the *innovation* quadrant. The owners of HH realize that there is a need for better data management as well as improved communication with donors and guests

and stakeholders. In attempting to move to the *coordination* and *collaboration* quadrants from their current state, HH is aware that the business will need to 1. Develop a website to get more exposure in the community and provide URL address to key stakeholders (increase customer base by reducing customer dominance and moving into the *coordination* quadrant); 2. Network with local education providers to allow guests to obtain needed training for the future (improve relationships with few customers i.e. local educational institutes through increased customer dominance by moving into the *collaboration* quadrant); 3. Work with local businesses to develop a community and a pool of potential job opportunities (improve relationships with few customers i.e. local businesses through increased customer dominance by moving into the *collaboration* quadrant); and 4. Present successful outcomes either in person through presentations or online through their website to stakeholders. In addition, the owners of HH want to go a step farther and maintain a strategic focus to drive them into the *innovation* quadrant. They would like to have innovative web-based applications that will enable online reservation capability. The website should also offer capabilities to allow referral

Figure 6. Focus-Dominance model mapping for HE

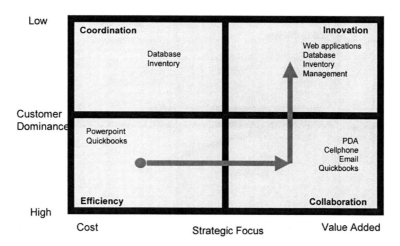

services to contact HH and eventually develop a treatment and payment plan online through a range of treatment options and payment types. Such an IS will tie in all of their business strategies to show relevant outcomes to stakeholders – thus moving them towards the *innovation* quadrant as a result of aligning IS with their overall business strategies (Levy et al., 2001).

HE: HE offers massage therapy services. The owner is seeking to diversify into the retail sale of a variety of natural health products.

Current state: The owner has technology already available to her, but needs help utilizing it. There was an unopened PDA, a laptop, and a desktop. The owner would like to get things organized between the two computers and the PDA. The owner wanted help learning QuickBooks and possibly setting up a company website. She needed security on her laptop and Microsoft Office 2003 installed on both computers. This business lies in the *efficiency* quadrant as it is only beginning to set-up the technology for the business and the primary focus of the IS will be for controlling the business by improving the efficiency of internal processes (Levy et al., 2001)

IT therapy: The ITD Innovators provided the following IT therapy interventions: installing

Microsoft Office 2003; setting up security on the laptop computer; connecting the PDA to both the laptop and desktop; installing a CD-backup system; helping the owner learn how to organize her contact information in Microsoft Outlook.

Future state: Since HE is only at the very early stages of incorporating technology into the business, the owner did not have a well thought out plan as to how the business would want to grow using the technology. The owner did express the intent to have a company website to eventually sell the company's products.

EP: EP is a modeling agency that provides models who reflect the diversity of "normal" (non-glamorous) Americans.

Current state: EP has two dimension of the concept of customer. There are the models who sign up online that can be seen as customers and EP as the agency. The companies who require models for shoots are also customers of EP. EP has low customer dominance since it deals with a large number of models as well as agencies and so very few customers can dominate EP. EP's current state makes it reside in the *coordination* quadrant of the focus-dominance model since according to Levy et al. (2001), the primary use of IS in the *coordination* quadrant is to maintain

Figure 7. Focus-Dominance model mapping for EP

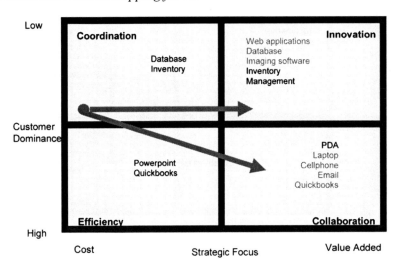

customer relationships – which is a function of the larger customer base. Typically, information systems in this context hold basic customer data.

IT therapy: A major task for the ITD innovators in this case was training the business owner to help her understand the strategic importance of technology in the business. Remote desktop was installed and demonstrated to show how greater mobility and convenience could be achieved through technology. Basic workstation maintenance such as ensuring critical patches and updates were current. The differences between critical and non-critical updates were explained. Desktop security and wireless security were explained to the users. Using QuickBooks to cut down on time spent on non-value added services was explained. Website ranking and place was also explained with possible solutions. It is important to mention here that an ITD innovators role was to increase the owner's comfort level with the technology.

Future state: EP is heading towards both the *collaboration* as well as the *innovation* quadrants. It is heading to the *collaborative* quadrant since the owner has to maintain close contact with current clients as in photographers, ad agencies and also the listed models. Laptop and cell phone

use allow the owner to have a mobile office when the owner travels, in addition to keeping in touch with clients that need models. This mode of operation is consistent with Levy et al.'s (2001) description whereby they state that businesses in the *collaboration* quadrant need to communicate and exchange information with major customers in a cost-efficient manner. In addition, EP is also heading to the *innovation* quadrant since the business model of EP relies on a web presence and is looking to be ahead of its competitors by enabling models to sign up online and get scheduled for photo shoots which will enable it to align its core business strategy with its online presence (Levy et al., 2001).

HC: HC is an on-line business that sells wedding cake toppers that reflect the ethnic diversity of customers.

Current state: The business started in the *efficiency* quadrant. The customer dominance is currently quite high as the business has only had a few sales and relies on a small number of customers. Although HC is an online business, the owner has minimal interaction with the business website and uses minimal ICT for day-to-day business operations. In addition, HC's current

Figure 8. Focus-Dominance model mapping for HC

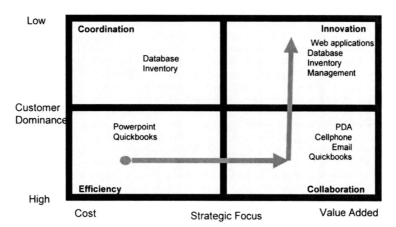

state can be considered to reside in the *collaboration* quadrant since the owner of HC interacts with a small number of suppliers to obtain the cake toppers. And this trend is consistent with Levy et al.'s (2001) description since in this quadrant, the businesses need to communicate with major customers (in the case of HC, its major customers are its suppliers).

IT therapy: Some of the significant IT therapy interventions that were carried out for HC are as follows: *New website* – A completely new website was developed. The new website has a more organized and efficient layout comparable to other leading online competitors of similar products. *Training* - Training for the owner has come in the form of providing her with a manual to help add/delete products on the website so that customers will always have the new and updated product list. And most importantly, the owner will not have to depend on someone else to change the products for her – she will be able to perform the changes herself by following the steps outlined in the manual. A couple of hands-on sessions were done with the ITD innovator so that any confusion could be cleared. *Perceptions and attitude changes* - One of the owner's needs is to have the business website look more "crisp" and professional. On doing some preliminary research

as to the look and feel of other comparable businesses, we had to suggest to the owner to change the colors and layout of her current site to help attract more customers. We had to persuade the owner to shift away from her inefficient current layout and existing bold colors (red and black) to a more "crisper" organized layout and softer colors to help attract more customers.

Future state: HC is primarily an internet business which entails web applications. The owner understands that in order to be competitive, the business will need to take a strategic focus to carrying out business online by selling its products through a professional looking website. The owner is looking to take the necessary steps to align HC's business strategy to its IS needs and the design and implementation of the newly developed website was the first step towards achieving that goal.

FD: FD specializes in the design of elegant, conservative women's clothing. The owner has aspirations of being a player in the global fashion market.

Current state: FD has a laptop and an electronic cash register with some back-office software. FD currently resides in the *efficiency* quadrant since the owner has been using the technology available to the business for primar-

Figure 9. Focus-Dominance model mapping for FD

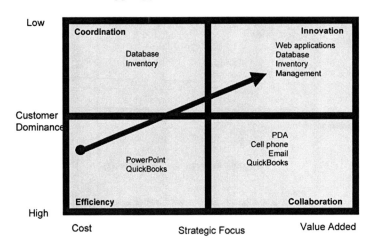

ily basic day-to-day operational activities (Levy et al., 2001).

IT therapy: On meeting with the owner of FD and analyzing the technology needs of the business, The ITD innovators came up with the following list of items to be carried out to assist in the growth of the business: develop a website to promote its products, a developer to update and to do maintenance, and training and technical support for FD's staff to be able to update the website regularly; FD may benefit from online free technical assistance programs.

Future state: FD's main objective is to grow and attract new customers. The owner realizes that the only way to effectively achieve that goal is to have a web presence on the internet through a business website. The owner would like the following goals to be accomplished through the website: 1. To use it as a place to target new customers by advertising the owner's fashion designs; 2. To sell and promote the business on the web; 3. To advertise and provide information about FD. Achieving these three goals will enable it to align its core business strategy with its IS (Levy et. al, 2001).

ANALYSIS

The results from the analysis indicate that five out of the seven micro-enterprises in this study start off in the *efficiency* quadrant in the focus-dominance model. According to Levy et al. (2001), this implies that the focus of the IS was to help reduce costs and achieve simple administrative efficiencies. On initial meetings with the microentrepreneurs, the researchers found that the business owners had no clear business strategy and was not aware of how they could derive the maximum benefit from the IS or technology that they had been awarded through the e-bay Techquity grant. Through the action research steps described in the methodology section, the researchers were able to instill an awareness and understanding of how the microentrepreneurs needed to align the goals of their business and how the available technology could help them reach that end state. The IT therapy process used with each of the micro-enterprises helped to address some of the immediate IT needs of the business. The immediate visible and measurable outcomes were in the area of improved day-to-day business administrative activities mainly through automation of many of the tedious manual activities. This form of outcome seems to support the view

Figure 10. Model of Micro-enterprise growth

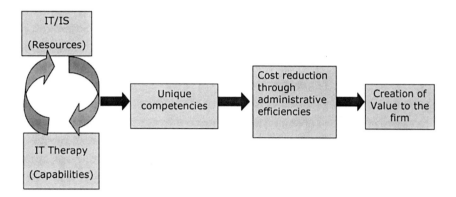

coming out from the strategic IT literature which states that one of the core ways in which IT may add value to a firm is by reducing costs incurred by the organization (Bakos and Treacy, 1986; McFarlan, 1984; Wiseman, 1988).

It can be seen that in all the micro-enterprises in this study, the final strategic position that resulted lay in the *innovation* quadrant of the focus-dominance model. The path to the *innovation* quadrant was different for each of the micro-enterprises. Depending on their context, some showed a tendency for a direct shift from the *efficiency* quadrant to the *innovation* quadrant. Whereas, others tended to take routes via either the *coordination* quadrant, or the *collaboration* quadrant, or via both. This implies that all the micro-enterprise owners are looking to integrate their IS with their business strategies by taking into consideration both internal (improving operational efficiency) as well as external (improved relationships with suppliers and customers) aspects of the business (Levy et al., 2001). This form of alignment of IS with business strategy will enable the micro-enterprises to reach a state whereby they will have a strong platform to be competitive with other businesses in their market.

The resource-based view of the firm (Clemons, 1991; Barney, 1991; Conner, 1991; Mata et al., 1995) to explain competitive advantage provides support for not only the outcomes from this study,

but also for the *process* by which IT therapy was used to assist the microeneterprises to have the potential to be competitive. In the resource-based view of the firm, resources and capabilities may provide a unique set of competencies that may serve to address either cost reduction or product differentiation strategies to eventually create value for the organization. Applying this perspective to the context of our study, the term *resources,* refers to the technology that was awarded to each of the micro-enterprises through the e-bay techquity grant program. The term, *capabilities,* refers to the context-sensitive technical assistance or the IT therapy that was provided by the ITD innovators in the case of each of the micro-enterprises.

Integrating the awarded IT (resources) with the IT therapy process (capabilities) produces certain context-sensitive competencies (for some of the micro-enterprises these were in the form of improved awareness of IT and for some others these were in the form of immediate solutions to technical problems that helped them clear the bottleneck that they were facing) for each of the micro-enterprises that as our results show, addressed cost reduction strategies through improved administrative efficiencies. Figure 3 shows a modified version of the resource-based view of the firm that incorporates the process of IT therapy. It shows how the integration of the IT therapy process with existing IT resources within the micro-enterprises creates added value to the firm – supporting and providing a means for competitiveness with other organizations. The effect of aligning the resources with the capabilities is illustrated in Figure 10.

This model illustrates how the IT therapy interventions bring about unique competencies that enable value to be created in the firm through cost reduction and administrative efficiencies. More specifically, the IT Therapy component of the work was focused on the entrepreneurs' strongly perceived issues and problems: LD's Internet connection was very unreliable; HH needed to provide better statistics to stakeholders; FD wanted to be able to show potential customers a PowerPoint show of her fashions; HE had customer information scattered in many different places; EP was frustrated by having to maintain duplicate accounting systems at work and at home; HC had ideas for enhancing her web site; CZ needed a more effective means of tracking tutors. In addition, the ITD innovators applied their skills and experiences to identify solutions to problems the entrepreneurs may not have been aware of.

The findings from this study also garner support from results carried out at country-level studies by various development researchers and practitioners. In a study by Hamdan (2004) carried out in Lebanon – where 88% of businesses are micro and small enterprises - the survey results and their corresponding policy recommendations suggest that in order to promote competitiveness in these enterprises, it is necessary to develop and enhance training schemes for micro-enterprises. Specifically, the researchers recommend that there is a need to *review the existing vocational and technical education courses* to assess how they could be adapted to assist the micro-enterprise sector and its institutions. Also, *access to formal and informal education and training* needs to be enhanced. Based on the findings of the survey, education and formal training enhances the development of micro and small enterprises and improves their performance. It is, thus, important

to concentrate more on the sustained investment in human resources and technical skills development if entrepreneurs are to lead effective sustained and profitable enterprises. In addition, *formal and informal training should be combined with business counseling.* A wide range of networks can be used for this purpose, including central and local government agencies, nongovernmental organizations, and others, where the training provider integrates training, coaching and consultancy in one single package. *It is recommended that training and counseling be sensitized to different factors.* Gender is one, the size of the micro-enterprise is another, and the type of business might be a third. Some sectors and types of micro-enterprises need to be provided with specialized tailor-made courses. In some micro-enterprises, especially family-run businesses, it may be necessary to focus on other issues, such as those pertaining to growth, including decision making and internal organization.

El-Mahdi (2004) carried out a similar extensive country-level survey study in Egypt – where 97% of the economy is comprised of small and micro-enterprises. Based on the survey results, a number of key recommendations arose. The one most relevant to this current study is the emphasis once again on training and building competencies of micro-entrepreneurs. El-Mahdi points out that in Egypt, the main source of training is provided by the private sector, and the micro-entrepreneurs themselves. They tend to offer their knowledge and skills to co-workers and apprentices. However, if the entrepreneur's skills are not up to the certain acceptable national or international standards of the profession, the result would be extending the same low levels of efficiency to the workers. Therefore, a reassessment of the role and quality of programs offered by the public training centers as well as the private ones is essential to ensure higher efficiency of the workers and entrepreneurs. Encouraging NGOs and the private sector to invest in the establishment of new modern specialized training centers and/or finance renovation and management of the existing public training centers could help in raising the skills of the workforce in the small and micro-enterprise sector.

Ozar (2004) reports on the state of micro-enterprises in Turkey and the possible steps that may be undertaken to make these small firms more competitive in today's economy. Over 75% of employment in Turkey is in small and micro-enterprises however, only 27% add value to the economy. Therefore the survey that was conducted gave way to two broad categories of policy recommendations: (1) Policies aiming to establish and sustain an enabling environment in which small and micro-enterprises can develop and expand their activities; (2) Policies aiming to enhance the capabilities and competence of entrepreneurs and the enterprises. In terms of enhancing competence and promoting competitiveness, Ozar (2004) states that most of the micro-enterprises in Turkey do not grow. And so policies for promoting micro-enterprises should not only focus on enhancing growth, but should also pay attention to developing the micro-enterprises in terms of both higher efficiency and decent work conditions. In this regard, the survey results showed that *trust building* was a core component. Over the years, the continuation of the adverse practices resulted in the accumulation of mistrust on the part of the entrepreneurs. They tend not to trust the aims and intentions of public institutions, professional organizations and business associations. This lack of confidence continues to affect the performance of the micro-enterprises. On the other hand, the public institutions attitude towards micro-enterprises also involves mistrust to a certain extent due to their participation in informal activities and relations. A trust building process should be initiated between micro-enterprises and public and professional institutions. Another core component is that of *education and training*. The survey revealed that most of the entrepreneurs lack entrepreneurial skills. Very few public and private organizations provide training for entrepreneurs. Moreover, it seems that the training given is not

fully compatible with the needs of the micro-enterprises. Appropriate training programs that meet the needs of the micro-entrepreneurs should be developed. In many cases, it was also seen that a lack of access to formal financial sources is a result of deficiencies in management and human capital on the part of micro-enterprises and their entrepreneurs. It is thus necessary for public policy processes to aim at raising the capacity of the enterprise by providing training and counseling.

It then appears from the aforementioned country studies that there is a dire need for context-sensitive assistance in ameliorating the various bottlenecks that micro-enterprises face in any country to enable them to be competitive. The IT therapy process that has been described in this study therefore, may be considered as an effective *tool* to accomplish this as it incorporates *trust building* between the micro-entrepreneur and the ITD innovator and it also provides the necessary *contextual training/education* that each micro-enterprise needs. Eventually, this would then pave unique competencies and add value to the firm making them competitive.

The resource based view of the firm suggests that sustaining the growth of these micro-enterprises would require sustaining the skills and experience developed through the IT therapy process. Competitive advantages that these micro-enterprises gain from the direction of their growth can be stimulated through additional interventions guided by the focus-dominance model. This research has also brought to light a unique set of skills and experiences that ITD innovators can bring to bear in helping micro-enterprises achieve sustained growth and competitive advantage.

CONCLUSION

This research suggests that while micro-enterprises have the potential to serve as the seedbed for economic development, they must overcome a number of challenges that obstruct their path.

Very few micro-enterprise entrepreneurs possess the technical skills or information systems necessary to streamline their business operations and help them compete and expand into new markets. This is why they need interventions by ITD innovators who can give them the skills that enable the micro-entrepreneurs to diagnose business problems, design IT and training interventions and implement processes to support IT adoption. An innovative approach was developed by integrating context-sensitive technical assistance, or in other words, "IT therapy" with existing IT resources in micro-enterprises to show how these small businesses may become competitive. This research has investigated how through the process of context-sensitive IT assistance has the potential to enable micro-enterprises to achieve competitiveness. This research is based on an interpretive field study method of inquiry as outlined by Klein and Myers (1999) with data collection being carried out using action research steps (Zuber-Skerrit, 1991; Avison et al., 1999). This paper used the Focus-Dominance model to investigate the adoption of ICT for competitive advantage by a set of seven micro-enterprises and the resource based view of the firm to develop a model of micro-enterprise growth. Further research needs to consider the effect of multiple interventions across a broader range of micro-enterprises over time through a longitudinal design.

REFERENCES

Avison, D. E., Lau, F., Myers, M., & Nielsen, P. A. (1999). Action Research. *Communications of the ACM, 42*(1), 94–97. doi:10.1145/291469.291479

Baark, E., & Heeks, R. (1998) *Evaluation of Donor-Funded Information Technology Transfer Projects in China: A Life-Cycle Approach.* Retrieved Dec 12, 2007, from http://idpm.man.ac.uk/wp/di/di_wp01.htm.

Bakos, J.Y. & Treacy, M.E. Information Technology and Corporate Strategy: A Research Perspective. *MIS Quarterly* (1 0:2), June 1986, pp. 107-1 19.

Barney, J. B. (n.d.). Firm Resources and Sustained Competitive Advantage, InBarney, J.B. (ed)Firm Resources and Sustained Competitive Advantage.

Barton, C., & Bear, M. (1999) *Information and Communications Technologies: Are they the Key to Viable Business Development Services for Micro and Small Enterprises? Report for USAID as part of the Microenterprise Best Practices Project. March.* Retrieved December 12, 2007, from http://www.mip.org/PUBS/MBP/ict.htm.

Bharati, P., & Chaudhury, A. (2006). Current Status of Technology Adoption: Micro, Small and Medium Manufacturing Firms in Boston. *Communications of the ACM, 49*(10), 88–93. doi:10.1145/1164394.1164400

Blili, S., & Raymond, L. (1993). Information technology: threats and opportunities for small and medium-sized enterprises. *International Journal of Information Management, 13*, 439–448. doi:10.1016/0268-4012(93)90060-H

Brown, D. H., & Lockett, N. (2004). Potential of critical e-applications for engaging SMEs in e-business: a provider perspective. *European Journal of Information Systems, 13*, 21–34. doi:10.1057/palgrave.ejis.3000480

Capon, N.& Glazer, R.(1987). Marketing and Technology: A Strategic Coalignment. *Journal of Marketing* 51,(3), pp. 1-1 4.

Checkland, P. (1981). *Systems Thinking, Systems Practice.* New York: John Wiley & Sons.

Checkland, P. (1991) "From Framework through Experience to Learning: The Essential Nature of Action Research. In Nissen, H.-E., Klein, H. &Hirschheim, R. (eds.) *Information Systems Research: Contemporary Approaches and Emergent Traditions* 397-403., North Holland: Elsevier Publishers.

Clemons, E. K. (1991). Corporate Strategies for Information Technology: A Resource-Based Approach. *Computer*, *24*(11), 23–32. doi:10.1109/2.116848

Clemons, E.K. & Row, M.C.(1991). Sustaining IT Advantage: The Role of Structural Differences. *MIS Quarterly* (1 5:3), September 1991 a, pp. 275-292.

Clemons, E.K. & Row, M.K. (1991). Information Technology at Rosenbluth Travel: Competitive Advantage in a Rapidly Growing Service Company. *Journal of Management Information Systems*, 8(2)pp. 53-79.

Conner, K.R.(1991). A Historical Comparison of Resource-Based Theory and Five Schools of Thought Within Industrial Organization Economics: Do We Have a New Theory of the Firm?. *Journal of Management* (1 7:1pp. 121-1 54.

Copeland, D.G. & McKenney, J.L.(1998). Airline Reservation Systems: Lessons from History.*MIS Quarterly* (12:3)pp. 353-370.

Cragg, P.B., & King, M. (1993). Small-Firm Computing: Motivators and Inhibitors. *Management Information Systems Quarterly*, *17*(1), 47–60. doi:10.2307/249509

DeLone, W. H. (1988). Determinants of Success for Computer Usage in Small Business. *Management Information Systems Quarterly*, *12*(1), 51–61. doi:10.2307/248803

Duncombe, R., & Heeks, R. (2003). An information systems perspective on ethical trade and self-regulation. *Information Technology for Development*, *10*(2), 123–139. doi:10.1002/itdj.1590100206

El-Mahdi, A. (2004). *MSES Potentials and Success Determinants in Egypt 2003-2004: Special Reference to Gender Differentials. Research report Series on Promoting Competitiveness in Micro and Small Enterprises in the MENA Region.* Economic Research Forum.

Feeny, D.F. & Ives, B. In Search of Sustainability: Reaping Long-Term Advantage from Investments in Information Technology,. *Journal of Management Information Systems* (7:1), Summer 1990, pp. 27-46.

Foong, S.-Y. (1999) Effect of end user personal and systems attributes on computer based information systems success in Malaysian SMEs. *Journal of Small Business Management*, July, 37(3), 81–87.

Galliers, R. D. (1992) Choosing Information Systems Research Approaches, In Galliers, R.D. (Ed.) *Information Systems Research: Issues, Methods and Practical Guidelines.* Henley-on-Thames: Alfred Waller, 144-162.

Grosh, B., & Somolekae, G. (1996). Mighty oaks from little acorns: Can micro-enterprise serve as the seedbed of industrialization? *World Development*, *24*(12), 1879–1890. doi:10.1016/S0305-750X(96)00082-4

Hamdan, K. (2004). *Micro and Small Enterprises in Lebanon. Research report Series on Promoting Competitiveness in Micro and Small Enterprises in the MENA Region.* Economic Research Forum.

Harrison, D. A., Mykytyn, P. P., Jr., & Riemenschneider, C. K.(1997). Executive Decisions About Adoption of Information Technology in Small Business: Theory and Empirical Tests. *Information Systems Research* (8:2), pp. 171-195.

Hashmi, M. S., & Cuddy, J. (1990) Strategic initiatives for introducing CIM technologies in Irish SMEs. In Faria, L. and Van Puymbroeck, W. (eds.) *Computer Integrated Manufacturing – Proceedings of the Sixth CIM-Europe Annual Conference*, (Springer Verlag, Lisbon).

Hazan, M. (2002) Virtual South: E-Commerce for unprivileged artisans. Retrieved Dec 12, 2007, from http://www.iicd.org/stories/.

Honig, B. (1998) What determines success? Examining the human, financial, and social capital of Jamaican microentrepreneurs *Journal of Business Venturing*, (13:5), pp.371-94.

Hyman, E.L. & Dearden, K.(n.d.). Comprehensive impact assessment systems for NGO microenterprise development programs. *World Development*, (26:2), pp. 261-276.

Igbaria, M., Zinatelli, N., Cragg, P. B.,& Cavaye, A. L. M.(1997) Personal Computing Acceptance Factors in Small Firms: A Structural Equation Model *MIS Quarterly* (21:3), pp. 279-305.

Ives, B., & Learmonth, G. P. (1984). The Information Systems as a Competitive weapon. *Communications of the ACM*, *27*(12), 1984. doi:10.1145/2135.2137

Klein, H. K., & Myers, M. D. (1999). A Set of Principles for Conducting and Evaluating Interpretive Field Studies in Information Systems. *Management Information Systems Quarterly*, *23*(1), 67–94. doi:10.2307/249410

Latchem. C. & Walker, D. (2001) Telecentres: Case Studies and Key Issues. Vancouver: The Commonwealth of Learning.

Lefebvre, L., & Lefebvre, E. (1993). Competitive positioning and innovative efforts in SMEs. *Small Business Economics*, *5*, 297–305. doi:10.1007/BF01516250

Lefebvre, L., & Lefebvre, L.A. (1996) Information and Telecommunication Technologies: The Impact of their Adoption on Small and Medium-sized Enterprises. Retrieved Dec, 12, 2007, from http://web.idrc.ca/en/ev-9303-201-1-DO_TOPIC.html.

Levy, M., & Powell, P. (1998). SME flexibility and the role of information systems. *Journal of Small Business Economics*, *11*, 183–196. doi:10.1023/A:1007912714741

Levy, M., Powell, P., & Yetton, P. (2001). (forthcoming). SMEs: Aligning IS and the Strategic Context. *Journal of Information Technology*. doi:10.1080/02683960110063672

Levy, M., Powell, P., & Yetton, P. (2002). The Dynamics of SME Information Systems. *Small Business Economics*, *19*, 341–354. doi:10.1023/A:1019654030019

Lichtenstein, G.A. and Lyons, T.S.(2001). The entrepreneurial development system: Transforming business talent and community economies, *Economic Development Quarterly*, (15:1),, pp.3-20.

Mansell, R., & Wehn, U. (1998). *Knowledge Societies: Information Technology for Sustainable Development*. Oxford: Oxford University Press.

Matthews, P. (2007). ICT Assimilation and SME Expansion. *Journal of International Development*, (19): 817–827. doi:10.1002/jid.1401

McFarlan, F.W.(1984) Information Technology Changes the Way You Compete. *Harvard Business Review* (62:3), pp. 98-1 03.

McFarlan, F. W., & McKenney, J. L. (1983). *Corporate Information Systems Management*. Homewood, Ill: Richard D. Irwin.

Montazemi, A. R. (1988). Factors Affecting Information Satisfaction in the Context of the Small Business Environment. *Management Information Systems Quarterly*, *12*(2), 239–256. doi:10.2307/248849

Moyi, E. D. (2003). Networks, information and small enterprises: New Technologies and the ambiguity of empowerment. *Information Technology for Development*, *10*, 221–232. doi:10.1002/itdj.1590100402

Naylor, J., & Williams, J. (1994). Successful Use of IT in SMEs. *European Journal of IS*, *3*(1), 48–56.

O'Farrell, C., Norrish, P., & Scott, A. (1999) *Information and Communication Technologies (ICTs) for Sustainable Livelihoods*. Burton Hall: Intermediate Technology Development Group.

Owen, W., & Darkwa, O. (1999). Role of Multipurpose Community Telecentres in Accelerating National Development in Ghana. *First Monday*, *5*(1), 1–23.

Ozar, S. (2004). *Micro and Small Enterprises in Turkey: Uneasy Development Research report Series on Promoting Competitiveness in Micro and Small Enterprises in the MENA Region*. Economic Research Forum.

Pateli, A.G., & Giaglis, G.M.(2004). A research framework for analyzing eBusiness models. *European Journal of Information Systems*, Vol. 13pp. 302 – 314.

Piscitello, L., & Sgobbi, F. (2004, June). Globalisation, E-Business and SMEs: Evidence from the Italian District of Prato. *Small Business Economics*, *22*(5), 333. doi:10.1023/B:SBEJ.0000022208.34741.55

Poon, S., & Swatman, P. (1999). An exploratory study of small business Internet commerce issues. *Information & Management*, *35*, 9–18. doi:10.1016/S0378-7206(98)00079-2

Porter, M. E. (1980). *Competitive Strategy: Techniques for Analyzing Industries and Competitors, New York*. New York, NY: Free Press.

Porter, M.E.& Millar, V.E.(1985). How Information Gives You Competitive Advantage. *Harvard Business Review* (63:4), July-August 1985, pp. 149-1 60.

Qiang, C. Z., Clarke, G. R., & Halewood, N. (2006). The Role of ICT. In World Bank (Ed.), *Doing Business Information and Communications for Development—Global Trends and Policies*. Washington, DC: World Bank.

Qureshi, S. (2005). "How does Information technology effect Development? Integrating Theory and Practice into a Process Model." *Proceedings of the eleventh Americas Conference on Information Systems*, Omaha, NE.

Qureshi, S., Kamal, M., & Wolcott, P. (2008). *Sustainability of Information Technology Therapy on Micro-enterprise Development*. HICSS.

Raymond, L. (1988). The Impact of Computer Training on the Attitudes and Usage Behaviour of Small Business Managers. *Journal of Small Business Management*, *26*(3), 9–13.

Raymond, L., Bergeron, F., & Blili, S. (2005). The assimilation of E-business in manufacturing SMEs: determinants and effects on growth and internationalization. *Electronic Markets*, *15*(2), 106–118. doi:10.1080/10196780500083761

Reid, G., & Jacobsen, C. (1988). *The Small Entrepreneurial Firm*. Aberdeen University Press.

Riemenschneider, C. Harrison, D. & P. Mykytyn. (2003) Understanding IT Adoption Decisions in Small Business: Integrating Current Theories. *Information and Management, Vol 40*.

Sanders, C.K.(2002). The impact of micro-enterprise assistance programs: A comparative study of program participants, non participants, and other low-wage workers*Social Service Review*, (76:2), pp.321-40.

Schreiner, M., & Woller, G. (2003). "Micro-enterprise Development Programs in the United States and in the Developing World," *World Development* (31:9pp 1567-1580.

Servon, L. J.& Doshna, J.P. (2000).Microenterprise and the economic development toolkit: A small part of the big picture" *Journal of Developmental Entrepreneurship.* (5:3), pp. 183.

Sethi, V., and King, W.R.(1994). "Development of Measures to Assess the Extent to Which an Information Technology Application Provides Competitive Advantage", *Management Science,* =40, (12). December 1994.

Southwood, R. (2004). ICTs and Small Enterprise: A Motor of Economic Development in Africa, IICD Research Briefs, IICD, The Hague: IICD Research Briefs 9.

Street, C. T., & Meister, D. B. (2004). Small Business Growth and Internal Transparency: The Role of Information Systems. *Management Information Systems Quarterly, 28*(3), 473–506.

Sullivan, B. C. "Economics of Information Technology" *International Journal of Social Economics.* Bradford. (12:1), 1985, pp. 37.

Thong, J., Yap, C., & Rahman, K. (1996). Top management support, external expertise and information systems implementation in small businesses. *Information Systems Research, 7*(2), 248–267. doi:10.1287/isre.7.2.248

Wiseman, C. (1988). *Strategic Information Systems.* Homewood, IL: Irwin.

Wolcott, P., Qureshi, S., & Kamal, M. (2007) "An Information Technology Therapy Approach to Micro-enterprise Adoption of ICTs" *Americas Conference on Information Systems (AMCIS*

Yap, C. (1989). Computerization problems facing small and medium enterprises: the experience of Singapore, in: *Proceedings of the 20th Annual Meeting of the Midwest Decision Sciences Institute,* Miami University, Miami. *OH. Osteopathic Hospitals, 19-21,* 128–134.

Zuber-Skerrit, O. (1991). *Action Research for Change and Development.* Aldershot: Gower Publishing.

Chapter 7
Privacy Factors for Successful Ubiquitous Computing

Linda Little
Northumbria University, UK

Pam Briggs
Northumbria University, UK

ABSTRACT

Certain privacy principles have been established by industry, e.g. the U.S. Public Policy Committee of the Association for Computing Machinery (USACM). Over the past two years, we have been trying to understand whether such principles reflect the concerns of the ordinary citizen. We have developed a method of enquiry which displays a rich context to the user in order to elicit more detailed information about those privacy factors that underpin our acceptance of ubiquitous computing. To investigate use and acceptance, Videotaped Activity Scenarios specifically related to the exchange of health, financial, shopping and e-voting information and a large scale survey were used. We present a detailed analysis of user concerns, firstly in terms of a modified Hertzberg model that identifies a set of constructs that might reflect user-generated privacy principles, secondly those factors likely to play a key role in an individuals cost-benefit analysis, and thirdly, longer-term concerns of the citizen in terms of the impact of new technologies on social engagement and human values.

INTRODUCTION

An individual has a right to determine how, when and to what extent information about the self will be released to another person – something commonly referred to as individual privacy (USACM, 2006). Not surprisingly, new developments in technology present challenges to the individual's

DOI: 10.4018/978-1-60960-132-4.ch007

rights in this respect (Price, Adam, & Nuseibeh, 2005) and so privacy issues are widely discussed by academics and designers alike (Kozlov, 2004; Dine & Hart, 2004), most of whom respect the individuals' right to control and protect their personal information (Nguyen & Truong, 2003).

Users are well aware of the need for informational privacy and frequently express concern about their rights. E-commerce consumers, for example, have major concerns about who has

Copyright © 2011, IGI Global. Copying or distributing in print or electronic forms without written permission of IGI Global is prohibited.

access to their personal data (Cranor, Reagle, & Ackerman, 1999; Jackson, et al., 2003; Earp, et al., 2005); and show a reluctance to disclose information to commercial web services (Metzger, 2004).

However, even those consumers who hold privacy in high regard are able to recognise the benefits of disclosing information (Hinz, et al., 2007). We need to understand why it is that users uphold their right to privacy whilst simultaneously giving away sensitive personal information (Malhotra, Kim, & Agarwal, 2004). In other words, we need to better understand the cost-benefit trade-off in which e-consumers will trade personal information online in order to achieve an improved service (something referred to as the 'privacy-personalisation paradox' (Awad & Krishnan, 2006)).

The perceived costs and benefits in any transaction inevitably reflect personal beliefs. People differ with respect to the value they place on privacy – and these individual differences are reflected in scales which have been designed to measure the strength of individual feeling in this regard. These include the Concern for Information Privacy (Smith, Milberg & Burke, 1996) and the Internet Users Information Privacy Concerns (Malhotra, et al., 2004).

In keeping with the concept of some kind of individualised privacy setting, designers are increasingly allowing users to manage their own concerns by setting privacy preferences. On the Internet, at least, various architectures have been suggested that allow personalized settings (Kobsa, 2003). For example the Platform for Privacy Preferences (P3P) allows users to set their own personal privacy preferences and if visited sites do not match these then warnings are shown – leaving responsibility ultimately with the individual user (Cranor, 2002). Guha, et al., (2008) propose a programme called 'none of your business (NOYB)' to protect privacy while online and have tested the system on social networking sites. NOYB provides fine-grained control over user privacy in online services while preserving

much of the functionality provided by the service. They argue NOYB is a first step towards a 'new design paradigm of online services where the user plays an active role in performing the sensitive operations on data, while the service takes care of the rest' (p.53).

Such tools are useful, but they are not future-proof. Specifically, they could not cope with the kinds of seamless, anywhere, anyplace exchanges of personal information that are anticipated by designers of ubiquitous computing systems. Systems that collect, process and share personal information are prerequisites for the creation of intelligent environments that can anticipate user's needs and desires (Dritsas, Gritzalis, & Lambrinoudakis, 2006). Pervasive technologies are expected to be responsive to different contexts and to act on the user's behalf seamlessly – but will privacy violations inevitably ensue?

Researchers disagree. On the one hand, (Olsen, Grudin, & Horvitz, 2005) argue that tools could be constructed to capture quite complex privacy preferences, preferences that are tailored to the context of the exchange, the sensitivity of the enquiry and the disclosure preferences of the individual. Such tools – if feasible - would prevent privacy violations in the day to day exchanges of ubiquitous computing. On the other hand, (Palen & Dourish, 2003) argue that a-priori privacy configurations and static rules will not work, but insist that the disclosure of information needs to be controlled dynamically and needs, essentially, to be passed into the hands of software agents designed to uphold general privacy preferences.

This begs the question of just what kinds of assurances software agents might look for before agreeing to the release of personal data. As a clue to this we might start by looking at established principles underpinning the right to privacy (Kobsa, 2007). For example, the U.S. Public Policy Committee of the Association for Computing Machinery (USACM) has laid down the following principles for privacy management:

1. **Minimization:** Store and use only essential data and delete it once no longer required.
2. **Consent:** Provide simple opt-in and opt-out procedures that ensure consent the storage and use of personal data is meaningful.
3. **Openness:** Ensure transparency in data collection and use – making salient the default procedures for the storage and use of data and being explicit about how it might be made available to others. Also ensure that privacy policies are communicated effectively.
4. **Access:** Provide the individual with the capacity to inspect their data and to determine how it has been made available to others, also how to repair any violation of privacy rights.
5. **Accuracy:** Ensure that personal information is sufficiently accurate and up-to-date and propagate corrections quickly to parties that have received or supplied inaccurate data.
6. **Security:** For all types of storage, maintain all personal information securely and protect it against unauthorized and inappropriate access or modification.
7. **Accountability:** Be accountable for data storage and proper adherence to privacy policies, ensuring that those responsible are trained, authorized, equipped, and motivated.

These are the kinds of privacy principles that have been established by the industry – but over the past two years, we have been trying to understand whether such principles reflect the concerns of the ordinary citizen. Some of the key research questions we have been addressing are: What are users' key concerns regarding privacy management in a ubiquitous context and do they reflect 'expert' privacy principles? Do these concerns vary as a function of context? Will users have enough confidence in privacy management procedures to hand-over management and administration of their privacy preferences?

Motahari, et al., (2007) argue people do not have a complete understanding of the threats to their privacy. While users of ubicomp systems are aware of inappropriate use of their personal information, legal obligations and inadequate security they are less aware of setting preferences for who has access and any social inferences that can be made by observations by other people. They further argue a holistic approach is needed as traditional approaches and current investigations are not enough to address privacy threats in ubiquitous computing. Recognising – in line with a number of other researchers (Harper & Singleton, 2001; Paine, et al., 2007) – that privacy concerns are likely to be highly situation-dependent, we have developed a method of enquiry which displays a rich context to the user in order to elicit more detailed information about those privacy factors that underpin our acceptance of ubiquitous computing.

METHOD

To communicate the concept of ubiquitous computing (ubicomp) to the ordinary citizen we engaged with a number of key stakeholders to generate detailed scenarios that communicated something about pervasive technologies and the privacy and identity issues they evoke. The stakeholders included relevant user groups, researchers, developers, businesses and government departments with an interest in ubicomp development. Working in conjunction with relevant stakeholders produced scenarios that were realistic and with high face validity.

Four scenarios were developed, related to health, e-voting, shopping and finance that included facts about the device, context of use, type of service or information the system would be used for.

The elicited scenarios were then professionally scripted and used to develop Videotaped Activity Scenarios (or VASc's). The VASc method is a tool for generating richly detailed and tightly focused group discussion and has been shown to be very effective in the elicitation of social rules (Little, Briggs, & Coventry, 2004). The VASc method allows individuals to discuss their own experiences, express their beliefs and expectations. This generates descriptions that are rich in detail and focused on the topic of interest.

For this research a media production company based in the UK was employed to recruit actors and videotape all scenarios. The production was overseen by both the producer and the research team to ensure correct interpretation. British Sign Language (BSL) and subtitles were also added to a master copy of the VASc's for use in groups where participants had various visual or auditory impairments.

The four scenarios are briefly described below:

Health Scenario:Bob is in his office talking on his personal digital assistant (PDA) to a council planning officer with regard to an important application deadline. Built into his PDA are several personalised agents that pass information seamlessly to respective recipients. A calendar agent records and alerts Bob of deadlines, meetings, lunch appointments and important dates. As Bob is epileptic his health agent monitors his health and can alert people if he needs help. An emergency management agent takes control in situations when a host of different information is needed; this agent has the most permissions and can contact anyone in Bob's contact list.

Bob is going to meet his friend Jim for lunch when he trips over a loose paving slab. He falls to the ground and looses consciousness. His health agent senses something is wrong and beeps, if Bob does not respond by pressing the appropriate key on the PDA the agent immediately informs the emergency services. Within seconds the emergency services are informed of Bob's current situation and his medical history. An ambulance is on its way. Paramedics arrive, examine Bob and then inform the hospital of Bob's condition on their emergency

device. The hospital staff is now aware of Bob's medical history and his present state, therefore on arrival he is taken straight to the x-ray department. A doctor receives the x-rays on her PDA. After examining Bob she confirms that he has a broken ankle, slight concussion and needs to stay in hospital overnight. After receiving treatment Bob is taken to a ward. His emergency management agent contacts John (Bob's boss) of his circumstance. The emergency management agent transfers the planning application files to John's PDA so the company do not miss the deadline. The agent also informs his parents letting them know his current state of health, exactly where he is so they can visit and that his dog needs to be taken care of. As Bob is also head coach at a local running club the agent informs the secretary Bob will not be attending training the following week. The secretary only receives minimal information through the permissions Bob has set.

Shopping Scenario: Anita arrives at the local supermarket grabs a trolley and slips her PDA into the holding device. A message appears on screen and asks her to place her finger in the biometric verification device attached to the supermarket trolley. Anita places her finger in the scanner and a personalised message appears welcoming her to the shop. She has used the system before and knows her personalised shopping list will appear next on the PDA screen. Anita's home is networked and radio frequency identification tags are installed everywhere. Her fridge, waste bin and cupboards monitor and communicate seamlessly with her PDA creating a shopping list of items needed. The supermarket network is set so that alerts Anita of special offers and works alongside her calendar agent to remind her of any important dates. As she wanders around the supermarket the screen shows her which items she needs in that particular aisle and their exact location. The device automatically records the price and ingredients of every item she puts into trolley and deletes the information if any item is removed. When Anita is finished she presses a button on the PDA and the total cost of her shopping is calculated. Anita pays for the goods by placing her finger on the biometric device and her account is automatically debited, no need to unpack the trolley or wait in a queue. The trolley is then cleared to leave the supermarket. Anita leaves the supermarket, walks to her car and places her shopping in the boot.

E-voting Scenario: Natasha decides she wants to vote in the next election using the new on-line system. She goes on-line and requests electronic voting credentials. Shortly before polling day a polling card and separate security card are delivered to Natasha's home. They arrive as two separate documents to reduce the risk of interception. Natasha picks up two of the letters from the doormat and puts the letters in her pocket as she rushes out of the door to head for work. While travelling on the local underground railway system Natasha decides to cast her vote on her way to work. The letters have provided her with a unique personal voting and candidate numbers which allows her to register a vote for her chosen candidate. She takes out her mobile phone and types her unique number into it. Her vote is cast by entering this unique number into her phone and sending it to a number indicated on the polling card. Her phone then shows a text message: THANK YOU FOR VOTING. YOU HAVE NOT BEEN CHARGED FOR THIS CALL. When Natasha arrives at work she logs on to the voting site to see if her vote has been registered. While at her computer with her polling cards on the desk in front of her a colleague looks over her shoulder, she can see that Natasha is checking her vote but can't see who she has voted for. Once the result of the election has been announced Natasha checks that the correct candidate name is published next to her unique response number to ensure that the system has worked properly.

Financial Scenario: Dave is at home writing a 'to do' list on his PDA. The PDA is networked and linked to several services that Dave has authorised. While writing his list he receives a reminder from his bank that he needs to make an appointment with the manager related to his yearly financial health check. He replies and makes an appointment for later that day. When he arrives at the bank he is greeted by the bank concierge system (an avatar presented on a large interface). The system is installed in the foyer of the bank where most customers use the banks facilities. The avatar tells Dave the manager, Mr Brown, will be with him soon. The avatar notes that Dave has a photograph to print on his 'to do' list and asks if he would like to print it out at the bank as they offer this service. The avatar also asks Dave to confirm a couple of recent transactions on his account prior to meeting Mr Brown.

Procedure

The four VASc's were shown to thirty-eight focus groups, with the number of participants in each group ranging from four to twelve people. Participants were drawn from all sectors of society in the Newcastle upon Tyne area of the UK, including representative groups from the elderly, the disabled and from different ethnic sectors. Prior to attending one of the group sessions participants were informed about the aims and objectives of the study. Demographic characteristics of all participants were recorded related to: age, gender, disability (if any), level of educational achievement, ethnicity, and technical stance. A decision was made to allocate participants to groups based on: age, gender, level of education and technical stance as this was seen as the best way possible for participants to feel at ease and increase discussions. As this study was related to future technology it was considered important to classify participants as either technical or non-technical. This was used to investigate any differences that might occur due to existing knowledge of technological systems and that heterogeneity of groups might have a negative impact on the social environment and impact upon group discussion due to incompatibility (Fern, 2001). Therefore participants were allocated to groups initially by technical classification i.e. technical/non-technical, followed by gender, then level of educational achievement (high = university education or above versus low = college education or below), and finally age (young, middle, old). Overall this categorization process culminated in 24 main groups. 180 male and 145 female participants took part with an age range of 16 – 89 years. For ethical and practical reasons only adults aged 16 or above took part in the study. Due to poor attendance at some group sessions these were run again at a later date. Although several participants with physical disabilities attended the main group sessions a group session for people with visual and auditory impairments was carried out at the Disability Forum in Newcastle. The forum was considered to have easier access and dedicated facilities for people with such disabilities.

Participants were told they would be asked to watch four short videotaped scenarios showing people using ubicomp systems and contribute to informal discussions on privacy and trust permissions for this type of technology. Once all the videos had been viewed an overall discussion took place related to any advantage/disadvantages, issues or problems participants considered relevant to information exchange in a ubiquitous society. Participant's attitudes in general towards ubicomp systems were also noted. The duration of the sessions was approximately ninety minutes.

QUALITATVE FINDINGS

A sentence-by-sentence analysis was applied to transcribed data using Atlas.ti™ qualitative software programme. Two members of the research team coded and compared the data for consistency,

good inter-rater reliability was found. The data was open coded using qualitative techniques and several categories were identified. Categories that frequently arose and reoccurred across the majority of groups are reported in this paper. Findings from all four scenarios have culminated in similar categories, however, data from the project is immense and therefore we have only provided findings from the health scenario in the qualitative section of this paper. For clarity and ease of interpretation the constructs were grouped into three categories. The first two were based on Hertzberg, et al., (1959) Two Factor Theory of Motivation in which hygiene factors (those factors indispensible to the acceptance or operation of a system) were divorced from motivating factors (those factors that played a more crucial role in assessing the costs or benefits of adoption). The first category we would describe in terms of principles that should underpin any technology; while the second simply describes the realities that are more likely to affect a user's decision to buy into a particular service. We also felt a number of constructs fell into a third category – related to the longer-term impact of new technologies on human values society. These categories and their underlying constructs are shown in Table 1.

Hygiene Factors

Credible

Participants discussed the ways in which source credibility would impact upon what information should or could be exchanged. In the health context, participants who visited their GP and/or hospital consultant on a regular basis discussed access and exchange of health information in terms of loyalty to a trusted physician and satisfaction with their performance over the years. However, participants raised concern over unknown stakeholders using ubiquitous systems to gather personal health information and then using this information to exploit people:

Table 1. Privacy constructs associated with use of a ubiquitous system and based on Hertzberg's (1959) two factor theory of motivation

Hygiene factors	Motivators	Longer-term Implications
Credible	Better healthcare	Over-reliance
Secure	Convenience	Dehumanisation
Reliable		Bystander apathy
Accurate		Reduced social interaction
Transparent		Enforced participation
Context aware		Health risks
Personalised	Inflexibility	Environmental issues
Easy to use	Profile Abuse	
Accessible	Surveillance	
	De-motivators	

'If you could do it through something like the BBC because it's typically British, you are going to trust the BBC, it's always been there, it's something tangible, but for a lot of older people, it's new and it's different, you know they don't trust it, whereas they trust their television because they have watched it all of their life.'

Secure

Security of ubiquitous systems for exchanging and storing health information emerged as key factor that would limit adoption and use. Fraudulent use, hacking, access by third parties, leakage and storage of information were all areas discussed. Participants agreed that being able to verify and access information stored on systems was needed.

'How secure would the information be? It could be that you have got a specific condition. You could have a drink problem or whatever and that could get back to your employer or it could get back, you know what I mean, I would have serious concerns, not that I've got a drink problem, not yet anyway!'

Reliable

Participants discussed the implications of system breakdown, recognising, for example, the problems inherent in a malfunctioning system that was effectively 'invisible'. How would the consequences of the breakdown be detected?

'The greater worry I think is that because you have then got a health system taking care of Bob on the basis of the information held in the system, is how correct is that, is the veracity of that information, because if there was a mistake in that information, then things could go awfully wrong. So it says, I see that you are allergic to aspirin, but say actually I was allergic to something else. If that was wrong then, although she verified that, you could verify that I suppose, but you would worry that there were going to be pieces of information that might be false, that people are acting upon.'

Accurate

Discussion highlighted human fallibility in keeping systems updated, entering the correct data and setting preferences for who has access to their health information. Data gathering and data mining by stakeholders would create profiles about a person that would contain false information.

'So it is all about the information, is all this information accurate or will they make mistakes? You know will it be useful? Some of it maybe is good, and some of it not. So I don't know for other people or for myself if RIFD would be accurate information. I don't think the information will be a hundred percent accurate.'

Transparent

Participants commented systems needed to be transparent and accessible so information could be verified and changed. Participants acknowledged that this was already a problem, since many stakeholders hold personal data files that are difficult or impossible to access. A sense of losing control over personal information emerged.

'I mean they don't really know where the information is going and what individuals are actually accessing it or is it just completely churned up by computers? I don't even know but the information is going somewhere and the customer, the consumer should actually have, be allowed to know where that information is going and it should be an open process, open to the consumer, if the consumer wants to know of course, some people might not want to know, but if the consumer wants to know how all that information is processed it should be open.'

Context Aware

Participants noted the dynamic and context-dependent nature of human behaviour, and questioned whether 'rules' for the disclosure of personal information could ever be sensitive enough. For example - a system programmed to alert parents to a minor accident would behave inappropriately if one of the parents was very ill or away on holiday.

Participants agreed that the ordeal of changing and resetting preferences would be tedious, time consuming and complex.

'Because if it makes a decision for you and you think to yourself, I've changed my mind, I'm not in the mood for that and therefore you have mucked your system up on your computer thing and you have to go in and tell it I've changed my mind, I don't want to do this, I want to change that.'

Personalised

Participants saw the benefits of a personalised service in certain contexts. For example, most agreed having a personalised electronic health record would bring benefits in terms of allergy alerts and reminders for people to take medication. The privacy-personalisation paradox was apparent with health information where data sensitivity was high, but the benefits were clear:

'I do think the hospital should have access to your information so say, If I do have a week heart, that should be able to convey to the hospital that plus your entire medical record.'

Discussion revealed participants concerns over systems being truly sensitive to circumstances under which health information could legitimately be exchanged. Leakage of sensitive information in inappropriate circumstances was seen as very problematic. Would the system only reveal what information was appropriate at that moment in time, or would boundaries be breached? For example, if a person was admitted to hospital with a broken foot, would a health professional have full access to a health record that revealed depression or a sexually transmitted disease?

Easy to Use

Participants, in particular in the older age group, discussed concern over the complexity of ubiquitous systems. Comments related to the fact existing technologies are difficult to use. Participants commented setting preferences for who has access to information time consuming and complicated. Comments related to the dynamic, complex nature of human behaviour and that we are not always predictable. Participants questioned whether in reality we could actually set preferences for all types of information. Discussion also focused on age differences in technology use, experience and familiarity.

'I think that is brilliant. To the younger generation they have been brought up with that technology. What about the minority groups, disabled, etc?'

Accessibility

Participants commented widespread exclusion would occur if people had to adopt ubiquitous systems. Exclusion would occur due to age, anxiety, ability, disability and socio-economic status.

'The thought of my Dad using that would cause more cognitive problems rather than solve them. It all depends on your technical ability to start off with.'

Motivators

Better Healthcare

The majority of participants discussed the concept of ubiquitous systems for exchanging health information as advantageous, and in particular for people with existing medical conditions. Advantages for personal use related to convenience, allergy alerts and health professionals having immediate access to patient records when needed. Stakeholder benefits were discussed in terms of monitoring, immediate access and updating patient records and marketing.

Participants agreed the type of information shared normally depends on who, what, where and why, but crucially is informed by the type of relationship they have with the other person. If their relationship is close e.g. a hospital consultant then the majority of information is shared quite freely. Participants agreed that electronic exchange of health information was beneficial and would create a more efficient service.

'I'm just thinking about the benefits of it you know like, you know the way things work now, I mean the only benefit I would say now is electronic exchange of information that the doctor or hospital sees.'

Convenience

All participants agreed the mobility of ubiquitous systems was advantageous and that through diffusion, adoption would probably occur. Participants discussed ubiquitous systems in terms of convenience related to their own use and the stakeholder.

'Yes, it was useful for him because he has epilepsy but if you don't have anything specific I don't know that it is that much use, that particular bit. For an elderly person who really wanted one, again you have somebody you trust, like a member of the family, to discuss what you want put in and if you don't want something put in, then you don't have it put in.'

De-Motivators

Inflexibility

Participants commented the pressure to adopt ubiquitous systems would increase and have a negative impact on behaviour. Participants were concerned about access to health information by third parties. These concerns were discussed in terms of screening people for jobs and insurance. Participants were concerned ubiquitous systems would become tools for marketing by various stakeholders e.g. advertising diets to people who are overweight.

'I think people who join are going to be pressurised into it. You know when there are facilities there and it gets a little bit pushed and all their friends are doing it and all of their family is doing it. Look at the time here, I've got to do this, I've got to do that and package it all into one. Let's just get it all out the way in one go'.

Profile Abuse

Concerns were raised over the probability that stakeholders would collect personal information in an ad hoc manner without informing the person. The concept of profile abuse was a major concern for all participants. Participants believed profiling would lead to untold consequence. For example, a person might be refused insurance as his or her profile states he has high blood pressure.

'I mean I do think that having all the information in one place and an exchange of information and the doctor and the hospital and maybe even the ambulance service being able to forward the information is good but I don't know whether I like it to that degree.'

Surveillance

Participants commented when using ubiquitous systems surveillance was a major issue. They discussed issues related to leakage of personal information in public settings and surveillance by others. Participants agreed surveillance would be beneficial for some people with certain medical conditions.

'It could work against you like at work for checking what you are doing and everything. Will your boss know what you are doing outside of work?'

'In fact I wouldn't mind being tracked if I had epilepsy, you know if I was in certain circumstances or had a heart condition. In that situation I wouldn't mind in fact but generally, no.'

Social Implications

Over-Reliance

Participants discussed relying too much on the system and/or themselves to exchange information and the responsibility associated with this as very problematic.

Concern arose over trust in the information exchanged. For example, how would the user be assured that his or her health information was actually secure and free from interference from others? Participants agreed stakeholders would have to be very responsible when dealing with any electronic system that contained health data. Stakeholders should only be made aware of the relevant health information, therefore access and exchange limited to pertinent others.

'The other thing is if you actually hand over all responsibility to automated systems you know if they make a mistake in your calculation and you are not actually paying any attention, you are just trusting this, you know it is essentially disempowering you.'

Dehumanisation

Participants found the concept of ubiquitous and the use of agent systems as dehumanising (in the scenario used in this study agent systems were portrayed with human-like features). Participants commented they would not trust such systems and found the concept very impersonal.

'It's all this de-humanisation is how I see it. Do his parents really want to know that he has had an accident, by? Why can they not wait until he can tell them himself? And alright he can't do his running club, but it's not the end of the world, they will realise something has happened, the message will get there somehow. Do we have to have everything working like clockwork?'

Bystander Apathy

Participants discussed how existing technology has changed the way we behave and were concerned that ubiquitous systems would have a greater impact. Reference was made to ubiquitous systems making people lazy, decreasing human cognitive ability and reducing the workforce.

'On the other hand, if you expected that everybody was like that and someone collapsed in the street, would it stop you going to help them, because you thought oh well the paramedics will be here in a minute, I'm not going to bother!'

Participants discussed the possibility that ubiquitous systems would foster social isolation as less human-human interaction would take place, this was considered very problematic. For example, after being admitted to hospital talking to a health professional about your symptoms and being reassured were considered beneficial. This type of interaction would be lost as there would be no need for personal contact or conversation. Participants also commented in our social world we already leak information to others in the form of visual cues e.g. a plaster on your foot, without any serious implications. In the physical world strangers knowing certain information about you is not problematic, however people do not want to share the same information with friends or even family e.g. your medical history.

'Yes you are losing contact with people if you are going to be somebody sat in a room by themselves with a machine like that, talking to people on this internet kind of thing, but there's no substitute for human contact. Its wonderful discourse with human beings face to face rather than through a machine I think.'

Reduced Social Interaction

Discussion highlighted how use of ubiquitous systems would result in less human-human interaction and this was considered very problematic.

'We are so anti-social anyway, unless Andrew has his friends to the house and I must admit I mean I communicate with a lot of my friends now by text messages whereas before you would have called to them or you know send an email but I see less of people that I care about because it's more convenient to send them a text or an email and I hate it, I really do hate it and I think that's going to encourage more because then you're not even going to have to make the effort to send the text message, your machine is going to be sending them a text message because you're overdue writing to them'

Enforced Participation

Participants commented little or even no choice would exist in a ubiquitous society. Comments suggested 'forced choice' would become the 'norm', making people use such systems for all forms of information exchange even if they did not want to. Participants expressed concern over the right not to reveal information having vast implications leading to exclusion in some circumstances.

Participants were concerned about reliance on ubiquitous systems for exchanging health information reducing personal control. Discussions revealed ubiquitous systems would create 'Big Brother' societies that lacked control and choice. Concern was raised over how information would be controlled by stakeholders, i.e. storage and transmission.

'You see all that information where is it going? And even if you say no I don't want you to pass my details on you never really know do you?'

Health Risks and Environmental Issues

Participants discussed concerns over health risks and environmental issues related to living in a ubiquitous society. Participants referred to problems with radiation from the systems and the global impact of such use. Comments related to development and cost of ubiquitous systems and the realisation that in parts of the world people were starving, therefore should we not focus resources on global problems.

'Also we are in a time when we are starting to think more and more about the materials we use and the amount of energy we are using and whether we shouldn't be thinking as humans how we should use our energy to think better, write lists rather than use the technology there.'

Older adults were concerned younger people would use ubicomp systems for exchanging information in an ad-hoc way, in particular if used for voting in political elections. Disabled participants discussed clear advantages in terms of independence and increased autonomy. Visually impaired participants commented they often had to ask others for help in social settings e.g. the supermarket and this can often lead to further problems, ubiquitous technologies where considered a way of having greater independence.

QUESTIONNAIRE DEVELOPMENT

From qualitative findings in the first phase of this research a questionnaire was developed. The questionnaire was posted to all participants who took part in the focus group sessions and promoted on Zoomerang.com website. The first section of the questionnaire addressed patterns of disclosure across different domains and these detailed disclosure patterns are not reported here.

The second part of the questionnaire was based in part on the qualitative findings above. Participants were asked to choose one of four contexts (health, lifestyle, finance and personal identity) and complete a number of questions regarding trust, privacy, usability and identity issues. Demographic variable were recorded related to age, gender, level of education, employment status and country of origin. When completing the questionnaire participants responded using 5-point Likert scales.

Participants

From an initial 1687 responses, the data set was cleaned up and any incomplete questionnaires were removed. A total of 505 replies were removed from the set (mainly through incomplete answers) leaving a total of 1182 respondents: 431 health, 309 shopping, 191 finance and 281 personal identity. Of the respondents, 623 were males and 559 females. Respondents reported locations from all over the world. As might be expected, the vast majority (1013) were from the United States, 158 from the UK and 11 were from other locations. This reflects the online population but also the bias as the survey was placed on Zoomerang.com a US site. Respondents reflected a wide range of ages. The majority falling in the 36-45 age group, though with a strong representation in all age groups from 18 to 65. Only the under 18 and over 75 groups showed any tailing off.

Materials

Sets of items related to trust, privacy, identity management and usability were constructed, based on findings from the qualitative phase of the project i.e. hygiene factors, motivators and de-motivators, longer-term implications (as outlined earlier) and known predictor variables in the current literature Sillence, et al., 2004). Participants were asked to indicate their responses on a 5-point scale. Items are detailed below:

- **Trust predictors:** When disclosing personal information it is important to me that the person accessing my information is *(1 not important to 5 very important):* 1. Credible, 2. Reputable, 3. Knowledgeable, 4. Expert, 5. Offers personalized service, 6. Predictable and consistent, 7. Responsible, 8. Will not pass in information about me to others without my consent, 9. Reliability of the system

- **Privacy predictors:** When using a system that exchanged and monitored personal information I would worry about the following (*1 not at all worried to 5 very worried*): 10. Fraudulent use, 11. Leakage of information, 12. Hacking, 13. Surveillance, 14. Being tracked, 15. Increase in social isolation, 16. Invading my privacy, 17. Having less contact with others, 18. Talking less to others, 19. Lack of control, 20. Reduction in choice

- **Privacy preferences:** (*1 not at all to 5 very*): 21. How concerned are you about the threat to your personal privacy? 22. How important is personal privacy to you? 23. How concerned are you about the misuse of your personal information?

- **Identity management:** When considering a system that exchanges and monitors personal information how important are the following *(1 not important to 5 very important)*: 24.Convenience, 25.Immediate access to information, 26.Ability to monitor funds, 27.Alert if account overdrawn, 28.Reminder to pay a bill, 29.Security of information, 30.No access by 3rd parties, 31.Secure storage of information, 32.I can access information stored about me, 33.I can verify information stored about me

- **Usability**: If a system existed that exchanged and monitored personal information the following tasks would be difficult *(1 not at all difficult to 5 very difficult)*: 34. Setting preferences for who has access, 35.

Keeping the system up to date, 36. Entering correct information, Setting preferences for a system that exchanged and monitored health information would be *(1 not at all to 5 very)* 37. Time consuming, 38. Tedious, 39. Difficult, 40. Dehumanising, 41. Impersonal way to communicate

A Principal Component Analysis with Varimax rotation indicated that information exchange in ubicomp contexts was predicted by seven factors. They accounted for 68% of the total variance and each had an eigenvalue index greater than 1.0. The interpretation of the factors was based on the grouping of variables from the original questionnaire.

- **Factor 1:** Security of information, privacy (informational, physical, social) and surveillance (10, 11, 12, 13, 14, 15, 17, and 20)
- **Factor 2:** Trust through credibility, responsibility and personalisation (1, 2, 3, 4, 5, 6, 7, 8, and 24)
- **Factor 3:** Design of system in relation to usability, reliability and human values (9, 34, 35, 36, 37, 38, 39, 40, and 41)
- **Factor 4:** Social concerns in relation to control and physical privacy (16, 18, and 19)
- **Factor 5**: Benefits of using Ubicomp systems (25, 26, 27, 28, and 29)
- **Factor 6**: Data management in relation to verification and access to information (30, 31, 32, and 33)
- **Factor 7**: Privacy preferences (21, 22, and 23)

Results

Stepwise regression analyses were conducted to establish those factors that predict information exchange within the four different contexts. The four dependent variables were health, finance, lifestyle

Table 2. Stepwise regression analysis for health information exchange in ubicomp contexts

Predictor factor	r^2	B	Std. error	β	t-value	p-value
Security	.042	.290	.048	.193	6.070	.000
Design	.056	-.197	.046	-.121	-4.231	.000
Trust	.064	-.274	.080	-.127	-3.416	.001
Data-management	.070	.256	.082	.116	3.114	.002
benefit	.074	-.093	.042	-.068	-2.219	.027

Table 3. Stepwise regression analysis for financial information exchange in ubicomp context

Predictor factor	r^2	B	Std. error	β	t-value	p-value
Security	.058	.318	.046	.214	6.854	.000
Data-management	.065	.336	.081	.155	4.146	.000
Benefit	.070	-.088	.041	-.065	-2.119	.034
Trust	**.073**	**-.157**	**.079**	**-.074**	**-1.980**	**.048**

and identity information and security, trust, design, social concerns, benefit, data-management and privacy preferences as the independent variables.

Health Model

The stepwise regression for the health model produced a fit (r 27.1%) of the variance explained. Security (20.5%), design (3.3%), trust (1.4%), data-management (1.2%) and benefit (.7%) were all found to be predictive factors for exchanging health information in ubicomp contexts. The Analysis of Variance (ANOVA) revealed that the overall model was significant (F 5, 1176 =18.66, p<0.001). (see Table 2)

Finance Model

The stepwise regression for the finance model produced a fit (r 27.1%) of the variance explained. Security (24.1%), trust (.6%), data-management (1.4%) and benefit (1%) were all found to be predictive factors for exchanging financial information in ubicomp contexts. The Analysis of Variance (ANOVA) revealed that the overall model

was significant (F 4, 1177 = 23.32, p<0.001). (see Table 3)

Personal Identity Model

The stepwise regression for the personal identity model produced a fit (r 23.5%) of the variance explained. Security (18.9%), design (3%) and data-management (1.6%) were all found to be predictive factors for exchanging identity information in ubicomp contexts. The Analysis of Variance (ANOVA) revealed that the overall model was significant (F 3, 1178 = 22.91, P<0.001). (See Table 4)

Lifestyle Model

The stepwise regression for the lifestyle model produced a fit (r 23.6%) of the variance explained. Social (16.3%), design (3.1%), security (1.7%) and trust (2.5%) were all found to be predictive factors for exchanging lifestyle information in ubicomp contexts. The Analysis of Variance (ANOVA) revealed that the overall model was significant (F 4, 1177 = 17.286; p<0.001). (See Table 5)

Table 4. Stepwise regression analysis for personal identifiable information exchange in ubicomp contexts

Predictor factor	r^2	B	Std. error	β	t-value	p-value
Security	.036	.257	.039	.207	6.588	.000
Design	.048	-.146	.039	-.109	-3.787	.000
Data-management	.055	-.169	.056	-.093	-3.015	.003

Table 5. Stepwise regression analysis for lifestyle information exchange in ubicomp contexts

Predictor factor	r^2	B	Std. error	β	t-value	p-value
Social	.027	.085	.026	.103	3.210	.001
Design	.037	-.122	.038	-.092	-3.199	.001
Security	.044	.168	.042	.138	4.024	.000
Trust	.055	-.198	.053	-.113	-3.712	.000

Social (16.3%), design (3.1%), security (1.7%) and trust (2.5%) were all found to be predictive factors for exchanging health information in ubicomp contexts (F 4, 1177 = 17.286; p<0.001).

Discussion

Earlier we described three key research questions as follows: 1. What are users' key concerns regarding privacy management in a ubiquitous context and do they reflect 'expert' privacy principles? 2. Do these concerns vary as a function of context? 3. Will users have enough confidence in privacy management procedures to hand-over management and administration of their privacy preferences?

In response to 1, we have presented a detailed analysis of user concerns firstly in terms of a modified Hertzberg model that identifies firstly a set of constructs that might reflect user-generated privacy principles; secondly those factors likely to play a key role in an individuals cost-benefit analysis and thirdly, that reflect longer-term concerns of the citizen in terms of the impact of new technologies on social engagement and hu-

man values. The hygiene factors listed in Table 1 and that are captured by the regression analyses above do not differ greatly from those USACM principles described earlier, save for two important constructs Firstly, trust is important as we are now talking about the dynamics of releasing information to one party rather than another. Trust is this respect is based on credibility, responsibility and personalisation and therefore crucial elements involved in adoption and use of ubiquitous systems. Secondly, usability emerges strongly (being part of the 'design' factor in three out of the four regression analyses). The fact usability emerged is an important message for developers and researchers – ease of use is potentially being overlooked as a crucial component of privacy management.

In response to 2, we have good reason to believe that while there are a number of universal privacy concerns, there is a residual effect of context. In the qualitative data people are more accepting of the seamless transmission of sensitive data in a health context because the benefits tend to outweigh the perceived costs. Also the presence and influence of privacy factors differs across the four contexts we presented. Different privacy models emerged in the quanttive data with, for example, the simplest model underpinning the management of personal identity and the most complex model underpinning health. These findings expand and support the work of Hong et al. (2004). Hong et al. in that designers of ubicomp systems need to deploy a privacy risk analysis considering social and organisational content. This type of analysis considers: Who are the users? What kind of personal information is being shared? How is personal information collected?

Finally – we asked about whether people are likely to have enough confidence in ubiquitous technologies to hand-over management of privacy preferences. In answer to this we turn to our interview data where it is clear that – providing the benefits are made apparent and the 'hygiene factors' are met, that users would be willing to hand-over to agent technologies in this way. One important point to note, however, is that members of the public are expressing concerns – about the de-humanising effects of new technologies – that are relatively rarely considered in the relevant literature. Such 'human values' issues are sometimes marginalized, but may form a key part of the ubiquitous computing agenda.

In conclusion, our findings provide evidence that established principles by industry e.g. US-CAM are inadequate. Basing principles on individual privacy or providing services that allow users to manage their own privacy preferences is not enough. Mohatari, et al., (2007) argue traditional approaches are not sufficient in addressing privacy threats in ubiquitous systems, we agree with this statement. More importantly development of privacy principles should incorporate situation, context and design.

REFERENCES

Awad, N. F., & Krishnan, M. S. (2006). The personalization privacy paradox: An empirical evaluation of information transparency and the willingness to be profiled online for personalization. *Management Information Systems Quarterly*, *30*(1), 13–28.

Cranor, L. (2002). *Web privacy with* (p. 3P). USA: O'Reilly & Associates.

Cranor, L. F., Reagle, J., & Ackerman, M. S. (1999). Beyond concern: understanding net users' attitudes about online privacy. In Vogelsang, I., & Compaine, B. (Eds.), *The Internet Upheaval: Raising Questions, Seeking Answers in Communications Policy* (pp. 47–60). USA: MIT Press.

Dinev, T., & Hart, P. (2004). Internet Privacy Concerns and their Antecedents - Measurement Validity and a Regression Model. *Behaviour & Information Technology*, *23*(6), 413–423. doi:10.1080/01449290410001715723

Dritsas, S., Gritzalis, D., & Lambrinoudakis, C. (2006). Protecting privacy and anonymity in pervasive computing trends and perspectives. *Telematics and Informatics*, *23*(3), 196–210. doi:10.1016/j.tele.2005.07.005

Earp, J. B., Anton, A. I., Aiman-Smith, L., & Stufflebeam, W. (2005). Examining Internet Privacy Policies within the Context of User Privacy Values. *IEEE Transactions on Engineering Management*, *52*(2), 227–237. doi:10.1109/TEM.2005.844927

Fern, E. F. (2001). *Advanced Focus Group Research*. London: Sage Publications.

Guha, S., Tang, K., & Francis, P. (2008). NOYB: Privacy in Online Social Networks. *WOSN'08, August 18, 2008*, Seattle, Washington, USA. 49-54

Harper, J., & Singleton, S. (2001). With a grain of salt: what consumer privacy surveys don't tell us. http://www.cei.org/PDFs/with_a_grain_of_salt.pdf

Herzberg, F., Mausner, B., & Snyderman, B. B. (1959). *The Motivation to Work* (2nd ed.). New York: John Wiley & Sons.

Hinz, O., Gertmeier, E., Tafreschi, O., Enzmann, M., & Schneider, M. (2007). *Customer Loyalty programs and privacy concerns. 20ʰ Bled eConference eMergence: Merging and Emerging Technologies, Processes and Institutions. June 406.* Slovenia: Bled.

Hong, J. I., Ng, J. D., Lederer, S., & Landay, J. (2004). Privacy risk models for designing privacy-sensitive ubiquitous computing systems, Proceedings of the 2004 conference on Designing interactive systems: processes, practices, methods, and techniques, Cambridge, MA, USA Jackson, L., von Eye, A., Barbatsis, G., Biocca, F., Zhao, Y., & Fitzgerald, H.E. (2003). Internet Attitudes and Internet Use: some surprising findings from the HomeNetToo project. *International Journal of Human-Computer Studies, 59,* 355–382.

Kobsa, A. (2003). Component architecture for dynamically managing privacy constraints in personalized web-based systems. In Proceedings of the Third Workshop on Privacy Enabling Technology, Dresden, (2003).Germany. Springer Verlag.

Kobsa, A. (2007). Privacy-Enhanced Personalisation. *Communications of the ACM, 50*(8), 24–33. doi:10.1145/1278201.1278202

Kozlov, S. (2004). *Achieving Privacy in Hyper-Blogging Communities: privacy management for Ambient Technologies.* http://www.sics.se/privacy/wholes2004/papers/kozlov.pdf

Little, L., Briggs, P., & Coventry, L. (2004). Videotaped Activity Scenarios and the Elicitation of Social Rules for Public Interactions. BHCIG UK Conference, Leeds, September

Maguire, M. C. (1998). A Review of User-Interface Guidelines for Public information kiosk Systems. *International Journal of Human-Computer Studies, 50,* 263–286. doi:10.1006/ijhc.1998.0243

Malhotra, N. K., Kim, S., & Agarwal, J. (2004). Internet users' information privacy concerns, IUIPC: the construct, the scale and a causal model. *Information Systems Research, 15,* 336–355. doi:10.1287/isre.1040.0032

Metzger, M. J. (2004). Exploring the barriers to electronic commerce: Privacy, trust, and disclosure online. *Journal of Computer-Mediated Communication, 9*(4). http://jcmc.indiana.edu/vol9/issue4/metzger.html.

Motahari, S., Manikopoulos, C., Hiltz, R., & Jones, Q. (2007). Seven privacy worries in ubiquitous social computing. *Symposium on usable privacy and security (SOUPS),* 171 – 172.

Nguyen, D. H., & Truong, K. N. (2003). PHEmail: Designing a Privacy Honoring Email System. *Proceedings of CHI 2003 Extended Abstracts,* Ft. Lauderdale, Florida, Olsen, K., Grudin, J., Horvitz, E. (2005). A study of preferences for sharing and privacy'. *CHI, 2005 extended abstracts on Human factors in computing systems.*

Paine, C. B., Stieger, S., Reips, U.-R., Joinson, A. N., & Buchanan, T. (2007). Internet users' perceptions of 'privacy concerns' and 'privacy actions'. *International Journal of Human-Computer Studies, 65*(6), 526–536. doi:10.1016/j.ijhcs.2006.12.001

Palen, L., & Dourish, P. (2003). Unpacking Privacy for a Networked World. *Proceedings of the ACM, CHI 2003, 5 (1), 129- 135.*

Price, B. A., Adam, K., & Nuseibeh, B. (2005). Keeping Ubiquitous Computing to yourself: a practical model for user control of privacy. *International Journal of Human-Computer Studies, 63*(1-2), 228–253. doi:10.1016/j.ijhcs.2005.04.008

Sillence, E., Briggs, P., Fishwick, L., & Harris, P. (2004). Trust and Mistrust of Online Health Sites. Proceedings of CHI'2004, April 24-29 2004, Vienna Austria, p663-670. ACM press

Smith, J. H., Milberg, S. J., & Burke, S. J. (1996). Information privacy: measuring individuals concerns about organizational practices. *Management Information Systems Quarterly*, 167–196. doi:10.2307/249477

Teltzrow M., & Kobsa, A. (2003). A. "Impacts of User Privacy Preferences on Personalized Systems - a Comparative Study", In Proc' *CHI2003*.

USACM. (2006). Policy Brief: USACM Policy Recommendations on Privacy, June 2006. http://usacm.acm.org/usacm/Issues/Privacy.htm

Westin, A. (1967). *Privacy and freedom*. New York: Atheneum.

This work was previously published in International Journal of E-Business Research (IJEBR), edited by In Lee, pp. 1-20, copyright 2009 by IGI Publishing (an imprint of IGI Global).

Chapter 8

Consumer Responses to the Introduction of Privacy Protection Measures:
An Exploratory Research Framework

Heng Xu
The Pennsylvania State University, USA

ABSTRACT

Information privacy is at the center of discussion and controversy among multiple stakeholders including business leaders, privacy activists, and government regulators. However, conceptualizations of information privacy have been somewhat patchy in current privacy literature. In this paper, we review the conceptualizations of information privacy through three different lenses (information exchange, social contract and information control), and then try to build upon previous literature from multiple theoretical lenses to create a common understanding of the organization-consumer information interaction in the context of Business-to-Consumer electronic commerce (B2C e-commerce). We argue that consumers' privacy beliefs are influenced by the situational and environmental cues that signal the level of privacy protections in a particular environment. The framework developed in this research should be of interest to academic researchers, e-commerce vendors, legislators, industry self-regulators, and designers of privacy enhancing technologies.

INTRODUCTION

As information technologies increasingly expand the ability for organizations to store, process, and exploit personal data, privacy is at the center of discussion and controversy among multiple stakeholders including business leaders, privacy activists, and government regulators. Studies sug-

gest that the loss of consumer confidence related to privacy fears has already hindered the growth of Business-to-Consumer electronic commerce (B2C e-commerce) by tens of billions of dollars (Cavoukian & Hamilton, 2002). Governments throughout the world are taking notice, and in many jurisdictions there has been a concerted effort to restore confidence in e-business with data protection legislation as a complement to industry self-regulation. As such, information privacy has

DOI: 10.4018/978-1-60960-132-4.ch008

Copyright © 2011, IGI Global. Copying or distributing in print or electronic forms without written permission of IGI Global is prohibited.

become a business issue, a social issue and a legal issue—increasingly difficult to ignore.

Although the term such as "Information Privacy in the E-Business" or "Consumer Online Privacy Concerns" has been considerably hyped in the media, conceptualizations of information privacy have been somewhat patchy. In the privacy literature, there are some difficulties in defining common ground of information privacy and such challenge will likely become more pronounced in the next few years. According to a 2007 study sponsored by the National Research Council (Waldo, Lin, & Millett, 2007), the relationship between information privacy and society is now under pressure due to several factors that are "changing and expanding in scale with unprecedented speed in terms of our ability to understand and contend with their implications to our world, in general, and our privacy, in particular" (p.27). Factors related to technological change (e.g., data collection, communications), to societal trends (e.g., globalization, cross-border data flow, increases in social networking) are combining to force a reconsideration of basic privacy concepts and their implications (Waldo et al., 2007). Therefore, rather than drawing on a monolithic concept of privacy from a single theoretical lens, we try to build upon previous literature from multiple theoretical lenses to create a common understanding of the organization-consumer information interaction in the B2C e-commerce context. Exploration of the influences and outcomes of the organization-consumer information interaction is particularly important in discussing organizational privacy protection strategies, as these are so often confused in technical design, websites' data collection practices and consumers' privacy perceptions.

Drawing on the marketing, social-psychology, and economics theories, we examine the information privacy phenomenon through three different theoretical lenses. The first lens, referred to as the *information exchange* lens, conceptualizes privacy as a "privacy calculus" which contributes to the understanding of the trade-offs that consumers are willing to make when they exchange their personal information for certain benefits. The second lens, referred to as the *social contract* lens, frames the discussion of the bond of trust between organizations and individuals over information privacy. The third lens, referred to as the *information control* lens, emphasizes the role of control perception in explaining the privacy phenomenon. We apply each lens separately to discuss the conceptualizations of information privacy and to explore factors influencing consumers' privacy concerns and their responses to the introduction of various privacy protection measures. This exploratory research framework will serve as a starting point for further research on conceptualizing information privacy in details.

INFORMATION PRIVACY IN B2C E-COMMERCE

Multiple Conceptualizations of Privacy

Continued advances in information technology in general and the growth in the adoption of e-commerce specifically, further facilitate the collection, storage, distribution, and use of personal information. The rise of identity theft and privacy breaches, along with highly publicized digital surveillance based on accessing public record files as well as personal profiles posted on social networking sites, makes the potential intrusion of privacy a more critical and acute concern (Westin, 2003). In the B2C e-commerce, "the technology-based business model of the 1990s—we must know you to serve you—came into fundamental collision with the now dominant consumer model—let me decide what you know about me, thanks" (Westin, 2003, p.442).

Although various definitions of privacy have been given in the literature, the notion of privacy is still fraught with multiple meanings and interpretations. Since 1960s, privacy has been generally defined as "the claim of individuals, groups, or institutions to determine for themselves when, how, and to what extent information about them is communicated to others" (Westin, 1967, p. 7). Westin's (1967) theory of privacy provided a framework for the landmark pieces of legislation enacted in U.S. and also made a significant contribution to the academic understanding of privacy. From the 1970s till present, researchers from a number of disciplines have examined the concept of privacy including psychology (e.g., Laufer & Wolfe, 1977), human resources (e.g., Stone & Stone, 1990), sociology (e.g., Etzioni, 1999), law (e.g., Solove, 2006), marketing (e.g., Sheehan & Hoy, 2000), and management information systems (e.g., Smith, Milberg, & Burke, 1996). With the wide scope of scholarly interests, it is not surprising to see that privacy theorists "...do not agree...on what privacy is or on whether privacy is a behavior, attitude, process, goal, phenomenal state, or what" (Margulis, 2003a, p.17). Privacy has been considered as a dynamic and dialectic concept which subsumes a wide variety of conceptualizations (Margulis, 2003a, 2003b). This rich ground of theoretical and empirical exploration has led to welcome efforts to synthesize various perspectives and identify common ground (Stone & Stone, 1990).

Approaches to Privacy Protection

The privacy literature describes three major privacy protection approaches: privacy-enhancing technology, industry self-regulation, and government legislation (Bellman, Johnson, Kobrin, & Lohse, 2004; Culnan & Bies, 2003; Fischer-Hüber, 2000; Tang, Hu, & Smith, 2008). In general, the public has been skeptical about the efficacy of privacy-enhancing technology and industry self-regulation for protecting information privacy. As a result, privacy advocates and individual activists continue to demand stronger government legislation to restrain abuses of personal information by merchants (Culnan, 2000; Milberg, Smith, &

Burke, 2000; Swire, 1997). We seek to contribute to this debate by investigating how technological solutions, industry self-regulation and government legislative solutions may influence consumers' privacy perceptions and privacy related construct, such as privacy concerns, trust, or perceived risks. Now we briefly review these three approaches to privacy protection in the e-business context.

Legislative Approaches to Privacy Protection

Privacy laws vary greatly throughout the world and the extent to which privacy laws are enforced also varies. The privacy laws of the European Union (E.U.) and the U.S. represent the two major privacy regulatory models—the comprehensive legislative approach and the self-regulatory approach, and the difference in privacy protection promoted by the two models has been the focus of heated debate in the recent past (Caudill & Murphy, 2000; Culnan, 2000; Culnan & Bies, 2003). These two different privacy regulatory models highlights two different views of privacy: a fundamental right view of privacy (i.e., "privacy as a human right") and an instrumentalist view of privacy (i.e., "privacy as a commodity"). The first camp views privacy as a fundamental human right, like the right to liberty or life (Sopinka, 1997; Walczuch & Lizette, 2001). Such fundamentalist position holds that privacy is tied to a cluster of rights, such as autonomy and dignity (Beaney, 1966). The second camp holds privacy to be of instrumental value rather than fundamental right; that is, the value of privacy comes because it sustains, promotes, and protects other things that we value (Waldo et al., 2007).

At the societal level, several studies pointed out that "human right" societies long approached privacy in an "omnibus" fashion by passing sweeping privacy bills that address all the instances of data collection, use and sharing (Bennett & Raab, 1997; Dholakia & Zwick, 2001; Smith, 2001). Some examples of countries in this category include Australia, Canada, New Zealand and countries in European Union (Smith, 2004). In contrast, in "commodity" societies, there are no "omnibus" laws governing collection, use, and sharing of personal information that transcend all types of data in all sectors of the economy (Smith, 2001). Some countries in this category have "patchwork" of sector-specific privacy laws that apply to certain forms of data or specific industry sectors (Bennett & Raab, 1997; Dholakia & Zwick, 2001; Smith, 2001). For instance, in the U.S., there are sector-specific laws for specific types of records such as credit reports, and video rental records, or for classes of sensitive information such as health information (Smith, 2004).

Industry Self-Regulatory Approaches to Privacy Protection

The major component of the U.S. self-regulatory approach to privacy protection is the influence of the private sector in safeguarding the electronic privacy of personal information. Self-regulation involves the setting of standards by an industry group or certifying agency and the voluntary adherence to the set standards by members or associates (Zwick & Dholakia, 1999). Under this self-regulatory approach, industries develop rules and enforcement procedures that substitute for government regulation (Swire, 1997) and often issue certifications in the form of seals of approvals which assure that the businesses indeed conform to the fair information practices they purport to (Culnan & Bies, 2003). The private sector approach to information privacy regulation consists of industry codes of conduct and the use of self-policing trade groups and associations to regulate information privacy. An examples of an industry self-regulator is the Direct Marketing Association (DMA) that made compliance with its privacy principles as a condition of membership (DMA, 2003). Other examples include privacy seals on e-commerce and e-service web sites such as those given by Online Privacy Alliance or TRUSTe, and whose effectiveness has been examined in prior

privacy studies (e.g., Xu, 2007; Xu, Teo, & Tan, 2005). In this situation, consumers and businesses collectively control personal information, with the industry self regulator acting as a facilitator for resolving any conflicts that may arise.

Technological Approaches to Privacy Protection

Researchers suggest that perhaps technology, although widely implicated for enabling companies to employ privacy invasive practices, could play a significant role in protecting privacy, particularly because of its ability to cross international political, regulatory, and business boundaries, much like the Internet itself (Turner & Dasgupta, 2003). PETs, also known as privacy-enhancing or privacy-enabling technologies, are broadly defined as any type of technology that is designed to guard or promote the privacy interests of individuals (Cavoukian & Hamilton, 2002). In the literature, a spectrum of systems and techniques has been proposed with the enterprise-level customer information protection at one end (Adams & Barbieri, 2006; Karjoth, 2003; Karjoth, Schunter, & Waidner, 2002), and individual PETs at the other end (Byers, Cranor, Kormann, & McDaniel, 2004; Cranor, 2002; Genkina & Camp, 2005). In this research, we focus on the discussion of PETs from the end-user perspective, and thus PETs refer to those tools implemented and deployed by e-commerce vendors to assist consumers in protecting their privacy online. Some popular end-user PETs include:

1. **Encryption tools** which prevent eavesdropping and protect data from unauthorized access (Ackerman, 2004). For example, the Secure Sockets Layer (SSL) is a general-purpose protocol for transmitting encrypted data over the Internet. It is used by all of the major web browsers for securely transmitting data to web sites that support SSL.

2. **Anonymity tools** can prevent online communications from being linked back to a specific individual and prevent eavesdroppers form learning with whom an individual is communicating (Ackerman, 2004; Kobsa, 2007). These anonymity tools, therefore, could help Internet users surf the Web anonymously.

3. **Cookie management tools** are available to prevent users' computers from exchanging cookies with web sites (Cranor, 2002). Most browsers have a parameter that can be set to either inform users when a site is attempting to install a cookie, allowing users the option to accept or decline it or to prevent any cookies from being installed (Cranor, 2002).

4. **The Platform for Privacy Preferences** provide a standard, computer-readable format for privacy policies and a protocol that enables web browsers to read and process privacy policies automatically (Ackerman, 2004; Cranor, 2002). Research on examining effectiveness of P3P criticized that, while P3P and its user agents provides users with the privacy options of notice (i.e., notifying users whether a Web site's privacy policy conflicts with their privacy preferences), P3P lacks the *enforcement* mechanism to ensure sites act according to their privacy policies (Ackerman, 2004; Xu et al., 2005). Recent studies have shown that few websites adopt P3P (Reay, Beatty, Dick, & Miller, 2007), which limits P3P's impact as a privacy enhancing approach. Reasons may include lack of enforcement (Turner & Dasgupta, 2003), lack of motivation to adopt stringent policy automation by commercial players (Hochheiser, 2002), and the lack of appropriate user interfaces for delivering the P3P policy to users and involving them in the decision processes (Ackerman, 2004).

Figure 1. Viewing information privacy through three theoretical lenses

VIEWING THE PHENOMENON THROUGH DIFFERENT LENSES

As shown in Figure 1, three domains of research inform our understanding of the nature of information privacy. Each incorporates a different conceptualization of information privacy: economic, psychological, and social. Each of these lenses looks at information privacy differently and therefore provides a valid basis upon which the factors influencing judgments about the degree of privacy concerns could be reasonably proposed.

Based on an extensive literature review, we develop a tentative organizing framework to synthesize results of prior privacy studies, outline major research issues, and identify future research opportunities (see Figure 2). Following Korba, Song, and Yee (2006), we highlight two main entities involved in the information flow: consumer and the e-commerce website. A long-term information exchange relationship is initiated when a consumer discloses personal information to an e-commerce website. As Figure 2 illustrates, consumers' information disclosure decision will be determined by four general factors: (1) privacy attitudes such as privacy concerns, (2) pri-

Figure 2. Conceptual model

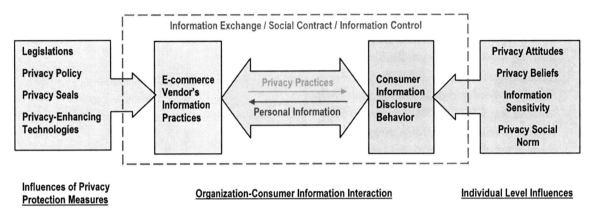

vacy related beliefs such as perceived risks, trust and perceived information control, (3) the type of personal information requested, and (4) social norm. On the other hand, in response to consumers' increasing privacy concerns, e-commerce websites implement privacy measures to comply with privacy laws, develop privacy policy and join privacy and security seal programs, and deploy privacy enhancing technologies to protect consumers' personal information.

The conceptual framework presented in Figure 2 depicts the information interaction between e-commerce websites and consumers, and shows the factors which may affect consumer information disclosure behavior and the website's information practices. To better understand privacy protection in B2C e-commerce, we identify three streams of privacy literature which may inform our understanding of the nature of information privacy. Each incorporates a different privacy conceptualization: information exchange, social contract, and information control. Each of these lenses looks at the information interaction between organization and consumer from different theoretical perspective and therefore provides a valid basis upon which the factors influencing judgments about the degree of privacy concerns could be reasonably proposed. These domains are presented as guiding propositions for future research.

Information Exchange Lens

One very important perspective views information privacy in terms of an *exchange* whereby personal information is given in return for certain benefits. This perspective is found in various works which viewed privacy as a *calculus* (e.g., Klopfer & Rubenstein, 1977; Stone & Stone, 1990). According to this perspective, Klopfer and Rubenstein (1977), for instance, found that the concept of privacy is not absolute but, rather, can be interpreted in "economic terms" (p.64). That is, as suggested in the literature on self-disclosure, individuals should make their decisions about the disclosure of information based on a "calculus of behavior" (Laufer & Wolfe, 1977, p.36) and should be willing to disclose personal information in exchange for some benefit, subject to an assessment that their personal information will subsequently be used fairly and that they will not suffer negative consequences in the future. Similarly, Stone and Stone (1990) developed an expectancy theory based model to identify the antecedents and consequences of the motivation to protect organizational privacy. The basis of this model echoed the idea of privacy calculus by incorporating prior research on expectancy theory models of motivation and the view that "individuals are assumed to behave in ways that they believe will result in the most favorable net level of outcomes" (Stone & Stone, 1990, p. 363).

This exchange perspective of information privacy is especially evident in works of analyzing consumer privacy concerns (e.g., Culnan, 2000; Culnan & Armstrong, 1999; Culnan & Bies, 2003; Milne & Gordon, 1993; Milne & Rohm, 2000; Milne, Rohm, & Boza, 1999; Sheehan & Hoy, 2000). It was noted that the findings of the self-disclosure literature perspective—the focus on the interpersonal context notwithstanding—can be applied to an impersonal commercial context as well (Culnan, 2000; Culnan & Armstrong, 1999; Milne & Gordon, 1993). Specifically, consumers often consider the nature of the benefit being offered in exchange for information when deciding whether an activity violates their privacy (Culnan, 1993; Goodwin, 1991; Milne & Gordon, 1993; Sheehan & Hoy, 2000). Such benefit could have a specific financial value (such as a cash payment, product, or service), and in some cases, the value could be information based (such as access to information that is of interest) (Sheehan & Hoy, 2000). In a study that attempted to measure the dollar value of information privacy, Hann et al. (2002) found that individuals are willing to trade off privacy concerns for economic benefits. In addition, the strategy of rewarding subjects in exchange for divulging personal attitudes or behaviors is well documented in the survey methodology literature as a means of increasing response rates (e.g., Barker, 1989; Chebat & Cohen, 1993). Overall, such exchange perspective of information privacy suggests the importance of rewarding consumers with benefits in return for the disclosure of their personal information.

Social Contract Lens

A second important perspective on information privacy views it through a social contract lens (e.g., Caudill & Murphy, 2000; Culnan, 1995; Culnan & Bies, 2003; Hoffman, Novak, & Peralta, 1999; Milne, 1996; Milne & Gordon, 1993; Phelps, Nowak, & Ferrell, 2000). The *Integrative Social Contract Theory* (ISCT) (Donaldson & Dunfee, 1994, 1995, 1999), the most widely used ethical theory in the context of information privacy, has been used to strengthen the bond of trust between corporations and consumers. ISCT posits that members of a given community or industry behave fairly if their practices are governed by social contracts[1] (Donaldson & Dunfee, 1994, 1995, 1999). ISCT is particularly appropriate for understanding the issues of consumer privacy as it provides a means for understanding the tensions between corporations and consumers over information privacy (Culnan, 1995). Specifically, it addressed the "context-specific complexity" of business situations by speaking directly to the shared understanding of the participants in a particular transaction, and thus it clearly corresponded to the exchange relationship central to marketing thought and practice (Donaldson & Dunfee, 1994, 1995, 1999; Dunfee, Smith, & Ross, 1999).

According to this ISCT perspective, a social contract is held to occur when consumers provide personal information to certain corporations, and the corporation in turn offers some benefits to the consumer (Caudill & Murphy, 2000; Culnan, 1995; Milne, 1996; Milne & Gordon, 1993; Phelps et al., 2000). "A social contract is initiated, therefore, when there are expectations of social norms (i.e., generally understood obligations) that govern the behavior of those involved" (Caudill & Murphy, 2000). For the corporation, one generally understood obligation accruing from entering into this social contract is that the corporation will undertake the responsibility to manage consumers' personal information properly (Caudill & Murphy, 2000; Culnan, 1995; Milne, 1996; Milne & Gordon, 1993; Phelps et al., 2000). This implied contract is considered breached if consumers are unaware that their information is being collected, if the corporation rents consumers' personal information to a third party without permission, or if the corporation shares consumers' personal information to unauthorized parties without consumers' consent, or if the corporation uses the consumers' personal information for other purposes without notifying consumers (Culnan, 1995; Milne, 1996; Phelps et al., 2000).

Thus, the social contract, dictating how corporations handle consumers' personal information in an implicit form (*not* in an economic or a legal form), involves unspecified obligations and requires consumers' trust on the corporation's compliance to this social contract (Caudill & Murphy, 2000; Culnan & Bies, 2003; Hoffman et al., 1999). Such social contract perspective of information privacy suggests the importance of consumer trust in the organization-consumer information interaction. In reviewing the extant online trust literature, it seems that the concept of privacy concern has been implicitly incorporated in various studies regarding issues of trust in the online environment. For instance, many trust researchers proposed various models of trust that consider the privacy policies and third party seals (e.g., TRUSTe seal) as the structural assurances built into a Web site which might affect trusting beliefs and trust related behaviors (e.g., Gefen, Karahanna, & Straub, 2003; McKnight & Chervany, 2002). However, the explicit involvement of privacy is somehow overlooked among these studies. Davison et al. (2003) feel "quite astonishing that a high proportion of the burgeoning literature on trust in the context of B2C fails to control for privacy, fails to meaningfully consider it, or even completely overlooks it" (p. 344). We attempt to address this gap by integrating the trust theories into privacy literature.

Information Control Lens

A third major perspective considers information privacy to be related to the control of personal information. This perspective is found in various prior works (Altman, 1977; Johnson, 1974; Laufer, Proshansky, & Wolfe, 1973; Westin, 1967) which

have contributed to and stimulated research and theory on privacy as a control related concept. By adopting the limited-access approach to privacy (i.e., individual controls the information access to herself), a number of privacy theorists have put emphases on the concept of *control* when defining privacy. For example:

- **Westin (1967):** "privacy is the right of the individual to decide what information about himself should be communicated to others and under what conditions".
- **Proshansky, Ittelson and Rivin (1970):** gaining privacy is to obtain freedom of choice or options to achieve goals, "... control over what, how, and to whom he communicates information about himself...".
- **Altman (1974):** "the selective control over access to the self or to one's group." "Privacy is an interpersonal boundary control process, designed to pace and regulate interactions with others".
- **Margulis (1977):** "privacy, as a whole or in part, represents control over transactions between person(s) and other(s), the ultimate aim of which is to enhance autonomy and/or to minimize vulnerability".
- **Stone et al. (1983):** "the ability (i.e., capability) of the individual to control personally (vis-à-vis other individuals, groups, organizations, etc.) information about one's self".
- **Margulis (2003b):** privacy is viewed as control over or regulation of or, more narrowly, limitations on or exemption from scrutiny, surveillance, or unwanted access.

From the above control-oriented definitions of privacy, it seems that privacy theorists have applied the term "control" widely in the privacy literature as the justification or motivation for defining privacy. Wolfe and Laufer (1974) suggested that "the need and ability to exert control over self, objects, spaces, information and behavior

Figure 3. Research framework

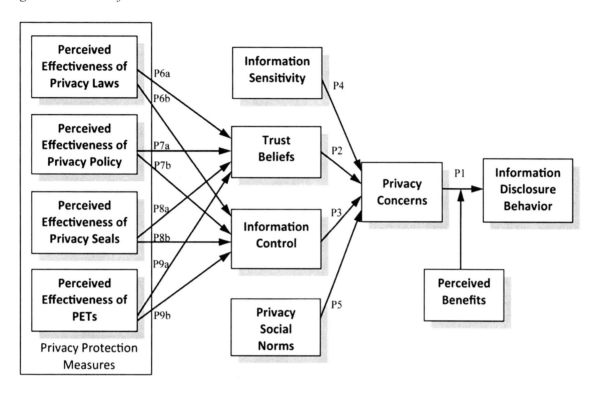

is a critical element in any concept of privacy" (p. 3). Westin's (1967) frequently cited "components" of privacy—solitude, anonymity, intimacy, and reserve—identify ways in which individuals control information about themselves.

The above view of privacy as a control related concept is also found in the works of a number of consumer privacy studies (e.g., Dinev & Hart, 2004; Goodwin, 1991; Nowak & Phelps, 1997; Phelps et al., 2000; Sheehan & Hoy, 2000). For instance, consumers perceive information disclosure as less privacy-invasive when, among other things, they believe that they will be able to control future use of the information (Culnan & Armstrong, 1999). It was further indicated that although much of the previous psychological, legal, and philosophical research has focused on control over physical intrusions, contemporary technology suggests that control over information represents the greater concern (Goodwin, 1991). This control perspective of information

privacy indicates that control should be one of the key factors which provides the greatest degree of explanation for privacy concern (Sheehan & Hoy, 2000).

SPURRING DEVELOPMENT OF PROPOSITIONS

The literature reviews in Section 3 presenting the importance of consumer privacy from the information exchange, social contract, and information control theoretical lenses provide the insightful theoretical foundations for the formulation of propositions for this research. Based on the three theoretical lenses described above, below we introduce the conceptual model and present research propositions concerning the relationships among the constructs. Figure 3 presents the research model.

Information Exchange Lens: Rational Choice and Bounded Rationality

According to the exchange lens of privacy, consumers can be expected to behave as if they are performing a privacy calculus in assessing the outcomes they will receive as a result of providing personal information to corporations (Culnan, 2000; Culnan & Armstrong, 1999; Culnan & Bies, 2003; Goodwin, 1991; Milne & Rohm, 2000; Milne et al., 1999). Hence, individuals will exchange their personal information as long as they perceive adequate benefits will be received in return—that is, benefits which exceed the perceived risks of the information disclosure (Culnan & Bies, 2003). In other words, consumers, when requested to provide personal information to corporations, would perform a risk-benefit analysis (i.e., 'privacy calculus') to assess the outcomes they would face in return for the information, and respond accordingly (Culnan, 1995; Culnan & Bies, 2003).

Consistent with the core ideas of a privacy calculus, the rational choice theory may further help predict how individuals make decisions regarding the revelation of personal information. This theory suggests that all action is fundamentally 'rational' in character and that consumers calculate the likely costs and benefits of any action before making a decision (Von Neumann & Morgenstern, 1947). Individuals tend to pursue outcomes that maximize positive valences, which can be directly enhanced by benefits provided, and minimize negative valences (Culnan & Bies, 2003; Stone & Stone, 1990). Along the line of rational choice theory, higher level of privacy concerns that viewed as the negative valences, would be expected to negatively influence a personal's information disclosure behavior.

The above arguments suggest the negative relationships between privacy concerns and information disclosure behavior; but recent privacy studies have highlighted the privacy attitude/behavior dichotomy (Acquisti, 2004; Acquisti & Grossklags, 2005). Although consumers may have a higher level of concerns for information privacy, they are willing to trade their personal information in exchange for some economic or social rewards (Culnan & Bies, 2003). Researchers who refer to these inconsistencies in individual privacy decision making argue that consumers' actual information disclosure behaviors may be different from their revealed privacy attitudes (Acquisti, 2004; Acquisti & Grossklags, 2005). "Either their behaviors reflect lower privacy concerns than polls and research would suggest, or other factors mitigate privacy concerns" (Dinev & Hart, 2006, p.61).

A plausible explanation for such privacy attitude/behavior dichotomy is that users' privacy decision processes are affected by bounded rationality (Acquisti & Grossklags, 2005). According to bounded rationality theory (Simon, 1982), human agents are unable to have *absolute rationality* because of the potential impacts of information processing capacity limitations and hyperbolic discounting effect. The economic literature suggest that individuals have a tendency to discount 'hyperbolically' future costs or benefits (O'Donoghue & Rabin, 2001; Rabin & O'Donoghue, 2000). Such hyperbolic discounting implies inconsistency of personal preference over time – future events may be discounted at different discount rates than near-term events (Acquisti, 2004). Hyperbolic discounting could be applied to the context of privacy decision making (Acquisti, 2004): the benefits of disclosing personal information may be immediate (e.g., convenience of placing orders online) but the risk of such information disclosure may be invisible or spread over time (e.g., identity theft). Individuals may genuinely want to protect their personal data, but because of bounded rationality, rather than carefully calculating long term risks of information disclosure, they may opt for immediate gratification instead (Acquisti, 2004).

Therefore, with the availability of immediate benefits of using e-commerce services (e.g., convenience, monetary rewards, and time savings), consumers are very likely to opt for immediate gratification by discounting the potential risks of information disclosure. Thus, we propose that perceived benefits will moderate the relationship between privacy concerns and information disclosure behavior:

Proposition 1: *With the perceived benefits available (e.g., convenience, monetary rewards, and time savings), the negative influences of privacy concerns on information disclosure behavior should be weaker.*

Social Contract Lens: The Role of Consumer Trust

The concept of social contract in the consumer privacy context means that consumers are willing to disclose personal information for certain benefits as long as they trust the corporation that it would uphold its side of social contract. Hence, the lack of consumer trust in customer-centric enterprises seems to be a critical barrier that hinders the efforts of these enterprises to collect personal information from consumers for the purpose of providing services. Trust has received a great deal of attention from scholars in the disciplines of social psychology (e.g., Lewicki & Bunker, 1995), sociology (e.g., Lewis & Weigert, 1985), management (e.g., Lane & Bachmann, 1996), and marketing (e.g., Moorman, Desphande, & Zaltman, 1993). In examining the published literature on trust, various definitions of trust have been proposed in many different ways. Nevertheless, across disciplines there is consensus that trust is a crucial enabling factor in relations where there is uncertainty, interdependence, risk, and fear of opportunism (Hoffman et al., 1999; Mayer, Davis, & Schoorman, 1995; McKnight & Chervany, 2002). "The need for trust only arises in a risky situation" (McKnight & Chervany, 2002), and trust could be an effective mechanism to reduce the complex-

ity of human conduct in situations where people have to cope with uncertainty (Luhmann, 1988).

Trust involves at least two entities in relation to each other—a trustor and a trustee. In the e-commerce context, the consumer is usually seen as the trustor, the party who places him or herself in a vulnerable situation; and the e-commerce vendor is the trustee, the party in whom trust is placed and who has the opportunity to take advantage of the trustor's vulnerability (Grabner-Kräuter & Kaluscha, 2003). Because of the absence of proven guarantees that the e-commerce websites will not engage in opportunistic behaviors in terms of information misuse, trust in an e-commerce website is crucial in helping consumers overcome their perceptions of uncertainty. If an e-commerce website is perceived to be caring about consumers' information privacy needs (trusting belief—benevolence), honest and consistent in its dealing with consumers' personal information (trusting belief—integrity), and capable of protecting their personal information (trusting belief—competence), the level of concerns over information privacy may be reduced. Therefore, we expect that the more trust a consumer has in an e-commerce vendor with regard to its information practice, the less likely he or she is to foresee the uncertainties associated with disclosing personal information to the e-commerce vendor.

Proposition 2: *Higher level of trust beliefs should lead to lower level of privacy concerns.*

Information Control Lens: The Construct of Perceived Control

As discussed above, more frequently than not, the element of control is embedded in most privacy conceptual arguments and definitions and has been used to operationalize privacy in numerous measurement instruments (Altman, 1975; Culnan, 1993; Kelvin, 1973; Margulis, 1977; Smith et al., 1996; Westin, 1967). Privacy scholars have linked the concept of privacy with control by either defining privacy as control, *per se*, or by positioning control as a key factor shaping privacy. Johnson (1974), for instance, defined privacy as "secondary control in the service of need-satisfying outcome effectance" (p. 91). Goodwin (1991) defined consumer privacy by two dimensions of control: control over information disclosure and control over unwanted physical intrusions into the consumer's environment. However, many researchers reason that control is actually one of the factors that shape privacy and that privacy is not control *per se* (Laufer & Wolfe, 1977; Margulis, 2003a, 2003b). For instance, Laufer and Wolfe (1977) conceptualized control as a mediating variable in the privacy system by arguing that "a situation is not necessarily a privacy situation simply because the individual perceives, experiences, or exercises control" (p. 26). Conversely, the individual may not perceive she has a control, yet the environmental and interpersonal elements may create perceptions of privacy (Laufer & Wolfe, 1977). Therefore, privacy should be more than control (Laufer & Wolfe, 1977; Margulis, 2003a) and control might be one of the factors which determine privacy state (Dinev & Hart, 2004).

In this research, "control" – defined as perceived control over information collection and use – is conceptualized as a related but separate variable from privacy concerns. Prior research has indicated that, in general, individuals will have fewer privacy concerns when they have a greater sense that they control the disclosure and subsequent use of their information (Culnan, 1993; Culnan & Armstrong, 1999; Milne & Boza, 1999; Stone & Stone, 1990). In other words, perceived control over disclosure and subsequent use of personal information is a contrary factor that is weighed against privacy concerns.

Proposition 3: *Higher level of control perceptions over disclosure and subsequent use of personal information should lead to lower level of privacy concerns.*

THE DIALECTIC NATURE OF INFORMATION PRIVACY

The individual decision process with respect to privacy is complex, multifaceted, and context-specific. Altman (1975) conceptualized privacy decision-making as a dialectic boundary regulation process which is conditioned by "individuals' own experiences and social expectations, and by those of others with whom they interact" (Palen & Dourish, 2003, p.129). Accordingly, it seems reasonable to argue that privacy beliefs should be better related to individuals' own information experiences and social expectations rather than be thought of as a global consequence of e-commerce use per se. Thus we believe that the constructs of information sensitivity and privacy social norm should have relevance for the current study. Below we develop the propositions about the relationships between information sensitivity, privacy social norm and privacy concerns, and elaborate on the reasoning supporting the causal relationships among these constructs in the research model.

Prior privacy literature has been shown that privacy attitude is a function of the type of personal information collected, stored, used, and released by an organization (Malhotra, Kim, & Agarwal, 2004; Milne & Gordon, 1993; Phelps et al., 2000; Sheehan & Hoy, 2000). All things being equal, individuals perceive greater vulnerability when disclosing more sensitive information than they do for disclosing less sensitive information. Generally, financial and healthcare information are found to be viewed more sensitive by consumers; while information such as shopping interests or lifestyle preferences are known to be less sensitive by consumers (Phelps et al., 2000; Sheehan & Hoy, 2000). Consequently, we propose that an e-commerce vendor's requests for more sensitive information, compared with less sensitive information, will exert a more negative effect on consumers' privacy attitudes. That is to say, when sensitive information is requested, the level of privacy concerns is proposed to increase:

Proposition 4:*Information sensitivity positively affects privacy concerns.*

As Laufer and Wolfe (1977) argue, the "mores of a community transmitted through language, tradition, and values constitute boundaries of consciousness about privacy" (p. 28). Patterns and forms of privacy have long been related to the cultural characteristics of the social group in which an individual lives (Altman, 1977; Roberts & Gregor, 1971). Several privacy studies have found that there are differences in information privacy concerns across difference societies (Bellman et al., 2004; Dinev et al., 2006a, 2006b; Milberg et al., 2000), the cultural dimension of individualism (Hofstede, 1980, 2003) being the most responsible factor for these differences. The concept of privacy is related to the extent that individualism is sought after and reinforced in a culture (Etzioni, 1999). In the U.S., a highly individualistic society, legal precedent and public opinion highly value privacy as an expression and a safeguard of personal dignity (Laufer & Wolfe, 1977) and individual right (Etzioni, 1999; Westin, 1967). Thus we posit that social norms shape the need for personal space and private information and thus are a predictor of the consumer's concerns for information privacy.

Proposition 5:*Privacy social norms positively affect privacy concerns.*

Perceived Effectiveness of Privacy Protection Measures

Consumers' privacy beliefs are influenced by the situational and environmental cues that signal the level of privacy protections in a particular environment (Belanger, Hiller, & Smith, 2002). This study examines the perceived effectiveness of four common privacy protection measures – privacy

enhancing technologies (PETs), privacy seals, privacy policy and privacy laws. Although not an exhaustive list of all privacy protection measures, the proposed factors represent popular market-driven institutional mechanisms (privacy policy and third party privacy seals), technology-driven mechanisms, and legal mechanisms. Perceived effectiveness of privacy protection measures are defined as the extent to which a consumer believes that the privacy protection measures existed in the transaction environment are able to protect their personal information from opportunistic firms in terms of information misuse. Accordingly, *perceived effectiveness* of privacy protection measures reflects the amount of consumers' subjective beliefs that the institutional setup allows for the privacy of their transaction to be maintained as promised. In the following paragraphs, we argue that privacy protection measures will affect consumers' perceived information control and trust, and elaborate on the reasoning supporting the causal relationships among these constructs in the research model.

Perceived Effectiveness of Privacy Legislations

The legislation approach that embodies the strong institutional structural assurances provided by government agencies (Zucker, 1986), has been proposed to have a strong impact on privacy related beliefs (Culnan, 2000). Some scholars have even suggested that the legal system is the most powerful mechanism for addressing privacy issues because it requires that offenders be punished in order to maintain its deterrent effectiveness (Spiro & Houghteling, 1981). The *perceived effectiveness of privacy legislations* is defined as the extent to which consumers believe that the relevant privacy laws will protect them from opportunistic firms. With the privacy legislation available, illegal behavior can be deterred through threat of punishment (Tittle, 1980). Recognizing the deterrent value of a legal system, consumers tend to believe that e-commerce vendors would abide by the law (Tittle, 1980), and would therefore collect and use personal information appropriately (Xu, 2007; Xu & Teo, 2004). Government legislation is also responsible for resolving conflicts that may occur. In privacy literature, limited studies have examined the role of privacy laws in increasing consumer trust beliefs and information control perceptions. Thus we predict that, in the presence of relevant privacy legislation, consumers are likely to believe that the legal assurance of their privacy rights should safeguard them from potential loss of their personal information, which will in turn lead to their trust beliefs in e-commerce vendors' information practices and confidence in controlling the disclosure and subsequent use of their personal information.

Proposition 6a:*The perceived effectiveness of privacy laws increases consumers' trust beliefs.*

Proposition 6b:*The perceived effectiveness of privacy laws increases consumers' perceived information control.*

Perceived Effectiveness of Privacy Policy

The industry self-regulatory approaches to privacy protections are predicated on the assumption that e-commerce vendors have an incentive to address privacy concerns of consumers because, if they fail to do so, they will suffer reputational losses. With this mechanism, when consumers disclose their personal information, the information moves to a collective domain where both consumers and e-commerce vendors become co-owners with joint responsibilities for keeping the information safe and private (Petronio, 2002). The result is that e-commerce vendors are responsible for protecting the information by implementing privacy policies based on fair information practices (Culnan & Bies, 2003). The *perceived effectiveness of privacy policy* is defined as the extent to which a consumer

believes that the privacy policy posted online is able to provide accurate and reliable information about the firm's information privacy practices.

Privacy literature suggests that an online firm's collection of personal information is perceived to be fair when the consumer is vested with notice and voice (Culnan & Bies, 2003; Malhotra et al., 2004). In other words, consumers want to influence changes in firms' polices that they find to be objectionable (Malhotra et al., 2004). Privacy policy is essentially a self-regulated organizational mechanism where consumers can be informed about the choices available to them regarding how the collected information is used, the safeguards in place to protect the information from loss, misuse, or alteration, and how consumers can update or correct any inaccurate information. Previous studies have shown that businesses that inform consumers about information handling procedures instill greater consumer confidence and trust perception (Culnan & Armstrong, 1999). It has been suggested that the prescription of notification of and consent by consumers effectively exemplifies procedural fairness and thus increases consumers' perceived control over their personal information (Culnan & Bies, 2003; Milne & Culnan, 2004). Therefore, we propose:

Proposition 7a:*The perceived effectiveness of privacy policy increases consumers' trust beliefs.*

Proposition 7b:*The perceived effectiveness of privacy policy increases consumers' perceived information control.*

Perceived Effectiveness of Privacy Seals

Frequently, the organizational privacy protection measure through privacy policy may need to be reinforced by having a trusted third party certify that the web sites indeed conform to the fair information practices they purport to (Culnan & Bies, 2003). Such third-party certification typically comes in the form of seals of approval such as those given by Online Privacy Alliance or TRUSTe. In such situation, consumers and web sites collectively control personal information, with the trusted third party acting as a facilitator for resolving any conflicts that may arise. The *perceived effectiveness of privacy seals* is defined as the extent to which consumers believe that third-party seal providers are able to guarantee that their information disclosed to firms will be protected in accordance with their expectations.

These seal programs should enhance the consumer's perceived control and trust beliefs because of two reasons. First, these institutional mechanisms could limit the firm's ability to behave in negative ways, allowing consumers to form and hold beliefs about expectations of positive outcomes (Johnson & Cullen, 2002). As Gefen et al. (2003) explain for the case of trust, having a third party like the reputable TRUSTe to vouch for a firm's trustworthiness should build trust in that such third party assurances have typically been one of the primary methods of building trust in business. Second, when violation occurs, these structures could provide mechanisms of voice and recourse for the betrayed (Johnson & Cullen, 2002; McKnight, Cummings, & Chervany, 1998), which could create strong incentives for firms to refrain from opportunistic behavior. Empirical studies have shown that companies that conform to the privacy seal programs could foster consumers' perceptions of control over their personal information (Culnan & Armstrong, 1999) and build consumer trust. Therefore, we propose:

Proposition 8a: *The perceived effectiveness of privacy seal programs increases consumers' trust beliefs.*

Proposition 8b: *The perceived effectiveness of privacy seal programs increases consumers' perceived information control.*

Perceived Effectiveness of Privacy Enhancing Technologies (PETs)

To the degree that privacy concerns represent a major inhibiting factor in consumers' usage of e-commerce applications (Chellappa & Sin, 2005), it is crucial for e-commerce vendors to implement and deploy privacy enhancing technologies (PETs) to address consumers' privacy concerns. The *perceived effectiveness of PETs* is defined as the extent to which consumers believe that the PETs implemented and deployed by e-commerce vendors are able to assist them in protecting their online privacy. As we discussed earlier, some popular end-user PETs in the context of B2C e-commerce include the Platform for Privacy Preference (P3P) and its user agents, features for consumers to opt-out from the marketing contacts, privacy management tools for consumers to access their personal information (e.g., update addresses, and delete credit card number from purchase history), and etc. In privacy literature, limited studies have examined the role of these PETs in increasing consumer trust. We predict that, introducing PETs should directly build consumers' trust beliefs toward an e-commerce vendor because of the nontrivial investment of time and resources made by the e-commerce vendor to design, implement and deploy the privacy-enhancing features (Xu et al., 2005). This action should be interpreted as a signal that the e-commerce vendor is proactively addressing consumers' privacy concerns and it will comply with the social contract by undertaking the responsibility to manage consumers' personal information properly (Xu et al., 2005). In other words, a particular e-commerce vendor's introduction of the PETs to consumers may enable them to believe that the e-commerce vendor cares about their information privacy needs (trusting belief—benevolence), and it is capable of protecting their personal information (trusting belief—competence).

Proposition 9a:*The perceived effectiveness of PETs increases consumers' trust beliefs.*

Privacy-enhancing technologies could empower consumers with primary control over the disclosure and access of their personal information that are gathered by e-commerce vendors. It has been found that end-user PETs help reduce individuals' privacy concerns through empowering their information control. For instance, to assuage employee perceptions of privacy invasion in the workplace, monitoring systems have been designed with features that allow employees to decide when their images can be displayed (Zweig & Webster, 2002). When employees are provided with means to delay or prevent performance monitoring, their perception of personal control increases (Stanton, 1996). Hence, when individuals are able to control the flow of their personal information to e-commerce vendors through using privacy enhancing technology, their level of perceived information control is likely to increase.

Proposition 9b:*The perceived effectiveness of PETs increases consumers' perceived information control.*

DISCUSSION AND CONCLUDING COMMENTS

In this paper, we have developed a theory-based conceptual framework which identified the factors affecting consumers' privacy concerns and how consumers' privacy concerns are influenced by these factors. To the best of our knowledge, the privacy literature has not seen a systematic theory-driven framework that can explain consumer responses to various privacy protection measures. Thus the framework developed in this research should be of interest to academic researchers, e-commerce vendors, legislators, industry self-regulators, and designers of privacy

enhancing technologies. Next, we present the contributions of this research and identify areas for future research.

Contributions to Research

To date, the conceptualizations of the phenomenon of information privacy are varied and somewhat confused. This study provides one of the first attempts to synthesize the conceptualizations of information privacy, which showed that the phenomenon of information privacy could be explained from at least three different theoretical perspectives (information exchange, social contract, and information control). We have developed a theoretical framework which not only explained how consumer trust, perceived information control, information sensitivity, privacy social norms, and various privacy protection measures may affect consumers' privacy concerns, but also describe how such privacy concerns may influence consumers' information disclosure behavior.

Using the conceptual model illustrated in Figure 3 as a starting point, we derived research propositions concerning the antecedents and outcomes of privacy concerns from multiple theoretical perspectives, including theories of rational choice and bounded rationality, the integrative social contract theory, the theory of trust, together with the notion of dialectic nature of privacy. We have also justified the propositions with existing empirical work in privacy (when available). Our conceptual model presented in Figure 3 is a causal model and its propositions should be best tested as such. The impacts of privacy protection measures, and various privacy belief factors on consumers' privacy concerns, as well as on their information disclosure behavior, would preferably be tested utilizing some innovative design where consumers' information disclosure behaviors can be observed. In this regard, longitudinal survey studies or field experiments with potential partnerships with e-commerce vendors would be recommended.

Suggestions for Future Research

Our research framework suggests opportunities for further theoretical development. First, this paper has investigated limited numbers of individual level factors. Future studies should investigate additional factors on individual differences which may have direct impacts on the research framework or may moderate some relationships in this framework. These factors may include age (Culnan, 1995), gender (Milne & Rohm, 2000), education level (Milne & Rohm, 2000), Internet usage experience (Sheehan & Hoy, 2000), and previous privacy experience (Culnan, 1995). For instance, it has been shown that consumers with higher education levels are more concerned about their online privacy than those with lower education levels (Milne & Rohm, 2000), and woman are shown to have more privacy concern than men (Sheehan & Hoy, 1999).

The current research framework can be expanded not only with including demographic variables either as covariates or moderators as discussed above, but also with some variables on personality traits. Future research can examine whether some personality traits may moderate the relationship between privacy protection measures and privacy related beliefs. For example, a potentially salient personality trait is locus of control, defined as the extent to which people believe they have the ability to change outcomes through their own actions (Rotter, 1966). Individuals with an internal locus of control (i.e., those who believe their own actions can produce predictable outcomes) are likely to prefer privacy protection measures that offer them personal control (e.g., privacy-enhancing technology) whereas people with an external locus of control (i.e., those who believe the actions of others can produce predictable outcomes) may prefer protection measures that provide them with proxy control (i.e., government legislation) (Yamaguchi, 2001).

Moreover, this research has focused on how privacy protection measures may individually influence privacy related beliefs without proposing the combinatory effects. Thus it is not clear that how different types of privacy protection measures may collectively influence privacy concerns through the effects on trust and information control. In practice, since these protection measures do not appear in isolation, their individual effects are less likely to be ecologically informative than their combinatory effects. Further theorization is needed to explore the interaction effects of various privacy protection measures with a view to answering the following question: What are the effects of different combinations of privacy protection measures on consumer trust and information control? Will the presence of some privacy protection measures (e.g., privacy seals) diminish the effects of other privacy protection measures (e.g., privacy legislation)?

In addition, since some scholars have suggested that the phenomenon of information privacy may be culturally dependent, future research should add another theoretical perspective – the cultural lens to the current research framework. The borderless nature of the new economy complicates the issue of information privacy because consumers in different countries vary widely in their opinions of what constitutes fair organizational information practices (Milberg et al., 2000; Milberg, Smith, & Kallman, 1995). Hence, to effectively build the information exchange relationships with consumers in each local market, it is essential that global marketers tailor for each country a proper practice of information collection and utilization. Prior privacy literature contains a few pioneering attempts at showing that the degree of privacy risk perceptions differs across countries (Bellman et al., 2004; Dinev et al., 2006b; Milberg et al., 2000; Milberg et al., 1995). However, few have examined whether these differences translate directly into higher or lower effectiveness of privacy protection measures. Future research could be designed to explore how consumers vary in their reactions to different privacy protection measures in different cultures. If systematic cross-cultural differences are found, further research should start building a theory of cross-cultural difference in mechanism for privacy protections.

Contributions to Practice

From a practical perspective, this study has implications for various players in the B2C e-commerce industry: e-commerce vendors, industry self-regulators, designers of PETs, privacy advocates and government legislators. First, given that the consumer's concerns for privacy are not absolute, but rather, can be traded off against benefits, there are ample opportunities for e-commerce vendors to address consumers' privacy issues. It follows that additional financial incentives need to be developed and provided to mitigate higher levels of privacy concerns. Second, it is important for practitioners to realize that, finding ways to increase consumers' control over their personal information disclosed online is crucial. It is very important for e-commerce vendors to develop improved privacy enhancing features with user-friendly interfaces for specifying privacy preferences to enhance consumers' control over their personal information.

Finally, this study shows that trust beliefs and information control beliefs are the important factors in consumers' interactions with e-commerce vendors. In this aspect, this study provides some insights into the different approaches that could be used by an e-commerce vendor to address privacy concerns by building trust and enhancing control perceptions. Incorporating organizational privacy interventions such as joining privacy seal programs or maintaining a good privacy policy into the management of information practices should be an important method for increasing users' trust beliefs and reducing their privacy concerns. In addition, it is important for an e-commerce vendor to develop privacy enhancing features with user-friendly interfaces for specifying privacy preferences to enhance trust and control beliefs, and to alleviate privacy concerns. To the extent

that information control is a key factor influencing privacy concerns, application developers should pay close attention to those measures that can increase the perceptions of information control. In sum, it is also important for practitioners to realize that, building trust and reducing privacy concerns could be the products of several aspects of the e-commerce vendors' interventions that could be well within the control of the e-commerce vendors.

ACKNOWLEDGMENT

The author likes to thank Prof. Hock Hai Teo, and Prof. Bernard C. Y. Tan for their valuable help on an earlier version of this research. This material is partially based upon work supported by the National Science Foundation under Grant No NSF-CNS 0716646. Any opinions, findings and conclusions or recommendations expressed in this material are those of the author and do not necessarily reflect the views of the National Science Foundation (NSF).

REFERENCES

Ackerman, M. S. (2004). Privacy in pervasive environments: next generation labeling protocols. *Personal and Ubiquitous Computing, 8*(6), 430–439. doi:10.1007/s00779-004-0305-8

Acquisti, A. (2004). *Privacy in Electronic Commerce and the Economics of Immediate Gratification.* Paper presented at the Proceedings of the 5th ACM Electronic Commerce Conference, New York, NY.

Acquisti, A., & Grossklags, J. (2005). Privacy and Rationality in Individual Decision Making. *IEEE Security & Privacy, 3*, 26–33. doi:10.1109/MSP.2005.22

Adams, C., & Barbieri, K. (2006). Privacy Enforcement in E-Services Environments. In Yee, G. (Ed.), *Privacy Protection for E-Services* (pp. 172–202). Hershey, PA: IDEA Group Publishing.

Altman, I. (1974). Privacy: A Conceptual Analysis. In D. H. Carson (Ed.), *Man-Environment Interactions: Evaluations and Applications (Part 2; Vol. 6: Privacy)* (pp. 3-28). Washington, DC: Environmental Design Research Association.

Altman, I. (1975). *The Environment and Social Behavior: Privacy, Personal Space, Territory, and Crowding*. Monterey, CA: Brooks/Cole Publishing.

Altman, I. (1977). Privacy Regulation: Culturally Universal or Culturally Specific? *The Journal of Social Issues, 33*(3), 66–84. doi:10.1111/j.1540-4560.1977.tb01883.x

Barker, L. B. (1989). Survey Research. In Emert, P., & Barker, L. B. (Eds.), *Measurement of Communication Behavior* (pp. 25–39). New York: Longman.

Beaney, W. M. (1966). Right to Privacy and American Law, The. *Law and Contemporary Problems, 31*, 253–271. doi:10.2307/1190670

Belanger, F., Hiller, J. S., & Smith, W. J. (2002). Trustworthiness in electronic commerce: the role of privacy, security, and site attributes. *The Journal of Strategic Information Systems, 11*(3-4), 245–270. doi:10.1016/S0963-8687(02)00018-5

Bellman, S., Johnson, E. J., Kobrin, S. J., & Lohse, G. L. (2004). International differences in information privacy concerns: A global survey of consumers. *The Information Society, 20*(5), 313–324. doi:10.1080/01972240490507956

Bennett, C. J., & Raab, C. D. (1997). The adequacy of privacy: The European Union data protection directive and the North American response. *The Information Society, 13*(3), 245–263. doi:10.1080/019722497129124

Byers, S., Cranor, L., Kormann, D., & McDaniel, P. (2004, 26-28 May). *Searching for Privacy: Design and Implementation of a P3P-Enabled Search Engine*. Paper presented at the The 2004 Workshop on Privacy Enhancing Technologies (PET2004), Toronto, Canada.

Caudill, M. E., & Murphy, E. P. (2000). Consumer Online Privacy: Legal and Ethical Issues. *Journal of Public Policy & Marketing, 19*(1), 7–19. doi:10.1509/jppm.19.1.7.16951

Cavoukian, A. H., & Hamilton, T. J. (2002). *The Privacy Payoff: How Successful Businesses Build Customer Trust*. Toronto: McGraw-Hill Ryerson.

Chebat, J.-C., & Cohen, A. (1993). Response Speed in Mail Survey: Beware of Shortcuts. *Marketing Research, 5*(2), 20–25.

Chellappa, R. K., & Sin, R. (2005). Personalization versus Privacy: An Empirical Examination of the Online Consumer's Dilemma. *Information Technology Management, 6*(2-3).

Cranor, L. F. (2002). *Web privacy with P3P*. Sebastopol, CA: O'Reilly.

Culnan, M. J. (1993). 'How Did They Get My Name'? An Exploratory Investigation of Consumer Attitudes toward Secondary Information Use. *Management Information Systems Quarterly, 17*(3), 341–364. doi:10.2307/249775

Culnan, M. J. (1995). Consumer Awareness of Name Removal Procedures: Implication for Direct Marketing. *Journal of Interactive Marketing, 9*, 10–19.

Culnan, M. J. (2000). Protecting Privacy Online: Is Self-Regulation Working? *Journal of Public Policy & Marketing, 19*(1), 20–26. doi:10.1509/jppm.19.1.20.16944

Culnan, M. J., & Armstrong, P. K. (1999). Information Privacy Concerns, Procedural Fairness and Impersonal Trust: An Empirical Investigation. *Organization Science*, *10*(1), 104–115. doi:10.1287/orsc.10.1.104

Culnan, M. J., & Bies, J. R. (2003). Consumer Privacy: Balancing Economic and Justice Considerations. *The Journal of Social Issues*, *59*(2), 323–342. doi:10.1111/1540-4560.00067

Davison, M. R., & Clarke, R., J., S. H., Langford, D., & Kuo, F.-Y. (2003). Information Privacy in a Globally Networked Society: Implications for IS Research. *Communications of the Association for Information Systems*, *12*, 341–365.

Dholakia, N., & Zwick, D. (2001). Contrasting European and American approaches to privacy in electronic markets: a philosophical perspective. *Electronic Markets*, *11*(2). doi:10.1080/101967801300197034

Dinev, T., Bellotto, M., Hart, P., Russo, V., Serra, I., & Colautti, C. (2006a). Internet users' privacy concerns and beliefs about government surveillance: An exploratory study of differences between Italy and the United States. *Journal of Global Information Management*, *14*(4), 57–93.

Dinev, T., Bellotto, M., Hart, P., Russo, V., Serra, I., & Colautti, C. (2006b). Privacy Calculus Model in E-commerce - a Study of Italy and the United States. *European Journal of Information Systems*, *15*(4), 389–402. doi:10.1057/palgrave.ejis.3000590

Dinev, T., & Hart, P. (2004). Internet Privacy Concerns and Their Antecedents - Measurement Validity and a Regression Model. *Behaviour & Information Technology*, *23*(6), 413–423. doi:10.1080/01449290410001715723

Dinev, T., & Hart, P. (2006). An Extended Privacy Calculus Model for E-Commerce Transactions. *Information Systems Research*, *17*(1), 61–80. doi:10.1287/isre.1060.0080

DMA. (2003, April 2003). Privacy Promise Member Compliance Guide. Retrieved April 1, 2005, from http://www.the-dma.org/privacy/privacypromise.shtml

Donaldson, T., & Dunfee, W. T. (1994). Towards a Unified Conception of Business Ethics: Integrative Social Contracts Theory. *Academy of Management Review*, *19*, 252–284. doi:10.2307/258705

Donaldson, T., & Dunfee, W. T. (1995). Integrative Social Contracts Theory: A Communication Conception of Economic Ethics. *Economics and Philosophy*, *11*, 85–112. doi:10.1017/S0266267100003230

Donaldson, T., & Dunfee, W. T. (1999). *Ties that Bind: A Social Contracts Approach to Business Ethics*. Cambridge, MA: Harvard Business School Press.

Dunfee, W. T., Smith, N. C., & Ross, T. W. J. (1999). Social Contracts and Marketing Ethics. *Journal of Marketing*, *63*, 14–32. doi:10.2307/1251773

Etzioni, A. (1999). *The limits of privacy*. New York: Basic Books.

Fischer-Hüber, S. (2000). *IT-Security and Privacy*. Berlin, Heidelberg: Springer-Verlag.

Gefen, D., Karahanna, E., & Straub, D. W. (2003). Trust and TAM in online shopping: an integrated model. *Management Information Systems Quarterly*, *27*(1), 51–90.

Genkina, A., & Camp, L. J. (2005, April 1). *Re-Embedding Existing Social Networks into Online Experiences to Aid in Trust Assessment*, Available at SSRN: http://ssrn.com/abstract=707139.

Goodwin, C. (1991). Privacy: Recognition of a Consumer Right. *Journal of Public Policy & Marketing*, *10*(1), 149–166.

Grabner-Kräuter, S., & Kaluscha, E. A. (2003). Empirical Research in Online Trust: A Review and Critical Assessment. *International Journal of Human-Computer Studies, Special Issue on ". Trust and Technology, 58*(6), 783–812.

Hann, I.-H., Hui, K. L., Lee, T., & L., P. I. P. (2002, December). *Online Information Privacy: Measuring the Cost-Benefit Tradeoff.* Paper presented at the Proceedings of the Twenty-Third Annual International Conference on Information Systems (ICIS), Barcelona, Spain.

Hochheiser, H. (2002). The platform for privacy preference as a social protocol: An examination within the US policy context. *ACM Transactions on Internet Technology, 2*(4), 276–306. doi:10.1145/604596.604598

Hoffman, D. L., Novak, T., & Peralta, M. A. (1999). Information Privacy in the Marketspace: Implications for the Commercial Uses of Anonymity on the Web. *The Information Society, 15*(2), 129–139. doi:10.1080/019722499128583

Hofstede, G. (1980). *Culture's consequences.* Beverly Hills, CA: Sage.

Hofstede, G. (2003). *Culture's Consequences: Comparing Values, Behaviors, Institutions and Organizations across Nations. Longdon.* Sage.

Johnson, C. A. (1974). Privacy as Personal Control. In D. H. Carson (Ed.), *Man-Environment Interactions: Evaluations and Applications: Part 2* (Vol. 6: Privacy, pp. 83-100). Washington, D.C.: Environmental Design Research Association.

Johnson, L. J., & Cullen, B. J. (2002). Trust in Cross-Cultural relationships. In Gannon, M. J., & Newman, K. L. (Eds.), *The Blackwell Handbook of Cross-Cultural Management* (pp. 335–360). Oxford, UK, Malden, Mass: Blackwell.

Karjoth, G. (2003). Access control with IBM Tivoli access manager. *ACM Transactions on Information and System Security, 6*(2), 232–257. doi:10.1145/762476.762479

Karjoth, G., Schunter, M., & Waidner, M. (2002). *The platform for enterprise privacy practices - privacy-enabled management of customer data.* Paper presented at the The 2nd Workshop on Privacy Enhancing Technologies (PET 2002), San Francisco, CA.

Kelvin, P. (1973). A social psychological examination of privacy. *The British Journal of Social and Clinical Psychology, 12,* 248–261.

Klopfer, P. H., & Rubenstein, D. L. (1977). The concept privacy and its biological basis. *The Journal of Social Issues, 33,* 52–65. doi:10.1111/j.1540-4560.1977.tb01882.x

Kobsa, A. (2007). Privacy-Enhanced Personalization. *Communications of the ACM, 50*(8), 24–33. doi:10.1145/1278201.1278202

Korba, L., Song, R., & Yee, G. (2006). Privacy Management Architectures for E-Services. In Yee, G. (Ed.), *Privacy Protection for E-Services* (pp. 234–264). Hershey, PA: IDEA Group Publishing.

Lane, C., & Bachmann, R. (1996). The social constitution of trust: supplier relations in Britain and Germany. *Organization Studies, 17*(3), 365–395. doi:10.1177/017084069601700302

Laufer, R. S., Proshansky, H. M., & Wolfe, M. (1973, June). *Some Analytic Dimensions of Privacy.* Paper presented at the Paper presented at the meeting of the Third International Architectural Psychology Conference, Lund, Sweden.

Laufer, R. S., & Wolfe, M. (1977). Privacy as a Concept and a Social Issue - Multidimensional Developmental Theory. *The Journal of Social Issues, 33*(3), 22–42. doi:10.1111/j.1540-4560.1977.tb01880.x

Lewicki, R. J., & Bunker, B. B. (1995). Trust in relationships: A model of trust development and decline. In Bunker, B. B., & Rubin, J. Z. (Eds.), *Conflict, Cooperation, and Justice* (pp. 133–173). San Francisco, CA: Jossey-Bass.

Lewis, J. D., & Weigert, A. J. (1985). Trust as a social reality. *Social Forces, 63*(4), 967–985. doi:10.2307/2578601

Luhmann, N. (1988). Familiarity, Confidence, Trust: Problems and Alternatives. In D. Gambetta, G. (Ed.), *Trust* (pp. 94-107). Basil Blackwell, New York.

Malhotra, N. K., Kim, S. S., & Agarwal, J. (2004). Internet Users' Information Privacy Concerns (IUIPC): The Construct, the Scale, and a Causal Model. *Information Systems Research, 15*(4), 336–355. doi:10.1287/isre.1040.0032

Margulis, S. T. (1977). Conceptions of Privacy-Current Status and Next Steps. *The Journal of Social Issues, 33*(3), 5–21. doi:10.1111/j.1540-4560.1977. tb01879.x

Margulis, S. T. (2003a). On the Status and Contribution of Westin's and Altman's Theories of Privacy. *The Journal of Social Issues, 59*(2), 411–429. doi:10.1111/1540-4560.00071

Margulis, S. T. (2003b). Privacy as a social issue and behavioral concept. *The Journal of Social Issues, 59*(2), 243–261. doi:10.1111/1540-4560.00063

Mayer, R. C., Davis, J. H., & Schoorman, F. D. (1995). An integrative model of organizational trust. *Academy of Management Review, 20*(3), 709–734. doi:10.2307/258792

McKnight, D. H., & Chervany, N. L. (2002). What trust means in e-commerce customer relationships: an interdisciplinary conceptual typology. *International Journal of Electronic Commerce, 6*(2), 35–59.

McKnight, D. H., Cummings, L. L., & Chervany, N. L. (1998). Initial Trust Formation in New Organizational Relationships. *Academy of Management Review, 23*(3), 472–490. doi:10.2307/259290

Milberg, S. J., Smith, H. J., & Burke, S. J. (2000). Information privacy: Corporate management and national regulation. *Organization Science, 11*(1), 35–57. doi:10.1287/orsc.11.1.35.12567

Milberg, S. J. B., J.S., Smith, H. J., & Kallman, A. E. (1995). Values, Personal Information Privacy Concerns, and Regulatory Approaches. *Communications of the ACM, 38*(12), 65–74. doi:10.1145/219663.219683

Milne, G. R. (1996). *Consumer Participation in Mailing Lists: A Field Experiment* (No. Report no. 96-107). Cambridge, Mass.: Marketing Science Instituteo.

Milne, G. R., & Boza, M.-E. (1999). Trust and Concern in Consumers' Perceptions of Marketing Information Management Practices. *Journal of Interactive Marketing, 13*(1), 5–24. doi:10.1002/ (SICI)1520-6653(199924)13:1<5::AID-DIR2>3.0.CO;2-9

Milne, G. R., & Culnan, M. J. (2004). Strategies for reducing online privacy risks: Why consumers read(or don't read) online privacy notices. *Journal of Interactive Marketing, 18*(3), 15–29. doi:10.1002/dir.20009

Milne, G. R., & Gordon, E. M. (1993). Direct Mail Privacy-Efficiency Trade-Offs Within an Implied Social Contract Framework. *Journal of Public Policy & Marketing, 12*(2), 206–215.

Milne, G. R., & Rohm, A. (2000). Consumer Privacy and Name Removal Across Direct Marketing Channels: Exploring Opt-in and Opt-out Alternatives. *Journal of Public Policy & Marketing, 19*(2), 238–249. doi:10.1509/jppm.19.2.238.17136

Milne, G. R., Rohm, A., & Boza, M.-E. (1999). Trust Has to Be Earned. In Phelps, J. (Ed.), *Frontiers of Direct Marketing* (pp. 31–41). New York: Direct Marketing Educational Foundation.

Moorman, C., Desphande, R., & Zaltman, G. (1993). Factors affecting trust in market research relationships. *Journal of Marketing, 57*(1), 81–101. doi:10.2307/1252059

Nowak, J. G., & Phelps, J. (1997). Direct Marketing and the Use of Individual-Level Consumer Information: Determining How and When "Privacy" Matters. *Journal of Direct Marketing, 11*(4), 94–108. doi:10.1002/(SICI)1522-7138(199723)11:4<94::AID-DIR11>3.0.CO;2-F

O'Donoghue, T., & Rabin, M. (2001). Choice and procrastination. *The Quarterly Journal of Economics, 116*, 121–160. doi:10.1162/003355301556365

Palen, L., & Dourish, P. (2003). *Unpacking "privacy" for a networked world.* Paper presented at the Proceedings of the SIGCHI conference on Human factors in computing systems, Ft. Lauderdale, Fl.

Petronio, S. S. (2002). *Boundaries of privacy: dialectics of disclosure.* Albany: State University of New York Press.

Phelps, J., Nowak, G., & Ferrell, E. (2000). Privacy Concerns and Consumer Willingness to Provide Personal Information. *Journal of Public Policy & Marketing, 19*(1), 27–41. doi:10.1509/jppm.19.1.27.16941

Proshansky, H. M., Ittelson, W. H., & Rivin, L. G. (1970). *Environmental Psychology: Man and His Physical Setting.* New York: Holt, Rinehart, and Winston.

Rabin, M., & O'Donoghue, T. (2000). The economics of immediate gratification. *Journal of Behavioral Decision Making, 13*, 233–250. doi:10.1002/(SICI)1099-0771(200004/06)13:2<233::AID-BDM325>3.0.CO;2-U

Reay, I., Beatty, P., Dick, S., & Miller, J. (2007). A Survey and Analysis of the P3P Protocol's Agents, Adoption, Maintenance and Future. *IEEE Transactions on Dependable and Secure Computing, 4*(2), 151–164. doi:10.1109/TDSC.2007.1004

Roberts, J. M., & Gregor, I. (1971). Privacy: A Cultural View. In Penncock, J., & Chapman, J. (Eds.), *Privacy* (pp. 199–225). New York: Atherton Press.

Rotter, J. B. (1966). *Generalized Expectancies for Internal Versus External Control of Reinforcement.* Unpublished manuscript.

Sheehan, K. B., & Hoy, G. M. (2000). Dimensions of Privacy Concern among Online Consumers. *Journal of Public Policy & Marketing, 19*(1), 62–73. doi:10.1509/jppm.19.1.62.16949

Sheehan, K. B., & Hoy, M. G. (1999). Using E-mail To Survey Internet Users In The United States: Methodology And Assessment. *Journal of Computer-Mediated Communication, 4*(3).

Simon, H. A. (1982). *Models of bounded rationality.* Cambridge, MA: The MIT Press.

Smith, H. J. (2001). Information privacy and marketing: What the US should (and shouldn't) learn from Europe. *California Management Review, 43*(2), 8–33.

Smith, H. J. (2004). Information Privacy and Its Management. *MIS Quarterly Executive, 3*(4), 201–213.

Smith, H. J., Milberg, J. S., & Burke, J. S. (1996). Information Privacy: Measuring Individuals' Concerns About Organizational Practices. *Management Information Systems Quarterly, 20*(2), 167–196. doi:10.2307/249477

Solove, D. J. (2006). A Taxonomy of Privacy. *University of Pennsylvania Law Review, 154*(3), 477–560. doi:10.2307/40041279

Sopinka, J. (1997). Freedom of speech and privacy in the information age. *The Information Society, 13*(2), 171–184. doi:10.1080/019722497129197

Spiro, W. G., & Houghteling, L. J. (1981). *The Dynamics of Law* (2nd ed.). New York: Harcourt Brace Jovanovich.

Stanton, J. M. B.-F., J. L. (1996). Effects of electronic performance monitoring on personal control, task satisfaction, and task performance. *The Journal of Applied Psychology, 81*, 738–745. doi:10.1037/0021-9010.81.6.738

Stone, E. F., Gueutal, G. H., Gardner, D. G., & McClure, S. (1983). A Field Experiment Comparing Information-Privacy Values, Beliefs, and Attitudes Across Several Types of Organizations. *The Journal of Applied Psychology, 68*(3), 459–468. doi:10.1037/0021-9010.68.3.459

Stone, E. F., & Stone, D. L. (1990). Privacy in Organizations: Theoretical Issues, Research Findings, and Protection Mechanisms. *Research in Personnel and Human Resources Management, 8*(3), 349–411.

Swire, P. P. (1997). Markets, Self-Regulation, and Government Enforcement in the Protection of Personal Information. In W. M. Daley & L. Irving (Eds.), *Privacy and Self-Regulation in the Information Age* (pp. 3-19). Washington, D.C.: Department of Commerce, U.S.A.

Tang, Z., Hu, Y. J., & Smith, M. D. (2008). Gaining Trust Through Online Privacy Protection: Self-Regulation, Mandatory Standards, or Caveat Emptor. *Journal of Management Information Systems, 24*(4), 153–173. doi:10.2753/MIS0742-1222240406

Tittle, C. R. (1980). *Sanctions and Social Deviance: The Question of Deterrence*. New York: Praeger.

Turner, C. E., & Dasgupta, S. (2003). Privacy on the Web: An Examination of User Concerns, Technology, and Implications for Business Organizations and Individuals. *Information Systems Management*, (Winter): 8–18. doi:10.1201/1078/43203.20.1.20031201/40079.2

Von Neumann, J., & Morgenstern, O. (1947). *Theory of Games and Economic Behavior* (2nd ed.). Princeton: Princeton University Press.

Walczuch, R. M., & Lizette, S. (2001). Implications of the new EU Directive on data protection for multinational corporations. *Information Technology & People, 14*(2), 142. doi:10.1108/09593840110695730

Waldo, J., Lin, H., & Millett, L. I. (2007). *Engaging Privacy and Information Technology in a Digital Age*. National Academies Press.

Westin, A. F. (1967). *Privacy and Freedom*. New York: Atheneum.

Westin, A. F. (2003). Social and Political Dimensions of Privacy. *The Journal of Social Issues, 59*(2), 431–453. doi:10.1111/1540-4560.00072

Wolfe, M., & Laufer, R. S. (1974). The Concept of Privacy in Childhood and Adolescence. In S. T. Margulis (Ed.), *Privacy as a Behavioral Phenomenon, Symposium Presented at the Meeting of the Environmental Design Research Association*. Milwaukee.

Xu, H. (2007). *The Effects of Self-Construal and Perceived Control on Privacy Concerns*. Proceedings of the 28th Annual International Conference on Information Systems (ICIS 2007), Montréal, Canada.

Xu, H., & Teo, H. H. (2004). *Alleviating Consumer's Privacy Concern in Location-Based Services: A Psychological Control Perspective*. Proceedings of the Twenty-Fifth Annual International Conference on Information Systems (ICIS 2004), Washington, D. C., United States.

Xu, H., Teo, H. H., & Tan, B. C. Y. (2005). *Predicting the Adoption of Location-Based Services: The Roles of Trust and Privacy Risk.* Proceedings of 26th Annual International Conference on Information Systems (ICIS 2005), Las Vegas, NV.

Yamaguchi, S. (2001). Culture and Control Orientations. In Matsumoto, D. (Ed.), *The Handbook of Culture and Psychology* (pp. 223–243). New York: Oxford University Press.

Zucker, L. G. (1986). Production of trust: Institutional sources of economic structure, 1840-1920. In Staw, B. M., & Cummings, L. L. (Eds.), *Research in Organizational Behavior* (*Vol. 8*, pp. 53–111). Greenwich, CT: JAI Press.

Zweig, D., & Webster, J. (2002). Where is the Line between Benign and Invasive? An Examination of Psychological Barriers to the Acceptance of Awareness Monitoring Systems. *Journal of Organizational Behavior, 23,* 605–633. doi:10.1002/job.157

Zwick, D., & Dholakia, N. (1999). *Models of Privacy in the Digital Age: Implications for Marketing and E-Commerce: Research Institute for Telecommunications and Information Marketing (RITIM).* University of Rhode Islando.

ENDNOTE

[1] ISCT encompasses two different types of social contracts (Donaldson & Dunfee 1999, p.19): 1) *the hypothetical or "macro" contract,* reflecting hypothetical agreement among rational members of a community. Such contract usually refers to broad, hypothetical agreements among rational people and it is designed to establish objective background standards for social interaction. 2) *The "extant" or "micro" contract,* reflecting an actual agreement within a community. Such contract usually refers to non-hypothetical, actual (although typically informal) agreements existing within and among industries, national economic systems, corporations, trade associations, and so on.

This work was previously published in International Journal of E-Business Research (IJEBR), edited by In Lee, pp. 21-47, copyright 2009 by IGI Publishing (an imprint of IGI Global).

Chapter 9
Business Associates in the National Health Information Network:
Implications for Medical Information Privacy

Edward J. Szewczak
Canisius College, USA

Coral R. Snodgrass
Canisius College, USA

ABSTRACT

This article examines the role of the business associate of healthcare providers (BAHP) in the National Health Information Network. Current Health Insurance Portability and Accountability legislation has little to say about BAHPs and their potential impact on medical information privacy. For the good of the business enterprise, managers who are BAHPs or who supervise BAHPs need to be aware of the potential pitfalls of ignoring medical information privacy and take a proactive stance in protecting medical information privacy within the National Health Information Network. Among the approaches that managers can adopt include creating legal contracts between a business and BAHPs, proactively adopting more effective transmission security technologies, and insuring that BAHPs properly dispose of medical information after their use. Such proactive approaches will help to insure that the business is protected against a serious data breach that may result in popular and/or legal challenges to the business.

INTRODUCTION

In his 2004 State of the Union address, President George W. Bush stated that, by computerizing health records, it would be possible to avoid dangerous medical mistakes, reduce medical costs, and improve medical care (The White House, 2006). Drawing on a report from the Institute of Medicine (2001) and on the conclusions of a panel of IT experts, Kaushal *et al.* (2005) reported that the creation of a national system of electronic health records and a National Health Information Network electronically connecting

DOI: 10.4018/978-1-60960-132-4.ch009

Copyright © 2011, IGI Global. Copying or distributing in print or electronic forms without written permission of IGI Global is prohibited.

electronic heath records to healthcare providers, insurers, pharmacies, laboratories and claims processors will be possible at a cost of $156 billion. Four companies (Accenture, Computer Science Corporation, IBM and Northrop Grumman) have been selected by the Department of Health and Human Services to develop regional versions of the National Health Information Network with a view toward developing interoperability in the near future. A report from the Office of the National Coordinator for Health IT (Rishel, Riehl & Blanton, 2007) suggests that the National Health Information Network will be a:

"network of networks" that will securely connect consumers, providers and others who have, or use, health-related data and services, while protecting the confidentiality of health information. The NHIN will not include a national data store or centralized systems at the national level. Instead, the NHIN will use shared architecture (services, standards and requirements), processes and procedures to interconnect health information exchanges and the users they support (p. 2).

Electronic health records contain an individual's medical information that can take many forms such as text, photographs, video, x-ray, sound, etc. One definition of information that is directly relevant to medical information privacy is data that have been evaluated to be relevant and useful for making particular decisions or classes of decisions (King and Epstein, 1976). Though the account was originally provided for the context of business management decision making, it is clearly applicable to the situation of various medical practitioners as well as a business associate of a healthcare provider (BAHP) such as an insurance agent, a billing agent, a consultant, or a transcriptionist. Generally speaking, a BAHP is anyone who works closely with a healthcare provider in non-treatment contexts in both healthcare related businesses as well as non-healthcare related businesses. (The term "private contractor" is also used to describe BAHPs in government,

for example, by the Veterans Administration.) For example, a BAHP may be interested in developing patient profiles with a view toward customized marketing aimed at a particular profile or class of related profiles.

Despite government efforts to ensure medical information privacy, no comprehensive national strategy to safeguard medical information privacy has been developed and implemented (Koontz & Melvin, 2007). As such, the National Health Information Network poses a real threat to individuals' medical information privacy (Szewczak, 2007). This paper considers the role of the BAHP in the context of the National Health Information Network, identifies potential threats to individuals' medical information privacy, and proposes solutions to management challenges presented by the current and future availability of medical information made possible by the National Health Information Network.

THE MEDICAL RECORD

Traditionally medical data were collected and stored as records in physician's offices and in hospitals. Often the data were recorded manually and retrieved manually. Patient data forms the medical record and its contents (Electronic Frontier Foundation, 1993). Medical records may contain patient personal data such as name, address, age, next of kin, names of parents, date and place of birth, marital status, religion, history of military service, Social Security number, and name of insurer. Medical records also contain medical data such as complaints and diagnoses, medical history, family history, previous and current treatments, an inventory of the condition of each body system, medications taken now and in the past, use of alcohol and tobacco, diagnostic tests administered, and findings, reactions and incidents. Records may also contain subjective information based on impressions and assessments by healthcare workers such as mental ability and psychological stability and status. In addition to data about the patient's current condition, a patient's medical record may also contain the results of genetic research and testing that enable predictions of future medical conditions and the prospects of developing specific medical problems.

Typically the creation and maintenance of medical records was done manually by healthcare professionals. But IT has changed this practice (Kilman and Forslund, 1997). Notes hand-written by doctors and nurses are being put into electronic form in the name of faster, more extensive access to needed information. Healthcare companies are competing to get doctors to write prescriptions over the Internet and to persuade people to place their personal health records on the Internet (Consumer Reports, 2000). Companies have made available software that an individual can use to create an Internet-based "personal health record" that can be used to organize family medical histories, including medical conditions, medications and allergies. These personal records may be transmitted to healthcare professionals over a computer network (Rubenstein, 2005; Lawton & Worthen, 2008).

Medical records are available online to medical practitioners for the purposes of decision making and improving healthcare as well as medical research. They are also available to other users and institutions in non-treatment contexts. Medical records are used to conduct federal government-mandated medical community audits of physician competency and performance. They are also used by insurance companies in the assessment of an applicant's eligibility for health and life insurance and in claims processing to detect medical fraud. Medical information is also used by private employers, educational institutions, credit investigators, and law enforcement agencies for a variety of non-medical reasons. It is in these non-treatment contexts that the BAHP plays an important role.

MEDICAL INFORMATION AND PRIVACY

Cate (1997) identified a number of conceptions of what constitutes privacy from the literature. Privacy has been viewed as an expression of one's personality or personhood, focusing on the right of the individual to define his or her essence as a human being; as autonomy – the moral freedom of the individual to engage in his or her own thoughts, actions, and decisions; as citizens' ability to regulate information about themselves, and thus control their relationships with other human beings; and as secrecy, anonymity and solitude. In the area of medical information, the definition of privacy as "the claim of individuals, groups, or institutions to determine for themselves when, how, and to what extent information about them is communicated to others" (Westin, 1967, p. 7) is appropriate. This paper will focus on medical information exclusively, though the problems and challenges of information privacy are not necessarily unique to medical information (Szewczak, 2009).

The Westin definition is consistent with the confidential relationship between doctor and patient. Confidentiality refers to how data collected for approved purposes will be maintained and used by the individual, group or institution that collected it, what further uses will be made of them, and when individuals will be required to consent to such uses. In this regard, privacy may be construed as a balance struck by society between an individual's right to keep information confidential and the societal benefit derived from sharing the information for the purposes of medical research and public health management, and how the balance is codified into legislation giving individuals the means to control information about themselves (Office of Technology Assessment, 1993; Rindfleisch, 1997).

As personal information, medical information has a special status. As Krzysztof & Moore (2002) observe:

Medical information about the individual patient is considered highly private, and the general public is extremely fearful about disclosure....We all enjoy the benefits of medical research conducted on other patients, but we are very often reluctant to contribute or release our own information for such purposes. When medical data are published it is expected that the researchers will maintain the dignity of the individual patient, and that the results will be used for socially beneficial purposes (p. 15).

This observation has been supported by various public opinion polls conducted since 1993 that have uncovered a basic concern people have about the privacy of their medical records and how these records may be used (Electronic Privacy Information Center, 2006). Major areas of concern are:

- Employment/career advancement. People are concerned that employers may use personal health information to limit job opportunities. They are also concerned that medical information will be used for many non-health purposes, such as determining promotions and job advancement.
- Insurance eligibility. People are concerned that insurance companies may use personal health information to deny an application for various kinds of insurance coverage (e.g. medical insurance such as long-term disability insurance).
- Computerized versus paper records. The trend toward computerizing the healthcare system and keeping records electronically threatens medical information privacy. People feel more secure when medical records are kept in paper form.
- Genetics research. People do not want medical researchers to be allowed to study an individual's genetic information without obtaining the individual's consent.

- Medical records security. People feel protecting the confidentiality of medical records is essential to healthcare reform. Weak data security may lead to leaks of sensitive health information. People also think that insurance companies get more information from doctors than is needed.
- Mistrust of government. People worry that existing federal health privacy rules protecting patient information may be reduced or ignored in the name of efficiency. In addition, people fear that government agencies and researchers are allowed to see medical records without a patient's permission.

One might think that legislation addressing the issues and problems of safeguarding medical information would have solved many of the problems involving the mishandling of medical information. However, the effectiveness of legislation in establishing and maintaining medical information privacy is questionable at best, despite legislative efforts to the contrary. Federal and state governments have attempted to deal with privacy issues in ways that satisfy the needs of various stakeholders such as doctors, insurance companies, researchers, law enforcement, and data processing firms as well as individuals. The result has been various legislative measures that provide legal compromise. For our purposes, the most significant measure is the Health Insurance Portability and Accountability Act (HIPAA) of 1996.

HIPAA provides the first comprehensive set of federal regulations of health information. It provides for two rules related directly to medical information privacy: the Privacy Rule (45 Code of Federal Regulations 164.500 – 164.534) (Federal Register, 2002) and the Security Rule (45 Code of Federal Regulations 164.103 – 164.318) (Federal Register, 2003). It is the Privacy Rule that is most relevant to the issue of medical information privacy. The Security Rule will be discussed briefly later in this paper in a discussion of transmission security technology as a management challenge. Interested readers are referred to the Health Information Technology website of the Department of Health and Human Services (www.hhs.gov/healthit/healthnetwork/background/) for current details of the National Health Information Network technical implementation.

The HIPAA Privacy Rule provides the federal floor of privacy of protected health information in the U.S. It only applies to medical records maintained by "covered entities" (healthcare providers, health plans, and health care clearinghouses/data processing firms) in any form (electronic or non-electronic, including oral). It allows more stringent state laws to continue in force. An individual has a number of rights under the Privacy Rule including the following (adapted and expanded from Electronic Privacy Information Center, 2008):

To access, inspect and copy protected health information held by hospitals, clinics, health plans and other "covered entities" with some exceptions

- To request amendments to protected health information held by covered entities
- To request an accounting of disclosures that have been made without authorization to anyone other than the individual for purposes other than treatment, payment and "health care operations" (i.e., medical practice evaluations for accreditation conducted by organizations such as the Joint Commission for the Accreditation of Healthcare Organizations and the National Committee for Quality Assurance)
- To request restrictions on uses and disclosures of protected health information

The HIPAA Privacy Rule does not prohibit the disclosure of protected health information when such disclosure is required or permitted by other federal law. For example, the Gramm-Leach-Bliley Act does not prohibit the sharing of information among affiliated companies (such as banks and brokerages, which are not covered entities). So an individual's credit card account transactions may include data about where an individual goes for healthcare, and this data may be shared among affiliated companies and is not protected by HIPAA. The HIPAA Privacy Rule also explicitly includes exceptions to the rules for use and disclosure. In fact, there are a number of uses and disclosures of information for which an authorization or opportunity to agree or object is not required (for example, for judicial and administrative proceedings, and for law enforcement purposes), including the use of protected health information for marketing purposes (which, according to the Department of Health and Human Services, may be too difficult to distinguish from treatment purposes) (Privacy Rights Clearinghouse, 2007).

The HIPAA Privacy Rule is particularly difficult to implement when it comes to managing BAHPs under contract who perform an action on the healthcare provider's behalf and to whom the healthcare provider is releasing protected health information. These business associates often have free access to a patient's protected health information. They include people such as insurance agents, billing agents, consultants, and transcriptionists. If a healthcare provider discovers that a BAHP has breached or violated a contract with respect to safeguarding protected health information, the healthcare provider must take reasonable steps to remedy the problem or terminate the contract. If the contract cannot be terminated, the healthcare provider must report the problem to the Office of Civil Rights, which may exact civil penalties against the business associate. Criminal penalties can approach $250,000 and/or 10 years imprisonment if the offense is committed with intent to sell, transfer or use protected health information for commercial or personal gain, or for malicious harm (Federal Register, 2006; Wilson, 2006).

However a healthcare professional may not know that a BAHP has breached or violated a contract with regard to safeguarding protected health information. Because HIPAA does not prohibit the sharing of protected health information among various covered entities or their BAHPs, protected health information could be used in ways other than for treatment or billing. For example, an individual could be charged higher loan rates because of some piece of data in his/her medical record, and it would be impossible to prove the data were shared because there is no required disclosure audit for non-covered entities.

In addition, data networks may be Internet-based and global in reach. Individual health records may be transmitted overseas and handled by a subcontractor (a kind of BAHP) in ways the individual is completely unaware of and would object to under any circumstances (Consumer Reports, 2006; Ferris, 2008).

Another related security challenge is the data breach. A hacker, a BAHP, an ex-employee, or even a trusted employee can steal data from a computer system and offer them for sale to interested parties. Data breaches are not all that uncommon in today's technology-oriented world. A case in point is the 2005 LexisNexis data breach with 310,000 possible consumers affected. In some cases computer programs were used to generate IDs and passwords matching those of legitimate customers. In other cases hackers used computer viruses to collect IDs and passwords from infected machines as they were being used (Washington Post, 2005). Another case is the 2007 TJX data breach with 45.6 million credit and debit card numbers stolen over a period of 18 months by an unknown number of intruders. TJX was hit by several lawsuits after disclosing the data breach. It settled many of the suits to a total of about $250 million (Computer World, 2007, 2008).

Finally, if the history of dotcom business is any guide, companies that run into financial difficulties may choose to sell customer data to meet obligations, even though the companies have published privacy policies. As the following details, such

customer data may contain individuals' medical information.

PUBLICLY AVAILABLE SOURCES OF MEDICAL INFORMATION

There are a number of sources of an individual's medical information, including medical databases, company and government databases, public records, and consumer volunteered information. In the case of databases, the information is structured formally so as to facilitate system organization and maintenance. In instances when database organization is lacking, the information will be stored in unrelated files. All of these sources will be accessible in the National Health Information Network.

Medical databases will be major sources of medical information on the National Health Information Network. However a database is implemented, the electronic health records comprising it will be accessed by many interested parties over the National Health Information Network.

One of the largest central databases of electronic health records is the Medical Information Bureau (MIB). It is shared by insurance companies to obtain information about life insurance and individual health insurance policy applicants. If the applicant reports a condition that the insurer considers significant, or if the results of a required examination, blood test, or urine test raise questions for the insurer, the insurer will report that information to the MIB. MIB electronic health records consist of codes indicating a particular condition or lifestyle (such as the individual smokes cigarettes). As such, MIB does not include the totality of an individual's medical record (Privacy Rights Clearinghouse, 2007).

Another example is the Children's Hospital of Philadelphia (CHOP). CHOP is collecting DNA profiles on as many as 100,000 child patients in order to develop an anonymous database that researchers can use to study children's genetic profiles. Research results may reveal which genes underlie problems affecting children such as diabetes, obesity, asthma and cancer. This research could lead to the development of diagnostic tests and drugs. By linking genetic information to electronic health records, CHOP may obtain research funds and patents and forge partnerships with drug companies (Regalado, 2006).

Another recent development in the storage of medical information is the creation of electronic warehouses by Microsoft and Google where individuals can store their health records and make them available to health care providers. Neither company is considered a covered entity, so neither is subject to HIPAA rules (Steinkraus, 2007).

There are a number of benefits as well as disadvantages of medical databases (U.S. Department of Education, 2006). Among the benefits are:

- A patient's medical information would be immediately available to an attending doctor, including life saving information
- Researchers would be able to track certain diseases as well as patients' responses to certain drugs
- Medical databases would allow for better organization and more legibility of medical files
- Electronic health records may be more secure than paper records since security systems can monitor medical databases

Among the disadvantages of medical databases are:

- Employers may access medical information about their employees which they might use to deny employment or job advancement
- Insurers may use medical information to deny insurance to people they consider to be high risk
- Digitizing medical records will allow many more people legitimate access to medical records, with the increased possibility that the information may be misused by one or more of them

It is important to note that, in general, inaccuracies in databases are widespread and that the ability of individuals to detect these inaccuracies is limited (Straub & Collins, 1990). In addition, the problem of missing values – values accidentally not entered or purposely not obtained for technical, economic or ethical reasons – is widely encountered in medical databases since medical data are collected as a byproduct of patient care activities rather than rigorously collected and evaluated for use in research (Krzysztof & Moore, 2002). These inaccuracies and omissions only accentuate the disadvantages of medical databases.

Inaccuracies also exist in non-medical databases. It appears likely that businesses may acquire medical information that is contained in company databases as a result of acquiring these databases in the course of merger/acquisition activities. It is also likely that they may also have access to medical information in other companies' databases in the course of maintaining friendly strategic alliances with these companies. In addition, BAHPs are in a position to collect and store medical information in company databases for use in business decisions (for example, determining loan rates). As was discussed earlier, HIPAA does not prohibit the sharing of protected health information among various covered entities or their BAHPs. There are a number of security risks to medical information may come from inside a business as well as from external sources. Though a BAHP may try to safeguard an individual's medical information privacy, it may be jeopardized by a number of internal security risks such as accidental disclosures, insider curiosity, releasing medical information to outsiders for revenge, spite or profit, and uncontrolled support functions (Rindfleisch, 1997).

Government databases at the federal, state and local levels contain personal (including medical) information. The federal government maintains electronic files on hundreds of millions of Medicare claims. State governments collect and store medical data on their citizens, including registries of births, deaths, immunizations, and communicable diseases. Many states mandate collection of electronic records of every hospital discharge, and maintain registries of every newly diagnosed case of cancer. Most of these databases are available to any member of the public who asks for them and can operate the database software required to read and manipulate them (Consumer Reports, 2000).

Although many of these government database records are stripped of information which could be used to identify individuals (such as Social Security numbers), it is still possible to link the records to private sector medical records using standard codes for diagnoses and procedures employed by the United States healthcare system. The codes are usually included on insurance claims and hospital discharge records. In addition, a patient's anonymity may be compromised by the fact that personally identifiable health information is needed for a variety of research purposes (e.g. to check for duplicate records or redundant cases, and for longitudinal studies) (Electronic Privacy Information Center, 1999). Straub & Collins (1990) relate how a user can retrieve information about a specific person from large statistical databases with a small number of unsophisticated queries. As a case in point, a computer privacy researcher at Carnegie Mellon University was able to retrieve the health records of the governor of Massachusetts from an "anonymous" database of state employee health insurance claims by knowing his birth date and ZIP code. The researcher demonstrated that she could do the same for 69% of the 54,805 registered voters on the Cambridge, MA voting list (Consumer Reports, 2000).

Electronically available public records (e.g. court records) are also a source of an individual's medical information (Ogles, 2004). An individual's medical record may be entered into court documents (say, if an individual sues over

payment claims) which are available on-line. Public records also have a connection to junk mail, since state counties have sold information from public records to commercial companies that then repackage it and resell it to other companies and individuals (Leach, 2004). Junk mail in itself may not be overly troublesome to an individual. But what these companies and individuals may do with public record information in addition to creating and sending junk mail is cause for some concern.

Much personal health information that is available to the public is volunteered by individuals themselves, by responding to 800 numbers, coupon offers, rebate offers and Web site registration. The information is included in commercial databases like Behavior-Bank sponsored by Experian, one of the world's largest direct-mail database companies. This information is sold to clients interested in categories of health problems, such as bladder control or high cholesterol. Drug companies are also interested in the commercial databases (Consumer Reports, 2000). With the implementation of the National Health Information Network, this interest will be heightened as hospitals link up electronically with doctor offices' records (Landro, 2006).

BAHP often want access to medical information for data mining purposes. Data mining of medical data offers the health care industry the ability to address issues related to fraud detection and abuse, to profitability analysis, to patient profiling, and to patient retention management (Payton, 2003). However, patients are often unaware that their medical information is being used for data mining purposes, making it unlikely that patients will object to the practice. The challenge to organizations that conduct data mining with medical information is how to respond when and if patients become aware of the data mining. For some patients, the awareness will make no difference; for others, the reaction may be very negative.

MANAGEMENT CHALLENGES OF MEDICAL INFORMATION

Since companies have relatively easy access to individuals' medical information, the adequate protection of the privacy of this information must be considered an important management challenge, especially in the context of the National Health Information Network.

For healthcare-related businesses, the requirement to safeguard patients' medical information is specified by HIPAA. In their dealings with BAHP, healthcare-related businesses should create legal contracts between the business and any BAHP given access to individually identifiable medical information requiring the BAHP to safeguard the data. Ongoing internal review of data access records should be performed in order to uncover possible security violations (Saul, 2000).

For businesses in industries other than healthcare, the challenges center on how to adequately safeguard an individual's medical information acquired in mergers/acquisitions, from public records, from customer volunteers, or simply in the course of doing business (for example, hiring new employees). Though it is not required by law, businesses should attempt to respect as much as is relevant and possible the rights of individuals under the HIPAA Privacy Rule. In particular, businesses should honor individual requests to restrict the use and disclosure of medical information. It is not simply a matter of behaving ethically. Calculating the impact of a potential loss of medical information from a security breach is very difficult. Customer backlash in response to a business' failure to safeguard medical information is a very real and potentially costly possibility (e.g. a grassroots protest in the form of a boycott of a company's goods and services). Another possibility is an expensive class action lawsuit that could last a protracted period of time and result in monetary damages. Given how strongly people feel about the privacy of their medical information, either form of customer reaction could also damage the business' public reputation, especially if the reaction attracts the attention of the various news reporting agencies.

In addition, proactive managers should take the initiative in surpassing HIPAA in two important areas: use of transmission security technology, and treatment of BAHPs. In fact, the proactive manager will intentionally surpass the baseline requirements of HIPAA, thereby realizing the enhancement of individual medical privacy protection.

Use of transmission security technology. The HIPAA Security Rule (45 Code of Federal Regulations 164.103-164.318) provides security standards and implementation specifications for three kinds of safeguards (administrative, physical and technical) to protect protected health information in electronic form. It also divides the implementation specifications into required and addressable (i.e., not required but recommended). Covered entities have a certain amount of flexibility in implementing addressable specifications. In deciding which security measures to adopt, the covered entity must consider its own size, complexity and capabilities, its technical infrastructure, hardware and software security capabilities, the costs of the security measures, and the probability and criticality of potential risks to electronic protected health information. For example, covered entities may choose to adopt encryption as a technical safeguard for the transmission security standard, but since encryption is given as an addressable implementation specification, it is not required by HIPAA but simply recommended.

HIPAA is not specific as to the exact technology that should be used to implement transmission security, since technology changes and progresses in ways that are difficult to predict. The current implementation of transmission security will most likely involve the use of firewalls, user authentication, encryption/decryption, anti-virus software, and anonymizers (Cheng & Hung, 2006). These implementation choices will be replaced as newer and more effective technologies become available.

The proactive manager should actively pursue the most effective transmission security technologies available, and not simply wait for Congress to update HIPAA with respect to more effective technological requirements.

Treatment of BAHPs. Any amended HIPAA legislation should explicitly consider the role of BAHPs in safeguarding medical information privacy. For healthcare-related businesses, the requirement to safeguard patients' medical information is specified by HIPAA. This includes the following activities (Saul, 2000):

- Develop policies to evaluate and certify that appropriate security measures are in place in the business
- Create legal contracts between the business and any business associates given access to individually identifiable medical information requiring the business associates to safeguard the data
- Develop contingency plans for response to emergencies, in a data backup plan and a disaster recovery plan
- Establish a system of access control that includes policies for the authorization, establishment and modification of access privileges
- Perform ongoing internal review of data access records in order to uncover possible security violations
- Supervise systems personnel responsible for systems maintenance activities
- Train system users in system security, including user education on virus protection, monitoring login failures, password management, and how to report discrepancies or suspicious activities
- Establish termination procedures for when an employee leaves the business (voluntarily or involuntarily) or whose data access privileges are revoked

For non-healthcare-related businesses, while BAHPs are bound by HIPAA regulations that limit their use of medical information to what they need to provide their services to the contracting agency, stricter rules are needed to ensure that the information is properly disposed of after use. Though data breaches are not always caused by BAHPs, the keeping of data long after their usefulness is ended could result in a data breach affecting many innocent people. Though BAHPs may be technologically savvy in their use of National Health Information Network technology, this may not always be the case. Despite a BAHPs best intentions, data breaches may be the result of a BAHP not having the technical or procedural skills to safeguard medical information in the environment of an emerging technology. Managers must be wary of a BAHP's technical competence and demand proof that the BAHP is qualified to effectively safeguard medical information.

Lastly, management of the relationship with BAHPs becomes even more problematic when the BAHP is located outside of the United States. There is ample evidence to show that there are substantial differences among nations concerning the value of privacy and the sanctity of respecting the legal obligations to control access to information. As an example, the most recent review by the United States Trade Representative's office on the protection of intellectual property rights cites continued and excessive violations of intellectual property in many of the same countries where many BAHPs are located (Office of the United States Trade Representative, 2008). This is in spite of years of work by the World Trade Organization to protect intellectual property and very stringent rules and penalties written into all new trade agreements. Thus it would seem unlikely that simply relying on written agreements to protect medical information would be prudent. Managers are advised to be very careful in choosing companies outside of the United States for the handling of medical information. There are sources of information that can be used to assess the potential for the loss of control of medical information. International organizations, such as the World Bank, maintain websites that report on assessments of riskiness for ventures in various parts of the world (World Bank, 2008). Universities, such as Michigan State University, also maintain websites that provide information on the state of international business activities around the world (Michigan State University, 2008). Trade Associations also maintain directories of subcontractors. Managers are well advised to visit all such sources of data before entering into a relationship with a firm outside the United States.

CONCLUSION

Given the potential for mishandling medical information acquired in the course of doing business, management must exercise vigilance in the safeguarding of this information. Though many businesses are not typically interested in acquiring and dealing with medical information, the possible negative consequences of mishandling medical information that is acquired from various sources cannot be ignored. This basic reality will only become magnified once the National Health Information Network is implemented, making it technologically possible to inadvertently disseminate medical information nationally as well as internationally. Companies whose employees act as BAHP in various capacities must be particularly vigilant to ensure the integrity of individuals' medical information. Management must move to preempt negative consequences before serious damage to the reputation of the business occurs as a result of BAHP mishandling medical information.

This work was previously published in International Journal of E-Business Research (IJEBR), edited by In Lee, pp. 48-62, copyright 2009 by IGI Publishing (an imprint of IGI Global).

REFERENCES

Cate, F. H. (1997). *Privacy in the information age.* Washington, D.C.: Brookings Institution Press.

Computer World. (2007). www.computerworld.com/action/article.do?command=viewArticleBasic&articleId=9014782; retrievedMarch26, 2008

Computer World. (2008). www.computerworld.com/action/article.do?command=viewArticleBasic&articleId=9070281&taxonomyId=148&intscr=kc_top; retrieved March 26, 2008

Electronic Frontier Foundation. (1993). www.eff.org/Privacy/Medical/1993_ota_medical_privacy.report; retrieved June 8, 2006.

Electronic Privacy Information Center. (1999). www.epic.org/privacy/medical/GAO-medical-privacy-399.pdf; retrieved May 17, 2006.

Electronic Privacy Information Center. (2006). www.epic.org/privacy/medical/polls.html; retrieved April 17, 2006.

Electronic Privacy Information Center. (2008). www.epic.org/privacy/medical; retrieved October 16, 2008.

Federal Register, 2002, 2003. (2006). www.archives.gov/federal-register/index.html retrieved June 10, 2006.

Ferris, N. (2008). Foreign hackers seek to steal American's health records. www.fcw.com/online/news/151334-1.html: etrieved February 4, 2008.

Institute of Medicine. (2001). *Crossing the quality chasm: A new health system for the 21st century.* Washington, D.C.: National Academy Press.

Kaushal, R., Blumenthal, D., Poon, E. G., Ashish, K. J., Franz, C., Middleton, B., et al., & the Cost of National Health Information Network Working Group. (2005). The costs of a national health information network. www.annals.org/cgi/reprint/143/3/165.pdf: retrieved February 4, 2008.

Kilman, D. G., & Forslund, D. W. (1997). An international collaboratory based on virtual patient records. *Communications of the ACM, 40*(8), 111–117. doi:10.1145/257874.257898

King, W. R., & Epstein, B. J. (1976). Assessing the value of information. *Management Datamatics, 5*(4), 171–180.

Koontz, L. D., & Melvin, V. C. (2007). Efforts continue but comprehensive privacy approach needed for national strategy. Testimony before the Subcommittee on Information Privacy, Census, and National Archive Committee on Oversight and Government Reform of the U.S. House of Representatives. www.gao.gov/new.items/d07988t.pdf: retrieved June 28, 2007.

Krzysztof, J. C., & Moore, J. C. (2002). Uniqueness of medical data mining. *Artificial Intelligence in Medicine, 26*(1/2), 1–24.

Landro, L. (2006). What drugs do you take? Hospitals seek to collect better data and prevent errors. *The Wall Street Journal.* May 23, D1.

Lawton, C., & Worthen, B. (2008). Google to offer health records on the web. *Wall Street Journal.* January 28, D1f.

Leach, S. L. (2004). Privacy lost with the touch of a keystroke? www.csmonitor.com/2004/1110/p15s02-stin.html: retrieved March 23, 2005.

Michigan State University. (2008). globalEDGE. msu.edu.

Office of Technology Assessment. (1993). Protecting privacy in computerized medical information. www.wws.princeton.edu/ota/disk1/1993/9342/9342.pdf: retrieved August 6, 2006.

Office of the United States Trade Representative. (2008). www.ustr.gov/assets/capitaldocument_Library/Reports_Publications/2008/2008_Special_301_Report; retrieved June 21, 2008.

Ogles, J. (2004). Court documents not fit for Web? www.wired.com/news/privacy/0,1848,65703,00.html; retrieved February 7, 2005.

Payton, F. C. (2003). Data mining in health care applications. In Wang, J. (Ed.), *Data mining: Opportunities and challenges* (pp. 350–365). Hershey: Idea Group Inc.

Privacy Rights Clearinghouse. (2007). www.privacyrights.org/fs/fs8a-hipaa.htm; retrieved June 16, 2006.

Regalado, A. (2006). Plan to build children's DNA database raises concerns. *The Wall Street Journal.* June 7, B1f.

Reports, C. (2000). Who knows your medical secrets? *Consumer Reports,* (August): 22–26.

Reports, C. (2006). The new threat to your medical privacy. *Consumer Reports,* (March): 39–42.

Rindfleisch, T. C. (1997). Privacy, information technology, and health care. *Communications of the ACM, 40*(8), 93–100. doi:10.1145/257874.257896

Rishel, W., Riehl, V., & Blanton, C. (2007). Summary of the NHIN prototype architecture contracts. www.hhs.gov/healthit/healthnetwork/resources/summary_report_on_nhin_Prototype_architectures.pdf: retrieved August 14, 2007.

Rubenstein, S. (2005). Next step toward digitized health records. *The Wall Street Journal.* May 9, B1f.

Saul, J. M. (2000). Legal policy and security issues in the handling of medical data. In Cios, K.J. (Ed.), *Medical data mining and knowledge discovery.* Heidelberg: Spring-Verlag, 17-31.

Steinkraus, D. (2007). Whose records? Does medical privacy law hinder privacy? www.journaltimes.com/articles/2007/11/14/life/doc-47372faec1ca6741856824.txt: retrieved December 7, 2007.

Straub, D. W., & Collins, R. W. (1990). Key information liability issues facing managers: Software piracy, proprietary databases, and individual rights to privacy. *Management Information Systems Quarterly*, (June): 143–156. doi:10.2307/248772

Szewczak, E. J. (2007). The national health information network and the future of medical information privacy. *Communications of the International Information Management Association*, *6*(4), 33–46.

Szewczak, E. J. (2009). E-technology challenges to information privacy. In Khosrow-pour, M. (Ed.), *Encyclopedia of information science and technology* (2nd ed., pp. 1438–1442). Hershey, PA: Idea Group, Inc.

U.S. Department of Education. (2006). www.lbl.gov/Education/ELSI/privacy-main.html; retrieved April 26, 2006.

Washington Post. (2005). www.washingtonpost.com/wp-dyn/articles/A45756-2005Apr12.html; retrieved March 26, 2008. The White House, www.whitehouse.gov/news/releases/2004/01/20040120-7.html; retrieved June 3, 2006

Westin, A. F. (1967). *Privacy and freedom*. New York: Atheneum.

Wilson, J. F. (2006). Health insurance portability and accountability act privacy rule causes ongoing concerns among clinicians and researchers. *Annals of Internal Medicine*, *145*(4), 313–316.

World Bank. (2008). www.worldbank.org.

This work was previously published in International Journal of E-Business Research (IJEBR), Volume 5, Issue 2, edited by In Lee, pp. 48-62, copyright 2009 by IGI Publishing (an imprint of IGI Global).

Chapter 10
Privacy Compliance Checking using a Model–Based Approach

Siani Pearson
Hewlett Packard Research Labs, UK

Damien Allison
Imagini Europe Limited, UK

ABSTRACT

Organisations are under pressure to be compliant to a range of privacy legislation, policies and best practice. At the same time many firms are using privacy as a key differentiator. There is a clear need for high-level management and administrators to be able to assess in a dynamic, customisable way the degree to which their enterprise complies with these. We outline a solution to this problem in the form of a model-driven automated privacy process analysis and configuration checking system. This system models privacy compliance constraints, automates the assessment of the extent to which a particular computing environment is compliant and generates dashboard-style reports that highlight policy failures. We have developed a prototype that provides this functionality in the context of governance audit; this includes the development of software agents to gather information on-the-fly regarding selected privacy enhancing technologies and other aspects of enterprise system configuration. This approach may also be tailored to enhance the assurance provided by existing governance tools, and to provide increased feedback to end users about the degree of privacy and security compliance that service providers are actually providing.

INTRODUCTION

In order to conduct business, organizations must try to assess and ensure compliance with privacy legislation, policies and regulations, as part of their IT governance initiatives. As well as these

DOI: 10.4018/978-1-60960-132-4.ch010

'data protection' concerns, there may be an intangible value in proposing an 'open' approach to privacy compliance, for example by showing all privacy-relevant information as is done within the Google dashboard (Google, 2009). Such privacy management is an important issue for e-business organizations since e-business can be defined as "the utilization of information and communica-

Copyright © 2011, IGI Global. Copying or distributing in print or electronic forms without written permission of IGI Global is prohibited.

tions technologies (ICT) in support of all the activities of business" (Wikipedia, 2010). This issue involves both operational aspects, related to the enforcement of privacy policies, and compliance aspects related to checking for compliance of these policies to expected business processes and their deployment into the enterprise IT infrastructures. A 'web of trust' may also be involved in order to determine when to share personal and sensitive information: for example, credit card details.

The Need for Automation

We address the problem of how to make privacy management more effective by introducing more technology and automation into the operation of privacy in e-business organizations. Enterprises are coming under increasing pressure to improve privacy management, both to satisfy customers and to comply with external regulation (Laurant, 2003) or internal policies. An alternative approach is to rely on the users 'voting with their feet', in the sense of using a company that they trust because they are familiar with it, but nevertheless this company still needs to be legally compliant. Not only are human processes prone to failure but the scale of the problem highlights the desire for additional technology to be part of the solution. The trend towards complexity and dynamism in system configurations heightens this need for automation to ensure that privacy and security properties are maintained as changes occur, and in addition to check that the privacy enhancing technologies are operating as desired (including 'always on' controls).

Automated Compliance Checking Requirements

Most of the technical work done in this space focuses on the provision of auditing and reporting solutions that analyse logged events and check them against privacy policies and process guidelines. These auditing systems usually operate at a low level of abstraction and do not take into account the overall compliance management process that involves both the refinement of privacy laws and guidelines within enterprise contexts, their mapping into the enterprise IT infrastructure and their subsequent checking against the enterprise's operational behaviour. 'Unit level' business model invariant solutions such as (Goossenaerts, 2009) rely on this type of approach without modelling higher level dependencies on low level issues.

At present there is a gap between the definition of high-level regulations, standards and best practices and what is actually happening in an enterprise at the level of application software, system software and middleware, processors, networks and data stores. The current approach is generally to fill this gap using people-based processes, but there are drawbacks to this, in terms of being slow, expensive, error-prone and leading to best-effort compliance due to limited resources. Our vision is to bridge this gap where possible with model-based technology and automation, as shown in Figure 1. On the one hand privacy policy enforcement technologies can be used to deliver compliance to privacy principles and goals; on the other hand (the focus of this chapter) we can use system monitoring technologies to continuously assess their actual performance and ability to deliver against the requirements of the policy. The key to this approach is to capture the tacit relations between low level signals and indicators and high level goals.

Our Approach

To address this problem we are developing a Policy Compliance Checking System. Key requirements of this system are to:

R1. *model privacy policies (based on company privacy policies, laws and guidelines or best practice).* A mechanism is needed that enables such models to be defined and viewed.

Figure 1. Model-based, policy-driven IT

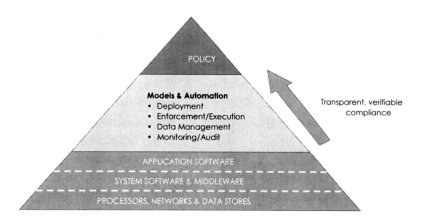

Predefined models should also be usable, and amendable by expert users if desired.

R2. *map these models at the IT level.* It is necessary to configure the models to the deployed system.

R3. *analyze related events.* The compliance checking system needs to monitor those properties of the deployed system that can affect satisfaction of the privacy policies.

R4. *generate meaningful reports highlighting compliance aspects and violations.* These reports should be understandable to non-experts, and allow drilling down to a greater level of detail.

One key advantage of an agent-based approach is that it does not rely on the application 'behaving', which could be a potential gain in the face of a security breach. The agent-based approach does not preclude the use of invariant-based assertions that are hard coded into the business model but it rather enhances their use as well as the confidence in their usefulness as indicators of compliance.

This system should supervise and report on the availability of other privacy enhancing technologies (PETs) – for example, privacy policy enforcement systems, obligation management systems and security technologies – and check for inconsistencies on enforced policies in real time, by comparing information coming from different sources.

For example, a privacy related goal an organisation could wish to attain is that personal data is only used for the purposes for which it was collected. This corresponds to a core privacy guideline (Information Commissioner's Office, 2007). A model may be built up which shows how this goal can be satisfied if a logical combination of subgoals may be satisfied. For instance, this goal can be partially satisfied by the subgoal that the organisation uses a technological control that enforces role-based access to data, where roles are associated with processes like marketing or customer support and a check is made such that the data can only be accessed if such processes are included in the allowed purpose of usage for the data but other related properties could also be crucial to the assertion that this property is a meaningful signal. There are numerous such invariant for key signals including system configuration. In addition, the system should check that the control is configured correctly, the control is available, the control has not been subverted and there is proper separation of the duties defined for specific roles. So, the goals are mapped to the IT level by means of real time monitoring and an implied 'chain of trust'. In addition to instrumentation and monitoring of the status of the data warehouse to ensure that the data is not accessed in a 'back door' way, by checking system updates, security software, firewall policies, system access and system processes, rootkit presence and indicators of potential system compromise such as process crashes or security logging.. it would be preferable to instrument the data client to ensure that it is following best practice policies (with respect to virus, passwords, user access, etc.).

To enhance the decision capability, further sub-checks might include for example how the access lists are controlled, who authorises the lists and what training they are given before they enter a username and password. If this technological control were not in place, an alternative method of satisfying the initial goal would be to check process, auditing logs and so on, but this can be very difficult to automate but the manual overrides should be cognisant rather than tacit

POLICY COMPLIANCE CHECKING SYSTEM

This work addresses the problem of explicitly assessing compliance of privacy policies; a similar approach applies to best practice guidelines, legislation and risk analysis. Our system verifies whether the data processing system is strong enough to automatically execute the privacy policies reliably: this involves assessment of the deployment of PETs and the underlying trust, security and IT infrastructure. We aim to allow organizations to check the trustworthiness of their system components, as well as those of their business partners to whom they may transfer personal data. For example, a service may be considered trustworthy if it has been accredited by an independent privacy inspector, (such as BBBOnLine or TRUSTe) (Cavoukian & Crompton, 2000), or a platform may be considered trustworthy if it is judged to be in a trusted state and is compliant with standards produced by the Trusted Computing Group (TCG) (2003).

Overview

This chapter describes the system we have developed to allow an organization to assess their policy compliance using a collection of information describing the organizations' resources. Our system will allow the description of a model defining the goals associated with satisfying its policy constraints. Our system can then monitor the organizational resources to verify that the goals described are being satisfied. The specific high level policy models may be templated for specific legislation which can then be analyzed locally and instrumented in specific properties of the modeled system.

With the aim of automating privacy process analysis and configuration checking for enterprises, we use functional decomposition of risks or policies defined by experts up-front, as shown in Figure 2, and then subsequently use this model to dynamically assess systems and generate reports, whenever required.

The system is intended to be used in the following way: first of all, predefined policy substructures would be input into our editing tool (shown below in Figure 4) by a privacy expert to form a generic privacy model (this only needs doing once, but can be updated subsequently). For each specific enterprise system on which the compliance checker is to be run, a privacy specialist and/or specialised administrator would tune the constraints and deploy the system. Next, agents would be deployed to resources based on information given in the model, and would gather information over a selected time period. Whenever desired, analysis could be triggered and a corresponding report generated (an example is shown below in Figure 5).

Our approach is novel: at the core the compliance checking system works by allowing a policy agent to identify key performance indicators of the live system that reflect attributes associated with goals. The system then monitors and reports in a real-time dashboard. The metrics used

Figure 2. Overview of the system

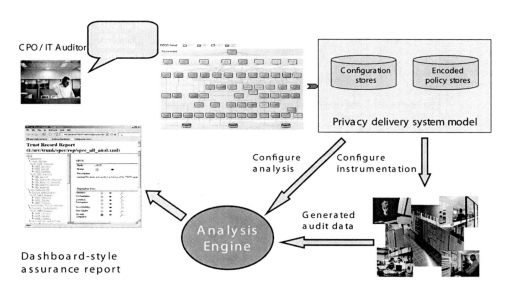

Figure 3. System architecture

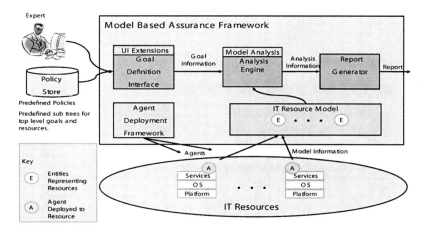

are often available in other domains, but have not before been pulled into one place for this purpose; they give the ability to instrument the lowest level checks. Furthermore, we use logical implication to aid policy modelers in investigating and stating what 'compliance' looks like.

Privacy Assurance Models

In order to automate privacy compliance the system assesses the extent to which IT controls (in-

cluding PETs such as privacy policy enforcement and obligation management systems) satisfy key privacy principles or goals. To do this the system uses a model that allows recursive decomposition of top-level properties down to specific requirements that technology can analyse, enforce and report on. We have already considered above an example of such technological control influence on a high level goal.

In general, there can be a many-many mapping between the goals and subgoals: for example,

Figure 4. Example privacy graph

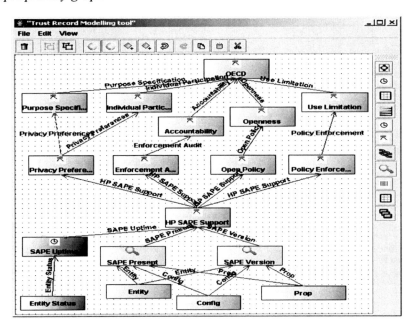

Figure 5. Example compliance report

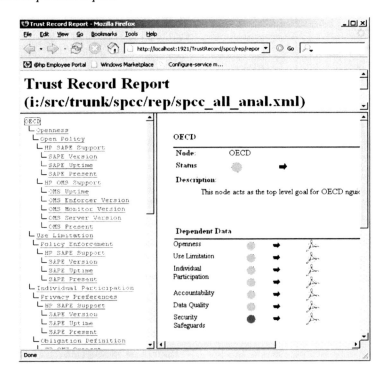

it may be necessary to satisfy a combination of subgoals in order to satisfy a higher level goal. At the same time, general subgoals associated with aspects of the system that influence it more widely may affect many supergoals.

The top-level goals can be, as desired, high level specification of privacy principles as suggested for example by Organisation for Economic Co-operation and Development (OECD) (1980) or APEC (Greenleaf, 2005), regulation such as European Directive 95/46/EC on the protection of personal data (European Parliament and Council, 1995) or even specific country legislation.

Implemented Models

In most of the models we have developed so far, the OECD (1980) principles for fair information usage are taken as the top layer within the model; there is an intermediate layer of information analysis nodes and a lower layer of technological input. The lowest layer assesses information provided by agents, as described further below, including the configuration, presence and availability of PETs, and other IT controls, and the degree of evidence provided for security and privacy technologies. Part of such a model will be discussed in detail in a later section and is displayed, via our tool model editing interface, in Figure 4.

The lower level checks performed on the system will be composed of a mixture of checking for specific technology availability and its configuration. For example, corresponding to Figure 1 the specific low level checks we specified and implemented include the following different kinds of check:

1. The organisation has a privacy seal.
   a. Presence of privacy seals for the back end system.
   b. Validity of privacy seals for the back end system.
2. Organisation key service host computers are secure.

   a. Key organisational services are patched up to the required level.
3. Organisation supports obligation management.
   a. Organisation has support for obligation management via known adequate systems.
   b. Systems version numbers are up to date.
   c. Systems are available at least a given percentage of the time.
4. Organisation supports role based data access.
   a. Organisation has support for role based data access via known adequate systems.
   b. System version numbers are up to date.
   c. Systems are available at least a given percentage of the time.
5. Organisation uses trusted hardware to enhance the security of key service hosts.
   a. Organisation trusted hardware is of sufficient version and produced by a reputable company.
   b. Organisation trusted hardware self test revealed no errors.
6. Key organisation services and resources operate in a safe environment.
   a. Key service hosts have trusted hardware installed.
   b. Key service hosts have adequate virus recognition in place.
   c. Key service hosts have properly configured firewall facilities.

Option to Focus on Specific Privacy Enhancing Technologies

Developing a comprehensive model is extremely complex, and so in many cases it makes sense to focus on specific privacy enhancing technologies and to be able to model the extent to which they contribute towards best practice, where the gaps remain, and whether they are deployed and operating correctly. For example, let us consider just two such technologies – privacy-enhanced access control (PAC), which puts a wrapper around "traditional" role-based access control, adding consideration of: the stated purpose to collect and hold personal information; data requestor's intent; data subject's consent details (Casassa Mont & Thyne, 2006) and a backend obligation management system (OMS), which provides a framework for monitoring, scheduling and enforcing responsibilities and duties related to personal information (Casassa Mont, 2005). The accountability provided by these technological controls with respect to the OECD principles would need to take account of the following:

- **Openness** Both PAC and OMS systems can contribute to this goal. Both systems provide a provisioning point for policy collection. As well as collection though, they also support the review and modification of those policies.
- **Use Limitation** PAC provides strong justification for use limitation as it allows the user to specify constraints on the usage of data by different roles. OMS also provides a weaker justification for use limitation as it can impose data retention restrictions on the organisation.
- **Individual Participation** The combination of PAC and OMS, as with openness, can provide justification for this goal as they provide participation from the user in the different areas of access and obligations.
- **Purpose Specification** PAC provides very strong justification for this goal as it defines a clear interface and enforcement of purpose specification.
- **Security Safeguards** Neither PAC or OMS provide any real justification for security safeguards. Other means must be used for the justification of this goal.
- **Accountability** PAC can support accountability by allowing an audit of the restrictions imposed by the data enforcer. PAC also supports logging of changes to policies.

- **Data Quality** OMS can provide some support for data quality through the use of notification of the user on data updates and active monitoring of obligation policies.
- **Collection Limitation** Neither PAC or OMS can be used to justify goals associated with this goal. Checking of collection limitation often requires an assessment process. There are possible ways that automated checks could be included but they could not, on their own provide comprehensive justification.

Model Specification

To make the analysis of the large set of fine grained information to be gathered from multiple heterogeneous sources, a comprehensive model needs to be developed. The model is flexible enough to encompass log or audit style information that is already generated by a number of products with a fine grained model of the configuration of resources. The modelling of resource configuration, in combination with the real time monitoring of the status of resources, allows a rich definition of the enterprise environment to be reasoned about.

In order to represent our assurance models we investigated two main types of approach: graphical notation and using the SmartFrog approach (an object oriented notation allowing representation of sets of attributes and values) (Hinde, 2005). In both cases there is an acyclic graph structure that links selected graph nodes, each of which has a type of information being modelled and a node-specific description of the desired state. This description can include properties such as controls, indicators, policies or the way system information should be processed. Information sources required for checking the state and the form of the output (resulting from matching the node description to the input) are defined for each node. The validity of the graph structure is checked using these inputs and outputs.

Our current approach to modelling is based upon a graphical modelling tool that has been developed. This tool allows the structure of the model to be created as a graph from low-level data source nodes being connected upwards to nodes representing high-level privacy concerns about the treatment of data. A Graphical User Interface (GUI) is used to permit different types of nodes and submodels to be placed in this graph. An initial set of node types allow various indicator statistics to be specified, along with policy combinations and control process definitions. Additional node types may be defined via extending the tool. The node inputs and outputs are described in terms of either a set of attribute value pairs or else columns, to give a better fit to a centralised enterprise database. The resultant model produced by the tool is in the form of an eXtensible Markup Language (XML) structure (XML, 2010) which can be input to the analysis engine, although it could be fairly easily modified to produce a model in the Smart Frog notation.

System Architecture

The architecture of our prototype system is shown in Figure 3. A full working prototype, based on this architecture, has been implemented.

The main components of the architecture can be described as follows:

1. **UI Extensions:** This part of the system allows the construction of constraints over the set of resources present in the organization. This allows the modeling of privacy policies (satisfying requirement R1).
2. **Model Analysis:** This part allows the constraints defined in the goal definition interface to be applied to the model of the organization's key resources. The analysis engine populates the measured system with the relevant agents to collect the information needed, which is then collected at the analysis/backend of the system. The reasoning engine continuously monitors the state of the 'measured environment' against the states

modeled. The top level goals are defined as a logical combination in order to specify the model and determine how to represent the effect in the dashboard. The analysis satisfies requirement R3 (analyzing relevant events).

3. **Agent Deployment Framework:** The agent framework is used to deploy software agents to the platforms' hosting resources that can monitor the events and configuration of the resources. The agents then map this information into the model of resources, thus helping satisfy requirement R3.
4. **IT Resource Model**: This provides a single model of the organization's IT resources. The model includes events captured from the resources, including from log files, and configuration information describing, for example, the setup of a host platform and runtime state. This is needed to satisfy R2 (the mapping of privacy models to IT infrastructure).
5. **Report Generator:** This generates reports, satisfying R4.

The architecture of the system is targeted at:

-   Allowing the maximum flexibility of the resources that can be modeled. This is achieved by using agents to map information into a standardized form that can be processed more easily by the analysis part of the system.
-   Avoiding the need to redevelop legacy systems to generate data – this can be achieved by using agents for data generation and sensing.
-   Providing a single information format that is used to record information; this is mapped into by the agents or other sources.
-   Providing an extensible framework for agent development.
-   Generic analysis allowing the formation of complex queries over resource properties.

As shown in Figures 2 and 3, this system examines distributed system configurations using an agent infrastructure deployed across IT resources, feeds the findings into a reasoning engine and reports the resulting findings in a tree-like structure that can be 'drilled down' to the level of detail required. It uses functional decomposition to model privacy and model-based reasoning to carry out the analysis and generate reports. More specifically, modeling of privacy goals is combined with modeling of organizational resources and the processes around these resources. If desired, semantic web technology can be used to create a common understanding of lower level checks that are carried out, but this is unnecessary if the compliance checking is for internal organizational purposes only.

In our implementation the privacy models are represented in an XML format and the analysis involves Java and SQL queries. The modelling of organisational resources is achieved using a set of agents deployed through a RMI deployment framework to monitor resources in real time. The locality of entities is defined in terms of a Uniform Resource Identifier (URI) that defines the deployment location for an agent allocated to monitor an entity. Although our implementation used a relatively simple RMI framework, as mentioned above a more advanced agent framework like Smart Frog (Hinde, 2005), could be deployed: such automated monitoring frameworks allow monitoring of complex and dynamic systems.

In order to avoid the approach consuming too much time so that the running applications in the environment will be affected, the granularity of the measurement of the state of the environment can be tailored: for each case a 'reasonable' polling interval could be proposed or eventing system introduced. The model once defined in the backend analysis system is 'efficient' as it is expressed as a database query, which is run on changes registered to the environment. For platforms that provide notification or events they can be utilised, e.g. FAM (File alteration monitor) or database events.

Agent Infrastructure

Once the privacy expert has defined the model, the compliance checking system identifies the resource properties that have to be monitored for satisfaction of the policy constraints in the model. Given a model of how the policy will be satisfied, the system deploys a collection of software agents to monitor specific properties of the enterprise system. The agents also perform data normalisation of the PET and system properties prior to analysis.

Once an agent has been deployed to the platform on which it is to monitor a given type of entity it uses the platform and information passed to it when it was created to monitor the entity at that location. In this way, a host's agent is deployed to every instance of entities of the type host stored in the entity model. The agent, having been deployed, can then monitor the properties of the entity it is monitoring and update the model of the entity.

Agents deployed in this way to monitor organisational resources that we implemented include:

1. **Host agent.** This provides patch information and other information about the host entities described in the model, as input to analyse the integrity of the host systems which support key organisational services.
2. **PET status agent.** Each monitors the activity of a particular PET application (for example, its execution time).
3. **PET configuration agent.** Each monitors the configuration of a particular PET entity instance (for example, its presence, version number, etc.)
4. **Trusted Platform Module (TPM) agent.** This monitors the status and configuration of trusted hardware devices used in key resource hosts (for example, information associated with the vendor and status of a TPM).

5. **Certificate agent.** This monitors the organisation's certificates to assess whether they are current and valid.

6. **Privacy seal agent.** This monitors the status of the privacy seal certification to check that it is valid. The checking of the privacy seal validity may involve submitting a HTTP request to the Certification Authority (CA) to verify its integrity, and checking of the CA against a predefined list of CAs trusted by the user or administrator of the Compliance Checking System.

This approach is flexible, in that agents are relatively generic: if for example one was used for reading a specific log file, it could be used on other similar log files (with different recognition patterns). It would be possible to reuse agents as the set of developed agents became more extensive. The actual number of possible agent types is not limited.

SPCC Organization Representation Model

Following the convention of object representations of entities (i.e. specific resources), the database schema to hold the model of the organization's resources mirrors the object model used to represent the resources.

The database schema storing the model of the organizational resources uses the following schema:

```
Entity(entity_id, name, type, info,
platform) PRIMARY KEY entity_id;
Config(config_id, eid, presence,
time) PRIMARY KEY config_id FOREIGN
KEY entity_id REFERENCES Entity.en-
tity_id;
Prop(prop_id, config_id, name, value)
PRIMARY KEY prop_id FOREIGN key con-
fig_id REFERENCES Config.config_id;
StatusEvents(status_event_id, en-
```

```
tity_id, status, time) PRIMARY KEY
status_event_id FOREIGN KEY entity_id
REFERENCES Entity.entity_id;
```

1. **Entity** The entity table holds information on each entity in the organization that is to be modeled.

2. **Config** The configuration table holds the configuration of entities described in the entity table. Configurations are stored for an entity and are relatively permanent. Example configuration details include operating system version number, virus recognition version number or TPM version/vendor.

3. **Prop** The prop table stores specific properties of configurations.

Using this association of entities with configurations and status-events allows the description of the properties of a specific resource to be arbitrarily large.

Interacting with the System

Figure 4 shows an example of the tool we developed to enable definition, input and customization of models that refine and transform privacy policies from high level statements to something that can be executed automatically at a lower level. In order to input the model, complete or partial graphs may be loaded. In addition, new nodes can be created via the buttons shown in the right hand side, each of which creates a different type of analysis node, and connections can be added via dragging and dropping arrow markers on the sides of the nodes. In order to configure these nodes, double-clicking on the nodes reveals windows appropriate to that type of node whose default settings can be changed. The models may be saved and/or exported for external usage.

Models can be created either in respect to a particular e-business process, or that incorporate multiple e-business processes in the same model, as desired. The model shown in Figure 4 focuses on assessing the deployment of a particular privacy policy enforcement system which is targeted at allowing both user preferences and enterprise policies to be taken into account when allowing access to personal information for a given purpose (blinded reference). We also developed other models, including analysis of a range of privacy and security-related IT controls and assurance information.

Figure 4 shows various types of agent that produce data that can populate a node in the graphical submodel; other 'logical' nodes can be used to combine measured states or other derived type node (inputs could also be mixed). In the prototype a minimal set of logical operations were available (not, or, and, in, etc). The model for the particular graphical substructure shown in Figure 4 includes analysis of the extent to which a particular technology for privacy policy enforcement can contribute strongly towards satisfaction of use limitation and purpose specification and to a limited extent also to openness, individual participation and accountability. The justification for this is very similar to that already given in a previous section. There is no contribution to other OECD goals that form the top level of our extended privacy compliance model. Each of these goals is shown in a box in the top part of Figure 4. Below these, subgoals can be defined, also in boxes, that can combine logically to satisfy these higher level goals, and where this is the case a link will be shown connecting the subgoal to the higher level goal. There can be multiple subgoals, but in Figure 4 only the part of the model structure is shown that relates to Select Access Privacy Enforcement (SAPE), which is a product that provides privacy-enhanced access control (PAC) (Casassa Mont & Thyne, 2006). Lower level boxes in the model shown are of different types, in that they correspond to modeling at the IT level the presence, version and availability of the product. This figure is an illustration of the general procedure, as it shows just part of the more complex model that we used.

A key role is played by the privacy expert(s) who is in charge of creating models. This expert must have knowledge of privacy laws; understand relevant enterprise processes, solutions and systems; author models describing the expected behavior. It is unlikely that one person can have all this knowledge, especially in complex scenarios such as enterprises. More realistically we are looking at teams of people whose complementary knowledge can cover these aspects. In an enterprise context we believe that "auditing teams" satisfy these requirements. The model graph need not be constructed each time by experts, because it is possible to use 'predefined' parts of the system that can then be instantiated with configuration. Nevertheless, a new type of skill is needed to understand how to instrument properties of the model in the system.

Figure 5 shows an example of the compliance report generated by our system using the model shown in Figure 4. This report is targeted at company executives, managers and auditors in order to provide information in a transparent way that can highlight areas that are a privacy concern in a dynamic and accountable way, and allow drilling down if desired to obtain further levels of detail.

The report can indicate areas of concern, as well as showing the extent to which these problems affect higher-level privacy goals. In Figure 5, there is a security vulnerability but this particular problem is not judged to affect overall privacy compliance to a great extent.

Current Status

The Policy Compliance Checking System described in this chapter is currently available as a prototype. There are a number of technical issues that would need to be addressed before this approach could be deployed, but the prototype presented does show our general methodology. The tool provides an (unchecked) high level reasoning framework that allows 'experts' to model the properties of a compliant system. Having the model means that it can at least be contested or 'approved' approaches may be suggested. The model then allows low level properties to be described and instantiated in the network. The model is in effect 'executed'. Changes in state are recorded in the backend. The model, when running is then evented on and changes reflected in the dashboard to register non-compliance. This does not have some of the properties that would be desirable in a productized version, for example a more reliable guaranteed agent communication mechanism, firewall traversal and encrypted communication using keys set up 'by hand' when the agent was installed and the system was considered to be in a secure initialization state. Instead, we focused our effort on trying to understand the usage of the interface to build our models. We are currently refining our modeling to reflect real-world scenarios, privacy regulation and best practice technologies.

For more detail about the prototype system design, see (Allison, 2005).

USAGE SCENARIOS

Our approach enables various usage cases that are centered around enterprise compliance with corporate governance legislation – such as Sarbanes-Oxley (SOX) and Health Insurance Portability and Accountability Act (HIPAA), enterprise policies and privacy legislation. It allows enterprises to determine whether system configurations or processes do actually conform to their assertions about privacy-respecting safeguards. This not only has an application in the auditing arena, but could also be used as a privacy expert system highlighting areas for improvement. Furthermore, there are certification service opportunities for development of the model and component substructures, agents and analysed systems, and opportunities for semi-automation of the provision of privacy seal or best practice certificates.

In addition, our solution could be adapted to increase user trust and willingness to engage in e-commerce. For example:

- Giving consumers the ability to determine whether unknown vendors on the Web are using IT systems and processes that can be trusted to execute their stated privacy policies.
- Automation of privacy assessment of the service side can be conveyed to the user in an open way (i.e. the compliance reports can be accessible to public) and with much more of a focus on evidence rather than having to rely on self-certification.

Overall, there can be seen to be two main benefits of our approach for enterprises. The first relates to the formalization of privacy models. Currently, documentation of compliance approval processes (especially privacy seals) is a manual process which is aided by intuition and tacit knowledge. Even without the monitoring aspects of our solution, this process of decomposing privacy satisfaction is extremely powerful and can have value for business, for example in allowing links to be made across different audits or in aiding consolidation of information during a merger.

There is additional business value using an approach like ours because it allows justifications to be audited rather than just the IT infrastructure, and furthermore allows assessment to be much more continuous and responsive to change. Combining this huge increase in functionality with automated analysis can save vast amounts of time and monitoring effort for large enterprises.

RELATED WORK

Our goal is to provide an automated policy compliance checking system that can include checks about trust and assurance properties and that takes into account changing information, including at the IT resource level. Our compliance checker is based upon a model-based assurance framework that provides generic assurance modeling and analysis; furthermore, it is focused on privacy and can model organizational resources and reason about system and application properties. We are not aware of products or solutions providing this type of model-driven assurance and compliance verification.

There has been a great deal of work done on defining privacy polices: policy specification, modeling and verification tools include EPAL (Ashley et al, 2003), OASIS XACML (2005), W3C P3P (Cranor, 2002), Datalog with constraints (Li & Mitchell, 2003) and Ponder (Damianou *et al*, 2001). In these policy frameworks the focus has been on access control based on conditional logic. The high-level goals associated with the upper levels of nodes in our models are not this kind of policy, and it is not appropriate to process them against some rule set to produce a decision on whether data should be released. Rather, they correspond to goals within a control framework: descriptions of desired privacy features, corresponding IT controls and possible implementations and configurations of these. The model itself would be the subject for agreement by a privacy or audit expert as to its validity, rather than something which is in itself automatically provable. The approach presented here is intended as an aid to locating gaps in compliance and potentially also to highlighting operational privacy problems; it would not be comprehensive, or fully automatable, or suitable to be the subject of formal method-type proofs. What the model does do is to drive the subsequent analysis and reporting, as described above.

P3P specifications (Cranor, 2002) allow people to describe their privacy expectations and match them against the level of privacy supported by an enterprise. This helps shape people's trust in enterprises. However, P3P only checks if their expectations are matched against promises made by the enterprise, and does not provide mechanisms to check and prove upfront compliance

with fine-grained constraints. As is the case with privacy seals, P3P cannot link the privacy practices expressed by the website and anything tangible on the back-end.

Our solution can actually be used to fill this gap, in that it is capable of providing assurances that are missing from the P3P model. That is to say, as already discussed in the usage scenarios section, the system described can be used internally within an organization to assess internal compliance, but could potentially as well be used to advertise that compliance to other parties as part of an assurance provision process. For example, it can be used to enhance the compliance checking system aimed at giving users control over compliance checking of organisations that they wish to interact with that is implemented as a subpart of the PRIME system (PRIME, 2008). More specifically, Elahi and Pearson (2007) describe a related approach to privacy compliance checking that is designed to enable EU citizens to scrutinize the stated claims of a service provider on safeguarding PII by interrogating their infrastructure. End users are provided with means to communicate their privacy concerns in a common language understood by the service provider, allowing them to set baseline privacy practices for service providers to adhere to, and providing a means of retrieving information from the service provider in this common language to base their PII release decisions. This approach uses pre-defined natural language clauses to simplify the definition of user policies: a previous approach that used a more complex ontological-based policy representation was proposed in (Pearson, 2006). Once the end user divulges their information we want them to be able to check that the service provider continues to adhere to their privacy practices. We can use the approach described in this chapter to provide a persistent service that monitors the end user's information and checks that the privacy practices are still in place. So with these two approaches working in concert, they can provide stronger evidence that the service provider is honoring its promises. We also integrated this approach with obligation management and trust management to further empower the user and enforce user preferences on the back end (Elahi & Pearson, 2007).

Although P3P has its limitations, its strength as a robust policy definition language and logic model allows it to translate complex privacy clauses into machine readable form. In fact, P3P's strengths could benefit our solution and could be incorporated as the gateway between human readable clauses and service provider result databases and back end models.

Projects like Privacy Bird (Cranor, 2003) from AT&T and Privacy Fox (Arshad, 2004) try to bring a simplified and more useful solution to end user by providing a graphical face to P3P. Our solution differs in that instead of just a single aggregate representation embodied by the bird icon we opted to give a more granular output so that the end user could have more context as to exactly what went wrong.

A model-driven regime for VAT-compliance in ERP systems has recently been proposed by Goossenaerts, Zegers & Smits (2009) that has some conceptual similarities to our approach: they use UML-like descriptions of the business objects and then define invariants over the properties of the objects, with 'leveling' as a function on the relations defined in that model, However, there seems to be no explanation about how to compose multi-level invariants, nor how to capture the implications of failure. In our system, we use a decomposition model with logical combinations of child states which are generated as a set of agents. Related work includes the COMET methodology (COMET, 2006), which addresses the modelling and verification of business systems, providing a use-case driven, model-focused approach aimed at supporting the process of developing and maintaining products. Both are oriented at business-object views of the world: this is acceptable as long as one can define a representation of the thing over which invariants are to be defined; agents (perhaps in the form of 'write sensors') could allow some

abstraction and independence from the issues of combining that with the object model. The main advantage of using an 'agent' based solution like the one proposed in this chapter rather than a model invariant based solution is that having a separation between the business logic and the implementation requirements allows the agents to monitor the solution without having to rely on the implementation upholding its invariants.

Our approach requires privacy experts to input the models by hand. There is therefore scope to improve this process by including more automation at this stage. Annie Anton and co-workers have spearheaded research into how to automatically extract rules and regulations from existing natural language text (Breaux & Anton, 2008), although it would require further research to assess how exactly that work might be used in the current context. Other related work is on policies and iconography, notably that of Mary Rundly to learn from creative commons licences and use icons to express different policies (Rundly, 2006).

The difficulty that exists in current business practice is in the enforcement of the requirements of law and regulation in business practice, and usually compliance and adherence to these requirements is attempted in an isolated fashion, separately from mainstream business processes and decision-making. It is currently understood that compliance mechanisms need to be integrated with normal business processes and enforced in an automated fashion as much as possible.

For this reason, software platforms for governance, risk and compliance (GRC) have become commonplace, and as evident in our list above, there exist many different flavours but all have the same goal: to ensure that legal requirements for the protection of customer and business data are met, while providing staff at different levels of an enterprise with suitable views and audit trails demonstrating compliance. Several major ERP vendors are now building GRC platforms. Typically compliance is handled with a special plug-in, or "module", that can be purchased separately and incorporated into an ERP/GRC product that has been deployed across an enterprise.

An integrated solution, of which compliance management is a part, can usefully track information emerging from several processes in an organisation together, including Health and Safety, Environment, Quality, Human Resources, IT Security and Commercial departments.

The relevant regulations and laws which these tools are designed to support are encoded as "templates" for a GRC system - this means that a GRC system is designed to be flexible, because templates can be rewritten, new ones built when new laws are created etc. There are a number of key regulatory & legal frameworks supported by the various tools for IT compliance:

- SOX (Sarbanes-Oxley Act).
- GLBA (Gramm-Leach-Bliley Act).
- HIPAA (Health Insurance Portability and Accountability Act of 1996).
- SB 1386 (California Security Breach Information Act).
- EU Data Protection Directive.
- PCI DSS (Payment Card Industry Data security Standard).

Note that the compliance tools are mostly designed for the US market so relevant regulations from other countries are not always covered.

A range of software tools support the management of compliance processes and in particular, support enterprises in conforming to business standards, regulations and legal constraints with regards to privacy of personally identifiable information.

These compliance checking products tend to hardcode their compliance checking process or at least cannot model privacy processes and IT components as we do. They are targeted at the definition and monitoring of compliance goals for all IT related organizational resources, whereas our system focuses on monitoring the privacy compliance of key resources. Some key examples include:

- *Agiliance Compliance Manager* (Agiliance, 2010): This product is based on the RiskVision GRC platform, and has out-of-the-box support for complying with regulations and standards such as the HIPAA (for health records) etc. The tool provides an integrated interface for all risk and compliance-related information of an enterprise. It is evident that the tool can monitor and manage policies for data gathering/collection, which is particularly relevant in the EnCoRe context. It provides support for privacy policies.
- *Archer SmartSuite* (Archer, 2010):This is a GRC platform with similar capabilities to RiskVision. The website for this platform explicitly mentions **testing** capabilities, which would be a useful and direct means of assessing that compliance requirements are met. It provides support for testing compliance.
- *Autonomy Information Governance Tools* (Autonomy, 2010): This is a very ambitious suite that attempts to cater for all aspects of information governance, of which compliance is but a part. The product does not pay particular attention to privacy or privacy-related legislation. It provides support for privacy policies and risk assessment.
- *Computer Associates Records Manager* (Computer Associates, 2010):This platform incorporates a policy-based engine, which is extensible in the sense that enterprises can carve out in-house policies in addition to any prevailing laws/regulations that need to be complied with. It provides support for privacy policies.
- *HP OpenView Compliance Manager* (Enterprise Management Associates, 2005): this is a report pack based on OpenView that provides metrics for internal audit at the infrastructure level.

- *IBM Security Compliance Manager* (IBM, 2008): early warning systems identify security vulnerabilities and security policy violations and support compliance definition and monitoring. This integrates with Tivoli's automated security management tools to help mediate security policy violation and risk and uses predefined policies based on SANS top risks to security and compliance.
- *Modulo Risk Manager* (Modulo, 2010): This tool provides means of analysing and reasoning about risk and so has a certain niche. It allows an enterprise to automate gap analyses and risk analyses over business processes. For the privacy domain, the possibility of doing risk analysis is particularly useful.
- *SenSage Compliance Solution* (SenSage, 2008): this system uses event log data for analytics, and provides reports for audit.
- *Sun Java System Identity Auditor* (Sun Microsystems, Inc., 2005): this aims to help compliance with internal and external regulatory requirements across critical enterprise applications and across the identity management infrastructure. It features a compliance dashboard, an audit scan and reports.
- *Synomos Compliance & Data Governance* (Synomos, 2006): this was a system for managing data policies and compliance. It was policy driven rather than model driven and was focussed on getting low level events. It cannot model processes or check with the level of granularity of our system. This system is no longer on the market.

Additional relevant products not already mentioned above include the following: BWise GRC Platform, Relational Security RSAM, Symantec Control Compliance Suite, Telos Xacta IA Manager, OpenPages ITG, Thomson Reuters Paisley Enterprise GRC, sOracle JD Edwards EnterpriseOne, MetricStream Compliance Management Tool, Cura Enterprise GRC Suite, Protiviti Governance Portal, Mega GRC Compliance and Control, Methodware ERA, Axentis Enterprise Platform, IDS Scheer ARIS, and Aline GRC Platform. Of these, Agilence Compliance Manager and Archer Technologies SmartSuite are regarded as lead products by Gartner (Gartner, 2009). These two, together with CA Records Manager, Modulo Risk Manager and Autonomy, provide support for demonstrating compliance with privacy legislation (although the emphasis is on US legislation).

Privacy Impact Assessments (PIAs) have been defined "as a systematic risk assessment tool that can be usefully integrated into decision-making processes" (Warren et al, 2008). In November 2007 the UK Information Commissioners Office (ICO) [7] (an organisation responsible for regulating and enforcing access to and use of personal information), launched a Privacy Impact Assessment (PIA) process (incorporating privacy by design) to help organizations assess the impact of their operations on personal privacy. This process assesses the privacy requirements of new and existing systems; it is primarily intended for use in public sector risk management, but is increasingly seen to be of value to private sector businesses that process personal data. Similar methodologies exist and can have legal status in Australia, Canada and the USA (Tancock et al, 2010). This methodology aims to combat the slow take-up of designing in privacy protections at the enterprise level, and could provide a high level framework for risk analysis.

There is ongoing research on security policies and end-user policy compliance (Tejaswini et al, 2009). Organizations are applying security technologies and practises to achieve information security; however, in order to achieve this goal, the use of technological tools should be combined with information security policies. Enterprises mainly focus their efforts on setting and monitoring such policies, yet if their employees do not comply with these policies, then these efforts are in vain.

Steps towards the provision of more assurance to people on privacy have been made by various privacy seals providers and verifiers (Cavoukian & Crompton, 2000). This approach provides general purpose information about the conformance of a service provider or an enterprise with certified, privacy compliant processes when handling and managing personal data. However, the information is nearly always produced by self-certification and cannot be checked dynamically.

In summary, the differentiating features of our technology are the following:

- it is privacy-focused
- it is model-based and uses functional decomposition of privacy goals and constraints
- it is an agent-based approach
- it allows checking of trust and assurance constraints
- it allows the combination of runtime state, process analysis, log data, resource and infrastructural models and other information sources into a explicit representation of how an enterprise satisfies its obligations
- it neither presupposes deployment of other proprietal products nor requires major changes to applications, services or data repositories
- it can provide stronger degrees of evidence
- it can provide a finer level of granularity
- it is not reliant on self-certification and people-driven processes

LIMITATIONS TO AUTOMATED REASONING FOR PRIVACY COMPLIANCE

In the course of this research, various constraints became apparent that limit the effectiveness of automating privacy compliance assessment:

First of all, we are able to provide partial automation only because of a lack of formal verifiable definitions of manual processes that are currently used to check the validity for example of privacy seals, and these are difficult to automate, and also because manual process entries are sometimes necessary, and in these cases the most we can do is to have a website automatically generated to request such information.

Second, there is complexity involved in the necessary modelling, and so it can be difficult. For example, back end infrastructures can be extremely complex: to reduce this problem we model just the key privacy-related subparts of such systems. It is also necessary to address the complexity of how subnodes within the privacy models relate to each other.

Third, there is some missing infrastructure currently. There is a need to standardise a meta-data format for machine-readable certificates because most machine-readable certificate information that is available is not very interesting from a privacy point of view, and other interesting information is not machine-readable or analysable.

In addition, there is no trusted infrastructure around agent deployment, and so the information obtained from the agents cannot be trusted. The problem is that malicious layered services could operate unknown to (our) monitoring services — there is a risk of administrators compromising the system and also a risk when checking external topologies. This problem is generally faced by compliance monitoring and reporting systems. Approaches to solve this include:

- Authentication between components (which may be enhanced by using trusted hardware to protect private keys)
- Next generation trusted computing and infrastructure, e.g. Trusted Computing Group (2003) integrity checking (if available, allowing the verification of a loaded system image to avoid system compromise), agents isolated in trusted compartments (Anderson, Moffie and Dalton, 2007), etc.
- Establishment of a 'process' for installing the agent platform which involves verification of the installation fingerprint with a Trusted Platform Module (TPM) that can

be used to verify it is correct; the chain can then be extended to the agents deployed on the platform. The agents' availability and monitoring is also a condition of compliance.

Further Development of Our Research

Given these issues, we see potential usage of this technology as developing over time in the following way:

- In the *immediate term*, basic system properties, such as presence, availability and properties of services, security hardware, etc., could be checked, together with configuration (e.g., patching). Also monitoring of changes to the infrastructure over time and assessment of logs. Where privacy enhancing technologies are not available due to lack of deployment or even availability in the marketplace, the equivalent manual processes can be included and monitored within the submodels. Additional agents could be used to establish the seciruty of the platform onto which they are deployed, for exampel a distributed store of binary fingerprints analogous to AIDE (AIDE, 2010).
- In the *intermediate term*, schema definitions could be provided for properties of IT controls, improve risk assessment models for privacy and audit what really happens against expected enforcement (for example, by checking failures in a specific PET).
- In the *longer term*, more PETs and technologies could be assessed as they reach the market (so that both these technologies and alternative human-driven processes for the same business processes are modeled), data flow could be modeled and instrumented and a trusted infrastructure could be used to protect the agents.

The technology would be particularly suitable for areas such as enhancing privacy for customer relationship management and enabling checks of compliance by partners with whom data is shared. It could also be applied in a focused way to situations such as identifying issues before an upcoming audit or before problems arise, trying to prevent fraud and internal threats and checking that important data (such as forensic data) is kept in a suitably protected way.

Since developing our initial prototype, we have integrated a privacy compliance checking approach within the EU PRIME project (2008) integrated prototype and are also building upon these ideas within the EnCoRe project (2010) in order to enhance a compliance framework for consent and revocation management.

CONCLUSION

This project has succeeded in demonstrating the feasibility of a model based privacy 'best practice' compliance checker by extending what is automatable. This was achieved by encoding a set of high level goals, based on guidelines defined by the OECD (1980) and linking these to system level enforcement technologies that may be used to satisfy these top level goals. We proposed a framework that helps experts reason about how privacy compliance may be satisfied, optionally using predefined/approved submodels. Once defined, the resultant model can then be executed and generates a 'compliance dashboard' that can be used by non-expert users.

Working prototypes have been fully implemented to demonstrate the feasibility of our approach. Even subparts of such a system prove useful.

The use of an agent framework has shown that it is possible to instrument the collection of fine grained data regarding organisational resources. This in combination with simulated data has allowed the demonstration of the failure of entities to pass constraints. The use of the reporting system has demonstrated how the information regarding failures can be reflected at a high level, whilst allowing the user of the system to explore the specific cause.

The development of a framework for the formal definition of privacy and security constraints forces the explicit description of satisfaction constraints. The use of such a system as part of a risk analysis and mitigation framework can be of significant benefit. The automation of analysis and reporting would provide a more specific measurable assessment of an organisation's compliance.

REFERENCES

Agiliance. (2010). *Compliance Manager*. Retrieved August 2010 from www.agiliance.com/assets/pdf/Agiliance_compliance_automation.pdf

AIDE. (2010). *Advanced Intrusion Detection Environment*. Retrieved August 2010 from http://www.cs.tut.fi/~rammer/aide.html

Allison, D. (2005). System Policy Compliance Checker. MSc. Thesis, University of Newcastle, UK.

Anderson, M. J., Moffie, M., & Dalton, C. I. (2007). *Towards Trustworthy Virtualisation Environments: Xen Library OS Security Service Infrastructure*. Tech. Rep. No. HPL-2007-69, HP Labs, Bristol. Retrieved June 2008 from http://www.hpl.hp.com/techreports/2007/HPL-2007-69.pdf

Archer. (2010). *Compliance Suite*. Retrieved August 2010 from www.archer.com/

Arshad, F. (2004). *Privacy Fox – A JavaScript-based P3P Agent for Mozilla Firefox*. http://privacyfox.mozdev.org/PaperFinal.pdf

Ashley, P., Hada, S., Karjoth, G., Powers, C., & Schunter, M. (2003). *Enterprise Privacy Authorization Language (EPAL 1.1)*. Research Report, IBM. Retrieved Jan 2008 from http://www.zurich.ibm.com/security/enterprise-privacy/epal

Autonomy. (2010). *Information Governance Tools*. Retrieved August 2010 from Breaux, T.D. & Anton, A.I. (2008). Analyzing Regulatory Rules for Privacy and Security Requirements. *IEEE Transactions on Software Engineering, 34*(1), 5-20.

Caldwell, F. Eid, T. & Casper, C.(2009) *Magic Quadrant for Enterprise Governance, Risk and Compliance Platforms*. Gartner RAS Core Research Note G00169604.

Casassa Mont, M. (2005). Handling privacy obligations in enterprises: important aspects and technical approaches. *Comput. Syst. Sci. Eng., 20*, 6.

Casassa Mont, M., & Thyne, R. (2006). In Danezis, G., & Golle, P. (Eds.), *A Systemic Approach to Automate Privacy Policy Enforcement in Enterprises. Privacy Enhancing Technologies 2006, LNCS 4258* (pp. 118–134). Springer.

Cavoukian, A., & Crompton, M. (2000). Web Seals: A review of Online Privacy Programs. 22nd International Conference on Privacy and Data Protection. Retrieved Dec. 2006 from http://www.privacy.gov.au/publications/seals.pdf

COMET. (2006). Component and model-based development methodology. Retrieved August 2010 from http://www.modelbased.net/comet/

Computer Associates. (2010). Policy and Configuration and Records Manager. Retrieved August 2010 from http://www3.ca.com/solutions/Product.aspx?ID=165

Cranor, L. F. (2002). *Web Privacy with* (p. 3P). O'Reilly and Associates.

Cranor, L.F. (2003). P3P: Making privacy policies more useful. *IEEE Security and Privacy*, 1:6, November, 50-55.

Damianou, N., Dulay, N., Lupu, E., & Sloman, M. (2001). *The Ponder Policy Specification Language*. Retrieved 2007 from http://www-dse.doc. ic.ac.uk/research/policies/index.shtml

Elahi, T. E., & Pearson, S. (2007). Privacy Assurance: Bridging the Gap Between Preference and Practice. TrustBus 2007, LNCS 4657, Springer-Verlag, 65-74.

EnCoRe. (2010). *Ensuring Consent and Revocation project*. Retrieved August 2010 from www. encore-project.info.

Enterprise Management Associates. (2005). HP Openview Compliance Manager: Integrating the Synergies of Management, Security and Compliance. Retrieved June 2008 from http://www. managementsoftware.hp.com/products/ovcm/ swp/ovcm_swp.pdf

European Parliament and Council (1995). Directive 95/46/EC on the protection of individuals with regard to the processing of personal data and on the free movement of such data. Official Journal of the European Communities. L. 28, 31.

Google. (2009). Transparency, choice and control – now complete with a dashboard! The Official Google Blog. Retrieved 2010 from http://google-blog.blogspot.com/2009/11/transparency-choice-and-control-now.html

Goossenaerts, J.B.M., Zegers, A.T.M. & Smits, T.M. (2009) A multi-level model driven regime for value-added tax compliance in ERP systems. *Computers in Industry, 60*:9, December, 709-727.

Greenleaf, G. (2005). APEC's Privacy Framework: A new low standard. *Privacy Law and Policy Reporter, 11(5)*. Retrieved 2008 from http:// www.aph.gov.au/Senate/committee/legcon_ctte/ completed_inquiries/2004-07/privacy/submissions/sub32ann_c.pdf

Hinde, S. (2005). *The SmartFrog Reference Manual*, v3.06. Retrieved Dec. 2006 from http:// cvs.sourceforge.net/viewcvs.py/*checkout*/ smartfrog/core/smartfrog/docs/sfReference.pdf

IBM. (2008). *Tivoli Security Compliance Manager*. Retrieved June 2008 from http://www-306. ibm.com/software/tivoli/products/security-compliance-mgr/

Information Commissioner's Office UK. (2007). PIA handbook. Retrieved November 2008 from http://www.ico.gov.uk/.

Laurant, C. (2003). Privacy and Human Rights 2003: an International Survey of Privacy Laws and Developments. *Electronic Privacy Information Center (EPIC), Privacy International*. Retrieved Dec. 2006 from http://www.privacyinternational. org/survey/phr2003/

Li, N., & Mitchell, J. C. (2003). Datalog with Constraints: A foundation for trust management languages. PADL'03. Springer Verlag, 58-73.

Modulo (2010). Risk Manager. Retrieved August 2010 from www.modulo.com/risk-manager

OASIS. (2005). eXtensible Access Control Markup Language (XACML). Version 2.0. Retrieved Feb. 2005 from http://docs.oasis-open. org/xacml/2.0/access_control-xacml-2.0-core-specs-os.pdf

OECD. (1980). OECD Guidelines on the Protection of Privacy and Transborder Flows of Personal Data. Retrieved Dec. 2006 from http://www1. oecd.org/publications/e-book/9302011E.PDF

Pearson, S. (2006). In Stolen, K. (Eds.), *Towards Automated Evaluation of Trust Constraints, iTrust 2006, LNCS 3986* (pp. 252–266). Springer-Verlag.

PRIME. (2008). Privacy and Identity Management for Europe. European RTD Integrated Project under the FP6/IST Programme. Retrieved June 2008 from http://www.prime-project.eu.org/

Rundly, M. (2006). International Personal Data Protections and Digital Identity Management Tools. W3C Workshop on Languages for Privacy Policy Negotiation and Semantics-Driven Enforcement. Retrieved Jan. 2008 from http://www.w3.org/2006/07/privacy-ws/papers/21-rundle-data-protection-and-idm-tools/

SenSage. (2008). SenSage 4.0 Product. Retrieved June 2008 from http://www.sensage.com/

Sun Microsystems, Inc. (2005). Identity Auditing: Taking Compliance Beyond the Baseline. White Paper. Retrieved Dec. 2006 from http://www.sun.com/software/products/identity_auditor/index.xml

Syed, A., Syed, N., Indulska, M., & Sadiq, S. (2009) A Study of compliance management in information systems research. 17th European Conference on Information Systems.

Synomos (2006) Synomos Align 3.0, Retrieved Dec. 2006 from http://www.synomos.com/

Tancock, D., Pearson, S., & Charlesworth, A. (2010). *Analysis of Privacy Impact Assessments within Major Jurisdictions. PST 2010.* Ottawa: IEEE.

Tejaswini, H., & Raghav, R. (2009). Protection motivation and deterrence: a framework for security policy compliance in organisations. *European Journal of Information Systems, 18*, 106–125. doi:10.1057/ejis.2009.6

Trusted Computing Group. (2003). TCG Main Specification, v1.1b. Retrieved Dec. 2006, from http://www.trustedcomputinggroup.org

Warren, A., Bayley, R., Charlesworth, A., Bennett, C., Clarke, R., & Oppenheim, C. (2008). Privacy Impact Assessments: international experience as a basis for UK guidance. *Computer Law & Security Report, 24*(3), 233–242. doi:10.1016/j.clsr.2008.03.003

Wikipedia (2010). *Electronic business.* Retrieved August 2010 from http://en.wikipedia.org/wiki/E-business

XML. (2010). Extensible Markup Language. Retrieved August 2010 from http://www.w3.org/XML/

Chapter 11
Towards a Model–Driven Approach for Process–Aware Web Applications

Davide Rossi
University of Bologna, Italy

Elisa Turrini
University of Bologna, Italy

ABSTRACT

Model-driven methods are always welcome when developing complex applications. Their availability is usually related to the problem domain that has to be addressed and to the software architectures that have to be supported. Process-aware Web applications are arguably the prominent examples of applications in which multi-user, coordinated work takes place and are, as the web evolves towards a Business System, strongly emerging as one of the main types of Web-applications. In this chapter the authors propose a model-driven approach to process-aware Web applications based on a graphical process modeling and execution language that eases the development process (from the design to the implementation) by promoting an effective separation of concerns. Driven by an emerging class of applications, the Web is evolving into a Business System. Web-based business applications allow the participation of several actors to complex enterprise-wide (or even multi-enterprise) business processes and pose new challenges to the software designers and software architects. The design models have to address both navigational and process-based interactions; the software architecture has to provide the components to enact the process and has to define how these components interoperate with the other components of the Web applications. In this chapter the authors show how, promoting an effective separation of concerns, a process modeling language and its enactment engine can be used in the modeling and implementation of process-aware Web applications.

DOI: 10.4018/978-1-60960-132-4.ch011

Copyright © 2011, IGI Global. Copying or distributing in print or electronic forms without written permission of IGI Global is prohibited.

INTRODUCTION

As the Web continues its evolution from a distributed hypermedia system to an Information System to a Business System, several recent proposals (Brambilla, Ceri, Fraternali, & Manolescu, 2006; Koch, Kraus, Cachero, & Meliá, 2004; Schmid & Rossi, 2004; Troyer & Casteleyn, 2003) have appeared with the aim of modeling and designing Web applications able to support not just simple navigation and data access activities but (potentially complex) business processes. One of the main shortcomings of most of the existing proposals is, in our opinion, the fact that they limit the business processes to the so called *transactions* (Distante, Rossi, & Canfora, 2007), functional activities related to the interaction with the Web application. They, in other words, aim at short-term business processes strongly contextualized within a specific Web application and limited to the interaction with a single user (like the check-out process in a e-commerce application) rather than as a complex orchestration of activities carried out by several actors and software components that could only partially take place by using the Web.

Our approach to face the issues that arise in this complex scenario is to consider this emerging class of Web applications as an instance of the more generic class of process-aware applications that include Workflow Management Systems, Web service orchestration platforms, Business Process Management support systems (like CRM and ERP), etc. This class of applications is characterized by having a *control-flow perspective* (also called *process perspective* (Jablonski & Bussler, 1996)), i.e. a dimension of concern that focuses on the coordination among actors. It is usual, for these applications, to address the control-flow perspective at the design level by using some kind of process modeling notation (that can be a visual one, like a diagram, or can be a specific language). At the software architecture level we can witness a quite obvious evolution trend, that started with the workflow languages and that now continues

in the Service Oriented Architecture era with service orchestration: the control-flow perspective is addressed by directly enacting the model developed at the design level by means of specific software systems (usually called *engines*). There are several advantages related to this approach:

- the guarantee that the enacted process will behave exactly as expected at the modeling stage;
- a smooth, effortless, transition from design to implementation;
- programmers do not have to reinvent the wheel and can rely on the non-functional software qualities of the engine.

The latter argument is of particular importance if we analyze what the alternative would be: without the executable language/enactment engine approach, the process modeled at the design level has to be refined into a set of components able to enforce the process behavior. Respecting the functional requirements for these components (i.e. assuring that the software systems respects the modeled behavior of the process) can already be quite troublesome since advanced synchronization operations can be challenging to implement. But this is just the easy part: non-functional requirements are where most of the effort is going to be spent. Addressing requirements like persistence, efficiency, availability, robustness, reliability and security can be very expensive. Assuming that an existing enactment engine is able to address them the cost-effectiveness of such a solution is clearly visible.

In this paper we investigate how to use the executable language/enactment engine approach (and enjoy its advantages) in the design and implementation of process-aware Web applications. In the following sections we first discuss existing approaches to address the integration of business processes within Web applications from both a design and a software architecture point of view; we then present our proposal based on a process modeling language, EPML, and its enactment engine. A discussion of the proposal and an outline of the future work conclude the article.

DESIGNING AND ARCHITECTING BUSINESS PROCESSES IN WEB APPLICATIONS

In this section we discuss the existing approaches to the design and implementation of process-aware Web applications. From the design perspective there are two rather obvious, and opposite, approaches that can be taken to address business processes in Web applications: extending the navigation model to capture the business workflow and extending the process modeling notation to generate a sequence of *views* dispatched to the user when interacting with the Web application. In the first approach, implicit process control by link topology, the hypertext structure is used to guide the user through a sequence of pages that correspond to the steps of the business process. This solution cannot address multi-party processes with complex synchronizations. In the second approach, process-enforced navigation, the navigational paths of the users are constrained by the status of the process they participate in. This solution is not feasible in contexts in which users can leave the process at any time by navigating to other pages, which is something that most of the users of a Web application take for granted. Moreover, in both cases, one model is overloaded trying to address two different concerns at the same time. To overcome this latter problem one of the aforementioned methods (UWE) maintains the separation of concerns at the design level by providing separate models for process and navigation concerns whereas the others take the first of the two approaches outlined above: the navigation model is extended in order to address process control. To achieve a reasonable separation of concerns, most of these methods do use a stand-alone process model of some sort (UML activity diagrams,

BPMN (http://www.bpmn.org/) diagrams and so forth) but this model is later merged with the navigation model. The main problems of this choice are related to the redesign that has to take place when the process model changes (something that happens in most evolutionary software systems) and to the fact that the ability to express complex interaction among actors in a process depends on the ability of the extended navigation model to support them. WebML (Brambilla, M., Comai, S., Fraternali, P., & Matera M.), for example, suggests the use of BPMN diagrams that have to be converted in a WebML extended notation from which a full navigation model and its related process reference models are derived. This means that WebML becomes the process modeling notation itself and the expressive power (with respect to the control-flow) of the modeled processes is that of WebML. This introduces a possible issue that arises frequently when transforming process models, since the expressive power of BPMN, the "stating" notation, is higher than that of WebML, the "target" notation. As a consequence, an interaction pattern that can be modeled with BPMN could not be supported by WebML, leading to a failure in the refinement process. The same applies to methods like OOHDM that use UML activity diagrams (which, especially in UML 1.4, are already constrained by their lack of expressive power (Wohed, van der Aalst, Dumas, Russell, & ter Hofstede, 2005)) and map them to elements of the conceptual and/or navigational schema.

From the software architecture/implementation strategies point of view the aforementioned methods largely differ. Some of them overlook the problem (since they are more focused on the design phase) suggesting some kind of "do-it-yourself" process management implemented inside the chosen Web applications framework (which is a feasible solution only in the case of very elementary processes). Some, like OOHDM, propose the use of existing state-machine frameworks like Expresso ("Expresso", n.d.) for managing the state of the process. It is worth noticing that even the documentation of Expresso reports: "Expresso offers a basic form of workflow", so, yet again, this is a feasible solution only for short-living, non critical business processes. Please notice that we are not arguing about the relevance or the merits of the existing proposals, we are just pointing out that some of them are targeted at a specific class of business processes and, as long as the business process to be addressed falls within this category, they are valuable solutions. WebML is the only proposal that offers advanced support for complex business processes and really stands out from the others in this respect. WebML can be used to model multi-actor processes with advanced synchronizations and can also be used to interact with other software systems by using Web services. As hinted before, WebML tries to be a "one fits all" solution since the very same notation is used to address the navigation perspective, the control-flow perspective and even to explicitly orchestrate Web services. The main plus of this approach is that it really takes advantage of model driven engineering for Web applications development and, in fact, the gap between the design model and the implementation in WebML, when used from within its own case tool, WebRatio, is very narrow. The drawback is that the use of WebML is really meaningful only when the intention is to adopt its software development process and its associated tools too. It should be noted that, in this case, a software component inside the WebRatio architecture is used to enact the processes modeled with WebML by operating on the process reference model stored in a relational DBMS. Once again, in most scenarios, WebML is a valuable solution with obvious merits and some limitations.

THE EPML APPROACH

For the reasons mentioned in the introduction, we decided to follow the executable language/ enactment engine approach. This decision leads to two possible scenarios: create a new language/

engine or use (and eventually adapt) an existing one. The first solution would result in yet another process modeling language for a very specific application domain. Moreover, given the focus on Web applications, it would have not been possible to address all the cases of large business processes spanning across different technologies. The second solution is equally troublesome since it turns out that most existing language/engine systems focus on a specific applications domain (workflow management, Web service orchestration, ...) and adapting them to be used in a Web application context is problematic to say the least.

EPML is a process modeling language (for which an enactment engine exists) that we created in the context of a past research project. The main design goal of EPML was to support the process perspective across a wide array of different application domains, overcoming the limitation that makes the second solution hard to implement. In the next subsections we briefly introduce EPML and we discuss how it can be used in the modeling and in the implementation of process-aware Web applications.

EPML: An Executable Process Modeling Language

With a good separation of concerns, software systems can be built by complementing sub-systems that address different perspectives. EPML has been designed to help this long-standing dream of software engineering turn into reality. To promote an effective separation of concerns, in fact, it has been designed with a minimalistic approach by only addressing the control-flow perspective. EPML is composed of a modeling language and an execution engine. The language is used to write specifications that model processes. The engine is used to enact processes given their specifications. To enhance the suitability of the language (and its related run-time system) across different application domains we pursued these goals:

Figure 1. The basic elements of EPML

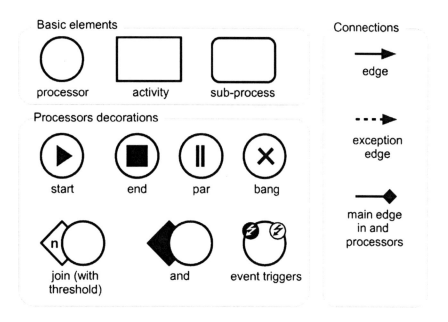

- (reasonably intuitive) graphical notation;
- executable language;
- high expressive power (or, better, *suitability*);
- formal semantics;
- modularity.

In the next few lines we will try to give a flavor of EPML, being an in-depth description out of the scope of this paper, the interested reader can refer to (Rossi & Turrini, 2007). A process specification in EPML is a diagram in which the elements depicted in Figure 1 are connected with directed edges (also called links).

Activities are elements of computation, and can be used to model either a service invocation or the assignment of a work item to an actor (being it a human or a system) participating in the process. Processors are elements of coordination; they are used to model the points in the process in which decisions about the flows (in a process several flows can execute concurrently) take place, from which concurrent flows can stem, or/and in

which flows have to be synchronized. The resulting network defines how process flows evolve during the process enactment. While an in-depth knowledge of the language is not uncomplicated, the very elementary use of it we do in this work should make this very terse introduction sufficient to understand the modeled examples to any reader familiar with one of the most used process modeling notations such as UML activity diagrams and BPMN.

Web Applications with EPML

While interacting with the Web application, users can navigate to pages that are not related to any process or can visit process-related pages. We refer to the former as *standard navigation mode* and to the latter as *process flow mode*. To enter process flow mode the users follow specific *process-aware* hyperlinks. Process-aware hyperlinks can be used to create a (sub)process, to resume a previously started process that has been left (probably by using navigation links that drove the user outside

Figure 2. A review process in EPML

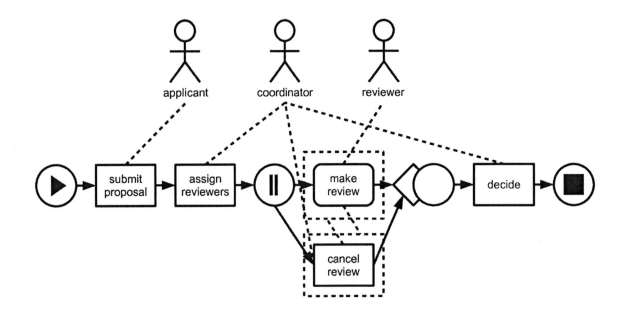

the process flow), or to join an existing process created by another actor. In process flow mode, the sequence of the pages that are dispatched to the users may depend on the control flow of the process rather than on the navigation structure of the Web application. Specifically, in our approach, the pages in process flow mode correspond to the tasks assigned to the users by the process. Consider the process depicted in Figure 2: it is a high level model of a simple project grant review process. Applicants submit their projects for review, the coordinator assigns the actual reviews to a given number of reviewers, and the reviewers make the reviews. A review is actually composed of two steps: a first evaluation is given considering an anonymous subset of the documents in the proposal; a second evaluation is given considering all the information related to the project, including the applicants' identity. While waiting for the reviewers to complete their work, the coordinator can decide to cancel a review (because it is delaying the process or for other reasons). When all the reviews have either been completed or

canceled, the coordinator decides to reject or to fund the project. Please notice that the modeled process is a highly simplified version of what actually takes place in the real word. EPML has been designed with a high expressive power right because the authors acknowledge that real world (business) processes are far more complex than what academic papers seem to suggest.

Nevertheless, given the focus of this work, an oversimplified example seems reasonable.

To decide if a proposal should be funded or rejected, coordinators have to join the flow of the process generated by the applicants when they submitted a proposal. In order to do that from within the Web application, coordinators have to follow a process-aware hyperlink that drives them to a page related to the *decide* activity. This page should be available only when the *decide* activity has been assigned to the coordinator and it is a reasonable design strategy to prevent the generation of process-aware hyperlinks related to processes for which no activity is assigned to the current user. In the specific case of the aforementioned

Figure 3. The make review sub-process

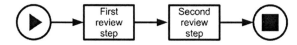

example, the *decide* hyperlink should be available from the proposal details page only when all the reviews have either been received or canceled. In general only process-aware hyperlinks used to start a new process can be always available. Even hyperlinks used to start sub-processes are not generally available (in the example, the make review sub-process can be started by reviewers only when they have been assigned the review of a proposal).

Consider now Figure 3: it depicts the make review sub-process.

As discussed above, this sub-process is composed of two steps and it is very well possible that reviewers leave the sub process when finished the first step, before completing the second. As a consequence the *make review* hyperlink that is available from the pending reviews page can lead reviewers to the forms associated to the first review step or to the second review step, depending on the state of the make review sub-process for that specific proposal.

Even from this elementary example we can point out a set of issues (related to both the modeling language and to the execution environment) that have to be faced by the process model and by the enactment engine:

- processes can require the interaction with several users;
- advanced synchronization between the workflows of several users may be required;
- users can participate in several processes at the same time;
- the Web application framework must be able to interface to the process enactment

engine in order to query the activities assigned to specific users and to signal the completion of activities;
- processes may have to be persistent.

It is our opinion that these issues can effectively be addressed by EPML and its enactment engine.

If we focus now on the issues that have to be addressed from the modeling point of view, we can list:

- the modeling of process-aware hyperlinks;
- the modeling of non-navigational sequences of views in process-flow mode and
- the modeling of associations between the pages in the navigation model and the related activities in the process model.

In Figure 4 is depicted a model for the make review sub-process that uses a simple extension of a WAE (Conallen, 2002) navigation diagram (a stereotyped UML class diagram that is part of the user experience model) and an EPML diagram. We decided to use WAE for mainly two reasons: first, to remain agnostics with respect to existing methods that we mentioned before and, second, because it is a quite "lightweight" method that easily allows simple extensions. This is mostly because WAE is not targeted at model driven development and, thus, the design models are not overloaded with details.

From this example it is easy to see how the aforementioned issues can be addressed. Process-aware hyperlinks are modeled with navigational associations that connect to a *process*-stereotyped class. In order to remark the specific behavior of these associations, we also used the *process link* stereotype, but it is not really essential. The *p.screen* stereotype is used (for inner classes inside a *process*-stereotyped class) to mark the entry points of sub-sequences related to an action in the EPML model. The active sub-sequence can be easily inferred since the names of the *p.screen*-stereotypes classes correspond to the names of

Figure 4. Modeling the review sub-process

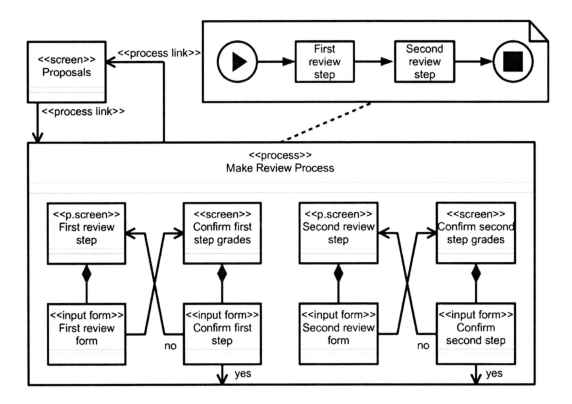

the actions in the process model. When a navigational subsequence in process-flow mode returns the control to the process-flow, a navigation connection is made between the last screen (or its aggregated forms) and the outer process class that contains it (as in the two input confirmation forms of the example). Process-stereotyped classes admit only one exit association that leads to the subsequent page (or process) that is visited when the (sub)process ends. In our example this association too is process link-stereotyped.

Please notice that, up to this point, this modeling approach does not necessarily assume the use of WAE and/or EPML. Most of these concepts can be applied to the methods we mentioned before.

As far as implementation strategies are concerned, several options are available, depending on the selected Web application framework. The solution we present here is based on Java Enterprise Edition (which is a natural choice, since the EPML engine is written in Java) and the Struts Model-View-Controller (MVC) framework; similar solutions, however, can be implemented with different technologies. Basically, the functions that have to be supported by the framework in order to address the issues related to process-aware Web applications that we mentioned above are:

- implement process-aware links to create, resume or join a process;
- dispatch the correct sequence of pages in process-flow mode;
- hide process-aware links that would lead to processes in which there are no actions (or

there is not a specific action) assigned to the current user.

When using a MVC framework like Struts these issues can be easily addressed by writing specific process-aware controllers that, interfacing with the engine, dispatch the correct view given the current user (in our implementation we assume this information can be extracted from the user's session data) and the process the link points to. In the case of processes in which more than one action can be associated to the same user (this is an event that does not show up in our example) an additional parameter specifies which, among the available actions, has to be used as a starting point for the current flow. Process-aware hyperlinks can then be created simply pointing to a process-aware controller. The same controller can be used to dispatch the correct sequence of pages in the process flow. Finally, generic parts of a Web page can be hidden by using a conditional custom tag that queries the engine about the availability of an action for the current user in the target process.

By assuming a target architecture based on Java Enterprise Edition (Java EE) and a framework like Struts it is possible to apply model driven engineering techniques to our method. We implemented a set of tools to create a Web application architecture as direct refinement of the EPML process models and of the WAE-based navigation (process-aware) models previously described. The resulting application skeleton is based on specific interface components created to mediate the interactions among the EPML engine and the Web application components.

The diagram in Figure 5 depicts the main elements of our method at both the design and the system level. (Process-aware) WAE is automatically refined into a Web application skeleton in which process-based navigation is already fully addressed by interfacing with the EPML engine.

The EPML engine has been designed using an event-driven approach: the engine consumes environment events (typically end activity events) and produces events for the environment (typically start activity events). A *WebMediator* object is used to record all the activation events and keep track of all the activities associated to the various actors during the execution of the processes enacted by the engine. It is also used to notify the engine about a completed activity and to obtain the subsequent activity for the same actor in the specified process. The *WebMediator* should never be accessed directly from the Web application components. Whenever a process link has activated by the user, or whenever the control from a navigational subsequence returns to the outer process class, the corresponding Struts action has to be implemented by the programmer: after having performed its non-process related operations, the action has to delegate to the predefined *Process* action that, by querying the *WebMediator* object, will dispatch the correct *p.screen* view for the current actor in the current process. The Struts configuration file that allows the creation of the correct navigational path for both the standard navigation mode and the process flow mode is automatically created by the model driven engineering tools. Technically the tool reads an XML description of the EPML diagram and the XMI version of the UML diagram and creates the *struts-config.xml* configuration file along with the skeletons of all the JSP pages and the Struts actions (the actions that connect to a process flow are already set up to delegate navigation control to the *Process* action). The programmer has to write the code to implement the navigation logic in the Struts actions (just like with any Web application) and has never to worry about addressing the process flow mode.

In Figure 6 a few screen-shoots show the actual process: the EPML modeling tool is used to create the EPML specification, an UML modeler (Topcased for Eclipse in this case) is used to create the extended WAE diagram. The Struts configuration (graphically depicted in the leftmost screen-shoot) is the one created by our tool.

Figure 5. From design to actual system: a model driven approach

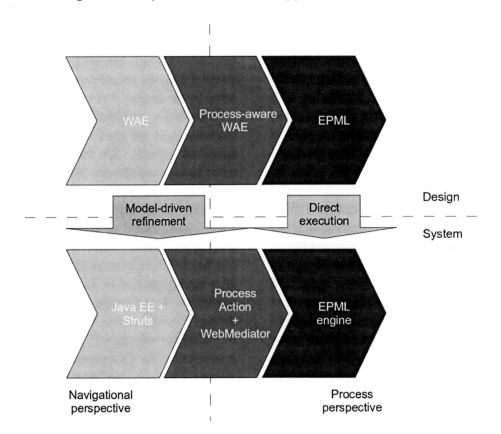

The model-driven tool and the graphics modelers are all available as Eclipse plug-ins providing an integrated environment for applications design and development.

The management of the data perspective introduces some subtle issues and, while it is slightly out of the main topic of this article, we are going to discuss possible solutions. The main problem, in this context, is that almost every software system has some kind of data perspective; this is the case for EPML too, since some kind of data management is considered necessary at least to allow the processors to take decisions when needed. It turns then out that we are trying to mix two sub-systems that have two distinct data perspectives. Duplicating the application data in both perspectives is unfeasible and error prone, so reasonable solutions are: using one of the two

data perspectives and adapting the other system (if possible) to interface to the selected data management solution or using an external sub-system that addresses the data perspective and adapting the remaining sub-systems to interface to it. The correct solution depends on the specific overall architecture. In our case, for example, if we are dealing with a large business process that interfaces with several systems and is just partially participated using a Web application, then using an ad hoc data management for the process-relevant data is arguably the best solution. In this case the Web application has to be designed in order to interface to that data management system. On the other side, if we are dealing with a fully Web-based business process, using the data perspective that is managed by the Web application framework (in the case of Java EE, request and session data for the Web

Figure 6. Screen shoots of the tools used during the development process

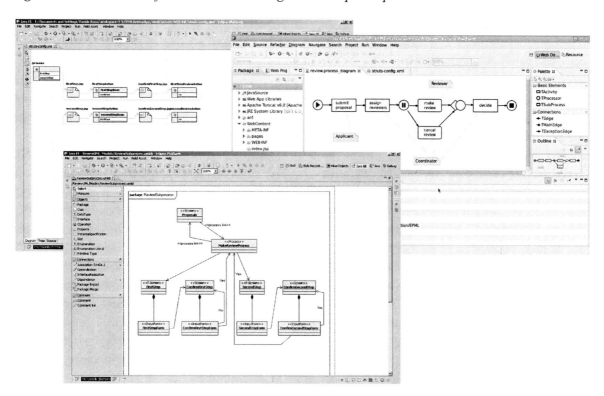

tier - persistent data via EJBs or Hibernate for the business tier) is a feasible solution. Assuming the second scenario in our example application, Java EE-based solutions are used to address the data perspective; in this case the process logic of the EPML processors has to be designed so that it can access the Web framework data (in other words the processors in EPML have to be able to interface to HTTPServletRequest-accessible data: query strings, form submitted-data, session data, etc., and to the model components). Designing this solution is trivial using Java EE and the EPML engine in which we simply have to add the relevant references into the flow data each time a terminate activity event is dispatched to the engine (typically when a process-aware controller is activated as a consequence of a process-related interaction returning the control to the process flow). In the project proposal review application this could happen, for example, when the review-

ers confirm the first review step. Suppose that a processor positioned between the *First review step* and the *Second review step* activities takes decisions about outgoing flows by accessing the form data filled by the reviewer (for example, the second step is not activated if the average score for the first step is below a certain threshold). In our prototype, to better separate the two sub-systems, the relevant Web framework data are used to create an XML document that is put in the flow data. The processor uses XQuery on these data to create a new document that is fed to a set of XPath expressions that are used to decide which output flow has to be enabled. By using this approach the process logic contained in the processors can be expressed by XQuery and XPath expressions without the need to write Java code. This results in incremented portability of the process model (if, in the future, the same process is used in a context which is not that of a Web application) and in improved readability.

Beyond Web Applications

One of the advantages of the approach we propose in this article is that a single process model can be used to address the enactment of processes also in complex applications for which only part of the interactions are carried out via the Web. This can be the case for large inter-organizations applications but also for smaller ones in which the process interacts with users via a Web interface and with other software components via Web Services.

By using EPML a single process model can be used for both the Web application (or even multiple Web applications) and for the Web Services orchestration; furthermore the same engine can support the enactment of both.

EPML.WS is a software architecture for Web Services orchestration (à la WS-BPEL) based on EPML. In order to support this specific applications class EPML.WS complements EPML with components that address the interaction with synchronous and asynchronous web services and allow a EPML-enacted process to be accessed as a web service.

EPML.WS is designed to be hosted inside a JEE architecture supporting JSR 109 (Implementing Enterprise Web services) and JSR 181 (Web Services Metadata for the Java Platform).

A very thin layer of software adapters have been provided in order to create the EPML.WS architecture.

This includes an adapter to transform incoming web services invocations (SOAP messages) into external events that are feed to the EPML engine, an *activity wrapper* to implement activities execution as web services invocation and a process logic wrapper (WSXQueryLogic) to use XQuery for routing decisions and to perform data management.

The WSXQueryLogic adapter first creates the XML document against which the provided

XQuery expression has to be run, it executes the XQuery expression and then parses the generated output to activate one or more exit edges and to modify the process data.

This allows to use well-known XML-related standards to orchestrate Web services, keeping the advantage of using the graphical notation of EPML to describe the process.

As a simple example of the usage of EPML. WS consider some steps of a process (part of which may be executed via a Web application) that invoke an external Web Service under specific conditions; in our example this is part of a loan approval sub-process. Assuming that an XML data mapping as previously described is used, a processor can receive the following information (possibly in the form of a Web Service invocation):

```
<body>
    <firstName>John</firstName>
    <name>Doe</name>
    <amount>1000</amount>
</body>
```

Please notice that namespace references have been omitted for clarity.

The processor can the apply the following XQuery-based process logic:

```
<xq_result>
    <edges>
    {
        if(data(//amount) > 10000)
        then <edge>yes</edge>
        else
            <edge>no</edge>
            <wsout>
            <param name="name">
            {data(//name)}</param>
            <param name="first name">
            {data(//firstName)}</param>
            <param name="amount">
            {data(//amount)}</param>
            </wsout>
    }
```

```
    </edges>
    <data>
        <entry name="name">
           {data(//name)}</entry>
            <entry name="first name">
            {data(//firstName)}</entry>
            <entry name="amount">
            {data(//amount)}</entry>
    </data>
</xq_result>
```

obtaining:

```
<xqresult>
    <edges>
        <edge>no</edge>
    </edges>
    <data>
        <entry name="name">Doe</entry>
        <entry name="first
name">John<entry>
        <entry name="amount">1000</en-
try>
    <data>
    <wsout>
        <param name="name">Doe</param>
        <param name="first
name">John<param>
        <param name="amount">1000</
param>
    </wsout>
</xqresult>
```

that means that the "no" outgoing edge has to be activated and that the next activity can invoke an external load assessor Web Service using, as invocation parameters, the data in the wsout element.

Further details of EPML.WS are omitted since they are outside the scope of this article, the simple example reported above is provided only to show how elements of EPML can correspond to views in a Web application and to invocations in a Web service choreography.

DISCUSSION AND CONCLUSION

In this paper we presented a proposal for the modeling and implementation of process-aware applications. Our approach addresses both short-term, single user, process-based interactions and complex business processes involving several users, spanning across systems and organizations' boundaries. The use of an executable modeling language at the design level and of its enactment engine at the system level guarantees the matching between the designed and the actual behavior of the system. Moreover, with respect to the "do-it-yourself" solutions, the resulting software architecture can rely on the enactment engine for managing aspects like integration with other systems, persistence, reliability, etc. (if the engine addresses them, of course). Several issues, however, merit to be discussed. First of all, the decision to use yet another (non-standard) modeling language and its execution engine can be perceived as a critical point.

Our solution is based on EPML because it is an executable language for which an enactment engine is available. BPMN, being an OMG-endorsed standard, would have been more reasonable for the modeling phase, but it is not an executable language (and also has no formal semantics). It is true that, by using MDA-like techniques, it is possible to transform a BPMN diagram into a WS-BPEL specification (Alves A., at al.), but this transformation suffers from several problems (Ouyang, Dumas, Breute, & ter Hofstede, 2006) such as, for instance, different expressive power between the two languages and unclear mapping methods. Moreover the usage of a WS-BPEL engine to address the control-flow perspective in a Web application appears troublesome, being WS-BPEL designed for Web service orchestration only (which means that it addresses also the operational perspective and does not concentrate on the control-flow one only as EPML does). BPMN could, however, complement our proposal with high-level business process design. Being EPML an executable language, it models processes with a high level of detail, which may not be needed at an early design stage or for documentation purposes.

YAWL (van der Aalst & ter Hofstede, 2005) is an executable workflow language for which an enactment engine is available. Yet again, YAWL addresses not only the control-flow perspective (which is perfectly reasonable, having been designed for workflow management), limiting its usability across application domains. Practical issues arise because the language assumes a specific XML-based data model and the engine addresses the operational perspective by only using Web services to interact with other systems. As of today EPML is the most reasonable solution (in fact it has been designed right because we felt it would have been filled an empty niche); the conceptual approach we developed in this paper should be applicable to (future) different modeling tools and enactment systems.

Windows Workflow Foundation (WWF), first released as a part of .NET Framework 3.0 (http://www.microsoft.com/net/), is a technology for defining, executing, and managing workflows. An XML-based language, XAML, can be used for declaring the structure of a workflow, while a workflow engine runtime provides common facilities for running and managing the workflow definition.

The same framework (.NET) also includes Windows Presentation Foundation (WPF), a technology that allows for the design of both windows applications and Rich Internet Applications (RIAs). Also in WPF, the application user interfaces can be defined using XAML. This suggests that, by combining the aforementioned technologies, a synergic solution could be adopted in order to support process-based RIAs. However, it should be noticed that such approach differs from the one we proposed mainly for two reasons.

First, the resulting application would be a RIA and not a regular Web application (it needs SilverLight plugin to run inside a browser). Second, WPF and WWF do not currently provide high-level support for designing process-based RIAs. The programmer should implement a specific dispatcher page that queries the workflow engine runtime in order to activate a specific page depending on the state of a process. This solution, at the system level, is similar to the solution we proposed. What is missing is the design level.

In fact, although both WPF and WWF allow high level design via XAML, WPF/XAML is not "process aware" unless the designer specifically introduces the aforementioned dispatcher directly in the navigational model, letting a system-level concern emerge at the design level. In our approach the dispatch component is not present at the design level and, more importantly, it is automatically refined with the proposed model-driven tools (this is the Process Action). Not code related to the interplay between the navigation and the process has to be handwritten.

Other issues are mostly related to technical details. For example, it is possible that the action corresponding to a process-related page is canceled by some concurrent process flow while the user is interacting with it. The actual solution we implemented dispatches to the users a (customizable) error page each time they try to submit data from a process-related page for which no active action exists (the corresponding check is added automatically by the transformation tool when creating the Struts actions skeletons). A similar problem is related to synchronization points in the workflow: if, while in process-flow mode, users finish an activity but the process has to wait before starting the next (typically because a synchronization has to be performed), the system assumes that the process has to be treated as suspended and the user is sent to the page connected to the process-stereotyped class with the outgoing process-stereotyped navigation link. While this solution could be improved (for example by using other specific outgoing links) the related problem, most of the times, arises because of design errors (joins with other process flows should not happen inside navigable sub-processes).

We are now extending our method to rich internet applications (that are mostly based on AJAX-like technologies and are not well-modeled with page-oriented design methods like WAE); initial work suggests that most of the concepts presented in this article are preserved.

REFERENCES

Alves A., & al. (2007). Web Services Business Process Execution Language Version 2.0. OASIS standard. Available at http://docs.oasis-open.org/wsbpel/2.0/wsbpel-v2.0.pdf

Brambilla, M., Ceri, S., Fraternali, P., & Manolescu, I. (2006). Process modeling in web applications. *ACM Transactions on Software Engineering and Methodology, 15*(4), 360–409. doi:10.1145/1178625.1178627

Brambilla, M., Comai, S., Fraternali, P., & Matera, M. (2007). *Designing Web applications with WebML and WebRatio, Web Engineering: Modeling and Implementing Web Applications*. Springer.

Conallen, J. (2002). *Building Web Applications with UML*. Boston, MA: Addison-Wesley Longman Publishing Co., Inc.

Distante, D., Rossi, G., & Canfora, G. (2007). Modeling business processes in web applications: an analysis framework. *Proceedings of the 2007 ACM Symposium on Applied Computing*, (pp. 1677-1682).

Expresso - java architectural framework. (n.d.). Retrieved June 23, 2008, from http://www.jcorporate.com/html/products/expresso.html

Jablonski, S., & Bussler, C. (1996). *Workflow Management: Modeling Concepts, Architecture and Implementation. London et al.* International Thomson Computer Press.

Koch, N., Kraus, A., & Cachero, C., & Meliá, S. (2004). Integration of business processes in Web application models. *Journal of Web Engineering, 3*(1), 22–29.

Ouyang, C., Dumas, M., Breutel, S., & ter Hofstede, A. H. (2006). Translating standard process models to BPEL. *Proceedings of the 18th International Conference on Advanced Information Systems Engineering*, (pp. 417-432).

Rossi, D., & Turrini, E. (2007). *EPML: Executable process modeling language*. (Report No. UBLCS-2007-22). Bologna: Department of Computer Science, University of Bologna.

Schmid, H. A., & Rossi, G. (2004). Modeling and designing processes in e-commerce applications. *IEEE Internet Computing, 8*(1), 19–27. doi:10.1109/MIC.2004.1260699

Troyer, O. D., & Casteleyn, S. (2003). Modeling Complex Processes for Web Applications using WSDM. *Proceedings of the Third International Workshop on Web-Oriented Software Technologies*.

van der Aalst, W. M., & ter Hofstede, A. H. (2005). YAWL: Yet another workflow language. *Information Systems, 30*(4), 245–275. doi:10.1016/j.is.2004.02.002

Wohed, P., van der Aalst, W. M., Dumas, M., Russell, N., & ter Hofstede, A. H. (2005). Pattern-based analysis of the control-flow perspective of UML activity diagrams. *Proceedings of the 24th International Conference on Conceptual Modeling, 3716*, 63-78.

Chapter 12
AGATHE-2:
An Adaptive, Ontology-Based Information Gathering Multi-Agent System for Restricted Web Domains

Bernard Espinasse
Aix-Marseilles University, France

Sébastien Fournier
Aix-Marseilles University, France

Fred Freitas
Universidade Federal de Pernambuco, Brazil

Shereen Albitar
Aix-Marseilles University, France

Rinaldo Lima
Universidade Federal de Pernambuco, Brazil

ABSTRACT

Due to Web size and diversity of information, relevant information gathering on the Web turns out to be a highly complex task. The main problem with most information retrieval approaches is neglecting pages' context, given their inner deficiency: search engines are based on keyword indexing, which cannot capture context. Considering restricted domains, taking into account contexts, with the use of domain ontology, may lead to more relevant and accurate information gathering. In the last years, we have conducted research with this hypothesis, and proposed an agent- and ontology-based restricted-domain cooperative information gathering approach accordingly, that can be instantiated in information gathering systems for specific domains, such as academia, tourism, etc. In this chapter, the authors present this approach, a generic software architecture, named AGATHE-2, which is a full-fledged scalable multi-agent system. Besides offering an in-depth treatment for these domains due to the use of domain ontology, this new version uses machine learning techniques over linguistic information in order to accelerate the knowledge acquisition necessary for the task of information extraction over the Web pages. AGATHE-2 is an agent and ontology-based system that collects and classifies relevant Web pages about

DOI: 10.4018/978-1-60960-132-4.ch012

Copyright © 2011, IGI Global. Copying or distributing in print or electronic forms without written permission of IGI Global is prohibited.

a restricted domain, using the BWI (Boosted Wrapper Induction), a machine-learning algorithm, to perform adaptive information extraction.

INTRODUCTION

Because of the size of the Web and the diversity of accessible information, to gather relevant information from the Web turns out to be a highly complex task. Without taking explicitly into account the search context, the majority of the current approaches of information retrieval (IR) let escape many forms of organized information of the Web, for example, specific domains or "clusters" of information.

However, the field known as Symbolic Artificial Intelligence (AI) has faced a similar challenge in the past. During the seventies, researchers from this field tried to produce systems that could cope with inference capabilities about everything. The lesson learned (Newell, Shaw, & Simon, 1959) was that the use of knowledge-based systems is feasible only over restricted domains, which led to the relative success of the expert systems. This policy is also valid for the IR field. Indeed, the evaluation of the IR systems is mainly carried out over homogeneous corpora, whose texts relates to only one subject and often come from the same source, and not from text sets with diverse contents and writing styles, as it is the case of those available on the Web. This fact is also besides at the origin of the development in IR of specialized search engines (Mc Callum et al, 1999).

Another argument pleading for a restricted domain in IR relates to Information Extraction (IE). Generally, IE works over textual documents collections (Muslea, Minton, & C. Knoblock, 1998). The task consists in extracting data starting from specific classes of Web pages (Gaizauskas & Robertson, 1997). It concerns the identification of specific fragments from a document, which should constitute the core of its semantic contents (Kushmerick, 1999a). The main goal of IE is to populate databases about specific domains - such

as Tourism, Academia, etc - regrouping information coming from many Web pages spread over geographically distributed sites. These databases save users' work on finding, checking and comparing the data which then can be easily queried by users.

Taking such a specific domain context into account enables better data processing (Etzioni et al., 2004). It is the case of the extraction of majority of information from a given class of pages (for example the value of the dollar from a currency exchange rates page, subjects of interest of a researcher from his homepage and so on). Another advantage is to make possible for the users to carry out queries combining, in particular, search keys relative to various classes of pages, allowing complex requests (the search of the papers published in a certain whole of conferences, for example). Thus, it is possible to build sophisticated applications in order to gather Web information from specific domains. With the "Tourism" cluster, for example, applications could retrieve, extract, and classify data about hotels, passage tickets, and cultural events.

On the other hand, it is widely known that Machine Learning (ML) algorithms simplify the development of IE programs; these algorithms have been utilized to automate extraction rules' production. In recent times, many IE systems had been developed following a three-step procedure: (1) Recognizing relevant information in the text (2) Extracting this information (3) Storing it in an organized structure or in a database (Kushmerick, 1999b; Siefkes & Siniakov, 2005).

In the last years, we have conducted research with these research hypotheses, and produced ontology-based restricted-domain cooperative information gathering software agents accordingly, that permit the development of a specific information gathering systems e.g. the MASTER-

Web system (Freitas & Bittencourt, 2003), and a first version of AGATHE system (Espinasse et al, 2008). According to this approach and based on previously-presented guiding ideas, this chapter presents a generic software architecture, named AGATHE-2, an extension of AGATHE system (Espinasse et al., 2008) that permits a more adaptive information gathering on restricted Web domains. As its predecessors, AGATHE-2 is an agent and ontology-based system that collects and classifies relevant Web pages from a restricted Web domain. Furthermore, it uses the BWI (Boosted Wrapper Induction) [ref], a machine-learning algorithm, to perform adaptive information extraction over the collected Web pages.

The chapter is organized as follows: section 2 introduces major notions of cooperative information gathering, and the interest of using agents and different kinds of ontologies to develop intelligent gathering systems on one or more restricted domains of the Web. Section 3 presents the AGATHE-2 system, a multi-agent architecture for the development of intelligent gathering systems on the Web, its objectives, its architecture with its three main subsystems, and its general functioning. Sections 4 to 6 present in detail these subsystems composing AGATHE-2 system: the Search Subsystem, the Extraction Subsystem and the User Subsystem. Section 7 presents some implementation details of the prototype in progress and some results. Finally, we conclude with some research perspectives.

COOPERATIVE INFORMATION GATHERING, ONTOLOGIES AND MACHINE LEARNING

Suggested by (Oates et al, 1994), the concept of "Cooperative Information Gathering" (CIG), is based on the distributed problem solving paradigm for the fields of multi-agent systems (MAS) and distributed artificial intelligence (DAI) (Huhns, 1994; Nwana, 1996). CIG involves concurrent, asynchronous discovery and composition of information spread across a network of information servers. The distributed resolution of problem is then a means for the agents to discover relevant clusters of information.

Other research works recommend the use of agents for information gathering. In (Ambite & Knoblock, 1997), in hierarchical classes the databases of a large numerical library, each class has its own agent with explicit knowledge about it. These agents build the research plans, which improve the effectiveness in the search process. Using such a tool on the Web requires a correct pairing of the pages discovered on the Web with these classes and to extract information from it to feed these databases.

(Decker et al, 1995) have proposed MACRON, an agent architecture adapted to Cooperative Information Gathering. In MACRON, the top-level user queries drive the creation of partially elaborated information gathering plans, resulting in the employment of multiple cooperative agents for the purpose of achieving goals and sub-goals within those plans. MACRON is composed of three types of autonomous agents: reasoning agents, low-level retrieval agents, and user interface agents.

(Lesser et al., 2000) have proposed the BIG system. This system is an informational agent, that plans to gather information to support a decision process, reasons about the resource trade-offs of different possible gathering approaches, extracts information from both unstructured and structured documents, and uses the extracted information to refine its search and processing activities.

Motivation of Using Ontologies for CIG

In order to take into account context for domain restricted CIGs, it is necessary to use knowledge related to the concerned domain. The use of ontologies in CIGs is justified by the advantages of using declarative solutions, due to a number of reasons.

First of all, declarative solutions provide closer integration of an ontological approach with a more direct translation of the domain knowledge.

Moreover, the tasks of extraction and classification on the Web, which deals with unstructured or semi-structured data, require frequent changes of their solutions. With declarative knowledge, defined in ontologies, such changes can be easily taken into account, without the needs of recompiling code or stop execution. In this way, the use of ontologies constitutes a notable advantage of extensibility. In more of the possibilities of inferences, concepts implied in these tasks (for example cluster entities, functional groups, representations of Web page, etc.) are defined in a declarative way in ontologies.

The use of ontologies brings many others advantages (Gruber, 1995). They permit multiple inheritances and take advantage of expressivity in comparison to using object-oriented implementations. They also enable the use of high level communication models, in which the defined concepts, like domain knowledge, are common to the communicating agents, playing the role of shared vocabulary for agents' communication. Finally, the use of ontology increases the flexibility of information gathering systems.

Different Types of Ontologies for CIG

In information gathering over restricted domains of the Web, the major tasks to perform are Web pages' retrieval, classification and information extraction. For the realization of these tasks, three types of ontologies can be used in a complementary way:

1. *Domain ontologies*: these are one or more ontologies related to the restricted domain. These ontologies should cover the concepts, relations, restrictions, terminology and valid axioms of the domain and can be used, e.g., to classify Web pages and extract relevant information from them.

2. *Linguistic ontologies*: the integration of natural languages processing techniques exploiting linguistic ontologies is relevant in particular for the tasks of classification and information extraction, in order to make them more powerful, in particular in clearing up a lot of ambiguity related to natural languages. Typical examples are co-reference resolution (e.g., to know at whom the pronoun "it" refers to in the phrases "My dog likes my cat. It purrs every morning to wake me up.") and passive voice phrases where simple extractors, such as wrappers (Kushmerick, 1999a) fail. Wordnet (Miller et al, 1990) and the ontologies from the GATE project (General Architecture for Text Extraction) are good examples of ontologies of this type.

3. *Operational ontologies*: they gather and organize knowledge used by a software tool, enabling this tool to perform the set of tasks for which it was designed. In such a tool, the main interest of using knowledge defined in an operational ontology is still related to its declarativity. This declarativity brings a greater extensibility to the tool by allowing many possibilities of evolution in the realization of its tasks.

Classification and information extraction tasks concerning semi- or unstructured information are very difficult to realize. They use, in general, heuristics, often developed in an empirical way, and require, in consequence, many adjustments. The exploitation of declarative knowledge defined in an operational ontology promises to facilitate the realization of these tasks.

Such operational ontologies concern knowledge that is not specific to the restricted domain considered, but associated to the manner to exploit Web page related to this domain, in particular in classification and extraction tasks. Such instrumental knowledge is not limited to terms, keywords and statistics like is usually done in common gathering systems. This knowledge can concern any fact that make possible, in page classification, to distinguish a class of pages from other classes, or in information extraction, to consider the structure of the page treated, of the probable areas of this page where to find suitable information to extract.

Machine Learning for Information Extraction: Adaptive Information Extraction

Rule-based IE systems, as AGATHE, used to be developed in an ad hoc manner; however the process of knowledge engineering required to come up with the rules is laborious and time consuming. Domain specific extraction rules or patterns, instead of being handcrafted for each application domain, can be learnt directly by generic domain-independent IE system using a tagged domain-specific training set (Etzioni et al, 2008). Enriched with natural language processing (NLP) and inductive logic programming (ILP) methods, a spectrum of generic architectures were proposed to realize supervised IE on Web pages (Turmo et al, 2006).

Recently, self-supervised IE systems, a new paradigm in the IE research domain, has come to life. In general, these systems depend on domain-independent patterns to label their training sets for each application domain (Etzioni et al., 2008). According to the under test performance of self-supervised systems, supervised IE systems are still more attractive. In order to evaluate and compare IE supervised algorithms, three measures are principally used: Precision, Recall and F-Measure (Maynard et al, 2006).

As for the task of text categorization, in the last decade, different classifications for adaptive information extraction methods were proposed (Siefkes & Siniakov, 2005; Tang et al 2007). According to the classification proposed in (Tang et al., 2007), the three distinguished classes of adaptative IE methods are: Rule Learning based methods, Classification based Methods, and Sequential Labeling based Methods.

AGATHE-2 has adopted the Boosted Wrapper Induction (BWI) algorithm (Freitag & Kushmerick, 2000; Kauchak et al 2004), a Rule Learning based method belonging to the Wrapper Induction category. The reason for which BWI was chosen for this work is its competence in information extraction from unstructured text in addition to structured and semi-structured text (Albitar et al., 2010; Lima et al, 2010)

AGATHE OVERVIEW

The AGATHE project is an international cooperation between France and Brazil. Its aim is proposing a generic software architecture that allows the development of information gathering systems on the Web, for one or for a few restricted domains. In the AGATHE architecture, cooperative agents exploit one (or more) domain ontologies, related to one (or more) restricted domains and an operational ontology to perform its various processing tasks over Web pages in a distributed and cooperative way, as any multi-agent-based solution.

AGATHE software architecture benefits from agent-oriented software engineering (which would be extended thereafter to Web services). Such software engineering ensures flexibility and reusability. The starting point of this architecture is the MASTER-Web system (Freitas & Bittencourt, 2003), which uses ontologies to carry out the tasks of classification and extraction of information on the Web on only one restricted domain of search at a time. AGATHE is enabled not only to perform over more than one domain at a time, but also to establish cooperations among different domains. For instance, a cooperation between the domains of Academia and tourism could be held in the following way: The academic research domain concerns relevant information about events, such as title, sponsors place, topics, important dates, program, title of sessions, etc contained in calls for papers (CFPs) and calls for participation pages. Information gathering over this domain will then be widened to another restricted domain. For instance, we can consider the tourism and transport domains in order to envisage a displacement related to participation in a particular scientific event (trips, lodging, touristical visits, etc.).

AGATHE-2, as its previous version AGATHE (Espinasse et al., 2008) is an extension of MASTER-Web, thus reusing the latter's ontologies (Frame ontologies) and deploys their use onto a complex and distributed organization of more effective software agents, with different types of specialized agents in interaction. Moreover, AGATHE allows for treating several fields of search simultaneously and has mechanisms of recommendation inter sophisticated fields, with an easier implementation. Lastly, in its agent-oriented implementation, AGATHE respects the recommendations defined by the FIPA ("FIPA," 2000).

As symbolic rules were domain dependent and arduously written, in particular for the information extraction task from collected Web pages, it seemed judicious to replace them by machine supervised learning techniques. Thus, in order to make more adaptive the AGATHE system, recent works relative to the use of machine learning techniques (and particularly the efficient and effective BWI algorithm [Kauchak et al 2004]) for information extraction tasks from Web pages, have lead to a new version of this system, a more adaptive version named AGATHE-2.

The main objective of the whole AGATHE project is to accomplish information gathering on restricted fields of the Web that can be gradually widened. For the development of AGATHE, the first restricted domain of search chosen is the academic search domain, more precisely scientific events (international conferences or workshops). With each of these search domains there is a specific ontology associated.

In this section, the general architecture and functioning of AGATHE-2 system are firstly presented, then the three main subsystems composing

Figure 1. General AGATHE architecture

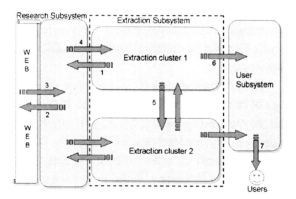

AGATHE-2 system are introduced. Finally, some implementation details are given.

Architecture and General Functioning of AGATHE-2 System

The AGATHE-2 general architecture, illustrated on Figure 1, is articulated around three principal subsystems in interaction: the *Search subsystem (SSS), the Extraction subsystem (ESS), and the User subsystem (USS).*

The three main subsystems of AGATHE-2 are themselves multi-agent systems (MAS), composed of software agents. Some of them use ontologies to carry out the tasks for which they were conceived.

The *Search subsystem (SSS)* is in charge of querying external Web search engines (such as Google) in order to obtain Web pages, which will be treated by the *Extraction subsystem (*ESS). This Subsystem is a multi-agent system (MAS), composed of different types of agents to search all the Web by the use of traditional search engines (Google, Altavista, Yahoo), to look in specific resource sites of the Web (DBLP, CITESEER,…).

The *Extraction subsystem (ESS)* is the heart of the whole architecture and is composed of different "extraction clusters" (EC), each one specialized in the processing of Web pages on a specific field (like that of academic search, or that of tourism).

Each cluster is associated to one domain ontology. This subsystem is a MAS composed of different agents performing different tasks of classification and information extraction, supported by different ontologies.

The *User subsystem (USS)* performs the storage of information extracted from the Web pages already treated by the Extraction subsystem, and provides a query interface for the users, which can be humans or other software agents. This subsystem is in charge of the user interactions within the AGATHE system.

The general functioning of AGATHE is illustrated on Figure 1. Below is description of the numbered arrows that represents the step-by-step interactions among its various constituent subsystems:

- 1: A cluster of extraction of the Extraction SubSystem (ESS) requires a search for pages particular to the Search Subsystem;
- 2 and 3: The SSS works like a meta-robot of search, seeking Web pages, by querying existing search engines like Google, Altavista or other;
- 4: These pages are then transmitted to the ESS, more precisely to the agent of the extraction cluster which has done the initial query (1);
- 5: If necessary, recommendations are sent by the cluster to other extraction clusters, in order to propose pages to them which can potentially interest them;
- 6: Extracted information is then transmitted to the Front-Office Subsystem (FOSS), in order to be stored in a specific database, which is accessible by users' queries (7).

Implementation Details

The AGATHE-2 system is deployed in the Eclipse environment in Java, and uses the Jade multi-agent platform ("Jade," 2006). The Search Subsystem (SSS) and the User Subsystem (USS)

are composed of agents developed in Java. In the Extraction subsystem (ESS), the agents using the domain ontology and/or the operational ontology to perform specific tasks, are developed with the Jess inference engine ("Jess," 2006). Currently, the Extraction subsystem works over only one extraction cluster without recommendation mechanism.

For the construction and the handling of ontologies, defined by Frames, the Protégé environment (Protégé, 2006) is used, and the exploitation of the ontologies by the Jess agents is done via the Protégé plugin JessTab (Eriksson, 2003).

The information extraction task, performed by the ESS subsystem, uses the WEPAIES system (Lima et al., 2010). This system integrates various software modules to clean, prepare, annotate and produce, by supervised learning, information extractors used in AGATHE-2. In order to clean the Web pages it uses the HTMLCleaner tool (Girardi, 2007). The Web pages, are annotated with POS (Part Of Speech) tags, by employing the QTAG tool (Tufis & Mason, 1998). Finally, capitalizing over the linguistic patterns, an automatic extractor based on extraction rules is produced using a specially tailored version of TIES system("TIES," 2004) developed by our group (Lima et al., 2010).

The classification results and information extracted are stored in a MySQL relational management database system according the RDF Format and use Jena framework ("Jena," 2006). Jena is a Java framework for building Semantic Web applications providing a programmatic environment for RDF, RDFS and OWL, SPARQL and includes a rule-based inference engine. Jena framework is used in AGATHE-2 to store in the database the classification results, and extracted information in RDF format. These tasks are performed by the Storage Agent of the Extraction Subsystem. Jena framework is also used to exploit this database in the User Subsystem.

The following section presents in detail the three subsystems composing AGATHE-2 system.

Figure 2. Internal architecture of the Search Subsystem

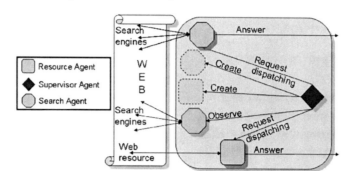

THE AGATHE SEARCH SUBSYSTEM

As illustrated in Figure 2, the Search Subsystem receives requests for Web pages from specific agents of a cluster. For instance, the Articles agent from the Science cluster asks for pages that contain keywords such as "introduction", "related work", "conclusion", and some others. Then the Search Subsystems forwards this query to existing search engines, gathers the Web pages returned by them and return these pages to the specific Extractor Agents from the Extractor Cluster that solicited them.

Three types of agents contribute to the information search process: (i) Search Agents, (ii) Resource Agents and (iii) Supervisor Agent. The Search Agent performs requests to existing search engines (Google, and\or others). It receives requests from a specific Extractor Agent. After having merged the different results obtained by the various engines, the Search Agent directly transmits them to the Extraction Subsystem.

The Resource Agent is similar to a Search Agent, but it performs requests only to specialized resources of the Web. For example, for information related to the academic research, such resources can be the CITESEER site for publications, the DBLP site for authors, a specific web service, or a specialized database. It is requested by the Supervisor Agent, and it transmits its results directly to a specific Extractor agent in the Extraction Subsystem.

The Supervisor Agent coordinates the activities of the Search Subsystem. It receives requests from the Extraction Subsystem and, aware of the workload of various Search and Resource Agents, it manages for the best allocation of these requests to be treated. According to the strain over these agents, it creates (or even deletes) Search and Resource Agents. For performance reasons, the Supervisor Agent can also decide to move these Search Agents to CPUs with less work. The Supervisor Agent manages also subscriptions, permitting the Extraction Subsystem to receive periodically results from a specific information request. The strategy used can be called "push" and the results are directly transmitted, without the necessity of formulating further requests.

THE AGATHE EXTRACTION SUBSYSTEM (ESS)

The general aim of the Extraction Subsystem is to classify Web pages transmitted by the Search subsystem, and to extract relevant information from them and finally to store this information in a database, to be accessed by the users in the User Subsystem.

In the following sections, we present the architecture of the Extraction Subsystem of AGATHE-2, the different ontologies used in this Subsystem to perform classification and extraction tasks, the way that agents employ these ontologies, and finally, we present in details each agent of this subsystem.

Extraction Subsystem Architecture

The AGATHE-2 system have to permit an information gathering concerning more than one restricted domain, the AGATHE Extraction Subsystem is composed of a set of extraction "clusters" (while MASTER-Web processes only one cluster at a time). Each of these extraction clusters is related to a specific domain, to which is associated a specific ontology. For example, considering scientific events deployed via Call for Papers (CFP) Web pages, these can be processed by classes of an academic research cluster, classes which are related to scientific events. However these Web pages usually bring information about trips, hotels, social and cultural events which are simultaneous or with dates near the conference, and so on. Other extraction clusters related to the tourism domain could also process these CFP Web pages.

In order to be more efficient, an extraction cluster is performed by several cooperating software agents, each agent being specialized in a specific task, like, searching the web for useful pages, pre-processing, extracting, supervising, recommending and storing. This distribution in AGATHE allows for a better performance when treating a very large number of pages. For example, several instances of a same type of agent could share the treatment of these pages running on the same machine or on different machines. This distribution allows distributing the Web page processing on several instances of different extractor agents specialized in the treatment of different parts of the domain ontology related to the cluster. This division is essentially designed for scalability purposes, while in MASTER-Web one agent is responsible for a class of pages (like CFPs, for instance) and could not scale to a better performance when a high number of pages have to be processed.

The Extraction Subsystem's functions are two-fold: first to ask for Web pages to the Search Subsystem, and then to process these pages (the Web pages that the Search Subsystem has deployed, which are supposed to belong to the class being processed by the Extractor agent which asked for them). This latter task constitutes the backbone of then whole system, and consists in the subtasks of page validation, functional classification, and information extraction.

The AGATHE-2 extraction subsystem is quite different from the AGATHE extraction subsystem, because it performs an adaptive information extraction based on supervised learning techniques. This new subsystem is composed of extraction clusters which are, in turn, composed of software agents that performs pages classification and information extraction.

Software agents using symbolic rules that exploit ontologies used to realize most tasks of information classification and extraction in the original AGATHE system (Espinasse et al., 2008). Since symbolic rules were domain dependent and had to be written manually at a high human-labour cost machine learning techniques seemed to us welcome to help develop extractors automatically in a faster way. Therefore, the aim of our recent work was to combine, in AGATHE-2, symbolic based classification and machine learning based information extraction in new extraction subsystem architecture.

Agents exploit a domain ontology using symbolic rules in order to realize the tasks of classification. For the information extraction task, for each relevant web page class of this ontology, an specific agent extracts information according to extractors obtained by a supervised learning phase realized by BWI algorithm (Albitar et al., 2010; Lima et al., 2010).

The new extraction cluster is presented in Figure 3. Every extractor agent wraps a running WEPAIES for IE, while the classifier agent realizes semantic classification only. An extractor master agent is introduced in this cluster in order

Figure 3. Internal architecture of an Extraction Cluster

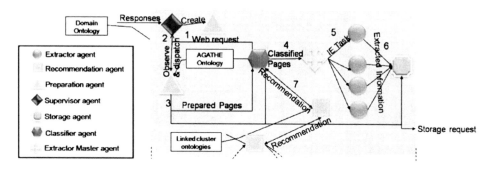

to ensure system modularity and agent specialization. This agent manages the allocation of IE tasks to extractor agents according to a predetermined strategy. Finally, the storage agent stores extracted information in a database for future analysis

As illustrated in Figure 3, each of these Extraction Clusters is a multi-agent system performing the classification of the Web pages, and information extraction from these pages. These agents perform specific tasks in the extraction cluster. Some of these agents use ontologies to perform their tasks. The various agents that compose the cluster are:

- a set of Preparation Agents,
- one Supervisor Agent,
- one Classifier Agent,
- one Extractor Master Agent,
- a set of Extractor Agents,
- one Recommendation Agent, and
- one or more Storage Agents.

The functioning of the Extraction Cluster is the following (Figure 3):

1. The classifier agent sends a demand for a web search to the supervisor agent.
2. The supervisor agent forwards the demand towards the search subsystem and then sends the retrieved pages to the preparation agent.

3. After filtering and functionally classifying (discarding emails and lists), preparation agent sends valid web pages to the classifier agent and sends preparation results to the storage agent.
4. Web pages belonging to the cluster's specific domain are sent by the classifier agent, after classifying them semantically, to the extractor master agent.
5. The extractor master agent dispatches IE task between multiple extractor agents according to a predetermined distribution strategy.
6. Each extractor agent realizes the assigned IE task and sends extracted information to the storage agent in order to be stored in the database.
7. If the classifier agent discovers that the web page doesn't belong to its domain, it forwards it to the recommendation agent who decides to which cluster the page must be sent.

Before presenting in detail these different agents composing the ESS, the following subsections introduce the different ontologies used by these agents and how they benefit from them.

Ontologies Used in the Extraction Subsystem

The cooperative agents composing the AGATHE Extraction Subsystem exploit two types of ontology to perform tasks of pages classification and

Figure 4. A part of the "Science ontology" concerning scientific events

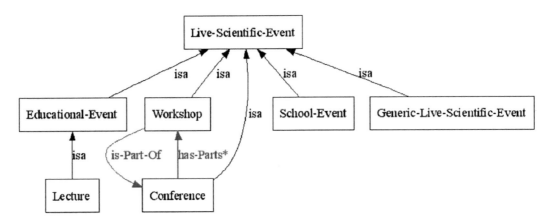

information extraction. The first one is an internal ontology, an operational ontology, called "Agathe Ontology", used to perform in a cooperative way, various information treatments on the Web pages. The second type are the domain ontology(ies), related to one or more restricted domain of search.

The current version of AGATHE does not use linguistic ontologies. The information extraction process is based only on the presence or absence of concepts belonging to the domain ontology. An upcoming version of AGATHE will use linguistic ontologies and natural languages processing techniques to improve classification and extraction tasks.

A domain ontology concerns the restricted domain considered for information gathering. Each extraction cluster is associated to such ontology. Figure 4 presents a part of the domain ontology, named "Science ontology", relative to the academic research field. This part concerns the live scientific events, concerning publication, CFP (Call For Papers).

The operational Agathe ontology is already defined and used in MASTER-Web system and named inside "Web ontology". This ontology specifies the main concepts used by AGATHE-2 for the classification and extraction tasks performed on Web pages. Figure 5 presents a subset of this ontology, related to the concept of Web

page and two specific concepts for information extraction (Slot-Recognizer and Slot-Extractor).

Both kinds of ontologies are defined in Frames using the Protégé environment (Protégé, 2006).

How Agents Use Ontologies

Agents of the Extraction Subsystem are cognitive agents and employ the Jess inference engine ("Jess," 2006) in their reasoning for the tasks of classification and extraction, using production rules written in Jess. The ontologies specified in the latter section are translated to Jess facts thanks to the JessTab (Eriksson, 2003) Protégé plugin. The general structure of such rules is:

1. Name of the rule
2. Precondition: presence in the facts base of concepts that belong to the operational Agathe ontology and associated attributes
3. Test on attributes obtained (begin by keyword test).
4. Action of the rule specific to the rule (begin by => symbol).

Here is an example of a specific extraction rule, in Jess/JessTab syntax, used by the Extractor agents:

Figure 5. Main classes, slots and relations of the operational ontology

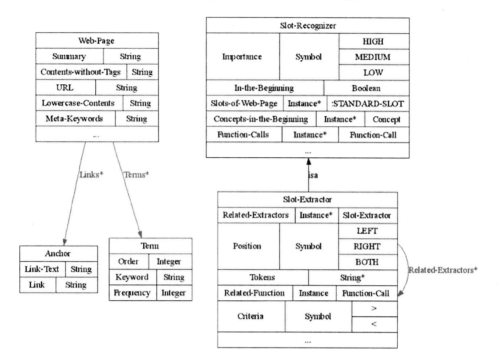

This specific rule permits to find interesting data in text associated to links that help to classify a page. The name of this rule is "r_454" and its purpose is to identify if a certain slot (?s, in the rule) is identified and it uses the Processing-Monitor and Slot-Recognizer concepts that are a part of the Agathe ontology (see Figure 5). It tests if the slot ?s has already been found (the condition (not (object (is-a Slot-Found) (Slot-in-Process ?s)))), and then, in the test part of the rule, it checks whether one of the concepts that should be present ($?cb, in the rule) in the text of a Web link and whether the absent concepts are not present ($?ca). If these conditions are met, the slot ?s is found so its name is stored in a list of slots found (the fact [SLOT-FOUND]). Note that rules used by agent referencing ontologies can be complex to develop, consequently a specific tool has been developed to permit to create them more easily.

The following subsections describe in detail each type of agent composing the ESS, in particular the tasks that they perform.

Preparation Agents

Preparation Agents receive Web pages from the Search Subsystem and perform some treatment on them that will be described below. These agents are created by the Supervisor Agent of the considered extraction cluster and are deleted by this same agent when they are not being used any more. These agents perform the first treatments, thus permitting more easily to reason with the Web pages. These preparation tasks are based in the treatment performed by any MASTER-Web agent, which are explained below (figure 6):

- *Validation.* This task verifies if the Web pages obtained are in HTML format, accessible, and if they are already stored in the database. Pages that do not meet these requirements will not be considered in following treatments.

- *Pre-processing.* This task collects contents (in various representations, for example,

Algorithm 1.

```
(defrule r_454
(object (Page-Status STORED) (is-a Processing-Monitor))
?f <- (object (Importance MEDIUM) (is-a Slot-Recognizer)
(Slot-in-Process ?s)
(Concepts $?cb&:(> (length$ $?cb) 0))
(Absent-Concepts $?ac)
(not (object (is-a Slot-Found) (Slot-in-Process ?s)))
(test (and
(= (count-occurs-once (words-of-concepts $?ac) (slot-get [LINKS-TEXTS] Val-
ues)) 0)
(> (count-occurs-once (words-of-concepts $?cb) (slot-get [LINKS-TEXTS] Val-
ues)) 0)))
=>
(slot-insert$ [SLOTS-FOUND] Instance-Values  ?s))
```

Figure 6. A Preparation Agent and its internal tasks

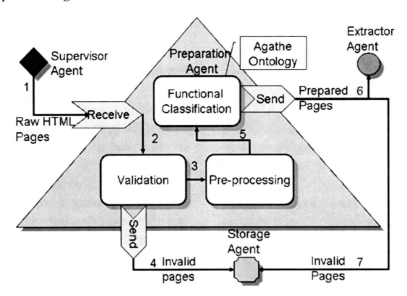

without stopwords, lowercase, without tags, etc), title, links, and emails from the Web pages, using information retrieval techniques and, if necessary, natural language techniques.

- *Functional classification.* This task is knowledge-based and uses the Jess inference engine exploiting the Agathe ontol-

ogy. Thanks to a specific knowledge base (production rules), the Preparation Agent uses this ontology to classify Web pages according to a functional aspect. The functional categories in which the pages will be classified are: messages, lists of links to potentially useful pages (e.g. a list of CFPs), auxiliary pages (pages that contain

Figure 7. The Classifier Agent and its internal tasks

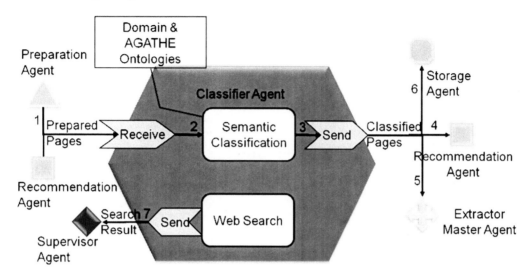

some pieces of information but don't represent an instance of an entity, e.g. a separate page of topics of a conference which has its own page), pages selected for extraction, and finally pages considered as invalid.

In order to achieve better performance and flexibility, it is possible to duplicate such preparation agents to reduce their strain.

The Classifier Agent

As defined in previous version of AGATHE, this agent classifies Web pages semantically, using symbolic Jess rules and exploiting the domain ontology; if the page belongs to a relevant class of the domain, it sends it to the extractor master agent, otherwise it sends it to the recommendation agent of its cluster. Moreover, the page's class (ex. Conference, workshop, journal, etc.), with its address as well as other details are sent by this agent to the storage agent to be eventually stored in the database. The Figure 7 presents the Classifier Agent and its internal tasks.

The Extractor Master Agent

Web pages belonging to a specific class of the considered domain might contain information related to different concepts in the domain ontology. While AGATHE has a multi-agent architecture, it appeared coherent and beneficial to distribute the IE load among multiple extractor agents according to user-defined strategies. Consequently, it was legitimate to introduce the extractor master agent to dispatch IE tasks: first, it receives a classified web page, then it resends it toward the extractor agents specialized in its class according to the defined distribution strategy. The Figure 8 presents the Extractor Master Agent and its internal tasks.

Figure 9 illustrates the class based distribution strategy actually adopted in AGATHE. Each extractor agent is specialized in extracting information from pages belonging to a specific class in the scientific domain.

The Extractor Agents

The Extraction Cluster is composed of several Extractor Agents associated to a specific domain ontology linked to the cluster. The task of these agents is to perform an adaptive information

Figure 8. The Extractor Master Agent and its internal tasks

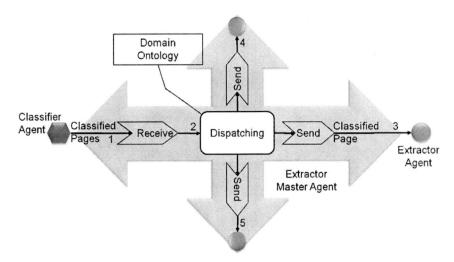

Figure 9. Distribution strategy in the extraction subsystem

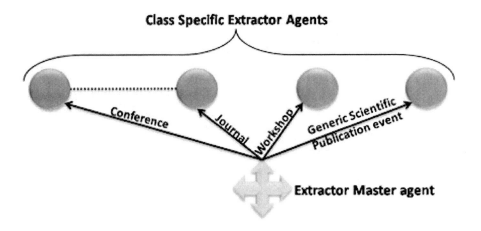

extraction on these pages by applying extractors obtained by supervised learning. This supervised learning is done using a training set of relevant annotated Web pages of the concerned domain. Corpus annotation, which can be done manually by domain experts, uses domain ontology's concepts, and might be completed automatically by POS (Part of Speech) tagging, that takes into account the morphosyntactic structure of the natural language. Each Extractor Agent is associated to a particular class (concept) of the domain ontology to extract.

This agent wraps WEPAIES (Lima et al, 2010), an IE system implementing BWI which is a supervised machine learning algorithm. It extracts relevant information from web pages by executing WEPAIES, using wrappers produced off-line during a training step and saved in XML files. Choosing a concept-based distribution strategy, a single domain concept is delegated to each extractor. Consequently, as soon as an extractor agent receives a message, it runs WEPAIES to extract specific concepts from the page specified in the message. Wrapped inside AGATHE,

Figure 10. An Extraction agent and its internal tasks

WEPAIES is always executed in "IE" mode; supervised training is carried out independently. The Figure 10 presents the Extractor Agent and its internal tasks.

Depending on the classification results for a Web page, and making use of ontologies, the Extractor agent performs the information extraction task. For example, the "Call For Papers" agent could classify different calls for papers for conferences, journals, book chapters and many other classes defined in the Science ontology (domain ontology), which are subclasses of the class Scientific-Events. After finishing the IE task according to the assigned class, the extracted information is then transmitted to the Storage Agent.

The Recommendation Agent

The Recommendation Agent (Figure 11) receives prepared pages from the Preparation Agent and dispatches them to other agents in the same cluster or to other clusters. It accomplishes three main tasks:

- *Inter-Domain recommendation*: it recommends pages/links that might have some interest to other Classifier Agents of the cluster.
- *Intra-Domain recommendation*: it recommends some pages/links to other Extraction Clusters, pages that could be interesting for them. For this task, the

Recommendation Agent needs to access ontologies from the different clusters involved. It dispatches these pages to the various Recommendation Agents of the cluster concerned. An example is briefly described below.

- *Dispatching*: it forwards pages that have been recommended by another Recommendation Agent of other Cluster.

Two clusters are linked if a contextual link exists between them. For instance, the agent responsible for scientific events can suggest for a Tourism cluster some information found on "call for papers" pages, which is related to accommodation and transport facilities to participate in such scientific events. It is typically available in these pages under the label "social program".

The Storage Agent

The Storage Agent is in charge of storing the extracted/classified information in the database of the User Subsystem. This agent prepares and performs the storage. It treats the received information so as to conform to the storage formats, according to the storage structure of the databases tables. It also saves the classification results and the extracted information in the database to be queried by the users via the User Subsystem.

More precisely, this Storage Agent stores in persistent memory the instances of the class "Slot-Found" of the Agathe ontology, class where the

Figure 11. Recommendation agent and its internal tasks

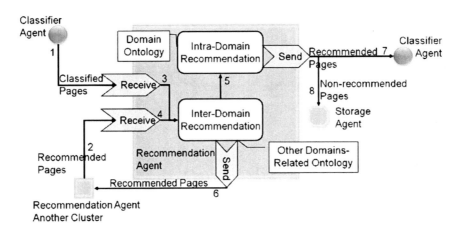

Figure 12. Storage agent

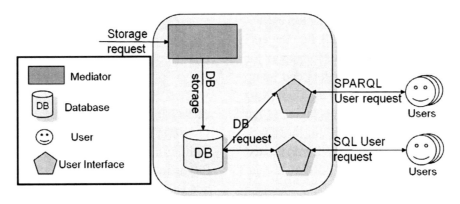

extracted information is stored by the Extraction Agent, and store these information in the RDF format in a relational data base. For this task, this agent uses the JENA (Jena, 2006) environment facilities. We use RDF format in order to work at knowledge level and to keep semantic information related to the ontology.

THE AGATHE USER SUBSYSTEM

The User Subsystem (USS) is the subsystem supporting user interactions with the AGATHE system. The USS is composed of two main components (Figure 12).

The first component concerns the coherence checking of the extracted information stored in the data base. Developed in the JENA environment and SPARQL language, it permits to the user, according an interactive way, to detect incoherence and update consequently the RDF data base of extracted information. Indeed, the extraction process is not always perfect, and some incoherencies can appear. Integration of techniques of natural languages processing in the information extraction task could reduce these incoherencies.

The second component supports user interactions with the AGATHE system to exploit with queries the extracted information stored in the data

Table 1. Frequencies' concepts in the CFP test corpus

Concepts to extract	Frequencies in the corpus			
	Learning	%	Test	%
workshopname	543	11.8	245	10.8
Workshopacronym	566	12.3	243	10.7
Workshophomepage	367	8.0	215	9.5
Workshoplocation	457	10.0	224	9.9
workshopdate	586	12.8	326	14.3
workshopsubmissiondate	590	12.9	316	13.9
Workshopnotificationacceptancedate	391	8.5	190	8.4
Workshopcamerareadycopydate	355	7.7	163	7.2
conferencename	204	4.5	90	4.0
Conferenceacronym	420	9.2	187	8.2
conferencehomepage	104	2.3	75	3.3
TOTAL	**4583**	**100**	**2274**	**100**

base. The SPARQL language and SQL language can be used for it.

FIRST RESULTS

The AGATHE system is currently under development between France and Brazil. To develop and test the AGATHE architecture, the restricted domain of the scientific events in academic research has been chosen. The prototype first performs a gathering of pages concerning Calls For Papers (CFP), then it filters these pages and classifies them into 8 CFP subclasses (conference, workshop, journal etc). Finally, it extracts relevant information and stores them into a database.

Experimental Conditions

In order to evaluate the AGATHE-2 system's performances, we used in our experiments the Call For Papers (CFP) test corpus of the Pascal Challenge (Pascal Challenge, 2005) (200 pages containing 2274 annotated fields) without taking into consideration text annotation. This corpus had been used earlier as a formal basis to evalu-

ate and compare the performance of different ML algorithms (Ireson et al., 2005). The majority of the 1100 documents (850 calls for workshops, 250 calls for conferences) constituting the CFP corpus come from the domain of computer science. Others were collected from the biomedicine and linguistics domains.

The 1100 documents were arranged in three different corpuses; the training corpus containing 400 calls for workshops, the test corpus containing 200 calls for workshops and the enrich corpus containing 250 calls for workshops and 250 calls for conferences. A call for workshop might include details regarding conferences as workshops might be related to other conferences.

In the corpus' pages, 11 information to extract corresponding to concepts of the domain ontology, are annotated: 8 for workshop class concepts and 3 for conference class concepts. Some concepts like dates can be shared between both classes. Conference concepts have lower frequencies in corpus compared to workshop concepts. Table 1 shows the 11 concepts' frequencies in both training and test corpuses.

Table 2. Classification results

Number of pages	Classified as conference	Classified as Workshop	Unclassified pages
199	28	169	2

Classification Results

According to the first version of AGATHE (Espinasse et al., 2008), classification task based on symbolic rules resulted in good precision and recall. For this reason, we maintained the symbolic approach based part for the semantic classification.

Statistical results presented in table 2 shows that AGATHE had some difficulties in classifying some test corpus' pages (200 calls for workshops) as both classes (workshop and conference) are very close. Anyway, AGATHE was able to classify most corpus pages as workshop as it obtained (86% and 85%) rates for the precision and the recall respectively.

Information Extraction

Here we demonstrate how AGATHE works taking as example the call for paper of the conference RCIS2010 presented in Figure 14.

First, the page was prepared and then classified as conference that is the correct class of the page. Then, the extractor agent extracted information from the page. The resulting information, highlighted in Figure 13, is presented in table 3. As workshop and conference classes are so close, they share many concepts like date, location etc. This was the case of last five extracted concepts.

Information Extraction Results

AGATHE (Espinasse et al., 2008) didn't deliver promising results concerning the IE task. This task was implemented in symbolic rules, which were costly to develop. This was the reason for which we adopted an adaptative IE algorithm in

Figure 13. IEEE RCIS 2010 CFP

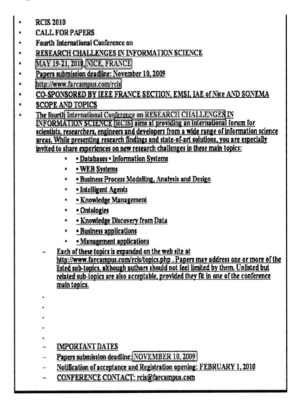

Figure 14. F-measure of extracted concepts in Pascal corpus

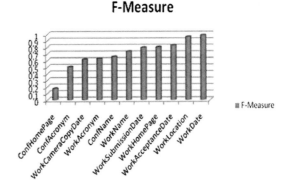

the new version that demonstrated considerably promising results.

After statistical analysis for about 10000 database entries retrieved from treating the test corpus, the average value of F-measure for work-

Table 3. Extracted information for IEEE RCIS 2010 CFP

Concept	Value	Start	End
Conferencename	International Conference on RESEARCH CHALLENGES	304	351
Conferenceacronym	RCIS)	376	381
Workshopdate	MAY 19 - 21, 2010	104	119
Workshophomepage	deadline: November 10, 2009 http:// www. farcampus. com / rcis	152	209
Workshoplocation	NICE, FRANCE	121	133
Workshoppapersubmissiondate	deadline: NOVEMBER 10	4488	4509
Workshopnotificationofacceptancedate	NOVEMBER 10, 2009	4498	4515

shop concepts was equal to (70%). Furthermore, for some concepts like *workshoplocation* and *workshopdate*, highest values (more than 85%) were observed for both precision and recall. Figure 13 illustrates F-measure values obtained during our experimentation concerning different domain concepts (Albitar et al., 2010). Lowest F-measure values were obtained for *conferenceacronym* and *conferencehomepage* concepts. Such low values come from the low frequency of these concepts in the training corpus; as it does not contain enough instances of both concepts so WEPAIES was not trained well to extract them (see Table 1).

Discussion

As a training corpus is used to learn how to extract information, similar information contexts are expected in pages to extract otherwise our system won't be able to extract target fields. This was the case for the concept *workshopnotificationofacceptancedate* that AGATHE-2 could not extract well. The reason to this error is that three words "and registration opening" were placed after "notification of acceptance" taking the place expected for the acceptance date as it was learned and registered in detectors' patterns. This kind of error is explainable as training corpus might not cover all possible cases.

Other sources of confusion might be in the length and the position of field. This was the case for the *conferencename* that was not entirely

extracted. Nevertheless, this kind of confusion might be resolved as AGATHE-2 permits user intervention to decide on the correct result.

In (Lima et al., 2010) an investigation was conducted in the direction of using the BWI algorithm as an IE method for unstructured natural language documents. Table 4 shows the results obtained using the WEPAEIS on 3 corpora: the Pascal challenge Call for Papers (CFP), Seminars, and Job (http://www.isi.edu/info-agents/RISE/repository.html). These corpora were chosen because they present decreasing levels of structuring, from the more structured corpus (Seminars) to the less structured one (CFP). The results are very slightly better than the original BWI algorithm without POS tagging.

Concerning the influence of the POS tagging in information extraction process with BWI algorithm, we note that they obtained the better results for the CFP Pascal Challenge Corpus. On the other hand, for the other corpora (Seminars and Jobs) there was practically no difference. These results were justified by analyzing the more structured nature of the documents in these corpora in which the inducted wrappers could achieve very good performance without POS annotation.

Additionally, (Lima et al. 2010) have also shown that the gain in performance (F-measure) for some concepts was more the 5%, which permitted them to conclude that the use of POS tagging combined with BWI pays off against highly unstructured texts.

Table 4. Influence of the POS tagging on 3 corpora information extraction

Corpus	P	R	F1	P	R	F1
Seminars	0.974	0.953	0.963	0.971	0.964	0.967
Jobs	0.945	0.778	0.853	0.939	0.780	0.853
CFP	0.891	0.571	0.696	0.896	0.591	0.712
	(a) no POS			**(b) with POS**		

RELATED WORK

Cooperative Information Gathering proposed by (Oates et al., 1994), apprehends information gathering as a problem solving process distributed on cooperative agents permitting discovery and integration of relevant information clusters.

Following the MACRON (Decker et al., 1995) and BIG (Lesser et al., 2000) systems and the works of Ambite and Knoblock (1997), agents are being more and more used in the development of information retrieval and recommender systems on the Web (Birukov et al, 2005; Lorenzi et al, 2005; Woerndl & Groh, 2005). The combined use of agents and ontologies for information gathering on the Web, as proposed in AGATHE, is more recent, and the works of Cesarano et allii (2003) and Jung (2007) are in this trend.

(Cesarano et al., 2003) propose a system coupling agents and ontologies to perform an on-line classification of Web pages resulting of a user request on the Web, which gives a ranking more relevant than the one given by the search engine. After a preparation phase, agents reclassify the Web pages, comparing the word they contain to an ontology previously defined. This new ranking, taking into account to the semantics of the user request is more relevant.

Jung (2007) proposes a system permitting to refine requests on the Web by automatically building and merging ontologies associated to specific areas of the Web (set of pages) with a mediator agent. Doing so, this mediator agent builds a consensual ontology which is then used by other agents to refine the requests.

Other information gathering systems have also adopted this approach, particularly the CROSS-MARC system (Karkaletsis et al., 2003) that was implemented for e-retail and job offers domains coupling symbolic rules with wrapper induction.

CONCLUSION AND FUTURE WORK

While being limited to restricted domains, our research hypothesis is that taking into account contexts leads to more relevant information gathering. In the last years, we have concentrated in these research issues and produced ontology-based restricted-domain cooperative information gathering software agents accordingly, that permit the development of a specific information gathering systems e.g. the MASTER-Web system (Freitas & Bittencourt, 2003), and a first version of AGATHE system, AGATHE (Espinasse et al., 2008). Furthermore, in the AGATHE-2 system we have employed machine learning techniques that simplified the development of IE; these algorithms have been utilized to automate rule production for extracting data, endowing with speed the instantiation of a solution for a new domain to be dealt by the system.

The use of supervised ML techniques in IE, Boosted Wrapper Induction (BWI), in information gathering on restricted web domains, improved the task of information extraction in terms of portability and performance. Indeed, the results obtained from this new version of AGATHE-2 system, combining agent and wrapper induction in its information extraction task, are very encouraging.

In a short-term perspective, for the IE task, we intend first to reduce its time, especially by using efficient distribution strategies to dispatch this task. Multiple class specialized extractor agents might be deployed in parallel distributing the information extraction load among them.

In a middle-term perspective, in order to improve the relevance of results, we intend to improve the classification task in particular by using pre and post treatments exploiting ontologies. The integration of techniques of natural languages processing in this task, could improve this SC task, by minoring typical linguistic problems like polysemy, passive voice, anaphora, among other language pitfalls. Then integration of learning techniques in this task could also accelerate knowledge acquisition and increase the adaptivity of the system

In more long-term perspective, we intend to use Web services (WS), perceived as components, which can be used to develop some informational agents. On this last point, the WS library defined for the travel industry in the Satine project (The Satine Project, 2006), could be used in a forthcoming version of AGATHE.

REFERENCES

Albitar, S., Espinasse, B., & Fournier, S. (2010). Combining Agents and Wrapper Induction for Information Gathering on Restricted Web Domains. *In Proceedings of the fourth international conference on research challenges in information science.*

Ambite, J. L., & Knoblock, C. A. (1997). Agents for Information Gathering. *IEEE Expert: Intelligent Systems and Their Applications, 12*(5), 2-4. doi:http://dx.doi.org/10.1109/64.621219

Birukov, E., Blanzieri, E., & Giorgini, P. (2005). *Implicit: A Recommender System that uses Implicit Knowledge to Produce Suggestions.* In Proceedings of the Workshop on Multi-Agent Information Retrieval and Recommender Systems at the 19th International Joint Conference on Artifical Intelligence (IJCAI-05)

Cesarano, C., d'Acierno, A., & Picariello, A. (2003). An intelligent search agent system for semantic information retrieval on the internet. In *WIDM '03: Proceedings of the 5th ACM international workshop on Web information and data management* (p. 111–117). New York ACM. doi:http://doi.acm.org.gate6.inist.fr/10.1145/956699.956725

Decker, K., Lesser, V., Prasad, M. V. N., & Wagner, T. (1995). MACRON: An Architecture for Multi-agent Cooperative Information Gathering. *In Proccedings of the CIKM-95 Workshop on Intelligent Information Agents.*

Eriksson, H. (2003). Using JessTab to Integrate Protégé and Jess. *IEEE Intelligent Systems, 18*(2), 43–50. doi:http://dx.doi.org.gate6.inist.fr/10.1109/MIS.2003.1193656

Espinasse, B., Fournier, S., & Freitas, F. (2008). Agent and ontology based information gathering on restricted web domains with AGATHE. In *SAC '08: Proceedings of the 2008 ACM symposium on Applied computing* (p. 2381–2386). New York: ACM. doi:http://doi.acm.org.gate6.inist.fr/10.1145/1363686.1364252

Etzioni, O., Banko, M., Soderland, S., & Weld, D. S. (2008). Open information extraction from the web. *Commun. ACM, 51*(12), 68-74. doi:http://doi.acm.org/10.1145/1409360.1409378

Etzioni, O., Cafarella, M., Downey, D., Kok, S., Popescu, A., Shaked, T., et al. (2004). Web-scale information extraction in knowitall: (preliminary results). In *WWW '04: Proceedings of the 13th international conference on World Wide Web* (p. 100–110). New York: ACM. doi:http://doi.acm.org.gate6.inist.fr/10.1145/988672.988687

FIPA. (2000). *The Foundation for Intelligent Physical Agents*. Retrouvé Juillet 13, 2010, from http://www.fipa.org/

Freitag, D., & Kushmerick, N. (2000). Boosted Wrapper Induction. Proceedings of the 17th National Conference on AI and 12th Conference on Innovative Applications of AI.

Freitas, F., & Bittencourt, G. (2003). An Ontology-Based Architecture for Cooperative Information Agents. In *International Joint Conference on Artificial Intelligence (IJCAI)* (p. 37-42). Acapulco, Mexico.

Freitas, F. L. G., & Bittencourt, G. (2003). An ontology-based architecture for cooperative information agents. In *IJCAI'03: Proceedings of the 18th international joint conference on Artificial intelligence* (p. 37–42). San Francisco: Morgan Kaufmann Publishers Inc.

Gaizauskas, R., & Robertson, A. M. (1997). Coupling Information Retrieval and Information Extraction: A New Text Technology for Gathering Information from the Web. *IN proceedings of the 5th computed-assisted information searching on internet conference (RIAO'97)* (p. 356–370).

Girardi, C. (2007). HTMLCleaner: Exracting relevant text from web pages.

Gruber, T. R. (1995). Toward principles for the design of ontologies used for knowledge sharing. *Int. J. Hum.-Comput. Stud., 43*(5-6), 907–928. doi:http://dx.doi.org.gate6.inist.fr/10.1006/ijhc.1995.1081

Huhns, M. (1994, Juin). *Distributed Artificial Intelligence for Information Systems*. Tutorial presented at Second International Conference on Cooperating Knowledge Based Systems (CKBS-94), Keele, UK.

Ireson, N., Ciravegna, F., Califf, M. E., Freitag, D., Kushmerick, N., & Lavelli, A. (2005). Evaluating Machine Learning for Information Extraction. Proceedings of the 22nd international conference on ML. doi:http://doi.acm.org/10.1145/1102351.1102395

Jade. (2006). *Java Agent DEvelopment Framework*. Accessed july 13th, 2010, from http://jade.tilab.com/

Jena. (2006). *Jena Semantic Web Framework*. Accessed july 13th, 2010, from http://jena.sourceforge.net/

Jess. (2006). *Jess the Rule Engine for the Java Platform*. Acessed July 13th, 2010, de http://www.jessrules.com/

Jung, J. J. (2007). Ontological framework based on contextual mediation for collaborative information retrieval. *Inf. Retr., 10*(1), 85–109. doi:http://dx.doi.org.gate6.inist.fr/10.1007/s10791-006-9013-5

Karkaletsis, V., Spyropoulos, C. D., Souflis, D., Grover, C., Hachey, B., Pazienza, M. T., et al. (2003). Demonstration of the CROSSMARC system. *Proceedings of the 2003 Conference of the North American Chapter of the Association for Computational Linguistics on Human Language Technology: Demonstrations* - Volume 4. doi:http://dx.doi.org/10.3115/1073427.1073434

Kauchak, D., Smarr, J., & Elkan, C. (2004). Sources of Success for Boosted Wrapper Induction. *Journal of Machine Learning Research, 5*, 499–527.

Kushmerick, N. (1999a). Gleaning the Web. *IEEE Intelligent Systems, 14*(2), 20–22. doi:http://dx.doi.org.gate6.inist.fr/10.1109/5254.757626

Kushmerick, N. (1999b). Gleaning the Web. *IEEE Intelligent Systems, 14*(2), 20-22. doi:http://dx.doi.org/10.1109/5254.757626

Lesser, V., Horling, B., Klassner, F., Raja, A., Wagner, T., & Zhang, S. X. (2000). Big: An agent for resource-bounded information gathering and decision making. *Artificial Intelligence, 118*, 197–244. doi:10.1016/S0004-3702(00)00005-9

Lima, R., Espinasse, B., & Freitas, F. (2010). Adaptive Information Extraction System based on Wrapper Induction with POS Tagging. In *Proceedings of SAC-ACM 2010, Sierre, Switzerland.*

Lorenzi, F., Santos, D. S., & Bazzan, A. L. C. (2005). Negotiation for task allocation among agents in case-base recommender systems: a swarm-intelligence approach. In E. Aimeur (Ed.), *Multi-Agent Information Retrieval and Recommender Systems - Nineteenth International Conference on Artificial Intelligence (IJCAI 2005)* (p. 23--27). Edimburgh, Scotland.

Maynard, D., Peters, W., & Li, Y. (2006). Metrics for evaluation of ontology-based information extraction. *WWW 2006 Workshop on "Evaluation of Ontologies for the Web" (EON)*, Edinburgh, Scotland.

Mccallum, A., Nigam, K., Rennie, J., & Seymore, K. (1999). *Building Domain-Specific Search Engines with Machine Learning Techniques.*

Miller, G. A., Beckwith, R., Fellbaum, C., Gross, D., & Miller, K. (1990). WordNet: An on-line lexical database. *International Journal of Lexicography, 3*, 235–244. doi:10.1093/ijl/3.4.235

Muslea, I., Minton, S., & Knoblock, C. (1998). STALKER: Learning extraction rules for semi-structured Web-based information sources. *Proceedings of the AAAI-98 Workshop on "AI & Information Integration".*

Newell, A., Shaw, J., & Simon, H. (1959). *Report on a General Problem-Solving Program.*

Nwana, H. S. (1996). Software Agents: An Overview.

Oates, T., Prasad, M. N., & Lesser, V. R. (1994). Cooperative information gathering: a distributed problem solving approach.

Pascal Challenge. (2005). Pascal Challenge. Accessed from http://nlp.shef.ac.uk/pascal/

Protégé. (2006). Protégé. *The Protégé Ontology Editor and Knowledge Acquisition System.* Accessed from http://protege.stanford.edu/

Siefkes, C., & Siniakov, P. (2005). An Overview and Classification of Adaptive Approaches to Information Extraction. *Journal on Data Semantics, IV*, 172–212.

Tang, J., Hong, M., Zhang, D., Liang, B., & Li, J. (2007). Information Extraction: Methodologies and Applications. Dans *Emerging Technologies of Text Mining: Techniques and Applications* (p. 1-33). Prado and Edilson Ferneda (Ed.), Idea Group Inc., Hershey, USA.

The Satine Project. (2006). The Satine Project. Accessed July 15th, 2010, from http://www.ve-forum.org/apps/pub.asp?Q=1275&T=Clusters%20and%20Projects

TIES. (2004). *TIES - Trainable Information Extraction System.* Accessed July 15th, 2010, from http://tcc.itc.it/research/textec/tools-resources/ties.html

Tufis, D., & Mason, O. (1998). Tagging Romanian Texts: a Case Study for QTAG, a Language Independent Probabilistic Tagger. In *Proceedings of the First International Conference on Language Resources and Evaluation (LREC* (p. 589–596).

Turmo, J., Ageno, A., & Catala, N. (2006). Adaptive information extraction. *ACM Comput. Surv., 38*(2), 4. doi:http://doi.acm. org/10.1145/1132956.1132957

Woerndl, W., & Groh, G. (2005). A proposal for an agent-based architecture for context-aware personalization in the Semantic Web. In *Multi-Agent Information Retrieval and Recommender Systems Proceedings of, IJCAI-2005 Workshop, 2005.*

Chapter 13

Personalizing News Services Using Semantic Web Technologies

Flavius Frasincar
Erasmus University Rotterdam, The Netherlands

Jethro Borsje
Erasmus University Rotterdam, The Netherlands

Frederik Hogenboom
Erasmus University Rotterdam, The Netherlands

ABSTRACT

This chapter describes Hermes, a framework for building personalized news services using Semantic Web technologies. The Hermes framework consists of four phases: classification, which categorizes news items with respect to a domain ontology, knowledge base updating, which keeps the knowledge base up-to-date based on the news information, news querying, which allows the user to search the news with concepts of interest, and results presentation, which shows the news results of the search process. Hermes is supported by a framework implementation, the Hermes News Portal, a tool that enables users to have a personalized access to news items. The Hermes framework and its associated implementation aim at advancing the state-of-the-art of semantic approaches for personalized news services by employing Semantic Web standards, exploiting and keeping up-to-date domain information, using advanced natural language processing techniques (e.g., ontology-based gazetteering, word sense disambiguation, etc.), and supporting time-based queries for expressing the desired news items.

INTRODUCTION

The simplicity, availability, reachability, and reduced exploitation costs have made the Web one of the most common platforms for information publishing and dissemination. This is particularly true for news agencies that use Web technologies to present emerging news regarding different types of events as for example business, cultural, sport, and weather events. Most of this information is published as unstructured text that is made available to a general audience by means of Web pages.

DOI: 10.4018/978-1-60960-132-4.ch013

Copyright © 2011, IGI Global. Copying or distributing in print or electronic forms without written permission of IGI Global is prohibited.

The heterogeneity of the Web audience and the diversity of the published information asks for more refined ways of delivering information that would enable users to access news items that interest them. For this purpose the Really Simple Syndication (RSS) (Winer, 2003) standard was developed that publishes information in a semi-structured format that supports machine processing. This format is based on metadata that (1) associates news items with channels (feeds) that have properties like categories (e.g., business, sport, politics, etc.), title, publication date, etc., and (2) describes news items by means of their properties as categories (e.g., online business, business system, Internet marketing, etc.), release time, title, abstract, link to the original published information, etc.

Most of the annotations supported by the RSS feeds are coarse-grained providing general news information. Fine-grained information, as for example the financial events depicted in news, is at the moment not available. Also, the current annotations are only partially processable by machines as the tags do not have formal semantics associated and hence have different interpretations. Being able to understand the semantic content of a news item would enable a fine-grained categorization of this information, thus better supporting the users (casual users, media analysts, stock brokers, etc.) information needs.

In order to make the Web data not only machine readable but also machine understandable the World Wide Web Consortium proposes the Semantic Web (Berners-Lee, Hendler, & Lassila, 2001), a set of technologies that allow for self-describing content. On the Semantic Web, metadata is defined using semantic information usually captured in ontologies. Some of the most popular formats to describe ontologies on the Semantic Web are RDF(S) (Klyne & Carroll, 2004) (Brickley & Guha, 2004) and OWL (Bechhofer et al., 2004).

A special class of users who make daily use of (emerging) news is that of stock brokers. Because

news messages may have a strong impact on stock prices, stock brokers need to monitor these messages carefully. Due to the large amounts of news information published on a daily basis, the manual task of retrieving the most interesting news items with respect to a given portfolio is a challenging one. Existing approaches such as Google Finance or Yahoo! Finance are developed to meet these personalization needs by supporting automatic news filtering on the Web.

Current approaches to news filtering are able to retrieve only the news that explicitly mention the companies involved, failing to deliver indirect information which is also deemed relevant for the considered portfolio. For example, for a portfolio based on Google shares, such systems fail to deliver news items related to competitors of Google, such as Yahoo! or Microsoft, which might have an indirect influence on the share price of Google. Exploiting the semantic contextual information related to companies such as its competitors, CEO's, alliances, products, etc., enables a more comprehensive overview of relevant news with respect to a certain portfolio.

Existing news filtering systems are not able to cope with delivering news items satisfying temporal constraints. The time aspect is of utmost importance when, for example, one considers the fact that news items usually have an immediate impact on stock prices, or when one desires to do a historical analysis of past news and stock price evolutions. Being able to exploit the timestamps associated to news items enables retrieving only news that obey user-determined time-related constraints.

Another limitation of existing news personalization services is that they fail to consider the dynamicity of the current world. In an economic context companies are created, disappear, or are bought by other companies, CEO's change positions or sometimes even companies, companies develop new products while other products become obsolete, etc. For a proper representation of the domain it is important that we cope with these changes and allow our world representations to dynamically change. It is only in this case that the user will be able to properly specify their interests and receive up-to-date news information that matches these interests.

In this chapter we propose the Hermes framework, a semantics-based approach for retrieving news items related, directly or indirectly, to concepts of interest from a domain ontology. In addition these news items might need to satisfy temporal constraints. For illustration purposes we focus here on the NASDAQ stock market domain (Kandel & Marx, 1997), but the genericity of our approach makes it applicable also to other domains, as, e.g., tourism or scientific domains. The Hermes News Portal (HNP) is an implementation of the Hermes framework, which allows the user to specify queries for the concepts of interest and temporal constraints, and retrieve the corresponding news items.

For HNP we make use of Semantic Web technologies like OWL (Bechhofer et al., 2004) for formally defining the semantics of the concepts of interest in the ontology. We employ natural language processing (NLP) technologies as, e.g., lexical analysis, gazetteering, word sense disambiguation, etc., for indexing news items based on ontology terms. The most popular Semantic Web query language SPARQL (Prud'hommeaux & Seaborne, 2008) is used for expressing queries using the previously identified concepts. In order to simplify the representation of temporal constraints we propose time-related extensions to SPARQL. HNP is a generic platform that could easily be applied to domains other than the financial one.

Compared to our pervious work on Hermes (Borsje, Levering, & Frasincar, 2008) (Frasincar, Borsje, & Levering, 2009) (Schouten et al., 2010), this chapter provides a complete description of Hermes as available at the current moment. It also enhances our previous presentations on the Hermes framework with additional details on the knowledge base updating and results presentation steps (e.g., refinement of the information extrac-

tion patterns, definition of concept importance in a news item with respect to a query, .etc.). Based on our latest insights in designing the framework, this chapter suggests additional future work that we have not previously identified.

The structure of the chapter is defined as follows. The first section discusses related approaches for news personalization services. The second section presents the Hermes framework identifying the proposed methodological steps. The third section describes HNP, an implementation of the proposed framework. The fourth section discusses future research directions. The last section concludes the chapter.

BACKGROUND

Among the methods that aim at personalizing news information we distinguish two types: non-semantic approaches and semantic approaches. In the followings we will present short descriptions of three non-semantic methods: SeAN, YourNews, and NewsDude, and three semantic methods: MyPlanet, SemNews, and QuickStep. For each presented method we give the differences compared to our approach and at the end of this section we highlight the main contributions of the Hermes framework.

Server for Adaptive News (SeAN) (Ardissono, Console, & Torre, 2001) enables a personalized access to news servers on the Web. The generated views are composed of sections, as in newspapers, on which customized news items are embedded. The news items are viewed as complex entities in which attributes define different components, e.g., title, abstract, text, photos, videos, commentaries, etc. The system employs a user model initialized using orthogonal stereotypes (interests, domain expertise, cognitive characteristics, and life styles) for which the user is asked to provide input and is further updated using rules that exploit the user behavior with the application. Taking into account the user model, the system builds a presentation based on relevant news items, each news item being shown at an appropriate level-of-detail (based on the user model). Differently than SeAN, our framework uses standard Semantic Web technologies for representing knowledge and employs NLP techniques for automatic annotation of news items, instead of a manual approach.

YourNews (Ahn, Brusilovsky, Grady, He, & Syn, 2007) proposes an open and editable user model for personalizing news items. The user model is open in the sense that users can view the list of keywords stored in the individual profiles. The user model is also editable as it allows users to add/delete keywords from their associated profiles. As an additional feature which also contributes to the transparency and control over adaptation, YourNews shows the key terms present in news items. The representation of news items is given by weighted vectors of terms (Salton, 1971), where the weights are computed using TF-IDF (Salton & McGill, 1983). The visited news items are used for building a weighted term vector which is the user model. The similarity between a news item and the user model is defined by the cosine metric between their associated vectors. This measure allows the system to recommend news items that are considered relevant for the user. Despite the users' interest to view and edit their profiles, there is a decrease in performance (e.g., precision, recall, etc.) for recommended items compared to the same system using a closed user model (where the user is not able to view/edit the user model). While YourNews uses a keyword-based approach for modeling news items and user interests, Hermes employs a semantic approach based on ontology concepts for modeling similar aspects.

NewsDude (Billsus & Pazzani, 1999) is a personal news agent. It uses a two step solution for personalization, at the beginning it employs the user's short term interests to discover relevant news items, and, if the result set is empty result, it filters news based on the user's long term interests. For the short term model construction, NewsDude employs TF-IDF in combination with Nearest

Neighbour (NN), which is able to represent user's multiple interests and takes in consideration the changing user's short term interests. Long term interests or user's general interests are modeled using a Naïve Bayes classifier. Compared to NewsDude, Hermes uses a semantic instead of lexical representation of the available data, and an unsupervised classification algorithm instead of a supervised one, eliminating thus the need of a training step.

MyPlanet (Kalfoglou, Domingue, Motta, Vargas-Vera, & Shum, 2001) aims at providing users with news items relevant for their topics of interest. MyPanet is an extension of PlanetOnto, an integrated suite of tools used to create, deliver, and query internal newsletters of the Knowledge Media Institute (KMi). Similar to our approach an ontology is used for classifying news items and allowing the user select his topics of interest. Nevertheless, the classification process is based on the heuristics of cue phrases attached to ontology concepts, while we have a more systematic approach to classification by employing NLP techniques (e.g., exploiting the WordNet term synonyms, performing word sense disambiguation, etc.) that improve classification results. Also, we support semi-automatic ontology updates, a feature missing from MyPlanet. In addition, our implementation is based on the standard ontology language OWL instead of the specific ontology language, OCML (Motta, 1999), used in myPlanet. We also did choose to present the ontology as a graph instead of a tree as it allows the user to have a more comprehensive overview of the ontology structure.

SemNews (Java, Finin, & Nirenburg, 2006) proposes a framework for understanding and querying news items. As in Hermes, the monitored news are made available by RSS feeds. The news items are analyzed by OntoSem (Nirenburg & Raskin, 2001), SemNews' natural language processing engine. OntoSem converts the textual representation of news into Text Meaning Representation (TMR), a specific format for knowledge representation. The TMR descriptions are subsequently converted to OWL and published on the Web. The OWL news representation can be used for querying using RDQL (Seaborne, 2004), one of the precursors of the SPARQL query language. Differently than SemNews, Hermes uses a semantic lexicon (e.g., WordNet) for performing word sense disambiguation, and allows for a more intuitive way of building queries by letting the user make his selections in a graphical way.

Quickstep (Middleton, Shadbolt, & Roure, 2004) is a recommender system for academic papers. Academic papers are classified by means of the boosted IBk classifier (Aha, Kibler, & Albert, 1991) which employs the k-Nearest Neighbour (k-NN) algorithm applied on a vector space encoding of papers. Paper topics are represented in an ontology and are also used for describing user interests. In addition this ontology is used for solving the user or item cold-start problems, by setting the initial user interests using the topics of authors' previous papers. The recommendation is based on the similarity between the user's topic of interest and the paper's topics. Differently than Quickstep, which considers only type relationships, Hermes takes into account also other ontology relationships (e.g., part-of, domain specific relationships, etc.) in the personalization process. Also, we used an unsupervised method for classification instead of supervised one, thus not requiring a training phase.

The contributions that Hermes brings to building news personalization services compared to existing approaches are sixfold. First, Hermes makes a strict distinction between the framework (Hermes framework) and its implementation (HNP), allowing for possible different technologies (as these evolve) to be used with the same framework. Second, Hermes uses an advanced NLP methodology (e.g., tokenization, part-of-speech tagging, word sense disambiguation, etc.) for news understanding employing a semantic lexicon (e.g., WordNet). Third, the implementation is based on the most up-to-date Semantic Web standards (OWL and SPARQL). Fourth, we

allow news querying using temporal constraints by providing temporal extensions to SPARQL. Fifth, the user is provided with a graphical query interface to specify the concepts of interest in a direct (using concept selections) or indirect manner (using relationship selections). Sixth, and the last contribution of Hermes, is the process of updating the domain knowledge based on real-time world changes (as given in news), such that the domain ontology is up-to-date.

HERMES FRAMEWORK

The Hermes framework proposes a sequence of steps to be followed in order to build a news personalization service. The input for the constructed system comprises RSS news feeds and the output consists of news items fulfilling user needs. The Hermes framework is centered around a domain ontology which is used for indexing news items and helping the user formulate queries based on his concepts of interest. In addition, the user can specify temporal constraints that news items need to satisfy. The resulting news items are sorted based on their relevance for the user queries.

For illustrative purposes we chose a financial domain example, i.e., a personalized news service which can help the stock brokers in their daily decisions. More precisely we opted for portfolios based on stocks of NASDAQ companies. For this purpose we developed a domain ontology, which captures companies, products, competitors, CEO's, etc. In addition we have developed a news ontology able to store news items and their metadata such as title, abstract, time stamp, etc.

The domain ontologies are developed by domain experts (in the example these are the financial domain experts). The process of developing the ontology is an incremental middle-out approach. First the most salient concepts are defined and then these are refined using generalization/specialization towards the top/bottom of the ontology. As the news information can contain additional

Figure 1. Hermes architecture

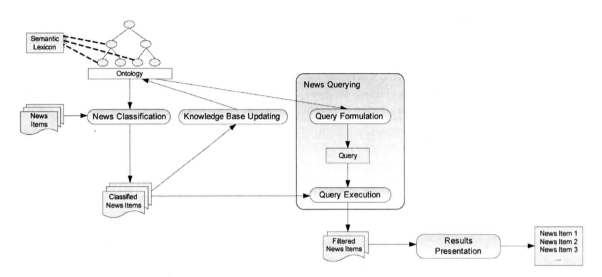

concepts not known a priori, the ontology needs to be regularly maintained by the domain experts. We validated our domain ontology using the On-toClean methodology (Guarino & Welty, 2002).

As news items might come from different RSS feeds, it is possible that the same news item has been published through different channels. After aggregating the news items one needs to remove the duplicate ones. In order to speed-up this process we employed the heuristics to use only the title for identifying news items, even so we acknowledge that in few cases news items might have the same title and still have different content, i.e., they represent different news items.

The architecture of the Hermes framework is described in Figure 1 and is composed of four main steps: *news classification, knowledge base updating, news querying,* and *results presentation. News classification* is responsible for indexing the news items based on ontology concepts. *Knowledge base updating* keeps the knowledge base (ontology instance) up-to-date. *News querying* consists of two substeps: *query formulation,* i.e., helping the user build the query that expresses the items of interest, and *query execution,* i.e.,

computing the results of query evaluation. In the last step, *results presentation* the computed news items are presented based on their relevance to the user interests.

News Classification

The ontology concepts used for news items classification are classes and individuals from the domain ontology. Concepts are linked to synsets, i.e., sets of synonyms, from a semantic lexicon, which identify their unique meaning. The synonyms stored in a synset in the semantic lexicon are used as lexical representations of the associated concept. In this case a lexical representation has a sense associated with it, i.e., the one given by the corresponding synset. As the ontology is specific to a domain, while the semantic lexicon is domain independent, we associate additional domain specific lexical representations to the concepts in our ontology. The lexical representations are composed only of word lemmas (the canonical word form appearing in dictionaries).

In addition, for classes without subclasses and for individuals we decided to consider the hyponyms associated to their corresponding semantic lexicon synset. For these classes and individuals, the domain expert, who devised the ontology, is probably not interested in more refined definitions of these. However, the lexical representations of these concepts can be enlarged by considering also the corresponding hyponyms synsets from the semantic lexicon.

The classification approach is *ontology-centric*, in the sense that the ontology concepts are loaded one at-a-time and their lexical representations are matched against the news items. This approach is different than a *news items-centric* one where the words in the news items are matched against the lexical representations of the concepts from the ontology. We opted for an ontology-centric approach in order to speed-up the classification process as in this case we need to traverse the ontology only once. The number of concepts in the ontology is considerably larger than the number of words in the news items (for batch processing of news items).

First the tokenization, sentence splitting, part-of-speech tagging, and morphological analysis are performed. The tokenization precedes sentence splitting as sentence splitting needs the identification of the punctuation signs from tokenization (as ".", ",", etc.). Morphological analysis follows part-of-speech tagging because the lemma of a word depends on its part-of-speech tag. For example "reading" as a verb has lemma "read" but as noun it has the lemma "reading". In this way, all words in a news item are reduced to their canonical form, a form shared also by the lexical representations of concepts stored in the domain ontology. For lexical representation identification we use the maximal group of words (compound words) found in sequence in a news item that stand for a concept's lexical representation. For example "European Central Bank" would be identified as a compound word representing the ECB concept, e.g., a longer match supersedes a shorter match.

Each time a lexical representation of a concept is matched a *word sense disambiguation* procedure takes place. As the same lexical representation can belong to different concepts (present or not in the ontology) this procedure checks if the match corresponds to the meaning of the found concept. If the check is positive a *hit* is stored in the ontology, i.e., a link between the news item and the corresponding concept is defined. The hit also stores the found lexical representation, as classification evidence.

For word sense disambiguation we use a variant of the SSI algorithm (Navigli & Velardi, 2005). In this process we also consider lexical representations for concepts that are not stored in the ontology but are present in the semantic lexicon as these are relevant when computing the sense of a found lexical representation from the ontology. These lexical representations help in better determining the context of a sentence and thus computing the sense of an ontology-based lexical representation.

The algorithm determines, per news sentence, the sense of a lexical representation (*lex*) by computing the sum of the distances between one of the senses of the considered lexical representation (s_j) and the senses of the previously disambiguated lexical representations from the context sentence (sc_j). The sense corresponding to the smallest sum is the chosen one (*selectedSense*). The algorithm starts with monosemous lexical representations (i.e., lexical representations which correspond to only one concept) and in case that such representations do not exist a guess is made by picking the most common sense for one of the found lexical representations. These senses are added to the context (*I*) of the sentence. For each remaining polysemous lexical representations two steps take place: a disambiguation step to find the correct sense and an insertion step which adds the newly computed sense to the context. In this way the context gets enlarged with new senses that model the meaning of the sentence. Formula (1) specifies what sense is selected for each lexical representation.

$$selectedSense(lex) = \arg \min_{s_j \in senses(lex)} \sum_{sc_i \in I} d(s_j, sc_i)$$

(1)

The distance between senses is defined as being inverse proportional with the length of the shortest path between the corresponding synsets ($sense_i$ and $sense_j$) in the semantic lexicon graph. The graph is based on the hypo/hypernyms relationships stored in the semantic lexicon. Path lengths larger than a predefined constant (e.g., 4 or 5) are not used (for these cases the distance is considered infinite). In this way we employ only semantically close concepts that truly help in the disambiguation procedure and we also improve the speed of the process by not using arbitrarily large paths. Formula (2) shows how to compute the distance between two senses. (see Box 1)

As the distances between synsets are not changing, one can pre-compute these, thus further reducing the time needed for the disambiguation step. The Hermes framework can be used with other methods for computing the similarity between concepts as for example string metrics (e.g., Levenshtein, Editex, etc.) or lexical co-occurrences in a corpus (e.g., pairwise mutual information, Google distance, etc.). Nevertheless, many of these methods are less precise than the graph-based method used here, as they do not take in account senses, comparing only the lexical representations of concepts.

Knowledge Base Updating

As the real world is continuously changing it is important for our framework to keep its internal world representation up-to-date. For this purpose we employ the information contained in news items as a source of possible changes in the real-world. In the Hermes framework news play a dual role (1) they are used to provide the user with the desired information, and (2) they are employed as a source of new information to be used for updating the knowledge base. Regarding updates, we recognize concepts known in the knowledge base in news items and detect changes related to these concepts that happen in the real-world (e.g., concepts can disappear, concept relationships might change, etc.).

In the Hermes framework the world changes are triggered by *events* that are modeled in the ontology and are detected in news items. Events have associated alternative lexico-semantic patterns for their detection, and a sequence of actions to be used for updating the knowledge base. Note that one event type (e.g., kb:newCEO, which represents the appointment of a new CEO) can correspond to many event instances detected in news items each triggering the associated list of actions. The *lexico-semantic patterns* associated to an event combine lexical arguments with ontology concepts (which have attached lexical representations). The list of actions associated to an event represent an ordered set of actions each being an insert or delete operation to be performed on the knowledge base. The lexico-semantic patterns communicate with the actions by means of variables bounded to ontology concepts during information extraction (event rules patterns execution). The events and their associated information (lexico-semantic patterns and actions) are maintained by the domain experts.

The knowledge base updating step is composed of five substeps: event rules patterns construction, i.e., building the alternative lexico-semantic patterns associated to events, event rules actions construction, i.e., building of action lists associated to events, event rules patterns execution, i.e., extraction of the event-related information (event instances) from news, event validation, i.e., allowing the domain expert to validate extracted event instances before updates, and event rules actions execution, i.e., updating the knowledge base with the event information.

Box 1.

$$d(sense_i, sense_j) = \frac{1}{length(shortestPath(synset(sense_i), synset(sense_j)))} \tag{2}$$

Event Rules Patterns Construction

Each event (type) has a set of lexico-semantic patterns (alternatives) that can trigger the detection of an event instance in a news item. The lexico-semantic patterns are based on triples (subject, predicate, object), each triple element being possibly annotated with variables. As triple elements one can use a knowledge base instance (concepts that represent instances) or a knowledge base concept (concepts that represent types).

We differentiate between types and instances by enclosing types in the square brackets ("[" and "]"). A type is a placeholder for all lexical representations of all instances of this type, while a concept instance stands only for the lexical representations associated to this particular instance. For example the type [kb:Company] represents all lexical representations of all company instances, i.e., "IBM", "International Business Machines", "EBay", "E-bay", "Ebay", etc., while the instance kb:IBM represents all lexical representations of IBM, i.e., "IBM", "International Business Machines", etc. Variables are represented by names prefixed with the "$" symbol. In addition to concepts and variables, lexico-semantic patterns can contain lexical representations enclosed in quotes as for example "is ruined".

There are two types of lexico-semantic patterns: SP patterns, i.e., patterns that have only a subject and a predicate, and SPO patterns, i.e., patterns that have a subject, a predicate, and an object. An example of an SP pattern associated to the kb:Bankruptcy event is:

```
$c:[kb:Company] kb:GoesBankrupt
```

```
p:[kb:Person] kb:BecomesCEO
$c:[kb:Company]
```

Event Rules Actions Construction

Each event (type) has a list of update actions (ordered set) that can fire when an event instance is found in a news item and has been validated by the user. These actions are used to update the knowledge base by deleting or adding concept relationships. There are two types of update actions: insert triples, i.e., add new triples to the knowledge base, and delete triples, i.e., remove triples from the knowledge base. For the kb:newCEO event the action list contains two actions given in the following order:

```
DELETE $c kb:hasCEO *
INSERT $c kb:hasCEO $p
```

In the actions list, the order of actions is important as it gives the execution order and the update results are sensitive to this order. Performing last a delete action would remove the newly inserted CEO leaving the company with the CEO undefined. The wildcard symbol '*' is a placeholder which stands for any concept (in the knowledge base). It is used to delete triples for which some of the components are not known in the query creation process.

Event Rules Patterns Execution

The event rules patterns execution is used for extracting information, more precisely events, from the news textual information. Each match represents an event instance. Variables are bound to the matched ontology concepts in news and are used in the event rules actions execution for possibly inserting the event instance in the knowledge base but more importantly they are used to implement the world state changes triggered by the found events.

Using the previous example, once the kb:newCEO event instance is found (triggered by the found relation kb:BecomesCEO), the variable $p is instantiated with the found instance of kb:Person and the variable $c is instantiated with the found instance of kb:Company. These variables are used in the event rules action execution to state that the found person is the new CEO of the found company. Note that for each found kb:newCEO event, the previous variables have different values unless the same event instance has been found multiple times.

Event Validation

As the event detection is not flawless, these events need to be validated by the domain expert. The validation step is necessary in order not to pollute the knowledge information with incorrect information. Polluting the ontology will have a negative impact in the next information extraction run. It is the domain expert who can acknowledge if the event has been properly extracted and if it represents a fact or an opinion (only facts are valid events).

The manual event validation process makes our framework semi-automatic, all the other steps besides this one being fully automatic. We assume that the domain expert has configured the system with the right input information (the domain ontology and the RSS feeds). It is the domain expert, and not the user, who controls the internal data of the system and thus is responsible for any changes made to the domain ontology.

Event Rules Actions Execution

After an event instance has been discovered, as a result of its validation, the Hermes framework will update the ontology with the event-triggered new information. The event instances are processed in the order they are found in the news items, and for each event instance the associated list of actions is executed in the list specified order. In the previous example it is important to first delete the old CEO from the knowledge base before inserting the new CEO. Swapping these two actions would make a company not have a CEO defined in the ontology.

By processing the events in the order they are found (chronological order) we make sure that the newest events are processed last. In this way, in case of conflicting updates, we will retain the most up-to-date ones in the knowledge base. After executing the actions in the proper order we have the event effects captured in the knowledge base. With an updated knowledge base the system is ready to classify the new news items as well as offer concepts for queries that better reflect reality.

News Querying

The user expresses the topics of interests by posing queries using concepts from the domain ontology. In addition the user can express constraints that the timestamps associated to news items need to satisfy. The news querying step consists of two substeps: query formulation, i.e., supporting the user to build queries, and query execution, i.e., computing the results of query evaluation.

Query Formulation

In order to assist the query construction process we present to the user the ontology graph. We decided to show a graph-based representation of the ontology instead of a tree-based representation, as it gives more insight in the overall structure of our domain. For example a graph representation captures more relationship types instead of a singular relationship type, often the subsumption relationship, from a tree-based representation. The user needs to understand the different relationship types in order to be able to build his query.

By using the ontology graph the user can select the *direct concepts of interest*. For each concept of interest, the framework considers all its lexical representations, which the user does not need to remember during the query specifications. In addition he is able to specify concepts of interest using a keyword search facility through the graph. For this purpose the input keyword is checked for possible inclusion in the lexical representations of concepts. If such inclusions are found the corresponding concepts are being returned as possible direct concepts of interest. It is the task of the user to accept these as direct concepts of interest or to reject them.

One of the important functionalities of the Hermes approach is that it allows for the selection of concepts indirectly linked to the selected ones, concepts which may not a priori be known to the user. We call these concepts *indirect concepts of interest*. For the selection of the indirect concepts of interest the user can state the type of the relationships that link the direct concepts of interest to the indirect concepts of interests or leave this undefined in which case all relationship types are being considered.

Suppose that the user has selected the direct concept of interest Google from the NASDAQ domain ontology. The user also specifies that he is interested in news related to the competitors of Google by selecting the kb:hasCompetitor relationship. That means that kb:Yahoo, kb:Microsoft, and kb:EBay will be selected as indirect concepts of interests, without the user having to know the exact names of Google's competitors. All this background information is being extracted from the ontology.

The direct, indirect, and keyword-based search concepts of interest, as well as the other concepts from the ontology are emphasized in a graph by using for example different colors. In this way the user is able to know, by analyzing the graph, why a certain concept is being highlighted. As the size of the graphs can be very large the user is provided with zooming/panning facilities for visualizing the ontology.

The original graph of the domain ontology is also called the *conceptual graph*. Based on the user selection, a new graph is generated, the so-called *search graph* that contains only the concepts and concept relationships relevant for the query. The user can go back and forth between the two graphs performing new selections and thus updating the search graph with new concepts.

The search graph is given by the subgraph of the conceptual graph that models the user interests. It contains all the user concepts of interests (directly or indirectly selected by the user) and the relationships among them. The search graph has generalized disjunctive semantics with respect to the included concepts which means that the user is interested in *any* of the search graph concepts to be found in news items. Also, the more query concepts are found in a news item, the more relevant is the news item with respect to the query.

Another crucial functionality of the Hermes approach is that it allows the specification of temporal constraints for news items. As news items appear at a certain moment in time and have certain time validity, it is important to be able to restrict the timestamps associated with the news. For this purpose the user can employ time comparison/arithmetic operators and retrieve the current time in order to build complex time expressions. In addition the system provides predefined temporal constraints such as: last day, last week, last two weeks, last three months, last quarter, last half year, and last year. The temporal conditions that model these constraints have conjunctive semantics as they need to be fulfilled in the same time.

Query Execution

Based on the previously selected concepts and specified temporal constraints the system can

Box 2.

$$relevanceDegree\,(news\ item) = \sum_{\substack{c_i\ found\ in\ title \\ c_i \in Q \cap news\ item}} w_{title}\ n_{title}(c_i) + \sum_{\substack{c_i\ found\ in\ body \\ c_i \in Q \cap news\ item}} w_{body}\ n_{body}(c_i) \qquad (3)$$

Box 3.

$$importanceDegree\,(c_i, news\ item) = \sum_{c_i\ found\ in\ title} w_{title}\ n_{title}(c_i) + \sum_{c_i\ found\ in\ body} w_{body}\ n_{body}(c_i) \qquad (4)$$

support the generation of the corresponding query in a semantic query language. This translation process involves mapping concepts and temporal constraints to query restrictions. After that, the user can trigger the query evaluation and the relevant news items are retrieved. The order of the retrieved news items is not relevant, at this stage.

Results Presentation

The results presentation is responsible for displaying the news items that match the user query. The results presentation is composed of two substeps: news sorting, i.e., sorting the news based on their relevance to the user query, and news presentation, i.e., displaying the news items in a visual appealing manner and explaining their relevance to the user query.

News Sorting

The results returned from query evaluation are presented in the order of their relevance for the user query. For this purpose, for each returned news item a *relevance degree* is computed based on all the hits between the news item and the query concepts. News items with a high relevance degree are placed at the top of the retrieved news items list.

Based on previous work (Micu, Mast, Milea, Frasincar, & Kaymak, 2008) the relevance degree is defined as a weighted sum of the number of hits ($n(c_i)$), where the weights (w) depend on hits location (*title* or *body* of a news item). From our experimental results we have determined as acceptable values for w_{title} to be *2* and for w_{body} to be *1*. Formula (3) presents how to compute the relevance degree. (see Box 2)

News items that have the same relevance degree are sorted in descending order based on the associated timestamps (the most recent news items are presented first).

News Presentation

For each news item a summary is given containing the title, source, date, and few lines from the news item. Also, the icon of the most important query concept found in each news item is displayed. Formula (4) shows how to compute the *importance degree* for each query concept c_i found in a news item. (see Box 3)

The most important query concept in a news item is the one with the highest importance degree. If several query concepts have the same importance degree in a news item, an arbitrary query concept from these ones is chosen as the most important concept.

In addition to presenting the relevant news items, the system shows the query concepts in order to provide cues of the current query for which the results are computed. Also, for each returned news item, the found lexical representations stored in the hits are emphasized in the news item text, thereby offering to the user an explanation of why a certain news item is considered to be relevant.

HERMES NEWS PORTAL

The Hermes News Portal (HNP) is an implementation of the Hermes framework, which allows the user to specify queries on the considered domain using temporal constraints and subsequently retrieve the relevant news items. The presentation of HNP follows closely the steps proposed by the Hermes framework. Note that HNP is one of the possible implementations of the Hermes framework, with specific design choices, query/programming languages, and libraries used.

Operating on the Semantic Web we chose as ontology language OWL due to its expressivity and standard status. We did not opt for RDFS because OWL specific features, as for example relationship inverses (hasCompetitor has as inverse isCompetitorOf), are exploited in the conceptual graph. Lacking a true OWL query language we used SPARQL (Prud'hommeaux & Seaborne, 2008) as the query language, an RDF query language that we extended with time-related functionality. This functionality is provided by implementing comparison/arithmetic time operators and functions for retrieving current time information.

The chosen implementation language is Java due to the availability of powerful libraries for manipulating, reasoning with, querying, and visualizing OWL ontologies. For manipulating and reasoning with OWL ontologies we used Jena (Jena Development Team, 2010a). For querying we employed ARQ (Jena Development Team, 2010b), the SPARQL implementation available in Jena. For updating the ontology we have used

SPARQL/Update (Seaborne et al., 2008) also supported by ARQ. For visualizing ontologies we adapted the generic graph visualization library Prefuse (The Berkeley Institute of Design, 2010) for visualizing OWL graphs (Borsje & Giles, 2010). For part-of-speech tagging we used the Stanford parser (The Stanford Natural Language Processing Group, 2010). As a semantic lexicon we employed WordNet (Princeton Cognitive Science Laboratory, 2010), the largest database available online for the English language. JWI (Finlayson, 2008) was used for the morphological analysis (finding lemmas of words) and the communication with WordNet. As natural language processing pipeline (e.g., tokenization, sentence splitting, gazetteering, etc.) we have used the A Nearly New Information Extraction System (ANNIE) pipeline from General Architecture for Text Engineering (GATE) (Cunningham, Maynard, Bontcheva, & Tablan, 2002) and for information extraction from news items we have used the Java Annotations Patterns Engine (JAPE) language and its implementation, also part of GATE.

We illustrate the HNP by means of the following user query: *retrieve all news items related to Google or one of its competitors that appeared in the last three months*. For this query we will go through all the different phases of Hermes: news classification, knowledge base updating, news querying, and results presentation. In the current HNP the news items duplicates removal has not been yet implemented.

News Classification

The news classification step is responsible for indexing news items based on the domain ontology. We present this process by means of the news item example depicted in

Figure 2. The first line describes the title, the second line shows the timestamp, and the remaining text represents the content of the news item.

The news classification step starts by identifying lexical representations of the ontology con-

Figure 2. News item example

> **Google to broker print ads in newspapers**
> 6 November 2006 17:41 CET
>
> SAN FRANCISCO (Reuters) - Google Inc. is set to begin helping customers buy advertisements in 50 U.S. newspapers in a test of how the Web search leader can extend its business into offline media, the company said on Sunday.

cepts in the news item. First the tokenization, sentence splitting, part-of-speech tagging, and morphological analysis take place. Then, the concepts from the ontology are traversed once and their lexical representations are matched against the content of the news item. The following lexical representations "Google", "extend", and "company" are found. Next, per sentence, for each of the lexical representations with multiple senses, the word sense disambiguation procedure takes place in order to identify the used senses. The noun "Google", having only one sense, does not undergo the word sense disambiguation procedure and is mapped to the kb:Google concept.

For "extend" and "company" a word sense disambiguation procedure is needed. In this process we do consider also lexical representations of concepts outside the ontology, as for example the nouns "customer" and "business", or the verb "buy" that do appear in the news item. We select the sense that yields the smallest sum of similarities to previously disambiguated lexical representations. "extend" is determined as representing the extend-verb-#1 concept with lemma extend, part-of-speech tag verb, and the first sense from WordNet. For "company" the corresponding concept is company-noun-#1. "customer", a lexical representation outside the ontology, is determined as having the sense customer-noun-#1.

After identifying an ontology concept in a news item, a hit is stored. This hit is defined as a link between the news item and the concept together with the found lexical representation. For this purpose we decided to model a hit as an instance of the Relation class, which uses different properties for storing the involved news item, concept, and found lexical representation. This modeling choice is based on a best practice for representing N-ary relations on the Semantic Web (Noy & Rector, 2006). A news item can have multiple hits associated, enabling thus its multiple classification.

Knowledge Base Updating

The knowledge base updating step makes sure that the knowledge base has an accurate representation of the real-world in HNP. It is composed of five substeps: event rules patterns construction, event rules actions construction, event rules patterns execution, event validation, and event rules actions execution, which are discussed below. In order to support the domain expert for the events definition process we have developed an event editor in the HNP.

Event Rules Patterns Construction

In the first step, event rules patterns constructions, the lexico-semantic patterns associated to event types are defined. These lexico-semantic patterns are used to discover event instances in news items. The lexico-semantic patterns have a subject, a relation, and an optional object. The subjects, relations, and objects are concepts from the knowledge base (instances or types), and are interpreted as placeholders for all the associated

Figure 3. The event editor: Lexico-semantic patterns example

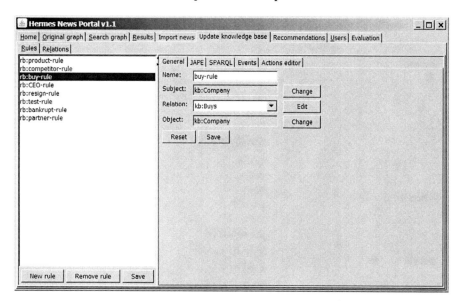

lexical representations (of instances or of all instances associated to a certain type).

Figure 3 shows the definition of a lexico-semantic pattern in the event editor. In this example the rb:buy-rule (the prefix rb stands for rule base, to differentiate from the prefix kb, which stands for knowledge base) is used to detect a buy event. The subject is of type [kb:Company], the object is of type [kb:Company], and the predicate is kb:Buys. At the current moment, HNP does not use a different notation for types than for individuals, as we have specified in the framework (types are never interpreted as individuals, i.e., instances of the meta-class owl:Class; in HNP, a type is a placeholder for all the individuals of this type). In the future we plan to update the HNP with the latest framework features, including the most recent information extraction pattern language developments.

The subject and the object can be changed by selecting new concepts. Figure 4 shows the selection of concepts. These concepts are selected from the graph representation of the knowledge base. The lexical representations associated to these concepts are defined in the knowledge base. The current version of HNP allows for the definition

of relations and their lexical representations. For example, Figure 5 shows the kb:Buys relation and its associated lexical representations: "purchase", "acquire", "acquires", etc.

Event Rules Actions Construction

Each event has a list of actions associated which are used to update the knowledge base with the event-based information. The actions are insert triples or delete triples in the knowledge base. Each action can contain multiple insert or delete operations. Figure 6 presents the action editor of the HNP. For example rb:buy-rule, which represents the new buy event, has one action associated rb:removeCompetesWith. The action removes one triple with the event subject (<event subject>, which in this case is a company), the predicate kb:hasCompetitor, and event object (<event object>, which in this case is a company), and another triple where the subject and object are swapped. The meaning of these actions is that after a company buys another company they cease to compete with each other.

The implementation does not yet make use of user-defined variables to pass information from

Figure 4. The event editor: concepts example

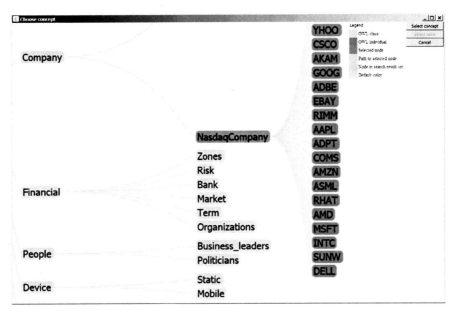

Figure 5. The event editor: relations example

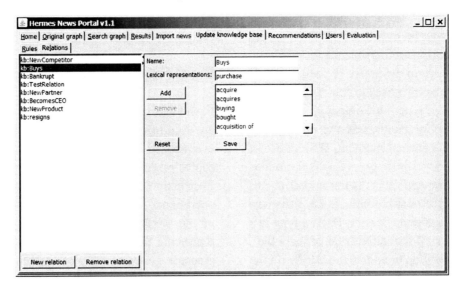

the information extraction step to the knowledge base updating step, and is based on a more rigid approach employing the predefines variables <event subject>, <event predicate>, and <event object>. The user-defined variables approach would allow the definition, in the future, of complex information extraction patterns based on regular expressions (e.g., optional, repetition,

sequence, etc.) where more than three entities are used. Also, the actions are expressed using SPARQL templates and do not make use yet of the action language defined in Hermes, which is implementation-independent (please note that "?" represents the optional operator in regular expressions, and we reserve this symbol for this functionality in a future HNP version).

Figure 6. The rule editor: actions example

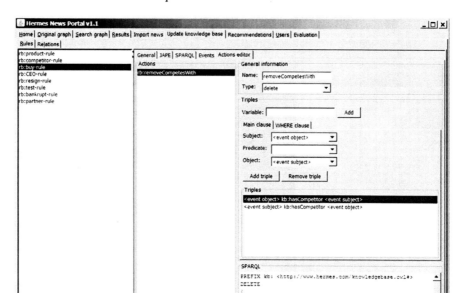

As can be noticed from Figure 6 we have created a graphical editor for SPARQL insert and delete queries, which allows users to specify the query type, the query triples, as well as inspect the constructed query. In order to support the domain expert during the query creation process for the subjects, predicates, and objects one makes selections from drop down lists filled with existing concepts from the knowledge base, or one of the predefined variables in the framework <event subject>, <event predicate>, or <event object>.

Event Rules Patterns Execution

In event rules patterns execution, the lexico-semantic patterns are executed on the news items and possibly yield to event instances being detected. For example for the kb:Buy event, this amounts to finding the subject and object and binding them to the predefined <event subject> and <event object> variables, respectively. The implementation of the information extraction patterns is based on Java Annotation Patterns Language (JAPE) rules.

JAPE rules have two parts: the left-hand side, which describes the patterns to be matched, and the right-hand side, which specifies the actions to be performed when a pattern is matched. The left-hand side language is based on regular expressions. The right-hand language allows for annotations of the matched piece of text. For advanced actions (e.g., deleting temporary annotations, manipulating annotations, complex control expressions, etc.) one can make use of Java code on the right-hand side.

For the running example, the JAPE rules will find the buyer and the buyee. In our domain these are both companies that are present in the knowledge base. It is important that these two companies are present in the ontology in order for the kb:Buy event to be discovered. After annotating the lexical representations with the corresponding knowledge base concepts, the event instance is discovered and ready for validation.

Figure 7. The rule editor: events validation example

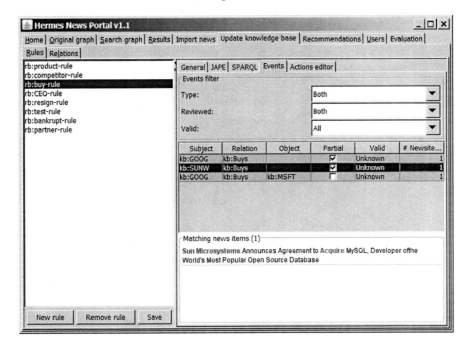

Event Validation

The knowledge base updating step is a semi-automatic process, the HNP allows the domain expert to validate the event (instance) before triggering the knowledge base updates based on the event information. The user is presented with the subject, relation (predicate), and optional object, as well as the news item(s) in which the event originated. The domain expert has the options to declare the event: valid, invalid, or unknown (unknown is used when the domain expert is not able to decide the validity of the event and defers the event for future processing). Figure 7 shows the event validation in the HNP. If the user validates the event the knowledge base is updated in the next substep. In the running example the user has to validate if Sun Microsystems has bought MySQL as suggested in the displayed news item.

Event Rules Actions Execution

The last step of knowledge base updating is the execution of the actions associated with the events found and validated by the user. HNP executes the actions in the order of the found events, and for each event in the specified action order. The actions are SPARQL queries that update the knowledge base with event-related information. At the end of this substep one should have a valid knowledge base with a proper representation of the reality at a given moment.

News Querying

The news querying is based on the graphical interface of the HNP. It is composed of two substeps: query formulation and query execution.

Query Formulation

Figure 8 shows the conceptual graph from which the user can select concepts of interest. Once a user selects a concept, the control panel gets activated by means of which the user can add to the search graph his concepts of interest.

The concepts of interest can only be the current concept, all related concepts including the current

Figure 8. Conceptual graph example

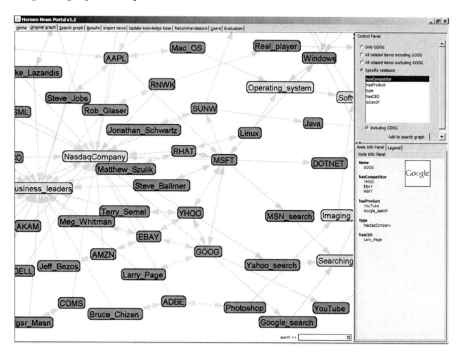

one, all related concepts excluding the current one, or all related concepts by means of specified relationships including/excluding the current concept. The node info panel shows information regarding the selected concept.

The local name of the different concepts is displayed using ovals. In order to emphasize the different types of concepts we use the following coloring scheme for ovals. The selected concepts are displayed in red, the concepts related to the selected one are shown in green, and the ones returned by the keyword search are presented in pink. The other concepts are displayed in yellow for classes and magenta for individuals.

In the example from Figure 8 the user has directly selected the kb:Google concept. In the node info panel all the information related to the kb:Google concept is displayed: name, competitors, CEO, etc. Then, the user can select the indirect concepts by specifying the kb:hasCompetitor relationship between the direct concept and the indirect ones. The user also specifies that the kb:Google concept should be kept in the search graph.

After selecting the concepts of interest the user can visualize the search graph. The user can refine its query by deleting some of the concepts, resetting the search, or adding new concepts from the conceptual graph to the search graph. After a number of iterations the user has added all the concepts of interests to the search graph.

Figure 9 shows the search graph, which presents the selected concepts, in this case kb:Google and its competitors: kb:Microsoft, kb:Yahoo, and kb:EBay. In the time constraint panel the user can specify the desired time restriction. The user can choose between predefined temporal constraints as the past hour, past day, past week, past two weeks, past three months, past quarter, past half year, and past year, and specific time/date constraints.

As before the node info panel displays information about the currently selected node. However, differently than in the previous situation, only the information given by the specified relationships, in this case the kb:hasCompetitor relationship, are displayed.

Figure 9. Search graph example

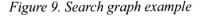
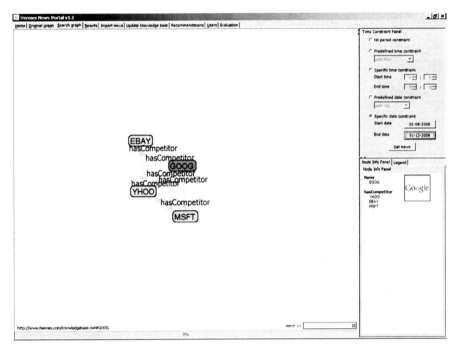

In this example the user has specified that the news items have to be between 1st of September 2009 and 1st of December 2009, where the current day is 1st of December 2009 (the *last three months* in the user query). Alternatively the user could have selected the past three months option from the predefined temporal constraints.

Query Execution

For each search graph a SPARQL query is generated. This query is a SELECT query as it retrieves the news items in which any of the search graph concepts are present. The disjunctive semantics of the search graph with respect to its embedded concepts is naturally specified as an 'or' filter in the SPARQL query. Also, we have decided to use filters to specify the time restrictions that news timestamps need to satisfy. Due to the conjunctive semantics of the time restrictions we modeled them as an 'and' filter in the SPARQL query.

Figure 10 shows the SPARQL query corresponding to the search graph given in Figure

9. This query is hard-coded with XML Schema xsd:dateTimes specifying the desired temporal boundaries of the interval in which the timestamps of the desired news items need to be contained.

The first part of the SPARQL query defines that the returned news items should be related to the concepts of interest. The second part of the query is composed of two filters. The first SPARQL filter defines the concepts of interest to be kb:Google, kb:Microsoft, kb:Ebay, and kb:Yahoo. The second SPARQL filter specifies that the timestamp of news items should be between 1st of September 2009 and 1st of December 2009, where 1st of December 2009 is the current day. Both dates are specified using XML Schema xsd:dateTime format.

In order to ease the specification of temporal constraints in queries we have extended SPARQL with custom functions. We call the SPARQL language extended with time functions tSPARQL. Please note that SPARQL does naturally support such extensions, tSPARQL being backwards compatible with SPARQL. Figure 11 shows the

Figure 10. SPARQL query example

```
PREFIX kb: <http://hermes-news.org/news.owl#>
SELECT ?title
WHERE {
    ?news kb:title ?title .
    ?news kb:time ?date .
    ?news kb:relation ?relation .
    ?relation kb:relatedTo ?concept .
    FILTER (
    ?concept = kb:Google ||
    ?concept = kb:Microsoft ||
    ?concept = kb:Ebay ||
    ?concept = kb:Yahoo
    ) .
    FILTER (
    ?date > "2009-09-01T00:00:00.000+01:00" &&
    ?date < "2009-12-01T00:00:00.000+01:00"
    )
}
```

signature of the time functions that we have added. These functions relate to retrieving the current xsd:date and xsd:time, the current xsd:dateTime, adding/subtracting to a xsd:dateTime instance a xsd:duration, and subtracting two xsd:dateTime instances (xsd:date, xsd:time, xsd:dateTime, and xsd:duration are defined by XML Schema).

These functions relate to retrieving the current xsd:date and xsd:time, the current xsd:dateTime instance, adding/subtracting to a xsd:dateTime instance a xsd:duration, and subtracting two xsd:dateTime instances.

Figure 12 depicts the same query as in Figure 10 but now written in tSPARQL. Differently than in the previous case the tSPARQL query is not hard-coded with times and dates, but makes use of custom functions and durations. The semantics of the query is closer to its representation, in our current example that is retrieving the news items *that appeared in the last three months*.

The tSPARQL query uses the dateTime-substract() to determine the xsd:dateTime of three months ago, now() is used to obtain the current xsd:dateTime, and it specifies that the news time-

stamps should be between these two xsd:dateTimes. P0Y3M is an XML Schema xsd:duration constant that specifies a period with 0 number of years and 3 months.

After its creation, the tSPARQL query is executed. As a result, the news items that match the query constraints (concepts of interest and temporal constraints) are being returned. The order of the results is not relevant here.

Results Presentation

The results presentation is based on the graphical interface of the HNP. It is composed of two substeps: news sorting and news presentation.

News Sorting

Figure 13 shows the results after the query execution. The news items are sorted based on their relevance degree with the user query. The relevance degrees have been displayed as relative percentages with respect to the best matching news

Figure 11. Custom time functions

```
      xsd:date currentDate()
      xsd:time currentTime()
  xsd:dateTime dateTime-add(xsd:dateTime A, xsd:duration B)
  xsd:dateTime dateTime-subtract(xsd:dateTime A, xsd:duration B)
  xsd:duration dateTime-subtract(xsd:dateTime A, xsd:dateTime B)
```

Figure 12. tSPARQL query example

```
PREFIX kb: <http://hermes-news.org/news.owl#>
SELECT ?title
WHERE {
    ?news kb:title ?title .
    ?news kb:time ?date .
    ?news kb:relation ?relation .
    ?relation hermes:relatedTo ?concept .
    FILTER (
    ?concept = kb:Google ||
    ?concept = kb:Microsoft ||
    ?concept = kb:Ebay ||
    ?concept = kb:Yahoo
    ) .
    FILTER (
    ?date > kb:dateTime-subtract(hermes:now(), P0Y3M) &&
    ?date < kb:now()
    )
}
```

item. The most relevant news items are presented at the top of the results list.

News Presentation

Figure 13 also lists the concepts of interest from the search graph (top). In addition, the system shows the found lexical representations of the concepts of interests in the returned news items using different colors. The user is able to deselect some of the concepts of interest in order to refine his query and thus limit the result set.

For each news item the system shows a summary containing the title, source, date of publication, and few beginning lines from the news item. Its also shows the icon of the most important query concept found in a news item. The icons correspond often to logos of companies that the user is interested in, and are retrieved from the knowledge base.

EVALUATION

In order to evaluate the performance of the implementation we measured the concept identification precision. Precision was defined as the number of concepts correctly identified in the news items divided by the number of concepts identified in news items. We define recall as the number of concepts correctly identified in the news items divided by the number of concepts that should have been identified in news item. For our current implementation, for concept identification,

Figure 13. Results presentation example

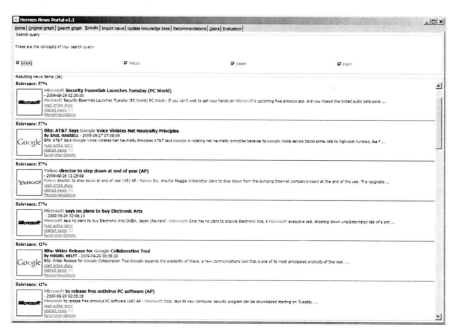

the precision is 85% and the recall is 81% for a given repository of around 200 news items. For event identification, which is based on a sequence of 2 or 3 concepts (contained in a pattern), we obtained a precision of 62% and recall of 53%.

Precision is based on cumulative errors through our application pipeline based on the HNP's part-of-speech recognition, morphological analysis, and word sense disambiguation algorithm. Despite using only WordNet as a semantic lexicon (compared to other approaches which combine several semantic lexicons, some domain specific (Navigli & Velardi, 2005)) we obtained high values for precision as many of our concepts' lexical representations are named entities (names of companies, CEO's, locations, etc.) that usually have only one meaning. The high value of recall can be explained by the fact that many of the concepts lexical representations found in news items are present also in the domain ontology and these lexical representations have been correctly disambiguated.

A different metric for the performance evaluation is the latency of a news item in the concept identification phase. The obtained average latency time is around 1s which represents the time needed to process a news item from tokenization to concept recognition. The bottleneck lies in the disambiguation step due to its computations. The sysnset distances are pre-computed (a limit of 4 for the shortest path length between synsets is used) in order to speed-up the disambiguation algorithm.

Regarding usability we have asked 9 users (students at Erasmus University Rotterdam following a course on Semantic Web technologies including RDF(S), OWL, and SPARQL) to find news items for 3 given natural language queries in two ways: (1) using the Hermes implementation and (2) a SPARQL engine. Most students were able to correctly build the search graph and specify the temporal constraints, as well as the corresponding SPARQL query. All queries were faster specified using the Hermes framework than using SPARQL. Note that we do not claim that it is easier to use Hermes instead of SPARQL for querying RDF graphs, but for expressing a certain set of RDF queries (the ones supported by the search graph with temporal restrictions, which we consider typical for news querying) Hermes seems to be easier to use than SPARQL. Among the features mostly appreciated by students in Hermes were the graphical representations of the conceptual graph, the predefined time functions, and the visual cues employed for emphasizing concepts in returned news items.

Compared with traditional keyword-based search engines for news items (e.g., YourNews, SeAN, Google News, Yahoo! News, etc.) our semantic approach benefits from better precision, as it is able to disambiguate (compound) words, query flexibility, because it allows the selection of indirect concepts (i.e., concepts not directly related to the items of interests), and the support for temporal constraints. A quantitative comparison with non-semantic based approaches is difficult to achieve due to the query limitations that these systems have and the impossibility of using the same news items as inputs in the compared systems.

In the tradeoff between expressivity and usability we decided to keep our queries simple with intuitive semantics so that a broad range of users (casual users, media analysts, stock brokers, etc.) should be able to use Hermes. Nevertheless, we acknowledge that an expert user might need more query expressivity (e.g., optional graph patterns, disjunctive semantics for temporal constraints, etc.) which contributes to the increase in complexity (and thus to the decrease in usability) of the framework. For this purpose we plan to extend the Hermes framework in the future with additional functionality that would enable the generation of a news personalization service family (services targeting novice, average, or expert users).

FUTURE RESEARCH DIRECTIONS

As future work, we would like to extend the Hermes framework by employing multiple semantic lexicons and adding new domain specific concepts to the ontology that are not captured in

existing semantic lexicons. Some domain specific concepts (e.g., domain neologisms) are used in news items while current semantic lexicons, which are not up-to-date, do not include them. We also plan to exploit the structure of the domain ontology in order to compute the similarity between concepts. In this way we are better equipped in determining concept (synset) similarity. For the knowledge base updating we would like to be able to discover new concepts (that go beyond the possibilities of a gazetteer) in news items and add them to our ontology. Also, we would like to distinguish between facts and opinions during event recognition and present to the user for validation only fact-based events, as these represent the true source of real-world updates.

At the current moment the lexico-semantic patterns are defined by the domain expert. We would like to automatically extract patterns for detecting events by using machine learning techniques (e.g., genetic algorithms (Castellanos, Gupta, Wang, & Umeshwar, 2010)). The expressivity of the information extraction language can be extended by using regular expressions (e.g., repetition, sequence, optional, etc.) over ontology concepts. The update language can also be extended by using a triggers-based mechanism as in current relational or recent ontology update languages (Losch, Rudolph, Vrandecic, & Studer, 2009). In addition, we would like to refine the expressivity of our query language by allowing the use of Boolean operators (AND, OR, and NOT) as well as pattern-based (sequence-based) queries.

Furthermore we would like to explore the possibilities to redefine the domain ontology as a time-based representation, where instances have a certain time validity associated with them (Milea, Frasincar, & Kaymak, 2008) (Frasincar, Milea, & Kaymak, 2010). These temporal extensions to the ontology would enable us to better reason with the temporal contextual information available for our domain. Regarding the news presentation we would like to include timelines that would allow the user to visualize results in a temporal dimension. Also, for news presentation we would like to experiment with the use of snippets of the news message that match the user query instead of the current few beginning lines from the returned news items.

Another direction that we would like to pursue is that of semantic adaptation of news items based on a user model. The user preferences now represented in the (temporary) search graph would be represented in a (stored) user model which is continuously adapted based on user behavior. In order not to bother the user with already seen content, we would like to be able to filter news items that provide new information by using a novelty control mechanism (Gabrilovich, Dumais, & Horvitz, 2004). We believe that our semantic approach can be successfully applied for modeling dissimilarities between news items and thus be able to recommend only news carrying novel content. In a different scenario, by measuring the similarities between news items, we would be able to recommend news items related to the same story but issued at different moments in time and/or by different institutions.

Regarding HNP we would like to implement news items duplicates removal, timestamps-based sorting of relevant news items, and the user-defined variables employed for communication between information extraction and knowledge base updating as proposed in the Hermes framework. Additionally, we also wish to implement the previously proposed extensions to the Hermes framework: enriching our knowledge sources with multiple lexicons and domain-specific concepts, adding a user model and employing it to adapt system functionality, and filtering news that provide novel content. Also, we would like to test the usage of data structures for fast data access (e.g., hash maps) for ontology access in a news-centric approach where the concept lexical representations are identified during a single news item traversal. Having a constant access time to concept lexical representations and taking in consideration that the number of lexical representations in a news item is smaller than in an ontology might reduce the time needed for the news classification step (for run-time processing of news items).

Additionally, we would like to conduct a more extensive evaluation procedure of the Hermes implementation. Based on detailed questionnaires we can obtain more evidence on the system usability. The accuracy of the proposed relevance degree (based on concept identification) could be determined by measuring the access order and reading time of news item in the result list (accessing the first items first and spending substantial time for reading them are good indications that the returned items are relevant). In addition, we want to experiment with other domains (e.g., politics, sports, etc.) and analyze the precision, recall, and latency of our implementation for these new fields. The genericity of our approach only asks for the definition of a new domain ontology and domain-specific news feeds that need to be plugged into our implementation.

CONCLUSION

The Hermes framework proposes a sequence of steps to be followed for building personalized news services. The input for these systems are RSS news feeds and the output are news items fulfilling user needs. The Hermes approach is based on a domain ontology used for classifying news items and to support the user define his concepts of interest. In addition to concepts and their relationships, the domain ontology stores for each entity lexical representations, some being retrieved from a semantic lexicon. Also, the user can specify temporal constraints that the news items need to obey. For this purpose we have proposed a number of custom functions to support the user during the query creation process. The knowledge base is updated in a semi-automatic fashion using news information. In order to facilitate the user browsing of results we have ordered the news items based on their relevance to the user query.

The Hermes News Portal (HNP) is an implementation of the Hermes framework. The domain ontology is specified in OWL and as a query language we used SPARQL. As a semantic lexicon we employed WordNet, one of the most popular English dictionaries available online. For the natural processing pipeline we have used ANNIE from GATE extended with our own ontology gazetteer and word sense disambiguation engine. For representing temporal constraints we have extended the SPARQL language with temporal functions. JAPE from GATE was used for implementing the lexico-semantic patterns for information extraction. For the knowledge base updates we employed SPARQL/Update.

Differently than Google News and Yahoo! News, Hermes is able to exploit the background information stored in ontologies for retrieving user's items of interest. In this way the user does not need to explicitly define all the instances involved in the query by making use of the concept relationships for specifying his concepts of interest. In addition to the concepts of interest, the user is able to specify temporal constraints in his query. Another key feature of Hermes is the word sense disambiguation procedure, which is not used in related approaches as SeAN, YourNews, NewsDude, MyPlanet, SemNews, or QuickStep. The word sense disambiguation step increases the accuracy of news classifications, by making sure that the found lexical representations indeed correspond to the meaning of the domain ontology concepts. Hermes is also the only personalization framework that to our knowledge allows for semi-automatic update of its knowledge base using news information.

ACKNOWLEDGMENT

The authors are partially supported by the NWO Physical Sciences Free Competition Project 612.001.009: Financial Events Recognition in News for Algorithmic Trading (FERNAT) and EU funded IST-STREP Project FP6-26896: Time-Determined Ontology-Based Information System for Real Time Stock Market Analysis (TOWL). Also, we would like to thank Kim Schouten, Philip Ruijgrok, Leonard Levering, Wouter Rijvordt, Maarten Mulders, and Hanno Embregts for their contribution to the Hermes framework.

REFERENCES

Aha, D. W., Kibler, D., & Albert, M. K. (1991). Instance-Based Learning Algorithms. *Machine Learning, 6*(1), 37–66. doi:10.1007/BF00153759

Ahn, J.-w., Brusilovsky, P., Grady, J., He, D., & Syn, S. Y. (2007). Open User Profiles for Adaptive News Systems: Help or Harm? In *16th International Conference on World Wide Web (WWW 2007)* (pp. 11-20). New York:ACM.

Ardissono, L., Console, L., & Torre, I. (2001). An Adaptive System for the Personalized Access to News. *AI Communications, 14*(3), 129–147.

Bechhofer, S., Harmelen, F. v., Hendler, J., Horrocks, I., McGuinness, D. L., Patel-Schneider, P. F., et al. (2004). *OWL Web Ontology Language Reference* W3C Recommendation 10 February 2004.

Berners-Lee, T., Hendler, J., & Lassila, O. (2001). The Semantic Web. *Scientific American, 284*(5), 34–43. doi:10.1038/scientificamerican0501-34

Billsus, D., & Pazzani, M. J. (1999). A Personal News Agent that Talks, Learns and Explains. In *Third International Conference on Autonomous Agents (Agents 1999)* (pp. 268-275). New York: ACM.

Borsje, J., & Giles, J. (2010). OWL2Prefuse. Retrieved from http://owl2prefuse.sourceforge.net/index.php

Borsje, J., Levering, L., & Frasincar, F. (2008). Hermes: a Semantic Web-Based News Decision Support System In *23rd Annual ACM Symposium on Applied Computing (SAC 2008)* (pp. 2415-2420). New York: ACM.

Brickley, D., & Guha, R. V. (2004). *RDF Vocabulary Description Language 1.0: RDF Schema*: W3C Recommendation 10 February 2004.

Castellanos, M., Gupta, C., Wang, S., & Umeshwar. (2010). Leveraging Web streams for Contractual Situational Awareness in Operational BI. In *International Workshop on Business intelligencE and the WEB (BEWEB 2010)*. New York: ACM.

Cunningham, H., Maynard, D., Bontcheva, K., & Tablan, V. (2002). GATE: A Framework and Graphical Development Environment for Robust NLP Tools and Applications. In *The 40th Anniversary Meeting of the Association for Computational Linguistics (ACL 2002)* (pp. 168–175). Morristown, NJ: ACL.

Finlayson, M. (2010). *The MIT Java Wordnet Interface (JWI)*. Retrieved from http://www.mit.edu/~markaf/projects/wordnet/

Frasincar, F., Borsje, J., & Levering, L. (2009). A Semantic Web-Based Approach for Building Personalized News Services. *International Journal of E-Business Research, 5*(3), 35–53.

Frasincar, F., Milea, V., & Kaymak, U. (2010). tOWL: Integrating Time in OWL. In R. D. Virgilio, F. Giunchiglia & L. Tanca (Eds.), *Semantic Web Information Management: A Model-Based Perspective* (pp. 225-246). Berlin Heidelberg, Germany: Springer.

Gabrilovich, E., Dumais, S., & Horvitz, E. (2004). Newsjunkie: Providing Personalized Newsfeeds via Analysis of Information Novelty. In *13th International Conference on World Wide Web (WWW 2004)* (pp. 482-490). New York: ACM.

Guarino, N., & Welty, C. A. (2002). Evaluating Ontological Decisions with OntoClean. *Communications of the ACM, 45*(1), 61–65.

Java, A., Finin, T., & Nirenburg, S. (2006). Text Understanding Agents and the Semantic Web. In *39th Hawaii International Conference on Systems Science (HICSS 2006)* (Vol. 3, pp. 62.62). Washington, DC: IEEE Computer Society.

Jena Development Team. (2010a). A Semantic Web Framework for Java (Jena). Retrieved from http://jena.sourceforge.net/

Jena Development Team. (2010b). A SPARQL Processor for Jena (ARQ). Retrieved from http://jena.sourceforge.net/ARQ/

Kalfoglou, Y., Domingue, J., Motta, E., Vargas-Vera, M., & Shum, S. B. (2001). *myPlanet: An Ontology-Driven Web-Based Personalized News Service*. Paper presented at the Workshop on Ontologies and Information Sharing (IJCAI 2001).

Kandel, E., & Marx, L. M. (1997). NASDAQ Market Structure and Spread Patterns. *Journal of Financial Economics, 45*(1), 61–89. doi:10.1016/S0304-405X(96)00894-X

Klyne, G., & Carroll, J. J. (2004). *Resource Description Framework (RDF): Concepts and Abstract Syntax*: W3C Recommendation 10 February 2004.

Losch, U., Rudolph, S., Vrandecic, D., & Studer, R. (2009). Tempus Fugit. In *6th European Semantic Web Conference (ESWC 2009)* (pp. 278-292). Berlin Heidelberg, Germany: Springer.

Micu, A., Mast, L., Milea, V., Frasincar, F., & Kaymak, U. (2008). Financial News Analysis Using a Semantic Web Approach. In Zilli, A., Damiani, E., Ceravolo, P., Corallo, A., & Elia, G. (Eds.), *Semantic Knowledge Management: An Ontology-Based Framework* (pp. 311–328). Hershey, PA: IGI Global.

Middleton, S. E., Shadbolt, N. R., & Roure, D. C. D. (2004). Ontological User Profiling in Recommender Systems. *ACM Transactions on Information Systems*, *22*(1), 54–88. doi:10.1145/963770.963773

Milea, V., Frasincar, F., & Kaymak, U. (2008). Knowledge Engineering in a Temporal Semantic Web Context. In *The Eighth International Conference on Web Engineering (ICWE 2008)* (pp. 65-74). Washington, DC: IEEE Computer Society Press.

Motta, E. (1999). *Reusable Components for Knowledge Modelling: Case Studies in Parametric Design Problem Solving* (*Vol. 53*). Amsterdam, the Netherlands: IOS Press.

Navigli, R., & Velardi, P. (2005). Structural Semantic Interconnections: a Knowledge-Based Approach to Word Sense Disambiguation. *IEEE Transactions on Pattern Analysis and Machine Intelligence*, *27*(7), 1063–1074. doi:10.1109/TPAMI.2005.149

Nirenburg, S., & Raskin, V. (2001). Ontological Semantics, Formal Ontology, and Ambiguity. In *Formal Ontology in Information Systems (FOIS 2001)* (pp. 151-161). New York: ACM.

Noy, N., & Rector, A. (2006). *Defining N-ary Relations on the Semantic Web*: W3C Working Group Note 12 April 2006.

Princeton Cognitive Science Laboratory. (2010). A Lexical Database for the English Language (WordNet). Retrieved from http://wordnet.princeton.edu/

Prud'hommeaux, E., & Seaborne, A. (2008). *SPARQL Query Language for RDF*: W3C Recommendation 15 January 2008.

Salton, G. (1971). *The SMART Retrieval System—Experiments in Automatic Document Processing*. Upper Saddle River, NJ: Prentice-Hall.

Salton, G., & McGill, M. J. (1983). *Introduction to Modern Retrieval*. New York: McGraw-Hill.

Schouten, K., Ruijgrok, P., Borsje, J., Frasincar, F., Levering, L., & Hogenboom, F. (2010). A Semantic Web-Based Approach for Personalizing News. In *25th Annual ACM Symposium on Applied Computing (SAC 2010)* (pp. 854-861). New York: ACM.

Seaborne, A. (2004). *RDQL - A Query Language for RDF*: W3C Member Submission 9 January 2004.

Seaborne, A., Manjunath, G., Bizer, C., Breslin, J., Das, S., Davis, I., et al. (2008). *SPARQL Update: A language for Updating RDF Graphs*: W3C Member Submission 15 July 2008.

The Berkeley Institute of Design. (2010). The Prefuse Visualization Toolkit. Retrieved from http://prefuse.org/

The Stanford Natural Language Processing Group. (2010). The Stanford Parser: A Statistical Parser. Retrieved from http://nlp.stanford.edu/software/lex-parser.shtml

Winer, D. (2003). *RSS 2.0 Specification*. Harvard Law School.

KEY TERMS AND DEFINITIONS

Domain ontology: A domain ontology is a formal shared specification of a domain conceptualization (includes both schema and instance of the represented domain). For example, a financial domain ontology can include the class kb:Company and its axioms (e.g., superclasses) and the instance kb:Google.

Knowledge base: A knowledge base is a domain ontology instance (includes also instance types but does not contain type axioms). For example, a financial knowledge base can include the class kb:Company and the instance kb:Google.

Concept: A concept is a class or instance from the knowledge base. For example, a financial knowledge base can include the concepts kb:Company (class) and kb:Google (instance).

Conceptual graph: The conceptual graph is the graph representation of the knowledge base. Nodes represent concepts and edges represent relationships.

Search graph: The search graph is a subgraph of the conceptual graph used to define the search query. It is composed of user-selected concepts and relationships from the conceptual graph.

News classification: News classification is the process of assigning concepts from the knowledge base to news items. A news item can have zero or more concepts associated depending on the number of concepts present in the news item.

Knowledge base updating: Knowledge base updating is the process of adding new instances and/or relationships to the knowledge base. For example in a financial domain when a company buys another company the competitor relationship between these companies ceases to exist.

Results presentation: Results presentation is the process of displaying the news items matching the search query. The news items are ranked based on their relevance to the query.

Lexico-semantic pattern: A lexico-semantic pattern is an information extraction pattern that uses lexical representations and/or concepts. An example of a lexico-semantic pattern (which uses only concepts) is kb:Google kb:Buys kb:YouTube.

tSPARQL: tSPARQL is SPARQL extended with temporal operators. Examples of temporal operators are retrieving the current xsd:date, adding a xsd:duration to a xsd:dateTime, substracting two xsd:dateTimes, etc.

Chapter 14
Study on E–Business Adoption from Stakeholders' Perspectives in Indian Firms

Ranjit Goswami
Indian Institute of Technology, Kharagpur, India

S K De
Indian Institute of Technology, Kharagpur, India

B. Datta
Indian Institute of Technology, Kharagpur, India

ABSTRACT

E-business adoption towards creating better stakeholders' values in any business organization should begin with corporate home pages, which is equivalent of the online identity of the physical firm. This paper, by taking two snapshot pictures of corporate homepages, one in 2005 and another in 2007, analyses e-business adoption levels in fifteen publicly-listed Indian firms of three different sizes and five sectors from four external stakeholders (Customers, Suppliers/Alliances, Shareholders and Society/Community) perspectives. We also measure overall e-business readiness levels from four stakeholders' perspectives in 2005 and 2007, and analyze the adoption as per Stages of Growth model. The measurement is based on presence of various categories of interactions, as commonly perceived, between the firm and respective stakeholder group.

INTRODUCTION

Creating an e-business strategy to support corporate functions is quite an intriguing task due to the evolving nature of e-business practices, technological innovations and also due to increasing reach of the Internet. Business organizations were still not in a position to effectively leverage real time queries from stakeholders until the turn of the twenty first century when Internet with its increased reach and acceptability made it possible for organizations to engage into real time capturing of information and conducting business transactions with various stakeholders, as and when wanted by the stakeholders. Effective e-business practices generate opportunities to create value

DOI: 10.4018/978-1-60960-132-4.ch014

Copyright © 2011, IGI Global. Copying or distributing in print or electronic forms without written permission of IGI Global is prohibited.

for the enterprise by reducing response time and costs due to reengineered business processes in one side, and by increasing market reach, thereby resulting in better satisfaction levels and financial performances.

E-business is defined as the use of Internet-based Information and Communication Technologies (ICTs) by organizations to conduct business transactions, to share information and to maintain relationships (Singh & George, 2005). We studied e-business adoption by studying the corporate portals of our sample, starting with the homepages. A portal is an application of information technology that facilitates complex business interactions by presenting them in an easy-to-use web based interface (Curran & Singh, 2001) whereas a homepage is the main page of a website, intended chiefly to greet visitors and provide information about the site or its owner. Reichinger & Baumgartner (2004) found that an entity can have multiple homepages, however there can be only one entity that has any particular homepage, i.e. not allowing two entities to have the same homepage. Normally we don't see business organizations having multiple homepages, they rather have one. A homepage in this sense is a public web document about that business entity, though parts of that public web document may have private access. For this work, we felt homepages did qualify to be part of corporate portals as well

Like the physical business of any organization that strives to meet the diverse needs of its various stakeholders, the homepages also addresses and informs different groups of stakeholders, thereby facilitating online/offline business and meeting their diverse online business needs. Through clearly demarcated sections in homepages, firms try to reach out to its various stakeholders like customers, alliances/suppliers, shareholders, government, potential employees and finally to the community (society). Addressing online the company initiatives, to foster a better community through Corporate Social Responsibility (CSR), can be an excellent tool for enhancing the legiti-

macy of the firm among its other stakeholders, and thereby helps towards development of a positive corporate image (Morimoto et al, 2004). Homepages can be the platform where the various other stakeholder-specific public or private portals of the firm can potentially converge.

This paper examines already adopted E-business practices in fifteen Indian firms for four groups of stakeholders - namely Customers, Suppliers/Alliances[1], Community and Shareholders over two time-periods. As adoption of e-business strategy is influenced by firm and industry level factors, the sample comprised five different segments (Banking, Chemical, Metal, FMCH and IT) and three different sizes (small, medium and large). E-business with Government as a stakeholder is not considered as that remains outside the purview of homepage functionalities - to whatever extent that happens over Internet. Similarly employees are also not considered for this study because e-business practices with employees may not be publicly accessible. Two categories of information flows are considered between firms and select four groups of stakeholders – one what the firm wants to communicate with the selected stakeholder groups through standardized open communications, and 2nd what customized queries the firm intends to entertain from the selected stakeholder groups based on their generic and specific interests in the firm.

To do so, we identified certain set of stakeholder specific hygiene and motivational factors, and checked for presence (or absence) of these factors in the corporate homepages of these fifteen firms to finally arrive at combined corporate e-business adoption level scorecard for these four categories of stakeholders. The studies were first initiated in 2005 (March), and again repeated in 2007 (December) to have two comparable periodic pictures on adoption levels. The overall scores of individual firms are added across segments and sizes to arrive at e-business readiness of that segment and size or that of the overall sample to

Figure 1. E-business stakeholders' model (Jutla et. al., 2001)

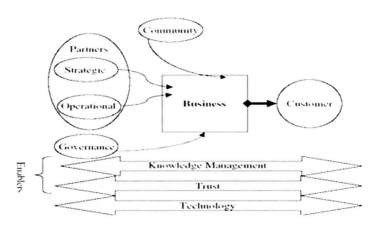

have an insightful understanding of adoption of e-business in Indian firms.

The overall contribution of our paper is to introduce two more variables (firm size and firms' prioritization of stakeholders' interests while adopting e-business practices) in the Stages of Growth Model (Nolan and Gibson, 1974; Nolan, 1979) based on our findings of these two surveys. The next section of the paper presents the literature review while the subsequent sections deal with the methodology, the findings and finally to the conclusions.

A REVIEW OF STAKEHOLDER THEORIES IN E-BUSINESS

Researchers identified indicators that reveal the nature of a website. As the data for research had to be easily accessible, therefore each criterion had to be either present or absent in that study, where the objective of the study was more in gauging transparency and openness (Beer, 2004). Models like e^3 value methodology (Gordijn, 2003) provided ontology to conceptualize and to visualize an e-business idea. Ontology as an area provides definitions, concepts, relations between the concepts, and rules, which are interpreted in the same way by stakeholders, to conceptualize a specific domain, so that multiple e-business actors and multiple stakeholders don't interpret things differently. Other notable e-business model ontology described the logic of a *"business system"* for creating value in the Internet era based on product innovation, infrastructure management, customer relationship and financial aspects (Osterwalder & Yves, 2002).

E-business stakeholder model (Figure 1) of Jutla et al (2001) is customer focused, arguing business stakeholders work together to meet customers' demand, and to improve customer acquisition, satisfaction and retention levels. The external stakeholders or linkages identified in this model are strategic partner, operational partner, customer community and governance. Stages-of-growth model (Caroline & Swatnam, 2004) proposed four stages for B2B e-commerce implementation, namely initial e-commerce, centralized e-commerce, looking inward for benefits and global e-commerce as e-commerce evolves to maturity in any organization.

The closest match to our studies came from Straub and Watson (2000) as they developed the *Hexagonal Model* to describe the organization's interactions with various stakeholders. They showed the firm's interactions with six stakeholders, namely: (1) suppliers, (2) intermediaries, (3) customers, (4) government, (5) employees, and

Figure 2. Hexagonal (Hex) model of firm interactions (Straub and Watson, 2000)

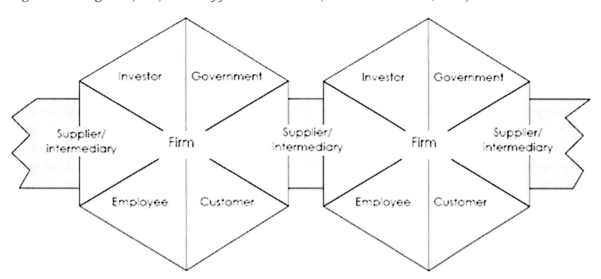

(6) investors whereas we retained three of the above group of stakeholders, adding society/community as its importance grows in business environment. We also excluded government, employees and intermediaries as our improvised methodology could not support applications predominantly based on intranets and/or applications meant for closed-user-groups. In our methodology, we not only tried to capture presence of these interactions; but also wanted to qualitatively measure exhaustiveness of these interactions (at least the intent or the promise, not what's being delivered). Online interactions between firm and its intermediaries, government and employees tend to follow Closed User Group (CUG) model which are less likely to have their initiations from the homepages. That's true for customers and suppliers as well, however firms always compete to attract new customers and better suppliers, the beginning of these two categories of interactions tend to be more publicly accessible in homepages.

On the geographical dimensions of e-business adoption across countries, it is closely linked with macro-economic factors like telecom and Internet infrastructure. Oyeyinka and Kaushalesh (2004), through firm-level data from three developing countries (India, Nigeria & Uganda) concluded that size of operation, export performance, profitability, significantly determine firm level e-business adoption. On E-business readiness and adoption studies in different countries, The Economist Intelligence Unit (EIU – 2004, in its fifth such annual rankings) in co-operation with IBM Institute of Business Value 'The 2004 e-readiness ranking' ranked India in 46th position (same in 2003 also) in terms of global e-readiness ranking with a score of 4.45 out of 10 (3.95 in 2003)[2]. It cited Indian business environment being indifferent to hostile to niches of programming, customer services & business process outsourcing. Another study of Rastogi (2003) also pointed similar observations. It identified some of the barriers to e-commerce adoption in India like limited Internet access among customers and SMEs, poor telecom and infrastructure for reliable connectivity, multiple gaps in the current legal and regulatory framework, and multiple issues of trust and lack of payment gateways. However The Economist study also talked about drastic increase in investments and bandwidth happening in India in 2004-05, results of which have been seen in subsequent years in tremendous growths in mobile telephony, and very lately in broadband penetrations as well. The EIU study was based on nearly 100 quantitative and qualitative criteria, organized into six distinct categories - (1) Connectivity & technology infrastructure (25% wt. in overall score), (2) Business environment (20%), (3) Consumer & business adoption (20%), (4) Legal & policy environment (15%), (5) Social & cultural environment (15%) & finally (6) Supporting e-services (5%). On a comparative basis, India's rank didn't see improvements in-spite of the earlier promise of investments as it slipped to 54th rank in the year 2007.

Another cross-country comparison among ten countries (India although not included in that sample) among developed, newly industrializing and developing nations by Gibbs et al (2002) found global, environmental and policy factors also influences e-commerce diffusion. It concluded that B2B e-commerce is driven by global forces through increasingly globalized competition and 'MNC push'.

METHODOLOGY

Stakeholders as such can be categorized into existing and potential ones. Existing stakeholders can be better served by user-identification protected intranets/extranets which may/may not have its origin/linkages from/with corporate homepages, accessible to all. However objective of corporate portal is to attract, acquire, retain and thereby engage the targeted potential stakeholders on an ongoing manner in line with company's business objectives. The paper makes an assumption that any e-business strategy therefore should begin from corporate homepages only – which is easily accessible by all existing and potential stakeholders without any entry barriers and easily identifiable with the corporate entity of the firm. Therefore for present study, corporate homepages are taken as the starting point from where organizations initiate and interact with these set of stakeholders, which essentially acts as a dissemination point for

company's orientation to different stakeholders, as a platform for sharing news and views with regular financial statements to target stakeholders as well as respond to customized queries from any of these existing or potential stakeholders. We argue that closed user group systems that firms may have with existing stakeholders is an outcome and a subsequent development resulting from corporate homepages, as existing stakeholders had also been potential ones at some point in past (and considering firms as ongoing entities).

This paper studied fifteen Indian organizations' corporate homepages and analyzed e-business practices and adoption levels for the selected four categories of stakeholders across a time-span of over two years. We follow a simple improvised methodology. First, we observed for specific presence of exclusive separate zones for these four categories of stakeholders on corporate homepage. Subsequently we looked for the necessary and sufficient features within the homepage-portal that facilitates two categories of interactions - from firm to stakeholders in Category I, and stakeholders to firm in Category II. Based on presence and absence of these features, and also based on a qualitative understanding on convenience and detailing of the need, as likely norms or as likely exceptions that these stakeholders may have with the firm; we assigned scores out of a pre-defined distributed weighing system.

We define Category I communications to be essentially the answer of the firm when following generic question is asked:

"What does the firm want to communicate with this group of stakeholders online?"

Whereas Category II communications, in turn, is the answer by the firm when following generic question is asked:

"What categories of online customized queries from this group of stakeholders do the firm entertain?"

Further, the paper identifies certain Hygiene factors and Motivational factors[3] in both categories of interactions, weight of Hygiene factors in determining e-readiness being more (50% for Hygiene against 25% for Motivational; balance 25% on exclusive stakeholder zones on homepage). Based on present practice of recognition of these four stakeholders' requirements in the priorities of the organization, we arrived at e-business readiness scores of firms, and subsequently of segments and sizes from a stakeholders' perspective and finally to an indicative measure of e-business readiness status for overall Indian industries (true, sample size and segments studied are small for this generalization). The specific types of Hygiene and Motivational factors across Category I and II are given in Table 2 of Appendix A.

Note of Caution on Characteristics of Variables, and on Their Measurements

With segment specific characteristics, stakeholders' expectations would vary. Like what customers value in Banks & Financial Institutes (Percival-Straunik, 2001) would be different from what buyers would value while buying industrial chemicals (Dennis, 2001). Zhu et al (2002) segregated manufacturing firms with high and low-IT intensity sectors towards accessing firm performance to e-commerce capabilities. Our study however follows same variables with same weigh, irrespective of segment-specific characteristics, except in two specific changes in stakeholder characteristics, namely as (1) 'Alliances' substituted 'Suppliers' in Information Technology firms, and (2) for Banks & Financial Institutions, 'Suppliers' are interchangeable with 'Customers'.

Also while measuring based on presence of these stakeholders' zones in the homepage itself, and subsequently by features enabling both way communications as identified, there exists significant scope of manual error/bias. There is a further

possibility of that bias being different during the two distant periods of study (one in March 2005 and the other in December 2007, and in e-business - that's a long time!). The measurement anyway represents a snapshot relative picture as firms often change their websites, and date of accessing the homepage for both the studies (2005 & 2007) were provided with respective scores in Appendix A & Appendix B. For any 'miss' or 'errors', the authors take their due responsibility and state omission/misinterpretation is purely unintentional. Any measurement of non-financial parameters and practices would be subjective to such errors.

There can also be information/interaction opportunities across stakeholders, like the already stated CSR practices or financial information, which can be used by customers, suppliers as well along with shareholders. The methodology we followed however didn't provide additional weigh for such provisions.

SAMPLE SURVEY

Sample characteristics

The objective of this study is to identify e-business readiness of firms and adoption level of e-enabled processes in meeting stakeholders' requirements across different segments and sizes of business organizations in India. In this paper, fifteen listed business organizations were selected from five different segments. A broad financial characteristic of the sample is given in Table 1 of Appendix A. Out of three firms from each segment, one was selected from BSE[4] 'Sensex' scripts (representative of large firm in segment), one from BSE 'A' group (representative of mid-sized firms in the segment) and last one was from BSE 'B' group (representative of small firm in the segment) leading to sample comprising five firms from 'Sensex' scripts, five from BSE 'A' group and five from BSE 'B' group from five different segments, namely

(1) Banks and Financial Institutes, (2) Chemicals/ Conglomerates within broader Chemicals segment, (3) Commodities (primarily Iron & Steel, though one player had power exposure as well), (4) FMCG and finally (5) Information Technology.

E-business readiness score at firm level and subsequently at segment or size level from the four identified groups of stakeholders' perspective, namely Customers, Suppliers/Alliances, Shareholders and Community are the dependent variables of this study. These are derived by surveying the homepages of the sample firms for presence (or absence) of exclusive stakeholder zones in homepages, and subsequently for presence (or absence) of Hygiene & Motivational features for Category I & II communications (as identified and listed in Table 2 of Appendix A). On a zero to one score, based on presence of exclusive stakeholder zones in homepage and subsequently based on the qualitative coverage of Hygiene and Motivational factors in Category I and II areas, this measurement is tabulated in Table 3 of Appendix A. Subsequent multiplication by the weigh of the respective categories gives the e-business readiness score (Table 4, Appendix A).

Independent variables are derived from exclusive stakeholders' zones in homepage (presence/ secondary presence/absence) in 1st level and subsequently from qualitative presence/absence of both way critical and desired Hygiene & Motivational factors for both-way (Category I & Category II) interactions. This essentially is a quantitative measurement in the form of 'Yes/In-between/ No' for stakeholders' zones for their exclusivity of presence in the homepage through 'presence/ presence with reduced priority/absence' practices.

Each of the four groups of stakeholders weigh is assumed to be uniform and therefore stands at 25%. One-fourth of that is assigned on presence/ absence of clearly marked zones – therefore 6.25% for each stakeholder specific zones on the homepage, a ½ rating indicates presence with reduced priority (e.g. no exclusive zone in homepage but clubbed under a broader heading like 'About Us'

which is interpreted as reduced priority/space allotment in homepage).

Out of balance 75%, 50% is on Hygiene factors and 25% on Motivational factors distributed equally over Category I and II interactions (37.5% each). Therefore 12.5% each is assigned for presence/absence of Hygiene factors for two-way effective communications (Category I & Category II each having 6.25% again) between firm and its each stakeholder group under study. Similarly 6.25% is the weigh assigned on each stakeholder group Motivational factors (totaling 25%) for both-way communications (Category I & Category II each having 3.125%). The score is based on combined presence (or absence) of any number of identified features, and therefore can take figures other than '1'/'0' binary forms. Scores in Categories (I & II) and Factors (Hygiene & Motivational) for a stakeholder get multiplied by assigned score of exclusivity in homepage. Therefore when Community as a stakeholder is missing from corporate homepage altogether (0 score in Stakeholders' zone for Community), subsequent Community scores for Hygiene and Motivational factors in both Category I and II (depicted as CO-CI-HF, CO-CII-HF, CO-CI-MF & CO-CII-MF) would all be zero (cell scores in Table 3, Appendix A are already multiplied by parent scores). Thereby Table 3 rates the respective homepages of the firms based on presence/ absence of stakeholders' specific exclusive zones, and also based on qualitative presence of pre-identified Hygiene & Motivational factors (Table 2 of Appendix A) across two categories – Category I & Category II communications respectively. The total firm level e-business readiness score is thereby arrived at from these four groups of stakeholders' perspectives, and tables accordingly to segments and for sizes in Table 4 in Appendix A as Summary Findings.

A similar exercise was repeated with same sample in December 2007, and findings of that are provided in Appendix B (Tables 9, 10, 11, & 12) with more of the scores and few company characteristics (like M-Cap) without as much detailing as Appendix A (for 2005) provided, as the methodology remained same.

Findings of our Study

Firm, segment and size related salient findings are:

- Majority of the studied companies already adopted certain practices towards better stakeholders' interactions management online; however they mostly took the communications as one way than both ways, focusing more on Category I interactions.
- Public Sector Unit like Balmer Lawrie (only PSU[5] firm in sample) had its tenders put on homepage which act as suppliers' interface to a certain extent (Category I partly covered for suppliers as a stakeholder). Otherwise suppliers' interface was missing from all other mid-sized and small manufacturing companies in 2005, and that mostly remained valid in 2007 as well..
- Firms in services sectors like B & FIs & IT companies have their homepages largely dedicated to customer services and knowledge practices respectively. ICICI Bank & Infosys had community as a category getting served with exclusive zones in 2005, however not in the homepage itself, but under 'About Us' category (2nd level if homepage is taken as 1st level), which we concluded as assigning them less priority ('shelf-space' not given in homepage in comparison to retail sector) in-spite of their managing this stakeholder interactions well otherwise.
- Large manufacturing companies like RIL & Tata Steel have online ordering/interactions with established large 'A' group customers, however it looked like they don't have online support/order acceptance from a new (potential) customer, or CRM for retail end consumer as expected for the

challenges of B2C nature of fulfillment and relationship issues (same with certain divisions of ITC, in FMCG sector as well).

- In Investors' Relations cell, most 'Sensex' companies have well-established processes, however we did not see future/upcoming schedule of analysts' meet in any site, which we took as one criterion in Category I Motivational Factor for shareholders as it enables all to know and follow that on a real time basis, making information available to all uniformly irrespective of reach and status irrespective of being in the firm's closed user group of 'analysts'.
- Suppliers' linkages with ITC is found to be nil (as the firm exhibits significant level of vertical integration) other than ambitious e-choupal initiatives of its International Business Division (IBD) where present and potential suppliers of certain agri-inputs for IBD are/can be millions of rural farmers. FMCG sector as such faces this fragmentation challenge in e-business supply chain management (both suppliers and customers are many in numbers, and thereby fragmented by nature of business), and this being true to a certain extent for other manufacturing companies as well who sell partly or mostly through retail distribution channels. Channel partners' interactions, vital for FMCG firms, are not specifically considered in this study where channel partners' have been clubbed with broader 'Customer' base as a stakeholder.
- Archies has joined hands with leading B2C portal indiatimes (media firm) to serve and fulfill customer registrations and order fulfillments online. Indiatimes could have been considered as a strategic partner/alliance, which however we didn't.
- Contact details of Registrar and Share Transfer agents (Category I Hygiene Factor for investor community) was not found in most IT firms, however these firms have a

feature on subscribing to company news. Hexaware didn't have Analysts' meet presentations, however it made available brokerage houses' outlook on the firm. This can also be explained by higher proportion of overseas listing of Indian IT firms (within our samples, two out of three had overseas listing; highest among the five segments; and that's in general true for IT sector in India).

- Other than the large firms from Sensex, the study shows that e-enabled business interactions of Community and Suppliers as stakeholders are significantly less for mid-sized (two out of five firms have some features for both Community & Suppliers) and small firms (none out of five for Community & two out of five for Suppliers having some features) in 2005.

- The broader trends of above (for 2005) was found to be true in 2007 studies as well, though we found Small and Medium Sized players to have improved significantly in matters of customers and investors communication categories.

E-Business Readiness Score Analysis

Simple analysis of scores was carried out in Table 4 to Table 8 for 2005 (Appendix A). These were primarily focused at:

1. Firm level e-business adoption for these stakeholders (Table 4) varied from 0 to 0.88 (out of 1) indicating practices from initial e-business to global e-business (Chan et al, 2004), surprisingly within same segment in our 2005 studies. The lower range remained same even in 2007.

2. Segment level (Table 5) e-business adoption score of these five segments in 1st study of 2005 varied from 0.37 (commodities/metals) to 0.69 (B & FIs), and size level (Table 6)

e-business adoption score for three different size-categories varied from 0.325 (small firms) to 0.7 (large firms). In our repeat study of 2007 (Table 10 of Appendix B), we found a degree of convergence across segments and sizes (segment scores varied from 0.39 for commodities to 0.66 for chemicals, and 0.37 for smaller firms to 0.7 for the larger ones).

3. Stakeholder wise adoption level of business interactions across sizes and segments (Table 7, Appendix A) varied from 0.06 (community) to customers (0.19) and the trend repeated even in 2007 (0.22 for customer and 0.07 for community) showing customer-centric adoption with community as most neglected stakeholder; and finally

4. Category-wise (Category I interactions from firm to stakeholders and Category II interactions from stakeholders to firms) and Factor-wise (Hygiene and Motivational factors of interactions desired) e-business readiness form sample and across sizes is presented in Table 8, Appendix A and Table 12 of Appendix B. The adoption level of Category I interactions and that of Hygiene Factors outscored Category-II interactions and Motivational factors in both the years. It's natural and as per expectations in terms of higher adoption of Hygiene factors, however that can't be true for Category I & II interactions as firms fail to make best use of listening to their stakeholders using Internet as a media.

Few of the salient findings, many in line with expectations but quite a few otherwise as well are noted below:

1. Tata Steel scored highest for e-business readiness (with 0.88 score) followed by a close 2nd ICICI Bank (0.87) followed by UTI Bank (72%) at 3rd place in our 1st survey (2005). The range of absolute score varied from 0

to 0.88 (out of 1) in terms of e-readiness adoption from four of these stakeholders' perspectives. The top order saw quite some changes in 2007, with Reliance occupying the top position followed by ITC and then followed by Tata Steel. All the three top rankers in 2007 essentially came from the large groups.

2. Interestingly, the least score (and 2nd least score also) comes from same commodity group (steel) segment that produced the overall winner (in 2005). In 2007 also, we find this segment having least adoption level due to extreme score of one sample within a sample size of three.

3. Overall e-business readiness of firms studied in 2005 had a mean e-business readiness score of 0.49, and a Standard Deviation (SD) of 0.24. Extremely small sample size is noted here. In 2007, we see small and medium firms making clear progress whereas large firms overall rating remaining same; leading the mean to go up to 0.55 and standard deviation to come down to 0.2, explaining convergence as time progressed.

4. Expectedly, low-touch standardized services segments like Banks & Financial Institutes had the highest mean in segment e-business readiness score (0.68) in 2005, although it could not retain that position in 2007 (mean score 0.59, as online banking alone is no longer a winning feature for banks). Chemicals/conglomerates segment ranked 2nd with 0.51 mean in 2005, and came on top in 2007 (0.66). Other than Monnet Ispat score of zero skewing mean score of commodity (steel) segment, making it the worst performing segment; FMCG segment also was a laggard in both the years. These findings are in line with Boston Consulting Group (shop.org, 2001) forecasts of US online transactions (1999) and Forrester Research findings on Leaders and Laggards.

5. From stakeholders' perspective, firms have maximum e-readiness in order of customers (0.19 out of 0.25 for each stakeholder's groups), shareholders (0.15), suppliers (0.1) and community (0.06) in 2005 with same order was repeated in 2007 as well (0.22 for customers followed by 0.18 for shareholders followed by 0.08 for suppliers and finally community scoring 0.07).

6. Other than a few exceptions, adoption of e-business decreased as we moved from Sensex companies (large ones) to BSE 'A' group (mid-sized) to BSE 'B' group (small ones) in both the surveys.

7. Expectedly, Standard Deviation of firms in mid-sized & smaller ones were higher compared to larger firms in 2005, meaning adoption level was more non-uniform across medium and small firms in our initial studies. However in 2007, we found SD of mid-sized firms to be the least (0.09 against 0.21 in 2005). The comparable scores for large firms were 0.12 (against 0.16 in 2005) and 0.25 (against 0.21 in 2005). *Size wise SD figures for 2007 not separately shown in Appendix B, though it was calculated and can be calculated from given values.*

8. We also found that large companies largely have similar scores towards Customers and Shareholders (true for broader sample also). Variance in score for Suppliers stakeholder is explained by segment dynamics and/or on scale of integration. Other than RIL, all large companies were engaged in significant e-enabled community development programs towards the CSR objectives in 2005, which surprisingly took a beating in 2007.

9. Mean scores on Category I (what firms communicate to stakeholders) and Category II communications (what customized queries from stakeholders' the firm encourages) show that firms in-general engage in more one-way communication (from firm to stakeholder) than they prefer to listen to what

Figure 3. Stages of Growth in e-Business Adoption: Size and Stakeholders' perspectives (amended from Nolan & Gibson, 1974)

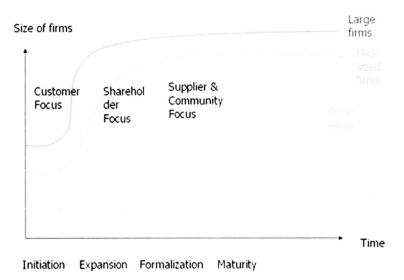

their stakeholders have to say. Category I mean score was 20% vis-à-vis Category II mean score of 13% in 2005 (2007 figures were 22.5% and 15.6% respectively). Both Categories have equal weight of 37.5% in determining e-business readiness in our model (balance 25% being stakeholder specific zone in homepage).

10. Similarly mean scores on Hygiene Factors (24.3% out of 50%) vis-à-vis Motivational Factors score (9.4% out of 25%) justify the focus to be more on essential than on desired features, and expectedly organizations adopt Hygiene Factors more and faster. The trend was similar in 2007 as well (26.8% and 10.9%).

11. Overall, the comparison of the e-readiness scores across two time periods showed an improved adoption level in overall scores (more so amongst the SMEs) and also in each of the sub-groups like stakeholder wise (except suppliers category), segment wise and size wise improvement; although the trend of neglecting community as a stakeholder or Category II communications remained intact.

Our Perspective on E-Business Adoption Across Sizes and Stakeholders

Aided by above findings and analysis, we present our model by incorporating two more variables in the Stages of Growth Model, namely size of firms and prioritization of stakeholders' interest in firms' operations (Figure 3).

We see here that firms' initially have a customer-centric approach as they adopt e-business, and large firms score higher in overall e-business adoption levels compared to small-and-mid-sized firms. However with time, the gap of e-business adoption level across firms from different sizes diminishes; and also as firms' move to maturity, they start paying attentions to other stakeholders' (namely suppliers and community). We also conclude that the initial drivers of e-business adoption that favor certain sectors (like Banking, as we found in our first survey of 2005) diminish as online banking percolates down to the very basics of banking business itself.

CONCLUSION

Stages-of-growth model (Nolan and Gibson) has been the most popular approach used for strategy development and implementation covering areas of new innovative practices. Going by four stage-of-growth models proposed for e-business implementations specifically and for Information Systems in Organizations from a more generalized perspective (Chan et al, 2004), fifteen Indian organizations studied here collectively display the characteristics of these four categories of evolution – from 'initial e-business' to 'global e-business' in both these two time-periods with a clear shift of progress in growth models, as scores improved in 2007. Community as a stakeholder gets least attention from Indian business organizations whereas customers and shareholders get the maximum attentions, in respective orders. As e-business increasingly resembles business itself, the study could throw insightful findings on Indian firms order of priorities related to different stakeholders in running their businesses. Customers and Shareholders came on top in order of priority. The paper also found similar sized firms show better uniformity in levels of e-business adoption, with smaller and medium sized firms learning fast and improving the gaps in e-business adoption practices against larger ones by copying best practices quickly (Porter, 2001). This again proves that learning in e-space to be real fast, even in a country like India with poor Internet infrastructures. While the study validated what was anyway expected on a generalized basis, it also provided quite a few meaningful new insights and surprises in understanding how firms prioritize stakeholders' interests in more details. In the background when e-business increasingly looks to be maturing as an application, we were surprised that firms, irrespective of their sizes and segments, use their homepages and features therein more to announce about themselves rather than using the interactivity rich feature of Internet to listen to the various customized queries that their stakeholders might have.

REFERENCES

Beer Michael. (2004). *Corporate Identity & the web: What your homepage tells about your organization.* Available: http://ui4all.ics.forth.gr/workshop2004/files/ui4all_proceedings/adjunct/organisational/72.pdf (Accessed: 2005, February 25).

Chan, C., & Swatnam, P. M. C. (2004). B2B E-commerce Stages of Growth: The Strategic Imperatives. *In 37th Hawaii International Conference on System Sciences.*

Curran, C., & Singh, G. (2001). Enterprise Portals: Building Value through Organizational knowledge. *DiamondCluster International Inc Centre for Technology Innovation, 2*(2).

Dennis, D. L. (2001). *New Study by Accenture Reveals Keys to Online Success for Chemicals Industry.* Available: http://www.accenture.com/xd/xd.asp?it=enweb&xd=_dyn%5Cdynamicpressrelease_305.xml (Accessed 2004, July 7).

Gibbs, J., Kraemer, K. L., & Dedrick, J. (2002). *Environment and Policy Factors Shaping E-commerce Diffusion: A Cross-Country Comparison. Center for Research on Information Technology & Organizations.* Irvine: University of California.

Gordijn, J. (2003). *Why visualization of e-business models matters. In 16th Bled Electronic Commerce Conference eTransformation,* Bled, Slovenia, June 9-11, 2003 http://www.cs.vu.nl/~obelix/publications/Why%20visualization%20of%20e-business%20models%20matters.pdf

Jutla, D. N., & Bodorik, C. J. (2001). A methodology for creating e-business strategy. *In The 34th Hawaii International Conference on System Sciences.*

Morimoto, R., Ash, J., & Hope, C. (2004). *Corporate Social Responsibility Audit: From Theory to Practice.* University of Cambridge, Judge Institute of Management, Working Paper No. 14/2004.

Nolan, R. (1979). Managing The Crisis In Data Processing. *Harvard Business Review, 57*(2), 115–126.

Nolan, R., & Gibson, C. F. (1974, January/February). Managing the four stages of EDP growth. *Harvard Business Review,* 76–88.

Osterwalder, A., & Pigneur, Y. (2002). An e-Business Model Ontology for Modelling e-Business. *In 15ᵗʰ Bled Electronic Commerce Conference e-Reality: Constructing the e-Economy,* Bled, Slovenia.

Oyelaran-Oyeyinka, B., & Lal, K. (2005). *Determinants of e-business Adoption: Evidence from firms in India, Nigeria Uganda.* Institute for New Technologies (INTECH), United Nations University, Available: http://www.intech.unu.edu/publications/discussion-papers/2004-14.pdf (Accessed: 2005 22nd February)

Percival-Straunik, L. (2001). *E-commerce.* London: Profile Books Ltd.

Percival-Straunik, L. (2001). Shop.org. In *E-Commerce, The Economist.*

Porter, M. (2001). Internet and the Strategy. *Harvard Business Review, 79*(3).

Rastogi, R. (2003). *India: Country report on E-commerce Initiatives.* http://www.unescap.org/tid/publication/part_three2261_ind.pdf (Accessed: 2005 February 20)

Reichinger, K., & Baumgartner, R. (2004). *SEMNUM RDF Vocabulary Specification v.01.* DBAI Technical Report. http://www.dbai.tuwien.ac.at/local/reports/semnum.pdf (Accessed: 2007 July 21ˢᵗ).

Singh, M., & Byrne, G. (2005). Performance evaluation of e-business in Australia. *Electronic Journal of Information Systems Evaluation, 8*(1). Available: http://www.ejise.com/volume-8/v8-iss-1/v8-i1-art8.htm (Accessed 2005, February 25).

Straub, D. W., & Watson, R. T. (2000). *Key issues in researching IT and electronic commerce: Research report of Georgia State University.*

The Economist Intelligence Unit in co-operation with IBM Institute of Business Value. *The 2004 e-readiness rankings.* Available: http://eb.eiu.com/site_info.asp?info_name=err2004 (Accessed on October 10, 2004), and *'The 2007 e-readiness rankings'* available at http://www.eiuresources.com/mediadir/default.asp?PR=2007042601 (accessed on March 25, 2008)

Zhu, K., & Kraemer, K. L. (2002). e-Commerce Metrics for Net-Enhanced Organizations: Assessing the Value of e-Commerce to Firm Performance in the Manufacturing Sector. *Information Systems Research, 13*(3), 275–295. doi:10.1287/isre.13.3.275.82

ENDNOTES

[1] One of the five sectors studied is banking industry, where, when money is taken as the primary input and output for banks; both the customers and suppliers are same. However, here the distinguishing factor is depositors and lenders. We could have taken suppliers of the banks to be the ATM manufacturers or systems suppliers; however we felt the other categories to be more suitable.

[2] Incidentally, in its 8ᵗʰ annual e-readiness ranking of 2007, Indian came in 54ᵗʰ position (53ʳᵈ in 2006) with a score of 4.66 (4.04 in 2006). http://www.eiuresources.com/mediadir/default.asp?PR=2007042601

[3] We use Hygiene factors and Motivational factors in the same sense as it's proposed

in Two-factor Theory by Frederick Hertzberg (1966). Satisfaction from e-business by stakeholder group is determined more by Motivational factors whereas lack of Hygiene factors in e-business features cause dissatisfaction in respective stakeholder groups.

[4] Bombay Stock Exchange is one of the two leading stock exchanges of India (other one being National Stock Exchange), and it's also the oldest in Asia.

[5] Public Sector Unit, where Government owns majority of the ownership in the firm.

APPENDIX A: DATA COLLECTION AND ANALYSIS

Table 1. Sample characteristics (2005 findings)

Measures	B & FIs			Chemicals/Cnglmts			Commodity/metal			FMCG			IT		
Financial/business characteristics	ICICI	UTI	SIB	RIL	TCL	BL	Tata Steel	Jindal Steel	Monnet Ispat	ITC	Dabur India	Archies	Infy	Hexaware	Tata Infotech
M-Cap (in Million US$)	6687	1236	72	18214	799	76	5430	843	141	7776	794	12	13776	411	165
Paid-up Equity Capital (in Million US$)	140.9	53.2	10.8	319.1	49.2	3.7	126.6	3.5	7.0	56.7	6.5	1.5	30.9	5.4	4.2
Net worth (in Million US$)	1831	260	90	7250	457	40	1032	196	34	1451	61	11	744	52	56
Overseas listing	Y	N	N	Y	N	N	N	N	N	Y	N	N	Y	Y	N
PE	15.9	17.7	10.6	12.0	14.3	16.6	7.3	7.6	6.5	19.1	26.6	8.8	35.8	41.0	11.5
RONW (%)	21.9	27.1	23.6	17.4	12.1	10.9	45.4	42.8	25.5	27.3	29.8	11.4	40.7	5.7	26.4
Plant Locations	NA	NA	NA	5	3	13	6	4	1	66	14	6	3	NA	3
URL	Icici-bank.com	Utibank.com	South-indian-bank.com	Ril.com	Tatachemi-cals.net	Bal-mer-law-ric.com	Tatasteel.com	Jindal-steel-power.com	Mon-net-group.com/com/iron_di-vision.html	Itc-por-tal.com	Dabur.com	Ar-chieson-line.com	Info-sys.com	Hexaware.com	Tatainfo-tech.com

Notes:

1. In FMCG segment Britannia Industries was initially chosen as BSE 'A' group company, however as its homepage was not accessible during the study period (britindia.com, as per group portal) which asked for user identification, we shifted to Dabur India Ltd.

2. Market-cap, Paid-up equity capital & P/E are as of 4th March 2005. Balance Figures are of FY2003-04 year-end figures as per audited statements. RONW figure is for preceding financial year. Source is Cyberline, Intranet version of Capitaline Corporate Database 2000. INR: US$ is taken as 43.75:1 as per prevalent market rate of 2005.

3. Scale of size and complexity of operations/degree of globalization could be analyzed by number of employees and global presence (in number of major economies) respectively. However information of these two was not easily available, therefore not presented in Table 1.

4. 'NA' stands for not available in Capitaline.

Table 2. Hygiene & Motivational factors for Category I & II interactions (Partly adopted from Jutla et al, 2001 and further developed by authors)

Stakeholders	Motivational & hygiene factors desired for Category I & II (75%)	Hygiene factor Category I (6.25%in each cell)	Hygiene factor Category II (6.25%)	Motivational factor Category I (3.125%)	Motivational factor Category II (3.125%)
Customers (CU)	Products, Prices, Places (3 Ps), Engage, Order, Fulfill, Support. However last two can be user defined.	Information on Products, Places	Customized query generations/form	Customer relationship management/ testimonials	Order placement with fulfillment supports/e-sales
Community (CO)	Engage, Community interaction, Community services, Community governance, Sustainability	Sustainability, CSR	Community interactions, Query generation	Community Governance, initiatives in local, & national levels	Online application and approval process
Suppliers/Alliances (SU)	Requirements, selection criterion, approval process, queries.	Selection criterion / values sought from alliances	Online application/ initiation and approval status.	Supplier requirements & approval process / list of alliances'	E-Procurement/ query from potential alliances
Shareholders (SH)	Financial statements, projections, analyst meets, press releases, news, credit rating, investor education & rights	Financial statements & news, Registrars & Share Transfer Agent	Queries to investor relation cell	Outlook, Analyst meets, Schedule of future analyst meets.	Feedback mechanisms from shareholders.

Table 3. Homepage survey: detailed scores. Exclusive zones for stakeholders and subsequent Hygiene & Motivational factors for Category I & II communications (based on March 5-March 7, 2005 findings)

Segments Measures	B & FIs			Chemical/Conglomerates			Commodity/metals			FMCG Firms			IT Firms		
Exclusive zones, HF & MF for CI-II	ICICI	UTI	SIB	RIL	TCL	BL	Tata Steel	Jindal Steel	Monnet Ispat	ITC	Dabur	Archies	Infy	Hexaware	Tata Info-tech
Customers	1	1	1	1	1	1	1	1	0	1	1	1	1	1	1
Community	1/2	0	0	0	1	0	1	1	0	1	0	0	1/2	0	0
Suppliers	1	1	1	1	0	1	1	0	0	1/2	0	0	0	1	1
Shareholders	1	1	0	1	1	1	1	0	0	1	1	0	1	1	1
CU-CI-HF	1	1	1	1	1	1	1	1	0	1	1	1	1	1	1
CU-CII-HF	1	1	1	1	0	0	1	0	0	1	0	1	1	0	0
CU-CI-MF	1	3/4	1/2	3/4	0	0	3/4	0	0	3/4	1	1	1	1	1
CU-CII-MF	1	1	1	3/4	0	0	3/4	0	0	3/4	0	1	0	0	0
CO-CI-HF	1/2	0	0	0	1	0	1	0	0	1	0	0	1/2	0	0
CO-CII- HF	1/2	0	0	0	0	0	1	0	0	0	0	0	0	0	0
CO-CI- MF	1/2	0	0	0	1	0	1	1	0	1	0	0	1/2	0	0
CO-CII – MF	1/2	0	0	0	0	0	0	0	0	0	0	0	0	0	0
SU-CI-HF	1	1	1	0	0	1	1	0	0	1/4	0	0	0	1	0
SU-CII-HF	1	1	1	0	0	0	0	0	0	1/4	0	0	0	0	0
SU-CI-MF	1	1/2	1/2	1	0	1	1	0	0	1/4	0	0	0	1	1
SU-CII-MF	1	1	1	1	0	0	1	0	0	1/4	0	0	0	1	0
SH-CI-HF	1	1	0	1	1	1	1	0	0	1	1	0	3/4	3/4	1
SH-CII-HF	1	1	0	1	1/2	1	1	0	0	1	1	0	3/4	0	0
SH-CI-MF	3/4	3/4	0	3/4	1	0	3/4	0	0	0	3/4	0	3/4	3/4	0
SH-CII-MF	1	1	0	1	1/2	0	1	0	0	0	0	0	0	0	0

Notes to Table 3:

1. While rating a homepage for presence of exclusive stakeholders' zones, if presence is on homepage and exclusive, rating of 1 is given. If presence is in the next level where stakeholder exclusivity is maintained, rating of ½ is given. If neither of above two is present, a rating of 0 is given.

2. For rating presence/absence of Category I & II Hygiene and Motivational factors, a combined score is assigned based on presence or absence of identified factors in Table 2. Nomenclature is first two letters of Stakeholder-Category (I or II) Hygiene Factors (Hygiene or Motivational). For example CO-CII-HF measures firms' web-based interactions with Community for Category II Hygiene Factors.

Table 4. Firm level score of e-business readiness (based on 2005 findings)

Firms Stake-holders	B & FIs			Chemical/ Conglomerate			Commodity/metal			FMCG			IT		
	ICICI	UTI	SIB	RIL	TCL	BL	Tata Steel	Jin-dal Steel	Mon-net Ispat	ITC	Dabur	Arc-hies	Infy	Hexa-ware	Tata Info-tech
Cus-tomers	0.25	0.24	0.23	0.23	0.13	0.19	0.23	0.13	0.00	0.23	0.16	0.25	0.22	0.16	0.16
Com-munity	0.13	0.00	0.00	0.00	0.16	0.00	0.22	0.09	0.00	0.16	0.00	0.00	0.13	0.00	0.00
Suppli-ers	0.25	0.23	0.23	0.09	0.00	0.16	0.19	0.00	0.00	0.08	0.00	0.00	0.00	0.19	0.09
Share-holders	0.24	0.24	0.00	0.24	0.20	0.19	0.24	0.00	0.00	0.19	0.21	0.00	0.20	0.20	0.13
Total (Rank)	0.87 (2)	0.72 (3)	0.47 (9)	0.57 (5)	0.48 (8)	0.53 (7)	0.88 (1)	0.22 (13)	0.00 (14)	0.66 (4)	0.37 (11)	0.25 (12)	0.54 (6)	0.54 (6)	0.38 (10)

Table 5. Segment level score of e-business readiness

Segment	Segment mean	Segment SD
B & FIs	0.69	0.20
Chemicals/Conglomerates	0.51	0.08
Commodities/metals	0.37	0.46
FMCG	0.43	0.21
IT	0.49	0.09

Table 6. e-business readiness score, as per size

Sample	Segment mean	Segment SD
Overall sample	0.49	0.24
Sensex (Large) firms	0.70	0.16
BSE 'A' group firms (Mid-size)	0.47	0.21
BSE 'B' group firms (small ones)	0.325	0.21

Table.7. Stakeholder wise e-business readiness score, as per size

Customers	Mean	SD	Community	Mean	SD	Suppliers	Mean	SD	Shareholders	Mean	SD
Sample	0.19	0.07	Sample	0.06	0.08	Sample	0.10	0.10	Sample	0.15	0.10
Sensex	0.23	0.01	Sensex	0.13	0.08	Sensex	0.12	0.10	Sensex	0.22	0.02
BSE 'A' Grp	0.16	0.05	BSE 'A' Grp	0.05	0.07	BSE 'A' Grp	0.08	0.12	BSE 'A' Grp	0.17	0.10
BSE 'B' Grp	0.17	0.10	BSE 'B' Grp	0	0	BSE 'B' Grp	0.10	0.10	BSE 'B' Grp	0.06	0.09

Table 8. Category-wise (I & II) & factor-wise (Hygiene & Motivational) readiness score

Categories of communications/factors of communications	Overall sample		Sensex		BSE 'A' Group		BSE 'B' Group	
	Mean	SD	Mean	SD	Mean	SD	Mean	SD
Category I mean score (wt. 37.5%)	20.4%	9.33%	27.5%	7.1%	20.6%	7.0%	13.1%	8.7%
Category II mean score (wt. 37.5%)	13.33%	10.66%	22.2%	8.0%	9.7%	10.8%	8.1%	8.1%
Hygiene factors mean score (wt. 50%)	24.37%	12.94%	35.3%	8.4%	21.6%	11.2%	16.2%	12.2%
Motivational factors mean score (wt. 25%)	9.37%	6.00%	14.4%	5.7%	8.7%	5.0%	5.0%	3.6%

APPENDIX B: DATA COLLECTION IN 2007 (DECEMBER 10-11 FOR HOMEPAGE SCORES)

Table 9. (for same sample group as in Table 1 of Appendix A) and comparison with 2005

Measures	B & FIs			Chemicals/Cnglmts			Commodity/metal				FMCG			IT		
Financial/business characteristics	ICICI	UTI	SIB	RIL	TCL	BL	Tata Steel	Jindal Steel	Monnet Ispat	ITC	Dabur India	Archies	Infy	Hexaware	Tata Infotech
M-Cap (in billion US$)	34	8	0.4	106	2	0.25	14	12	0.4	18	3	0.024	24	0.3	Please see notes to Appendix B below (point 2)
% rise since 2005, Table 1	506	675	552	581	254	335	263	1402	280	237	329	196	172	69	
Score & Rank* as per Table 4, Appendix A (2005 studies)	0.87 (2)	0.72 (3)	0.47 (9)	0.57 (5)	0.48 (8)	0.53 (7)	(0.88) (1)	0.22 (13)	0 (14)	0.66 (4)	0.37 (11)	0.25 (12)	0.54 (6)	0.54 (6)	
Score in 2007 & Rank	0.625 (5)	0.66 (4)	0.5 (10)	0.84 (1)	0.58 (7)	0.56 (8)	0.70 (3)	0.45 (11)	0 (13)	0.8 (2)	0.45 (11)	0.41 (12)	0.55 (9)	0.59 (6)	

Overall mean at 0.55 in 2007 against mean of 0.49 in 2005 (Std. dev in 2007 is at 0.20 against 0.24 in 2005). Sample size in 2007 14

Notes to Table 9

1. Market-cap figures are of 6th December, 2007. INR: US$ is taken as 39.5:1 as per prevalent market rate.

2. UTI Bank was renamed as Axis Bank, and url thereby changed to www.axisbank.com/, RIL went through a demerger process in the end of 2005, Tata Chemicals also had tatachemicals.com (along with with.net homepage url as in 2005), Monnet Ispat changed its name to Monnet Ispat and Energy Ltd. in 2006, though the homepage remained same; and Tata Infotech was amalgamated into one of the larger IT services company within same Tata group, TCS in 2005. It meant that 2007 survey of ours had 14 samples, and only 2 from IT.

3. Balmer Lawrie, as the only PSU in our sample, had provisions made on its homepage related to Rights to Information Act (2005). It also had the content in one of the local official languages (Hindi), the only firm in our sample to have local language content.

4. Though the name of Monnet Ispat changed as per stock-exchange information and media information, a visit to its web-site reflected no such distinctions in terms of its various identities (as sponge iron & steel, and power and ferroalloys were into two different domains). Therefore the rating still remained poor.

5. ITC has a list of divisional and group companies' website on its home page, due to its diverse nature of business interests. Similar practice was found in Tata Steel as well (as it acquired few other entities globally).

6. The above sites were studied on 10th & 11th of December 2007 following same methodology as in 2005, as done for Table 3. The total and sector-wise/size-wise and stakeholder-wise scores have been given here, avoiding detailed markings as was done in Table 3. However we calculated these total scores and other break-ups of it using same methodology.

7. We acknowledge that relative marking on presence/absence of features/communications for stakeholders in 2007 may not be uniform as it was followed in 2005. Expectedly the individual bias would vary across these two time-period of studies, though it's likely to be uniform across any single period of study. Though same set of individuals performed this-survey, the uniformity in qualitative measurements is difficult to be exactly replicated after more than 2-years.

8. We were also interested to see if there exists any meaningful correlations between m-cap gains of firms (an indicator of overall and financial performances) with e-business adoption levels; however we didn't find any significant linkages. However the gain in e-Business adoption level (between 2007 and 2005) had better correlations with gain in m-caps rather than the individual stand-alone scores over these two timeperiods.

* Rank in 2007 means e-business readiness rank in 2007 in a repeat survey following same methodology as followed in 2005 (Table 3 & 4 of Appendix A).

Table 10. Segment and size wise comparison of e-business readiness score (2007 with 2005)

Segment	Segment mean, 2007 (2005)	Size	Mean in 2007 (2005 fig)
B & FIs	0.59 (0.69)	Sensex (Large) firms	0.70 (0.70)
Chemicals/Conglomerates	0.66 (0.51)	BSE 'A' group firms (Mid-size)	0.54 (0.47)
Commodities/metals	0.39 (0.37)		
FMCG	0.55 (0.43)	BSE 'B' group firms (small ones)	0.37 (0.325)
IT	0.57 (0.49)		

Table 11. Stakeholder wise e-business readiness score & comparison with 2005

	Average for customers	Average for community	Average for suppliers	Average for shareholders
Sample (in 2007, 14)	0.22	0.07	0.08	0.18
Sample (in 2005)	0.19	0.06	0.10	0.15

Table 12. Category-wise (I & II) & factor-wise (Hygiene & Motivational) readiness & comparison with 2005

Categories of communications/factors of communications	Overall sample (2007)	In 2005
	Mean	Mean
Category I mean score (wt. 37.5%)	22.5%	20.4%
Category II mean score (wt. 37.5%)	15.6%	13.33%
Hygiene factors mean score (wt. 50%)	26.8%	24.37%
Motivational factors mean score (wt. 25%)	10.9%	9.37%

The studies were done following our methodology, and the findings have not been shared with the real life firms. As explained in the limitations of the study, subjective elements in scoring cannot be ruled out; though there's been no deliberate bias of researchers.

This work was previously published in International Journal of E-Business Research (IJEBR), edited by In Lee, pp. 54-77, copyright 2009 by IGI Publishing (an imprint of IGI Global).

Chapter 15
Product Choice and Channel Strategy for Multi-Channel Retailers

Ruiliang Yan
Indiana University Northwest, USA

John Wang
Montclair State University, USA

ABSTRACT

With the explosive growth of online sales, multi-channel retailers are increasingly focused on finding ways of integrating the online channel with traditional retail stores. The need for the development of effective multi-channel strategies is strongly felt by the retailers. The present research normatively addresses this issue and using a game theoretic approach, derives optimal strategies that maximize profits under different competitive market structures. Managerial implications are discussed and probable paths of future research are identified.

INTRODUCTION

According to Comscore Networks, online retail spending in 2006 reached $102.1 billion, marking a 24 percent increase over 2005's $82.3 billion. An estimated 6 percent of all non-travel consumer retail spending (excluding expenditures for autos, gasoline, and food) is spent online. Also, according to Forrester Research, European e-commerce is forecasted to surge to €263 billion in 2011, with travel, clothes, groceries, and consumer electronics all reaching the €10 billion per year mark. Consequently, the rapid development of commerce on the Internet has made it attractive for many marketers to engage in direct online sales. As a result, many firms are using or pursuing both direct and distributor-based approaches to sell products. In real business world, it is not uncommon for many brick and mortar firms to create e-commerce channels that operate independently from existing physical outlets (Steinfield, Mahler and Bauer 1999; Useem 1999; Venkatesh 1999). However, recent trends indicate that an increasing number of firms have started to integrate the physical and online channels together to avoid channel conflict and gain benefits from channel integration (Ward 2001; Steinfield et al. 2002).

DOI: 10.4018/978-1-60960-132-4.ch015

Copyright © 2011, IGI Global. Copying or distributing in print or electronic forms without written permission of IGI Global is prohibited.

When a retailer employs a mixed online and traditional retail channel to sell products, an important question is how the optimal channel strategy should be identified by the retailer using a mixed online and traditional retail channel, so as to maximize its profit. In our research we use a game theoretical model to specifically examine how the product categories impact the channel strategy of retailer using a mixed channel approach under different competitive markets: two retailers and more than two retailers in the competitive market. Based on our analytical results, we determine optimal strategies for the retailers using a mixed channel approach in a competitive market.

The rest of our paper is organized as follows. Section 2 provides a summary of the relevant literature. Section 3 presents our modeling framework. In section 4, we determine optimal product categories and channel strategies for the retailer using a mixed online and traditional retail channel approach under a two-retailer competitive market. In section 5, we further analyze the optimal product categories and channel strategies for this retailer when the competitive market consists of n ($n > 2$) retailers. In section 6, we illustrate our findings by means of numerical examples. In section 7, we extend our model by investigating the impact of internet coverage rate on the product categories and channel strategies. Concluding remarks are presented in section 8.

LITERATURE REVIEW

Multi-Channel Retailing

Multi-channel marketing allows multiple contact points between customers and marketers and affords the customers the ability to choose the time and mode of contact. In this paper, the focus is on multi-channel retailing where the retailer-customer interactions take place across multiple channels even within a single purchase. The growth of multi-channel retailing is an off-shoot of the growth of online marketing. The proportion of multi-channel shoppers has gone up in recent years (Wallace et al 2004). A recent analysis of online retail sales by the management consulting firm McKinsey indicates that multi-channel retailers accounted for over 50 per cent of internet sales, compared to the 31 per cent garnered by the retailers with an exclusively internet presence (Grosso et al 2005).

The growing popularity of multi-channel retailing can be attributed to the benefits received by the consumers as well as the retailers. The greater utilitarian value of internet stores in the context of information search and price comparisons has been hypothesized by Noble et al (2005). However, their empirical results indicated that while customers derived greater utility from the internet stores in comparison to catalogs, physical stores provided the greatest utility in regard to price comparisons. But it is possible for consumers to use the different channels in order to maximize the utility. The portfolio of service outputs expected by customers of multi-channel retailers in fact increases as customers gain more experience (Wallace et al 2004). Rangaswamy and Van Bruggen (2005) have linked the increased service outputs of multi-channel retailing to stronger customer relationships.

The benefits accruing to the retailers have been discussed by many marketing scholars. The review of online price dispersion by Pan et al (2004) provides theoretical as well as empirical evidence regarding the higher prices charged by multi-channel retailers in comparison to pure-play internet retailers. The price differentiation is justified by the higher service outputs provided by multi-channel retailers. According to the empirical study conducted by Kumar and Venkatesan (2005), the benefits provided by multi-channel customers include higher revenues, higher share of the wallet, greater profits as well as the likelihood of future purchases. The multi-channel loyalty framework proposed by Wallace et al (2004) suggests that the greater service outputs provided by the multi-channel retailers lead to greater customer satisfaction, which, in turn, results in greater customer loyalty to the retailer.

Benefits aside, multi-channel retailing gives rise to several managerial issues that need to be addressed. The decision to adopt a multi-channel retailing model itself can be considered to be a dilemma faced by the manufacturers (Lee et al 2003), since its adoption can turn the manufacturer into a competitor in the eyes of the retailers. The complexity of retail strategy decisions increases with the adoption of a multi-channel retailing format (Noble et al 2005). While multiple decisions are involved, pricing has been identified by several scholars as an important issue that needs to be addressed in the context of multi-channel retailing. Rangaswamy and Van Bruggen (2005) have identified the need for academic research on the impact of the adoption of multi-channel retailing on channel relationships. They argue that the 'new price dynamics' introduced by the adoption of multi-channel retailing will affect power balance and channel relationships. The research by Hughes (2006) has identified pricing and product type as important drivers of the decision to adopt multi-channel retailing.

Multiple-Channel Firms

There is a long marketing tradition of studying issues pertaining to the practice of selling across multiple channels. With the emergence of the Internet as a viable channel of distribution, study of multi-channel competition has acquired additional importance. Previous Research has examined a variety of issues. Balasubramanian (1998) reported the strategic implications of information diffusion. A hybrid channel, where customers are segmented into price-sensitive and service-sensitive segments, was studied by Rhee and Park (1999). Their results show that such a channel design is optimal when the service valuation is similar in both segments. The fact that the dual channel (hybrid of physical and e-tail channels)

holds most promise for the future was proclaimed by Levary and Mathieu (2000). Geyskens et al. (2002) found that powerful companies with a few direct channels achieve better financial performance than less powerful companies with broader direct market offerings. King, Sen and Xia (2004) used a game-theoretic approach to study the impact of Web-based e-commerce on a retailer's distribution channel strategy. They showed that the multi-channel strategy followed by retail firms is an equilibrium outcome of the game resulting from competitive pressure by other retailers and this strategy is not the only possible short-run outcome. Chiang, Chhajed, and Hess (2003) used a game theoretic model to study the channel competition between a manufacturer's direct channel and its traditional channel. They argue that the independent direct channel allows a manufacturer to constrain its retailer's pricing behavior and this may not always be detrimental to the retailer because it may be accompanied by wholesale price reduction.

Furthermore, some researchers argue that traditional enterprises have moved to integrate e-commerce into their mix, using the Internet to supplement traditional brick and mortar retail channels, and the channel integration of traditional physical and e-commerce channels has a great potential for future. For example, Steinfield et al. (1999), Steinfield and Whitten (1999), and Gulati and Garino (2000) all argued that integration among channels can be a more successful strategy. Based on an empirical examination of retailer profitability, Kumar et al (2006) have recently called for attention to the design of multi-channel marketing strategies.

Product Categories Sold through Online Channel

Prominent among the drivers for the adoption of new channels are pricing and product type (Hughes, 2006). There is a substantial body of literature (e.g., Chiang et al, 2003), which indicates that when the same product is purchased on the Internet, it is of less value to the consumer. Liang and Huang (1998) did an empirical study to show that some products are more suitable for marketing on the web than others. Kwak et al. (2002) conducted an empirical study to examine the following products for sells on the web: books, information, or magazines; communications services (e.g., internet phone services); computer-related products and services; education; electronics; entertainment; internet-related products and services; music and videos; and travel and vacations. They observed that computer-related products and services and books, information, and magazines were the most frequently purchased products, whereas electronics and entertainment were least frequently purchased online. Bhatnagar, Misra and Rao (2000) identified some of the product characteristics that decrease the value of a product when it is purchased on the Web as compared to from a traditional retail channel. Consumers perceive high degree of risk when a product is technologically complex, satisfies ego-related needs, has a high price, and when 'touch and feel' is important. The increase in risk lowers the consumer value. According to Lal and Sarvary (1999), consumers need to gather information about two types of product attributes: digital attributes (which can be communicated on the Web at very low cost) and non-digital attributes (for which physical inspection of the product is necessary). Evidently, consumers would be less willing to buy products with high proportion of non-digital attributes. It is also difficult to return products on the Web. According to Wood (2001), consumer purchase on the Web is more risky because of lack of experiential information about product return policy. According to Korgaonkar, Silverblatt and Girard (2006), credence products are less likely to sell on the Web as compared to search or experience products.

However, none of these papers ever considered the important effect of product categories on the channel strategy. Our paper fills a conceptual and practical gap for a structured analysis of the current state of knowledge about the effect of product categories on the channel strategy of multi-channel retailers. In this paper, we will examine the effect of product categories on the channel strategy of multi-channel retailers under different types of competitive market structures. Generally, this paper addresses the following research questions. In a two retailers competitive market, when the retailer using a mixed channel adopts channel integration or decentralized channel strategy, what is the optimal sales policy for its online channel? What are the product categories and the channel strategy the retailer should select in order to maximize its profit? Furthermore, what are the appropriate product categories and channel strategy if the competitive market consists of more than two retailers? If the factor of internet coverage rate is considered, what are the appropriate product categories and channel strategy? Based on our results, we propose optimal marketing strategies for the retailers who are using a mixed online and traditional retail channel.

MODEL FRAMEWORK

In this section, we lay out the basic market structure underlying our analysis of the channel strategy problem.

The Demand Functions of Online and Traditional Channels

We consider a market setting where two traditional brick and mortar retailers competitively sell the same product and one of the retailers opens an online store to sell through a mixed channel. We assume that this market involves a circular spatial setting (Salop, 1979) and that the two retailers are located at equal distances from each other on the circle. Consumers incur transaction costs at a rate *t* per unit distance when purchasing from a traditional retailer. This transaction costs include travel distance, shopping process time and shopping inconvenience. Transaction costs can be interpreted broadly and measure the ease of retail shopping in different stores. We also assume that the online store is located at the center of the circle. When consumers purchase from the online store, we assume that the store uses the system of "make to order" or "just in time" to fill out the orders. That means that the online store uses an independent delivery medium to transmit the product to consumers, which makes the physical location irrelevant.

In this market, customers can purchase the product from either the online channel or the traditional channel. We assume that consumers have complete information about product availability and prices. When customers purchase a product from the online or traditional channel, they are assumed to be heterogeneous in the value v that they obtain from this purchase. When one of the retailers opens an online store, this online store not only draws some consumers from its own traditional channel but also draws some consumers from its competitor.

When consumers purchase from a traditional retailer, the product attributes are transparent to a consumer and the gratification is instant, such as the fit of a pair of trousers, shoes, etc. However, when the consumers purchase online, the product attributes are hidden on the Web, gratification is delayed and also it is difficult to return products on the Web. Thus, the consumers are forced to forgo these advantages at a cost, called monetary disutility, denoted by the parameter θ. The parameter θ measures the lack of fit of the product to the online store. When the product is perfectly suited to the online store, θ will be zero (for product categories such as air-tickets, music, CDs, etc.). When the product is not well suited to the online store or product's freight charges are high, in case of products such as bed, mattress, furniture, and food, θ will be high. Kacen et al. (2002) did an empirical study to find some product categories value for θ (Table 1).

Figure 1. Spatial setting of the circular market with two retailers

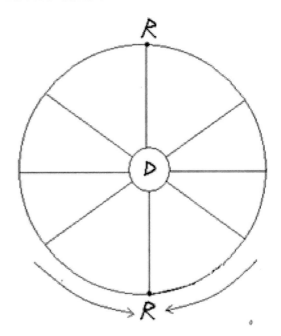

Suppose the product is sold in online channel at price p_1 and in traditional channel at price p_2. Therefore, the consumer surplus in the traditional channel would be $v - p_2 - xt$ and the consumer surplus in the online channel would be $v - p_1 - \theta$. All consumers whose consumer surplus in the traditional channel is positive (i.e., $v - p_2 - xt \geq 0$) will consider buying from the traditional channel. Similarly, all consumers whose consumer surplus in the online channel is positive (i.e., $v - p_1 - \theta \geq 0$) would consider buying from the online channel. Since in our model, consumers can buy from either channel, they would prefer the channel where they derive more surplus (i.e., in the online channel or the traditional channel depending upon the comparison of $v - p_1 - \theta$ versus $v - p_2 - xt$). If $v - p_2 - xt \geq v - p_1 - \theta$, then the traditional channel would be weakly preferred to the online channel. The marginal consumer would be one who is indifferent between the two channels when $p_2 + xt = p_1 + \theta$. Therefore, in the interval [0,

Table 1. Product lack of fit θ for web-based online market

Category	Book	Shoes	Toothpaste	DVD player	Flowers	Food items
Lack of fit	0.096	0.231	0.114	0.213	0.208	0.216

Note: All product categories have θ below 1.0 at the 1% significance level.

x] Consumers will buy the product from traditional channel. Since we assume a circular spatial market, thus the demand in the traditional channel will be [0, 2x] and the demand in the online channel will be $2(\frac{1}{2} - 2x)$. Balasubramanian (1998) used a similar market structure and he shows the demand for the two channels to be,

$$d_2 = \frac{2(p_1 - p_2 + \theta)}{t} \qquad (1)$$

$$d_1 = 2(\frac{1}{2} - \frac{2(p_1 - p_2 + \theta)}{t}) \qquad (2)$$

Where, d_1 is the demand of online channel and d_2 is the demand of traditional channel.

Profit Functions of Retailers

For the sake of simplicity, we assume that the marginal costs of production and retailing are identical for the two channels and without loss of generality can be assumed to be zero. Therefore, in a given period, the retailer's profit with an online channel is given by

$$\pi_1 = p_1 d_1 + p_2 d_2 \qquad (3)$$

And the other retailer's profit without online channel is given by

$$\pi_2 = p_2 d_2 \qquad (4)$$

PRODUCT CATEGORY AND CHANNEL STRATEGY

The Strategy of Channel Integration

Here we focus on the channel strategy for the retailer using a mixed online and traditional retail channel. If the retailer adopts a channel integration strategy (the two channels are vertically integrated), the decision-making in the channel integration is centralized with the retailer. Therefore, the retailer would seek unified and centralized price solutions to maximize its total profit, which can be expressed as the following maximization problem:

$$Max\pi_1 = p_1 d_1 + p_2 d_2$$

Given the above structure, we can obtain the online and traditional retail prices, demand, and profit with channel integration strategy. All of results are summarized as follows.

From Table 2, it can be seen that the online demand under channel integration is zero. Thus, we have the proposition 1.

Proposition 1:*No matter how well the product category is suited to online channel, it is most profitable for the retailer with a mixed channel approach to sell nothing through its online channel when this retailer adopts a channel integration strategy.*

Proposition 1 shows that when a retailer with a mixed channel adopts a channel integration strategy in a competitive market, the first and optimal

Table 2. Market strategies of the retailer under channel integration

Price	
Online channel, p_1	$p_1 = \theta - t$
Traditional channel, p_2	$p_2 = \theta - \dfrac{t}{2}$
Demand	
Online channel, d_1	$d_1 = 0$
Traditional channel, d_2	$d_2 = \dfrac{2\theta}{t} - 1$
Profit	
Retailer with mixed channel, π_1	$\pi_1 = \dfrac{(2\theta - t)^2}{2t}$

For the proof, please see Appendix A.

Table 3. Market strategies of the retailer under decentralized channel

Price	
Online channel, p_1	$p_1 = \dfrac{t - 2\theta}{6}$
Traditional channel, p_2	$p_2 = \dfrac{t + 4\theta}{12}$
Demand	
Online channel, d_1	$d_1 = \dfrac{2(t - 2\theta)}{3t}$
Traditional channel, d_2	$d_2 = \dfrac{t + 4\theta}{6t}$
Profit	
Retailer with mixed channel, π_1	$\pi_1 = \dfrac{t}{8} - \dfrac{\theta}{3} + \dfrac{2\theta^2}{3t}$

For the proof, please see Appendix B

way of selling products is through the traditional physical channel. Our finding is consistent with Chiang, et al (2003) that it is most profitable for an integrated firm to arrange prices so that nothing is ever sold through its own online channel.

The Strategy of Decentralized Channel

However, if the retailer adopts a decentralized channel strategy (the two channels work independently), the online channel determines its price p_1 to maximize its profit. Similarly, the traditional retailer determines its retail price p_2 to maximize its profit. There is no price leader in this market, and both channel members make price decisions independent of each other. Given the above structure, we obtain the online and traditional retail prices, demand, and profit as follows.

From Table 3, it is evident that when a retailer with a mixed channel adopts a decentralized channel strategy to sell product through a competitive market, the optimal demand through online chan-

nel decreases with θ. Therefore, we advance the next proposition.

Proposition 2:*Under the decentralized channel, it is most profitable for the retailer with a mixed channel to sell as much as possible through its online channel, especially when the product category is more suited to an online channel.*

For the proof, please see Appendix C.

Our finding is consistent with the business reality that the independent online channel always looks forward to selling as much as possible through the online store when the product category is more suited to the online channel.

If we assume profit to be the primary goal of the retailer, it is critical to find out under which channel strategy the retailer using a mixed channel can derive larger profits. Since the product category has a strategic impact on the retailer's decision to centralize or not, this can be determined by comparing the retailer's profit in Table 2 with the retailer's profit in Table 3. We find out the threshold value, θ, to determine which channel strategy is more profitable to the retailer with a mixed channel. The results are summarized in the following proposition.

Proposition 3: *When $\theta > t$, the optimal channel strategy for the retailer with a mixed channel to adopt is channel integration; when $0 \leq \theta < \dfrac{t}{2}$, the optimal channel strategy for the retailer with a mixed channel to adopt is decentralized channel strategy; when $\dfrac{t}{2} \leq \theta \leq t$, there is no optimal channel strategy for this retailer.*

For the proof, please see Appendix D.

Proposition 3 has some important implications. First, when t is a regular constant, and if the product category is poorly suited to the online channel, the channel integration will provide a competitive advantage to the retailer using a mixed channel. The rationale is that if the product category is poorly suited to the online channel, the retailer would like consumers to purchase the product through the physical store and the online channel is used to merely provide information and support sales through the traditional physical channel. However, when t is a regular constant, and if the product category is highly or moderately suited to the online channel, the optimal channel strategy for the retailer using a mixed channel is the decentralized channel strategy. The rationale is that the highly and moderately suited products can draw the maximum possible number of consumers to the online channel. Second, when t decreases and is close to zero, the channel integration strategy will have a better competitive advantage than the decentralized channel strategy. The rationale is that when t decreases and approaches zero, the retailer effectively improves the competitive capability of the traditional channel and pushes consumers to purchase through the physical store.

Figure 2. Spatial setting of the circular market with N (n > 2) retailers

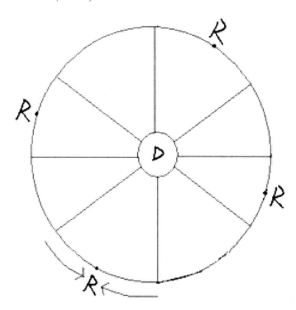

N (*N* > 2) RETAILERS MARKET

In this section, we extend our model by investigating the case of n ($n > 2$) independent retailers who are identical and directly compete with each other in this circular spatial market.

We also assume one of the retailers opens an online store and uses a mixed online and traditional channel to sell products. Our intention is to see how the channel strategy will be impacted by the product category. With this in mind, we use a similar analysis as the one employed before. Thus we have the online and traditional retailer demand functions, which can be expressed as follows.

$$d_2 = \frac{2(p_1 - p_2 + \theta)}{t} \tag{5}$$

$$d_1 = N\left(\frac{1}{N} - \frac{2(p_1 - p_2 + \theta)}{t}\right) \tag{6}$$

Again, in a given period, the retailer's profit with an online channel is given by

$$\pi_1 = p_1 d_1 + p_2 d_2 \qquad (7)$$

And the other retailer's profit without online channel is given by

$$\pi_2 = p_2 d_2 \qquad (8)$$

The Strategy of Channel Integration under N Retailers

When there are N retailers in the competitive market, one of the retailers opens an online channel and adopts the channel integration strategy. Given the above structure, we do the same analysis as in the previous section. We obtain the optimal results summarized in Table 4 as follows.

We saw in proposition 1 that under the competitive market of two retailers, when the retailer with a mixed channel adopts a channel integration strategy, it is most profitable for this retailer to sell nothing through its online channel. It turns out that this result holds for the competitive market of more than two-retailer case as well and the reason is the same.

Decentralized Channel Strategy under N Retailers

When there are N retailers in the competitive market and one of the retailers opens an online channel and adopts the decentralized channel strategy, we do the same analysis as in the case of the two retailer competitive market. We obtain the optimal results summarized in Table 5.

We saw in proposition 2 that under the competitive market of two retailers, it is most profitable for the retailer with a mixed channel to sell

Table 4. Market strategies of the retailer under channel integration

Price	
Online channel, p_1	$p_1 = \dfrac{(n-1)\theta - t}{(n-1)^2}$
Traditional channel, p_2	$p_2 = \dfrac{n\theta(n-1) - t}{2(n-1)^2}$
Demand	
Online channel, d_1	$d_1 = 0$
Traditional channel, d_2	$d_2 = \dfrac{n\theta(n-1) - t}{(n-1)^2 t}$
Profit	
Retailer with mixed channel, π_1	$\pi_1 = \dfrac{(n\theta(n-1) - t)^2}{2(n-1)^4 t}$

For the proof, please see Appendix E

as much as possible through its online channel, especially when the product category is more suited to the online channel. It turns out that these results hold for the competitive market of more than two retailer case for essentially the same reason. Next, we compare the retailer's profit under different channel strategies and identify the channel strategy that the retailer with a mixed channel should employ in order to obtain greater profits.

By comparing the retailer's profit between the channel integration and decentralized channel strategies, we find out the threshold value, θ, to determine which channel strategy is more profitable to the retailer with a mixed channel. The results are summarized in the following proposition.

Proposition 4: *When* $\theta > \dfrac{t}{n-1}$ *, the optimal channel strategy for the retailer with a mixed channel is*

Table 5. Market strategies of the retailer under decentralized channel

Price	
Online channel, p_1	$p_1 = \dfrac{t}{3n} - \dfrac{\theta}{3}$
Traditional channel, p_2	$p_2 = \dfrac{t}{6n} + \dfrac{\theta}{3}$
Demand	
Online channel, d_1	$d_1 = \dfrac{2(t - n\theta)}{3t}$
Traditional channel, d_2	$d_2 = \dfrac{t + 2n\theta}{3nt}$
Profit	
Retailer with mixed channel, π_1	$\pi_1 = \dfrac{4n^2(n+1)\theta^2 + (1+4n)t^2 - 4(2n-1)nt\theta}{18n^2 t}$

For the proof, please see Appendix F

channel integration; however, when $0 \le \theta < \dfrac{t}{n}$, the optimal channel strategy for the retailer with a mixed channel is decentralized channel strategy; when $\dfrac{t}{n} \le \theta \le \dfrac{t}{n-1}$, there is no optimal channel strategy for the retailer.

For the proof, please see Appendix G.

We saw in proposition 3 that when t is a regular constant and the product category is poorly suited to the online channel, the channel integration will provide a competitive advantage to the retailer using a mixed channel; when t is a regular constant and the product category is highly or moderately suited to online channel, the optimal channel strategy for the retailer using a mixed channel to adopt is the decentralized channel strategy. Also, when t decreases and close to zero, the channel integration strategy will have a better competitive advantage than the decentralized channel strategy. It turns out that these results hold for the competi-

tive market of more than two retailer case as well for the same reason.

Furthermore, from the proposition 4, we find that when the number of the retailers in a competitive market increases, the value of the cannibalistic threshold decreases, and the value approaches zero as the number of retailers becomes very large. That is, the competitive advantage from channel integration increases with market competition. When the market competition is perfect (n is large and the threshold value approaches zero), the channel integration strategy provides a dominant competitive advantage to the retailer using a mixed channel. The rationale is that when the number of retailers in a competitive market increases, the channel conflict increases, which could bring about a "price war" among the retailers. However, channel integration effectively moderates this conflict, leading to larger profits than in the decentralized channel.

Table 6. Various parameters and retailer's profit

Parameters	N	θ	t	π_1^I	π_1^d	Profit comparison
$\theta > t$	2	0.3	0.2	0.4	0.23	$\pi_1^I > \pi_1^d$
$0 \le \theta < \dfrac{t}{2}$	2	0.08	0.2	0.004	0.02	$\pi_1^I < \pi_1^d$
$\dfrac{t}{2} \le \theta \le t$	2	0.15	0.2	0.025	0.05	$\pi_1^I < \pi_1^d$
$\dfrac{t}{2} \le \theta \le t$	2	0.2	0.2	0.1	0.09	$\pi_1^I > \pi_1^d$

Where π_1^I is the retailer's profit with channel integration; π_1^d is the retailer's profit with decentralized channel.

NUMERICAL EXAMPLES

In this section, we do some numerical analysis to illustrate our analytical results and give us more managerial insights. The values we used for the various parameters are shown in Table 6. We vary some values of the parameters to examine the retailer's performances in the business market.

The retailer's profit in Table 6 shows that when $\theta > t$, the optimal channel strategy for the retailer with a mixed channel to adopt is channel integration; when $0 \le \theta < \dfrac{t}{2}$, the optimal channel strategy for the retailer with a mixed channel to adopt is a decentralized channel strategy; when $\dfrac{t}{2} \le \theta \le t$, there is no optimal channel strategy for this retailer.

IMPACT OF INTERNET COVERAGE RATE

In this section, we still consider two traditional retailers competitively sell the same product and one of two retailers opens an online store to sell through a mixed channel. We extend our model by considering the internet coverage rate in this circular spatial market. We assume that a fraction λ of consumers receiving the internet have the option to purchase from online or traditional channel and the fraction of consumers is evenly distributed over the circular spatial market. Consumers who have no internet are constrained to purchase between the two channels and only can purchase product from the traditional channel. Our intention is to see how the channel strategy will be impacted by the internet coverage rate. With this in mind, we do a similar analysis as the one employed before. We then obtain the optimal results summarized in Tables 7 and 8.

We saw in proposition 1 that under the competitive market of two retailers, when the retailer with a mixed channel adopts a channel integration strategy, it is most profitable for this retailer to sell nothing through its online channel. It turns out that for the competitive market of two retailer case with the factor of the internet coverage rate. We saw in proposition 2 that under the competitive market of two retailers, it is most profitable for the retailer with a mixed channel to sell as much as possible through its online channel, especially when the product category is more suited to the online channel. It turns out that these

Table 7. Market strategies of the retailer with factor of internet coverage rate under channel integration

Price	
Online channel, p_1	$p_1 = \dfrac{(1+\lambda)(t-\theta)}{2+2\lambda-6\lambda^2}$
Traditional channel, p_2	$p_2 = \dfrac{t(1-\lambda+\lambda^2)+2\theta\lambda(1-2\lambda)}{2+2\lambda-6\lambda^2}$
Demand	
Online channel, d_1	$d_1 = 0$
Traditional channel, d_2	$d_2 = \dfrac{t(1+\lambda^3)+2\lambda\theta(1-\lambda+2\lambda^2)}{2t(1-\lambda+3\lambda^2)}$
Profit	
Retailer with mixed channel, π_1	$\pi_1 = \dfrac{(1+\lambda)(t(1-\lambda+\lambda^2)+2\lambda\theta(1-2\lambda))^2}{4t(1-\lambda+3\lambda^2)^2}$

For the proof, please see Appendix H

Table 8. Market strategies of the retailer with factor of internet coverage rate under decentralized channel

Price	
Online channel, p_1	$p_1 = \dfrac{t(3+\lambda)-4\theta(1+\lambda)}{8+16\lambda}$
Traditional channel, p_2	$p_2 = \dfrac{2t-t\lambda+4\lambda\theta}{4+8\lambda}$
Demand	
Online channel, d_1	$d_1 = \dfrac{\lambda(t(3+\lambda)-4\theta(1+\lambda))}{2t+4t\lambda}$
Traditional channel, d_2	$d_2 = \dfrac{(1+\lambda)(t(2-\lambda)+4\theta\lambda)}{4t+8t\lambda}$
Profit	
Retailer with mixed channel, π_1	$\pi_1 = \dfrac{1}{18t(1+2\lambda)^2}(t^2(4+17\lambda+11\lambda^2+2\lambda^3)$ $-8t\theta\lambda(1+\lambda)+16\lambda\theta^2(1+3\lambda+2\lambda^2))$

For the proof, please see Appendix I

results hold for the competitive market of two retailer case with the factor of the internet coverage rate.

Next, by comparing the retailer's profit between the channel integration and decentralized channel strategies, we also find out the threshold value, θ, to determine which channel strategy is more profitable to the retailer with a mixed channel when the factor of internet coverage rate, λ, is considered. The results are summarized in the following proposition.

Proposition 5: *When* $\dfrac{t(3+\lambda)}{4(1+\lambda)} \leq \theta \leq t$ *with*

$0 < \lambda < \dfrac{1+\sqrt{13}}{6}$ *or* $\theta > t$ *with* $\lambda > \dfrac{1+\sqrt{13}}{6}$, *the*

optimal channel strategy for the retailer with a mixed channel is channel integration; when

$0 \leq \theta < \dfrac{t(3+\lambda)}{4(1+\lambda)}$, *the optimal channel strategy*

for the retailer with a mixed channel is decentralized channel strategy.

For the proof, please see Appendix J.

Proposition 5 shows that when $0 < \lambda < \dfrac{1+\sqrt{13}}{6}$ and this internet coverage rate increases, the competitive advantage from channel integration increases. However, when $\lambda > \dfrac{1+\sqrt{13}}{6}$, the competitive advantage from the decentralized channel strategy increases, thus the channel integration strategy only benefits from the product categories which are poorly suited to the online channel in this internet coverage rate. Note that substituting $\lambda = 1$ yields the results in proposition 3.

CONCLUDING REMARKS

The contributions of this study are both theoretical and substantive in nature. In this paper, we

demonstrate that optimal channel strategy exists for different product categories when the retailer uses a mixed online and traditional retail channel to sell products in a competitive market. We first derive the results of channel integration and decentralized channel strategies for the retailer using a mixed channel under a two retailer competitive market, and then we do a comparison to determine optimal channel strategy decisions. Our results indicate that in a two retailer competitive market, when t is a regular constant and the product category is poorly suited to online channel, the channel integration will provide a competitive advantage to the retailer using a mixed channel. However, when t is a regular constant and the product category is highly or moderately suited to online channel, the optimal channel strategy for the retailer using a mixed channel is the decentralized channel strategy. Also, when t decreases and approaches zero, the channel integration strategy will have a better competitive advantage than the decentralized channel strategy. Furthermore, we show that if the number of retailers in a competitive market increases, the channel integration strategy will have a better competitive advantage than the decentralized channel strategy. Under the conditions of perfect competition, the channel integration strategy will offer a dominant competitive advantage for the retailer using a mixed channel. Also, when the factor of internet coverage rate is considered, the internet coverage rate plays a strategic impact on the channel strategy design. These results from our research provide important insights for marketing managers how to manage the mixed channel efficiently according to different product categories in a competitive market.

Our research can be extended in several directions in future work. First, in this paper, we assumed that consumers have perfect information. However, information with the consumers could be incomplete, and we can explore the competitive equilibrium under incomplete information settings. Second, our analysis is based on a single period model. Therefore, for future research, it is a good idea to examine the channel strategy in a dynamic, multi-period environment. Finally, the coordination of online and traditional retail channels is of interest to both researchers and practitioners. Further research can be carried out on the advanced methods and plans used by online channels to coordinate with traditional channels, such as information sharing, cooperative advertising, etc.

Next, we summarize the managerial implications of the research. In today's business environment, with the rapid development of Internet, firms and individuals are increasingly using the Internet to sell directly to customers. The rise of dual channel competition provides a motivation for many firms to better understand the importance of channel strategy. Since the online sales do compete with the traditional retail sales and this competition is becoming more and more intense with the rapid development of Internet, it is managerially important for the retailer using a mixed channel to deploy an optimal channel strategy in order to maximize its profit. Our paper provides a very useful model framework for business managers to design optimal channel strategy, when they are using a mixed online and traditional retail channel to sell their products in a competitive market. For example, when the product is poorly suited to online channel, the optimal channel strategy is channel integration. RoomStore and RoomToGo are using this strategy for selling their products for mattresses and furniture. However, when the product is highly or moderately suited to online channel, the optimal channel strategy is decentralized channel. For instance, the book retailer Barnes & Noble and the clothing retailer Kohl's are some examples of retailers with such a strategy.

REFERENCES

Balasubramanian, S. (1998). Mail versus Mall: A strategic analysis of competition between direct marketers and conventional retailers. *Marketing Science, 17*(3), 181–195. doi:10.1287/mksc.17.3.181

Bhatnagar, A., Misra, S., & Rao, H. R. (2000). On Risk, Convenience and Internet shopping. *Communications of the ACM, 43*(11), 98–105. doi:10.1145/353360.353371

Chiang, W. Y., Chhajed, D., & Hess, J. D. (2003). Direct marketing, indirect profits: A strategic analysis of dual-channel supply chain design. *Management Science, 49*(1), 1–20. doi:10.1287/mnsc.49.1.1.12749

Geyskens, I., Gielens, K., & Dekimpe, M. G. (2002). The market valuation of Internet channel additions. *Journal of Marketing, 66*, 102–119. doi:10.1509/jmkg.66.2.102.18478

Grosso, C., McPherson, J., & Shi, C. (2005). Retailing: what's working online? *The McKinsey Quarterly, 3*, 18.

Gulati, R., & Garino, J. (2000). Get the right mix of bricks & Clicks. *Harvard Business Review, 78*(3), 107–114.

Hughes, T. (2006). New channels/old channels: Customer management and multi-channels. *European Journal of Marketing, 40*(1/2), 113–129. doi:10.1108/03090560610637347

Kacen, J., Hess, J., & Chiang, W. K. (2002). Bricks or Clicks? Consumer Attitudes toward Traditional Stores and Online Stores. (Working Paper). University of Illinois, Champaign, IL

King, R. C., Sen, R., & Xia, M. (2004). Impact of Web-based e-commerce on channel strategy in retailing. *International Journal of Electronic Commerce, 8*(3), 103–130.

Korgaonkar, P., Silverblatt, R., & Girard, T. (2006). Online retailing, product classifications, and consumer preferences. *Internet Research, 16*(3), 267–287. doi:10.1108/10662240610673691

Kumar, V., Shah, D., & Venkatesan, R. (2006). Managing retailer profitability – one customer at a time! *Journal of Retailing, 82*(4), 277–294. doi:10.1016/j.jretai.2006.08.002

Kumar, V., & Venkatesan, R. (2005). Who are the Multichannel Shoppers and how do They Perform? Correlates of Multichannel Shopping Behavior. *Journal of Interactive Marketing, 19*(2), 44–62. doi:10.1002/dir.20034

Kwak, H., Fox, R. J., & Zinkhan, G. M. (2002). What products can be successfully promoted and sold via the Internet? *Journal of Advertising Research, 2*, 23–38.

Lal, R., & Sarvary, M. (1999). When and how is the internet likely to decrease price competition. *Marketing Science, 18*(4), 485–503. doi:10.1287/mksc.18.4.485

Lee, Y., Lee, Z., & Larsen, K. R. T. (2003). Coping with Internet Channel Conflict. *Communications of the ACM, 46*(7), 137–142. doi:10.1145/792704.792712

Levary, R., & Mathieu, R. G. (2000). Hybrid retail: integrating e-commerce and physical stores. *Industrial Management (Des Plaines), 42*(5), 6–13.

Liang, T., & Huang, J. (1998). An empirical study on consumer acceptance of products in electronic markets: A transaction cost model. *Decision Support Systems, 24*, 29–43. doi:10.1016/S0167-9236(98)00061-X

Noble, S. M., Griffith, D. A., & Weinberger, M. G. (2005). Consumer derived utilitarian value and channel utilization in a multi-channel context. *Journal of Business Research, 58*, 1643–1651. doi:10.1016/j.jbusres.2004.10.005

Pan, X., Ratchford, B. T., & Shankar, V. (2004). Price dispersion on the internet: A review and directions for future research. *Journal of Interactive Marketing, 18*(4), 116–135. doi:10.1002/dir.20019

Rangaswamy, A., & Van Bruggen, G. H. (2005). Opportunities and Challenges in Multichannel Marketing: An Introduction to the Special Issue. *Journal of Interactive Marketing, 19*(2), 5–11. doi:10.1002/dir.20037

Rhee, B., & Park, S. (1999). Online store as a new direct channel and emerging hybrid channel system. (Working Paper), Hong Kong University of Science and Technology, Clear Water Bay, Kowloon, Hong Kong

Salop, S. (1979). Monopolistic competition with outside goods. *The Bell Journal of Economics, 10*, 141–156. doi:10.2307/3003323

Steinfield, C., Bouwman, H., & Adelaar, T. (2002). The dynamics of click and mortar e-commerce: Opportunities and management strategies. *International Journal of Electronic Commerce, 7*(1), 93–119.

Steinfield, C., Mahler, A., & Bauer, J. (1999). Electronic commerce and the local merchant: Opportunities for synergy between physical and web presence. *Electronic Markets, 9*(2), 51–57.

Steinfield, C., & Whitten, P. (1999). Community level socio-economic impacts of electronic commerce. *Journal of Computer-Mediated Communication, 5*(2).

Useem, J. (1999). Internet defense strategy: Cannibalize yourself. *Fortune, 140*(121).

Venkatesh, A. (1999). Virtual models of marketing and consumer behavior. ESRC Virtual Society Program Workshop: E-Commerce and the Restructuring of Consumption, London.

Wallace, D. W., Giese, J. L., & Johnson, J. L. (2004). Customer retailer loyalty in the context of multiple channel strategies. *Journal of Retailing, 80*, 249–263. doi:10.1016/j.jretai.2004.10.002

Ward, M. R. (2001). Will online shopping compete more with traditional retailing or catalog shopping? *NETNOMICS: Economic Research and Electronic Networking, 3*(2), 103–117. doi:10.1023/A:1011451228921

Wood, S. T. (2001). Remote Purchase Environments: The influence of return policy leniency on two-state decision processes. *JMR, Journal of Marketing Research, 38*(2), 156–169. doi:10.1509/jmkr.38.2.157.18847

APPENDIX A

$$d_2 = \frac{2(p_1 - p_2 + \theta)}{t}$$

$$d_1 = 2(\frac{1}{2} - \frac{2(p_1 - p_2 + \theta)}{t})$$

Thus in a given period, the retailer's profit with an online channel is given by

$$\pi_1 = p_1 d_1 + p_2 d_2$$

And the other retailer's profit without online channel is given by

$$\pi_2 = p_2 d_2$$

When the retailer using a mixed channel employs a channel integration strategy, by differentiating π_1 on p_1 and p_2, simultaneously, and letting $(\partial \pi_1 / \partial p_1) = 0$ and $(\partial \pi_1 / \partial p_2) = 0$, we obtain:

$$p_1 = \theta - t$$

$$p_2 = 2\theta - \frac{3t}{2}$$

However, by differentiating π_2 on p_2, and letting $(\partial \pi_2 / \partial p_2) = 0$, we obtain:

$$p_2^* = \theta - \frac{t}{2}$$

Since in a competitive market, the lower price always has a competitive advantage. Thus, the retailer with a higher price has to drop its price p_2 and approach p_2^*. We then substitute p_1 and p_2^* into demand and profit function to yield all results in Table 2.

APPENDIX B

When the retailer using a mixed channel employs a decentralized channel strategy, each channel will take independent price policies to maximize individual profit. Thus, the profit of online channel is

$$\pi_{online} = p_1 d_1$$

And the profit of traditional channel is

$$\pi_{traditional} = p_2 d_2$$

Thus, the total profit of retailer with a mixed channel is

$$\pi_1 = p_1 d_1 + p_2 d_2$$

The profit of retailer with only a traditional retail is

$$\pi_2 = p_2 d_2$$

By differentiating π_{online} on p_1 and $\pi_{traditional}$ on p_2, simultaneously, and letting $(\partial \pi_{online} / \partial p_1) = 0$ and $(\partial \pi_{traditional} / \partial p_2) = 0$, we obtain:

$$p_1 = \frac{t - 2\theta}{6}$$

$$p_2 = \frac{t + 4\theta}{12}$$

Substituting $p_1 = \dfrac{t - 2\theta}{6}$ and $p_2 = \dfrac{t + 4\theta}{12}$ into demand and profit functions, we obtain all results summarized in Table 3.

APPENDIX C

When the retailer with a mixed channel employs the decentralized channel strategy, the demand in the online channel is

$$d_1 = \frac{2(t - 2\theta)}{3t}$$

And because $\theta < \frac{t}{2}$, thus $d_1 = \frac{2(t - 2\theta)}{3t} > 0$

Also, $\frac{\partial d_1}{\partial \theta} = -\frac{4}{3t} < 0$,

Thus, proposition 2 is proved

APPENDIX D

When the retailer with a mixed channel employs a channel integration strategy, its profit is $'\pi_1 = \frac{(2\theta - t)^2}{2t}$

When the retailer with a mixed channel employs a decentralized channel strategy, its profit is

$$\pi_1 = \frac{t}{8} - \frac{\theta}{3} + \frac{2\theta^2}{3t}$$

Let $'\pi_1 = \pi_1$, we obtain $\theta > \frac{1}{8}(5 + \sqrt{7})t$ or $\theta < \frac{1}{8}(-5 - \sqrt{7})t$ for channel integration and other for decentralized channel strategy. However, because channel integration only works under $\theta > t$ and decentralized channel strategy works under $\theta < \frac{t}{2}$, thus we show that when $\theta > t$, the optimal channel strategy is channel integration; when $0 \leq \theta < \frac{t}{2}$, the optimal channel strategy is decentralized channel. Thus, proposition 3 is proved.

APPENDIX E

When there are n ($n > 2$) retailers in a competitive market,

$$d_2 = \frac{2(p_1 - p_2 + \theta)}{t}$$

$$d_1 = n(\frac{1}{n} - \frac{2(p_1 - p_2 + \theta)}{t})$$

Thus in a given period, the retailer's profit with an online channel is given by

$$\pi_1 = p_1 d_1 + p_2 d_2$$

And the other retailer's profit without online channel is given by

$$\pi_2 = p_2 d_2$$

When the retailer using a mixed channel employs a channel integration strategy, by differentiating π_1 on p_1 and p_2, simultaneously, and letting $(\partial \pi_1 / \partial p_1) = 0$ and $(\partial \pi_1 / \partial p_2) = 0$, we obtain:

$$p_1 = \frac{n\theta - \theta - t}{(n-1)^2}$$

$$p_2 = \frac{2n\theta(n-1) - (n+1)t}{2(n-1)^2}$$

However, by differentiating π_2 on p_2, and letting $(\partial \pi_2 / \partial p_2) = 0$, we obtain:

$$p_2^* = \frac{n\theta(n-1) - t}{2(n-1)^2}$$

Since in a competitive market, the lower price always has a competitive advantage. Thus, the retailer with a higher price has to drop its price p_2 and approach p_2^*. We then substitute p_1 and p_2^* into demand and profit function to yield all results in Table 4.

APPENDIX F

In the n $(n > 2)$ retailers competitive market, when the retailer using a mixed channel employs a decentralized channel strategy, each channel will take independent price policies to maximize individual profit. Thus, the profit of online channel is

$$\pi_{online} = p_1 d_1$$

And the profit of traditional channel is

$$\pi_{traditional} = p_2 d_2$$

Thus, the total profit of retailer with a mixed channel is

$$\pi_1 = p_1 d_1 + p_2 d_2$$

The profit of retailer with only a traditional retail is

$$\pi_2 = p_2 d_2$$

By differentiating π_{online} on p_1 and $\pi_{traditional}$ on p_2, simultaneously, and letting $(\partial \pi_{online} / \partial p_1) = 0$ and $(\partial \pi_{traditional} / \partial p_2) = 0$, we obtain:

$$p_1 = \frac{t}{3n} - \frac{\theta}{3}$$

$$p_2 = \frac{t}{6n} + \frac{\theta}{3}$$

Substituting $p_1 = \frac{t}{3n} - \frac{\theta}{3}$ and $p_2 = \frac{t}{6n} + \frac{\theta}{3}$ into demand and profit functions, we obtain all results summarized in Table 5.

APPENDIX G

When the retailer with a mixed channel employs a channel integration strategy, its profit is

$$^I\pi_1 = \frac{(n\theta(n-1)-t)^2}{2(n-1)^4 t}$$

When the retailer with a mixed channel employs a decentralized channel strategy, its profit is

$$\pi_1 = \frac{4n^2(n+1)\theta^2 + (1+4n)t^2 - 4(2n-1)nt\theta}{18n^2 t}$$

Let $^I\pi_1 = \pi_1$, and because channel integration only works under $\theta > \dfrac{t}{n-1}$ and decentralized channel strategy works under $\theta < \dfrac{t}{n}$, thus we show that when $\theta > \dfrac{t}{n-1}$, the optimal channel strategy is channel integration; when $0 \le \theta < \dfrac{t}{n}$, the optimal channel strategy is decentralized channel. Thus, proposition 4 is proved.

APPENDIX H

When the factor of internet coverage rate is included in our model, let p^r is the price charged by retailer, and p_1 is the price charged by online market. Thus consumers in the fraction of internet coverage rate, λ, can purchase from traditional retail market and online market, where $p^r + tx = p_1 + \theta$. In the fraction of $(1-\lambda)$ only can purchase from traditional retail market, where $p^r + tx' = p_2 + t(\dfrac{1}{2} - x')$. Therefore, the demand functions for online and traditional retail market are defined as follows.

$$d_2 = (1-\lambda)(\frac{p_2 + \frac{t}{2} - p^r}{t}) + \frac{2\lambda(p_1 - p^r + \theta)}{t}$$

$$d_1 = 2\lambda(\frac{1}{2} - \frac{2(p_1 - p_2 + \theta)}{t})$$

Thus, the total profit of retailer with a mixed channel is

$$\pi_1 = p_1 d_1 + p^r d_2$$

When the retailer with a mixed channel employs the channel integration strategy, we differentiate π_1 on p_1 and p^r, respectively, and setting the differentials to zero, and then optimal prices p_1 and p^r are obtained. Further, since the retail market is symmetric, $p_2 = p^r$. We substitute p_2 for p^r and eliminate p^r yield optimal prices in Table 7. Market demand and profits are obtained by further substitution.

APPENDIX I

When the retailer with a mixed channel employs a decentralized channel strategy, the profit of online channel is

$$\pi_{online} = p_1 d_1$$

And the profit of traditional channel is

$$\pi_{traditional} = p_2 d_2$$

By differentiating π_{online} on p_1 and $\pi_{traditional}$ on p^r, simultaneously, and letting $(\partial \pi_{online} / \partial p_1) = 0$ and $(\partial \pi_{traditional} / \partial p^r) = 0$, and we further substitute p_2 for p^r and eliminate p^r yield optimal prices in Table 8. Market demand and profits are obtained by further substitution.

APPENDIX J

By comparing the profits of retailer with a mixed channel in Tables 5 and 6, and because channel integration only works under $\dfrac{t(3+\lambda)}{4(1+\lambda)} \le \theta \le t$ with $0 < \lambda < \dfrac{1+\sqrt{13}}{6}$ or under $\theta > t$ with $\lambda > \dfrac{1+\sqrt{13}}{6}$ and decentralized channel strategy works under $0 \le \theta < \dfrac{t(3+\lambda)}{4(1+\lambda)}$, thus proposition 5 is proved.

This work was previously published in International Journal of E-Business Research (IJEBR) Volume 5, Issue 3, edited by In Lee, pp. 78-99, copyright 2009 by IGI Publishing (an imprint of IGI Global).

Chapter 16
Web Services Communities:
From Intra-Community Coopetition to Inter-Community Competition

Zakaria Maamar
Zayed University, UAE

Philippe Thiran
University of Namur, Belgium

Jamal Bentahar
Concordia University, Canada

ABSTRACT

This chapter discusses the structure and management of communities of Web services from two perspectives. The first perspective, called coopetition, shows the simultaneous cooperative and competitive behaviors that Web services exhibit when they reside in the same community. These Web services offer similar functionalities, and hence are competitive, but they can also cooperate as they share the same savoir-faire. The second perspective, called competition, shows the competition that occurs not between Web services but between their communities, which are associated with similar functionalities. To differentiate such communities, a competition model based on a set of metrics is discussed in this chapter.

INTRODUCTION

For the World Wide Web Consortium, a Web service "*is a software application identified by a URI, whose interfaces and binding are capable of being defined, described, and discovered by XML artifacts and supports direct interactions with other software applications using XML-based messages via Internet-based applications*". For the last few years, the development pace of Web services has been impressive (Di Martino, 2009; Maamar et al., 2008; Maaradji et al., 2010; Khosravifar et al., 2010a). On the one hand, several standards have been developed to deal for example with Web services definition, discovery, and security. On the other hand, several projects have been initiated to examine among other things Web services composition, personalization, and contextualization.

Nowadays, competition between businesses does not stop at goods, services, or software products, but includes as well Web services. In-

DOI: 10.4018/978-1-60960-132-4.ch016

Copyright © 2011, IGI Global. Copying or distributing in print or electronic forms without written permission of IGI Global is prohibited.

dependent providers develop several Web services that sometimes offer the same functionality such as weather forecast and currency exchange. It is reported in (Bui, 2005) that although Web services are heterogeneous, the functionalities they offer are sufficiently well defined and homogeneous enough to allow for market competition to happen. To ease and improve the process of Web services discovery in an open environment like the Internet, we gather similar Web services into communities (Maamar et al., 2009). Acknowledging the efforts that service engineers need to put into designing and managing communities, we put forward guidelines that define how to specify and set up a community, how to manage the Web services that reside in a community, and how to reconcile conflicts within a community and between communities. In a community, the Web services are simultaneously in competition and in cooperation, i.e., they compete to participate in composite Web services since they all offer the same functionality with different non-functional properties (or QoS) and at the same time cooperate when they substitute for each other in case of failure.

As several communities of Web services come online and in line with today's economy featured by competition, there, also, exist relationships between communities that offer the same functionality. This increases the competition among communities of Web services and potential users of Web services. On the one hand, providers are interested in finding the communities that give better exposure to their respective Web services. On the other hand, users are interested in binding to the best communities that host the appropriate Web services as per their respective needs. The development of a reputation model is deemed appropriate for both parties.

The remainder of this chapter is organized as follows. The next section introduces the definitions of some concepts upon which communities of Web services are built. The intra-community coopetition and inter-community competition

are discussed after that. Finally some concluding remarks are drawn.

SOME DEFINITIONS

Community. It means different things in different settings. In Longman Dictionary, community is "*a group of people living together and/or united by shared interests, religion, nationality, etc.*" In the field of knowledge management, communities of practice constitute groups within (or sometimes across) organizations who share a common set of information needs or problems (Davies, 2003). Communities are not formal organizational units but networks with common interests and concerns. When it comes to Web services, Benatallah et al. define community as a collection of Web services with a common functionality although these Web services have distinct non-functional properties (Benatallah, 2003). Medjahed and Bouguettaya use community to provide an ontological organization of Web services sharing the same domain of interest (Medjahed, 2005). Medjahed and Atif use community to implement rule-based techniques for comparing context policies of Web services (Medjahed, 2007). Maamar et al. define community as a means to provide a description of a desired functionality without explicitly referring to any concrete Web service that will implement this functionality at run-time (Maamar et al., 2009). Finally, Wan et al. define communities of Web services as virtual spaces that can dynamically gather different Web services having complementary or related functionalities (Wan et al., 2010).

Reputation. It is "*the opinion (more technically, a social evaluation) of the public toward a person, a group of people, or an organization*" (Wikipedia). Reputation, besides other selection criteria, has been widely used for evaluating and ranking participants in social networks, online collaborations, agent-based systems, or in e-business platforms (like e-Bay). Nowadays, opinions and user ratings are no longer sufficient for assessing the reputation of computer systems as Elnaffar stresses out in (Elnaffar 2006). Opinions/Ratings are subjective and can be easily tampered. A reputation system that solely relies on the temporal perspective of humans (i.e., clients) can expose the system, intentionally or unintentionally, to dishonest ratings caused by the following types of users:

- Emotional reactors: clients who give non-subjective, inaccurate ratings influenced by some personal (could be temporal) issues with the system being used.
- Bad mouthers: clients who unfaithfully exaggerate by giving negative ratings to service providers. These clients might plan to collude with the competitors of these providers.
- Ballot stuffers: clients who unfaithfully exaggerate by giving positive ratings to service providers. Like for bad mouthers, these clients plan to collude with these providers.

Coopetition. It is kind of combination between cooperation and competition (Bengtsson and Kock, 2000). Simultaneously, actors are engaged in cooperative and competitive relationships. Actors have, on the one hand, conflicts of interests (competition) and, on the other hand, common interests (cooperation). In a shopping mall retailers that display the same merchandise exhibit a competitive behavior, but at the same time cooperate to attract the maximum number of customers since they are in the same mall. They aim at providing customers with more choices (also known as externalities) and compete since each retailer is a profit maximizer.

INTRA-COMMUNITY COOPETITION

In a community, competition and cooperation coexist among Web services. Competition appears because each Web service aims at maximizing its participation rate in Web services composition. Cooperation takes place because Web services need each other to sustain the growth of their community by for example maintaining a good reputation level and substituting each other in case one of them fails. Web services are part of a two-side market (Roson, 2005). The benefits of one side from interacting through the community depend on the size of the other side that consists of Web services contributing together to the attractiveness of their community. As a result, a community must make itself attractive to users by encouraging and managing the competition and cooperation (i.e., coopetition) of its Web services. The community therefore cares about the interactions between the two sides and the management of its members.

Architecture

Figure 1 represents the architecture of Web services communities. The components of this architecture are the internal structure of communities, providers of Web services and UDDI registries (or any type of registry like ebXML). Communities are established and dismantled according to specific scenarios and protocols that are detailed in the next section. UDDI registries receive advertisements of Web services from providers for posting purposes. Figure 1 offers some characteristics that need to be stressed out. First, the common way to describing, announcing, and invoking Web services is still the same as described in the standard service-oriented architecture although Web services are now associated with communities. Second, the regular facilities that UDDI registries offer are still the same; no extra facilities are required to accommodate communities' needs. Finally, the selection of Web services out of communities is transparent to users and independent of the way they are gathered into communities. Two communities of Web services are shown in Figure 1. They could have airfare quotation and

Figure 1. Architecture of single Web services communities per functionality

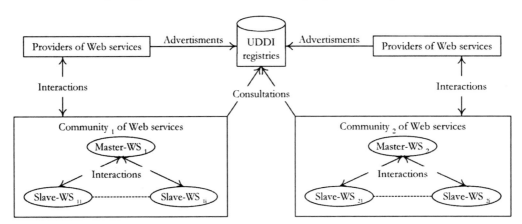

hotel booking as examples of functionalities, respectively. A master component always leads a community. This master could itself be implemented as a broker Web service (like shown in Figure 1) for compatibility purposes with the rest of Web services in a community, which are now denoted as slaves. Master-Slave Web services relationship in a community is regulated using the well-known Contract Net protocol (Smith, 1980) (*CNProtocol*). However, more advanced protocols involving negotiations based on argumentation can also be used (Bentahar et al. 2007).

One of the responsibilities of the master Web service is to attract Web services to make them sign up for its community using rewards (Maamar et al., 2009). As a result, the master Web service checks regularly the UDDI registries so that it is kept updated about the latest changes like new advertisements in their respective contents. The master also checks the credibility of the potential members, so only trustful Web services are invited (Khosravifar et al., 2010b). More responsibilities of the master Web service include nominate the slave Web service out of several peers to participate in a composite Web service, and run the *CNProtocol* to nominate this Web service.

In a community, the master Web service is designated in two different ways. The first way is to have a dedicated Web service playing the role of master for the time being of a community. Since the master Web service never participates in any composition, it is only loaded with community management mechanisms like Web services attraction and retention. The second way is to identify a Web service from the list of available Web services to act as a master. This identification happens on a voluntary basis or by running an election process among the Web services. Because of the temporary no-participation restriction of a master Web service in compositions, the nominated Web service is compensated (Bentahar et al., 2008). The call for elections in a community takes place regularly and in a democratic way, so that the burden on the same Web services to lead a community is either minimized or avoided.

Operation

Community operation is about developing a new community, dismantling an existing community, attracting new Web services to a community, retaining existing Web services in a community, and selecting slave Web services in a community to take part in a composition.

Community development. A community gathers similar Web services using a two-step process. The first step is to define the functionality, e.g., flight booking, of the community. The second step is to deploy the master Web service that will lead the community and take over the aforementioned responsibilities. One of them is to invite and convince Web services to sign up for its community. The survivability of a community, i.e., to avoid dismantlement, depends on the performance of the community, which in turn depends to a certain extent on the performance of the existing Web services in this community. Another responsibility is to check the credentials (e.g., announced QoS) of Web services before they are admitted in a community. This checking has a dual advantage: boost the security level among the peers in a community and enhance the trustworthiness level of a master Web service towards the slave Web services it manages. The first advantage avoids dealing with malicious Web services that could attempt to alter other peers' data and behaviors. The second advantage shows the reliance of the master Web service on the slave Web services in completing the prescribed operations. Enhancing the security of a community is an important factor that contributes towards its reputation (Khosravifar et al., 2010a). Such a reputation is fundamental to attract both new Web services to sign up and users to request Web services (Elnaffar, 2008). It should be noted that slave Web services could turn out "lazy"1 after joining a community, which calls for their immediate ejection from the community.

Dismantling a community happens upon request from the master Web service. This one oversees the events in a community such as arrival of new Web services, departure of some Web services, and sanctions on Web services because of misbehavior. When a master Web service notices that the community has poor performance over a certain period of time, the community designer can decide to dismantle it. This performance can be measured using the number of Web services that are registered in the community and the number of participation requests in composite Web services. Ultimately, the performance over a period of time $[t_1, t_2]$ can be measured from an economical perspective as follows:

$$Performance^{[t_1,t_2]} = Incomes^{[t_1,t_2]} - Rewards^{[t_1,t_2]}$$

where incomes are generated from the participation in composite Web services and rewards are expenses used to establish and manage the community by attracting and retaining good Web services. Consequently, the community has a good performance when the number of active Web services is high and close to the number of its members. However, the performance is poor when the number of active Web services is low compared to the number of registered Web services.

Web services attraction and retention. Attracting new Web services to and retaining existing Web services in a community fall into the responsibilities of the master Web service. A community could vanish if the number of active Web services that reside in it drops below a certain threshold that is set by the community designer.

Web services attraction makes the master Web service consult regularly the different UDDI registries looking for new Web services. When a candidate Web service is identified based on the functionality it offers, the master Web service interacts with its provider (Figure 1). The purpose is to ask the provider to register its Web service with the community of this master Web service. Some arguments to convince the provider include high participation-rate of the existing Web services in composite Web services (it shows the visibility of the community and the reputation of Web services (Maximilien, 2002)), short response-time when handling user requests, and efficiency of the security mechanisms against malicious Web services (Khosravifar et al., 2010a).

Retaining Web services to remain committed to a community for a long period of time is a good indicator of the following elements:

- As mentioned earlier, although Web services in a community are competitive, they expose a cooperative attitude (i.e., they are coopetative). For instance, Web services have not been subject to attacks from peers in the community (because all Web services would like to participate in composition scenarios, some of them could try to make other peers less competitive by illegally altering their execution properties). This backs the security argument that the master Web service uses again to attract Web services and convince their providers.

- A Web service provider is satisfied with its participation rate in composite Web services. This is in line with the participation-rate argument that the master Web service uses to attract new Web services.
- Web services are, through the master Web service, aware of some peers in the community that could replace them in case of failure, with less impact on the composite Web services in which they are involved.

Web services attraction and retention shed the light on a third scenario, which is Web services being invited to leave a community as briefly reported earlier. A master Web service could issue such a request upon assessment of the following criteria:

- The Web service is unreliable. On different occasions the Web service failed to participate in composite Web services due to recurrent operation problems.
- The credentials of the Web service were "beefed up" to enhance its participation opportunities in composite Web services. Large differences between a Web services' advertised QoS and delivered QoS indicate performance degradation (Ouzzani, 2004).

Web services selection. In a community, selection of Web services to participate in composition rely on the Contract-Net protocol, namely job contracting and subcontracting between two types of agents known as initiator (master Web service) and participant (slave Web service). At any time an agent can be initiator, participant, or both. The sequence of steps in the contract-net protocol, which we slightly extend, is as follows: (1) initiator sends participants a call for proposals with respect to a certain job to carry out; (2) each participant reviews the call for proposals and bids if interested (i.e., feasible job); (3) initiator chooses the best bid and awards a contract to that participant; and (4) initiator rejects other bids.

Mapping the contract-net protocol onto the operation of a community occurs as follows. When a user (through some assistance (Schiaffino, 2004)) selects a community based on its functionality, the master Web service of this community is contacted in order to identify a specific slave Web service that will implement this functionality at run-time. The master Web service sends all slave Web services a call for bids (CNStep 1). Prior to getting back to the master Web service, the slave Web services assess their status by checking their ongoing commitments in other compositions and their forthcoming maintenance periods (Maamar, 2006) (CNStep 2). Only the slave Web services that are interested in bidding inform the master Web service. This latter screens all the bids before choosing the best one (CNStep 3)2. The winning slave Web service is notified so that it can get itself ready for execution when requested (CNStep 3). The rest of the slave Web services that expressed interest but were not selected, are notified as well (CNStep 4).

INTER-COMMUNITY COMPETITION

In this section, we extend our previous discussion by considering that a functionality can be offered by more than one community. Hence, both providers and users have to decide whether or not to use or subscribe to a specific community. A party considers the incentive provided by the other party. For providers, a major incentive is the participation rate that the community can offer to them. For the users, the main factor is

Figure 2. Architecture of multiple Web services communities per functionality

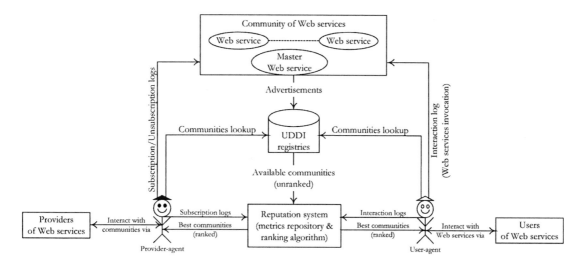

their satisfaction about the provided service. We argue in this chapter that these incentives can be captured through reputation.

Architecture

Figure 2 depicts an augmented Web services community architecture that takes into consideration the notion of community reputation. As shown, the architecture consists of the following main components:

- UDDI registry: In addition to Web services' descriptions that are posted on the UDDI descriptions of available communities are posted, as well.
- User Agent: It is a proxy between the user and other parties namely, UDDI registry, Web services communities, and the reputation system.
- Provider Agent: Akin to the user agent, a provider agent is a proxy between the provider and other parties, namely, UDDI registry, Web services communities, and the reputation system.
- Reputation System: It maintains a repository of run-time operational data, called

logs below, that are needed to compute the performance metrics of a community, and ranks communities by their reputation.

To compute reputation from the perspective of users or providers, user agents should intercept the following time-stamped logs for each event that happens during the interaction with the community

1. Received Requests log tracks all requests directed to the community by the user agents. This log is needed to compute *inDemand, selectivity,* and *satisfaction* metrics.
2. Response Time log tracks how long it took a community's Web service master to find and nominate a Web service slave to handle a user's request, the time needed by the Web service to provide the service back to the user, plus the extra time needed in case of substitution. This log is required to compute the *responsiveness* metric.
3. Advertized Response Time log tracks the community's advertized response time needed to provide the service back to the user. This log is used to compute the *satisfaction* metric in an objective way.

339

4. Invocations log tracks all received requests that have been accepted by the community master and invoked by the designated Web service slave. This log is required when computing the *fairness* metric.
5. Users log tracks the user agents that requested services from the community. This log contributes in the calculation of the *satisfaction* metric.

In addition to these logs, and to compute the provider-perceived performance metrics, provider agents should intercept the following additional time-stamped logs:

1. Subscriptions/Unsubscriptions logs track providers signing up/off to a community. These logs are needed to compute the *market share* metric as they can tell how many Web service members are presently there in the community.
2. Leave log tracks Web services that leave the community. This log is used to compute the stability metric of the community.

The different logs permit to compute performance metrics in order to assess a community reputation. Data stored in these logs are monitored and collected by agents independent of the three key players in the computing platform (users, providers and community masters). This is aimed at fostering the trust between them.

Reputation-Based Operation

In the following, C_i denotes Community i that is under consideration by either provider or user, and $|C_i|$ denotes the number of Web services residing in C_i. We examine the role of a community reputation model from the perspectives of users of and providers of Web services.

Reputation from the user's perspective. As perceived by users, a community reputation model would help them select communities that can offer

Web services that meet their quality expectations. The reputation model for communities would drive the discovery process that is based on aggregating and operating on historical performance metrics. In general, most of these metrics are monitored over an observation window, w, which is measured using different units like days or weeks, and recorded in run-time logs. Next, we outline some of the performance metrics that can play a role in assessing the reputation of a community as seen by users.

Responsiveness metric: is one of the important qualities that users care about when selecting a community. It is the metric that determines how fast a community master is at nominating a Web service slave from this community that can handle the user's request, how fast the slave is at providing back the service, and how fast the substitution is performed. The responsiveness of community C_i, denoted by $Responsiveness_{C_i}$, is measured by computing the average of the n response times to the requests that took place throughout the observation window w. To simplify the formulas, the window w, which is supposed to be fixed, is omitted. So,

$$Responsiveness_{C_i} = \frac{1}{n} \sum_{k=1}^{n} rt_{C_i}^k$$

where $rt_{C_i}^k$ is the response time taken to fulfill the user's request number k in C_i.

InDemand metric: assesses the interest of users in a specific community by the percentage of requests that a community receives to the total requests submitted to all communities throughout w. That is,

$$InDemand_{C_i} = \frac{ReceivedRequests_{C_i}}{\sum_{k=1}^{M} ReceivedRequests_k}$$

where *M* denotes the number of communities that are under consideration and $ReceivedRequests_{C_i}$ is the number of requests that C_i receives over *w*.

Satisfaction metric: represents the objective opinion of clients who dealt with a community recently, i.e., over the observation window *w*. It is computed in terms of the difference between the advertized (promised) response time $art_{C_i}^k$ and the provided one $rt_{C_i}^k$ for each interaction *k* over *n* interactions during window *w*:

$$Satisfaction_{C_i} = e^{-\sum_{i=1}^{n}|rt_{C_i}^k - art_{C_i}^k|}$$

Notice that with this function the satisfaction is 1 when the difference between the two times is null. The satisfaction decreases with the increase of this difference.

Reputation from the provider's perspective. A reputation model would here support providers of Web services identify the communities where their Web services will sign up. Below we list some performance metrics that we conceive important to the final assessment of the community's reputation.

Selectivity metric: any provider wishes to join communities in which the provider has the maximum likelihood of being selected for fulfilling user's request compared to other communities. Assuming that the community master adopts fair (uniform) selection policy among Web services, the selectivity of community C_i is the average number of requests that are assigned to a Web service member inside a community and is computed as follows:

$$Selectivity_{C_i} = \frac{ReceivedRequests_{C_i}}{|C_i|}$$

MarketShare metric: is the ratio of the Web services subscribed to a community to the total number of Web services subscribed to all communities:

$$MarketShare_{C_i} = \frac{|C_i|}{\sum_{k=1}^{M}|C_k|}$$

where $\sum_{k=1}^{M}|C_k|$ represents the total number of Web services that signed up in all the *M* communities. From the provider's perspective, $MarketShare_{C_i}$ factor may be a double-edged sword. On the positive side, the larger $MarketShare_{C_i}$ the more powerful the candidate community is, which means a better chance of having it more often selected by clients. On the negative side, small $MarketShare_{C_i}$ means a lower selectivity rate and a tougher competition for the provider.

Stability metric: is the metric allowing to measure how stable the community is in terms of the portion of Web services that leave the community during the window time $w\,Leave_{C_i}$ to the total number of members of this community:

$$Stability_{C_i} = e^{-\frac{Leave_{C_i}}{|C_i|}}$$

CONCLUSION

The notion of Web services communities is presented in this chapter where Web services providing the same functionality are put together in one or many communities. In these communities two behaviors emerge: intra and inter. The intra behavior is coopetative, which means Web services are supposed to be at the same time competitive since they offer users the same functionalities and cooperative since they serve the benefits of the same community. The inter behavior is a market-oriented behavior where communities operating in the same activity domains compete to attract the maximum number of users and providers of Web services. In such a competitive setting, providers of Web services use reputation metrics to decide about the community where to subscribe their Web services. Users use other reputation metrics to identify the community that offer the Web services they need.

ACKNOWLEDGMENT

The authors would like to thank Djamal Benslimane, Said Elnaffar, Chirine Ghedira, Michael Mrissa, Subramanian Sattanathan, Wei Wan, and Hamdi Yahyaoui, for their contributions to the early stages of the Web services community project. Jamal Bentahar would like to thank the Natural Sciences and Engineering Research Council of Canada (NSERC) and Fonds québécois de recherche sur la société et la culture (FQRSC).

REFERENCES

Benatallah, B., Sheng, Q. Z., & Dumas, M. (2003). The Self-Serv Environment for Web Services Composition. *IEEE Internet Computing*, *7*(1). doi:10.1109/MIC.2003.1167338

Bengtsson, M., & Kock, S. (2000). *Coopetition in Business Networks to Cooperate and Compete Simultaneously. Industrial Marketing Management*, *29*(5). doi:10.1016/S0019-8501(99)00067-X

Bentahar, J., Maamar, Z., Benslimane, D., & Thiran, Ph. (2007). An Argumentation Framework for Communities of Web Services. *IEEE Intelligent Systems*, *22*(6), 75–83. doi:10.1109/MIS.2007.99

Bentahar, J., Maamar, Z., Wan, W., Benslimane, D., Thiran, P., & Subramanian, S. (2008). Agent-based Communities of Web Services: An Argumentation-driven Approach. *Service Oriented Computing and Applications*, *2*(4), 219–238. doi:10.1007/s11761-008-0033-4

Bui, T., & Gacher, A. (2005). Web Services for Negotiation and Bargaining in Electronic Markets: Design Requirements and Implementation Framework. *Proceedings of the 38th Hawaii International Conference on System Sciences (HICSS'2005), Big Islands, Hawaii, USA.*

Davies, J., Duke, A., & Sure, Y. (2003). OntoShare - A knowledge Management Environment for Virtual Communities. *Proceedings of the Second International Conference on Knowledge Capture (K-CAP'2003).*

Di Martino, B. (2009). Semantic Web Services Discovery based on Structural Ontology Matching. *International Journal of Web and Grid Services*, *5*(1).

Elnaffar, S., Maamar, Z., Yahyaoui, H., Bentahar, J., & Thiran, Ph. (2008). Reputation of Communities of Web services - Preliminary Investigation. *Proceedings of the International Symposium on Web and Mobile Information Services (WA-MIS'2008) held in conjunction of the 22nd International Conference on Advanced Information Networking and Applications (AINA'2008).*

Khosravifar, B., Bentahar, J., & Moazin, A. (2010b). Analyzing the Relationships between some Parameters of Web Services Reputation. In *Proceedings of the 8th IEEE International Conference on Web Services (ICWS'2010)*, Miami, Florida, USA.

Khosravifar, B., Bentahar, J., Moazin, A., & Thiran, Ph. (2010a). Analyzing Communities of Web Services Using Incentives [IJWSR]. *International Journal of Web Services Research*, *7*(3).

Maamar, Z., Benslimane, D., Mostefaoui, G. M., Subramanian, S., & Mahmoud, Q. H. (2008). Toward Behavioral Web Services Using Policies, *IEEE Transactions on Systems, Man, and Cybernetics, Part A*, 38(6).

Maamar, Z., Benslimane, D., & Narendra, N. C. (2006). What Can Context do for Web Services? *Communications of the ACM, 49*(12). doi:10.1145/1183236.1183238

Maamar, Z., Subramanian, S., Thiran, P., Benslimane, D., & Bentahar, J. (2009). Communities of Web Services -Concepts, Architecture, Operation, and Deployment. [Hershey, PA: IGI Global Publishing]. *International Journal of E-Business Research, 5*(4), 1–12.

Maaradji, A., Hacid, H., Daigremont, J., & Crespi, N. (2010). Towards a Social Network Based Approach for Services Composition, in *the Proceedings of the 2010 IEEE International Conference on Communications (ICC'2010)*, Cape Town, South Africa.

Maximilien, M., & Singh, M. (2002). Concept Model of Web Service Reputation. *SIGMOD Record, 31*(4). doi:10.1145/637411.637417

Medjahed, B., & Atif, Y. (2007). Context-based Matching for Web Service Composition. *Distributed and Parallel Databases, Springer, 21*(1).

Medjahed, B., & Bouguettaya, A. (2005). A Dynamic Foundational Architecture for Semantic Web Services. *Distributed and Parallel Databases, Kluwer Academic Publishers*, 17(2).

Ouzzani, M., & Bouguettaya, A. (2004). Efficient Access to Web Services. *IEEE Internet Computing, 8*(2).

Schiaffino, S., & Amandi, A. (2004). User - Interface Agent Interaction: Personalization Issues. *International Journal of Human Computer Studies, Elsevier Sciences Publisher*, 60(1).

Smith, R. (1980). The Contract Net Protocol: High Level Communication and Control in Distributed Problem Solver. *IEEE Transactions on Computers*, 29. Roson, R. (2005). Two-Sided Markets: A Tentative Survey. *Review of Network Economics, 4*(2).

Wan, W., Bentahar, J., & Ben Hamza, A. (2010). Modeling and Verifying Agent-based Communities of Web Services, *Proceedings of the 23rd International Conference on Industrial, Engineering and Other Applications of Applied Intelligent Systems (IEA-AIE 2010)*, Cordoba, Spain.

ENDNOTES

[1]   Web services that do not satisfy the QoS that a master Web service advertises and guarantees to potential users.

[2]   In case there are several tied bids, different selection opportunities are offered to the master Web service like randomly, firstly received, etc.

Chapter 17
Tana and the Handbag:
Extending the Model of Factors Influencing the Final Price in Online Auctions

Val A. Hooper
Victoria University of Wellington, New Zealand

Sid L. Huff
Victoria University of Wellington, New Zealand

Jon McDonald
Trade Me, New Zealand

ABSTRACT

Research into the determinants of online auction prices has tended to group them into buyer factors, seller factors and site factors. A case is presented which recounts how a $30 handbag was sold for $ 22,750 in an online auction shortly after a national sport event. Analysis of the case indicates that, in addition to the three groups of factors already identified, other factors can exert a considerable influence on the final auction price. A model is proposed which depicts five groups of factors impacting the final price: buyer factors, seller factors, site factors which are expanded to include timing of the auction, and site brand strength; product factors which include product features, brand strength, and brand extension/ association; and promotion, which includes media publicity. While not all factors will impact on every auction, due consideration should be accorded each of them by both buyers and sellers.

INTRODUCTION

The emergence of the Internet has given rise to a number of new models, or models which have been adapted from the traditional to suit the online environment. An example of the latter is online auctions. Not only has this business model been adapted for the online environment but the latter has served to facilitate the widespread participation in online auction participation. Few people are unaware of auction sites such as eBay.

However, the online environment has also served to highlight certain aspects of auction behaviour which differ from those in the offline environment, and which are unique to the online environment.

This chapter presents the case of how a vinyl handbag containing a broken cellphone was sold

DOI: 10.4018/978-1-60960-132-4.ch017

Copyright © 2011, IGI Global. Copying or distributing in print or electronic forms without written permission of IGI Global is prohibited.

in an online auction in New Zealand for $22,750 (all prices refer to New Zealand dollars). Similar handbags could be bought from retailers for $20-$30, and similar new cellphones cost about $100. An exploration of the factors surrounding, and events leading up to the sale serves to identify the reasons for this extraordinary outcome.

First, a review of the research literature examining the factors which influence the outcomes of online auctions is presented. This literature is summarized in a "standard model" of online auction factors of influence. The history of events leading up to the sale of the vinyl handbag is then presented. As will become evident from the case, certain additional factors exercised an even more important influence than did the conventional factors embodied in the standard model. Finally, an extension to the standard model is presented. It takes into account additional factors that may influence the outcomes of online auctions - factors illustrated in the case of Tana and the handbag.

ONLINE AUCTIONS

The rise of the Internet and e-commerce has seen the emergence of a number of new business models, and adaptations of others (Rappa, 2004). One important example of a successful adaptation is the online auction.

Most traditional auctions attracted attention from limited numbers, e.g., the very wealthy (Bazerman, 2001), or specific-interest groups such as used car salesmen, real estate developers, or fresh produce and livestock dealers. In contrast, online auctions have changed the profile of interested parties significantly (Hu & Elliott, 2010; Gilkeson & Reynolds, 2003).

Online auctions based on the Internet have resulted in lowered barriers to entry, improved flow of information, enhanced power of buyers, increased efficiencies, and intensified competition (Ibeh, Luo & Dinnie, 2005). Accessibility has also dramatically increased: the ubiquity of the Internet means that many more people have access to online auctions and to the information relating to any specific auction, than would be the case for traditional fixed-time-and-place auctions.

However, in many ways, online auctions follow the approaches of traditional auctions. Online auctions can be open or sealed bid, single or multiple item lots, a seller can set a reserve price or not, and either the first in descending order (Dutch auction) or the last bid in ascending order (English auction) can be the winning one. Bidding can open at zero with a hidden price reserve, or the seller can predetermine the opening bid price (Massad & Tucker, 2000).

Implicit in auctions is the element of risk. Hofacker (1999) noted five categories of risk associated with auctions: time between purchase and delivery, vendor trustworthiness, security, brand integrity, and privacy. All of these apply to online auctions as well as traditional auctions. However, despite the risks, online auctions have been found to exceed in-person auctions both with regard to opening bid prices and average final prices (Massad & Tucker, 2000).

In any auction, final prices paid for the goods being auctioned are the ultimate indication of success. Stern and Stafford (2006) identified three groups of factors which determine final prices in online auctions: buyer factors, seller factors, and site factors. Other auction research literature also supports these three groups. Each group of factors is examined below.

Determinants of Price in Online Auctions

Buyer Factors

Psychological factors are extremely important in influencing the prices paid at auctions (Kagel, 1995). This applies to online auctions as well (Gilkeson & Reynolds, 2003). However, as yet the individual and collective psychology of bidders is not well understood – especially those aspects that lead to higher bids and higher profits (Stern & Stafford, 2006).

Motivation is a strong determinant of buyer behaviour and it can be argued that both cognitive motivations as well as hedonistic motivations help to explain bidding behaviour (Bosnjak, Obermeier & Tuten, 2006). Recognizing the importance of hedonism, Higgs and Worthington (2005) developed a hedonic price index with regard to art auctions. The hedonic value of online auctions was similarly found to be a significant contributor to bidder satisfaction, by Wu, Lin and Cheng(2009). In addition, Bosnjak et al. (2006) pointed out the desire for entertainment with online auctions – either as an observer or as a participant – while Hou and Elliott (2010) found bargain hunting and convenience to be further motivators.

There is also a competitive aspect to auctions. The desire to compete with others is a strong motivation (Stern & Stafford, 2006) and the competitive dynamic which develops during online auctions, especially consumer-to-consumer (C2C) auctions, has been seen to drive price escalation. Overpayment for a good may result (Dolan & Moon, 2000; Liang & Doong, 2000; Lucking-Reiley, Bryan, Prasad & Reeves, 2000).

Reference group influence can also be a strong driver of price escalation (Moschis, 1987; Goethals, 1976). Bidders are often driven by both group behaviour and competitive gamesmanship (Stern & Stafford, 2006). One version of this is termed "herd behaviour." This is particularly noticeable in online auctions where early bids on an item set off a chain reaction. Other bidders appear to perceive that good as desirable and thus gravitate towards it, irrespective of comparable available alternatives (Stern & Stafford, 2006). Dholakia and Soltysinski (2001) also studied "herd behaviour bias" in online auctions and came to the conclusion that items which attracted many bidders became coveted. Gilkeson and Reynolds (2003) demonstrated that, although bidders have their own private information, they are still influenced by the actions of other bidders.

Buyers' perceptions of the value of the good for which they are bidding also affects their motivations. However, what exactly constitutes "value" in the eyes of any particular consumer has been shown to be personal and idiosyncratic (Zeithaml, 1988). There are four very general categories of value: value is low price; value is whatever I want in a product, or the benefits I seek; value is the quality I get for the price I pay; and value is what I get for what I give (Zeithaml, 1988). In this fourth interpretation of value, perceived value is the result of a trade-off between perceived benefits and perceived sacrifices (Zeithaml, 1988; McDougall & Levesque, 2000). This is exemplified in the desire to "get a steal" (Holt, 1997, p.334) where the perceived benefits are much greater than the perceived sacrifices.

As indicated, perceived quality can be seen as one dimension of the construct of perceived value. Perceived quality, in turn, is influenced by price (Zeithaml, 1988). In fact, most research on perceived quality has focused on price as being the key extrinsic signal of quality (Zeithaml, 1988; Harcar et al., 2006). However, Mazursky and Jacoby (1985) and Harcar, Kara and Kucukemiroglu (2006) all found brand name to be used more frequently than other information to assess quality of goods.

Seller Factors

One of the drawbacks of online auctions has been the inability to physically check the good before purchasing, resulting in a degree of uncertainty regarding the quality of the good. Consequently, buyers seek reassurance elsewhere and rely on other indicators of expected quality. One key indicator is the seller's reputation (Snijders & Zijdeman, 2004). This reputation can be built up by means of feedback mechanisms on the auction site whereby buyers rate sellers. Brinkman and Siefert (2001) found that such feedback mechanisms formed the foundation of strong perceptions of trust. As a seller builds up a favourable reputation, buyers come to trust that seller. Because it tends to have strong emotional aspects, trust in a seller's reliability and integrity is very important (Hsu & Wang, 2008; Bejou, Ennew & Palmer, 1998; Pedersen & Nysveen, 2001). The seller's overall positive reputation impacts a buyer's willingness to pay higher prices (Resnick & Zeckhauser, 2002; Ba & Pavlou, 2002), and this reputation becomes even more important when there is uncertainty about the quality of the good (Melnick & Alm, 2005).

Site Factors

Two aspects of the auction web site are especially important: the features of the site, and the context which the site creates for the bidders.

With regard to the site itself, Stern and Stafford (2006) found that it was imperative for a site to capture the attention of potential buyers. With the multitude of offerings available over the Internet, buyers are subject to selective exposure and only attend to certain stimuli. Items such as the key words of a listing, or an item's label, are particularly important. Even more important are images: pictures provide greater vividness and a more distinct impact than words (Nisbett & Ross, 1980; Taylor & Thompson, 1982). Furthermore, viewers attend more eagerly to information-rich pictorial listings (Janiszewski, 1998). One of the explanations for this phenomenon is that visual stimuli are encoded both in terms of mental pictures and visual traces (Stern & Stafford, 2006); the greater the possibilities for decoding, the stronger the impact of the message.

Stern and Stafford (2006) explored the influence of pictorial visual cues on final prices of online auctions and found an indirect link which was mediated by the number of first day bids and bidders. The latter act as an associative reference group, signalling the value and the desirability of the good to other bidders. A snowball effect results with bidders relying on the valuation of others

to indicate the worth of the good (Burnkrant & Cousineau, 1975).

Snijders & Zijdeman (2004) suggested that the form of the auction could have an influence on final prices, with a last bid winner being preferred over a first (Dutch auction) bid simply because no upper limit is set.

Reserve prices also play an important role in online auctions, although it's not clear whether they exert positive or negative influences. Lucking-Reiley et al. (2000) reported that reserve prices exert a positive (upward) influence on final prices, because bidders regarded it as a competing bidder. However, Katkar and Lucking-Reiley (2000) found that reserve prices in online auctions reduced the final price of items sold. They also found that the reserve price acted as a deterrent to actually selling the good.

Lucking-Reiley et al. (2000) found that longer auctions usually achieved higher final prices. Unfortunately, as noted by Rafaeli and Noy (2002), no distinction was made in their study between the time spent analyzing the auction data and the time spent actually participating. However, Roth and Ockenfels (2002) found that auctions with a "soft" ending time discouraged last minute bidding or sniping.

Auctions are social events. In online auctions, given the absence of physical competitors, buyers relate to the virtual presence of other bidders. A phenomenon termed "social facilitation" occurs in an online auction: both sellers and buyers prefer a high volume of bidders (Wilcox, 2000; Gilkeson & Reynolds, 2003), and bidders improve their results and stay longer in situations of higher virtual presence (Rafaeli & Noy, 2002). This could be explained by the need for affiliation which Rafeali and Noy (2002) found to be manifested in bidders remaining online for longer in online auctions.

In general, the overall bidder satisfaction is significantly influenced by both the quality of the information systems as well as the service quality that the site provides (Wu et al. 2009).

Figure 1. A "standard model" of factors influencing the final price in online auctions

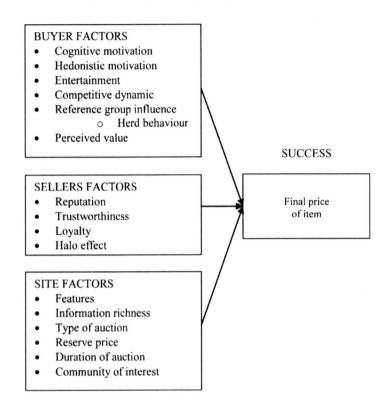

A "Standard Model" of Online Auction Price Outcomes

The above discussion is summarized in Figure 1, the "standard model" of online auction outcomes.

Given this model and the component groups of factors, it could have been expected that they would account for the final price obtained in an online auction. However, final price influences, which were not attributable to these factors alone, emerged in the following case.

TANA AND THE HANDBAG

Rugby

Many nations claim a national sport. However, only a few nations – regardless of size - are ac-knowledged as being world-dominant in a major sport. New Zealand is arguably one nation that can lay claim to such a status, in rugby. New Zealand's national rugby team is known as the All Blacks.

"Everyone in New Zealand and every rugby fan in the world knows the All Blacks, the most dominant team in all of rugby history. New Zealand rugby is part of the national identity." (New Zealand Tourism Online, 2006). Selection for the All Blacks is considered "the highest honour that a New Zealand athlete can achieve" (All Blacks, 2006). Played predominantly by males, all schoolboys are encouraged to participate in rugby and parents support these school games avidly. In the words of Mike Miller, the International Rugby Board Chief executive: "It is their national sport, they live and breathe rugby" (IRB World Cup Rugby, 2006).

Rugby was introduced to New Zealand in the late 1860s and in 1882 New Zealand participated in its first round of international competitions. In 1905 the first tour of Britain took place and it was during that tour that the All Blacks got their name - all their sports clothes were black.

The All Blacks have arguably become New Zealand's best-known brand. The depth of feelings which New Zealanders hold for their national rugby team is tantamount to national patriotism. Constant media coverage of all national rugby matches fans the passion of the support of that brand. This media coverage is provided in a number of forms – television, newspapers, magazine articles, and Internet features – all featuring a selection of news items, documentaries, panel discussions and interviews. New Zealanders are continuously updated on the potential players, the selection process of team members, their training progress, their private lives, and debates about the team merits vis-à-vis their opponents. Shops abound in All Blacks memorabilia. So strong is the promotional marketing that New Zealanders come to feel as if they know many of the players on a personal level. Because New Zealand is a small country of just over 4 million people, this sense of personal relationship is further enhanced, because average New Zealanders do in fact occasionally find themselves in face-to-face contact with All Black players – in restaurants, pubs, social events, fundraising activities and so forth.

The Super 14

Apart from international test matches in which composite national teams participate, there are also international competitions involving provincial teams. The Super 14 is such a competition. Established in 1996 and played on an annual basis, it is the largest rugby union championship in the southern hemisphere. It consists of fourteen competing provincial teams from Australia (4), New Zealand (5) and South Africa (5).

The Super 14 has been dominated by a New Zealand team, the Crusaders, who have played in eight finals and won six. The most recent final was played in Christchurch, New Zealand, the home of the Crusaders. They played another New Zealand side, the Hurricanes from Wellington. In the final on 27 May 2006, interest in the game was heightened even further by the two players who captained the two opposing sides. Captain of the Crusaders was Richie McCaw, one of the finest players in the game and the new All Blacks captain. Captain of the Hurricanes was Tana Umaga, the immediate past captain of the All Blacks, a player who had been variously described as "a hero," "a mentor" and "a legend."

Tana Umaga

Tana Umaga was first selected to play for the All Blacks in 1997, and assumed the captaincy in 2004. In 2005 he led the All Blacks to their victory over the touring Lions from the United Kingdom, the Tri-Nations victory, and the Bledisloe Cup. Not only his captaincy but also his playing shone and that year he was short-listed as the World Player of the Year. In addition, Tana was instrumental in New Zealand's being awarded host nation status for the World Cup Rugby competition in 2011. His impassioned speech was broadcast around the world.

Despite having manifested some wild behaviour in his youth, Tana demonstrated a compassion and caring that was well-known among his teammates and opponents alike. In 2003 he took the highly unusual step of stopping play in an international match against Wales, to attend to the Welsh captain who had been knocked out in a tackle. He was awarded the Pierre de Coubertin trophy by the International Committee for Fair Play that year.

In addition to his humble upbringing, he was the first All Black captain born of Polynesian (Samoan) heritage. These two facts demonstrated to many in New Zealand and the world that fame and glory were possible for all, and not the prerogative of the wealthy or the members of a majority ethnic group (Spratt, 2006).

Tana had become a national icon – a national brand. He epitomized many of the New Zealand core values, and consistently delivered on the promise of his brand.

The Super 14 Final

It was thus with considerable excitement and passion that New Zealanders either turned out, or turned on their television sets, to watch the Super 14 final in May 2006. The fact that two New Zealand teams were playing meant that New Zealand as a country had already won, but it remained to determine which team within New Zealand was the best.

On the one hand, the Crusaders with their excellent track record, their captain being the new All Black captain, and playing on their home ground seemed like the favourites. On the other hand, the Hurricanes had had a very good season - and they had Tana as captain.

The build-up in the media had been enormous, but as the crowds poured into the stadium and as viewers watched preliminary events on television, less and less became visible. A thick fog had descended on the stadium. The players could barely see each other or the ball, and the crowd could hardly see anything unless it was not happening "close enough for them to smell the liniment" (Birkett, 2006). Goal kicking was done more by instinct than sight. Nevertheless, the game continued with the fog easing slightly in the middle. Eventually, the Crusaders won 19-12 in "a contest which can only be described as bizarre" (Birkett, 2006).

After the Match

As is the routine, after the match the teams each gathered to discuss the game, celebrate their success or drown their sorrows with their fans. The Hurricanes chose a tavern called The Jolly Poacher.

Patronized by a number of people, an incident took place, the repercussions of which were to prove even more newsworthy than the game. Hurricanes team member Chris Masoe tripped over a patron's feet. Perceiving this as deliberate action, he punched the patron. Tana then grabbed a female patron's handbag and smacked Chris over the head with it, with the intention of bringing him to order. A cellphone which was in the handbag was broken. Masoe himself – the 230 pound All Blacks loose forward - was quickly hustled out of the bar by his teammates.

The event was much publicized with ribald comments and cartoons being made of such a masculine hero as Tana resorting to using such a feminine accessory to settle a spat. A few days later Chris Masoe was fined $3000 by the New Zealand Rugby Union. Tana received no blame as he was seen to be trying to restore order to the situation.

However, the matter did not rest there. Prompted by her friends, the owner of the handbag, Nichole Davis, decided to auction the bag – on the New Zealand online auction site, TradeMe. On Thursday June 1st 2006, five days after the Super 14 final, the handbag appeared on Trade Me with the auction due to close at 6:59pm on June 3rd. The identity of the seller was not initially disclosed.

TradeMe

In the few short years of its existence, Trade Me had grown into a major New Zealand success story.

Founded in 1999 by Sam Morgan, an IT consultant who had dropped out of university, TradeMe offered New Zealand what e-Bay failed to – a trusted site for buying and selling goods in an auction format, geographic proximity of buyers and sellers, and a common cultural base.

In 1999, struggling to find a second-hand electric heater and frustrated by the lack of relevant information, it occurred to Sam that this might present a possible business opportunity. Being IT-savvy, he set about building the initial TradeMe classified ads website. Although it was slow to take off, Morgan slowly built up his business, staffing it in the early days with family and friends whom he could trust implicitly.

By the end of March 2000, TradeMe was running 6000 auctions a month, and the potential was evident. In 2001 e-Bay tried to break into the New Zealand market but was unsuccessful. TradeMe had already secured its homegrown advantage – "a site by New Zealanders for New Zealanders" (Absolutely Positively Wellington. Entrepreneurs – Trade Me, 2006).

Trade Me Ltd. continued to grow, to become New Zealand's largest online auction business. It operates a variety of websites, including TradeMe, Find Someone, Old Friends and Safe Trader, and offers members the opportunity to report fraud by means of the Community Watch. In 2005 it limited its membership to New Zealand and Australian residents in order to further reduce fraud and minimize payment problems. To improve the safety and trustworthiness of its auction environment even further, TradeMe prohibited the sale of a number of categories of items.

With the number of members and the volume of sales growing rapidly, TradeMe soon became recognized and trusted throughout New Zealand. By March 2003 250,000 auctions were being held each month. By July 2006 the number of active members exceeded 1.3 million, with an average number of 333,596 people visiting the site each day – over 8 percent of the entire population!

Just like Tana Umaga, TradeMe had become an iconic New Zealand success story. The fact that a local entrepreneur could build up a multi-million dollar business in less than eight years appealed to the entrepreneurial spirit of many New Zealanders, and also highlighted the fact that success and fortune were within everyone's grasp. Enhanced by media coverage of many of its activities, TradeMe had become a well-known brand (Hickey, 2006).

The Auction

Nichole Davis's handbag was made of vinyl, carried the Roxy label and retailed for around $30. The description of the item on TradeMe appeared as:

"These are the genuine articles.

Handbag was used by Tana Umaga to hit Chris Masoe at the Jolly Poacher in Christchurch after the Super 14 final. Cellphone that was broken in this bar incident is also included.

This can be verified as the genuine articles at time of purchase."

A photograph of the articles accompanied the description, a nickname for the seller was provided, and her location was reported as being Christchurch. The undisclosed reserve price was $1,500.

Bidding opened at $150 in the evening of May 31st. The next day the price rose to $260. On June 2nd the momentum built, and the bids began pouring in. These included many bogus bids which exceeded $1 million. (When they couldn't be verified they were excluded by TradeMe). By 08:15 the price had broken through the $1,000 ceiling and by 18:08 it had exceeded $10,000. By the end of the day, the highest bid was $17,000. The next day bidding started slowly; the first new bid was $21,569, entered at 11:19 a.m. However, a completely different group of players was participating, and within the last 35 minutes the eventual winner became a contender along with some seven other players.

Almost as soon as the handbag was offered up for auction, the media coverage began. On June 2nd, 17 newspapers, both national and provincial, carried articles about the auction. In 12 instances the title referred to Tana, and invariably the articles were on the front or second page and accompanied by a picture of either Tana or the handbag and the cellphone (as it appeared on the TradeMe site).

On June 3rd, 18 newspapers carried reports of the bidding. As on the previous day, the articles usually appeared on either of the first two pages. However, the article titles focused more on the auction than on Tana. Nine titles referred to the bidding frenzy, e.g. "Bidding through the roof…" and "Bidding for bashing bag goes ballistic". Seven titles referred to the value or price of the handbag, e.g. "Bidding leaps to $1 million for Umaga handbag" – reflecting one of the bogus bids. In addition, not only did some newspapers report on the number of hits, as had been done the previous day, but they also reported the total value of all the bids, which was often incorrectly noted as being $100 million or more.

In addition to the press, the various radio stations in New Zealand carried constant updates on the status of the bidding. Television news, both national public television as well as the commercial channels, featured the status of the bidding prominently in their peak time news reports. Even radio and television news programmes in the US, Australia, South Africa and the UK carried reports on the auction. Search engines, such as Google, frequently updated the details of the auction.

The ultimate winning bid – for the $30 handbag and the $100 broken cellphone – was $22750.

Thousands of contributions in the 'Comments on this auction' section appeared on the site. The comments included:

"Is there any blood on the handbag?"

"I think some of your profits should go to charity"

"This is so funny…I love the entrepreneurial aspect, good on you!"

"Hi. I called one network news as this is great. You are currently getting about 15 hits a second. This is your windfall, so go for it and get as much exposure as possible. It is all good clean fun and hurting no one."

"omg im never leaving home without a bag ever"

""OMG!!! Clever girls, good on you, enjoy the rewards, wahoo congratulations ☺ well done"

"How very NZ number 8 wire of you!" [reference to the New Zealand entrepreneurial approach of fixing everything with No 8 fencing wire]

"This is a great way to get famous quick, for the buyer I mean, they'll almost certainly be on the news tonight"

ANALYSIS AND DISCUSSION

In analyzing the case, two expert researchers worked closely with TradeMe in order to identify themes that emerged. Details of all aspects of the auction process and related media coverage had been recorded and/or collected by TradeMe, and in-depth analysis of these records was conducted by the researchers and members of the TradeMe company. This facilitated triangulation of the findings, and enhanced the interpretation of the various phenomena, as well as the value of the conclusions drawn.

With regard to the "standard model" of factors which determine final online auction prices, the case certainly demonstrated support for many of these factors. However, it also highlighted the even stronger influence of certain other factors, which are not part of the standard model. First, though, the support for the "standard model" factors is discussed.

Buyer Factors

The buyer factors which are supported are those which indicate both cognitive and hedonistic motivations. Obviously the bidders logically assessed the perceived value of the handbag and thus embarked on their auction participation.

The hedonistic influences came in the form of ownership of a trophy, the handbag (Bosnjak et al., 2006; Hou & Elliott, 2006). By association this ownership would bring them closer to the national hero, Tana Umaga. Even participation in the auction would reflect some small portion of that glory on the bidder.

"Does the bag still contain Tana DNA?"

"If I win the bid who will deliver the hand bag to me... Tana?"

The entertainment provided by the handbag auction was clearly an important aspect (Bosjnak et al., 2006; Hou & Elliott, 2010). Many of the comments on the TradeMe site alluded to the fun that the auction was providing, both for the participants and the viewers, and national media coverage ensured and enhanced the entertainment value.

"Good for you!:) You deserve every penny just for entertainment value!!!"

Clearly this wasn't a bargain hunting exercise (Hou & Elliott, 2010).

The competition element was also obvious as bids, as well as the number of hits on the site, soared higher and higher. Participation in the bidding was encouraged by comments on the TradeMe site.

"Come on New Zealand – make the auction have 1 million views, surely that has to be a world record for the internet"

The media also reported frequently on the auction progress. Some degree of "herd behaviour" was evident: the phrase "bidding frenzy" was used on numerous occasions by the media. This led to the many bogus bids of over $ 1 million as viewers and participants became swept up in the excitement.

The findings of Harcar et al. (2006) notwithstanding, the brand name of the handbag, Roxy, does not appear to have exerted any influence on the bidding, in terms of brand loyalty or perceived quality. The bag was made of vinyl and retailed for a low price. It was also easily available from retail stores. The eventual purchaser of the handbag certainly didn't pay over $22,000 because of the high quality of the bag itself (although it was noted that, while the cellphone inside the bag did break from the impact, the bag itself did not).

Seller Factors

With regard to the seller factors, contrary to some literature (Snijders & Zijdeman, 2004) but in agreement with others regarding e-tailing (Saastamoinen, 2009), the seller's reputation appears to have been completely irrelevant. The seller's name, Nichole Davis, was initially unknown but when it was disclosed, it made no apparent difference to the bidding. Consequently, there was no evidence of trust in, or loyalty to the seller. However, the bidders did appear to trust that the handbag was the genuine article. Also, the fact that the seller recognized the importance of the handbag to rugby fans classed her as someone who had regard for rugby in New Zealand. As such, the halo effect of the associative reference group of fellow supporters may have resulted in a transfer of loyalty to the seller, and also that she could be trusted with claiming that it was "the" handbag.

Site Factors

The site factors which appear to have exerted an influence were similar to those noted in the literature. The key words referring to Tana Umaga and the handbag on the auction site were sufficient triggers to cause the bidding frenzy which ensued (Stern & Stafford, 2006). The additional pictorial illustration further enhanced the informational quality of the listing (Janiszewski, 1998).

The auction type of last bid as opposed to a Dutch auction presented no ceiling to the bidding and thus provided the opportunity for an extraordinarily high final price Snijders & Zijdeman, 2004).

In addition, the virtual presence of many other online bidders comprised a strong reference group and appears to have led to an increased perceived value of the handbag (Gilkeson & Reynolds, 2003). Furthermore, this generated a degree of herd behaviour with regard to the bidding, with the comments on the site reflecting the enormous attractiveness of the auction and its progress.

"Holy Cow. There have been more than 3,500 viewings since I found the listing at 10:15 till now at 10:35. You will have all the techos at trademe going frantic to stop the site from crashing. This is so funny.... You go girl!!"

Obviously, the information system quality appeared sufficiently robust (Wu et al., 2009).

However, the existence of a reserve price, and a longer auction period, did not appear to have had any effect on the bidding and the final price. In fact, most of the auction's "action" took place in a relatively short time period.

Given the evidence of the existence of some of the more "standard" factors and their possible impact on the final price, the question arises as to whether other factors were present which could also have contributed to the high final price and the overall success of the auction.

AN EXTENDED MODEL

Clearly the price of the handbag and broken cellphone cannot be entirely understood in terms of the "standard model" of factors influencing the price of an auctioned item.

In order to understand the additional factors at play here, we draw upon the basic 4 Ps of the traditional marketing mix – product, place, promotion, price (McCarthy, 1960). Some have argued for extensions to the traditional marketing mix, e.g. Judd (1987) proposed "people" as the fifth P, and Kotler (1986) proposed "public relations" and "politics" as yet other Ps. Some have felt that the traditional marketing mix was outdated as a paradigm and should make place for the more recently developed relationship marketing (Webster, 1992). However, the original 4 Ps provide a tried-and-trusted basis for a marketing transaction, particularly in a situation such as this type of online auction where the focus is less on building a long term relationship with a customer. They are thus used as the point of departure for examining the case.

Product – Branding

As mentioned earlier, one of the drawbacks of online auctions is the inability for potential bidders to inspect the physical good prior to bidding. Ways in which this can be overcome are by means of extensive product descriptions and pictures (Snijders & Zijdeman, 2004) and by means of branding. Branding is an important contributor to perceived value and trust.

A brand is a name, term, design, symbol or any other feature that identifies one seller's good or service as distinct from those of other sellers (Bennett, 1988). Apart from commercial products and services, many things or people may be viewed as brands – universities, museums, medical practices, television stations, and people, either living or dead (Schmitt, 2000). Aaker (1992) identified four dimensions of strong brands: awareness, associations, perceived quality, and brand loyalty. Good branding thus focuses on understanding, communicating and delivering on the value proposition which is most important to a certain group of stakeholders (Lynch & De Chernatony, 2004). Consumers' familiarity and memory associations of the brand exert a strong influence on brand perception (Gwee, Hui and Chau, 2002), and because affective characteristics of brands are important in brand building, those brands which are based on trust, reassurance, responsiveness, a good reputation, and a strong image are seen to be more durable and less prone to competitive erosion (Aaker, 1998; Doyle, 2002).

Undoubtedly, brand strength played a major role in the handbag auction. However, it was not the branding of the auctioned item itself, but of a number of external or associated factors which played the pivotal roles. Strongest among these was the brand of Tana Umaga. It could be argued that the handbag, by virtue of having been "used" by him, became a brand extension and thus assumed some of the perceived value of Tana himself. This highlights the importance of acknowledging brand extensions, specifically, in contributing to final prices in auctions. There have been many examples of items used by celebrities attracting high auction prices.

In addition, the branding of rugby as a national sport in New Zealand and the branding of the Super 14, especially the final match, further enhanced the attraction of the auction and contributed to the final price.

Place (Site) - Branding

Another very important branding influence was that of TradeMe. Almost as iconic as rugby and Tana, the placement of the handbag up for auction on this website, aggregated the effect of many strong brands and resulted in a synergistic effect on the bidding prices.

Place (Site) - Timing

A further influential factor was the timing of placement of the item on the auction site. A minimal amount of time lapsed between The Jolly Poacher incident on 27 May and when the handbag first appeared on TradeMe on 31 May. Memories were still very vivid so that the seller could exploit that recency of that event to the maximum effect. Had she waited for a month or more, other events would have eclipsed the incident and it is doubtful whether the final price would have been nearly as high.

Furthermore, the auction only lasted for three calendar days and commenced in the middle of a week when it could be argued people were gearing up for weekend entertainment. Had the auction run for longer, it is possible that interest would have abated. Also, had the final day of the auction been a weekday, it is likely that the "action" at the end would not have been nearly so strong.

Promotion - Publicity

In marketing terms, promotion includes a number of strategies such as paid advertisements, sponsorships, trade promotions, direct mail, public relations, and publicity. Unlike public relations - which is what a person or an organization reports himself - publicity is what others report about the organization or individual (Kotler, 1986). One of the measures of promotional/publicity effectiveness is the extent of reach (number of relevant individuals reached), and the frequency (number of times that those individuals were reached) (Krugman, 1972).

In this case, a very important and very effective factor was the role that the media played in promoting and publicizing the auction, and in fanning the interest in its progress and enthusiasm to participate. The continuous stream of coverage, whether in the newspapers, on radio, on television or on the Internet, including the TradeMe site, forced an awareness of the auction event into nearly all New Zealand homes, to say nothing of additional homes worldwide.

"Watching from the USA. Congratulations on your windfall. Take the money and KEEP IT!"

"Watching from London"

The wording used in the captions and titles further inflamed the enthusiasm, e.g., "bidding frenzy," or "bidding on handbag goes through the roof." In addition, references to Tana Umaga ("Tana's handbag goes up for auction," "Umaga's handbag takes on a value of its own") further enhanced the brand extension. In addition, reference to TradeMe in the titles ("Infamous handbag a hit on TradeMe") embraced another famous New Zealand brand which had received wide media coverage from its recent sale.

The foregoing analysis suggests that the "standard model" of factors which determine the final prices, and thus the success, of online auctions, be extended to adequately accommodate instances such as this one. Specifically, our analysis suggests that certain adjustments to the "standard model" be made. Depending on what is being auctioned, different groups of factors will play a greater or lesser influential role. Buyer and seller factors remain unchanged. Site factors should be extended to include consideration of timing (e.g., when the good was first listed in relation to any relevant event, if applicable, and the specific start and end dates/times of the auction) and the brand strength of the auction site itself. Product factors need to be specifically included in the model. Although these would refer predominantly to the physical features of the product, there is also the need to accommodate the influence of brand strength, and brand extensions and associations with regard to both personalities and the event. Finally, Promotion should be included in the model, and should comprise media publicity and coverage of the events leading up to the auction, as well as the auction itself.

The proposed extended model is depicted in Figure 2.

CONCLUDING COMMENTS

Factors that have been seen to exert an influence on the final price in online auctions have typically fallen into one of three groups: buyer factors, seller factors and site factors. These were depicted in the "standard model" of online auction final price

Figure 2. An extended model of factors influencing the final price in online auctions

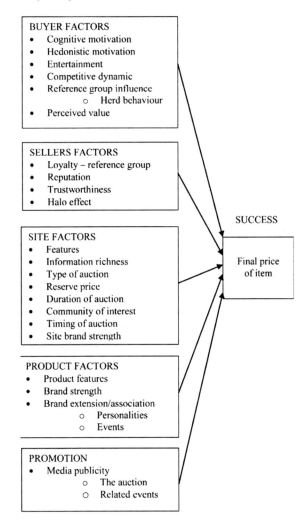

determinants. However, the case of The Rugby Player and the Handbag has clearly illustrated that in some cases, additional factors need to be considered as well.

Using the traditional marketing mix as the point of departure, the additional groups of factors which were identified were product factors (product features, brand strength, and brand extension/association) and promotion (media publicity). Two additional site factors (timing of "action", and site brand strength) were also identified as playing an important role. Together with the more standard three groups of factors, an extended model is proposed which depicts five groups of factors exerting an influence on the final price.

Although this case focused on a C2C auction, the same groups of factors can be applied to B2C and B2B auctions. It would be advisable for managers to consider the potential impact of each of these factors prior to an auction so that strategies could be devised for obtaining the optimal final price.

This extended model contains a number of important practical implications. From the perspective of sellers in an online auction, these additional factors provide points of leverage with which sellers may be able to influence the price others are willing to pay. Sellers should be aware of the potential opportunity to "capitalize" on these seemingly irrational influences. Similarly, buyers need to understand the potential price-escalating impacts of the extended model factors so that they can rationally weigh the various drivers of price, and decide whether they want to continue to compete in the auction. In some ways this is similar to investors in the stock market needing to differentiate the intrinsic value of a stock as compared to its current market value (which may be influenced by factors similar to those in the extended model). Finally, there are lessons here for operators of online auction sites such as Trade Me. Events such as the auctioning of the handbag generate huge interest in the auction site as well as the auction itself – a kind of free publicity. Opportunities may emerge for the auction site managers to enhance the reputation of the site in conjunction with the publicity surrounding the actual auction.

Additional research focusing on the proposed extensions to the standard auction outcome model would be useful. The effect of other aspects of promotion such as sponsorship and advertising, would be worth exploring. Also, insights into the relative importance of the various factors in the extended model as contingent on the specific situation, would provide valuable insights. This might take the form of a weighting scheme whereby the influence of the various factors of an online auction be weighted according to their significance and the estimated final price be calculated accordingly; or perhaps a contingency model suggesting situations in which certain factors would be more important than others.

While the case of the handbag auction is obviously unusual, it is by no means unique. Similar behaviours can be commonly witnessed in auctions of items of celebrity clothing and artefacts, or items related to specific events. The extended model accommodates both these types of auctions as well as the more standard types. The value of this model is that it raises the awareness of additional factors which can exert a considerable influence on the final price, and which should always be considered.

REFERENCES

Aaker, D. (1998). *Strategic Market Management*. New York: Wiley.

Aaker, D. A. (1992). Managing the most important asset: Brand equity. *Planning Review, 20*, 56–58.

Absolutely Positively Wellington. (2006*). Entrepreneurs – Trade Me*. Retrieved June 5, 2006 from http://www.wellington.govt.nz/aboutwgtn/ innovation/ details/trademe.html.

All Blacks. (2006).Retrieved July 23, 2006, from http://en.wikipedia.org/wiki/ All_Blacks.

Ba, S., & Pavlou, P. A. (2002). Evidence of the effect of trust building technology in electronic markets: price premiums and buyer behaviour. *Management Information Systems Quarterly, 26*, 243–266. doi:10.2307/4132332

Bejou, D., Ennew, C., & Palmer, A. (1998). Trust, ethics and relationship satisfaction. *International Journal of Bank Marketing, 16*(4), 276–286. doi:10.1108/02652329810220729

Bennett, P. D. (1988). *Dictionary of Marketing Terms*. Chicago, IL: The American Marketing Association.

Birkett, G. (2006). *McCaw's cup runneth over*. Fairfax New Zealand. Retrieved July 23, 2006, from http://www.stuff.co.nz/stuff/print/0,1478,3682753a1823,00.html.

Bosnjak, M., Obermeier, D., & Tuten, T. L. (2006). Predicting and explaining the propensity to bid in online auctions: A comparison of two action-theoretical models. *Journal of Consumer Behaviour, 5*(2), 102–116. doi:10.1002/cb.38

Brinkman, U., & Siefert, M. (2001). Face-to-interface - the establishment of trust in the Internet: The case of e-auctions. *Journal of Sociology (Melbourne, Vic.), 30*, 2347.

Burnkrant, R. E., & Cousineau, A. (1975). Informational and normative social influence in buyer behaviour. *The Journal of Consumer Research, 2*(3), 206–215. doi:10.1086/208633

Dholakia, U. M., & Soltysinski, K. (2001). Coveted or overlooked? The psychology of bidding for comparable listings in digital auctions. *Marketing Letters, 12*(3), 225–237. doi:10.1023/A:1011164710951

Dolam, R. J., & Moon, Y. (2000). Pricing and market-making on the internet. *Journal of Interactive Marketing, 14*(2), 56–73.

Doyle, P. (2002). *Marketing Management and Strategy. Financial Times*. Harlow, England: Prentice Hall.

Gilkeson, J. H., & Reynolds, K. (2003). Determinants of Internet auction success and closing price: An exploratory study. *Psychology and Marketing, 20*(6), 537–542. doi:10.1002/mar.10086

Goethals, G. R. (1976). An attributional analysis of some social influence phenomena. In Harvey, J. H., Ickes, W. J., & Kidd, R. F. (Eds.), *New Directions in Attribution Research* (*Vol. 1*, pp. 291–310). Hillside, NJ: Lawrence Erlbaum.

Gwee, J.-T., Hui, K.-L., & Chau, P. Y. K. (2002). Determinants of brand equity in e-businesses: An exploratory study. *Proceedings of the Twenty-Third International Conference on Information Systems,* Barcelona, 617-627.

Harcar, T., Kara, A., & Kucukemiroglu, O. (2006). Consumer's perceived value and buying behavior of store brands: An empirical investigation. *Business Review (Federal Reserve Bank of Philadelphia), 5*(2), 55–62.

Hickey, B. (2006). *Fairfax acquires Trade Me for $700m*. Retrieved July 5, 2006, from http://www.stuff.co.nz/stuff/print/0,1478,3594845a10,00.html.

Higgs, H. & Worthington, A. (2005). Financial returns and price determinants in the *Australian art market*, 1973-2003.

Hofacker, C. (1999). *Internet Marketing*. Dripping Springs, TX: Digital Spring.

Holt, B. (1997). Poststructuralist lifestyle analysis: conceptualizing the social pattern of consumption in postmodernity. *The Journal of Consumer Research, 23*(3), 326–350. doi:10.1086/209487

Hou, J., & Elliott, K. (2010). Profiling online bidders. *Journal of Marketing Theory and Practice, 18*(2), 109–126. doi:10.2753/MTP1069-6679180201

Hsu, L.-C., & Wang, C.-H. (2008). A study of e-trust in online auctions. *Journal of Electronic Commerce Research, 9*(4), 310–321.

Ibeh, K. I. N., Luo, Y., & Dinnie, K. (2005). E-branding strategies of internet companies: Some preliminary insights from the UK. *Journal of Brand Management, 12*(5), 355–373. doi:10.1057/palgrave.bm.2540231

Janiszewski, C. (1998). The influence of display characteristics on visual exploratory search behaviour. *The Journal of Consumer Research, 25*(3), 290–301. doi:10.1086/209540

Judd, V. C. (1987). Differentiate with the 5th P: people. *Industrial Marketing Management, 16*, 241–247. doi:10.1016/0019-8501(87)90032-0

Kagel, J. H. (1995). Auctions: a survey of experimental research. In Kagel, J., & Roth, A. (Eds.), *Handbook of Experimental Economics* (pp. 501–585). Princeton, NJ: Princeton University Press.

Katkar, R., & Lucking-Reiley, D. (2000). *Public versus secret reserve prices in eBay auctions: Results from a Pokemon field experiment*. Unpublished paper. Arizona State University.

Kotler, P. (1986). Megamarketing. *Harvard Business Review, 64*(2), 117–124.

Liang, T. P., & Doong, H. S. (2000). Effect of bargaining in electronic commerce. *International Journal of Electronic Commerce, 4*(3), 23–43.

Lucking-Reiley, D., Bryan, D., Prasad, N., & Reeves, D. (2000). *Pennies from eBay: the determinants of price in online auctions*. Working paper, Vanderbilt University.

Lynch, J., & De Chernatony, L. (2004). The power of emotion: Brand communication in business-to-business markets. *Journal of Brand Management, 11*(5), 403–419. doi:10.1057/palgrave.bm.2540185

Massad, V. J., & Tucker, J. M. (2000). Comparing bidding and pricing between in-person and online auctions. *Journal of Product and Brand Management, 9*(5), 32–44. doi:10.1108/10610420010347128

Mazursky, D., & Jacoby, J. (1985). Forming impressions of merchandise and service quality. In Jacoby, J., & Olson, J. (Eds.), *Perceived Quality* (pp. 139–154). Lexington, MA: Lexington Books.

McCarthy, E. J. (1960). *Basic Marketing*. Homewood, Ill: Irwin.

McDougall, G., & Levesque, T. (2000). Customer satisfaction with services: putting perceived value into the equation. *Journal of Services Marketing, 14*(5), 392–410. doi:10.1108/08876040010340937

Melnick, M. I., & Alm, J. (2005). Seller reputation, information signals, and prices for heterogeneous coins on eBay. *Southern Economic Journal, 72*(2), 305–328. doi:10.2307/20062113

Moschis, G. M. (1976). Social comparison and informal group influence. *JMR, Journal of Marketing Research, 13*(3), 237–244. doi:10.2307/3150733

Moschis, G. M. (1987). *Consumer Socialization*. Lexington, Mass: D.C. Health.

New Zealand Tourism Online. (2006). Retrieved July 23, 2006, from http://www.tourism.net.nz/featured-events/all-blacks/.

Nisbett, R. E., & Ross, I. (1980). *Human Inference: Strategies and Shortcomings of Social Judgment*. Engelwood Cliffs, NJ: Prentice-Hall.

Pedersen, P. E., & Nysveen, H. (2001). Shopbot banking: an exploratory study of customer loyalty effects. *International Journal of Bank Marketing, 19*(4), 146–155. doi:10.1108/02652320110392518

Rafaeli, S., & Noy, A. (2002). Online auctions, messaging, communication and social facilitation: a simulation and experimental evidence. *European Journal of Information Systems, 11*, 196–207. doi:10.1057/palgrave.ejis.3000434

Rappa, M. A. (2004). The utility business model and the future of computing services. *IBM Systems Journal, 43*(1), 32–42. doi:10.1147/sj.431.0032

Resnick, P., & Zeckhauser, R. (2002). *Trust among strangers in Internet transactions: Empirical analysis of eBay's reputation system. The economics of the Internet and e-commerce* (pp. 127–157). Amsterdam: Elsevier Science.

Roth, A., & Ockenfels, A. (2002). Last-minute bidding and the rules for ending second-price auctions: Evidence from eBay and Amazon auctions on the Internet. *The American Economic Review, 92*, 1093–1103. doi:10.1257/00028280260344632

Rugby World Cup, I. R. B. (2006). Retrieved July 24, 2006, from http://www.rugbyworldcup.com/EN/Home/News/051117+dk+rwc2011.htm.

Schmitt, B. (2000). Branding puts a high value on reputation management. *Financial Times (North American Edition), 13*(June), 6–9.

Snijders, C., & Zijdeman, R. (2004). Reputation and internet auctions: eBay and beyond. *Analyse & Kritik, 26*(1), 158–184.

Spratt, A. (2006). Tana – the man behind the legend. *The New Zealand Herald*. Retrieved July 13, 2006, from http://www.nzherald.co.nz/topic/story.cfm?c_id=116&ObjectID=10363762.

Stern, B. B., & Stafford, M. R. (2006). Individual and social determinants of winning bids in online auctions. *Journal of Consumer Behaviour, 5*(1), 43–55. doi:10.1002/cb.47

Taylor, S. E., & Thompson, S. C. (1982). Stalking the elusive "vividness" effect. *Psychological Review, 89*, 155–181. doi:10.1037/0033-295X.89.2.155

Webster, F. E. Jnr. (1992). The changing role of marketing in the corporations. *Journal of Marketing, 56*(Oct), 1–17. doi:10.2307/1251983

Wilcox, R. T. (2000). Experts and amateurs: The role of experience in Internet auctions. *Marketing Letters, 11*, 363–374. doi:10.1023/A:1008141313927

Wu, W.-H., Lin, B., & Cheng, C.-F. (2009). Evaluating online auction strategy: A theoretical model and empirical exploration. *Journal of Computer Information Systems, 49*(3), 22–30.

Zeithaml, V. A. (1988). Consumer perceptions of price, quality, and value: A means-end model and synthesis of evidence. *Journal of Marketing, 52*(3), 2–22. doi:10.2307/1251446

Chapter 18

Critical Factors to Successful Website Development:
Opinions of Website Designers and Developers

Pradeep Korgaonkar
Florida Atlantic University, USA

Bay O'Leary
Nova Southeastern University, USA

Ronnie Silverblatt
Florida International University, USA

Kevin Korgaonkar
University of Rochester, USA

ABSTRACT

This study was conducted to help understand the factors involved in building a successful website. A national survey of professionals in the areas of website design and development were contacted. Based on past published writings in the literature eight factors were identified as critical to the success of website functionality. The factors that are consistently posited in the literature are: 1) Entertainment and Visual Appeal, 2) Reliability, 3) Cost Reductions Attained, 4) Back-End Processes Enabled, 5) Personalization, 6) Information Quality, 7) User Empowerment, and 8) Privacy/Security. Study results are based on the analysis of 349 responses and provide support for the research hypotheses.

INTRODUCTION

The field of electronic commerce is registering significant and sustainable growth in the U.S.A. Originally, the primary purpose of a website was to provide information about a company and its products/services. Today, companies utilize websites as an efficient and convenient way to provide these products and services to their customers in addition to helping them develop and maintain long term relationships with these customers. In the United States alone, there are over 210 million users of the Internet; this equates to almost

DOI: 10.4018/978-1-60960-132-4.ch018

Copyright © 2011, IGI Global. Copying or distributing in print or electronic forms without written permission of IGI Global is prohibited.

70% of the population. Worldwide, over 1 billion people (World Internet Usage, 2007) are surfing the the millions of websites on the Web (http://www.geekpedia.com; http://www.ciadvertising.org). With new websites being created every minute, it is impossible to know the precise number of websites. The plethora of Web development tools available has simplified the launching of new websites; this has led many entrepreneurs and businesses to rush website development, often at the cost of quality issues. Clearly, the old axiom, "If you build it, they will come" may no longer be applicable to website design. For many businesses, the problem is two-fold; they do not: (1) fully understand how a successful website gives them a competitive advantage, and (2) know how to produce a successful website (Eisammani, Hackney, and Scown, 2004). In a study conducted by Forrester Research (cited in Neilson, 1998b), it was found that 50% of lost sales were due to inadequate website design. Lost sales were attributed to customers who left the website because they either (a) couldn't navigate the site to complete a purchase, or (b) were not able to find what they wanted on the site even though the item was listed. Similarly, Schaffer (2000), states that one reason consumers leave a website without making a purchase is because they are unable to navigate their way through the site. In addition, once a consumer has had a negative experience on a website, they are less prone to return to the site resulting in an even greater loss of potential revenue. Unless a site can convince a visitor to remain on the website it is difficult to establish a rapport with the visitor. Myspace.com and Yahoo.com are the first and second most popular websites because of their fast and simplistic design (http://internet.seekingalpha.com/article/25309). Similarly, in the U.K., consumers voted Profile-heaven.com the best website of 2006 because of its content, navigation, and design; this suggests that designing a successful website improves a company's standing in the marketplace (http://www.websiteoftheyear.co.uk/winners.php).

Clearly, a website is an interface between an organization and its stakeholders such as customers, financial community, suppliers, etc. The interface is strategically important so as to gain a competitive advantage both locally as well as globally. As a consequence, a few studies have attempted to determine how consumers evaluate websites. However, little is known about what those who actually create, operate, and maintain the website operations think regarding the key issues of website design. Although consumers' opinions are important, we believe it is equally important to seek the opinion of the professionals in the field regarding the factors they think make or break website operations. For most establishments, it is either too difficult or cost prohibitive to seek the opinions of consumers. As a result, companies are forced to rely on the expertise of Web designers. For example, in a survey of small and medium size businesses, over 80% sought assistance of Web designers and developers outside their organizations before activating their websites (Eisammani, Hackney, Scown, 2004).

Thus, this study fills an important void in the existing literature. This void is filled by (1) surveying professionals in the area of website design and development, (2) polling a national sample of Web designers and developers instead of using convenience samples of past studies, and (3) building upon past exploratory studies by focusing on the factors reported to be significant in more than one study.

Published writings in the literature suggest eight factors are critical to website functionality success; these factors are the basis for this study and are discussed in the next section.

LITERATURE REVIEW

Electronic commerce continues to grow rapidly and has reached almost all sectors of the economy. Still, online commerce often lacks the physical touch, feel, and smell, associated with traditional off-line businesses. As a consequence, the website performs the function of a salesperson, helping to build trust in customers' minds about the company and its offerings (Del Giudice & del Giudice, 2003). As suggested by Reichheld and Schefter (2000), a successful website should encourage customer loyalty. This is easier said than done as customers have literally millions of websites from which to choose. Recognizing the arduous task that businesses have of attracting and retaining repeat visitors to websites, a number of past academic studies and trade books have attempted to offer solutions addressing the issue of successful website development and creation (e.g. Nielsen, 2000; Nielsen, 2003; Ranganathan & Ganapathy, 2002; Ranganathan & Grandon, 2005; Palmer, 2002). These studies and professional books provide useful insights regarding the factors that may influence the success or failure of websites. Still, as correctly pointed out by Lin and Lu (2000) and Dhyani et al. (2002), implicit assumptions about successful websites and factors responsible for their success are not clearly known. A large portion of past studies have been conducted primarily using convenience sampling to survey customers (e.g. Light & Wakeman, 2001; Pollard and Blyth, 1999). The studies have either focused on the content or the functions of websites. For example, the studies have looked at the issues of relevance or quality of content (Perkowitz & Etzioni, 1999; Bhatii et al., 2000) and functions such as interface and search engine (Slatin, 2001; Thelwall, 2000). A large number of studies have been exploratory rather than confirmatory in nature (Liu & Arnett, 2000; Simeon, 1999). Adding to the confusion is the fact that a variety of different factors have been studied in the past with studies not consistently identifying and building on previous work of others (see for example Zang & Myers, 2005, Cao & Zhang, 2005, Nour & Fadlalla, 2000; Nielsen, 2003; Ranganathan & Ganapathy, 2002; Palmer, 2002; Jones, Clarke-Hill, Shears, & Hillier, 2001). Given the plethora of variables studied in the past, our study builds upon previ-

ous research and focuses on those key factors that have been reported to be significant in more than one study. The factors that are consistently posited in the literature are: 1) Entertainment and Visual Appeal, 2) Reliability, 3) Cost Reductions Attained, 4) Back-End Processes Enabled, 5) Personalization, 6) Information Quality, 7) User Empowerment, and 8) Privacy/Security. These factors have been statistically supported in the published studies (e.g. Chakraborty, 1 Lala, Warren, 2003; Zhuang & Giesel M. von Dran, 2000; Nielsen, 2003; Ranganathan & Ganapathy, 2002; Ranganathan & Grandon, 2005; Palmer, 2002).

Each of the eight factors is discussed below:

1)Entertainment and Visual Appeal: This factor relates to the aesthetic and affective aspect of the website design. It refers to how well the website is designed in terms of visual as well as audio characteristics and the creative elements embodied within the site. Web designers such as Nigel Homes approach the design of a site using a 'point of view.' He takes information and translates it into understandable forms. No matter how accurate and usable a design needs to be, that won't come through to the user unless the visual is able to attract them into the site (Mok, 1996). Website design faces the challenge of orienting the user to the meaning and flow of the site as well as creating an immediate relationship between the user and the information presented. It must address the issues of the color, text, font size, videos and sound, all of which contribute to the appeal of the website.

The visuals refers to how well the graphic design principles are adhered to so as not to detract from the informational content on the website. User gratification literature in the mass communication discipline suggests that entertainment and visuals are important in drawing a visitor to a website (Anderson & Meyer, 1975; King, 1998; Katterattanakul, 2002). The Korgaonkar and Wolin (1999) study suggest that entertainment is one of the major gratifications sought by consumers for surfing on the Web. Humor has also been found to play a part in the entertainment aspect of a website (Katterattanakul, 2002). A study on the acceptance of hand held Internet devices found that the attribute of how much 'fun' the device offered was even more important than the utilitarian feature of 'usefulness' of the device (Bruner & Kunar, 2005). Many examples in the virtual world bear out these assumptions. Bingo players return again and again to riverbellebingo.com to play bingo in a highly social and fun environment. Chat rooms are available where players can take a break and socialize with other visitors, creating a 'bingo' community (PR Newswire, 2007). Universal Pictures has recently launched a visually rich and compelling interactive mobile web (WAP) that consumers can enjoy on their mobile phones. Universal is a pioneer in integrating technology with its marketing strategy (PR Newswire, 2007). Therefore, we hypothesize:

H1: *The entertainment and visual appeal factor will be positively associated with successful websites.*

2) *Reliability*: This factor refers to the ability of the user to order a product/service or retrieve information from the website on a consistent basis. Reliability is a key factor in any product/service transaction. In one study it was rated as the most important factor in the deliverability of services (Parasuraman, Zeithaml & Barry, 1993). When transferring the concept of reliability to the design of a website, it is often difficult to convince customers that their transaction will be performed as they expect. A reliable website allows for error free transactions and, correspondingly, results in users developing trust with the company and their website. The site must be able to deliver accurate computing and error free transactions if it is to be viewed as a reliable site (Katterattanakul, 2002). Another study found that the type of processing system utilized was important to the integrity of the site (DeLone & MacLean, 1992).

Several companies' measure reliability as an aspect of the site's ranking. Despite providing users with fast response times, many mobile sites still had problems with reliability issues and outages (Wireless Week, Sept. 1, 2005). The head of marketing and communications for the financial website TrustNet, found that reliability of service and ease of use were the crucial elements linked to the success of TrustNet (Money Marketing, Nov. 20, 2003). The American Accreditation Healthcare Commission will only give its seal of approval to heath-related websites, such as WebMD, if the site assures the reliability of online health information and protects users' privacy (Pharmaceutical Executive, Jan. 2002). In order to create a trustworthy website a company needs sufficient technical, financial, and managerial resources. Without the necessary resources the reliability of the website would be doubtful and there would be the possibility of failure. So we hypothesize:

H2: *The higher the reliability of the website, the higher the probability the website will be successful.*

3) *Costs Reductions*: One of the benefits of the Internet is its ability to provide business performance efficiencies. For example, the disintermediary function provided by website operations allows a company to deliver its goods directly to customers, thus enabling the company to achieve significant costs reductions in procurement, distribution, and marketing. Firms place 'cookies' on user's customers; 'cookies" are small files firms designed to allow them to track the customer (Laudon, 2004). When the customer returns to the website, the firm retrieves the data placed on the cookie and can respond to the customer in a personalized manner. Popular travel websites such as Travelocity, Expedia and Orbitz are helping companies reduce the skyrocketing cost of air travel by setting fare parameters and routing employees to less expensive flights and hotels.

Memorial Health System has been experimenting with best supply chain practices. It anticipates saving over \$2 million per year. On average, hospitals using GHX software report 25% fewer ordering errors and 80% reduction in order discrepancies (Hospital Materials Management, 2005). The success of online companies such as E-bay is directly related to the cost reductions that are attainable because of their successful website operations.

A recently published study designed to measure the business benefits of electronic commerce (Zhuang & Lederer, 2003) reports cost reductions and back-end efficiencies as the two important benefits of e-commerce. Some firms view their website as a way to reduce both their number of employees and compensation costs as well as flatten their management structure. As a result of these moves, the company becomes more flexible and increases their competitive advantage. We hypothesize that:

H3: *The higher cost reductions achieved by the website operation, the greater the chances of creating a successful website.*

4) *Back End Operations*: In addition to cost reductions, the website operation allows a company to improve efficiencies in the company's backend operation. For example, in a published study of users versus nonusers of electronic data interchanges the authors found a significant difference in the backend improvement of the two groups. Specifically, the user group, when compared to the nonusers, had improvement in back end operations such as customer service, data control, less clerical errors, etc. Tiwana and Ramesh (1999), suggest that one of the key benefits of e-commerce investment is improving internal business process. We expect that by providing electronic tracking services of shipped products/services and electronic billing services, the company is able to improve its customer service. Additionally, electronic auditing and data control operations contribute to improving the efficiency and effectiveness of the website. With functionalities such as extranet designed into the website, vendors can access the portion of the site suitable to their needs. They can determine in real time how much stock the company has and when to refill stock. The globalization of business has infiltrated website design by allowing instant communications with and between regional offices. Tools such as intranets are allowing companies to 'meet' through the firm's website. Software such as Trackpoint allows easy tracking of the real-time status of projects and is especially useful to subcontractors (Contractor, 2005). Broadband Internet connections are revamping back-end systems in warehousing. The new systems connect shippers faster to their inventory and transportation information (Traffic World, 2006). Curt Barry, an operations consultant, states, "Back-end technology is so pervasive today that without it even the most resourceful operations executive would find it tough to perform basic warehouse tasks" (Catalog Age, 2003). This leads us to hypothesize:

H4: *The greater the improvements in back end operations, the higher the chances are of creating a successful website.*

5) *Personalization*: As defined by Chakrabory, Lala and Warren (2003), personalization means treating Web visitors as individuals as opposed to grouping them together. As suggested by Bakos (1991, 1997), one of the important ways to reduce customers' frustrations and search costs is by providing customized information. The personalization features allow the website developer to overcome the impersonal nature of the Internet. In addition, personalizing a customer's website allows the customer to interact with the site in a quick, efficient manner. A purchase can be made using a 'one-click' technology such as that used by Amazon.com, or a user can make a one-time purchase using only a password for access to the users file.

Companies such as Changing World are marketing software that will personalize ad campaigns to ensure relevance to the customer. Clixsmart is an example of personalization technology that is currently available (Business Wire, 2007). Specific customer segments are being targeted by personalized sites such as BOOMj.com. This is a social network geared toward the Baby Boomers (PR Newwire, 2007). Ellen T. Fisher, who spearheaded websites for women, thinks that the future of websites is about filters, buying recommendations and creative personalization" (Knight Ridder Tribune Business News, 2007). Hence, we hypothesize:

H5: *The higher the degree of personalization, the higher the chance of success.*

6) *Information Quality*: Early critics of the Internet posited that the information on the Web consisted mainly of advertising and personal promotion. As such, the medium was looked at as being of "dubious quality." They suggested that things such as the standing and professional qualifications of the site's author be identified as well as identifying the source of the content (Wilkinson, Bennett & Oliver, 1997). Increasingly, the quality of information is becoming more important to web surfers than the quantity of information. As stated by Lohse and Spiller (1998), web surfers want careful, continuous, useful communication across geographic boundaries. It is important that the website users know that the information posted on the site is reliable, accurate, and trustworthy. This is validated in a study of hygiene and motivating factors used in website evaluations reported by Zhang and von Dran (2000). The researchers surveyed website users to find out the biggest motivating factor in the users' evaluation of the websites; the users indicated the level of learning and/or new skills acquired from the website as the most important factors leading to a positive evaluation. Another study validated that the quality of the website was

instrumental in the success of the site (Palmer, 2002). Functionalities such as order taking, delivery and customer knowledge need to be accurate in order for a firm to succeed. Laudon (2004) sees the quality of information as a direct link to the quality of decision making. He offers seven dimensions of information quality on a website. These dimensions are accuracy, integrity, consistency, completeness, validity, timeliness and accessibility. If the underlying information is wrong, decision-making suffers. Yang, Hung, Sung and Farn (2006) found third party seals and product information quality positively affected consumers' trust and led to more high involvement. A website called Internet Detective provides an introduction to issues of information quality and teaches users how to evaluate the quality of a website (Pack, 1999). Since there is relatively no quality control on the Internet, Donald Hawkins offers advice on how to determine what information is credible. He advises the use of site reviews, considering links to and from the site, and the use of WWW Virtual Library on information quality to view selected sites (Hawkins, 1999). Hence, we hypothesize:

H6: *As the quality of the information content improves, so does the success of websites.*

7) *User Empowerment*: One of the pivotal features of the Internet is the fact that it allows the surfer to interactively choose when and how to surf the net (Korgaonkar & Wolin, 1999). The organization of the pages on the website should make logical sense to the surfers thereby improving their ability to navigate (Porter, 2003; Eleniak, 2003). An excellent example is the electronic auctioneer Ebay.com. Ebay's system allows the prospective bidder to find out all the details of the ongoing bid for a product or service. Additionally, it provides a safeguard of security of payments via its trademark system called Paypal. The prospective purchaser has multiple opportunities to change the bidding price up until last minute. Thus, the user feels he/she is in charge

of his/her bidding strategy. The attribute of easy navigability further reinforces the idea that the surfer is in charge (Lawton, 2007). Websites such as YouTube and MySpace are empowering users to display their personal information. A recent study by Chakraborty, Lala, and Warren (2003) of business customers suggested that interactivity with the website as one of the top two important factors in their assessments of the websites. The factor of interactivity relates to the control the surfer has in navigating the website. This leads us to hypothesize:

H 7: *As the degree of user empowerment increases, so does the success of websites.*

8) *Privacy and Security*. The fact that personal information is transmitted through many different systems and servers before it reaches the final destination has website designers incorporating as many security systems into the site as deemed necessary. There are many ways to access and penetrate a website, such as through the users' computer, the actual communications lines and the corporate servers. Users can experience unauthorized access, worms and viruses. The lines that transmit data are vulnerable to theft, fraud and message alteration. Corporate servers can experience hacking, viruses, worms and denial of service attacks (Laudon, 2004). Almost every week there is a story in the popular media related to the issues of breach of privacy and security from federal government computers. For example, data on millions of veterans was stolen and private businesses such as AOL have reported accidentally releasing subscriber data (InformationWeek, Feb.12, 2007). In May 2007, banking giant J.P. Morgan 'lost' data containing information on 47,000 high-end accounts in the Chicago area. In September 2006, 2.6 million Circuit City account holders were notified that their data had been accidentally discarded. John's Hopkins University and John's Hopkins Hospital lost data on more than 135,000 patients (WSJ, 2007). The constant

barrage of stories related to Internet fraud due to stolen identities and consumer financial records have made this issue of major concern (Yoon, 2002; Korgaonkar & Wolin, 1999). A recent poll by the Pew organization validates that the respondents were worried about the lack of control over the collection, use, and sharing of personal information over the Internet.

Secure websites are necessary for e-commerce to thrive (Fallows, 2005; Fox, 2000). A company called Truste, which certifies over 1,500 websites, found that consumers are more likely to feel comfortable using a site that has a seal of security much akin to the old Good Housekeeping Seal. New websites such as newegg.com proudly display the Truste symbol (Stark & Wind, 2005). Several privacy protection laws have been enacted to aid in the fight against illegal use of information. The Gramm-Leach-Bliley Act of 1999 includes protection for customers of financial services. The Health Insurance Portability and Accountability Act of 1996 (HIPAA) protects against a person's medical records being released to unauthorized individuals (Laudon, 2004). Several studies have found that the ability to provide a site that employs a secure accessing message such as e-trust will have a better chance at convincing a potential customer to buy from that site than other sites. (Ba, Winston & Zang, 999; Javenpaa & Todd, 1997; Guay & Ettwein, 1998). Thus we hypothesize

H8: *As the privacy and security issues are addressed successfully, it will improve the websites' chances of success.*

The next section details the method used to test the aforementioned hypotheses.

METHOD

The data for the study was collected by surveying 3000 national Web designers and developers. The data collection was conducted in three phases. First, a pre-notification letter was sent indicating the purpose of the project and seeking their cooperation. Second, each respondent was mailed two identical questionnaires except one was clearly titled and labeled as successful and the other unsuccessful. They were requested to respond to either or both questionnaires based on their past experiences. The respondents were assured of both confidentiality and anonymity. Several weeks later, the same two questionnaires were mailed again to the respondents urging them to respond only if they had not done so previously. A total of 349 usable responses were obtained from the mailing.

Measurement

SUCCESS/UNSUCCESS: The dependent variable of successful vs. unsuccessful was measured as a dichotomous (1) success, and (2) unsuccessful variable. The measurement was consistent with the past research in e-commerce as well as in other business areas and provide nomological validity (e.g., Tai, 2007; Cooper, 1979 ; Smith, 2003; Macmillan, Zemann &. Subbanarasimha, 1987; Korgaonkar & Bellenger, 1985; Korgaonkar, Moschis & Bellenger, 1984, Korgaonkar & O'Leary, 2006). Additionally, the respondents were asked to provide criteria used to determine if the website was a success or failure based on checking one or more of the following six options: online sales, usability of the site, post purchase service, customers' comments, number of clicks on the website, and other. The Chi Square test indicated no significant difference (6.01 with 5 degrees of freedom, p<. 75) between the six types of success/failure responses and overall success/failure. Hence, the hypothesis testing was carried out with the overall success/failure measures as the dependent variable.

Sample Profile

Pertinent background information was collected regarding the company, the market, the product, and the degree of involvement of the respondents in the website development. The data related to these variables is shown in Table 1.

Independent Variables

The survey instrument for the study was developed based on published studies in the area (e.g. Chakraborty, Lala & Warren 2003; Zang & von Dran 2000; Zhung & Lederer 2003; Ranganathan & Ganapathy 2002; Palmer, 2002). As stated earlier, each survey was clearly marked as either "successful" or "unsuccessful" on the top of each questionnaire. Additionally, the caption pertaining to the survey statements read as follows, "Below you will find statements about successful (unsuccessful) Web site that you were involved with". Please indicate the level of agreement with each statement on a scale of (1) completely disagree, (2) strongly disagree, (3) somewhat disagree, (4) neutral, (5) somewhat agree (6) strongly agree (7) completely agree." This was followed by the statements designed to tap the eight factors of visual appeal, reliability, cost reductions, backend operations, personalization, information quality, user empowerment, privacy and security. The items designed to tap the eight factors were factor analyzed via varimax rotation. The results of the factor analysis are reported in Table 2. The results indicated the presence of hypothesized eight factors with Eigen values greater than one and explaining almost 75 percent variance. Table 2 shows each factor and statements that clearly loaded on only one factor with loading values of 0.5 or higher. A scale for each individual construct from the factor analysis was created by summing up the responses to the corresponding items. The factor analysis provided the construct validity of

Table 1.Profile of the survey respondents

Possible Responses	Percent
How involved were you with the Web site development?	
Very Involved	34
Somewhat involved	27
Slightly involved	18
Not involved	21
Did the company have a physical presence?	
Yes	75
No, it was purely e-business	23
No response	2
Were the products/services digital, physical or both?	
Digital	30
Physical	42
Physical	42
Would you consider the company financially sound?	
Yes	86
No	14
The company's market was:	
Consumer	43
Business	27
Both	30
The company size was:	
Large, 250 or more employees	53
Medium, 100-249 employees	30
Small, less than 100 employees	17
The company's market scope was primarily:	
Local	26
Regional	31
National	33
International	10
*What criteria did you use to determine if the website was a success/failure?**	
Online Sales	24.1
Usability of the site	31.1
Post-purchase service	3.1
Customer comments	13.6
Number of Clicks on the site	22.6
Other	5.5
*Check all that apply. Multiple responses possible	

Table 2. Factor Analysis of the Statements Designed to Measure the Eight Constructs* and the reliability coefficient Alpha of the composite scales

Construct	Statements	Loadings	Reliability Alpha
1) Entertainment and Visual Appeal	The website was fun to explore	0.701	
	The website design made use of appropriate multimedia.	0.708	0.912
	The website was entertaining	0.729	
	The website had eye-catching images and/or title on the homepage.	0.815	
	The website had attractive screen background and pattern.	0.812	
2) Reliability	The website enabled error-free transactions	0.659	
	The website was reliable from the users' perspectives	0.606	0.894
	The website was supported with sufficient technical resources.	0.638	
	The website was supported with sufficient financial resources.	0.715	
	The website was supported by trained personnel	0.685	
3) Cost Reductions Attained	The website reduced administrative costs	0.737	
	The website reduced customer support costs	0.787	0.901
	The website reduced information processing costs	0.699	
	The website reduced marketing costs	0.690	
4) Back End Processes Enabled	The website facilitated shipment tracing for the company	0.804	
	The website facilitated billing function of the company	0.819	0.853
	The website facilitated electronic auditing for the company	0.785	
5) Personalization	The website gave personal attention to the user	0.692	
	The website had features that made it easier to personalize it to the User's needs	0.825	0.884
	The website stored users' preferences and offered them service or information based on the preferences	0.701	
	The level of personalization at this website was about right, not too much or too little	0.742	
6) Information Quality	The website was for organization of good reputation	0.691	
	The website provided objective information	0.705	0.800
	The website helped the users research products/services	0.681	
	The information presented on the web site was fair and accurate	0.736	
7) User Empowerment	The website user could control opportunities for interaction	0.816	
	The website user could control how fast to go through the website	0.768	0.883
	The website users could control order and or sequence of information access	0.793	
8) Privacy and Security	The website had adequate security features.	0.693	
	The website assured that user data was encrypted	0.815	0.877
	The website made sure customers could feel safe conducting transactions	0.681	

*Only the statements with loadings on only one factor with the values of 0.50 or higher are included.

Table 3. Results of the Discriminant Analysis (A)

Test of Equality of Group Means between Successful Versus Unsuccessful for each of the eight discriminating variables. *					
Independent Variables	Wilks' Lambda	F statistics	Degrees of Freedom1	Degrees of Freedom2	Significance level
Entertainment	0.468	370.904	1	326	0.001
Reliable	0.541	276.741	1	326	0.001
Cost Reduced	0.585	231.358	1	326	0.001
Back End	0.882	43.488	1	326	0.001
Personalization	0.670	160.425	1	326	0.001
Information Quality	0.791	86.142	1	326	0.001
User Empowerment	0.823	70.274	1	326	0.001
Privacy/Security	0.838	63.176	1	326	0.001
Sample size is 328 as 21 cases had at least one missing discriminating variable.					

Table 4. Test of Canonical Discriminating Function (B)

Wilk's Lambda	Chi-square	Degrees of freedom	Significance level
0.335	351.815	8	0.001

Table 5. Classification Results Based on the Eight Factors (C)*

Predicted Group Membership					
		Success	Failure	Total	
Original count	Actual				
	Success	186	23	209	
	Failure	10	130	140	
Percent Classified as	Success	89%	11%	100%	
	Failure	7.1%	92.9%	100%	
*90.5% of original grouped cases correctly classified.					

the scales. Additionally, the reliability coefficient alpha for each of the summated scale is reported in Table 2. The values for the eight scales were in the range of 0.80 to 0.91 which suggests high reliability.

After establishing the validity and reliability of the scales, the hypotheses were tested by employing multiple discriminate analyses. The dependent variable in the analysis was the variable of successful versus unsuccessful web site. The predictor variables were the eight hypothesized

factors measured by the summated scales. The results of multiple discriminate analyses are reported in Table 3, 4, and 5.

The results indicate that each of the hypothesized eight factors is significantly ($p<.001$) related to the success of the website operation. Additionally, the discriminate function is significant at $p<.001$ level. The high statistically significant relationship of each of the eight factors is also confirmed by the high "hit" rate or the 90.5 percent rate of correct classification of the cases as successful or unsuccessful. Thus the analysis was in support of our hypothesized relationships between the eight factors and the success of websites. The next section provides the implications of the study results.

DISCUSSION

The results suggest that all eight factors have a significant and positive influence on the successful development of a website. The respondents agree that a website that is entertaining and fun to explore is more likely to be successful over a bland and boring website. Similarly, the use of multimedia which is designed judiciously and tastefully so as not to overload the system and cause delays, is more likely to lead to success. Eye-catching images and attractive background are preferred over dull and boring ones by these respondents.

However, it is important that the visual appeal of the site does not distract the visitor from the central purpose of the website and that the website should be attractive and useful. A reliable site backed with sufficient resources of talented personnel, financial, and technical infrastructure will pave the way towards success. Alba et. al (1997) posit that reliability is one of the four important features considered by consumers in their evaluation of websites. These resources could be directed towards developing a website that puts the Internet surfer in the driver's seat. The control afforded the surfer allows him or her opportunities for interactions as well as the speed of interactions of the surfer's choosing. For example, Smith and Brynjolfsson (2001) found that reliability was an important factor for consumers who use comparison websites with shop bots. As the international audience for the websites continues to grow, so does the reliability factor (Internet World Stats, 2005).

Another important factor leading to success is the degree of personalization made possible by the website. One of the characteristics of the Internet is the impersonal environment in which the buyers and sellers find themselves communicating and transacting. Impersonal interaction contributes to a less trusting relationship between the parties exchanging information and/or products and/or services. As a result, more successful websites are attempting to find ways of personalizing their presence on the Internet. For example, a recent article in the Wall Street Journal (Gaiter and Brecher, 2006) reports on the success of a few wine sellers who have made efforts to personalize their websites and as a result found new customers. However, attempts to personalize a website may sometimes lead to seeking information that may jeopardize the privacy and security of the surfers. As the Internet continues to grow in its popularity, it also attracts unscrupulous individuals determined to steal consumers' identity and money. For example, in the aftermath of Hurricane Katrina dozens of unauthorized websites were soliciting donations under the Red Cross logo (Bulkeley, 2006). Recent incidents such as of the theft of personal data from the US Veterans administration and the theft of U.S. Census laptops containing personal information have significantly raised the concerns of consumers regarding the safeguards of their personal data. A successful website needs to balance the need for personalization with the safety of the data obtained from the surfers and users of the site.

The Internet has become successful in providing massive quantity of data easily and cheaply on virtually any topic or subject. However, getting access to good and reliable information is not always easy. A recent study indicates that getting quality information about a wide variety of products is important to increasing number of shoppers (Shop.org, 2005). As a result, the quality of the information content is becoming as or more important than quantity. The respondents in this study clearly support the importance of this issue by agreeing that to be successful a website has to provide information that is relevant, up to date, as well as accurate.

Finally, the survey respondents suggest that a successful website should also assist the organization in controlling costs as well as improving backend functions. The improvements in backend operations could lead to providing better customer service and operational efficiencies enabling the organization to serve its constituencies in a superior way. Lederer et. al (2000) found that consumers are more inclined to use a website if it saved them time and effort. A good example is the Dell Computers website that allows the shopper to customize the computer to his or her needs, order and pay for it online, and trace the shipment status online. It significantly reduces the transaction costs for the buyers and sellers.

The results of this national sample study improve the usefulness of the findings for those who are aiming to create successful websites. To build a successful website, a designer must focus on the eight factors investigated here: 1) Entertainment and Visual Appeal, 2) Reliability, 3) Cost Reductions Attained, 4) Back-End Processes Enabled, 5) Personalization, 6) Information Quality, 7) User Empowerment, 8) Privacy/Security. With millions of websites to choose from, the challenge to create successful websites has perhaps gone stiffer.

REFERENCES

Alba, J., Lynch, J., Weitz, B., & Janiszewsk, C. (1997). Interactive home shopping: consumer, retailer, and manufacturer incentives to participate in electronic marketplaces. *Journal of Marketing*, *61*(July), 38–53. doi:10.2307/1251788

Anderson, J., & Meyer, T. (1975). Functionalism and the mass media. *Journal of Broadcasting*, *19*(1), 11–22.

Ba, S., Whinston, A. B., & Zang, H. (1999). Building trust in the electronic market through an economic incentive mechanism. In *Proceedings of the Twentieth International Conference on Information Systems*, (December), 13-15.

Baby boomers and generation Jones find a home online. *PR Newswire* (July 17, 2007).

Bakos, J. Y. (1991). A strategic analysis of electronic marketplaces. *Management Information Systems Quarterly*, (September): 295–310. doi:10.2307/249641

Bakos, J. Y. (1997). Reducing buyer search costs: Implications for electronic marketplaces. *Management Science*, *43*(12), 1676–1692. doi:10.1287/mnsc.43.12.1676

Bhatti, N., Bouch, A., Kuchinsky, A. (2000). Integrating user- perceived quality into web server design. *Computer Networks, 33*(1-6), 1-16.

Bruner, G. C. II, & Kunar, A. (2005). Explaining consumer acceptance of hand held Internet devices. *Journal of Business Research*, *58*(5), 553. doi:10.1016/j.jbusres.2003.08.002

Bulkeley, W. M. (2006). Should owners of web sites be anonymous? *Wall Street Journal*, (April 27), B1, B4. Retrieved from http://www.ciadvertising.org

Cao, M., & Zang, Q. (2005). Web site quality and usability in e-commerce. In Gao, Y. (Ed.), *Web systems Design and online consumer behavior* (pp. 107–124). Hershey, PA: Idea Group Publishing.

Chakraborty, G., Lala, V., & Warren, D. (2003). What do customers consider important in B2B websites? *Journal of Advertising Research*, *40*(March), 50–61.

Chang, L., & Arnett, K. P. (2000). Exploring the factors associated with web site success in the context of electronic commerce. *Information & Management*, *38*(1), 23–33. doi:10.1016/S0378-7206(00)00049-5

Cook, B. L. (2007). Tapping into pocketbook power; Ellen T. Fisher proved her knack for getting female entrepreneurs together, now, on to the Internet. *Knight Ridder Business News*, (May 13), 1.

Cooper, R. G. (1979). The dimensions of industrial new product success and failure. *Journal of Marketing, 43*(3), 93–103. doi:10.2307/1250151

Customer Data plus Carelessness Equals Pink Slip at AOL. InformationWeek, retrieved February 12, 2007 from General Reference Center Gold via Thomson Gale.

DeJohn, P. (2005). E-commerce stats refine search for supply savings. *Hospital Materials Management, 30*(9), 1–3.

Del Franco, M. (2003). The back end comes to the forefront. *Catalog Age, 20*(5), 31–33.

Del Giudice, M., & del Giudice, F. (2003). Locking-in the customer: how to manage switching costs to stimulate e-loyalty and reduce churn rate. In Sharma, S. K., & Gupta, J. (Eds.), *Managing e-business of the 21st century*. Heidelberg: Heidelberg Press.

DeLone, W. H., & MacLean, E. R. (1992). Information systems success; the quest for the dependent variable. *Information Systems Research, 3*(1), 60–95. doi:10.1287/isre.3.1.60

Dhyani, D., Ng, W., & Bhowmick, S. (2002). A survey of web metrics. *ACM Computing Surveys, 34*(4), 469–503. doi:10.1145/592642.592645

Doyle, John. (2007). Network operators deliver personalized mobile adverts with ClixSmart Ad-Personalizer. *Business Wire*, (June 20), 3.

Eisammani, Z. A., Hackney, R., & Scown, P. (2004). SME adoption and implementation process of websites in the presence of change agents. In Al-Qirim, N. A. Y. (Ed.), *Electronic Commerce in Small to Medium-Sized Enterprises: Frameworks, Issues, and Implications* (pp. 146–164). Hershey, PA: Idea Group Publishing.

Eleniak, M. (2003). *Essential navigation checklists for web design*. Sitepoint. www.sitepoint.com/articles/checklists-web-design.

Fallows, D. (2005). *How men and women use the Internet*. Pew Internet and American life project available at www.pewinternet.org.

Feldman, W., & Feldman, P. (2005). Solutions for service and project Management. *Contractor, 52*(4), 40–42.

Fox, S. (2000). Trust and privacy online: why Americans want to rewrite the rules. available at www.pewinternet.org.

Gaiter, D., & Brecher, J. (2006). A fine year for web wine. *Wall Street Journal*, (April 28), W1, W10.

Geekpedia. (n.d.). Retrieved from http://www.geekpedia.com

Guay, D., & Ettwein, J. (1998). Internet commerce basics. *International Journal of Electronic Markets, 8*(1), 12–15. doi:10.1080/10196789800000004

Hawkins, D. (1999). What is credible information? *Online, 23*(5), 86–90.

Hoffman, W. (2006). Technology, off the shelf. *Traffic World*, (July 17), 1.

Katz Ian. (2007). ID theft fell in '06, FTC study finds. *Sun-Sentinel*,(February,8), 3D.

Internet World Stats. (2005). Internet usage statistics--the big picture. Available at www.internetworldstats.com/stats.htm.

Javenpaa, S. L., & Todd, P. A. (1997). Is there a future for retailing on the Internet? In Peterson (ed.), *Electronic Marketing and the Consumer*, 139-154. Thousand Oaks, CA; SAGE.

Jones, P., Clarke-Hill, C., Shears, P., & Hillier, D. (2001). The eighth 'C' of (R) etailing: Customer Concern. *Management Research News, 24*(5), 11–16. doi:10.1108/01409170110782397

Katerattanakul, P. (2002). Framework of effective web site design for business-to-consumer Internet commerce. *INFOR, 40*(1), 57–71.

King, R. E. (1998). *The uses and gratifications of the World Wide Web: an audience analysis for local television broadcasters.* Unpublished doctoral dissertation, University of Tennessee.

Korgaonkar, P., & O'Leary, B. (2006). Management, market, and financial factors separating winners and losers in e-Business. *Journal of Computer-Mediated Communication, 11*(4). doi:10.1111/j.1083-6101.2006.00311.x

Korgaonkar, P., & Wolin, L. (1999). A multivariate analysis of web usage. *Journal of Advertising Research, 39*(Mar/Apr), 53–68.

Korgaonkar, P. K., & Bellenger, D. N. (1985). Correlates of successful advertising campaigns: managers' perspectives. *Journal of Advertising Research, 25*(4), 34–39.

Korgaonkar, P. K., Moschis, G. P., & Bellenger, D. N. (1984). Correlates of successful advertising campaigns: a survey of advertising agency executives. *Journal of Advertising Research, 24*(1), 47–53.

Laudon, K. C. (2006). *Management information systems: managing the digital firm.* Upper Saddle River, NJ: Pearson Prentice Hall.

Lawton, C. (2007). PC shopping: online vs. in store: web retailers pile on videos, reviews, pricing tool To lure consumers back from the mall. *Wall Street Journal,* (July, 25), D1, D3.

Lederer, A. L., Maupin, D. J., Sena, M. P., & Zhung, Y. (2000). The technology acceptance model and the world wide world. *Decision Support Systems, 29*(1), 269–282. doi:10.1016/S0167-9236(00)00076-2

Light, A., & Wakeman, I. (2001). Beyond the interface: Users' perceptions of interaction and audience on websites. *Interacting with Computers, 13*(3), 325–351. doi:10.1016/S0953-5438(00)00044-8

Lin, C. J., & Lu, H. (2000). Towards an understanding of the behavioral intention to use a Web site. *International Journal of Information Management, 20*(3), 197–208. doi:10.1016/S0268-4012(00)00005-0

Liu, C., & Arnett, P. K. (2000). Exploring the factors associated with Web site success in the context of electronic commerce. *Information & Management, 38*(1), 23–33. doi:10.1016/S0378-7206(00)00049-5

Lohse, G.L. & Spiller P. (1998). Electronic shopping. *Communications of the ACM, 41*(7), .81-90.

Macmillan, I. C., Zemann, L., & Subbanarasima, P. N. (1987). Criteria distinguishing successful from unsuccessful ventures in the venture screening process. *Journal of Business Venturing,* (2): 123–137. doi:10.1016/0883-9026(87)90003-6

Mok, C. (1996). *Designing Business.* San Jose, CA: Adobe Press.

PR Newswire. (2007). *Bingo Players Flock to River Belle for New Online Chat Games.* Accessed online August 8, 2007.

PR Newswire. (2007). *Universal Pictures Partners with MINICK to Launch Mobile Film Portals Worldwide.* Accessed online August 8, 2000.

PR Newswire. (2007). *Second Life Invaded by Greenies-Avatars Shrink to Size of Mice.* Accessed online August 8, 2007.

Nielsen, J. (1998a). *The web usage paradox: why do people use something this bad?* Alertbox, accessed on February 11, 2007 @ http://www.useit.com/alertbox/980809.html.

Nielsen, J. (1998b). *Failure of corporate websites.* Alertbox, accessed on February 11, 2007 @ http://www.useit.com/alertbox/981018.html.

Nielsen, J. (2000). *Designing web usability.* Indianapolis, IN: New Riders Publishing.

Nielsen, J. (2003). *Top ten web design mistakes of 2003.* Alterbox, http://useit.com/alterbox/20040119.html

Nour, M., & Fadlalla, A. (2000). A framework for web marketing strategies. *Information Systems Management,* •••, 41–50.

Pack, T. (1999). Can you trust Internet information? *Link-Up, 16*(6), 24.

Palmer, J. W. (2002). Web site usability, design, and performance metrics. *Information Systems Research, 13*(2), 151–167. doi:10.1287/isre.13.2.151.88

Parasuraman, A., Berry, L., & Zeithaml, V. (1993). Research note: more on improving quality measurement. *Journal of Retailing, 69*(1), 140–148. doi:10.1016/S0022-4359(05)80007-7

Perkowitz, M. & Eitzioni, O. (1999). Towards adaptive web sites: conceptual framework and case study. *Computer Networks, 31*(11-16), 1245-1258.

Pollard, K., & Blyth, R. (1999). User-centered design of web sites and the redesign of line one. *BT Technology Journal, 17*(1), 69–75. doi:10.1023/A:1009622925010

Porter, J. (2003). *Testing the three-click rule. User Interface Engineering.* www.uie.com/articles/three_click_rule/

Ranganathan, C., & Ganapathy, S. (2002). Key dimensions of business-to-consumer Web sites. *Information & Management, 39*(6), 457–465. doi:10.1016/S0378-7206(01)00112-4

Ranganathan, C., & Grandon, E. (2005). Converting browsers to buyers: key considerations in designing business to consumer web sites. In Yuan Gao (Ed) *Web Systems Design and Online Consumer Behavior,* 177-191. Hershey, PA: Idea Group Publishing.

Reichfeld, F. F., & Schefter, P. (2000). E-Loyalty: Your secret weapon on the Web. *Harvard Business Review, 78*(4), 105–113.

Schaffer, E. (2000). A better way for web design. *InformationWeek, 784,* 194.

Seal of Approval. *Pharmaceutical Executive,* (Jan. 2002, 22), (1). Accessed online August 7, 2007.

Shop.org. (2005). *Statistics: U.S. Online Shoppers.* Shop.org, Washington D.C. Available at www.shop.org/learn/stats.

Simeon, R. (1999). Evaluating domestic and international Web site strategies. *Internet Research: Electronic Networking Applications and Policy, 9*(4), 297–308. doi:10.1108/10662249910286842

Slatin, M. J. (2001). The art of ALT: Toward a more accessible Web. *Computers and Composition, 18*(1), 73–81. doi:10.1016/S8755-4615(00)00049-9

Smith, M. D., & Brynjolfsson, E. (2001). Consumer decision-making at an Internet shopbot: brand still matters. *The Journal of Industrial Economics, 49*(4), 541–558. doi:10.1111/1467-6451.00162

Smith, M. E. (2003). Changing an organization's culture: correlates of successful and failure. *Leadership and Organization Development Journal, 24*(5), 249–261. doi:10.1108/01437730310485752

Stark, D., & Wind, G. (2005). TNS/Truste holiday shopping survey shows identity theft, spam and spyware to be top concerns with shopping online. Available at www.truste.org.

Tai, S. H. C. (2007). Correlates of successful brand advertising in China. *Asia Pacific Journal of Marketing and Logistics, 19*(1), 40–56. doi:10.1108/13555850710720894

Thelwall, M. (2000). Commercial web sites: Lost in cyberspace? *Internet Research: Electronic Networking Applications and Policy, 10*(2), 150–159. doi:10.1108/10662240010322939

Tiwana, A. (1998). Interdependency factors influencing the World Wide Web as a channel of interactive marketing. *Journal of Retailing and Consumer Services, 5*(4), 254–253. doi:10.1016/S0969-6989(97)00038-6

Tiwana, A., & R. B. (1999). *Towards a composite metric for electronic commerce ROI: An extension of the balanced scorecard.* In Conference on the Measurement of Electronic Commerce, (December, 6-8), Singapore, available at www.singstat.gov.sg/EC/papers.html.

Top-20 Websites- Ranked by total time spent (in minutes, December 2006) at http://internet. seekingalpha.com/article/25309. UK's Website of Year 2006: Winners are revealed at http://www. websiteoftheyear.co.uk/winners.php

TrustNet website offers extra services. *Money Marketing* (2003, November 20. Accessed online August 3, 2007.

Week, W. (2005). *Measuring online experience.* Accessed online wwww.wirelessweek.com. August 1, 2007.

Wilkinson, G. L., Bennett, L. T., & Oliver, K. M. (1997). Evaluation criteria and indicators of quality for Internet resources. *Educational Technology*, (May-June): 88.

Wolfinbarger, M., & Gilly, M. C. (2002). *ComQ: dimensionalizing, measuring and predicting quality of the e-tail experience.* Working paper. Center for Research on Information Technology and Organizations, University of California, Irvine, CA.

World Internet Usage. (2007), Retrieved from February 11 from http://www.internetworldstats.com/stats.htm.

Yang, S., Hung, W., Sung, K., & Cheng-Kiang, F. (2006). Investigating initial trust toward e-tailers form the elaboration likelihood model perspective. *Psychology and Marketing, 23*(5), 429. doi:10.1002/mar.20120

Yoon, S. J. (2002). The antecedents and consequences of trust in online-purchase decisions. *Journal of Interactive Marketing, 16*(2), 47–63. doi:10.1002/dir.10008

Zhang, X., & Myers, M. (2005). Web design and e-commerce. In Gao, Y. (ed.). Web systems design and online consumer behavior, 205-221.Hershey, PA: Idea Group Publishing.

Zhuang, P., & von Dran, M. (2000). Satisfiers and dissatisfiers: A two-factor model for website design and evaluation. *Journal of the American Society for Information Science American Society for Information Science, 51*(14), 1253–1268. doi:10.1002/1097-4571(2000)9999:9999<::AID-ASI1039>3.0.CO;2-O

Zhuang, Y., & Lederer, A. L. (2003). An instrument for measuring the business benefits of e-commerce retailing. *International Journal of Electronic Commerce, 7*(3), 65–99.

Chapter 19

Still Watching Other People's Programmes?
The Case of Current TV

Theodoulos Theodoulou
Newcastle University, UK

Savvas Papagiannidis
Newcastle University, UK

ABSTRACT

In this paper, the authors adapt a value chain analysis framework used in the music industry and apply it to the television industry, in order to probe the television value creation and distribution mechanisms and examine how they were affected by technology. More specifically, they examine how viewers can effectively become producers by repositioning themselves in the value chain and the implications of such a shift. Their discussion takes place in the context of a case study, that of Current TV, in order to illustrate in practice the opportunities and implications for the content producers, the broadcasters, and the viewers themselves.

INTRODUCTION

The rapid development of the Internet and related technologies allowed organisations to conduct their business operations in ways not possible before. The opportunities offered and the challenges set by the Internet encouraged, and in many cases even forced, organisations to explore and develop new strategies and business models by utilising technology, in order to create competitive advantages. Although electronic business spawned evolutionary and revolutionary transformations in most industries, many were left relatively unaffected. One such industry is the television/video broadcasting one.

Using the Internet as their distribution channel, traditional channels could now broadcast beyond their geographical boundaries, while new broadcasters had an economically viable platform to distribute their content. At the same time professional and amateur producers capitalised on the popularity of services like YouTube and the audience's changing viewing habits to share their creation far beyond the narrow boundaries of their close social network. Technology did not only provide the means for distributing content, though;

DOI: 10.4018/978-1-60960-132-4.ch019

Copyright © 2011, IGI Global. Copying or distributing in print or electronic forms without written permission of IGI Global is prohibited.

it also affected its creation and consumption. The ever increasing available computing resources and the relatively inexpensive capturing and editing facilities meant that producing content of good quality was not beyond reach any more. At the same time, viewers started consuming video content when they wanted, rather than when it was broadcast, often outside their living rooms using portable devices such as the iconic iPods. Place and time shifting had changed the expectations of viewers for ever.

The above are facets of a rapidly changing industry that has experienced significant, if not fundamental, changes within a relatively short period of time, due to the introduction of new technologies. In this paper, we will be using a value chain analysis framework to probe the television value creation and distribution mechanisms and examine how they were affected by technology. In particular, we will examine how viewers can effectively become producers by repositioning themselves in the value chain. Our discussion will take place in the context of a case study, that of Current TV (http://www.current.com), in order to illustrate in practice the opportunities and implications for content producers, broadcasters, and the viewers themselves.

Our discussion will start with an outline in the next section of the conceptual framework we will be using in the case study. Before doing so, we should first highlight that when referring to the broadcasting of television, or video content in general, over the Internet we will be referring to the content distribution and not necessarily to a continuous stream of programmes (i.e. similarly to what happens with 'traditional' television). This is a more inclusive approach when compared to the definition by Papagiannidis *et al* (2006), who defined Internet-only TV channels as channels that broadcast continuous streams only over the Internet. After all, an answer to the question 'what is television' may simply be that the question actually does not matter any more (Papagiannidis and Berry, 2007) as technological advances have

enabled users to circumvent the restrictions posed by the conventional television box found in the living room and consume content as they please.

BUSINESS MODELS AND VALUE CHAINS: FROM AUDIO TO VIDEO

Many definitions of business models exist (Applegate, 2001; Mansfield and Fourie, 2004; Osterwalder and Pigneur, 2002; Rappa, 2006; Timmers, 1998; Yip, 2004). For this study we will be adopting the one by Afuah and Tucci (2003), who define a business model as the method by which a firm builds and uses its resources to offer its customers better value than its competitors and to make money doing so. This is a generic definition that emphasises value creation and profit extraction.

When it comes to business models of television broadcasters Chan-Olmsted and Ha (2003) proposed a number of different ways they can generate revenues online depending on their competencies. A television broadcaster can profit by advertising and sponsorship deals or ecommerce (i.e. merchandise or per unit content). In addition, broadcasters can charge a subscription fee to customers for accessing premium content. They can also sell their content to other websites or receive affiliate fees from them, often a percentage of the total sales spawned from customers that have been directed to those external websites from the broadcaster's one. Still, despite the potential to generate revenues online Chan-Olmsted and Ha found that television stations have focused their online activities on building audience relationships: "The Internet is mostly used by television broadcasters as a support mechanism to complement the stations' offline core products" (Chan-Olmsted and Ha, 2003). In addition to revenue generation, the Internet has all the potential to play a critical role in value generation for television broadcasters. For example, Waterman (2001) identified five improvements the Internet can make to the cost and efficiency of established broadband media. These include lower delivery costs and reduced capacity constraints, more efficient interactivity, more efficient advertising and sponsorship, more efficient direct pricing and bundling, and finally lower costs of copying and sharing. These, put together, can allow "creating new ways of working [and creating value in general] that are significantly different from, and often far superior to, what was possible (or conceivable) in the past" (Li, 2007).

Taking the above into consideration, in order to appreciate how value is created when Internet-based models and practices are applied we need to examine the individual value chain links. Amit and Zott (2001) observed that value creation in e-business goes beyond the value that can be realized through the configuration of the value chain (Porter, 1985). Still, a value chain analysis can be helpful in examining value creation in virtual markets in which opportunities to create value "may result from new combinations of information, physical products and services, innovative configurations of transactions, and the reconfiguration and integration of resources, capabilities, roles and relationships among suppliers, partners and customers" (Amit and Zott, 2001). When it comes to the entertainment value chain, Loebbecke and Powell (2002) state that it comprises four distinct activities that are carried out in a linear manner. The first activity of the value chain consists of the 'originators' creating the ideas, while during the next stage a 'transformation' takes place with companies purchasing the rights from the creators in order to develop them into content. During the next stage 'production' takes place, which is finally followed by the distribution stage. Writz (1999), similarly, divided the multimedia value chain into five different stages. During the first one content and service creators provide the program contents and services which are then combined by the content/services aggregators in order to create multiple program bundles. Then, the value added service providers develop and offer new services on existing

platforms. The final two stages are the access/connecting stage, during which the transmission of the content and services to the customer takes place and finally the navigation/interfacing stage, which provides the customer navigation tools. The Content Creators for Writz (1999) (for example, film studios, TV-producer, publisher, retailer) in their role as information suppliers constitute a core component of the value chain. Finally, Krueger and Swatman (2003) divided the content market value chain into four component parts: the creation of content, the adding of value to content, the distribution of content, and its consumption.

This type of value chain configuration can be very linear and end up not capturing the richness of the value generating activities and transactions. Normann and Ramírez argue that this linear approach to value creation is outmoded: "in a world where value occurs not in sequential chains but in complex constellations, the goal of the business is not so much to make or do something of value for customers as it is to mobilize customers to take advantage of proffered density and create value themselves" (Normann and Ramírez, 1993). This has also been proposed for the music industry by Papagiannidis and Berry (2007). As they explained, the music industry was a market dominated by a small number of sellers that were solely dependent on a copyright framework. These big firms that controlled the market would invest in artists and copyright laws would ensure their revenues. Artists relied on the big labels for manufacturing, promoting and distributing their work, which resulted in a linear value chain framework. The introduction of the Internet and related technologies radically transformed the industry by creating shorter and often direct links between creators and consumers and by empowering both to influence all links of the chain, as shown in Figure 1.

Papagiannidis and Berry (2007) also proposed that television business models could be seen as evolutionary models spawned from the music industry. "If bandwidth is considered as a core

Figure 1. Artists and consumers repositioning themselves on the value chain. Adopted from Papagiannidis and Berry (2007).

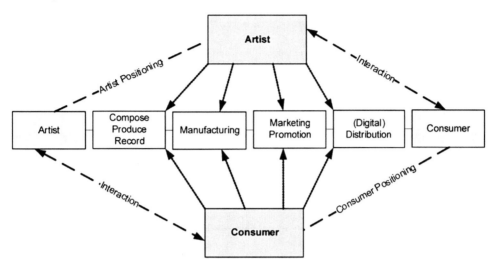

element of the value generated by e-business models, one could argue that the video broadcasting business models and subsequently television business models could be seen as evolutionary models spawned from the music industry". (Papagiannidis and Berry, 2007) Then, the new business models and the altered value chains of the music industry could be adapted to the television industry, which will be used in the case study presented in the next sections. As the framework proposed for the music value chain was a non-linear one, the television broadcasting one would also be non-linear, as illustrated in Figure 2. A notable difference between Figures 1 and 2 is that the latter not only considers the content creators, but also the TV broadcasters too. Both of them and the viewers, though, experience a similar repositioning along the value chain, enabling them to affect each link. In doing so, numerous opportunities for interactions among them emerge. A curly line between content producers and viewers is used in order to draw attention to the fact that viewers could be potentially active creators too, as we will see in the case study we will be presenting in the following section.

METHODOLOGY

In this paper we will present a qualitative methodology that is based on a single case study, that of Current TV (or simply Current). Yin (1994) proposes the case study as "the preferred strategy when 'how' and 'why' questions are being posed, when the investigator has little control over events and when the focus is on a contemporary phenomenon within some real-life context". He also argues that a single case study is appropriate when it represents the 'critical case' in testing a formulated theory (Yin, 1994). The case of Current is an ideal candidate that meets all the conditions for testing all the constituent parts of the transformed value chain framework as presented in the previous section. In fact, Current appears to be the only case that can be used for testing the framework. There are broadcasters who have a presence in both traditional and Internet distributions channels, but these lack innovative content acquisition methods and viewer interaction. On the other hand, there are online broadcasters who provide more interactive solutions, encouraging viewers to engage on different levels, but these tend to lack the visibility and reach of Current.

Figure 2. Producers/Television broadcasters and consumers, repositioning themselves on the value chain. Adapted from Papagiannidis and Berry (2007).

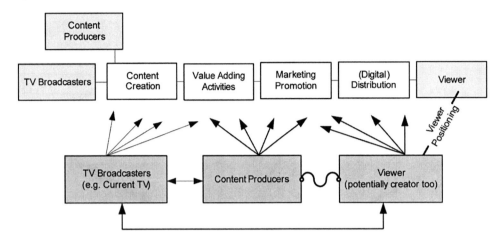

Consequently, Current has been selected not only because it can provide a platform on which to stage the framework's discussion, but more importantly because it has uniquely placed itself in the market. The above renders a case study approach an appropriate research instrument for this research.

On the other hand, a case study will challenge our ability to generalise any findings. After all, as Stake (1995) argues, case study research is not sampling research: "We do not study a case primarily to understand other cases. Our first obligation is to understand this one case." (Stake, 1995) Hence, the case study approach aims to facilitate the in-depth exploration of cases and to provide rich knowledge of a specific context (Eisenhardt, 1989; Patton, 1990). Still, although the case of Current is unique in that the constituent links of value chain are linked together, the individual links provide insights for other cases that employ similar practices, and hence there are lessons to be learnt.

More specifically, we will be using the framework developed above (Figure 2) in order to analyse the business activities and processes that make up Current's value chain and use them to determine how the content creators, the viewers, the company and the content itself have been influenced by the business model used. This is in

alignment with Cutler (2004), who suggested that "research cases are used to investigate activities or complex processes that are not easily separated from the social context within which they occur". The data used for the case study consisted mainly of information collected from Current's web site, other secondary online sources and personal communications with Current.

THE CASE STUDY: CURRENT TV

Current TV is a cable and satellite channel established in August 2005. Its founders are former United States Vice President Al Gore, who is the chairman, and Joel Hyatt, who is the chief executive officer. Although they mainly raised money for the channel's start up costs from a Democratic base, Hyatt stated that politics are not going to influence the content presented to viewers San Francisco Chronicle, 2005). Current targets an audience that ranges between eighteen to thirty four years old or, as one of its executives put it, "a media-grazing audience" (Young, 2007), that plays a central role in the station's business model. More specifically, for its broadcasting content Current primarily relies on short videos called 'pods' (Current TV, 2007a) that are submitted and uploaded by the viewers onto its network. In addition, the viewers have the opportunity to choose what is aired, by visiting its website and voting for the pods they like the most. In this way, Current goes well beyond the boundaries of the one-way communication model that traditional television offers, allowing viewers to influence what is broadcast, by actively participating in the creation and filtering of the content. Certainly, the above would not have been possible if it had not been for the Internet and related technologies, which changed the way organisations and consumers interact. Even though Current has not employed a pure dot-com business model, the Internet is an important aspect of its infrastructure and offering, since it is the medium used for viewers to upload, watch, vote for and comment on the videos.

Current enjoyed significant success with its innovative processes and activities, which added value to its content and one year after launching it managed to reach thirty million houses in the US, increasing its carriage by 70% (Current TV, 2006a). In addition, as of October 2006, it had broadened its market and launched in the UK and the Republic of Ireland (Current TV, 2006a). Current estimates its reach via cable and satellite TV networks at about 52 million homes around the world (Current TV, 2007a).

In the following sections we will examine Current's business model, by using the adapted television value chain framework shown in Figure 2.

The First Link in the Value Chain: Content Creation

The first step in the value chain involves the content creation and its acquisition by Current. Current utilises the Internet to efficiently acquire the content directly from the creators, many of whom are part of the audience itself. Content submitted by viewers is referred to as 'viewer contributed content' or in Current's terminology 'VC^2'. The topics for the pods could be selected by the creators themselves or picked from among the 'assignments' listed on the Current web site.

As only about a third of the content broadcast comes solely from the viewers (Current TV, 2007b), Current also needs other distinctive ways to create or acquire content. Following their innovative approach to obtaining content, Current approached news broadcasting in a similarly way, by partnering with Google. With Google being the most popular search engine, Current came up with the initiative to broadcast news covering topics relevant to the most popular searches on the web (Shim, 2005). The television program is called 'Google Current' and is broadcast every half hour, offering a unique approach to news broadcasting. An interesting point here is that Google's users indirectly decide what will be covered during the programme. Current also collaborated with Yahoo and launched the 'Yahoo Current Network' (Hansell, 2006) in an attempt to enhance its content and its network. At the Yahoo Current Network website, both professional and user-generated short clips are presented, split into different channels that are divided onto diverse specialised topics, such as travel, action sports, and cars.

Another Internet-based source of content that Current uses is that of viral video clips. The clips broadcast during the 'Current Virals' (Current TV, 2007c) television program are every day's most popular viral videos that get circulated on the web or appear on sites such as YouTube, Metacafe, MySpaceTV. Finally, in between the video-clips, short advertisements are shown. In line with Current's philosophy, viewers can create their own ad messages for well-known brands, called 'VCAM' (Current TV, 2007f), short for viewer contributed ad message. This is an inexpensive way for brands to tap into the creative flair of the audience, while potentially from the 'traditional' advertising stand point with the content broadcast being segmented into specific thematic areas advertisers can better target consumers and promote their products and services more successfully.

Internet services like YouTube have allowed users to upload and share their creations on the web. Current took this a step further and now content producers can appear on cable or satellite television too. This serves Current well, not only because it gets a significant percentage of its content in this way, but also because it can indirectly identify talent that has established a rapport with the audience. For example, a content producer called Joe Hanson became very famous with the pods he uploaded onto Current's network. Eventually, he got an offer to work for Current and host his own show called 'Joe Central' (Current TV, 2007e). Those producers who are successful in getting their content to appear on television programmes also get to benefit by a licence fee that Current pays depending on the content. Pod prices are negotiated on a per-piece basis. Current V-CAM submissions are paid at a flat rate of $1000 per V-CAM (separate fees may be paid out if the sponsor decides to use the clip elsewhere), while promos are purchased for a flat rate of $250 per promo (Current TV, 2007d).

The above clearly demonstrates the move of viewers from the end of the value chain, i.e. the consumption of the content stage, towards its left links, i.e. the creation and distribution stages, and their transformation to content producers in the process. They are not passive receivers of whatever content broadcasters throw at them, but can actively participate by submitting their own content.

The Second Link in the Value Chain: Adding Value to Content

The second link in the chain aims to add value to the content and the overall experience and Current in collaboration with the content producers and the viewers achieves this in a number of different ways.

First of all, Current's website offers online training and tips for content producers explaining how to shoot, edit and upload their pods. Users with no prior producing experience can apply the tips provided, hopefully producing better quality pods. Even experienced users may find the 'Producers Resources' section useful. For example, one of the biggest challenges Current was facing from user-generated content was copyright issues, and, more specifically, the music used in the pods. Every time users uploaded a video clip, Current would have to find the songs or music used in that pod and then contact the company which owned the copyright in order to receive permission to use it. This could result in delays and increased production costs. Current's solution to this was to partner with APM Music, one of the biggest companies that offer music for films, television and radio productions (Mayberry, 2006). Producers interested in creating content for Current now have online access to the music library of APM for free. Therefore, they can easily, and more importantly legally, download and use music that best suits their pods. Current also offers samples and sound effects from Sony Media Software in a variety of popular music genres that could be used too when producing pods. Another important legal issue that Current offers support with is video releases of people and places that appear on pods. Creators can download and use release documents protecting themselves and Current against any legal claims.

When it comes to filtering, viewers can log on to the website and not only watch, but also vote for, thousands of 'promos' (very short video clips developed by users that refer to and promote Current) and pods, which are categorised by genre, with the ones receiving the most votes making it on air. By allowing its audience to vote, Current benefits by saving time and resources that would have otherwise been spent on searching for quality content to broadcast. Also, by categorising them, it can learn which genres are most watched and potentially divert more resources towards them. The consumers also benefit, as by voting, they are effectively in control of the content broadcast. It is worth noting that although the content and information available on the US and UK/Ireland versions of Current's website are the same, there is a difference in that when a user from the US votes for a pod, it is rated only in the US website (Current TV, pers. comms). In this way, Current is able to localise its content, as pods which will eventually make it on air may be different in the USA from the ones broadcast in the UK and Ireland.

Moreover, in order for users to vote, they need to register and create an account, which effectively creates a community of creators and viewers. These accounts are not just a mechanism for uploading content or voting for pods, but represent a social entity within a very active community. This was reflected in the way voting worked, until Current changed their web site in autumn 2007. Users could vote by green-lighting pods, meaning that they were good enough to be put on air, or red-lighting them. Users that green-lighted uploaded pods and eventually made it on air were rewarded by achieving a higher voting rank, which meant that their green-lights counted more points towards a pod being aired. If users green-lighted a pod and it did not make it on air, then they lost points and they might even drop down the voting ranks. Consequently, users had a strong incentive to be very careful when they voted, as their votes could improve or damage their standing within the community and affect their ability to influence the filtering of the content.

Users can also write comments or give recommendations for the pods that content creators may find useful when producing future pods. So even though this does not add value directly to the pods for which the recommendations were made, the audience's 'wisdom' and their preferences can in the future help produce better targeted and higher quality pods. A good example of this can also be observed in how Current aimed to cover the 2007 New Year's Celebrations. Two members of Current's community suggested giving the network's viewers an unprecedented look at New Year's from all corners of the globe (Current TV, 2007b).

The concept spread through the Current message boards and many users decided to contribute to it. Current picked this up and decided on "New Year's Around the World" on New Year's Day, which included footage from all over the world. The community features that Current's web site offer also play an important role in helping viewers follow their favourite producers and their topics of interest using the '*My Current*' section.

Finally, Current exploits the very nature of its business model by using its website as a delivery mechanism for all its content irrespective of whether it gets aired or not. This may not be innovative as a service, but it does differ significantly from the typical use of television broadcasters' web sites, which are mostly used as a means to promote their organisations and their programmes. Interestingly, the more users contribute by adding more content, the more valuable the web site becomes in its own right, as it can then attract even more visitors.

The Third Link in the Value Chain: Marketing and Promoting Content

Current provides content producers with an opportunity to see their work on television. Professional and amateur producers have the opportunity to reach national television and also make money out of it, with the only requirement being that their content is good enough to find support from the viewers who will vote for it. Although publishing video content online is now open to all, programmes that get broadcast on TV still carry kudos for both the content and the producer. This is a significant differentiating factor between Current and services like YouTube.

Content producers and the viewers themselves can also promote the content by embedding it in web sites they have access to, increasing the exposure it gets. In doing so, they also promote Current and indirectly the community around it and the rest of the content available.

In addition to Current's partnerships with Google and Yahoo!, Current has also partnered with Flavourpill, a company that distributes eleven different email-magazines about cultural happenings to more than 500,000 subscribers, in an attempt by both companies to promote and market their content. With the direct relationships that the Internet offers, Current is able to promote its content to all Flavourpill subscribers, and encourage them to develop and upload pods about cultural events onto a Flavourpill page available on Current's website. As Mark Mangan, Flavourpill's co-founder, claimed, this is "[a] brilliant merging of user-generated content with the television experience, Current is the perfect forum for our creative community to showcase their stories to millions" (Current TV, 2006b). The partnership allows Flavourpill to promote its content to a wider audience and broadens its distribution horizons, as with Flavorpill's weekly RADAR feed broadcast on Current the company is able to offer its events listings.

The Fourth Link in the Value Chain: Digital Distribution

The final link of the proposed value chain framework is the distribution of content. This consists of all the mechanisms used by Current, the content producers and the audience in order to distribute the content among them and then consume it.

Current offers three ways of watching its programme and clips. The first one is via cable and satellite TV. As stated above, this service is only available in the United States, UK and Ireland. Also, its web site acts as repository for all its content that is available for users to view as individual clips. In this way, Current manages to potentially decrease its distribution costs, increase its geographic reach and even achieve long tail economics (Anderson, 2006). In fact, Current is a good example of how long tail economics in television could work through a democratisation of the tools of production, the democratisation of

distribution due to reduced costs and how finally supply and demand can be connected in new ways. In addition, viewers can watch clips on the Current web site. Finally, users can embed clips in their own web sites (e.g. blogs) by adding a piece of code to load the clip, allowing viewers to consume individual clips relevant to that particular web site.

DISCUSSION

"The strategic importance of the Internet is especially evident for the television industry as television and the Internet develop a symbiotic relationship with significant financial implications." (Chan-Olmsted and Ha, 2003) In this paper we have illustrated, using the case of Current, how the Internet could be used not only as a distribution mechanism, but also as a platform for a non-linear value chain for the video broadcasting industry. Our case study findings are summarised in Table 1, in which we treat content creation and value adding activities as one link, due to their very tight relationship and how one affects the other.

The Current case study provides strong evidence of how this re-orientation of channels, content producers and viewers and the strong direct links among them gives rise to an array of new activities that can enhance the viewing experience. The viewers have a say in what is aired, producers can get feedback and support on their work, while Current gets a constant supply of audience-filtered content. If considered separately, the above may not be very innovative, especially as they have appeared in various other services. However, when they come together in the context of broadcasting television, especially when the broadcasting barriers for individuals are considered, they are facets of a potential paradigm shift. Until now, technology may have allowed place-shifting and time-shifting, but it never offered the opportunity to influence the content itself. It could be argued that in fact even that is not 'innovative', as it is the natural evolution of

Table 1. Summary of the findings for each one of the stakeholders

Value chain link	Stakeholders		
	Current	Creators	Viewers
Content creation	Inexpensively, obtain content from various sources. Help improve content and provide effective mechanisms for filtering it.	Receive direct feedback from viewers when it comes to producing content and improving its quality. Receive support in order to improve content quality.	Can influence creation directly via providing feedback and indirectly based on what they watch.
Value adding activities			
Marketing promotion	Provide tools for creators and viewers to participate in the promotion.	Can utilise online distribution channels for promotion of their content.	Can actively support and promote their favourite content. Can influence what is aired.
(Digital) Distribution	Extended utilisation of offline and online distribution methods.	Access to Current's platform, especially when it comes to 'traditional' television broadcasting.	Can participate in the distribution of their favourite content, e.g. via blogs.

how broadcasting coupled with technology, and more specifically with the Internet, would have driven the market. Hence, it was just a matter of time until a broadcaster would have brought the distribution channels, the content and the people together. This does not suggest that all broadcasters will opt for a model similar to Current's because their existing models are under threat or because this model is more effective or efficient. It is, though, a reminder that the rules of the game have changed and existing models will need to be re-evaluated. Electronic business has been gradually spreading its influence within the television industry and it seems that we are getting closer to a tipping point.

Finally, perhaps a more pressing question is whether Current is really a television broadcaster that happens to utilise Internet technologies more effectively than the typical broadcaster or whether it is a social networking company that happens to broadcast part of its content on television. In the latter case, Current effectively creates a value network that evolves around the content, employing mediating technologies to facilitate the exchange relationships among the stakeholders (Stabell and Fjeldstad, 1998). If the Current platform is considered as a value network platform, then according to Stabell and Fjeldstad (1998) the primary activities for the stakeholders would consist of:

- Network promotion and contract management, i.e. activities promoting the network, inviting potential 'customers' to join it and the facilitation and management of contracts governing service provisioning.
- Service provisioning, i.e. undertaking activities associated with establishing, maintaining, and terminating links between 'customers' and billing for value received.
- Network infrastructure, which entails the network's maintenance and alertness in order to be ready to service 'customer' requests.

In Current's case the 'customer' is not just the viewer as the final consumer, but also the content producers and Current itself, as all three stakeholders can actively be engaged in the network's promotion and contract management and in the service provisioning. For example, viewers provide a service to Current by filtering the content and a service to the producers by providing feedback and promoting their clips. Current, though, plays a central role in bringing everything together by maintaining the network and facilitating the interactions.

FUTURE RESEARCH

The model used in this paper is primarily concerned with the four key links in the value chain. Potentially, a typology could be developed based on them which could be used to describe and evaluate other broadcasters' business models. This would render the constituent parts of the model easier to specify and allow comparisons among the different models in use. It could also provide useful insights as to which combinations, and hence which models, are the most popular ones. The above would extend the model and its applicability, making it easier to better identify other case studies for undertaking comparative analysis, especially as using a single case study limits our ability to generalise the findings.

Future research could also potentially look at each value link of the value chain in more detail by examining the stakeholders' (more specifically the broadcasters', the content producers' and the viewers') views of the perceived benefits, opportunities and challenges. Both quantitative and qualitative approaches could be used. For example, new and traditional broadcasters could be interviewed about their current and future strategies and how they impact on their business models. Content producers and viewers could participate in focus groups or be surveyed using a questionnaire, in order to gain an insight in the complex relationships among them and how they impact on the quality of the content produced. In addition, future research could survey the business models of broadcasters, evaluating their constituent parts against the framework or perhaps even a specific model, in order to identify the extent to which certain value adding activities take place. Finally, the filtering and rating mechanisms should be studied as they effectively decide what is broadcast or not. The above would provide valuable information as to potential ways of refining Current's business and operational model or even come up with new ones.

REFERENCES

Afuah, A., & Tucci, C. L. (2003). *Internet Business Models and Strategies: Text and cases* (2nd ed.). Boston: McGraw-Hill.

Amit, R., & Zott, C. (2001). Value creation in e-business. *Strategic Management Journal, 22,* 493–520. doi:10.1002/smj.187

Anderson, C. (2006). *The long tail: How endless choice is creating unlimited demand.* London: Random House Business Books.

Applegate, L. M. (2001). E-business Models: Making sense of the Internet business landscape. In G. Dickson, W. Gary and G. DeSanctis (Eds.), *Information Technology and the future enterprise: New models for managers.* Upper Saddle River, N.J.: Prentice Hall.

Chan-Olmsted, S. M., & Ha, L. S. (2003). Internet Business Models for Broadcasters: How Television Stations Perceive and Integrate the Internet. *Journal of Broadcasting & Electronic Media, 47,* 597–616. doi:10.1207/s15506878jobem4704_7

Current, TV (2006a). *Current to launch TV channel on Sky Digital in UK and Ireland.* Retrieved: 8th October, 2007, from http://www.current.tv/pdf/BSkyB_Oct2006.pdf

Current, TV (2006b). *Flavorpill partners with Current TV to generate viewer created video content for web and broadcast.* Retrieved: 2nd November, 2007, from http://current.com/pdf/Current_Flavorpill_Oct2006.pdf

Current, TV (2007a). *About Current TV.* Retrieved: 8th October, 2007, from http://current.com/s/about.htm

Current, TV (2007b). *Current Tv Viewer-Producers Usher In The New Year Capturing Celebrations From Around The Globe.* Retrieved: 5th November, 2007, from http://current.com/pdf/NewYears2007.pdf

Current, TV (2007c). *Current Virals*. Retrieved: 18th October, 2007, from http://uk.current.com/virals

Current, TV (2007d). *FAQ*. Retrieved: 19th October, 2007, from http://current.com/s/faq.htm

Current, TV (2007e). *Joe Central*. Retrieved: 15th June, 2007, from http://www.current.tv/pods/issue/PD03487?section=about

Current, TV (2007f). *XM Satellite Radio VCAM*. Retrieved: 18th October, 2007, from http://uk.current.com/make/vc2/vcam

Cutler, A. (2004). Methodical failure: The use of case study method by public relations researchers. *Public Relations Review, 30*(3), 365–375. doi:10.1016/j.pubrev.2004.05.008

Eisenhardt, K. M. (1989). Building theories from case study research. *Academy of Management Review, 14*(4), 532–550. doi:10.2307/258557

Hansell, S. (2006). Al Gore's Current TV Joins With Yahoo for a Video Venture. *New York Times*. Retrieved: 18th October, 2007, from http://www.nytimes.com/2006/09/20/business/20gore.html?ei=5088&en=4642a6c8ba35a6c5&ex=1316404800&adxnnl=1&partner=rssnyt&emc=rss&adxnnlx=1187694015-HGl7CuZdSkcOp26+zlBcVQ

Krueger, C. C., & Swatman, P. M. C. (2003). *Who are the Internet content providers? Identifying a realistic taxonomy of content providers in the online news sector*. Paper presented at the 3rd IFIP Conference on eBusiness, eCommerce and eGovernment, Sao Paolo, Brazil.

Li, F. (2007). *What is e-Business? How the Internet Transforms Organisations*. Oxford: Blackwell.

Loebbecke, C., & Powell, P. (2002). E-business in the entertainment sector: the Egmont case. *Journal of International Management, 22*, 307–322.

Mansfield, G. M., & Fourie, L. C. H. (2004). Strategy and business models - strange bedfellows? A case for convergence and its evolution into strategic architecture. *South African Journal of Business Management, 33*(1), 35–44.

Mayberry, C. (2006). *Current TV, APM Music pact on music use*. Retrieved: 18th October, 2007, from http://www.hollywoodreporter.com/hr/search/article_display.jsp?vnu_content_id=1003122553

Normann, R., & Ramirez, R. (1993). From value chain to value constellation: designing interactive strategy. *Harvard Business Review, 71*, 65–77.

Osterwalder, A., & Pigneur, Y. (2002). *An e-Business Model Ontology for Modeling e-Business*. Paper presented at the 15th Bled Electronic Commerce Conference e-Reality: Constructing the e-Economy, Bled, Slovenia.

Papagiannidis, S., & Berry, J. (2007). What has been learned from emergent music business models? *International Journal of E-Business Research, 3*(3), 25–42.

Papagiannidis, S., Berry, J., & Li, F. (2006). Well beyond streaming video: IP6 and the next generation television. *Technological Forecasting and Social Change, 73*(5), 510–523. doi:10.1016/j.techfore.2005.06.003

Patton, M. (1990). *Qualitative Data Analysis*. Thousand Oaks: Sage.

Porter, M. E. (1985). *Competitive Advantage: Creating and Sustaining Superior Performance*. New York: Free Press.

Rappa, M. (2006). *Business Models on the Web*. Retrieved: July 25, 2006, from http://digitalenterprise.org/models/models.html

San Francisco Chronicle. (2005). *On the Record: Joel Hyatt*. Retrieved: 8th October, 2007, from http://www.sfgate.com/cgi-bin/article.cgi?f=/c/a/2005/11/13/BUGM8FM6041.DTL

Shim, R. (2005). *Gore's TV network set to launch with Google tie-in*. CNET.com. Retrieved: 18th October, 2007, from http://www.news.com/2100-1047_3-5653913.html

Stabell, C. B., & Fjeldstad, Ø. D. (1998). Configuring value for competitive advantage: On chains, shops, and networks. *Strategic Management Journal*, *19*, 413–437. doi:10.1002/(SICI)1097-0266(199805)19:5<413::AID-SMJ946>3.0.CO;2-C

Stake, R. E. (1995). *The art of case study research*. Thousand Oaks: Sage Publications.

Timmers, P. (1998). Business models for electronic markets. *Electronic Markets*, *8*(2), 3–8. doi:10.1080/10196789800000016

Waterman, D. (2001). The economics of internet TV: New niches vs mass audiences. *Info*, *3*, 215. doi:10.1108/14636690110801932

Writz, B. W. (1999). Convergence Processes, Value Constellations and Integration Strategies in the Multimedia Business. *The International Journal on Media Management*, *1*(1), 14–22.

Yin, R. K. (1994). *Case Study Research: Design and Methods* (2nd Edition ed.). London: Sage Publications.

Yip, G. S. (2004). Using strategy to change your business model. *Business Strategy Review*, *15*(2), 17–24. doi:10.1111/j.0955-6419.2004.00308.x

Young, K. (2007). *The TV channel without programmes* Retrieved: 8th October, 2007, from http://news.bbc.co.uk/1/hi/entertainment/6442567.stm

This work was previously published in International Journal of E-Business Research (IJEBR), edited by In Lee, pp. 55-67, copyright 2009 by IGI Publishing (an imprint of IGI Global).

Chapter 20

Extending TAM and IDT to Predict the Adoption of the Internet for B-to-B Marketing Activities:
An Empirical Study of UK Companies

Riyad Eid
Wolverhampton University, UK

ABSTRACT

There has been considerable Research into the usage of the Internet for Business-to-Business (B-to-B) marketing activities in recent years. The need to understand how and why B-to-B companies utilize the Internet is important for researchers and practitioners alike. This study combines Davis' model-the Technology Acceptance Model (TAM)- and Roger's Theory- the Innovation diffusion Theory (IDT) to understand the process of Internet adoption for marketing purposes. It makes a comprehensive review of information technology, information systems, and marketing literature to locate factors that predict Internet use for marketing purposes. Moreover, it extends both TAM and IDT to find out factors that affect relative advantage, ease of use and compatibility of using the Internet for B-to-B marketing activities. Using a sample of 123 UK companies utilize the Internet, we found a substantial positive effect of the proposed factors on the Internet usage for B-to-B marketing activities.

INTRODUCTION

A number of theories that explain the adoption of different IS/IT applications have appeared in the last two decades (Eid, 2005). These theories provide managers with careful reasoned arguments and enable them to better influence the evaluation, adoption and use of Internet technology

DOI: 10.4018/978-1-60960-132-4.ch020

(Karahanna and Straub, 1999). Moreover, current research into the adoption of end user technologies has been encouraged by the great need to find out factors that affect the success of IT application in the marketing context (Rose and Straub, 1998).

However, Internet marketing as a technological innovation in B-to-B companies has not been studied rigorously from the perspective of diffusion, although there are issues such as compatibility,

Copyright © 2011, IGI Global. Copying or distributing in print or electronic forms without written permission of IGI Global is prohibited.

complexity, and top management support can affect its adoption (Cooper and Zmud, 1990; Drury and Farhoomand, 1996; Eid and Trueman, 2004; Rose and Straub, 1998). Consequently, the main aim of this research is to investigate two theories that have been extensively used over the past twenty years to understand the adoption of IS/IT applications and links them to the marketing context. Firstly, technology acceptance model (TAM) and secondly, the diffusion of innovation theory (IDT). These models give different, though overlapping perspectives on how companies use new technologies. TAM focuses on attitudes toward using a particular IT based on perceived benefits (usefulness) and ease of use (Davis, 1989). IDT focuses on the relationship between "perceived attributes" of technology and "rate of adoption of technology" (Rogers, 1983; 1995).

Undoubtedly, this study uses TAM and IDT for predicting the adoption of the Internet in B-to-B international marketing because of their solid theoretical foundation and the fact that they have been proven successful in numerous studies. Furthermore, it extends both TAM and IDT to find out factors that affect relative advantage, ease of use and compatibility of using the Internet for B-to-B marketing activities. Therefore, this study uses exogenous, external variables such as "drivers" and "barriers" of International Internet marketing since these variables can affect behaviour and attitudes towards this technology.

OBJECTIVES OF THE PAPER

To analyze the adoption of the Internet by B-to-B companies, the following main question has been developed:

- What are the factors that affect the adoption of the Internet for B-to-B international marketing?

This was the overall question to be answered by the current study; defined by the following three objectives:

- To explore the factors that influence the adoption of the Internet by B-to-B companies,
- To develop and clarify a conceptual model integrating these adoption constructs, and its consequences on B-to-B companies' usage of the Internet for their marketing activities and,
- To specify and test hypothesised relationships derived from the conceptual framework.

In the following sections, first the development of the conceptual model and the hypotheses of the study are presented. Next, the methodology of the study is discussed followed by the analysis and results. More specifically, the conceptual model is tested using path analysis, and data collected by mail survey of 123 B-to-B UK companies. Finally, the conclusions and their implications are discussed.

Background and Literature Review

Technology Acceptance Model (TAM)

System usage is one of the basic dependent variables of information systems (DeLone and McLean, 1992). Researchers and practitioners often use the Technology Acceptance Model (TAM) to gain a better understanding of the use of IT/IS application (Lederer, *et al.*, 2000; Straub, *et al.*, 1997. It is one of the most important models that studies factors that affect the adoption of IS/IT applications.

Davis introduced an adoption of Theory of Reasoned Action (TRA), an especially well-researched intention theory that has explained the intended behaviour across a wide variety of IS/IT applications, but the Technology Acceptance

Figure 1. Technology acceptance model (TAM) (Davis 1985; Davis et al., 1989)

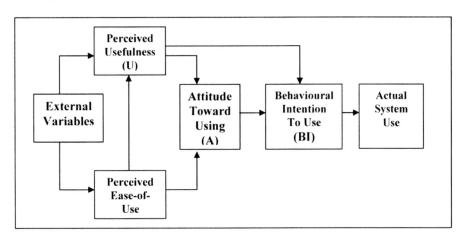

Model (TAM) was originally introduced to explain the cause/effect relationship between external variable and user acceptance of PC-based applications (Fenech, 1998). Davis states that TAM uses TRA as a theoretical basis for determining the cause/effect relationships between two key beliefs: Perceived usefulness (PU), and perceived ease of use (PEU), and how these benefits relate to users' attitudes, intentions and actual computer adoption behaviour (Davis et al., 1989).

According to TAM (see Figure 1) the usage of IT i.e. Internet is affected by beliefs a user has about its perceived usefulness (PU) and its perceived ease-of-use (PEU) (Karahanna and Straub, 1999). PU is defined as the degree to which a person believes that the use of an application can improve his/her performance (Davis, 1989). On the other hand, PEU is degree to which a person believes that using a particular application will be effortless (Davis, 1989). However, although PU and PEU were significantly correlated with usage, Davis (1989) found that PU mediates the effect of PEU on IT adoption (Karahanna and Straub, 1999). In other words, any IT/IS application will be used if it is believed to improve the performance, even if it is at first difficult to be used. The model has been very successful in explaining the adoption of various IT/IS applications including E-Mail and WWW (Fenech, 1998; Gefen and Straub, 1997).

Many researchers stated that usefulness is the strongest argument in favour of companies' use of the Internet (Davis, et al, 1989; Igbaria, et al, 1997; Lin and Lu, 2000; Teo, et al, 1999). As the level of technology advances in the near future, that perceived usefulness which is gained by the adoption of IT/IS application will increase.

However, many authors have extended the TAM by using other concepts in an attempt to improve its ability to predict the IT application usage. For example Chau (1996) has extended TAM to include both long-term and short-term perceived usefulness. The results reflect that perceived short-term usefulness has the greatest effect on the behavioural intention to adopt technology. Similarly, Igbaria, *et al.* (1995) have extended it to include individual, organisational and system characteristics. Their results confirm that individual, organisational, and system characteristics have a great influence on perceived ease of use and perceived usefulness. Gefen and Straub (1997) have extended this to include gender. They found that gender and IT diffusion models should be included along with other cultural factors.

Innovation Diffusion Theory (IDT)

Currently, researchers have started to rely on the innovation diffusion theory to study IT application

Figure 2. Innovation decision process (Rogers, 1983)

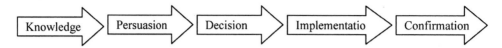

usage. Rogers (1983; 1995) has defined eight types of diffusion research from "earliness of knowing about innovation. and "rate of adoption in different social systems. to "opinion leadership. and "diffusion networks". communication channel use. and "consequences of innovation" are also considered. These issues may have particular significance from a marketing perspective (Eid, 2005).

The first contribution of IDT is the innovation decision process, which starts with one's knowledge about the innovation existence and ends with the confirmation of the adoption/rejection decision (Rogers, 1983, 1995). Figure 2 explains the five stages that are involved in innovation decision process developed by Rogers (1995). At the knowledge stage, users are first exposed to the innovation and gain initial understanding of it. In the second and third stages, managers move from persuasion to the decision to adopt/ reject the innovation. The fourth and final stages are implementation and use followed by the adoption/rejection decision to confirm or reserve the system from a usefulness or fitness perspective (Eid, 2005).

The second contribution of IDT is the group of innovation characteristics it provides that predict the rate of adoption. The attributes include relative advantage, compatibility, complexity, trialability, visibility, and observability (Rogers, 1983). The five attributes are reported to explain 49 to 87 percent of the variance rate of adoption (Rogers, 1995).

A stream of research on innovation diffusion has been based on these characteristics. They appear to have different relative importance on the adoption of innovation. For example, Cooper and Zmud (1990) found that the degree of com-

plexity of IT/IS application is a significant factor inhibiting successful adoption and the degree of compatibility is a critical factor in explaining the new IT/IS application adoption. Moore and Benbasat (1991) introduce seven different criteria of innovation diffusion: relative advantage, compatibility, trialability, observability, complexity, image and voluntariness of use. Each measure was needed to assess users' perception of an IT/ IS innovation. They also developed measurement scales, which can be applied to any innovation and have been adapted in subsequent research papers (see: Moore, 1996; Karahanna and Straub, 1999).

Combining TAM and IDT

Undoubtedly, Internet marketing is a new type of end-user information application of Electronic Commerce, and EC is heavily based on telecommunication technologies (Kalakota and Whinston, 1996). However, few recent studies have adopted TAM to study the adoption of telecommunication technologies such as E-mail and WWW (Cheung, *et al.*, 2000; Fenech, 1998; Gefen and Straub, 1997; Lederer, *et al.*, 2000; Lin and Lu, 2000; Moon and Kim, 2001). Chan and Swatman (2000) state that

...there is very little literature that discusses the process of Internet-based marketing. Therefore, researchers must start with the literature concerning more general IS/IT implementation and hope to develop a body of theory, which is more explicitly focused on the area of Internet marketing.

TAM and IDT are among the most effective models in predicting and explaining IT/IS usage, user evaluation of systems and innovation diffusion, respectively (Chen and Tan, 2004). They are chosen as the bases for predicting the adoption of the Internet in B-to-B international marketing because of their solid theoretical foundation and the fact that they have been proven successful in numerous studies (see for example Antonides et al., 1999; Cooper & Zmud, 1990; Davis et al., 1989; Drury & Farhoomand, 1996; Fenech, 1998; Ghorab, 1997; Higgins & Hogan, 1999; Igbaria et al., 1997; Karahanna & Straub, 1999; Rose & Straub, 1998; Straub et al., 1995; Straub, Keil, & Brenner, 1997; Teo *et al.*, 1999; Lederer, et al., 2000; Lin & Lu, 2000; Moon & Kim, 2001).

Undoubtedly, TAM and IDT often compliment each other. IDT involves the formation of a favourable or unfavourable attitude toward an innovation, but does not provide any information about the relationship between the attitudes and the actual accept/reject decision. TAM, on the other hand, provides theoretical linkage about beliefs, attitudes, intention, and action (Karahanna and Straub, 1999). In other words TAM is an IT theory that focuses more on the technology's end user and IDT is an IT theory that focuses more on the technology itself. Hence, combining TAM and IDT will help us to get an in-depth understanding of the adoption of the Internet by B-to-B companies.

TAM is specifically designed to understand human behaviour in the domain of information system, and most of research projects in the recent years deal with technology innovation (Eid, 2005). Based on the more general theory of reasoned action, TAM has been modified to predict computer usage (Rose and Straub, 1998). Lin and Lu (2000) found that TAM was able to explain behavior even in an Internet environment, accounting for 64% of the variance in usage. Consequently, it would appear that TAM can be used to study companies' acceptance of the Internet in B-to-B international marketing is a highly valid approach.

IDT, on the other hand, is a theory that has a long history of research in a great diversity of disciplines including sociology, anthropology, marketing, and information system. The theory

helps us to understand how and why an innovation is diffused into a social system (Rogers, 1995). B-to-B IIM is considered to be innovative because it has completely altered traditional marketing practice. Since this trend is still in its infancy, a well-researched theory, such as, IDT will help us to understand the process of using the Internet in B-to-B marketing (Eid, 2005; Eid & Elbeltagi, 2006).

However, Researchers working with TAM and IDT have discovered a similar relationship between the two constructs, namely (relative advantage and complexity) on one side, and (perceived usefulness and perceived ease of use) on the other side. Moore and Benbasat (1991) stated that Davis's Technology Acceptance Theory is quite similar to the Diffusion of Innovations Model. Davis included two constructs "Perceived Usefulness" and "Perceived Ease of Use".

Moore and Benbasat (1991) have raised a question about the appropriate terminology to use for Perceived Usefulness Construct. They suggest instead using the term Relative Advantage as it is a road term. Besides, Davis' definition of Perceived Usefulness is in relative terms. On the other hand, the term "Relative Advantage" has a very important spontaneous appeal, as it is a very generalisable term (Moore and Benbasat, 1991; Tornatzky and Klein, 1982). Therefore, the main constructs of interest in this research are the three previously mentioned characteristics of using an innovation namely, Perceived Ease of Use, Perceive Relative Advantage (Usefulness), and Perceived Compatibility.

Extending TAM and IDT

To improve its predictive value for the Internet marketing, additional constructs, *B-to-B IIM Drivers and B-to-B IIM Barriers*, were included in the model as mentioned earlier, many authors have extended the TAM in an attempt to improve its ability to predict use (Chau, 1996; Igbaria, *et al.*, 1995; Gefen and Straub, 1997; Karahanna and Straub, 1999).

B-to-B IIM Drivers

External drivers, internal drivers, or both motivate B-to-B IIM. Naturally, external drivers relate to the increased level of global competition, the changes in the international customers' needs, recent developments in IT, and competition (Chan & Swatman, 2000; Cronin, 1996b; Hollensen, 2001; Fillis et al., 2004; Poon and Jevons, 1997; Skinner, 1999; Venkatraman & Zaheer, 1990). Internal drivers are mainly related to changes in the organisational strategies and cost savings (Akinci et al., 2004; Chan & Swatman, 2000; Cronin, 1996b; Mattila et al., 2003; Mougayer, 1998; Simeon, 1999; Skinner, 1999).

Firstly, one of the strongest drivers is the increasing level of competition in the global markets has emphasised the need for organisations to innovate if they are to cope with global standards of products and services. Therefore, companies approach the Internet as a tool to dramatically improve businesses performance and gain or maintain a competitive position. Secondly, Chan and Swatman (2000), Berezai (2000), Poon and Jevons (1997) and Skinner, (1999) also believe that Internet marketing is driven by the never-ending needs of customers who are looking for better services and products. Thirdly, competitors' use of the Internet and their ability to respond to customers has a strong effect on the adoption of the Internet for marketing purposes. Fourthly, technology drives organisational change at process, communications, and strategic level. Changes in organisational strategy may involve Internet use to bring about new strategic goals. Finally, reducing costs by substituting the Internet for other communications channels with vendors, customers, information providers, and business partners is another driver for Internet use (Cronin, 1996a) since it is associated with cost savings.

B-to-B IIM Barriers

The Internet can do many things today and more opportunities are likely to be available in the future. However, this does not mean that the Internet is a magic stick that can solve all marketing problems. Many authors have argued that the Internet has a number of limitations that need to be addressed in marketing strategy (Evans & King, 1999; Hollensen, 2001; Porter, 2001; Skinner, 1999; Soh et al., 1997). These barriers include language barriers, cultural barriers, limited Internet access, different legislation, and logistical barriers (Hollensen, 2001).

When entering the global market there may be different barriers in each country: such as language barriers, cultural barriers, limited Internet access, different legislation, and logistical barriers (Hollensen, 2001:365). Furthermore, the Internet is not policed adequately and messages and credit card numbers can sometimes be intercepted. Though some devices such as firewall may protect internal data from theft, web users have fewer resources available for data protection. Another major problem of the Internet is information overload. The volume of information and sites on the Internet is growing exponentially.

Research Model and Hypotheses

The model for this research **(Figure 3)** is an extension of both TAM and IDT. B-to-B IIM drivers and barriers, the extended part of the model, is the construct of interest because it operationalises the question of how the adoption of the Internet by B-to-B companies is affected by external variables.

The basic assumption is that B-to-B basic drivers and barriers will have both direct effect on the use of the Internet and indirect effect through their influence on perceived relative advantage toward using the Internet.

The first hypothesis examines the link between B-to-B basic drivers to use the Internet and perceived relative advantage. The former has been found to influence B-to-B Internet usage directly or indirectly via perceived relative advantage. (Chan

Figure 3. Research model

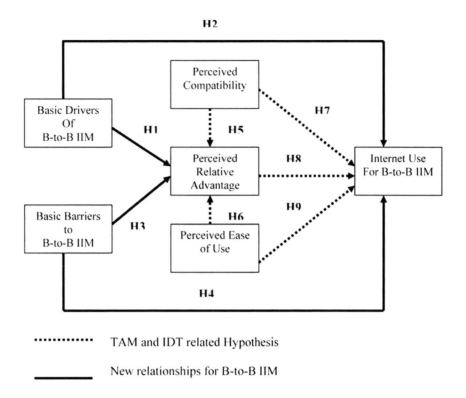

& Swatman, 2000; Cronin, 1996b; Hollensen, 2001; Mougayer, 1998; Poon & Jevons, 1997; Simeon, 1999; Skinner, 1999; Venkatraman & Zaheer, 1990). Venkatraman & Zaheer (1990:377) stated that it could be reasonably argued that major reason for the consideration of IT-based applications as potential sources of strategic advantages lies in the capability for electronic integration among a set of firms that could potentially change the basis of competition in a market place. Therefore, B-to-B IIM drivers are expected to have both direct and indirect influence on B-to-B Internet usage.

- **Hypothesis 1:** Basic drivers of B-to-B IIM affect the perceived relative advantage of using the Internet for B-to-B international marketing.
- **Hypothesis 2:** B-to-B IIM basic drivers positively affect B-to-B usage of the Internet.

Like B-to-B IIM drivers, B-to-B IIM basic barriers are expected to affect B-to-B usage of the Internet Both directly and indirectly via perceived relative advantage. When entering the global market there may be different barriers in each country: such as language barriers, cultural barriers, limited Internet access, different legislation, and logistical barriers (Hollensen, 2001:365). Furthermore, the Internet is not policed adequately and messages and credit card numbers can sometimes be intercepted. Though some devices such as firewall may protect internal data from theft, web users have fewer resources available for data protection. Visa, MasterCard, and others are working to define a better understanding way to secure payments based on encryption technology. Another major problem of the Internet is information overload. The volume of information and sites on the Internet is growing exponentially.

- **Hypothesis 3:** Basic barriers of B-to-B IIM negatively affect the perceived relative advantage of using the Internet for B-to-B international marketing.
- **Hypothesis 4:** B-to-B IIM basic barriers negatively affect B-to-B usage of the Internet.

Undoubtedly, stream of research on innovation diffusion has been based on TAM and IDT attributes. They appear to have different relative importance on the adoption of innovation. For example, Cooper and Zmud (1990) found that technological complexity is a significant factor inhibiting successful implementation and task-technology compatibility is a major factor in explaining the new technology adoption. Similarly, Tornatzky and Klein (1982) based on a meta-analysis of 105 diffusion studies; found that relative advantage, compatibility and ease of use were strongly related to the adoption of innovation (Fenech, 1998; Lederer et al., 2000; Lin & Lu, 2000; Moon & Kim, 2001; Stefansson, 2002). Based on the above and because TAM and IDT are used as the foundation model, the following hypotheses are offered to be verified in the context of B-to-B IIM.

- **Hypothesis 5:** There is a positive relationship between compatibility and perceived relative advantage in the B-to-B IIM context.
- **Hypothesis 6:** There is a positive relationship between ease of use and perceived relative advantage in the B-to-B IIM context.
- **Hypothesis 7:** Use of the Internet for B-to-B international marketing is dependent upon its compatibility.
- **Hypothesis 8:** Use of the Internet for B-to-B international marketing is dependent upon its relative advantage.
- **Hypothesis 9:** Use of the Internet for B-to-B international marketing is dependent upon its ease of use.

Research Methodology

The generalisability of the study relied on the representativeness of the respondents. Therefore, a representative selection of companies was made from a database of B-to-B companies. The selection included Aerospace, Agriculture, Chemical and Allied Products, Computers, Industrial Supplies and Textile companies. All the selected companies had implemented the Internet marketing. A research packet, which contained a covering letter and an anonymous [self-administering] questionnaire, was mailed to the head of marketing departments; customer services officers or sales managers [250 in total].

Of the 250 companies, a total of 161 questionnaires were returned. This included 9 returned not completed with a label stating "Gone Away-Please Remove From Mail List". A further 24 were returned with a covering letter explaining why they had not been completed the questionnaire. Most of the responses indicated that it was not company policy to participate in surveys or lack of time due to work pressures. Therefore, the number of returned completed questionnaires was 128 (including 5 unusable questionnaires, usable questionnaire = 123). Therefore, this procedure resulted in 123 useful responses or a 58.98% overall response rate. The response rate was calculated using the method proposed by De Vaus (1991: 99)

The sample can be described as follows: a majority of the respondents hold the position of marketing manager [64.2%], most were younger than 40 years old [52%], and a few respondent [approximately 2.4%] were more than 60 years old.. In terms of company size (44.7%) of the respondents have less than 100 employees, 37.4% have 100-500 employees, 13% have 501-1000 employees and (4.9%) have more than 1000 employees. Finally, 6.5% of the sample was Aerospace companies, 11.4% Agriculture companies, 6.5% Chemical and Allied Products companies,

Table 1. Measure of constructs

Constructs	Number of Items	Mean	Standard Deviation	Alpha
Internet: perceived ease of use	7	3.8103	.7201	.8938
Internet: perceived relative advantage	9	3.8879	.8162	.9487
Internet: perceived compatibility	7	3.8042	.6979	.8550
Internet use for marketing purposes	7	3.9512	.7285	.8754
B-to-B IIM Drivers	6	3.6867	.9344	.9206
B-to-B IIM Barriers	7	1.9600	.6454	.8058

32.5% Computers companies, 33.3% Industrial Supplies and 9.8% Textile companies.

To ensure that the valid responses were representatives of the larger population, a non-response bias test was used to compare the early and late respondents. χ^2 tests show no significant difference between the two groups of respondents at the 5% significance level, implying that a non-response bias is not a concern.

Research Instrument Development—Measures

The development of the research instrument was based mainly on new scales, because we could not identify any past studies directly addressing all of the issues in this research. However, and where possible, we used validated measures that have been previously applied. The constructs, scale items and factor loadings obtained from exploratory factor analysis are presented on the data analysis section.

Two consecutive rounds of pre-testing were conducted in order to insure that respondents could understand the measurement scales used in the study: First, the questionnaire was reviewed by six academic researchers experienced in questionnaire design and next, the questionnaire was piloted with two Internet marketing experts known to the researchers. The pilot took the form of an interview where the participants were first handed a copy of the questionnaire and asked to

complete it and then discuss any comments or questions they had. The outcome of the pre-testing process was a slight modification and alteration of the existing scales, in light of the scales context under investigation.

Analysis and Results

This section presents the statistics and analytic results of the research model and hypotheses.

Scale Reliability and Descriptive Statistics

The reliability of all constructs was assessed by the Cronbach alpha reliability coefficient (Cronbach, 1951). These coefficients are represented for each of the constructs in Table 1. Cronbach's alpha range, from 0.8085 for B-to-B IIM barriers to 0.9487 for Internet: perceived relative advantage, exceeded Nunnally's standards for research (Nunally, 1978).

Table 2 demonstrate the interrelation among all constructs. The bi-variate relationships indicate that all the variables were significantly correlated with each other.

Hypothesis Testing

The data were analysed using path analysis. Path analysis is a multivariate analytical methodology for empirically examining sets of relationships in

Table 2. Correlation matrix

	Perceived ease of use	Perceived relative advantage	Perceived compatibility	Internet use for marketing purposes	B-to-B IIM Drivers	B-to-B IIM Barriers
Perceived ease of use	1.000					
Perceived relative advantage	.734**	1.000				
Perceived compatibility	.729**	.764**	1.000			
Internet use for marketing purposes	.757**	.622**	.714**	1.000		
B-to-B IIM Drivers	.535**	.758**	.771**	.772**	1.000	
B-to-B IIM Barriers	-.533**	-.550**	-.568**	-.571**	-.419**	1.000

** Correlation is significant at the 0.01 level (2-tailed).

Table 3. Direct, indirect and total effect of different constructs on Internet use

Dependent Variables	Internet Use for B-to-B IIM		
	Direct Effect	Indirect Effect	Total Effect
Internet: perceived ease of use	0.124	0.116	0.240
Internet: perceived relative advantage	0.527	0.000	0.527
Internet: perceived compatibility	0.226	0.254	0.480
B-to-B IIM Drivers	0.116	0.128	0.244
B-to-B IIM Barriers	-0.038	-0.026	-0.064

the form of linear causal models (Duncan, 1966; Li, 1975).

In the regression analysis, we checked the multicollinearity of independent variables. Variance Inflation Factor (VIF) for the all independent was less than 10, indicating that we did not have any significant mulicolinearity problems with any of the independent variables (Neter et al, 1990). Besides, the correlation between independent variables are all less than 0.8 (Emory and Cooper, 1991). Furthermore, the scatter plots of the standardised residuals by the standardised predicted scores were also examined to verify the assumption of linearity.

Many researchers recommended calculating the overall impact of variables on B-to-B Internet use (Bryman & Cramer, 2001). Calculating the direct and indirect effect of each variable would

do this. The following table (Table 3) shows direct, indirect and total effects of all variables.

In terms of goodness-of-fit indicators, the model account for 89% of the variance in the use of the Internet by B-to-B companies. In addition, B-to-B IIM Drivers and Barriers account for 79.5% of the variance in perceived relative advantage of the Internet.

Figure (4) shows the regression results from testing the determinants of Internet use. B-to-B IIM drivers **H2** (Path coefficient=0.116 P< 0.01), compatibility **H7** (Path coefficient=0.226 P< 0.05), Relative advantage **H8** (Path coefficient=0.527 P< 0.01), and ease of use **H9** (Path coefficient=0.124 P< 0.01) are all positively related to the use of the Internet for B-to-B marketing. B-to-B IIM drivers **H1** (Path coefficient=0.244 P< 0.01), compatibility **H5** (Path coefficient=0.483 P< 0.01) and ease

Figure 4. Internet use: Path analysis

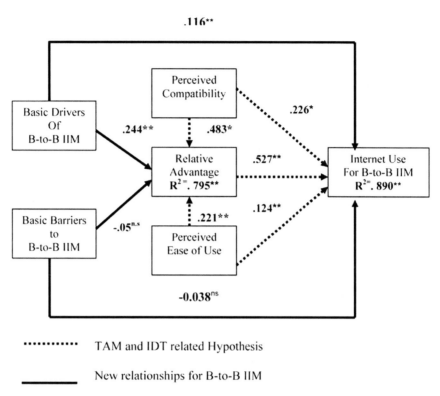

.... TAM and IDT related Hypothesis

———— New relationships for B-to-B IIM

** Significant at 0.01. *Significant at 0.05 and n.s not significant

of use **H6** (Path coefficient=0.221 P< 0.01) are positively related to relative advantage. Finally, although B-to-B IIM has a negative effect on both relative advantage (Path coefficient= -0.05) and Internet usage (Path coefficient= -0.038), these relations were not significant.

Discussion

This study extended both TAM and IDT in the Internet environment by adding B-to-B IIM drivers and barriers as external variables. B-to-B use of the Internet is significantly affected by their perception about Relative Advantage (Usefulness), Compatibility and Ease of Use respectively (Eid and Trueman, 2002). In fact the regression analysis shows that perceived relative advantage has the large effect on the Internet usage for

marketing purposes and perceived ease of use has the smallest (but significant) effect on it. These findings support the previous researches that show that perceived relative advantage (Usefulness) is significantly more strongly linked to IT usage (Davis, et al, 1989; Igbaria, et al, 1997; Lin and Lu, 2000; Teo, et al, 1999).

This study found that perceived compatibility is the second most important determining factor affecting the use of the Internet for B-to-B marketing. This means that when marketers feel that the Internet is compatible with their B-to-B activities, they are more likely to use it. This supports the finding of Cooper and Zmud (1990) that IT/IS application should be compatible with the organisation and its activities. We also find that the effect of perceived compatibility is mediated by perceived relative advantage (usefulness). Therefore, the more compatable the Internet application is, the greater the relative advantage (usefulness) perceived by marketers, which, in turn, increases the Internet usage for marketing purposes.

On the other hand, perceived ease of use had a less significant effect on Internet usage than perceived relative advantage and perceived compatibility. Therefore, to encourage Internet usage, top management should promote the Internet's relative advantage (usefulness) more than its ease of use. The results of our study further support previous findings in that the effect of perceived ease of use is mediated by perceived relative advantage (Usefulness) (Davis, 1989; Davis et al, 1989; Lin and Lu, 2000). That is to say, the less complex the Internet application is, the more relative advantage it is perceived by marketers to do their marketing activities, which, in turn, increase the usage of the Internet for marketing purposes.

Furthermore, B-to-B IIM drivers have a significant direct positive impact and indirect positive impact via perceived relative advantage on B-to-B Internet usage. This result is consistent with previous studies. For instance, Chan and Swatman (2000); Berezai (2000); Poon and Jevons (1997); Skinner, (1999) agreed that Internet marketing is driven by the never-ending needs of customers to look for better services and products. Competitors' use of the Internet and response to customers has a great impact on the adoption of the Internet for marketing purposes (Skinner, (1999). Chan and Swatman (2000:81) stated that:

IT developments are also forcing organisations to be up-to-date in their use of advanced technologies regarding delivery of speedy and high quality information, as well as facilitating greater degrees of communication and integration across business units and external partners

The increasing awareness of the gains that B-to-B can obtain from using the Internet is a key driver as well (Berezai, 2000). Changes in organisational strategy may involve some Internet uses to bring about the new business desires. The organisation may set up a strategy that makes intensive use of existing IT/IS trading facility to include the Internet as an alternative medium to bring about the new business wants (Chan and Swatman, 2000). Reducing costs by substituting the Internet for other communications channels with vendors, customers, information providers, and business partners is a strong motive for many companies to use the Internet (Cronin, 1996a: 21)

It was a surprise, however, to find that B-to-B barriers were not significantly related to both perceived relative advantage and Internet adoption. However, upon closer examination of our study, this should not have been unexpected. Many B-to-B IIM barriers have been addressed. For example, language barriers have launched a new Web-oriented translation industry (Eid et al., 2002). For instance, World Point (www.worldpoint.com) introuced a Web-based "customisation" service that translates and edits documents such as annual reports, manuals, and marketing materials into eighteen languages- not just text, but also currencies, dates, and even colour conventions (Kotab & Helsen, 2000:611). On the other hand, Quelch and Klein, (1996) note that the extensive use of the Internet for marketing activities will accelerate the trend for English to become the *Lingua Franca* of commerce. Besides, the security requirements have already been addresses within the electronic community and a number of technologies have been developed to satisfy different elements (Eid *et al.*, 2006). For example, Secure Sockets Layer (SSL) protocol developed by Netscape, which allows encryption of messages, can be used to transfer all data in encrypted form (Furnell and Karweni, 1999). Therefore, it is reasonable to find that B-to-B IIM barriers have no significant impact on the Internet usage.

CONCLUSION AND MANAGERIAL IMPLICATIONS

Understanding the theoretical determinants of the adoption of the Internet by B-to-B companies is an important step. The research has extended both TAM and IDT in an attempt to improve their ability to predict use of the Internet by B-to-B companies. Only B-to-B IIM drivers which include factors such as customer demand (requirement), reduced operating costs (marketing and production), reduced sales and purchasing costs, improving the range and quality of services, take advantage of being an early adopter and avoiding losing market share to competitors who are already using Internet marketing have been found to significantly affect B-to-B Internet usage for marketing purposes (Eid, 2005).

However, understanding the key constructs in TAM and IDT namely perceived relative advantage (usefulness), perceived ease of use and perceived compatibility is crucial to understand the adoption of the Internet by B-to-B companies. Therefore, this study represents one such step by testing these constructs and proposing and empirically testing the antecedents of these constructs in the field of Internet marketing. The results revealed a number of areas for future research.

Based on TAM and IDT, this study proposes factors that affect the adoption of the Internet for B-to-B international marketing activities. It also extended them to include factors that are more closed to B-to-B IIM. It thus helps researchers understand the relationships between relative advantage (usefulness), ease of use and compatibility, and the adoption of the Internet by B-to-B companies. It confirms that the use of the Internet depends on the perceptions of marketers about its usefulness, ease of use and compatibility. It also helps to understand the predictors of relative advantage of the Internet.

Moreover, this study has potential for managerial application in the adoption and use of the Internet for marketing purposes. By confirming the IT theories (TAM and IDT) in the field of Internet Marketing, it suggests that companies should provide usefulness, compatibility and ease of use for their Web sites to encourage their customer to revisit their sites. It also suggests both specific factors and items that companies might emphasise when they create their Web sites. These factors could be useful for both Web site managers and Web site developers in companies that encourage employees to use specific applications of the Internet (especially Intranet). Those developers and manager should consider these factors on the design of such application if they are to improve those applications and guarantee a wide use of them.

However, as with any study, there are certain limitations that should be recognized. First, the present study relied on a sample of UK companies and, consequently, we cannot afford to generalize the findings. Second, the data are cross-sectional in nature and hence it is not possible to determine causal relationships. An additional limitation of the study is the reliance on the subjective, self-report indicators to measure the research constructs in the survey questionnaire. For example, constructs measures such as perceived relative advantage, perceived ease of use, perceived compatibility and Internet usage were self-reported as opposed to objectively measured and therefore do not necessarily reflect objective reality. However, as suggested by Davis (1989) on the adoption of a new technology studies, beliefs are seen as meaningful variables in their own right. He further noted that, even if an application would objectively improve performance, if users do not perceive it as useful, they are unlikely to use it (Davis, 1989). Consequently, the above limitation notwithstanding, the results represent a promising step toward the establishment of improved measures for those important variables.

Recommendations for Future Research

By combining TAM and IDT, the study provides a new instrument tailored to the Internet. On one hand, future researchers could use this instrument for assessing the adoption of all types of Internet applications such as; Business-to-Customer, Business-to- Administration, Consumer-to-Administration. On the other hand, the instrument developed in this research could call for more research to be done. Alternative wording of the items might be tried. With further refinement of the Internet-specific items, greater variance explained might be achieved.

This work was previously published in International Journal of E-Business Research (IJEBR), edited by In Lee, pp. 68-85, copyright 2009 by IGI Publishing (an imprint of IGI Global).

ACKNOWLEDGMENT

The author sincerely thanks the editor and the anonymous IJEBR reviewers for their constructive and valuable comments and suggestions.

REFERENCES

Akinci, S., Aksoy, S., & Atilgan, E. (2004). Adoption of Internet banking among sophisticated consumer segments in an advanced developing country. *International Journal of Bank Marketing*, *22*(3), 212–232. doi:10.1108/02652320410530322

Antonides, G., Amesz, H. B., & Hulscher, I. C. (1999). Adoption of payment systems in ten countries-A case study of diffusion of innovations. *European Journal of Marketing*, *33*(11/12), 1123–1135. doi:10.1108/03090569910292302

Avlonitis, G. J., & Karayanni, D. A. (2000). The Impact of Internet Use on Business-to-Business Marketing: Examples from American and European Companies. *Industrial Marketing Management*, *29*(5), 441–459. doi:10.1016/S0019-8501(99)00071-1

Berezai, P. (2000). *B2B on the Internet: 2000-2005*. London: Datamonitor PLC.

Borders, A. L., Jonston, W. J., & Rigdon, E. E. (2001). Beyond the Dyad: Electronic Commerce and Network Perspectives in Industrial Marketing Management. *Industrial Marketing Management*, *30*(2), 199–205. doi:10.1016/S0019-8501(00)00143-7

Chan, C., & Swatman, P. M. C. (2000). From EDI to Internet Commerce: The BHL Steel Experiences. *Internet Research: Electronic Networking Applications and Policy*, *10*(1), 72–82. doi:10.1108/10662240010312039

Chau, P. Y. (1996). An Empirical Assessment of a Modified Technology Acceptance Model. *Journal of Management Information Systems*, *13*(2), 185–204.

Chen, L., & Tan, J. (2004). Technology Adaptation in E-commerce: Key Determinants of Virtual Stores Acceptance. *European Management Journal*, *22*(1), 74–86. doi:10.1016/j.emj.2003.11.014

Cheung, W., Chang, M. T., & Lia, V. S. (2000). Prediction of Internet and World Wide Web Usage at Work: a Test of an Extended Triandis Model. *Decision Support Systems*, *30*(1), 83–100. doi:10.1016/S0167-9236(00)00125-1

Cooper, R. B., & Zmud, R. W. (1990). Information Technology Implementation Research: A Technological Diffusion Approach. *Management Science*, *36*(2), 123–139. doi:10.1287/mnsc.36.2.123

Cronin, M. J. (1996a), *Global Advantage on the Internet*, New York: Van Nostrand Reinhold.

Cronin, M. J. (1996b). *The Internet Strategy Handbook: Lessons from the New Frontier of Business.* Boston, MA: Harvard Business School Press.

Davis, F. D. (1989). Perceived Usefulness, Perceived Ease of Use, and User Acceptance of Information Technology. *MIS Quarterly, 13*(3), 319–340. doi:10.2307/249008

Davis, F. D., Bagozzi, R. P., & Warshaw, P. R. (1989). User Acceptance of Computer Technology: A Comparison of Two Theoretical Model. *Management Science, 35*(8), 982–1003. doi:10.1287/mnsc.35.8.982

DeLone, W. H., & McLean, E. R. (1992). Information Systems Success: The Quest for The Dependent Variable. *Information Systems Research, 3*(1), 60–95. doi:10.1287/isre.3.1.60

Drury, D. H., & Farhoomand, A. (1996). Innovation Adoption of EDI. *Information Resources Management Journal, 9*(3), 5–13.

Duncan, O. D. (1966). Path Analysis: Sociological Example. *American Journal of Sociology, 72*(1), 1–16. doi:10.1086/224256

Eid, R. (2005). International Internet Marketing: a Triangulation Study of Drivers and Barriers in the Business-to-Business Context in the United Kingdom. *Marketing Intelligence & Planning, 23*(3), 266–280. doi:10.1108/02634500510597300

Eid, R., & Elbeltagi, I. (2006). The Influence of the Internet on B-to-B International Marketing Activities: An Empirical Study of the UK Companies. *Journal of Euromarketing, 15*(2), 51–73. doi:10.1300/J037v15n02_04

Eid, R., Elbeltagi, I., & Zairi, M. (2006). Making B2B International Internet Marketing Effective: A Study of Critical Factors Using a Case Study Approach. *Journal of International Marketing, 14*(4), 87–109. doi:10.1509/jimk.14.4.87

Eid, R., & Trueman, M. (2002). *The Adoption of the Internet for B-to-B International Marketing: A theoretical model.* Bradford University School of Management Working Paper Series, No 02/10.

Eid, R., & Trueman, M. (2004). Factors affecting the success of business-to-business international Internet marketing (B-to-B IIM): an empirical study of UK companies. *Industrial Management & Data Systems, 104*(1), 16–30. doi:10.1108/02635570410514061

Eid, R., Trueman, M., & Ahmed, A. (2002). A Cross-Industry Review of B2B Critical Success Factors. *Internet Research: Electronic Networking Applications and Policy, 12*(2), 110–123. doi:10.1108/10662240210422495

Emory, C. W., & Cooper, D. R. (1991). *Business Research Methods* (4th ed.). Boston: Irwin.

Evans, J. R., & King, V. E. (1999). Business to Business Marketing and the World Wide Web: Planning, Marketing and Assessing Web Sites. *Industrial Marketing Management, 28*(4), 343–358. doi:10.1016/S0019-8501(98)00013-3

Fenech, T. (1998). Using Perceived Ease of Use and Perceived Usefulness to Predict Acceptance of the World Wide Web. *Computer Networks & ISDN Systems, 30*(1-7), 629-630.

Fillis, I., Ulf, J., & Beverly, W. (2004). Factors impacting on e-business adoption and development in the smaller firm. *International Journal of Entrepreneurial Behaviour and Research, 10*(3), 178–191. doi:10.1108/13552550410536762

Gefen, D., & Straub, D. W. (1997). Gender Differences in the perception and use of E- mail: An Extension to the Technology Acceptance Model. *MIS Quarterly, 21*(4), 389–400. doi:10.2307/249720

Ghorab, K. E. (1997). The Impact of Technology Acceptance Consideration on System Usage, and Adopted Level of Technological Sophistication: An Empirical Investigation. *International Journal of Information Management, 17*(4), 249–259. doi:10.1016/S0268-4012(97)00003-0

Higgins, S. H., & Hogan, P. T. (1999). Internal Diffusion of High Technology Industrial Innovations: An Empirical Study. *Journal of Business and Industrial Marketing, 14*(1), 61–75. doi:10.1108/08858629910254157

Hoffman, D. L., Novak, T. P., & Chatterjee, P. (1995). Commercial Scenarios for the Web: Opportunities and Challenges. *Journal of Computer-Mediated Communication, 1*(3), 1–19.

Hollensen, S. (2001). *Global Marketing: A market-responsive approach* (2nd ed.). England: Pearson Education Limited.

Igbaria, M., Guimaraes, T., & Davis, G. B. (1995). Testing the Determinants of Microcomputer Usage via a Structure Equation Model. *Journal of Management Information Systems, 11*(4), 87–114.

Igbaria, M., Zinatelli, N., Gragg, P., & Cavaye, A. (1997). A Personal Computing Acceptance Factors in Small firms: A Structural Equation Model. *MIS Quarterly, 28*(2), 357–389.

Kalakota, R., & Whinston, A. B. (1996). *Frontiers of Electronic Commerce*. Addition- Wesley Publishing Company, Inc.

Karahanna, E., & Straub, D. W. (1999). The Psychological Origins of Perceived Usefulness and Ease-of-Use. *Information & Management, 35*(4), 237–250. doi:10.1016/S0378-7206(98)00096-2

Lederer, A. L., Maupin, D. J., Sena, M. P., & Zhuang, Y. (2000). The Technology Acceptance Model and the World Wide Web. *Decision Support Systems, 29*, 269–282. doi:10.1016/S0167-9236(00)00076-2

Li, C. C. (1975). *Path Analysis: A Primer*. Pacific Grove, CA: The Boxwood Press.

Lin, J. C., & Lu, H. (2000). Towards an Understanding of the Behavioural Intention to Use a Web Site. *International Journal of Information Management, 20*(3), 197–208. doi:10.1016/S0268-4012(00)00005-0

Mattila, M., Karjaluoto, H., & Pento, T. (2003). Internet banking adoption among mature customers: early majority or laggards? *Journal of Services Marketing, 17*(5), 514–528. doi:10.1108/08876040310486294

Moon, J., & Kim, Y. (2001). Extending the TAM for a World-Wide-Web Context. *Information & Management, 38*(4), 217–230. doi:10.1016/S0378-7206(00)00061-6

Moore, G. C. (1996). Integration Diffusion of Innovations and Theory of Reasoned action Models to predict Utilization of information Technology by End-Users. In *Diffusion and Adoption of Information Technology*. London: Chapman&Hall.

Moore, G. C., & Benbasat, I. (1991). Development of an Instrument to Measure the Perceptions of Adopting an Information Technology Innovation. *Information Systems Research, 2*(3), 192–223. doi:10.1287/isre.2.3.192

Mougayer, W. (1998). *Opening Digital Markets: Battle Plans and Strategies for Internet Commerce* (2nd ed.). New York: Commerce Net Press, McGraw-Hill.

Neter, J., Kutner, M. H., Nachtsheim, C. L., & Wasserman, W. (1990). *Applied Linear Regression Models*. Chicago: Irwin Inc.

Poon, S., & Jevons, C. (1997). Internet Enabled International Marketing: A Small Business Network Perspective. *Journal of Marketing Management, 13*(1-3), 29–42.

Poon, S., & Swatman, P. M. C. (1998). A Combined Method Study of Small Business Internet-Commerce. *International Journal of Electronic Commerce, 2*(3), 31–46.

Porter, M. E. (2001). Strategy and the Internet. *Harvard Business Review, 79*(3), 63–78.

Rogers, E. M. (1983). *The Diffusion of Innovations* (3rd ed.). New York: Free Press.

Rogers, E. M. (1995). *The Diffusion of Innovations* (4th ed). New York: Free Press.

Rose, G., & Straub, D. (1998). Predicting General IT Use: Applying TAM to the Arabic World. *Journal of Global Information Management, 6*(3), 39–47.

Simeon, R. (1999). Evaluating Domestic and International Web-Site Strategies. *Internet Research: Electronic Networking Applications and Policy, 9*(4), 297–308. doi:10.1108/10662249910286842

Skinner, S. (1999). *Business-to-Business E-Commerce: Investment Perspective*. London: Durlacher Ltd.

Soh, C., Mah, Q. Y., Gan, F. J., Chew, D., & Reid, E. (1997). The Use of the Internet for Business: Experience of Early Adaptors in Singapore. *Internet Research: Electronic Networking Applications and Policy, 7*(3), 217–228. doi:10.1108/10662249710171869

Stefansson, G. (2002). Business-to-Business Data Sharing: A Source for Integration of Supply Chains. *International Journal of Production Economics, 75*(1-2), 135–146. doi:10.1016/S0925-5273(01)00187-6

Straub, D. W., Keil, M., & Brenner, W. (1997). Testing the technology acceptance model across cultures: A three country study. *Information & Management, 33*(1), 1–11. doi:10.1016/S0378-7206(97)00026-8

Straub, D. W., Limayen, M., & Karahanna, E. (1995). Measuring System Usage:Implecations for IS Theory Testing. *Management Science, 41*(8), 1328–1342. doi:10.1287/mnsc.41.8.1328

Teo, T. S. H., Tan, M., & Buk, W. K. (1999). Intrinsic and Extrinsic Motivation in Internet Usage. *Omega, 27*(1), 25–37. doi:10.1016/S0305-0483(98)00028-0

Tornatzky, L. G., & Klein, K. J. (1982). Innovation Characteristics and Innovation Adoption-Implementation: A Meta Analysis of Findings. *IEEE Transactions on Engineering Management, 29*(1), 28–45.

Venkatraman, N., & Zaheer, A. (1990). Electronic Integration and Strategic Advantage: A Quasi-Experimental Study in the Insurance Industry. *Information Systems Research, 1*(4), 377–393. doi:10.1287/isre.1.4.377

APPENDIX

Table 4. Scale items and sources

Construct	Measures Used to Capture Constructs	Source
Internet Usage for B-to-B IIM	-Internet and its applications is used extensively in my organisation -Internet customers are strategically important to my company -The Internet will have an increasing role in B-to-B international marketing in the future -We expect our relationship with our Internet customer to strengthen over time -We expect to increase our sales via the Internet in the future -We have invested a lot of effort in the relationship with our Internet customers	New scale based on Davis,1989 and Davis et al., 1989, Eid and Elbeltagi, 2005
B-to-B IIM Drivers	-Customer demand (requirement) -Reduced operating costs (marketing and production) -Reduced sales and purchasing costs -Improving the range and quality of services we can offer to customers online -Take advantage of being an early adopter -Avoiding losing market share to competitors who are already using Internet Marketing	Adapted from Eid, 2005
B-to-B IIM Barriers	-Your company has concerns about confidentiality -The technology costs associated with further Internet marketing development are too high -Language barriers -The poor public telecommunications infrastructure hinders your technological advancement -Lack of management willingness to adopt IT is an obstacle to further Internet Marketing development -Cultural barriers -Further Internet Marketing development offers no tangible benefits to your company	Adapted from Eid, 2005
Perceived ease of Use	-Learning to use the Internet for marketing to other companies is easy for me -I find it easy to get the Internet to do what I want to do -The Internet is not rigid and flexible to interact with -It is easy for me to remember how to perform tasks using the Internet -Interacting with the Internet requires very little mental effort -My interaction with the Internet for marketing to other companies is clear and understandable	New scale based on Davis,1989 and Davis et al., 1989
Perceived Relative Advantage	-Using the Internet improves the quality of the marketing activities -Using the Internet gives me greater control over my work -The Internet enables me to accomplish marketing activities more quickly -The Internet supports critical aspects of my job -Using the Internet increases my marketing productivity -Using the Internet improves my marketing performance -Using the Internet allows me to accomplish more marketing work than would otherwise be possible -Using the Internet enhances my marketing effectiveness	New scale based on Davis,1989, Davis et al.,1989 and Soh et al., 1997
Perceived Compatibility	-The Internet is consistent with the values, beliefs, and business needs of my company -There is sufficient support for Internet marketing from top management -There is no (or only minimal) resistance to changes that the Internet requires from staff -My company exchange more information now with Internet customers than we did before the Internet was used -The Internet is compatible with all aspects of the work of the marketing department -Using the Internet improves our operations regarding to (Order Status- Stock Level- Production Schedule)	New scale based on Soh et al., 1997

This work was previously published in International Journal of E-Business Research (IJEBR), edited by In Lee, pp. 68-85, copyright 2009 by IGI Publishing (an imprint of IGI Global).

Compilation of References

Aaker, D. (1998). *Strategic Market Management*. New York: Wiley.

Aaker, D. A. (1992). Managing the most important asset: Brand equity. *Planning Review, 20*, 56–58.

Absolutely Positively Wellington. (2006*). Entrepreneurs – Trade Me*. Retrieved June 5, 2006 from http://www.wellington.govt.nz/aboutwgtn/innovation/ details/trademe.html.

Ackerman, M. S. (2004). Privacy in pervasive environments: next generation labeling protocols. *Personal and Ubiquitous Computing, 8*(6), 430–439. doi:10.1007/s00779-004-0305-8

Acquisti, A., & Grossklags, J. (2005). Privacy and Rationality in Individual Decision Making. *IEEE Security & Privacy, 3*, 26–33. doi:10.1109/MSP.2005.22

Acquisti, A. (2004). *Privacy in Electronic Commerce and the Economics of Immediate Gratification*. Paper presented at the Proceedings of the 5th ACM Electronic Commerce Conference, New York, NY.

Adams, C., & Barbieri, K. (2006). Privacy Enforcement in E-Services Environments. In Yee, G. (Ed.), *Privacy Protection for E-Services* (pp. 172–202). Hershey, PA: IDEA Group Publishing.

Afuah, A., & Tucci, C. L. (2003). *Internet Business Models and Strategies: Text and cases* (2nd ed.). Boston: McGraw-Hill.

Agiliance. (2010). *Compliance Manager*. Retrieved August 2010 from www.agiliance.com/assets/pdf/Agiliance_compliance_automation.pdf

Aha, D. W., Kibler, D., & Albert, M. K. (1991). Instance-Based Learning Algorithms. *Machine Learning, 6*(1), 37–66. doi:10.1007/BF00153759

Ahn, J.-w., Brusilovsky, P., Grady, J., He, D., & Syn, S. Y. (2007). Open User Profiles for Adaptive News Systems: Help or Harm? In *16th International Conference on World Wide Web (WWW 2007)* (pp. 11-20). New York:ACM.

AIDE. (2010). *Advanced Intrusion Detection Environment*. Retrieved August 2010 from http://www.cs.tut.fi/~rammer/aide.html

Aiken, L. S., & West, S. G. (1991). *Multiple Regression: Testing and Interpreting Interactions*. Thousand Oaks, CA: Sage Publications.

Ajzen, I. (1991). The theory of planned behavior. *Organizational Behavior and Human Decision Processes, 50*(2), 179–211. doi:10.1016/0749-5978(91)90020-T

Akinci, S., Aksoy, S., & Atilgan, E. (2004). Adoption of Internet banking among sophisticated consumer segments in an advanced developing country. *International Journal of Bank Marketing, 22*(3), 212–232. doi:10.1108/02652320410530322

Alavi, M., & Leidner, D. E. (2001). Review: Knowledge management and knowledge management systems: Conceptual foundations and research issues. *MIS Quarterly, 25*(1), 107–136. doi:10.2307/3250961

Alba, J., Lynch, J., Weitz, B., & Janiszewsk, C. (1997). Interactive home shopping: consumer, retailer, and manufacturer incentives to participate in electronic marketplaces. *Journal of Marketing, 61*(July), 38–53. doi:10.2307/1251788

Copyright © 2011, IGI Global. Copying or distributing in print or electronic forms without written permission of IGI Global is prohibited.

Albert, S., & Whetten, D. (1985). Organizational Identity. In Cummings, L. L., & Staw, B. (Eds.), *Research in Organizational Behavior, (7)* (pp. 263–295). Greenwich, CT: JAI Press.

Albitar, S., Espinasse, B., & Fournier, S. (2010). Combining Agents and Wrapper Induction for Information Gathering on Restricted Web Domains. *In Proceedings of the fourth international conference on research challenges in information science.*

All Blacks. (2006).Retrieved July 23, 2006, from http://en.wikipedia.org/wiki/ All_Blacks.

Allison, D. (2005). System Policy Compliance Checker. MSc.Thesis, University of Newcastle, UK.

Altman, I. (1975). *The Environment and Social Behavior: Privacy, Personal Space, Territory, and Crowding.* Monterey, CA: Brooks/Cole Publishing.

Altman, I. (1977). Privacy Regulation: Culturally Universal or Culturally Specific? *The Journal of Social Issues, 33*(3), 66–84. doi:10.1111/j.1540-4560.1977.tb01883.x

Altman, I. (1974). Privacy: A Conceptual Analysis. In D. H. Carson (Ed.), *Man-Environment Interactions: Evaluations and Applications (Part 2; Vol. 6: Privacy)* (pp. 3-28). Washington, DC: Environmental Design Research Association.

Alves A., & al. (2007). Web Services Business Process Execution Language Version 2.0. OASIS standard. Available at http://docs.oasis-open.org/wsbpel/2.0/wsbpel-v2.0.pdf

Ambite, J. L., & Knoblock, C. A. (1997). Agents for Information Gathering. *IEEE Expert: Intelligent Systems and Their Applications, 12*(5), 2-4. doi:http://dx.doi.org/10.1109/64.621219

Amit, R., & Schoemaker, P. J. H. (1993). Strategic assets and organizational rent. *Strategic Management Journal, 14*(1), 33–46. doi:10.1002/smj.4250140105

Amit, R., & Zott, C. (2001). Value creation in e-business. *Strategic Management Journal, 22*(6/7), 453–520.

Anderson, J., & Meyer, T. (1975). Functionalism and the mass media. *Journal of Broadcasting, 19*(1), 11–22.

Anderson, C. (2006). *The long tail: How endless choice is creating unlimited demand.* London: Random House Business Books.

Anderson, M. J., Moffie, M., & Dalton, C. I. (2007). *Towards Trustworthy Virtualisation Environments: Xen Library OS Security Service Infrastructure.* Tech. Rep. No. HPL-2007-69, HP Labs, Bristol. Retrieved June 2008 from http://www.hpl.hp.com/techreports/2007/HPL-2007-69.pdf

Ang, J. S. (1992). On the theory of finance for privately held firms. *Journal of Small Business Finance, 1*(3), 185–203.

Ang, J. S., Cole, R. A., & Lin, J. W. (2000). Agency costs and ownership structure. *The Journal of Finance, 55*(1), 81–106. doi:10.1111/0022-1082.00201

Antonides, G., Amesz, H. B., & Hulscher, I. C. (1999). Adoption of payment systems in ten countries-A case study of diffusion of innovations. *European Journal of Marketing, 33*(11/12), 1123–1135. doi:10.1108/03090569910292302

Applegate, L. M. (2001). E-business Models: Making sense of the Internet business landscape. In G. Dickson, W. Gary and G. DeSanctis (Eds.), *Information Technology and the future enterprise: New models for managers.* Upper Saddle River, N.J.: Prentice Hall.

Archer. (2010). *Compliance Suite.* Retrieved August 2010 from www.archer.com/

Ardissono, L., Console, L., & Torre, I. (2001). An Adaptive System for the Personalized Access to News. *AI Communications, 14*(3), 129–147.

Argyris, C., & Schon, D. (1978). *Organizational learning: A theory of action perspective.* Reading, MA: Addison-Wesley.

Arshad, F. (2004). *Privacy Fox – A JavaScript-based P3P Agent for Mozilla Firefox.* http://privacyfox.mozdev.org/PaperFinal.pdf

Ashley, P., Hada, S., Karjoth, G., Powers, C., & Schunter, M. (2003). *Enterprise Privacy Authorization Language (EPAL 1.1)*. Research Report, IBM. Retrieved Jan 2008 from http://www.zurich.ibm.com/security/enterprise-privacy/epal

Autonomy. (2010). *Information Governance Tools*. Retrieved August 2010 from Breaux, T.D. & Anton, A.I. (2008). Analyzing Regulatory Rules for Privacy and Security Requirements. *IEEE Transactions on Software Engineering, 34*(1), 5-20.

Avison, D. E., Lau, F., Myers, M., & Nielsen, P. A. (1999). Action Research. *Communications of the ACM, 42*(1), 94–97. doi:10.1145/291469.291479

Avlonitis, G. J., & Karayanni, D. A. (2000). The Impact of Internet Use on Business-to-Business Marketing: Examples from American and European Companies. *Industrial Marketing Management, 29*(5), 441–459. doi:10.1016/S0019-8501(99)00071-1

Awad, N. F., & Krishnan, M. S. (2006). The personalization privacy paradox: An empirical evaluation of information transparency and the willingness to be profiled online for personalization. *Management Information Systems Quarterly, 30*(1), 13–28.

Ba, S., & Pavlou, P. A. (2002). Evidence of the effect of trust building technology in electronic markets: price premiums and buyer behaviour. *Management Information Systems Quarterly, 26*, 243–266. doi:10.2307/4132332

Ba, S., Whinston, A. B., & Zang, H. (1999). Building trust in the electronic market through an economic incentive mechanism. In *Proceedings of the Twentieth International Conference on Information Systems*, (December), 13-15.

Baark, E., & Heeks, R. (1998) *Evaluation of Donor-Funded Information Technology Transfer Projects in China: A Life-Cycle Approach*. Retrieved Dec 12, 2007, from http://idpm.man.ac.uk/wp/di/di_wp01.htm.

Bagozzi, R. P., & Yi, Y. (1988). On the evaluation of structural equation models. *Journal of the Academy of Marketing Science, 16*(1), 74–94. doi:10.1007/BF02723327

Baker, T., & Nelson, R. E. (2005). Creating something from nothing: Resource construction through entrepreneurial bricolage. *Administrative Science Quarterly, 50*(3), 329–366. doi:10.2189/asqu.2005.50.3.329

Bakos, J. Y. (1991). A strategic analysis of electronic marketplaces. *Management Information Systems Quarterly*, (September): 295–310. doi:10.2307/249641

Bakos, J. Y. (1997). Reducing buyer search costs: Implications for electronic marketplaces. *Management Science, 43*(12), 1676–1692. doi:10.1287/mnsc.43.12.1676

Balasubramanian, S. (1998). Mail versus Mall: A strategic analysis of competition between direct marketers and conventional retailers. *Marketing Science, 17*(3), 181–195. doi:10.1287/mksc.17.3.181

Ballantine, J., Levy, M., & Powell, P. (1998). Evaluating information systems in small and medium-sized enterprises: issues and evidence. *European Journal of Information Systems, 7*(4), 241–251. doi:10.1057/palgrave.ejis.3000307

Balmer, J.M.T. (1998) Corporate Identity and Advent of Corporate Marketing. *Journal of Marketing Management,* (14), 963-996.

Barclay, I. (2006). Benchmarking best practice in SMEs for growth. *International Journal of Technology Management, 33*(2-3), 234–254. doi:10.1504/IJTM.2006.008313

Bargh, J. A. (1984). Automatic and Conscious Processing of Social Information. In Wyer, R. S. Jr, & Srull, T. K. (Eds.), *Handbook of Social Cognition* (pp. 1–43). Hillsdale, NJ: Erlbaum.

Barker, L. B. (1989). Survey Research. In Emert, P., & Barker, L. B. (Eds.), *Measurement of Communication Behavior* (pp. 25–39). New York: Longman.

Barley, S. R., & Tolbert, P. S. (1997). Institutionalization and Structuration: Studying the Links between Action and Institution. *Organization Studies, 18*(1), 93–117. doi:10.1177/017084069701800106

Barney, J. (1991). Firm resources and sustained competitive advantage. *Journal of Management, 17*(1), 99–120. doi:10.1177/014920639101700108

BarNir, A., Gallaugher, J. M., & Auger, P. (2003). Business process digitization, strategy, and the impact of firm age and size: The case of the magazine publishing industry. *Journal of Business Venturing, 18*(6), 789–814. doi:10.1016/S0883-9026(03)00030-2

Barton, C., & Bear, M. (1999) *Information and Communications Technologies: Are they the Key to Viable Business Development Services for Micro and Small Enterprises? Report for USAID as part of the Microenterprise Best Practices Project. March.* Retrieved December 12, 2007, from http://www.mip.org/PUBS/MBP/ict.htm.

Barua, A., Konana, P., Whinston, A. B., & Yin, F. (2004). An empirical investigation of net-enabled business value. *Management Information Systems Quarterly, 28*(4), 585–620.

Bassellier, G., Reich, B. H., & Benbasat, I. (2001). Information technology competence of business managers: A definition and research model. *Journal of Management Information Systems, 17*(4), 159–182.

Baumol, W. J. (2002). Entrepreneruship, innovation and growth: The David-Goliath Symbiosis. *Journal of Entrepreneurial Finance and Business Ventures, 7*(2), 1–10.

Beaney, W. M. (1966). Right to Privacy and American Law, The. *Law and Contemporary Problems, 31*, 253–271. doi:10.2307/1190670

Bechhofer, S., Harmelen, F. v., Hendler, J., Horrocks, I., McGuinness, D. L., Patel-Schneider, P. F., et al. (2004). *OWL Web Ontology Language Reference* W3C Recommendation 10 February 2004.

Beck, R., Wigand, R. T., & Konig, W. (2005). The diffusion and efficient use of electronic commerce among small and medium sized enterprises: An international three industry survey. *Electronic Markets, 15*(1), 38–52. doi:10.1080/10196780500035282

Beckinsale, M., Levy, M., & Powell, P. (2006). Exploring internet adoption drivers in SMEs. *Electronic Markets, 16*(4), 361–370. doi:10.1080/10196780600999841

Beer Michael. (2004). *Corporate Identity & the web: What your homepage tells about your organization.* Available: http://ui4all.ics.forth.gr/workshop2004/files/ui4all_proceedings/adjunct/organisational/72.pdf (Accessed: 2005, February 25).

Bejou, D., Ennew, C., & Palmer, A. (1998). Trust, ethics and relationship satisfaction. *International Journal of Bank Marketing, 16*(4), 276–286. doi:10.1108/02652329810220729

Belanger, F., Hiller, J. S., & Smith, W. J. (2002). Trustworthiness in electronic commerce: the role of privacy, security, and site attributes. *The Journal of Strategic Information Systems, 11*(3-4), 245–270. doi:10.1016/S0963-8687(02)00018-5

Bellman, S., Johnson, E. J., Kobrin, S. J., & Lohse, G. L. (2004). International differences in information privacy concerns: A global survey of consumers. *The Information Society, 20*(5), 313–324. doi:10.1080/01972240490507956

Benatallah, B., Sheng, Q. Z., & Dumas, M. (2003). The Self-Serv Environment for Web Services Composition. *IEEE Internet Computing, 7*(1). doi:10.1109/MIC.2003.1167338

Bengtsson, M., & Kock, S. (2000). *Coopetition in Business Networks to Cooperate and Compete Simultaneously. Industrial Marketing Management, 29*(5). doi:10.1016/S0019-8501(99)00067-X

Bennett, C. J., & Raab, C. D. (1997). The adequacy of privacy: The European Union data protection directive and the North American response. *The Information Society, 13*(3), 245–263. doi:10.1080/019722497129124

Bennett, P. D. (1988). *Dictionary of Marketing Terms.* Chicago, IL: The American Marketing Association.

Bentahar, J., Maamar, Z., Benslimane, D., & Thiran, Ph. (2007). An Argumentation Framework for Communities of Web Services. *IEEE Intelligent Systems, 22*(6), 75–83. doi:10.1109/MIS.2007.99

Bentahar, J., Maamar, Z., Wan, W., Benslimane, D., Thiran, P., & Subramanian, S. (2008). Agent-based Communities of Web Services: An Argumentation-driven Approach. *Service Oriented Computing and Applications, 2*(4), 219–238. doi:10.1007/s11761-008-0033-4

Berezai, P. (2000). *B2B on the Internet: 2000-2005.* London: Datamonitor PLC.

Berg, P. O. (1985). Organization Change as a Symbolic Transformation Process. In Frost, P., Moore, L., Louis, M. R., Lundberg, C., & Martin, J. (Eds.), *Reframing Organizational Culture* (pp. 281–300). Beverly Hills, CA: Sage.

Berger, A. N., Frame, W. S., & Miller, N. H. (2005). Credit scoring and the availability, price, and risk of small business credit. *Journal of Money, Credit and Banking, 37*(2), 191–222. doi:10.1353/mcb.2005.0019

Berger, P. L., & Luckmann, T. (1967). *The Social Construction of Reality.* New York: Anchor Books.

Berners-Lee, T., Hendler, J., & Lassila, O. (2001). The Semantic Web. *Scientific American, 284*(5), 34–43. doi:10.1038/scientificamerican0501-34

Bharadwaj, A. S. (2000). A resource-based perspective on information technology capability and firm performance: An empirical investigation. *MIS Quarterly, 24*(1), 169–196. doi:10.2307/3250983

Bharadwaj, P. N., & Soni, R. G. (2007). E-commerce usage and perception of e-commerce issues among small firms: Results and implications from an empirical study. *Journal of Small Business Management, 45*(4), 501–521. doi:10.1111/j.1540-627X.2007.00225.x

Bharadwaj, A. S., Sambamurthy, V., & Zmud, R. W. (2000). *IT capabilities: theoretical perspectives and empirical operalization.* Paper presented at the 21st International Conference on Information Systems, Brisbane, Australia.

Bharati, P., & Chaudhury, A. (2006). Studying the current status of technology adoption. *Communications of the ACM, 49*(10), 88–93. doi:10.1145/1164394.1164400

Bhatnagar, A., Misra, S., & Rao, H. R. (2000). On Risk, Convenience and Internet shopping. *Communications of the ACM, 43*(11), 98–105. doi:10.1145/353360.353371

Bhatti, N., Bouch, A., Kuchinsky, A. (2000). Integrating user-perceived quality into web server design. *Computer Networks, 33*(1-6), 1-16.

Bierly, P. E., & Daly, P. S. (2007). Sources of external organisational learning in small manufacturing firms. *International Journal of Technology Management, 38*(1/2), 45–68. doi:10.1504/IJTM.2007.012429

Bierly, P., & Chakrabarti, A. (1996). Generic knowledge strategies in the us pharmaceutical industry. *Strategic Management Journal, 17*, 123–135.

Billsus, D., & Pazzani, M. J. (1999). A Personal News Agent that Talks, Learns and Explains. In *Third International Conference on Autonomous Agents (Agents 1999)* (pp. 268-275). New York: ACM.

Birkett, G. (2006). *McCaw's cup runneth over.* Fairfax New Zealand. Retrieved July 23, 2006, from http://www.stuff.co.nz/stuff/print/0,1478,3682753a1823,00.html.

Birukov, E., Blanzieri, E., & Giorgini, P. (2005). *Implicit: A Recommender System that uses Implicit Knowledge to Produce Suggestions.* In Proceedings of the Workshop on Multi-Agent Information Retrieval and Recommender Systems at the 19th International Joint Conference on Artifical Intelligence (IJCAI-05)

Blili, S., & Raymond, L. (1993). Information technology: threats and opportunities for small and medium-sized enterprises. *International Journal of Information Management, 13*, 439–448. doi:10.1016/0268-4012(93)90060-H

Boland, R. (1986). Phenomenology: A Preferred Approach to Research in Information Systems. In E. Mumford, R. Hirschheim, G. Fitzgerald, and T. Wood-Harper (eds.), *Proceedings of the IFIP WG8.2 Colloquium,* Manchester Business School, Manchester: Elsevier Science.

Bollen, K. A. (1989). *Structural equations with latent variables*. Wiley-Interscience.

Borders, A. L., Jonston, W. J., & Rigdon, E. E. (2001). Beyond the Dyad: Electronic Commerce and Network Perspectives in Industrial Marketing Management. *Industrial Marketing Management, 30*(2), 199–205. doi:10.1016/S0019-8501(00)00143-7

Borsje, J., & Giles, J. (2010). OWL2Prefuse. Retrieved from http://owl2prefuse.sourceforge.net/index.php

Borsje, J., Levering, L., & Frasincar, F. (2008). Hermes: a Semantic Web-Based News Decision Support System In *23rd Annual ACM Symposium on Applied Computing (SAC 2008)* (pp. 2415-2420). New York: ACM.

Bosnjak, M., Obermeier, D., & Tuten, T. L. (2006). Predicting and explaining the propensity to bid in online auctions: A comparison of two action-theoretical models. *Journal of Consumer Behaviour, 5*(2), 102–116. doi:10.1002/cb.38

Boudreau, M.-C., Loch, K. D., Robey, D., & Straud, D. (1998). Going global: Using information technology to advance the competitiveness of the virtual transnational organization. *The Academy of Management Executive, 12*(4), 120–128.

Bourgeois, L. J. (1981). On the measurement of organizational slack. *Academy of Management Review, 6*, 29–39. doi:10.2307/257138

Bourgeois, L. J., & Singh, J. V. (1983). Organizational slack and political behavior within top management teams. *Academy of Management Proceedings,* 43-47.

Brambilla, M., Ceri, S., Fraternali, P., & Manolescu, I. (2006). Process modeling in web applications. *ACM Transactions on Software Engineering and Methodology, 15*(4), 360–409. doi:10.1145/1178625.1178627

Brambilla, M., Comai, S., Fraternali, P., & Matera, M. (2007). *Designing Web applications with WebML and WebRatio, Web Engineering: Modelling and Implementing Web Applications*. Springer.

Brancheau, J. C., & Wetherbe, J. C. (1990). The adoption of spreadsheet software: Testing innovation diffusion theory in the context of end-user computing. *Information Systems Research, 1*(2), 115–143. doi:10.1287/isre.1.2.115

Brickley, D., & Guha, R. V. (2004). *RDF Vocabulary Description Language 1.0: RDF Schema*: W3C Recommendation 10 February 2004.

Brinkman, U., & Siefert, M. (2001). Face-to-interface - the establishment of trust in the Internet: The case of e-auctions. *Journal of Sociology (Melbourne, Vic.), 30*, 2347.

Bromiley, P. (1991). Testing a causal model of corporate risk taking and performance. *Academy of Management Journal, 34*(1), 37–59. doi:10.2307/256301

Brown, D. H., & Lockett, N. (2004). Potential of critical e-applications for engaging SMEs in e-business: a provider perspective. *European Journal of Information Systems, 13*, 21–34. doi:10.1057/palgrave.ejis.3000480

Bruner, G. C. II, & Kunar, A. (2005). Explaining consumer acceptance of hand held Internet devices. *Journal of Business Research, 58*(5), 553. doi:10.1016/j.jbusres.2003.08.002

Bryan, J. (2006). Training and Performance in Small Firms. *International Small Business Journal, 24*(6), 635–660. doi:10.1177/0266242606069270

Bryman, A. (2001). *Social Research Methods*. Oxford: Oxford University Press.

Brynjolfsson, E., & Hitt, L. M. (1998). Beyond the productivity paradox. *Communications of the ACM, 41*(8), 49–55. doi:10.1145/280324.280332

Bui, T., & Gacher, A. (2005). Web Services for Negotiation and Bargaining in Electronic Markets: Design Requirements and Implementation Framework. *Proceedings of the 38th Hawaii International Conference on System Sciences (HICSS'2005), Big Islands, Hawaii, USA*.

Bulkeley, W. M. (2006). Should owners of web sites be anonymous? *Wall Street Journal,* (April 27), B1, B4. Retrieved from http://www.ciadvertising.org

Burke, K. (2005). The impact of firm size on Internet use in small businesses. *Electronic Markets*, *15*(2), 79–93. doi:10.1080/10196780500083738

Burke Jarvis, C., Mackenzie, S. B., & Podsakoff, P. M. (2003). A Critical Review of Construct Indicators and Measurement Model Misspecification in Marketing and Consumer Research. *The Journal of Consumer Research*, *30*(September), 199–218. doi:10.1086/376806

Burnkrant, R. E., & Cousineau, A. (1975). Informational and normative social influence in buyer behaviour. *The Journal of Consumer Research*, *2*(3), 206–215. doi:10.1086/208633

Byers, S., Cranor, L., Kormann, D., & McDaniel, P. (2004, 26-28 May). *Searching for Privacy: Design and Implementation of a P3P-Enabled Search Engine*. Paper presented at the The 2004 Workshop on Privacy Enhancing Technologies (PET2004), Toronto, Canada.

Caldeira, M. M., & Ward, J. M. (2003). Using resource-based theory to interpret the successful adoption and use of information systems and technology in manufacturing small and medium-sized enterprises. *European Journal of Information Systems*, *12*(2), 127–141. doi:10.1057/palgrave.ejis.3000454

Caldwell, F. Eid, T. & Casper, C.(2009) *Magic Quadrant for Enterprise Governance, Risk and Compliance Platforms*. Gartner RAS Core Research Note G00169604.

Caloghirou, Y., Protogerou, A., Spanos, Y., & Papagiannakis, L. (2004). Industry- versus firm-specific effects on performance: Contrasting SMEs and large-sized firms. *European Management Journal*, *22*(2), 231–243. doi:10.1016/j.emj.2004.01.017

Cao, M., & Zang, Q. (2005). Web site quality and usability in e-commerce. In Gao, Y. (Ed.), *Web systems Design and online consumer behavior* (pp. 107–124). Hershey, PA: Idea Group Publishing.

Capon, N.& Glazer, R.(1987). Marketing and Technology: A Strategic Coalignment. *Journal of Marketing* 51,(3), pp. 1-1 4.

Capron, L., & Pistre, N. (2002). When do acquirers earn abnormal returns? *Strategic Management Journal*, *23*(9), 781–794. doi:10.1002/smj.262

Casassa Mont, M. (2005). Handling privacy obligations in enterprises: important aspects and technical approaches. *Comput. Syst. Sci. Eng.*, *20*, 6.

Casassa Mont, M., & Thyne, R. (2006). In Danezis, G., & Golle, P. (Eds.), *A Systemic Approach to Automate Privacy Policy Enforcement in Enterprises. Privacy Enhancing Technologies 2006, LNCS 4258* (pp. 118–134). Springer.

Castellanos, M., Gupta, C., Wang, S., & Umeshwar. (2010). Leveraging Web streams for Contractual Situational Awareness in Operational BI. In *International Workshop on Business intelligencE and the WEB (BEWEB 2010)*. New York: ACM.

Cate, F. H. (1997). *Privacy in the information age*. Washington, D.C.: Brookings Institution Press.

Caudill, M. E., & Murphy, E. P. (2000). Consumer Online Privacy: Legal and Ethical Issues. *Journal of Public Policy & Marketing*, *19*(1), 7–19. doi:10.1509/jppm.19.1.7.16951

Cavalluzzo, K., & Wolken, J. (2005). Small business loan turndowns, personal wealth, and discrimination. *The Journal of Business*, *78*(6), 2153–2177. doi:10.1086/497045

Cavoukian, A. H., & Hamilton, T. J. (2002). *The Privacy Payoff: How Successful Businesses Build Customer Trust*. Toronto: McGraw-Hill Ryerson.

Cavoukian, A., & Crompton, M. (2000). Web Seals: A review of Online Privacy Programs. 22nd International Conference on Privacy and Data Protection. Retrieved Dec. 2006 from http://www.privacy.gov.au/publications/seals.pdf

Cesarano, C., d'Acierno, A., & Picariello, A. (2003). An intelligent search agent system for semantic information retrieval on the internet. In *WIDM '03: Proceedings of the 5th ACM international workshop on Web information and data management* (p. 111–117). New York ACM. doi:http://doi.acm.org.gate6.inist.fr/10.1145/956699.956725

Chakraborty, G., Lala, V., & Warren, D. (2003). What do customers consider important in B2B websites? *Journal of Advertising Research, 40*(March), 50–61.

Chan, Y. E., Bhargava, N., & Street, C. T. (2006). Having arrived: The homogeneity of high-growth small firms. *Journal of Small Business Management, 44*(3), 426–440. doi:10.1111/j.1540-627X.2006.00180.x

Chan, M. F. S., & Chung, W. W. C. (2002). A framework to development an enterprise information portal for contract manufacturing. *International Journal of Production Economics, 75*(1/2), 113–126. doi:10.1016/S0925-5273(01)00185-2

Chan, C., & Swatman, P. M. C. (2000). From EDI to Internet Commerce: The BHL Steel Experiences. *Internet Research: Electronic Networking Applications and Policy, 10*(1), 72–82. doi:10.1108/10662240010312039

Chan, C., & Swatnam, P. M. C. (2004). B2B E-commerce Stages of Growth: The Strategic Imperatives. *In 37th Hawaii International Conference on System Sciences.*

Chang, L., & Arnett, K. P. (2000). Exploring the factors associated with web site success in the context of electronic commerce. *Information & Management, 38*(1), 23–33. doi:10.1016/S0378-7206(00)00049-5

Chan-Olmsted, S. M., & Ha, L. S. (2003). Internet Business Models for Broadcasters: How Television Stations Perceive and Integrate the Internet. *Journal of Broadcasting & Electronic Media, 47*, 597–616. doi:10.1207/s15506878jobem4704_7

Chau, P. Y. (1996). An Empirical Assessment of a Modified Technology Acceptance Model. *Journal of Management Information Systems, 13*(2), 185–204.

Chebat, J.-C., & Cohen, A. (1993). Response Speed in Mail Survey: Beware of Shortcuts. *Marketing Research, 5*(2), 20–25.

Checkland, P. (1981). *Systems Thinking, Systems Practice.* New York: John Wiley & Sons.

Checkland, P. (1991) "From Framework through Experience to Learning: The Essential Nature of Action Research. In Nissen, H.-E., Klein, H. &Hirschheim, R. (eds.) *Information Systems Research: Contemporary Approaches and Emergent Traditions* 397-403., North Holland: Elsevier Publishers.

Chellappa, R. K., & Sin, R. (2005). Personalization versus Privacy: An Empirical Examination of the Online Consumer's Dilemma. *Information Technology Management, 6*(2-3).

Chen, L., & Tan, J. (2004). Technology Adaptation in E-commerce: Key Determinants of Virtual Stores Acceptance. *European Management Journal, 22*(1), 74–86. doi:10.1016/j.emj.2003.11.014

Cheng, J., & Kesner, I. (1997). Organizational slack and response to environmental shifts: The impact of resource allocation patterns. *Journal of Management, 23*, 1–18. doi:10.1177/014920639702300101

Cheung, W., Chang, M. T., & Lia, V. S. (2000). Prediction of Internet and World Wide Web Usage at Work: a Test of an Extended Triandis Model. *Decision Support Systems, 30*(1), 83–100. doi:10.1016/S0167-9236(00)00125-1

Chiang, W. Y., Chhajed, D., & Hess, J. D. (2003). Direct marketing, indirect profits: A strategic analysis of dual-channel supply chain design. *Management Science, 49*(1), 1–20. doi:10.1287/mnsc.49.1.1.12749

Chin, W. W. (1998). The Partial Least Squares Approach for Structural Equation Modelling. In Marcoulides, G. A. (Ed.), *Modern Methods for Business Research*. Hillsdale, NJ: Lawrence Erlbaum Associates.

Chin, W. W. (2001). PLS-Graph User's Guide, Version 3.0: Unpublished.

Chin, W. W., Marcolin, B. L., & Newsted, P. R. (1996). *A Partial Least Squares Latent Variable Modeling Approach for Measuring Interaction Effects: Results from a Monte Carlo Simulation Study and Voice Mail Emotion/Adoption Study.* Paper presented at the Seventeenth International Conference on Information Systems.

Chow, C. W., Haddad, K. M., & Williamson, J. E. (1997). Applying the Balanced Scorecard to small companies. *Strategic Finance, 79*(2), 21–28.

Christian, R. C. (1959). Industrial Marketing. *Journal of Marketing*, 79–80. doi:10.2307/1248856

Chung, S., Singh, H., & Lee, K. (2000). Complementarity, status similarity and social capital as drivers of alliance formation. *Strategic Management Journal, 21*(1), 1–22. doi:10.1002/(SICI)1097-0266(200001)21:1<1::AID-SMJ63>3.0.CO;2-P

Churchill, N. C., & Lewis, V. L. (1983). The five stages of small business growth. *Harvard Business Review, 61*(3), 30–39.

Chwelos, P., Benbasat, I., & Dexter, A. S. (2001). Research report: Empirical test of an EDI adoption model. *Information Systems Research, 12*(3), 304–321. doi:10.1287/isre.12.3.304.9708

Clarke, R. (2003). If e-business is different, then so is reseach in e-business. In Viborg Andersen, K., Elliott, S., Swatman, P., Trauth, E. M., & Bjørn-Andersen, N. (Eds.), *Seeking success in e-business*. Boston, Massachusetts: Kluwer Academic Publishers.

Claver, E., Llopis, J., Garcia, D., & Molina, H. (1998). Organizational culture for innovation and new technological behavior. *The Journal of High Technology Management Research, 9*(1), 55. doi:10.1016/1047-8310(88)90005-3

Clemons, E. K., & Row, M. C. (1991). Sustaining IT advantage: The role of structural differences. *Management Information Systems Quarterly, 15*(3), 275–292. doi:10.2307/249639

Clemons, E. K. (1991). Corporate Strategies for Information Technology: A Resource-Based Approach. *Computer, 24*(11), 23–32. doi:10.1109/2.116848

Clemons, E.K. & Row, M.K. (1991). Information Technology at Rosenbluth Travel: Competitive Advantage in a Rapidly Growing Service Company. *Journal of Management Information Systems*, 8(2)pp. 53-79.

Cohen, W. M., & Levinthal, D. A. (1990). Absorptive-capacity - a new perspective on learning and innovation. *Administrative Science Quarterly, 35*(1), 128–152. doi:10.2307/2393553

COMET. (2006). Component and model-based development methodology. Retrieved August 2010 from http://www.modelbased.net/comet/

Compeau, D. R., Higgins, C. A., & Huff, S. (1999). Social cognitive theory and individual reactions to computing technology: A longitudinal study. *Management Information Systems Quarterly, 23*(2), 145–158. doi:10.2307/249749

Computer Associates. (2010). Policy and Configuration and Records Manager. Retrieved August 2010 from http://www3.ca.com/solutions/Product.aspx?ID=165

Computer World. (2007). www.computerworld.com/action/article.do?command=viewArticleBasic&articleId=9014782; retrievedMarch26, 2008

Computer World. (2008). www.computerworld.com/action/article.do?command=viewArticleBasic&articleId=9070281&taxonomyId=148&intscr=kc_top; retrieved March 26, 2008

Conallen, J. (2002). *Building Web Applications with UML*. Boston, MA: Addison-Wesley Longman Publishing Co., Inc.

Conner, K. R. (1991). A historical comparison of resource-based theory and 5 schools of thought within industrial-organization economics - do we have a new theory of the firm. *Journal of Management, 17*(1), 121–154. doi:10.1177/014920639101700109

Cook, B. L. (2007). Tapping into pocketbook power; Ellen T. Fisher proved her knack for getting female entrepreneurs together, now, on to the Internet. *Knight Ridder Business News*, (May 13), 1.

Cooper, M. J., Upton, N., & Seaman, S. (2005). Customer relationship management: A comparative ananlysis of family and nonfamily business practices. *Journal of Small Business Management, 43*(3), 242–257. doi:10.1111/j.1540-627X.2005.00136.x

Cooper, R. G. (1979). The dimensions of industrial new product success and failure. *Journal of Marketing, 43*(3), 93–103. doi:10.2307/1250151

Cooper, R. B., & Zmud, R. W. (1990). Information Technology Implementation Research: A Technological Diffusion Approach. *Management Science, 36*(2), 123–139. doi:10.1287/mnsc.36.2.123

Copeland, D.G. & McKenney, J.L.(1998). Airline Reservation Systems: Lessons from History.*MIS Quarterly* (12:3)pp. 353-370.

Cormican, K., & O'Sullivan, D. (2004). Auditing best practice for effective product innovation management. *Technovation, 24*, 819–829. doi:10.1016/S0166-4972(03)00013-0

Cosh, A., Duncan, J., & Hughes, A. (1998). *Investment in Training and Small Firm Growth and Survival: An Empirical Analysis for the UK 1987-95*: Dfee Publivations Research Report No. 36.

Cousins, P. D., & Spekman, R. (2003). Strategic supply and the management of inter- and intra-organisational relationships. *Journal of Purchasing and Supply Management, 9*, 19–29. doi:10.1016/S1478-4092(02)00036-5

Cox, L. W., Camp, S. M., & Sexton, D. L. (2000). The Kauffman Financial Statements Database. In Katz, J.A.(ed): Databases for the Study of Entrepreneurship. *Advances in Entrepreneurship Research, 4*, 305-334.

Cragg, P. B., & King, M. (1993). Small-Firm Computing: Motivators and Inhibitors. *Management Information Systems Quarterly, 17*(1), 47–60. doi:10.2307/249509

Cranor, L. F., Reagle, J., & Ackerman, M. S. (1999). Beyond concern: understanding net users' attitudes about online privacy. In Vogelsang, I., & Compaine, B. (Eds.), *The Internet Upheaval: Raising Questions, Seeking Answers in Communications Policy* (pp. 47–60). USA: MIT Press.

Cranor, L. F. (2002). *Web privacy with P3P*. Sebastopol, CA: O'Reilly.

Cranor, L.F. (2003). P3P: Making privacy policies more useful. *IEEE Security and Privacy,* 1:6, November, 50-55.

Culnan, M. J. (1993). 'How Did They Get My Name'? An Exploratory Investigation of Consumer Attitudes toward Secondary Information Use. *Management Information Systems Quarterly, 17*(3), 341–364. doi:10.2307/249775

Culnan, M. J. (1995). Consumer Awareness of Name Removal Procedures: Implication for Direct Marketing. *Journal of Interactive Marketing, 9*, 10–19.

Culnan, M. J. (2000). Protecting Privacy Online: Is Self-Regulation Working? *Journal of Public Policy & Marketing, 19*(1), 20–26. doi:10.1509/jppm.19.1.20.16944

Culnan, M. J., & Armstrong, P. K. (1999). Information Privacy Concerns, Procedural Fairness and Impersonal Trust: An Empirical Investigation. *Organization Science, 10*(1), 104–115. doi:10.1287/orsc.10.1.104

Culnan, M. J., & Bies, J. R. (2003). Consumer Privacy: Balancing Economic and Justice Considerations. *The Journal of Social Issues, 59*(2), 323–342. doi:10.1111/1540-4560.00067

Cunningham, H., Maynard, D., Bontcheva, K., & Tablan, V. (2002). GATE: A Framework and Graphical Development Environment for Robust NLP Tools and Applications. In *The 40th Anniversary Meeting of the Association for Computational Linguistics (ACL 2002)* (pp. 168–175). Morristown, NJ: ACL.

Curran, C., & Singh, G. (2001). Enterprise Portals: Building Value through Organizational knowledge. *DiamondCluster International Inc Centre for Technology Innovation, 2*(2).

Cutler, A. (2004). Methodical failure: The use of case study method by public relations researchers. *Public Relations Review, 30*(3), 365–375. doi:10.1016/j.pubrev.2004.05.008

Cyert, R. M., & March, J. G. (1963). *A behavioral theory of the firm*. Englewood Cliffs, NJ: Prentice-Hall.

Daft, R. L., & Weick, K. E. (1984). Toward a model of organizations as interpretation systems. *Academy of Management Review, 9*(2), 284–295. doi:10.2307/258441

Damanpour, F. (1991). Organizational innovation: A meta-analysis of effects of determinants and moderators. *Academy of Management Journal, 34*(3), 555–590. doi:10.2307/256406

Damanpour, F., Szabat, K. A., & Evan, W. M. (1989). The relationship between types of innovation and organizational performance. *Journal of Management Studies, 26*(6), 587–601. doi:10.1111/j.1467-6486.1989.tb00746.x

Damanpour, F., & Wischnevsky, J. D. (2006). Research on innovation in organizations: Distinguishing innovation-generating from innovation-adopting organizations. *Journal of Engineering and Technology Management, 23*(4), 269–291. doi:10.1016/j.jengtecman.2006.08.002

Damianou, N., Dulay, N., Lupu, E., & Sloman, M. (2001). *The Ponder Policy Specification Language.* Retrieved 2007 from http://www-dse.doc.ic.ac.uk/research/policies/index.shtml

Dandridge, T. C. (1979). Children are not little grown-ups: Small business needs its own organizational theory. *Journal of Small Business Management, 17*(2), 53–57.

Daniel, E., Wilson, H., & Myers, A. (2002). Adoption of e-commerce by SMEs in the UK. *International Small Business Journal, 20*(3), 253–270. doi:10.1177/0266242602203002

Daniel, F., Lohrke, F. T., Fornaciari, C. J., & Turner, R. A. (2004). Slack resources and firm performance: a meta-analysis. *Journal of Business Research, 57*, 565–574. doi:10.1016/S0148-2963(02)00439-3

Dans, E. (2001). IT investment in small and medium enterprises: paradoxically productive? *The Electronic Journal of Information Systems Evaluation, 4*(1).

Darwell, C., Sahlman, W. A., & Roberts, M. J. (1998) *DigitalThink: Startup (Case # 9-898-186).* Cambridge, MA: Harvard Business School Publishing.

Davenport, T. H. (1993). *Process Innovation: Reengineering Work Through Information Technology.* Boston: Harvard Business School Press.

Davies, J., Duke, A., & Sure, Y. (2003). OntoShare - A knowledge Management Environment for Virtual Communities. *Proceedings of the Second International Conference on Knowledge Capture (K-CAP'2003).*

Davis, F. D. (1989). Perceived Usefulness, Perceived Ease of Use, and User Acceptance of Information Technology. *MIS Quarterly, 13*(3), 319–340. doi:10.2307/249008

Davis, F. D., Bagozzi, R. P., & Warshaw, P. R. (1989). User Acceptance of Computer Technology: A Comparison of Two Theoretical Model. *Management Science, 35*(8), 982–1003. doi:10.1287/mnsc.35.8.982

Davison, M. R., & Clarke, R., J., S. H., Langford, D., & Kuo, F.-Y. (2003). Information Privacy in a Globally Networked Society: Implications for IS Research. *Communications of the Association for Information Systems, 12*, 341–365.

Dean, T. J., Brown, R. L., & Bamford, C. E. (1998). Differences in large and small firm responses to environmental context: Strategic implications from a comparative analysis of business formations. *Strategic Management Journal, 19*(8), 709–728. doi:10.1002/(SICI)1097-0266(199808)19:8<709::AID-SMJ966>3.0.CO;2-9

Dean, J., Holmes, S., & Smith, S. (1997). Understanding Business Networks: Evidence from Manufacturing and Service Sectors in Australia. *Journal of Small Business Management, 35*(1), 79–84.

Debreceny, R., Putterill, M., Tung, L. L., & Gilbert, A. L. (2002). New tools for the determination of e-commerce inhibitors. *Decision Support Systems, 34*(2), 177–195. doi:10.1016/S0167-9236(02)00080-5

Decker, K., Lesser, V., Prasad, M. V. N., & Wagner, T. (1995). MACRON: An Architecture for Multi-agent Cooperative Information Gathering. *In Proccedings of the CIKM-95 Workshop on Intelligent Information Agents.*

DeJohn, P. (2005). E-commerce stats refine search for supply savings. *Hospital Materials Management, 30*(9), 1–3.

Del Franco, M. (2003). The back end comes to the forefront. *Catalog Age*, *20*(5), 31–33.

Del Giudice, M., & del Giudice, F. (2003). Locking-in the customer: how to manage switching costs to stimulate e-loyalty and reduce churn rate. In Sharma, S. K., & Gupta, J. (Eds.), *Managing e-business of the 21ˢᵗ century*. Heidelberg: Heidelberg Press.

DeLone, W. H. (1988). Determinants of Success for Computer Usage in Small Business. *Management Information Systems Quarterly*, *12*(1), 51–61. doi:10.2307/248803

DeLone, W. H., & MacLean, E. R. (1992). Information systems success; the quest for the dependent variable. *Information Systems Research*, *3*(1), 60–95. doi:10.1287/isre.3.1.60

Dembla, P., Palvia, P., & Brooks, L. (2007). Organizational adoption of web-enabled services for information dissemination. *Journal of Information Science and Technology*, *3*(3), 24–49.

Dennis, D. L. (2001). *New Study by Accenture Reveals Keys to Online Success for Chemicals Industry*. Available: http://www.accenture.com/xd/xd.asp?it=enweb&xd=_dyn%5Cdynamicpressrelease_305.xml (Accessed 2004, July 7).

Denzin, N. K. (1989). *The Research Act: A Theoretical Introduction to Sociological Methods*. Englewood Cliffs, NJ: Prentice Hall.

Dess, G. G. (1987). Consensus on strategy formulation and organizational performance: Competitors in a fragmented industry. *Strategic Management Journal*, *8*(3), 259–277. doi:10.1002/smj.4250080305

Dess, G. G., & Davis, P. S. (1984). Porter's (1980) generic strategies as determinants of strategic group membership and organizational performance. *Academy of Management Journal*, *27*(3), 467–488. doi:10.2307/256040

Devaraj, S., Krajewski, L., & Wei, J. C. (2007). Impact of e-business technologies on operational performance: The role of production information integration in the supply chain. *Journal of Operations Management*, *25*(6), 1199–1216. doi:10.1016/j.jom.2007.01.002

Devins, J., & Johanson, S. (2003). Training and Development Activities in SMEs: Some Findings from an Evaluation of the OSF Objective 4 Programme in Britain. *International Small Business Journal*, *22*(2), 205–218.

Dholakia, R. R., & Kshetri, N. (2004). Factors impacting the adoption of the Internet among SMEs. *Small Business Economics*, *23*(4), 311–322. doi:10.1023/B:SBEJ.0000032036.90353.1f

Dholakia, N., & Zwick, D. (2001). Contrasting European and American approaches to privacy in electronic markets: a philosophical perspective. *Electronic Markets*, *11*(2). doi:10.1080/101967801300197034

Dholakia, U. M., & Soltysinski, K. (2001). Coveted or overlooked? The psychology of bidding for comparable listings in digital auctions. *Marketing Letters*, *12*(3), 225–237. doi:10.1023/A:1011164710951

Dhyani, D., Ng, W., & Bhowmick, S. (2002). A survey of web metrics. *ACM Computing Surveys*, *34*(4), 469–503. doi:10.1145/592642.592645

Di Martino, B. (2009). Semantic Web Services Discovery based on Structural Ontology Matching. *International Journal of Web and Grid Services*, *5*(1).

Dickerson, M. D., & Gentry, J. W. (1983). Characteristics of adopters and non-adopters of home computers. *The Journal of Consumer Research*, *10*, 225–235. doi:10.1086/208961

DiMaggio, P. J., & Powell, W. W. (1983). The Iron Cage Revisited: Institutional Isomorphism and Collective Rationality in Organizational Fields. *American Sociological Review*, *48*, 147–160. doi:10.2307/2095101

Dinev, T., & Hart, P. (2004). Internet Privacy Concerns and their Antecedents - Measurement Validity and a Regression Model. *Behaviour & Information Technology*, *23*(6), 413–423. doi:10.1080/01449290410001715723

Dinev, T., & Hart, P. (2004). Internet Privacy Concerns and Their Antecedents - Measurement Validity and a Regression Model. *Behaviour & Information Technology*, *23*(6), 413–423. doi:10.1080/01449290410001715723

Dinev, T., & Hart, P. (2006). An Extended Privacy Calculus Model for E-Commerce Transactions. *Information Systems Research*, *17*(1), 61–80. doi:10.1287/isre.1060.0080

Distante, D., Rossi, G., & Canfora, G. (2007). Modeling business processes in web applications: an analysis framework. *Proceedings of the 2007 ACM Symposium on Applied Computing*, (pp. 1677-1682).

DMA. (2003, April 2003). Privacy Promise Member Compliance Guide. Retrieved April 1, 2005, from http://www.the-dma.org/privacy/privacypromise.shtml

Dolam, R. J., & Moon, Y. (2000). Pricing and market-making on the internet. *Journal of Interactive Marketing*, *14*(2), 56–73.

Donaldson, T., & Dunfee, W. T. (1994). Towards a Unified Conception of Business Ethics: Integrative Social Contracts Theory. *Academy of Management Review*, *19*, 252–284. doi:10.2307/258705

Donaldson, T., & Dunfee, W. T. (1995). Integrative Social Contracts Theory: A Communication Conception of Economic Ethics. *Economics and Philosophy*, *11*, 85–112. doi:10.1017/S0266267100003230

Donaldson, T., & Dunfee, W. T. (1999). *Ties that Bind: A Social Contracts Approach to Business Ethics*. Cambridge, MA: Harvard Business School Press.

Donaldson, L. (2001). *The contingency theory of organizations*. Thousand Oaks, CA: Sage Publications.

Dougherty, D., & Hardy, C. (1996). Sustained product innovation in large, mature organizations: Overcoming innovation-to-organization problems. *Academy of Management Journal*, *39*(5), 1120–1153. doi:10.2307/256994

Doyle, P. (2002). *Marketing Management and Strategy. Financial Times*. Harlow, England: Prentice Hall.

Doyle, John. (2007). Network operators deliver personalized mobile adverts with ClixSmart AdPersonalizer. *Business Wire*, (June 20), 3.

Drazin, R., & Schoonhoven, C. B. (1996). Community, population, and organization effects on innovation: A multilevel perspective. *Academy of Management Journal*, *39*(5), 1065–1083. doi:10.2307/256992

Dritsas, S., Gritzalis, D., & Lambrinoudakis, C. (2006). Protecting privacy and anonymity in pervasive computing trends and perspectives. *Telematics and Informatics*, *23*(3), 196–210. doi:10.1016/j.tele.2005.07.005

Drury, D. H., & Farhoomand, A. (1996). Innovation Adoption of EDI. *Information Resources Management Journal*, *9*(3), 5–13.

Duncan, O. D. (1966). Path Analysis: Sociological Example. *American Journal of Sociology*, *72*(1), 1–16. doi:10.1086/224256

Duncombe, R., & Heeks, R. (2003). An information systems perspective on ethical trade and self-regulation. *Information Technology for Development*, *10*(2), 123–139. doi:10.1002/itdj.1590100206

Dunfee, W. T., Smith, N. C., & Ross, T. W. J. (1999). Social Contracts and Marketing Ethics. *Journal of Marketing*, *63*, 14–32. doi:10.2307/1251773

Dutton, J., & Dukerich, J. (1991). Keeping an Eye on the Mirror: Image and Identity in Organizational Adaptation. *Academy of Management Review*, (34): 517–554.

Earp, J. B., Anton, A. I., Aiman-Smith, L., & Stufflebeam, W. (2005). Examining Internet Privacy Policies within the Context of User Privacy Values. *IEEE Transactions on Engineering Management*, *52*(2), 227–237. doi:10.1109/TEM.2005.844927

Easton, A. (1966). Corporate Style versus Corporate Image. *JMR, Journal of Marketing Research*, *3*, 168–174. doi:10.2307/3150206

Eid, R. (2005). International Internet Marketing: a Triangulation Study of Drivers and Barriers in the Business-to-Business Context in the United Kingdom. *Marketing Intelligence & Planning*, *23*(3), 266–280. doi:10.1108/02634500510597300

Eid, R., & Elbeltagi, I. (2006). The Influence of the Internet on B-to-B International Marketing Activities: An Empirical Study of the UK Companies. *Journal of Euromarketing, 15*(2), 51–73. doi:10.1300/J037v15n02_04

Eid, R., Elbeltagi, I., & Zairi, M. (2006). Making B2B International Internet Marketing Effective: A Study of Critical Factors Using a Case Study Approach. *Journal of International Marketing, 14*(4), 87–109. doi:10.1509/jimk.14.4.87

Eid, R., & Trueman, M. (2004). Factors affecting the success of business-to-business international Internet marketing (B-to-B IIM): an empirical study of UK companies. *Industrial Management & Data Systems, 104*(1), 16–30. doi:10.1108/02635570410514061

Eid, R., Trueman, M., & Ahmed, A. (2002). A Cross-Industry Review of B2B Critical Success Factors. *Internet Research: Electronic Networking Applications and Policy, 12*(2), 110–123. doi:10.1108/10662240210422495

Eid, R., & Trueman, M. (2002). *The Adoption of the Internet for B-to-B International Marketing: A theoretical model*. Bradford University School of Management Working Paper Series, No 02/10.

Eikebrokk, T. R., & Olsen, D. H. (2007). An empirical investigation of competency factors affecting e-business success in European SMEs. *Information & Management, 44*(4). doi:10.1016/j.im.2007.02.004

Eisammani, Z. A., Hackney, R., & Scown, P. (2004). SME adoption and implementation process of websites in the presence of change agents. In Al-Qirim, N. A. Y. (Ed.), *Electronic Commerce in Small to Medium-Sized Enterprises: Frameworks, Issues, and Implications* (pp. 146–164). Hershey, PA: Idea Group Publishing.

Eisenhardt, K. M. (1989). Building theories from case study research. *Academy of Management Review, 14*(4), 532–550. doi:10.2307/258557

Ekanem, I. (2005). 'Bootstrapping': The investment decision-making process in small firms. *The British Accounting Review, 37*(3), 299–318. doi:10.1016/j.bar.2005.04.004

Elahi, T. E., & Pearson, S. (2007). Privacy Assurance: Bridging the Gap Between Preference and Practice. TrustBus 2007, LNCS 4657, Springer-Verlag, 65-74.

Electronic Frontier Foundation. (1993). www.eff.org/Privacy/Medical/1993_ota_medical_privacy.report; retrieved June 8, 2006.

Electronic Privacy Information Center. (1999). www.epic.org/privacy/medical/GAO-medical-privacy-399.pdf; retrieved May 17, 2006.

Electronic Privacy Information Center. (2006). www.epic.org/privacy/medical/polls.html; retrieved April 17, 2006.

Electronic Privacy Information Center. (2008). www.epic.org/privacy/medical; retrieved October 16, 2008.

Eleniak, M. (2003). *Essential navigation checklists for web design*. Sitepoint. www.sitepoint.com/articles/checklists-web-design.

El-Mahdi, A. (2004). *MSES Potentials and Success Determinants in Egypt 2003-2004: Special Reference to Gender Differentials. Research report Series on Promoting Competitiveness in Micro and Small Enterprises in the MENA Region*. Economic Research Forum.

Elnaffar, S., Maamar, Z., Yahyaoui, H., Bentahar, J., & Thiran, Ph. (2008). Reputation of Communities of Web services - Preliminary Investigation. *Proceedings of the International Symposium on Web and Mobile Information Services (WAMIS'2008) held in conjunction of the 22nd International Conference on Advanced Information Networking and Applications (AINA'2008)*.

Elsbach, K. D., Sutton, R. I., & Principe, K. E. (1998). Averting Expected Challenges Through Anticipatory Impression Management: A Study of Hospital Billing. *Organization Science, 9*(1), 68–86. doi:10.1287/orsc.9.1.68

Emory, C. W., & Cooper, D. R. (1991). *Business Research Methods* (4th ed.). Boston: Irwin.

EnCoRe. (2010). *Ensuring Consent and Revocation project*. Retrieved August 2010 from www.encore-project.info.

Enterprise Management Associates. (2005). HP Openview Compliance Manager: Integrating the Synergies of Management, Security and Compliance. Retrieved June 2008 from http://www.managementsoftware.hp.com/products/ovcm/swp/ovcm_swp.pdf

Eriksson, H. (2003). Using Jess Tab to Integrate Protégé and Jess. *IEEE Intelligent Systems, 18*(2), 43–50. doi:http://dx.doi.org.gate6.inist.fr/10.1109/MIS.2003.1193656

Espinasse, B., Fournier, S., & Freitas, F. (2008). Agent and ontology based information gathering on restricted web domains with AGATHE. In *SAC '08: Proceedings of the 2008 ACM symposium on Applied computing* (p. 2381–2386). New York: ACM. doi:http://doi.acm.org.gate6.inist.fr/10.1145/1363686.1364252

Etzioni, A. (1999). *The limits of privacy*. New York: Basic Books.

Etzioni, O., Banko, M., Soderland, S., & Weld, D. S. (2008). Open information extraction from the web. *Commun. ACM, 51*(12), 68-74. doi:http://doi.acm.org/10.1145/1409360.1409378

Etzioni, O., Cafarella, M., Downey, D., Kok, S., Popescu, A., Shaked, T., et al. (2004). Web-scale information extraction in knowitall: (preliminary results). In *WWW '04: Proceedings of the 13th international conference on World Wide Web* (p. 100–110). New York: ACM. doi:http://doi.acm.org.gate6.inist.fr/10.1145/988672.988687

European Commission. (2004). *SME definitions*. Retrieved 23.03.2004, 2004, from http://europa.eu.int/comm/enterprise/enterprise_policy/sme_definition/index_en.htm

European Parliament and Council (1995). Directive 95/46/EC on the protection of individuals with regard to the processing of personal data and on the free movement of such data. Official Journal of the European Communities. L. 28, 31.

Evans, J. R., & King, V. E. (1999). Business to Business Marketing and the World Wide Web: Planning, Marketing and Assessing Web Sites. *Industrial Marketing Management, 28*(4), 343–358. doi:10.1016/S0019-8501(98)00013-3

Expresso - java architectural framework. (n.d.). Retrieved June 23, 2008, from http://www.jcorporate.com/html/products/expresso.html

Fallows, D. (2005). *How men and women use the Internet*. Pew Internet and American life project available at www.pewinternet.org.

Feeny, D. F., & Willcocks, L. P. (1998). Core IS capabilities for exploiting information technology. *Sloan Management Review, 39*(3), 9–21.

Feeny, D.F. & Ives, B. In Search of Sustainability: Reaping Long-Term Advantage from Investments in Information Technology,. *Journal of Management Information Systems* (7:1), Summer 1990, pp. 27-46.

Feindt, S., Jeffcoate, J., & Chappel, C. (2002). Identifying success factors for rapid growth in SME e-Commerce. *Small Business Economics, 19*(1), 51–62. doi:10.1023/A:1016165825476

Feldman, M. S. (1989). *Order without design: Information production and policymaking*. Stanford, CA: Stanford University Press.

Feldman, M. S. (1995). *Strategies for Interpreting Qualitative Data*. Thousand Oaks, CA: Sage Publications.

Feldman, M. S., & March, J. G. (1981). Information in Organizations as Signal and Symbol. *Administrative Science Quarterly, 26*(2), 171–186. doi:10.2307/2392467

Feldman, W., & Feldman, P. (2005). Solutions for service and project Management. *Contractor, 52*(4), 40–42.

Fenech, T. (1998). Using Perceived Ease of Use and Perceived Usefulness to Predict Acceptance of the World Wide Web. *Computer Networks & ISDN Systems, 30*(1-7), 629-630.

Fern, E. F. (2001). *Advanced Focus Group Research*. London: Sage Publications.

Fernandez, Z., & Nieto, A. J. (2006). The internet: competitive strategy and boundaries of the firm. *International Journal of Technology Management*, 35(1-4), 182–195. doi:10.1504/IJTM.2006.009234

Ferris, N. (2008). Foreign hackers seek to steal American's health records. www.fcw.com/online/news/151334-1.html: etrieved February 4, 2008.

Fichman, R. (2000) The Diffusion and Assimilation of Information Technology Innovations. In R. Zmud (ed.) *Framing the Domains of IT Management: Projecting the Future Through the Past*.pp. 105-104. Cincinnati, OH: Pinnaflex Educational Resources.

Fillis, I., Johannson, U., & Wagner, B. (2003). A conceptualisation of the opportunities and barriers to e-business developemnt in the smaller firm. *Journal of Small Business and Enterprise Development*, 10(3), 336–341. doi:10.1108/14626000310489808

Fillis, I., Ulf, J., & Beverly, W. (2004). Factors impacting on e-business adoption and development in the smaller firm. *International Journal of Entrepreneurial Behaviour and Research*, 10(3), 178–191. doi:10.1108/13552550410536762

Finlayson, M. (2010). *The MIT Java Wordnet Interface (JWI)*. Retrieved from http://www.mit.edu/~markaf/projects/wordnet/

Fiol, C. M. (1996). Squeezing harder doesn't always work: Continuing the search for consistency in innovation research. *Academy of Management Review*, 21(4), 1012–1021.

FIPA. (2000). *The Foundation for Intelligent Physical Agents*. Retrouvé Juillet 13, 2010, from http://www.fipa.org/

Fischer-Hüber, S. (2000). *IT-Security and Privacy*. Berlin, Heidelberg: Springer-Verlag.

Fishbein, M., & Ajzen, I. (1975). *Belief, attitude, intention, and behavior: An introduction to theory and research*. Reading, MA: Addison-Wesley.

Fiske, S.T. & Taylor, S.E. (1991) *Social Cognition (2nd ed.)*. NY: McGraw Hill.

Foong, S.-Y. (1999) Effect of end user personal and systems attributes on computer based information systems success in Malaysian SMEs. *Journal of Small Business Management*, July, 37(3), 81–87.

Fornell, C. (1982). *A Second generation of multivariate analysis*. New York: Praeger.

Fornell, C., & Larcker, D. F. (1981). Evaluating Structural Equation Models with Unobservable Variables and Measurement Error. *JMR, Journal of Marketing Research*, 28, 39–50. doi:10.2307/3151312

Fox, S. (2000). Trust and privacy online: why Americans want to rewrite the rules. available at www.pewinternet.org.

Frame, W. S., Srinivasan, A., & Woosley, L. (2001). The effect of credit scoring on small-business lending. *Journal of Money, Credit and Banking*, 33(3), 813–825. doi:10.2307/2673896

Frasincar, F., Borsje, J., & Levering, L. (2009). A Semantic Web-Based Approach for Building Personalized News Services. *International Journal of E-Business Research*, 5(3), 35–53.

Frasincar, F., Milea, V., & Kaymak, U. (2010). tOWL: Integrating Time in OWL. In R. D. Virgilio, F. Giunchiglia & L. Tanca (Eds.), *Semantic Web Information Management: A Model-Based Perspective* (pp. 225-246). Berlin Heidelberg, Germany: Springer.

Freeman, J., Carroll, G. R., & Hannan, M. T. (1983). The liability of newness: Age dependence in organizational death rates. *American Sociological Review*, 48(5), 692–710. doi:10.2307/2094928

Freitag, D., & Kushmerick, N. (2000). Boosted Wrapper Induction. Proceedings of the 17th National Conference on AI and 12th Conference on Innovative Applications of AI.

Freitas, F. L. G., & Bittencourt, G. (2003). An ontology-based architecture for cooperative information agents. In *IJCAI'03: Proceedings of the 18th international joint conference on Artificial intelligence* (p. 37–42). San Francisco: Morgan Kaufmann Publishers Inc.

Fuller-Love, N. (2006). Management development in small firms. *International Journal of Management Reviews, 8*(3), 175–190. doi:10.1111/j.1468-2370.2006.00125.x

Futrell, R. (1998). Performance Governance: Impression Management, Teamwork, and Conflict Containment in City Commission Proceedings. *Journal of Contemporary Ethnography, 27*(4), 494–529. doi:10.1177/089124199129023316

Gabrilovich, E., Dumais, S., & Horvitz, E. (2004). Newsjunkie: Providing Personalized Newsfeeds via Analysis of Information Novelty. In *13th International Conference on World Wide Web (WWW 2004)* (pp. 482-490). New York: ACM.

Gaglio, C. M., Cechini, M., & Winter, S. J. (1998). *Gaining Legitimacy: The Symbolic Use of Technology by New Ventures* (pp. 203–215). Frontiers of Entrepreneurship Research.

Gaiter, D., & Brecher, J. (2006). A fine year for web wine. *Wall Street Journal*, (April 28), W1, W10.

Gaizauskas, R., & Robertson, A. M. (1997). Coupling Information Retrieval and Information Extraction: A New Text Technology for Gathering Information from the Web. *IN proceedings of the 5th computed-assisted information searching on internet conference (RIAO '97)* (p. 356–370).

Galliers, R. D. (1992) Choosing Information Systems Research Approaches, In Galliers, R.D. (Ed.) *Information Systems Research: Issues, Methods and Practical Guidelines*. Henley-on-Thames: Alfred Waller, 144-162.

Gardner, W. L. (1992). Lessons in Organizational Dramaturgy: The Art of Impression Management. *Organizational Dynamics, 21*(1), 33–46. doi:10.1016/0090-2616(92)90084-Z

Gardner, W. L., & Avolio, B. J. (1998). The Charismatic Relationship: A Dramaturgical Perspective. *Academy of Management Review, 23*(1), 32–58. doi:10.2307/259098

Garfinkel, H. (1967). *Studies in Ethnomethodology*. Cambridge, MA: Polity.

Garud, R., & Rappa, M. A. (1994). A Socio-cognitive Model of Technology Evolution: The Case of Cochlear Implants. *Organization Science, 5*(3), 344–362. doi:10.1287/orsc.5.3.344

Garvin, D. (1988). *Managing Quality*. New York: Free Press.

Gefen, D., Karahanna, E., & Straub, D. W. (2003). Trust and TAM in online shopping: an integrated model. *Management Information Systems Quarterly, 27*(1), 51–90.

Gefen, D., & Straub, D. W. (1997). Gender Differences in the perception and use of E- mail: An Extension to the Technology Acceptance Model. *MIS Quarterly, 21*(4), 389–400. doi:10.2307/249720

Geiger, S. W., & Cashen, L. H. (2002). A multidimensional examination of slack and its impact on innovation. *Journal of Managerial Issues, 14*(1), 68–85.

Genkina, A., & Camp, L. J. (2005, April 1). *Re-Embedding Existing Social Networks into Online Experiences to Aid in Trust Assessment*, Available at SSRN: http://ssrn.com/abstract=707139.

George, G. (2005). Slack resources and the performance of privately held firms. *Academy of Management Journal, 48*(4), 661–676.

Geyskens, I., Gielens, K., & Dekimpe, M. G. (2002). The market valuation of Internet channel additions. *Journal of Marketing, 66*, 102–119. doi:10.1509/jmkg.66.2.102.18478

Ghorab, K. E. (1997). The Impact of Technology Acceptance Consideration on System Usage, and Adopted Level of Technological Sophistication: An Empirical Investigation. *International Journal of Information Management, 17*(4), 249–259. doi:10.1016/S0268-4012(97)00003-0

Gibbs, J., Kraemer, K. L., & Dedrick, J. (2002). *Environment and Policy Factors Shaping E-commerce Diffusion: A Cross-Country Comparison. Center for Research on Information Technology & Organizations*. Irvine: University of California.

Gilkeson, J. H., & Reynolds, K. (2003). Determinants of Internet auction success and closing price: An exploratory study. *Psychology and Marketing, 20*(6), 537–542. doi:10.1002/mar.10086

Gioia, D. A., Shultz, M., & Corley, K. G. (2000). Organizational Identity, Image, and Adaptive Instability. *Academy of Management Review, 25*(1), 63–81. doi:10.2307/259263

Gioia, D. A. (1986). Symbols, Scripts, and Sensemaking: Creating Meaning in the Organizational Experience. In Sims, H. P. Jr, & Gioia, D. A. (Eds.), *The Thinking Organization: Dynamics of Organization Cognition* (pp. 49–74). San Francisco: Jossey Bass.

Girardi, C. (2007). HTMLCleaner: Exracting relevant text from web pages.

Glaser, B. G., & Strauss, A. L. (1967). *The Discovery of Grounded Theory*. Chicago, IL: Aldine.

Goethals, G. R. (1976). An attributional analysis of some social influence phenomena. In Harvey, J. H., Ickes, W. J., & Kidd, R. F. (Eds.), *New Directions in Attribution Research* (*Vol. 1*, pp. 291–310). Hillside, NJ: Lawrence Erlbaum.

Golden, P. A., & Dollinger, M. (1993). Cooperative Alliances and Competitive Strategies in Small Manufacturing Firms. *Entrepreneurship Theory and Practice*, 43-56.

Goodwin, C. (1991). Privacy: Recognition of a Consumer Right. *Journal of Public Policy & Marketing, 10*(1), 149–166.

Google. (2009). Transparency, choice and control – now complete with a dashboard! The Official Google Blog. Retrieved 2010 from http://googleblog.blogspot.com/2009/11/transparency-choice-and-control-now.html

Goossenaerts, J.B.M., Zegers, A.T.M. & Smits, T.M. (2009) A multi-level model driven regime for value-added tax compliance in ERP systems. *Computers in Industry, 60*:9, December, 709-727.

Gordijn, J. (2003). *Why visualization of e-business models matters. In 16th Bled Electronic Commerce Conference eTransformation,* Bled, Slovenia, June 9-11, 2003 http://www.cs.vu.nl/~obelix/publications/Why%20visualization%20of%20e-business%20models%20matters.pdf

Grabner-Kräuter, S., & Kaluscha, E. A. (2003). Empirical Research in Online Trust: A Review and Critical Assessment. *International Journal of Human-Computer Studies, Special Issue on ". Trust and Technology, 58*(6), 783–812.

Grandon, E. E., & Pearson, J. M. (2004). Electronic commerce adoption: an empirical study of small and medium US businesses. *Information & Management, 42*(1), 197–216.

Grant, R. M. (1996). Toward a knowledge-based theory of the firm. *Strategic Management Journal, 17*, 109–122. doi:10.1002/(SICI)1097-0266(199602)17:2<109::AID-SMJ796>3.0.CO;2-P

Grayson, K., & Shulman, D. (2000). Impression Management in Services Marketing. In Swatz, T., & Iacobucci, D. (Eds.), *Handbook of Services Marketing and Management* (pp. 51–67). Thousand Oaks, CA: Sage.

Greenbaum, T. L. (1998). *Handbook of Focus Group Research*. Thousand Oaks, CA: Sage.

Greenleaf, G. (2005). APEC's Privacy Framework: A new low standard. *Privacy Law and Policy Reporter, 11*(5). Retrieved 2008 from http://www.aph.gov.au/Senate/committee/legcon_ctte/completed_inquiries/2004-07/privacy/submissions/sub32ann_c.pdf

Gregor, S., Martin, M., Fernandez, W., Stern, S., & Vitale, M. (2006). The Transformational Dimension in the Realization of Business Value from Information Technology. *The Journal of Strategic Information Systems, 15*, 249–270. doi:10.1016/j.jsis.2006.04.001

Greve, H. R. (2003). A behavioral theory of R&D expenditures and innovations: Evidence from shipbuilding. *Academy of Management Journal, 46*(6), 685–702. doi:10.2307/30040661

Grosh, B., & Somolekae, G. (1996). Mighty oaks from little acorns: Can micro-enterprise serve as the seedbed of industrialization? *World Development, 24*(12), 1879–1890. doi:10.1016/S0305-750X(96)00082-4

Grosso, C., McPherson, J., & Shi, C. (2005). Retailing: what's working online? *The McKinsey Quarterly, 3*, 18.

Grove, S. J., & Fisk, R. P. (1989). Impression Management in Services Marketing: A Dramaturgical Perspective. In Giacalone, R. A., & Rosenfeld, P. (Eds.), *Impression Management in the Organization* (pp. 427–438). Hillsdale, NJ: Lawrence Erlbaum.

Gruber, T. R. (1995). Toward principles for the design of ontologies used for knowledge sharing. *Int. J. Hum.-Comput. Stud., 43*(5-6), 907–928. doi:http://dx.doi.org.gate6.inist.fr/10.1006/ijhc.1995.1081

Guarino, N., & Welty, C. A. (2002). Evaluating Ontological Decisions with OntoClean. *Communications of the ACM, 45*(1), 61–65.

Guay, D., & Ettwein, J. (1998). Internet commerce basics. *International Journal of Electronic Markets, 8*(1), 12–15. doi:10.1080/10196789800000004

Guha, S., Tang, K., & Francis, P. (2008). NOYB: Privacy in Online Social Networks. *WOSN '08, August 18, 2008*, Seattle, Washington, USA. 49-54

Gujarati, D. N. (1995). *Basic Econometrics* (3rd ed.). New York: McGraw-Hill.

Gulati, R., & Garino, J. (2000). Get the right mix of bricks & Clicks. *Harvard Business Review, 78*(3), 107–114.

Gwee, J.-T., Hui, K.-L., & Chau, P. Y. K. (2002). Determinants of brand equity in e-businesses: An exploratory study. *Proceedings of the Twenty-Third International Conference on Information Systems,* Barcelona, 617-627.

Hair, J. F., Anderson, R. E., Tatham, R. L., & Black, W. C. (1992). *Multivariate Data Analysis.* New York: Macmillan Publishing Company.

Hall, R. (1993). A framework linking intangible resources and capabilities to sustainable competitive advantage. *Strategic Management Journal, 14*(8), 607–618. doi:10.1002/smj.4250140804

Hamdan, K. (2004). *Micro and Small Enterprises in Lebanon. Research report Series on Promoting Competitiveness in Micro and Small Enterprises in the MENA Region.* Economic Research Forum.

Hammer, M. (1990). Reengineering work: Don't Automate, Obliterate. *Harvard Business Review, 68*(4).

Hann, I.-H., Hui, K. L., Lee, T., & L., P. I. P. (2002, December). *Online Information Privacy: Measuring the Cost-Benefit Tradeoff.* Paper presented at the Proceedings of the Twenty-Third Annual International Conference on Information Systems (ICIS), Barcelona, Spain.

Hannan, M. T., & Freeman, J. H. (1984). Structural inertia and organizational change. *American Journal of Sociology, 89*, 149–164.

Hannan, M. T., & Freeman, J. (1984). Structural inertia and organizational change. *American Sociological Review, 49*(2), 149–164. doi:10.2307/2095567

Hansell, S. (2006). Al Gore's Current TV Joins With Yahoo for a Video Venture. *New York Times.* Retrieved: 18th October, 2007, from http://www.nytimes.com/2006/09/20/business/20gore.html?ei=5088&en=4642a6c8ba35a6c5&ex=1316404800&adxnnl=1&partner=rssnyt&emc=rss&adxnnlx=1187694015-HGl7CuZdSkcOp26+zlBcVQ

Hansen, J. A. (1992). Innovation, firm size, and firm age. *Small Business Economics, 4*(1), 37–44.

Harcar, T., Kara, A., & Kucukemiroglu, O. (2006). Consumer's perceived value and buying behavior of store brands: An empirical investigation. *Business Review (Federal Reserve Bank of Philadelphia), 5*(2), 55–62.

Harper, J., & Singleton, S. (2001). With a grain of salt: what consumer privacy surveys don't tell us. http://www.cei.org/PDFs/with_a_grain_of_salt.pdf

Harrison, D. A., Mykytyn, P. P., Jr., & Riemenschneider, C. K.(1997). Executive Decisions About Adoption of Information Technology in Small Business: Theory and Empirical Tests. *Information Systems Research* (8:2), pp. 171-195.

Hashmi, M. S., & Cuddy, J. (1990) Strategic initiatives for introducing CIM technologies in Irish SMEs. In Faria, L. and Van Puymbroeck, W. (eds.) *Computer Integrated Manufacturing – Proceedings of the Sixth CIM-Europe Annual Conference*, (Springer Verlag, Lisbon).

Hatch, M. J., & Schultz, M. (1997). Relations between Organizational Culture, Identity, and Image. *European Journal of Marketing*, 5(6), 356–365.

Hawawini, G., Subramanian, V., & Verdin, P. (2003). Is performance driven by industry- or firm-specific factors? New look at the old evidence. *Strategic Management Journal*, 24(1), 1–16. doi:10.1002/smj.278

Hawkins, D. (1999). What is credible information? *Online*, 23(5), 86–90.

Hazan, M. (2002) Virtual South: E-Commerce for un-privileged artisans. Retrieved Dec 12, 2007, from http://www.iicd.org/stories/.

Heijden, H. d. (2000). *Measuring IT core capabilities for electronic commerce: results from a confirmatory analysis.* Paper presented at the 21st International Conference on Information Systems, Brisbane, Australia.

Henderson, A. D. (1999). Firm strategy and age dependence: A contingent view of the liabilities of newness, adolescence, and obsolescence. *Administrative Science Quarterly*, 44(2), 281–314. doi:10.2307/2666997

Henderson, J. C., & Venkatraman, N. (1993). Strategic alignment: Leveraging information technology for transforming organizations. *IBM Systems Journal*, 32(1), 4–16.

Herold, D. M., Jayaraman, N., & Narayanaswamy, C. R. (2006). What is the relationship between organizational slack and innovation? *Journal of Managerial Issues*, 18(3), 372–392.

Herzberg, F., Mausner, B., & Snyderman, B. B. (1959). *The Motivation to Work* (2nd ed.). New York: John Wiley & Sons.

Hickey, B. (2006). *Fairfax acquires Trade Me for $700m.* Retrieved July 5, 2006, from http://www.stuff.co.nz/stuff/print/0,1478,3594845a10,00.html.

Higgins, S. H., & Hogan, P. T. (1999). Internal Diffusion of High Technology Industrial Innovations: An Empirical Study. *Journal of Business and Industrial Marketing*, 14(1), 61–75. doi:10.1108/08858629910254157

Higgs, H. & Worthington, A. (2005). Financial returns and price determinants in the *Australian art market*, 1973-2003.

Hillman, A. J., Shropshire, C., & Cannella, A. A. (2007). Organizational predictors of women on corporate boards. *Academy of Management Journal*, 50(4), 941–952.

Hinde, S. (2005). *The SmartFrog Reference Manual*, v3.06. Retrieved Dec. 2006 from http://cvs.sourceforge.net/viewcvs.py/*checkout*/smartfrog/core/smartfrog/docs/sfReference.pdf

Hinz, O., Gertmeier, E., Tafreschi, O., Enzmann, M., & Schneider, M. (2007). *Customer Loyalty programs and privacy concerns. 20th Bled eConference eMergence: Merging and Emerging Technologies, Processes and Institutions. June 406.* Slovenia: Bled.

Hochheiser, H. (2002). The platform for privacy preference as a social protocol: An examination within the US policy context. *ACM Transactions on Internet Technology*, 2(4), 276–306. doi:10.1145/604596.604598

Hofacker, C. (1999). *Internet Marketing.* Dripping Springs, TX: Digital Spring.

Hoffman, D. L., Novak, T., & Peralta, M. A. (1999). Information Privacy in the Marketspace: Implications for the Commercial Uses of Anonymity on the Web. *The Information Society*, *15*(2), 129–139. doi:10.1080/019722499128583

Hoffman, D. L., Novak, T. P., & Chatterjee, P. (1995). Commercial Scenarios for the Web: Opportunities and Challenges. *Journal of Computer-Mediated Communication*, *1*(3), 1–19.

Hoffman, W. (2006). Technology, off the shelf. *Traffic World*, (July 17), 1.

Hofstede, G. (1980). *Culture's consequences*. Beverly Hills, CA: Sage.

Hofstede, G. (2003). *Culture's Consequences: Comparing Values, Behaviors, Institutions and Organizations across Nations*. Longdon. Sage.

Hollensen, S. (2001). *Global Marketing: A market-responsive approach* (2nd ed.). England: Pearson Education Limited.

Holt, B. (1997). Poststructuralist lifestyle analysis: conceptualizing the social pattern of consumption in postmodernity. *The Journal of Consumer Research*, *23*(3), 326–350. doi:10.1086/209487

Hong, J. I., Ng, J. D., Lederer, S., & Landay, J. (2004). Privacy risk models for designing privacy-sensitive ubiquitous computing systems, Proceedings of the 2004 conference on Designing interactive systems: processes, practices, methods, and techniques, Cambridge, MA, USA Jackson, L., von Eye, A., Barbatsis, G., Biocca, F., Zhao, Y., & Fitzgerald, H.E. (2003). Internet Attitudes and Internet Use: some surprising findings from the HomeNet-Too project. *International Journal of Human-Computer Studies*, *59*, 355–382.

Honig, B.(1998)What determines success? Examining the human, financial, and social capital of Jamaican microentrepreneurs *Journal of Business Venturing*, (13:5), pp.371-94.

Hou, J., & Elliott, K. (2010). Profiling online bidders. *Journal of Marketing Theory and Practice*, *18*(2), 109–126. doi:10.2753/MTP1069-6679180201

Hsu, L.-C., & Wang, C.-H. (2008). A study of e-trust in online auctions. *Journal of Electronic Commerce Research*, *9*(4), 310–321.

Huang, X., Soutar, G. N., & Brown, A. (2002). New product development processes in small and medium-sized enterprises: Some Australian evidence. *Journal of Small Business Management*, *40*(1), 27–42. doi:10.1111/1540-627X.00036

Hughes, T. (2006). New channels/old channels: Customer management and multi-channels. *European Journal of Marketing*, *40*(1/2), 113–129. doi:10.1108/03090560610637347

Huhns, M. (1994, Juin). *Distributed Artificial Intelligence for Information Systems*. Tutorial presented at Second International Conference on Cooperating Knowledge Based Systems (CKBS-94), Keele, UK.

Iacovou, A. L., Benbasat, I., & Dexter, A. (1995). Electronic data interchange and small organizations: adoption and impact of technology. *Management Information Systems Quarterly*, *19*(4), 465–485. doi:10.2307/249629

Ibeh, K. I. N., Luo, Y., & Dinnie, K. (2005). E-branding strategies of internet companies: Some preliminary insights from the UK. *Journal of Brand Management*, *12*(5), 355–373. doi:10.1057/palgrave.bm.2540231

IBM. (2008). *Tivoli Security Compliance Manager*. Retrieved June 2008 from http://www-306.ibm.com/software/tivoli/products/security-compliance-mgr/

Igbaria, M., Zinatelli, N., Cragg, P., & Cavaye, A. (1997). Personal computing acceptance factors in small firms: a structural equation model. *Management Information Systems Quarterly*, *21*(3), 279–302. doi:10.2307/249498

Igbaria, M., Guimaraes, T., & Davis, G. B. (1995). Testing the Determinants of Microcomputer Usage via a Structure Equation Model. *Journal of Management Information Systems*, *11*(4), 87–114.

Igbaria, M., Zinatelli, N., Cragg, P. B.,& Cavaye, A. L. M.(1997) Personal Computing Acceptance Factors in Small Firms: A Structural Equation Model*MIS Quarterly* (21:3), pp. 279-305.

Ihlström, C., & Nilsson, M. (2003). E-business adoption by SMEs - Prerequisites and attitudes of SMEs in a Swedish network. *Journal of Organizational Computing and Electronic Commerce, 13*(3-4), 211–223. doi:10.1207/S15327744JOCE133&4_04

Ind, N. (1992). *The Corporate Image*. London: Kogan Page.

Information Commissioner's Office UK. (2007). PIA handbook. Retrieved November 2008 from http://www.ico.gov.uk/.

Institute of Medicine. (2001). *Crossing the quality chasm: A new health system for the 21ˢᵗ century*. Washington, D.C.: National Academy Press.

Internet World Stats. (2005). Internet usage statistics-the big picture. Available at www.internetworldstats.com/stats.htm.

Ireson, N., Ciravegna, F., Califf, M. E., Freitag, D., Kushmerick, N., & Lavelli, A. (2005). Evaluating Machine Learning for Information Extraction. Proceedings of the 22nd international conference on ML. doi:http://doi.acm.org/10.1145/1102351.1102395

Ives, B., & Learmonth, G. P. (1984). The Information Systems as a Competitive weapon. *Communications of the ACM, 27*(12), 1984. doi:10.1145/2135.2137

Ivis, M. (2001). *Analysis of barriers impeding e-business adoption among Canadian SMEs*. Canadian E-Business Opportunities Roundtable.

Jablonski, S., & Bussler, C. (1996). *Workflow Management: Modeling Concepts, Architecture and Implementation. London et al.* International Thomson Computer Press.

Jackson, M. H., Poole, M. S., & Kuhn, T. (2002). The Social Construction of Technology in Studies of the Workplace. In Lievrouw, L., & Livingstone, S. (Eds.), *Handbook of New Media: Social Shaping and Consequences of ICTs* (pp. 236–253). Thousand Oaks, CA: Sage.

Jade. (2006). *Java Agent DEvelopment Framework*. Accessed july 13th, 2010, from http://jade.tilab.com/

Janiszewski, C. (1998). The influence of display characteristics on visual exploratory search behaviour. *The Journal of Consumer Research, 25*(3), 290–301. doi:10.1086/209540

Jarratt, D. G. (1998). A Strategic Classification of Business Alliances: A Qualitative Perspective Built from a Study of Small and Medium-sized Enterprises. *Qualitative Market Research: An International Journal, 11*(1), 39–49. doi:10.1108/13522759810368442

Jarvis, C. B., Mackenzie, S. B., & Podsakoff, P. M. (2003). A critical review of construct indicators and measurement model misspecification in marketing and consumer research. *The Journal of Consumer Research, 30*(september), 199–218. doi:10.1086/376806

Java, A., Finin, T., & Nirenburg, S. (2006). Text Understanding Agents and the Semantic Web. In *39th Hawaii International Conference on Systems Science (HICSS 2006)* (Vol. 3, pp. 62.62). Washington, DC: IEEE Computer Society.

Javenpaa, S. L., & Todd, P. A. (1997). Is there a future for retailing on the Internet? In Peterson (ed.), *Electronic Marketing and the Consumer*, 139-154. Thousand Oaks, CA; SAGE.

Jena. (2006). *Jena Semantic Web Framework*. Accessed july 13th, 2010, from http://jena.sourceforge.net/

Jensen, M. C. (1986). Agency costs of free cash flow, corporate finance, and takeovers. *The American Economic Review, 76*, 323–329.

Jensen, M. C., & Meckling, W. H. (1976). Theory of the firm: Managerial behavior, agency costs, and ownership structure. *Journal of Financial Economics, 3*, 305–360. doi:10.1016/0304-405X(76)90026-X

Jess. (2006). *Jess the Rule Engine for the Java Platform*. Acessed July 13th, 2010, de http://www.jessrules.com/

Johansson, N., & Mollstedt, U. (2006). Revisiting Amit and Zott's model of value creation sources: The SymBelt Customer Center case. *Journal of Theoretical and Applied Electronic Commerce Research, 1*(3), 16–27.

Johnson, L. J., & Cullen, B. J. (2002). Trust in Cross-Cultural relationships. In Gannon, M. J., & Newman, K. L. (Eds.), *The Blackwell Handbook of Cross-Cultural Management* (pp. 335–360). Oxford, UK, Malden, Mass: Blackwell.

Johnson, C. A. (1974). Privacy as Personal Control. In D. H. Carson (Ed.), *Man-Environment Interactions: Evaluations and Applications: Part 2* (Vol. 6: Privacy, pp. 83-100). Washington, D.C.: Environmental Design Research Association.

Johnston, D. A., Wade, M., & McClean, R. (2007). Does e-business matter to SMEs? A comparison of the financial impacts of Internet business solutions on European and North American SMEs. *Journal of Small Business Management, 45*(3), 354–361. doi:10.1111/j.1540-627X.2007.00217.x

Johnston, K., Shi, J., Dann, Z., & Barcay, I. (2006). Knowledge, power and trust in SME e-based virtual organisations. *International Journal of Networking & Virtual Organizations, 3*(1), 42–59. doi:10.1504/IJNVO.2006.008784

Jones, C. (2004). An alternative view of small firm adoption. *Journal of Small Business and Enterprise Development, 11*(3), 362–370. doi:10.1108/14626000410551618

Jones, P., Clarke-Hill, C., Shears, P., & Hillier, D. (2001). The eighth 'C' of (R) etailing: Customer Concern. *Management Research News, 24*(5), 11–16. doi:10.1108/01409170110782397

Jöreskog, K. G., & Wold, H. (1982). *Systems under indirect observation: Causality, structure, prediction*. North-Holland.

Judd, V. C. (1987). Differentiate with the 5th P: people. *Industrial Marketing Management, 16*, 241–247. doi:10.1016/0019-8501(87)90032-0

Jung, J. J. (2007). Ontological framework based on contextual mediation for collaborative information retrieval. *Inf. Retr., 10*(1), 85–109. doi:http://dx.doi.org.gate6.inist.fr/10.1007/s10791-006-9013-5

Jutla, D. N., & Bodorik, C. J. (2001). A methodology for creating e-business strategy. *In The 34th Hawaii International Conference on System Sciences*.

Kacen, J., Hess, J., & Chiang, W. K. (2002). Bricks or Clicks? Consumer Attitudes toward Traditional Stores and Online Stores. (Working Paper). University of Illinois, Champaign, IL

Kagel, J. H. (1995). Auctions: a survey of experimental research. In Kagel, J., & Roth, A. (Eds.), *Handbook of Experimental Economics* (pp. 501–585). Princeton, NJ: Princeton University Press.

Kalakota, R., & Whinston, A. B. (1996). *Frontiers of Electronic Commerce*. Addition- Wesley Publishing Company, Inc.

Kalfoglou, Y., Domingue, J., Motta, E., Vargas-Vera, M., & Shum, S. B. (2001). *myPlanet: An Ontology-Driven Web-Based Personalized News Service*. Paper presented at the Workshop on Ontologies and Information Sharing (IJCAI 2001).

Kandel, E., & Marx, L. M. (1997). NASDAQ Market Structure and Spread Patterns. *Journal of Financial Economics, 45*(1), 61–89. doi:10.1016/S0304-405X(96)00894-X

Kane, G. C., & Alavi, M. (2007). Information technology and organizational learning: An investigation of exploration and exploitation processes. *Organization Science, 18*(5), 796–812. doi:10.1287/orsc.1070.0286

Karahanna, E., & Straub, D. W. (1999). The Psychological Origins of Perceived Usefulness and Ease-of-Use. *Information & Management, 35*(4), 237–250. doi:10.1016/S0378-7206(98)00096-2

Karjoth, G. (2003). Access control with IBM Tivoli access manager. *ACM Transactions on Information and System Security, 6*(2), 232–257. doi:10.1145/762476.762479

Karjoth, G., Schunter, M., & Waidner, M. (2002). *The platform for enterprise privacy practices - privacy-enabled management of customer data.* Paper presented at the The 2nd Workshop on Privacy Enhancing Technologies (PET 2002), San Francisco, CA.

Karkaletsis, V., Spyropoulos, C. D., Souflis, D., Grover, C., Hachey, B., Pazienza, M. T., et al. (2003). Demonstration of the CROSSMARC system. *Proceedings of the 2003 Conference of the North American Chapter of the Association for Computational Linguistics on Human Language Technology: Demonstrations* - Volume 4. doi:http://dx.doi.org/10.3115/1073427.1073434

Katerattanakul, P. (2002). Framework of effective web site design for business-to-consumer Internet commerce. *INFOR, 40*(1), 57–71.

Katila, R., & Shane, S. (2005). When does lack of resources make new firms innovative? *Academy of Management Journal, 48*(5), 814–829.

Katkar, R., & Lucking-Reiley, D. (2000). *Public versus secret reserve prices in eBay auctions: Results from a Pokemon field experiment.* Unpublished paper. Arizona State University.

Katz Ian. (2007). ID theft fell in '06, FTC study finds. *Sun-Sentinel,*(February,8), 3D.

Kauchak, D., Smarr, J., & Elkan, C. (2004). Sources of Success for Boosted Wrapper Induction. *Journal of Machine Learning Research, 5*, 499–527.

Kaushal, R., Blumenthal, D., Poon, E. G., Ashish, K. J., Franz, C., Middleton, B., et al., & the Cost of National Health Information Network Working Group. (2005). The costs of a national health information network. www.annals.org/cgi/reprint/143/3/165.pdf: retrieved February 4, 2008.

Keen, P. (1993). Information technology and the management difference: A fusion map. *IBM Systems Journal, 32*(1), 17–39. doi:10.1147/sj.321.0017

Keen, P. G. W. (1991). Redesigning the organization through Information Technology. *Planning Review, 19*(3).

Keller Johnson, L. (2002). New views on digital CRM. *MIT Sloan Management Review, 44*(1), 10–27.

Kelvin, P. (1973). A social psychological examination of privacy. *The British Journal of Social and Clinical Psychology, 12*, 248–261.

Khosravifar, B., Bentahar, J., Moazin, A., & Thiran, Ph. (2010a). Analyzing Communities of Web Services Using Incentives [IJWSR]. *International Journal of Web Services Research, 7*(3).

Khosravifar, B., Bentahar, J., & Moazin, A. (2010b). Analyzing the Relationships between some Parameters of Web Services Reputation. In *Proceedings of the 8th IEEE International Conference on Web Services (ICWS'2010),* Miami, Florida, USA.

Kilman, D. G., & Forslund, D. W. (1997). An international collaboratory based on virtual patient records. *Communications of the ACM, 40*(8), 111–117. doi:10.1145/257874.257898

King, W. R., & Epstein, B. J. (1976). Assessing the value of information. *Management Datamatics, 5*(4), 171–180.

King, R. C., Sen, R., & Xia, M. (2004). Impact of Web-based e-commerce on channel strategy in retailing. *International Journal of Electronic Commerce, 8*(3), 103–130.

King, R. E. (1998). *The uses and gratifications of the World Wide Web: an audience analysis for local television broadcasters.* Unpublished doctoral dissertation, University of Tennessee.

Kinkaide, P. (2000). *The New Frontier: SME's Enterprise and E-Business in Western Canada.*Unpublished manuscript, Edmonton.

Kishore, R., & McLean, E. R. (2007). Reconceptualizing innovation compatibility as organizational alignment in secondary IT adoption contexts: An investigation of software reuse infusion. *IEEE Transactions on Engineering Management, 54*(4), 756–775. doi:10.1109/TEM.2007.906849

Kivimaki, M., & Lansisalmi, H. (2000). Communication as a determinant of organizational innovation. *R & D Management, 30*(1), 33–42. doi:10.1111/1467-9310.00155

Klein, H. K., & Myers, M. D. (1999). A Set of Principles for Conducting and Evaluating Interpretive Field Studies in Information Systems. *Management Information Systems Quarterly, 23*(1), 67–94. doi:10.2307/249410

Klopfer, P. H., & Rubenstein, D. L. (1977). The concept privacy and its biological basis. *The Journal of Social Issues, 33*, 52–65. doi:10.1111/j.1540-4560.1977.tb01882.x

Klyne, G., & Carroll, J. J. (2004). *Resource Description Framework (RDF): Concepts and Abstract Syntax*: W3C Recommendation 10 February 2004.

Kobsa, A. (2007). Privacy-Enhanced Personalisation. *Communications of the ACM, 50*(8), 24–33. doi:10.1145/1278201.1278202

Kobsa, A. (2003). Component architecture for dynamically managing privacy constraints in personalized web-based systems. In Proceedings of the Third Workshop on Privacy Enabling Technology, Dresden, (2003).Germany. Springer Verlag.

Koch, N., Kraus, A., & Cachero, C., & Meliá, S. (2004). Integration of business processes in Web application models. *Journal of Web Engineering, 3*(1), 22–29.

Kogut, B., & Zander, U. (1992). Knowledge of the firm, combinative capabilities, and the replication of technology. *Organization Science, 3*(3), 383–397. doi:10.1287/orsc.3.3.383

Koontz, L. D., & Melvin, V. C. (2007). Efforts continue but comprehensive privacy approach needed for national strategy. Testimony before the Subcommittee on Information Privacy, Census, and National Archive Committee on Oversight and Government Reform of the U.S. House of Representatives. www.gao.gov/new.items/d07988t.pdf: retrieved June 28, 2007.

Korba, L., Song, R., & Yee, G. (2006). Privacy Management Architectures for E-Services. In Yee, G. (Ed.), *Privacy Protection for E-Services* (pp. 234–264). Hershey, PA: IDEA Group Publishing.

Korgaonkar, P., Silverblatt, R., & Girard, T. (2006). Online retailing, product classifications, and consumer preferences. *Internet Research, 16*(3), 267–287. doi:10.1108/10662240610673691

Korgaonkar, P., & O'Leary, B. (2006). Management, market, and financial factors separating winners and losers in e-Business. *Journal of Computer-Mediated Communication, 11*(4). doi:10.1111/j.1083-6101.2006.00311.x

Korgaonkar, P., & Wolin, L. (1999). A multivariate analysis of web usage. *Journal of Advertising Research, 39*(Mar/Apr), 53–68.

Korgaonkar, P. K., & Bellenger, D. N. (1985). Correlates of successful advertising campaigns: managers' perspectives. *Journal of Advertising Research, 25*(4), 34–39.

Korgaonkar, P. K., Moschis, G. P., & Bellenger, D. N. (1984). Correlates of successful advertising campaigns: a survey of advertising agency executives. *Journal of Advertising Research, 24*(1), 47–53.

Kotler, P. (1986). Megamarketing. *Harvard Business Review, 64*(2), 117–124.

Kozlov, S. (2004). *Achieving Privacy in Hyper-Blogging Communities: privacy management for Ambient Technologies.* http://www.sics.se/privacy/wholes2004/papers/kozlov.pdf

Kracaw, W. A., Lewellen, W. G., & Woo, C. Y. (1992). Corporate growth, corporate strategy, and the choice of capital structure. *Managerial and Decision Economics, 13*, 515–526. doi:10.1002/mde.4090130607

Krishnan, H. A., Miller, A., & Judge, W. Q. (1997). Diversification and top management complementarity: Is performance improved by merging similar or dissimilar teams? *Strategic Management Journal, 18*(5), 361–374. doi:10.1002/(SICI)1097-0266(199705)18:5<361::AID-SMJ866>3.0.CO;2-L

Krueger, R. A. (1998). *Developing Questions for Focus Groups.* Thousand Oaks, CA: Sage.

Krueger, C. C., & Swatman, P. M. C. (2003). *Who are the Internet content providers? Identifying a realistic taxonomy of content providers in the online news sector.* Paper presented at the 3rd IFIP Conference on eBusiness, eCommerce and eGovernment, Sao Paolo, Brazil.

Krzysztof, J. C., & Moore, J. C. (2002). Uniqueness of medical data mining. *Artificial Intelligence in Medicine, 26*(1/2), 1–24.

Kshetri, N. (2007). The adoption of e-business by organizations in china: An institutional perspective. *Electronic Markets, 17*(2), 113–125. doi:10.1080/10196780701296022

Kuan, K. K. Y., & Chau, P. Y. K. (2001). A perception-based model for EDI adoption in small businesses using a technology-organization-environment framework. *Information & Management, 38*, 507–521. doi:10.1016/S0378-7206(01)00073-8

Kumar, V., Shah, D., & Venkatesan, R. (2006). Managing retailer profitability – one customer at a time! *Journal of Retailing, 82*(4), 277–294. doi:10.1016/j.jretai.2006.08.002

Kumar, V., & Venkatesan, R. (2005). Who are the Multichannel Shoppers and how do They Perform? Correlates of Multichannel Shopping Behavior. *Journal of Interactive Marketing, 19*(2), 44–62. doi:10.1002/dir.20034

Kwak, H., Fox, R. J., & Zinkhan, G. M. (2002). What products can be successfully promoted and sold via the Internet? *Journal of Advertising Research, 2*, 23–38.

Kwon, D., & Watts, S. (2006). IT Valuation in Turbulent Times. *The Journal of Strategic Information Systems, 15*(4), 327–354. doi:10.1016/j.jsis.2006.07.003

Lal, R., & Sarvary, M. (1999). When and how is the internet likely to decrease price competition. *Marketing Science, 18*(4), 485–503. doi:10.1287/mksc.18.4.485

Landro, L. (2006). What drugs do you take? Hospitals seek to collect better data and prevent errors. *The Wall Street Journal*. May 23, D1.

Lane, C., & Bachmann, R. (1996). The social constitution of trust: supplier relations in Britain and Germany. *Organization Studies, 17*(3), 365–395. doi:10.1177/017084069601700302

Latchem. C. & Walker, D. (2001) Telecentres: Case Studies and Key Issues. Vancouver: The Commonwealth of Learning.

Laudon, K. C. (2006). *Management information systems: managing the digital firm.* Upper Saddle River, NJ: Pearson Prentice Hall.

Laufer, R. S., & Wolfe, M. (1977). Privacy as a Concept and a Social Issue - Multidimensional Developmental Theory. *The Journal of Social Issues, 33*(3), 22–42. doi:10.1111/j.1540-4560.1977.tb01880.x

Laufer, R. S., Proshansky, H. M., & Wolfe, M. (1973, June). *Some Analytic Dimensions of Privacy.* Paper presented at the Paper presented at the meeting of the Third International Architectural Psychology Conference, Lund, Sweden.

Laurant, C. (2003). Privacy and Human Rights 2003: an International Survey of Privacy Laws and Developments. *Electronic Privacy Information Center (EPIC), Privacy International.* Retrieved Dec. 2006 from http://www.privacyinternational.org/survey/phr2003/

Lawrence, K. L. (1997). *Factors Inhibiting the Utilisation of Electronic Commerce Facilities in Tasmanian Small-to-Mediun Sized Enterprises.* Paper presented at the 8th Australasian Conference on Information Systems.

Lawton, C. (2007). PC shopping: online vs. in store: web retailers pile on videos, reviews, pricing tool To lure consumers back from the mall. *Wall Street Journal*, (July, 25), D1, D3.

Lawton, C., & Worthen, B. (2008). Google to offer health records on the web. *Wall Street Journal*. January 28, D1f.

Leach, S. L. (2004). Privacy lost with the touch of a keystroke? www.csmonitor.com/2004/1110/p15s02-stin.html: retrieved March 23, 2005.

Lederer, A. L., Maupin, D. J., Sena, M. P., & Zhung, Y. (2000). The technology acceptance model and the world wide world. *Decision Support Systems*, *29*(1), 269–282. doi:10.1016/S0167-9236(00)00076-2

Lee, C., Lee, K., & Pennings, J. M. (2001). Internal capabilities, external networks, and performance: A study on technology-based ventures. *Strategic Management Journal*, *22*(6/7), 615–640. doi:10.1002/smj.181

Lee, H. J., Ahn, H. J., Kim, J. W., & Park, S. J. (2006). Capturing ans reusing knowledge in engineering change management: A case of automobile development. *Information Systems Frontiers*, *8*(5), 375–395. doi:10.1007/s10796-006-9009-0

Lee, R. P., & Grewal, R. (2004). Strategic responses to new technologies and their impact on firm performance. *Journal of Marketing*, *68*, 157–171. doi:10.1509/jmkg.68.4.157.42730

Lee, J. (2004). Discriminant analysis of technology adoption behavior: A case of Internet technologies in small businesses. *Journal of Computer Information Systems*, *44*(4), 57–66.

Lee, A. S. (1991). Integrating Positivist and Interpretive Approaches to Organizational Research. *Organization Science*, *2*, 342–365. doi:10.1287/orsc.2.4.342

Lee, C. S. (2001). An analytical Framework for Evaluting E-commerce Business Models and Strategies. *Internet Research: Electronic Network Applications and Policy*, *11*(4), 349–359. doi:10.1108/10662240110402803

Lee, D. M. S., Trauth, E. M., & Farwell, D. (1995). Critical Skills and Knowledge Requirements of Is Professionals - a Joint Academic-Industry Investigation. *Management Information Systems Quarterly*, *19*(3), 313–340. doi:10.2307/249598

Lee, J.-N. (2001). The impact of knowledge sharing, organizational capability and partnership quality on IS outsourcing success. *Information & Management*, *38*, 323–335. doi:10.1016/S0378-7206(00)00074-4

Lee, S., & Lim, G. G. (2005). The impact of partnership attributes on EDI implementation success. *Information & Management*, *42*, 503–516. doi:10.1016/S0378-7206(03)00153-8

Lee, Y., Lee, Z., & Larsen, K. R. T. (2003). Coping with Internet Channel Conflict. *Communications of the ACM*, *46*(7), 137–142. doi:10.1145/792704.792712

Lefebvre, L., & Lefebvre, E. (1993). Competitive positioning and innovative efforts in SMEs. *Small Business Economics*, *5*, 297–305. doi:10.1007/BF01516250

Lefebvre, L., & Lefebvre, L. A. (1996) Information and Telecommunication Technologies: The Impact of their Adoption on Small and Medium-sized Enterprises. Retrieved Dec, 12, 2007, from http://web.idrc.ca/en/ev-9303-201-1-DO_TOPIC.html.

Lesser, V., Horling, B., Klassner, F., Raja, A., Wagner, T., & Zhang, S. X. (2000). Big: An agent for resource-bounded information gathering and decision making. *Artificial Intelligence*, *118*, 197–244. doi:10.1016/S0004-3702(00)00005-9

Letaifa, S., & Perrien, J. (2007). The impact of E-CRM on organisational and individual bahavior: The effect of the remuneration and reward system. *International Journal of E-Business Research*, (3): 2–13.

Levary, R., & Mathieu, R. G. (2000). Hybrid retail: integrating e-commerce and physical stores. *Industrial Management (Des Plaines)*, *42*(5), 6–13.

Levy, M., & Powell, P. (1998). SME flexibility and the role of information systems. *Journal of Small Business Economics*, *11*, 183–196. doi:10.1023/A:1007912714741

Levy, M., Powell, P., & Yetton, P. (2001). (forthcoming). SMEs: Aligning IS and the Strategic Context. *Journal of Information Technology*. doi:10.1080/02683960110063672

Levy, M., Powell, P., & Yetton, P. (2002). The Dynamics of SME Information Systems. *Small Business Economics*, *19*, 341–354. doi:10.1023/A:1019654030019

Lewicki, R. J., & Bunker, B. B. (1995). Trust in relationships: A model of trust development and decline. In Bunker, B. B., & Rubin, J. Z. (Eds.), *Conflict, Cooperation, and Justice* (pp. 133–173). San Francisco, CA: Jossey-Bass.

Lewis, R., & Cockrill, A. (2002). Going global-remaining local: the impact of e-commerce on small retail firms in Wales. *International Journal of Information Management, 22*(3), 195–209. doi:10.1016/S0268-4012(02)00005-1

Lewis, J. D., & Weigert, A. J. (1985). Trust as a social reality. *Social Forces, 63*(4), 967–985. doi:10.2307/2578601

Li, C. C. (1975). *Path Analysis: A Primer*. Pacific Grove, CA: The Boxwood Press.

Li, F. (2007). *What is e-Business? How the Internet Transforms Organisations*. Oxford: Blackwell.

Li, N., & Mitchell, J. C. (2003). Datalog with Constraints: A foundation for trust management languages. PADL'03. Springer Verlag, 58-73.

Liang, T., & Huang, J. (1998). An empirical study on consumer acceptance of products in electronic markets: A transaction cost model. *Decision Support Systems, 24*, 29–43. doi:10.1016/S0167-9236(98)00061-X

Liang, T. P., & Doong, H. S. (2000). Effect of bargaining in electronic commerce. *International Journal of Electronic Commerce, 4*(3), 23–43.

Lichtenstein, G.A. and Lyons, T.S.(2001). The entrepreneurial development system: Transforming business talent and community economies, *Economic Development Quarterly*, (15:1),, pp.3-20.

Light, A., & Wakeman, I. (2001). Beyond the interface: Users' perceptions of interaction and audience on websites. *Interacting with Computers, 13*(3), 325–351. doi:10.1016/S0953-5438(00)00044-8

Lima, R., Espinasse, B., & Freitas, F. (2010). Adaptive Information Extraction System based on Wrapper Induction with POS Tagging. In *Proceedings of SAC-ACM 2010, Sierre, Switzerland*.

Lin, C. J., & Lu, H. (2000). Towards an understanding of the behavioral intention to use a Web site. *International Journal of Information Management, 20*(3), 197–208. doi:10.1016/S0268-4012(00)00005-0

Little, L., Briggs, P., & Coventry, L. (2004). Videotaped Activity Scenarios and the Elicitation of Social Rules for Public Interactions. BHCIG UK Conference, Leeds, September

Liu, C., & Arnett, P. K. (2000). Exploring the factors associated with Web site success in the context of electronic commerce. *Information & Management, 38*(1), 23–33. doi:10.1016/S0378-7206(00)00049-5

Loebbecke, C., & Powell, P. (2002). E-business in the entertainment sector: the Egmont case. *Journal of International Management, 22*, 307–322.

Lohse, G.L. & Spiller P. (1998). Electronic shopping. *Communications of the ACM, 41*(7),.81-90.

Lord, R. G., & Foti, R. J. (1986). Schema Theories, Information Processing and Organizational Behavior. In Sims, H. P. Jr, & Gioia, D. A. (Eds.), *The Thinking Organization: Dynamics of Organization Cognition* (pp. 20–48). San Francisco, CA: Jossey Bass.

Lorenzi, F., Santos, D. S., & Bazzan, A. L. C. (2005). Negotiation for task allocation among agents in case-base recommender systems: a swarm-intelligence approach. In E. Aimeur (Ed.), *Multi-Agent Information Retrieval and Recommender Systems - Nineteenth International Conference on Artificial Intelligence (IJCAI 2005)* (p. 23--27). Edimburgh, Scotland.

Losch, U., Rudolph, S., Vrandecic, D., & Studer, R. (2009). Tempus Fugit. In *6th European Semantic Web Conference (ESWC 2009)* (pp. 278-292). Berlin Heidelberg, Germany: Springer.

Love, P. E. D., & Irani, Z. (2004). An exploratory study of information technology evaluation and benefits management practices of SMEs in the construction industry. *Information & Management, 42*, 227–242.

Lucking-Reiley, D., Bryan, D., Prasad, N., & Reeves, D. (2000). *Pennies from eBay: the determinants of price in online auctions.* Working paper, Vanderbilt University.

Luhmann, N. (1988). Familiarity, Confidence, Trust: Problems and Alternatives. In D. Gambetta, G. (Ed.), *Trust* (pp. 94-107). Basil Blackwell, New York.

Lumpkin, G. T., & Dess, G. G. (2004). E-business strategies and Internet business models: How the Internet adds value. *Organizational Dynamics, 33*(2), 161–173. doi:10.1016/j.orgdyn.2004.01.004

Lynch, J., & De Chernatony, L. (2004). The power of emotion: Brand communication in business-to-business markets. *Journal of Brand Management, 11*(5), 403–419. doi:10.1057/palgrave.bm.2540185

Ma, X., & Loeh, H. (2007). Closing the gap: How should Chinese companies build the capabilities to implement ERP-driven process innovation? *International Journal of Technology Management, 39*(3/4), 380–395. doi:10.1504/IJTM.2007.013501

Maamar, Z., Benslimane, D., & Narendra, N. C. (2006). What Can Context do for Web Services? *Communications of the ACM, 49*(12). doi:10.1145/1183236.1183238

Maamar, Z., Subramanian, S., Thiran, P., Benslimane, D., & Bentahar, J. (2009). Communities of Web Services -Concepts, Architecture, Operation, and Deployment. [Hershey, PA: IGI Global Publishing]. *International Journal of E-Business Research, 5*(4), 1–12.

Maamar, Z., Benslimane, D., Mostefaoui, G. M., Subramanian, S., & Mahmoud, Q. H. (2008). Toward Behavioral Web Services Using Policies, *IEEE Transactions on Systems, Man, and Cybernetics, Part A, 38*(6).

Maaradji, A., Hacid, H., Daigremont, J., & Crespi, N. (2010). Towards a Social Network Based Approach for Services Composition, in *the Proceedings of the 2010 IEEE International Conference on Communications (ICC'2010)*, Cape Town, South Africa.

MacGregor, R. C. (2004). The Role of Strategic Alliances in the Ongoing Use of Electronic Commerce Technology in Regional Small Business. *Journal of Electronic Commerce in Organizations, 2*(1), 1–14.

Mach, T.L. & Wolken, J.D. (2006). Financial services used by small businesses: Evidence from the 2003 Survey of Small Business Finances. *Federal Reserve Bulletin*, October, A167-A195.

Macmillan, I. C., Zemann, L., & Subbanarasima, P. N. (1987). Criteria distinguishing successful from unsuccessful ventures in the venture screening process. *Journal of Business Venturing*, (2): 123–137. doi:10.1016/0883-9026(87)90003-6

Maguire, M. C. (1998). A Review of User-Interface Guidelines for Public information kiosk Systems. *International Journal of Human-Computer Studies, 50*, 263–286. doi:10.1006/ijhc.1998.0243

Malhotra, N. K., Kim, S. S., & Agarwal, J. (2004). Internet Users' Information Privacy Concerns (IUIPC): The Construct, the Scale, and a Causal Model. *Information Systems Research, 15*(4), 336–355. doi:10.1287/isre.1040.0032

Mansell, R., & Wehn, U. (1998). *Knowledge Societies: Information Technology for Sustainable Development.* Oxford: Oxford University Press.

Mansfield, G. M., & Fourie, L. C. H. (2004). Strategy and business models - strange bedfellows? A case for convergence and its evolution into strategic architecture. *South African Journal of Business Management, 33*(1), 35–44.

March, J. G. (1991). Exploration and exploitation in organizational learning. *Organization Science, 2*, 71–87. doi:10.1287/orsc.2.1.71

Margulis, S. T. (1977). Conceptions of Privacy - Current Status and Next Steps. *The Journal of Social Issues, 33*(3), 5–21. doi:10.1111/j.1540-4560.1977.tb01879.x

Markus, H., & Zajonc, R. B. (1985). The Cognitive Perspective in Social Psychology. In Lindzey, G., & Aronson, E. (Eds.), *Handbook of Social Psychology* (pp. 137–230). NY: Random House.

Marlow, S. (1998). So Much Opportunity -- So Little Take-up: The Case of Training in Small Firms. *Small Business and Enterprise Development*, *5*(1), 38–47. doi:10.1108/EUM0000000006729

Martin, P. Y., & Turner, B. A. (1986). Grounded Theory and Organizational Research. *The Journal of Applied Behavioral Science*, *22*(2), 141–157. doi:10.1177/002188638602200207

Massad, V. J., & Tucker, J. M. (2000). Comparing bidding and pricing between in-person and online auctions. *Journal of Product and Brand Management*, *9*(5), 32–44. doi:10.1108/10610420010347128

Mata, F. J., Fuerst, W. L., & Barney, J. B. (1995). Information technology and sustained competitive advantage: A resource-based analysis. *MIS Quarterly*, *19*(4), 487–505. doi:10.2307/249630

Maton, K. (1999). *Evaluation of Small Firms Training Loans*. UK Research Partnerships Ltd., Dfee Publications.

Matthews, P. (2007). ICT Assimilation and SME Expansion. *Journal of International Development*, (19): 817–827. doi:10.1002/jid.1401

Mattila, M., Karjaluoto, H., & Pento, T. (2003). Internet banking adoption among mature customers: early majority or laggards? *Journal of Services Marketing*, *17*(5), 514–528. doi:10.1108/08876040310486294

Maximilien, M., & Singh, M. (2002). Concept Model of Web Service Reputation. *SIGMOD Record*, *31*(4). doi:10.1145/637411.637417

Mayberry, C. (2006). *Current TV, APM Music pact on music use*. Retrieved: 18th October, 2007, from http://www.hollywoodreporter.com/hr/search/article_display.jsp?vnu_content_id=1003122553

Mayer, R. C., Davis, J. H., & Schoorman, F. D. (1995). An integrative model of organizational trust. *Academy of Management Review*, *20*(3), 709–734. doi:10.2307/258792

Maynard, D., Peters, W., & Li, Y. (2006). Metrics for evaluation of ontology-based information extraction. *WWW 2006 Workshop on "Evaluation of Ontologies for the Web" (EON)*, Edinburgh, Scotland.

Mazursky, D., & Jacoby, J. (1985). Forming impressions of merchandise and service quality. In Jacoby, J., & Olson, J. (Eds.), *Perceived Quality* (pp. 139–154). Lexington, MA: Lexington Books.

Mccallum, A., Nigam, K., Rennie, J., & Seymore, K. (1999). *Building Domain-Specific Search Engines with Machine Learning Techniques*.

McCarthy, E. J. (1960). *Basic Marketing*. Homewood, Ill: Irwin.

McDougall, G., & Levesque, T. (2000). Customer satisfaction with services: putting perceived value into the equation. *Journal of Services Marketing*, *14*(5), 392–410. doi:10.1108/08876040010340937

McFarlan, F. W., & McKenney, J. L. (1983). *Corporate Information Systems Management*. Homewood, Ill: Richard D. Irwin.

McFarlan, F.W. (1984) Information Technology Changes the Way You Compete. *Harvard Business Review* (62:3), pp. 98-1 03.

McKnight, D. H., & Chervany, N. L. (2002). What trust means in e-commerce customer relationships: an interdisciplinary conceptual typology. *International Journal of Electronic Commerce*, *6*(2), 35–59.

McKnight, D. H., Cummings, L. L., & Chervany, N. L. (1998). Initial Trust Formation in New Organizational Relationships. *Academy of Management Review*, *23*(3), 472–490. doi:10.2307/259290

Medjahed, B., & Atif, Y. (2007). Context-based Matching for Web Service Composition. *Distributed and Parallel Databases, Springer*, *21*(1).

Medjahed, B., & Bouguettaya, A. (2005). A Dynamic Foundational Architecture for Semantic Web Services. *Distributed and Parallel Databases, Kluwer Academic Publishers*, *17*(2).

Mehrtens, J., Cragg, P. B., & Mills, A. M. (2001). A model of internet adoption by SMEs. *Information & Management*, *39*, 165–176. doi:10.1016/S0378-7206(01)00086-6

Melewar, T. C., & Karaosmanoglu, E. (2006). Seven Dimensions of Corporate Identity: A Categorisation from the Practitioners' Perspectives. *European Journal of Marketing*, *40*(7/8), 846–869. doi:10.1108/03090560610670025

Melnick, M. I., & Alm, J. (2005). Seller reputation, information signals, and prices for heterogeneous coins on eBay. *Southern Economic Journal*, *72*(2), 305–328. doi:10.2307/20062113

Melville, N., Kraemer, K. L., & Gurbaxani, V. (2004). Information Technology and Organizational Performance: An Integrative Model of IT Business Value. *Management Information Systems Quarterly*, *28*(2), 283–322.

Merono-Cerdan, A. L., & Soto-Acosta, P. (2006). Examining e-business impact on firm performance through website analysis. *International Journal of Electronic Business*, *3*(6), 1–1.

Metzger, M. J. (2004). Exploring the barriers to electronic commerce: Privacy, trust, and disclosure online. *Journal of Computer-Mediated Communication*, *9*(4). http://jcmc.indiana.edu/vol9/issue4/metzger.html.

Meyer, J., & Rowan, B. (1977). Institutionalized Organizations: Formal Structure as Myth and Ceremony. *American Journal of Sociology*, *83*, 340–363. doi:10.1086/226550

Micu, A., Mast, L., Milea, V., Frasincar, F., & Kaymak, U. (2008). Financial News Analysis Using a Semantic Web Approach. In Zilli, A., Damiani, E., Ceravolo, P., Corallo, A., & Elia, G. (Eds.), *Semantic Knowledge Management: An Ontology-Based Framework* (pp. 311–328). Hershey, PA: IGI Global.

Middleton, S. E., Shadbolt, N. R., & Roure, D. C. D. (2004). Ontological User Profiling in Recommender Systems. *ACM Transactions on Information Systems*, *22*(1), 54–88. doi:10.1145/963770.963773

Milberg, S. J., Smith, H. J., & Burke, S. J. (2000). Information privacy: Corporate management and national regulation. *Organization Science*, *11*(1), 35–57. doi:10.1287/orsc.11.1.35.12567

Milberg, S. J. B., J.S., Smith, H. J., & Kallman, A. E. (1995). Values, Personal Information Privacy Concerns, and Regulatory Approaches. *Communications of the ACM*, *38*(12), 65–74. doi:10.1145/219663.219683

Milea, V., Frasincar, F., & Kaymak, U. (2008). Knowledge Engineering in a Temporal Semantic Web Context. In *The Eighth International Conference on Web Engineering (ICWE 2008)* (pp. 65-74). Washington, DC: IEEE Computer Society Press.

Miller, D. (1982). Evolution and revolution - a quantum view of structural-change in organizations. *Journal of Management Studies*, *19*(2), 131–151. doi:10.1111/j.1467-6486.1982.tb00064.x

Miller, G. A., Beckwith, R., Fellbaum, C., Gross, D., & Miller, K. (1990). WordNet: An on-line lexical database. *International Journal of Lexicography*, *3*, 235–244. doi:10.1093/ijl/3.4.235

Milne, G. R., & Boza, M.-E. (1999). Trust and Concern in Consumers' Perceptions of Marketing Information Management Practices. *Journal of Interactive Marketing*, *13*(1), 5–24. doi:10.1002/(SICI)1520-6653(199924)13:1<5::AID-DIR2>3.0.CO;2-9

Milne, G. R., & Culnan, M. J. (2004). Strategies for reducing online privacy risks: Why consumers read(or don't read) online privacy notices. *Journal of Interactive Marketing*, *18*(3), 15–29. doi:10.1002/dir.20009

Milne, G. R., & Gordon, E. M. (1993). Direct Mail Privacy-Efficiency Trade-Offs Within an Implied Social Contract Framework. *Journal of Public Policy & Marketing*, *12*(2), 206–215.

Milne, G. R., & Rohm, A. (2000). Consumer Privacy and Name Removal Across Direct Marketing Channels: Exploring Opt-in and Opt-out Alternatives. *Journal of Public Policy & Marketing*, *19*(2), 238–249. doi:10.1509/jppm.19.2.238.17136

Milne, G. R., Rohm, A., & Boza, M.-E. (1999). Trust Has to Be Earned. In Phelps, J. (Ed.), *Frontiers of Direct Marketing* (pp. 31–41). New York: Direct Marketing Educational Foundation.

Milne, G. R. (1996). *Consumer Participation in Mailing Lists: A Field Experiment* (No. Report no. 96-107). Cambridge, Mass.: Marketing Science Instituteo.

Mirchandani, A. A., & Motwani, J. (2001). Understanding small business electronic commerce adoption: an empirical analysis. *Journal of Computer Information Systems, 41*(3), 70–73.

Moch, M. K., & Morse, E. V. (1977). Size, centralization, and organizational adoption of innovations. *American Sociological Review, 42*(5), 716–725. doi:10.2307/2094861

Modulo (2010). Risk Manager. Retrieved August 2010 from www.modulo.com/risk-manager

Mohan-Neill, S. I. (1995). The influence of firm's age and size on its environmental scanning activities. *Journal of Small Business Management, 33*(4), 10–21.

Mok, C. (1996). *Designing Business*. San Jose, CA: Adobe Press.

Montazemi, A. R. (1988). Factors Affecting Information Satisfaction in the Context of the Small Business Environment. *Management Information Systems Quarterly, 12*(2), 239–256. doi:10.2307/248849

Moon, J., & Kim, Y. (2001). Extending the TAM for a World-Wide-Web Context. *Information & Management, 38*(4), 217–230. doi:10.1016/S0378-7206(00)00061-6

Moore, G. C., & Benbasat, I. (1991). Development of an Instrument to Measure the Perceptions of Adopting an Information Technology Innovation. *Information Systems Research, 2*(3), 192–223. doi:10.1287/isre.2.3.192

Moore, G. C. (1996). Integration Diffusion of Innovations and Theory of Reasoned action Models to predict Utilization of information Technology by End-Users. In *Diffusion and Adoption of Information Technology*. London: Chapman&Hall.

Moorman, C., Desphande, R., & Zaltman, G. (1993). Factors affecting trust in market research relationships. *Journal of Marketing, 57*(1), 81–101. doi:10.2307/1252059

Morgan, G., Frost, P. J., & Pondy, L. R. (1983). Organizational Symbolism. In Pondy, L. R., Frost, P. G., Morgan, G., & Dandridge, T. C. (Eds.), *Organizational Symbolism*. Greenwich, CT: JAI Press.

Morimoto, R., Ash, J., & Hope, C. (2004). *Corporate Social Responsibility Audit: From Theory to Practice*. University of Cambridge, Judge Institute of Management, Working Paper No. 14/2004.

Moschis, G. M. (1976). Social comparison and informal group influence. *JMR, Journal of Marketing Research, 13*(3), 237–244. doi:10.2307/3150733

Moschis, G. M. (1987). *Consumer Socialization*. Lexington, Mass: D.C. Health.

Motahari, S., Manikopoulos, C., Hiltz, R., & Jones, Q. (2007). Seven privacy worries in ubiquitous social computing. *Symposium on usable privacy and security (SOUPS)*, 171 – 172.

Motta, E. (1999). *Reusable Components for Knowledge Modelling: Case Studies in Parametric Design Problem Solving (Vol. 53)*. Amsterdam, the Netherlands: IOS Press.

Mougayar, W. (1998). *Opening Digital Markets: Battle Plans and Strategies for Internet Commerce* (2nd ed.). New York: Commerce Net Press, McGraw-Hill.

Mowshowitz, A. (1997). Virtual Organization. *Communications of the ACM, 40*(9). doi:10.1145/260750.260759

Moyi, E. D. (2003). Networks, information and small enterprises: New Technologies and the ambiguity of empowerment. *Information Technology for Development, 10*, 221–232. doi:10.1002/itdj.1590100402

Murphy, K. E., & Simon, S. J. (2007). Intangible Benefits Valuation in ERP Projects. *Information Systems Journal, 12*, 301–320. doi:10.1046/j.1365-2575.2002.00131.x

Muslea, I., Minton, S., & Knoblock, C. (1998). STALKER: Learning extraction rules for semistructured Web-based information sources. *Proceedings of the AAAI-98 Workshop on "AI & Information Integration"*.

Navigli, R., & Velardi, P. (2005). Structural Semantic Interconnections: a Knowledge-Based Approach to Word Sense Disambiguation. *IEEE Transactions on Pattern Analysis and Machine Intelligence, 27*(7), 1063–1074. doi:10.1109/TPAMI.2005.149

Naylor, J., & Williams, J. (1994). Successful Use of IT in SMEs. *European Journal of IS, 3*(1), 48–56.

Nelson, R. R., & Winter, S. G. (1982). *An evolutionary theory of economic change.* Cambridge, MA: Harvard University Press.

Neter, J., Kutner, M. H., Nachtsheim, C. L., & Wasserman, W. (1990). *Applied Linear Regression Models.* Chicago: Irwin Inc.

New Zealand Tourism Online. (2006). Retrieved July 23, 2006, from http://www.tourism.net.nz/featured-events/all-blacks/.

Newbert, S. L. (2007). Empirical research on the resource-based view of the firm: An assessment and suggestions for future research. *Strategic Management Journal, 28*(2), 121–146. doi:10.1002/smj.573

Newell, A., Shaw, J., & Simon, H. (1959). *Report on a General Problem-Solving Program.*

Nguyen, D. H., & Truong, K. N. (2003). PHEmail: Designing a Privacy Honoring Email System. *Proceedings of CHI 2003 Extended Abstracts*, Ft. Lauderdale, Florida, Olsen, K., Grudin, J., Horvitz, E. (2005). A study of preferences for sharing and privacy'. *CHI, 2005 extended abstracts on Human factors in computing systems.*

Nielsen, J. (2000). *Designing web usability.* Indianapolis, IN: New Riders Publishing.

Nielsen, J. (2003). *Top ten web design mistakes of 2003.* Alterbox, http://useit.com/alterbox/20040119.html

Nielson, J. F., Host, V., & Mols, N. P. (2005). Adoption of internet-based marketing channels by small- and medium-sized manufacturers. *International Journal of E-Business Research, 1*(2), 1–23.

Nirenburg, S., & Raskin, V. (2001). Ontological Semantics, Formal Ontology, and Ambiguity. In *Formal Ontology in Information Systems (FOIS 2001)* (pp. 151-161). New York: ACM.

Nisbett, R. E., & Ross, I. (1980). *Human Inference: Strategies and Shortcomings of Social Judgment.* Engelwood Cliffs, NJ: Prentice-Hall.

Noble, S. M., Griffith, D. A., & Weinberger, M. G. (2005). Consumer derived utilitarian value and channel utilization in a multi-channel context. *Journal of Business Research, 58*, 1643–1651. doi:10.1016/j.jbusres.2004.10.005

Nohria, N., & Gulati, R. (1996). Is slack good or bad for innovation? *Academy of Management Journal, 39*(5), 1245–1264. doi:10.2307/256998

Noir, C., & Walsham, G. (2007). The Great Legitimizer: ICT as Myth and Ceremony in the Indian Healthcare Sector. *Information Technology & People, 20*(4), 313–333. doi:10.1108/09593840710839770

Nolan, R. (1979). Managing The Crisis In Data Processing. *Harvard Business Review, 57*(2), 115–126.

Nolan, R., & Gibson, C. F. (1974, January/February). Managing the four stages of EDP growth. *Harvard Business Review*, 76–88.

Nonaka, I. (1994). A dynamic theory of organizational knowledge creation. *Organization Science, 5*(1), 14–37. doi:10.1287/orsc.5.1.14

Normann, R., & Ramirez, R. (1993). From value chain to value constellation: designing interactive strategy. *Harvard Business Review, 71*, 65–77.

Nowak, J. G., & Phelps, J. (1997). Direct Marketing and the Use of Individual-Level Consumer Information: Determining How and When "Privacy" Matters. *Journal of Direct Marketing, 11*(4), 94–108. doi:10.1002/(SICI)1522-7138(199723)11:4<94::AID-DIR11>3.0.CO;2-F

Noy, N., & Rector, A. (2006). *Defining N-ary Relations on the Semantic Web*: W3C Working Group Note 12 April 2006.

Nunnally, J. C. (1978). *Psychometric theory* (2nd ed.). New York: McGraw-Hill.

Nwana, H. S. (1996). Software Agents: An Overview.

OASIS. (2005). eXtensible Access Control Markup Language (XACML). Version 2.0. Retrieved Feb. 2005 from http://docs.oasis-open.org/xacml/2.0/access_control-xacml-2.0-core-specs-os.pdf

Oates, T., Prasad, M. N., & Lesser, V. R. (1994). Cooperative information gathering: a distributed problem solving approach.

O'Donoghue, T., & Rabin, M. (2001). Choice and procrastination. *The Quarterly Journal of Economics, 116*, 121–160. doi:10.1162/003355301556365

OECD. (1980). OECD Guidelines on the Protection of Privacy and Transborder Flows of Personal Data. Retrieved Dec. 2006 from http://www1.oecd.org/publications/e-book/9302011E.PDF

O'Farrell, C., Norrish, P., & Scott, A. (1999) *Information and Communication Technologies (ICTs) for Sustainable Livelihoods*. Burton Hall: Intermediate Technology Development Group.

Office of Technology Assessment. (1993). Protecting privacy in computerized medical information. www.wws.princeton.edu/ota/disk1/1993/9342/9342.pdf: retrieved August 6, 2006.

Office of the United States Trade Representative. (2008). www.ustr.gov/assets/capitaldocument_Library/Reports_Publications/2008/2008_Special_301_Report; retrieved June 21, 2008.

Ogles, J. (2004). Court documents not fit for Web? www.wired.com/news/privacy/0,1848,65703,00.html; retrieved February 7, 2005.

Oliver, C. (1991). Strategic Responses to Institutional Processes. *Academy of Management Review, 16*, 145–179. doi:10.2307/258610

Orlikowski, W. J., & Iacono, C. S. (2001). Research Commentary: Desperately Seeking the "IT" in IT Research – A Call to Theorizing the IT Artifact. *Information Systems Research, 12*(2), 121–134. doi:10.1287/isre.12.2.121.9700

Orlikowski, W. J., & Iacono, C. S. (2000). The Truth is Not Out There: An Enacted View of the 'Digital Economy. In Brynjolfsson, E., & Kahin, B. (Eds.), *Understanding the Digital Economy: Data, Tools, and Research Cambridge*. Cambridge, MA: EMIT Press.

Ornstein, S. (1989). Impression Management Through Office Design. In Giacalone, R. A., & Rosenfeld, P. (Eds.), *Impression Management in The Organization*. Hillsdale, NJ: Erlbaum.

Ortega, B. H., Marinez, J. J., & Hoyos, M. (2008). The role of information technology knowledge in b2b development. *International Journal of E-Business Research, 4*(1), 40–54.

Osterwalder, A., & Pigneur, Y. (2002). An e-Business Model Ontology for Modelling e-Business. *In 15th Bled Electronic Commerce Conference e-Reality: Constructing the e-Economy*, Bled, Slovenia.

Ouyang, C., Dumas, M., Breutel, S., & ter Hofstede, A. H. (2006). Translating standard process models to BPEL. *Proceedings of the 18th International Conference on Advanced Information Systems Engineering*, (pp. 417-432).

Ouzzani, M., & Bouguettaya, A. (2004). Efficient Access to Web Services. *IEEE Internet Computing, 8*(2).

Oviatt, B. M., & McDougall, P. P. (1994). Toward a theory of international new ventures. *Journal of International Business Studies, 25*(1), 45–64. doi:10.1057/palgrave.jibs.8490193

Owen, W., & Darkwa, O. (1999). Role of Multipurpose Community Telecentres in Accelerating National Development in Ghana. *First Monday, 5*(1), 1–23.

Oyelaran-Oyeyinka, B., & Lal, K. (2005). *Determinants of e-business Adoption: Evidence from firms in India, Nigeria Uganda.* Institute for New Technologies (INTECH), United Nations University, Available: http://www.intech.unu.edu/publications/discussion-papers/2004-14.pdf (Accessed: 2005 22nd February)

Ozar, S. (2004). *Micro and Small Enterprises in Turkey: Uneasy Development Research report Series on Promoting Competitiveness in Micro and Small Enterprises in the MENA Region.* Economic Research Forum.

Pack, T. (1999). Can you trust Internet information? *Link-Up, 16*(6), 24.

Paine, C. B., Stieger, S., Reips, U.-R., Joinson, A. N., & Buchanan, T. (2007). Internet users' perceptions of 'privacy concerns' and 'privacy actions'. *International Journal of Human-Computer Studies, 65*(6), 526–536. doi:10.1016/j.ijhcs.2006.12.001

Palen, L., & Dourish, P. (2003). Unpacking Privacy for a Networked World. *Proceedings of the ACM, CHI 2003, 5 (1), 129- 135.*

Pallant, J. (2002). *SPSS Survival manual.* Buckingham: Open University Press.

Palmer, J. W. (2002). Web site usability, design, and performance metrics. *Information Systems Research, 13*(2), 151–167. doi:10.1287/isre.13.2.151.88

Pan, X., Ratchford, B. T., & Shankar, V. (2004). Price dispersion on the internet: A review and directions for future research. *Journal of Interactive Marketing, 18*(4), 116–135. doi:10.1002/dir.20019

Papagiannidis, S., & Berry, J. (2007). What has been learned from emergent music business models? *International Journal of E-Business Research, 3*(3), 25–42.

Papagiannidis, S., Berry, J., & Li, F. (2006). Well beyond streaming video: IP6 and the next generation television. *Technological Forecasting and Social Change, 73*(5), 510–523. doi:10.1016/j.techfore.2005.06.003

Parasuraman, A., Berry, L., & Zeithaml, V. (1993). Research note: more on improving quality measurement. *Journal of Retailing, 69*(1), 140–148. doi:10.1016/S0022-4359(05)80007-7

Parker, C. M., & Castleman, T. (2007). New directions for research on SME-eBusiness: insights from an analysis of journal articles from 2003 to 2006. *Journal of Information Systems and Small Business, 1*(1-2), 21–40.

Pascal Challenge. (2005). Pascal Challenge. Accessed from http://nlp.shef.ac.uk/pascal/

Pateli, A.G., & Giaglis, G.M. (2004). A research framework for analyzing eBusiness models. *European Journal of Information Systems,* Vol. 13pp. 302 – 314.

Patton, D., Marlow, S., & Hannon, P. (2000). The Relationship Between Training and Small Firm Performance, Research Frameworks and Lost Quests. *International Small Business Journal, 19*(1), 11–27. doi:10.1177/0266242600191001

Patton, M. (1990). *Qualitative Data Analysis.* Thousand Oaks: Sage.

Payton, F. C. (2003). Data mining in health care applications. In Wang, J. (Ed.), *Data mining: Opportunities and challenges* (pp. 350–365). Hershey: Idea Group Inc.

Pearson, S. (2006). In Stolen, K. (Eds.), *Towards Automated Evaluation of Trust Constraints, iTrust 2006, LNCS 3986* (pp. 252–266). Springer-Verlag.

Pedersen, P. E., & Nysveen, H. (2001). Shopbot banking: an exploratory study of customer loyalty effects. *International Journal of Bank Marketing, 19*(4), 146–155. doi:10.1108/02652320110392518

Penrose, E. (1959). *The Theory of Growth of the Firm.* London: Basil Blackwell.

Peppard, J., Ward, J., & Daniel, E. (2007). Managing the Realization of Business Benefits from IT Investments. *MISQ Executive, 6*(1), 1–11.

Peppard, J., Lambert, R., & Edwards, C. (2000). Whose job is it anyway? organizational information competencies for value creation. *Information Systems Journal, 10,* 291–322. doi:10.1046/j.1365-2575.2000.00089.x

Percival-Straunik, L. (2001). *E-commerce.* London: Profile Books Ltd.

Percival-Straunik, L. (2001). Shop.org. In *E-Commerce, The Economist.*

Perkowitz, M. & Eitzioni, O. (1999). Towards adaptive web sites: conceptual framework and case study. *Computer Networks, 31*(11-16), 1245-1258.

Petersen, M. A., & Rajan, R. G. (1994). The benefits of lending relationships: Evidence from small business data. *The Journal of Finance, 49*(1), 3–37. doi:10.2307/2329133

Petronio, S. S. (2002). *Boundaries of privacy: dialectics of disclosure.* Albany: State University of New York Press.

Pfeffer, J., & Salancik, G. R. (1978). *The External Control of Organizations: A Resource Dependence Perspective.* New York: Harper and Row.

Phelps, J., Nowak, G., & Ferrell, E. (2000). Privacy Concerns and Consumer Willingness to Provide Personal Information. *Journal of Public Policy & Marketing, 19*(1), 27–41. doi:10.1509/jppm.19.1.27.16941

Piscitello, L., & Sgobbi, F. (2004, June). Globalisation, E-Business and SMEs: Evidence from the Italian District of Prato. *Small Business Economics, 22*(5), 333. doi:10.1023/B:SBEJ.0000022208.34741.55

Pollard, C., & Diggles, A. (2006). The role of trust in Business-to-Business e-Commerce collaberation in a unique environment in Australia. *International Journal of E-Business Research, 2*(3), 71–88.

Pollard, K., & Blyth, R. (1999). User-centered design of web sites and the redesign of line one. *BT Technology Journal, 17*(1), 69–75. doi:10.1023/A:1009622925010

Poon, S., & Swatman, P. (1999). An exploratory study of small business Internet commerce issues. *Information & Management, 35,* 9–18. doi:10.1016/S0378-7206(98)00079-2

Poon, S., & Jevons, C. (1997). Internet Enabled International Marketing: A Small Business Network Perspective. *Journal of Marketing Management, 13*(1-3), 29–42.

Poon, S., & Swatman, P. M. C. (1998). A Combined Method Study of Small Business Internet-Commerce. *International Journal of Electronic Commerce, 2*(3), 31–46.

Porter, M. E. (1991). Towards a dynamic theory of strategy. *Strategic Management Journal, 12,* 95–117. doi:10.1002/smj.4250121008

Porter, M. E. (1980). *Competitive Strategy: Techniques for Analyzing Industries and Competitors, New York.* New York, NY: Free Press.

Porter, M. E. (2001). Strategy and the Internet. *Harvard Business Review, 79*(3), 63–78.

Porter, J. (2003). *Testing the three-click rule. User Interface Engineering.* www.uie.com/articles/three_click_rule/

Porter, M.E. & Millar, V.E.(1985). How Information Gives You Competitive Advantage. *Harvard Business Review* (63:4), July-August 1985, pp. 149-1 60.

Powell, T. C., & Dent-Micallef, A. (1997). Information technology as competitive advantage: The role of human, business and technology resources. *Strategic Management Journal, 18*(5), 375–405. doi:10.1002/(SICI)1097-0266(199705)18:5<375::AID-SMJ876>3.0.CO;2-7

Powell, W. W., & DiMaggio, P. J. (1991). Introduction. In W.W. Powell a& P.J. DiMaggio (eds.), *The New Institutionalism in Organizational Analysis.* London: University of Chicago Press.

PR Newswire. (2007). *Bingo Players Flock to River Belle for New Online Chat Games.* Accessed online August 8, 2007.

PR Newswire. (2007). *Universal Pictures Partners with MINICK to Launch Mobile Film Portals Worldwide.* Accessed online August 8, 2000.

PR Newswire. (2007). *Second Life Invaded by Greenies-Avatars Shrink to Size of Mice.* Accessed online August 8, 2007.